£17.99
NW8942
HIST/99

REVOLUTIONARY EUROPE, 1780–1850

WITHDRAWN

N 0101890 6

LONGMAN HISTORY OF MODERN EUROPE

General Editors: M.J. Rodriguez-Salgado and H.M. Scott

The Longman History of Modern Europe is innovative in including works covering the mainstream political narrative together with regional and thematic volumes.

FORTHCOMING TITLES

Reformation Europe, 1480–1580
Ronnie Po-Chia Hsia

Europe 1580–1690
Robert Frost

Europe 1650–1780
H.M. Scott

Europe since 1929
Harold James

Mediterranean Europe, 1450–1800
M.J. Rodriguez-Salgado

Transformation of East Central Europe 1525–1815
Edgar Melton

Europe and the New World 1350–1820
Joan-Pau Rubies

The Rise and Fall of Communist Europe
Evan Mawdsley

REVOLUTIONARY EUROPE, 1780–1850

JONATHAN SPERBER

University of Missouri

NEWMAN COLLEGE
BARTLEY GREEN
BIRMINGHAM B32 3NT

CLASS   940.27
BARCODE 01018906
AUTHOR   SPE

Longman

An imprint of **Pearson Education**

Harlow, England · London · New York · Reading, Massachusetts · San Francisco · Toronto · Don Mills, Ontario · Sydney
Tokyo · Singapore · Hong Kong · Seoul · Taipei · Cape Town · Madrid · Mexico City · Amsterdam · Munich · Paris · Milan

Pearson Education Limited
Edinburgh Gate
Harlow
Essex CM20 2JE
England

and Associated Companies throughout the world

Visit us on the World Wide Web at:
http://www.pearsoneduc.com

First published 2000

© Pearson Education Limited 2000

The right of Jonathan Sperber to be identified as author of
this Work has been asserted by him in accordance with
the Copyright, Designs and Patents Act 1988.

All rights reserved; no part of this publication may be reproduced, stored
in a retrieval system, or transmitted in any form or by any means, electronic,
mechanical, photocopying, recording, or otherwise without either the prior
written permission of the Publishers or a licence permitting restricted copying
in the United Kingdom issued by the Copyright Licensing Agency Ltd.,
90 Tottenham Court Road, London W1P OLP.

ISBN 0 582 29446 0
ISBN 0 582 29447 9

British Library Cataloguing-in-Publication Data
A catalogue record for this book is available from the British Library

Library of Congress Cataloging-in-Publication Data
A catalog record for this book is available from the Library of Congress

10 9 8 7 6 5 4 3 2 1
04 03 02 01 00

Typeset by 35 in 11/13.5pt Columbus
Produced by Pearson Education Asia Pte Ltd.
Printed in Singapore

To the memory of David Wakefield—scholar, teacher, colleague and friend

CONTENTS

CONTENTS

CONTENTS

LIST OF PLATES

LIST OF MAPS

LIST OF TABLES

ACKNOWLEDGEMENTS

We are grateful to the following for permission to reproduce copyright material:

Table 5.2 from *European Historical Statistics 1750–1970*, New York, pp. 391–2, 434–5 (Mitchell, B.R., 1975); Plate 1 Engraving by French School (Eighteenth century), Private Collection, Bridgeman Art Library, Credit: Roger-Viollet, Paris; Plate 2 Engraving by unnamed artist, Mary Evans Picture Library; Plate 3 George Cruickshank illustration in *Maxwell's History*, Mary Evans Picture Library; Plate 4 Robert Lefevre, engraved by Henry Wolf in the 'Century' magazine, November 1895, p. 25, Mary Evans Picture Library; Plate 5 W. Lee in London Interiors, Mary Evans Picture Library; Plate 6 George Walker, Mary Evans Picture Library; Plate 7 George Cruickshank, Mary Evans Picture Library; Plate 8 Lithograph by A. Bayot in *Paris dans sa splendeur*, Mary Evans Picture Library.

Whilst every effort has been made to trace the owners of copyright material, in a few cases this has proved impossible and we take this opportunity to offer our apologies to any copyright holders whose rights we may have unwittingly infringed.

THE AGE OF REVOLUTION SEEN FROM THE TWENTY-FIRST CENTURY

A t the beginning of the twenty-first century, Europe in the age of revolution seems a long way off. A quick collage of images from the years 1780–1850 can only support such an assertion: those bewigged and powdered revolutionaries singing the *Marseillaise*, taking an oath to conquer or die at the 'altar of the fatherland'; Napoleon, mostly seen today on brandy bottles and remembered in 'not tonight Josephine' jokes; textbook figures, like Metternich, Peel, Mazzini. Social and economic developments appear equally distant. The large and bulky steam engines of the industrial revolution look a lot less revolutionary when microelectronics is the leading sector; the rise of factory work is less exciting when ever more people are employed in services. The famines and bread riots of revolutionary Europe (with Marie Antoinette telling the Parisians without bread to eat cake) might be relevant to life in underdeveloped countries of the southern hemisphere, but in the economically advanced countries agricultural policy seems to be mostly about finding a way to unload the excess of foodstuffs farmers produce over what consumers can eat.

To view revolutionary Europe as distant and irrelevant is not the only possible approach. A growing number of academics see the era as relevant but sinister. One scholarly tradition, that has gained new life with the end of communist regimes in Europe, castigates the French Revolution as the birth of genocidal, totalitarian Stalinism. In recent years, feminist and postmodernist scholars have decided that the Enlightenment and the French Revolution marked new heights of sexism and racism, steps in the direction of the oppression of women and people of colour, that were all the more insidious because these intellectual and political movements seemed to be about emancipation. Indeed, the French Revolution has been blamed for both fascism and communism.

Such viewpoints might discourage one from writing any history of revolutionary Europe. If an author had the nerve to continue under these

[2]   circumstances, the resulting book might treat the era like medieval Europe or classical antiquity: a fundamentally different epoch connected to our own only by the most abstract of cultural and intellectual ties. Or perhaps a book of denunciation might emerge, castigating the pernicious trends of the period, seeing it as the origin of much of the worst in the tormented first half of the twentieth century, and source of contemporary iniquities.

Before accepting such a pessimistic view, it might be well to note some counter-currents. The political bookends of the age of revolution, the French Revolution of 1789, and the European revolutions of 1848, have recently celebrated important anniversaries: the bicentenary of the French Revolution in 1989, and the 150th anniversary of the 1848 uprisings in 1998. Both were marked by lively scholarly debate and a surprising amount of interest on the part of the general public. Perhaps some life remains in these far-off events.

This was demonstrated to an astonishing extent in the autumn of 1989. No sooner had many scholarly commentaries on the bicentenary of the French Revolution suggested that revolutions were impossible in the present, and a good thing too, because in the past they had brought nothing but bad results, than great crowds of demonstrators appeared in the streets of Leipzig, Prague and Bucharest, waving tricolour flags, demanding an end to dictatorial regimes, and calling for the realization of liberty, equality and fraternity. If, as the eminent historian E.J. Hobsbawm has suggested, the revolutions of 1989 marked the end of an era beginning in 1914, that he dubbed the 'short twentieth century', then we might have to conclude that the age of revolution is strikingly contemporary. In some ways, symbols and ideals developed during it have led to the beginning of the twenty-first century.

In this book, I will adopt a little of both approaches, seeing the age of revolution as part of the more distant past but also still close to the present, noting its crimes and forms of oppression, but including the aspirations to liberation and emancipation that were articulated then, and even, sometimes, practised, however feebly and inconsistently. This balance between distance and closeness, between continuity and discontinuity in considering the relationship between past and present is characteristic of the historical enterprise in general, and consideration of every particular epoch will result in a distinct balance of these two elements. For revolutionary Europe, it seems to me that we can note a continuity in form, but something of a discontinuity in content. Politics was divided along a left–right spectrum into radicalism, liberalism and conservatism, as it is today, but each of these political tendencies had quite different meanings then than is the case in the present. Democracy and citizenship were important and contested ideals, but the understanding of democracy in the radical phrase of the French Revolution, or the nationalist conception of citizenship was quite distinct from the way these ideals are understood at the beginning of the twenty-first century. Feminism emerged as an aspiration in the 1830s and 1840s, involving a notion of the emancipation of women, but it was a noticeably different conception from the one held by feminists of the late twentieth and early twenty-first centuries.

In a different way, a similar point can be made about social and economic developments. Contemporaries of the first half of the nineteenth century were worried about poverty and social inequality; they debated the possibility of and prospects for economic growth; they considered government policies to deal with economic problems. These are certainly strikingly similar concerns to those raised today. However, the causes of poverty and social inequality – indeed, the nature of the society in which these appeared – was quite different from the industrial and post-industrial economy and society of the early twenty-first century. The government measures proposed, and even the conception of the place of the government in economy and society were also strikingly different.

Another problem emerges in writing any general history, and is particularly noticeable in considering such an event-filled period as the age of revolution. What is there to keep all the material together? How can one prevent a history from turning into a succession of spectacular but unrelated events or processes: the French Revolution, the Industrial Revolution, the Napoleonic Wars, the Great Reform Bill, Romanticism, the Revolutions of 1830 and 1848. They may all be written with capital letters, showing their individual importance, but how does one provide a thematic unity, analytic consistency, a narrative cohesion to these many, different, significant items?

Obviously, one has to choose some major themes, some issues that run throughout the book. Any choice of themes is, frankly, arbitrary, and, involves emphasizing some aspects of the past and downplaying or dealing more superficially with others. There are four such themes that will provide a framework for this book.

One major theme relates to economics. Here, the main motif is the Malthusian challenge, the threat posed to a not terribly productive economic system by the substantial population increase in most European countries after the middle of the eighteenth century. There will be discussions of the many possible responses to this challenge, the many ways in which the agrarian/artisan economy of the old regime was transformed: changes in demographic patterns, improvements in agricultural productivity, improvements in transport and communication, changes in the organization of

[4] production (such as outworking), and, of course, the introduction of steam-powered machinery. By discussing economic developments in this framework, we will get away from the sometimes exaggerated notions of an 'Industrial Revolution', and point out how, before 1850 at least, mechanization was one possible development of many, all of which might be best summed up under the general heading of the expansion of the market and of market forces.

The second major theme centres on the changes occurring in society, the movement from the old regime society of orders to a civil society of property owners. This was a complex development, sometimes violent and abrupt, as was the case with the French Revolution and the Napoleonic era, or the revolution of 1848, sometimes more peaceful, as was generally the case in Great Britain, and often true in the decades after 1815 in continental Europe. This development involved a series of changes. There were changes in the actual ownership of property, but perhaps even more in the legal and conceptual relations of property. Along with such changes in property went similar ones in the legal and conceptual relations of labour. Finally, there were changes in the nature of public life, in the institutions by which people could participate in it, and in the identity of people who did. Such changes proved to have a considerable effect on gender relations as well, and a discussion of such relations will be part of this theme. Finally, in the context of this theme, there will be a discussion of the adherents of different kinds of social order, other than those of the old regime or a society of property owners: the early proponents of a socialist society, and the supporters of a society of small producers and proprietors.

The third theme of this book is the expansion and transformation of the power of the state. We begin with old regime governments that were characterized by dichotomies between an absolutist monarch and constituted bodies of the society of orders, and between claims of the government to unlimited power and competence, and actual circumstances little short of anarchy. At the end of the process is a unitary, bureaucratically administered state, whose powers were usually restricted by a constitution or other legal framework. While it was a more limited government than its old regime predecessor, in those areas where it did intervene, it could do so with much greater effect and intrusiveness. This is a pattern that can be observed, with many different national variations, in a whole range of areas, from finance to the judiciary, to the military, to public education, to poor relief.

Finally, the fourth theme is the development of and conflict over political participation. One key aspect here is the question of the ordering of government: absolutist regimes or ones with a division of powers; a government

based on historical, chartered privilege, versus one based on a constitution,   [5]
with a legislature and guaranteed civil liberties; monarchy versus republic; a
franchise based on the old regime orders, versus one based on property, or a
democratic suffrage. Another, related and equally important way to consider
the history of political participation in this period is to consider the bases of
political legitimacy, to see the clash between the idea of a regime counting on
dynastic and confessional loyalties, and a state drawing on nationalist or
republican ones. In this context, we will consider the broader cultural outlines of political ideologies: the clash between the old regime culture of
confessionalism and the counter-culture of the Enlightenment; the movement
from a classical to a romantic cultural sensibility.

Now, none of the four themes mentioned were unique to the era of revolutionary Europe; developments mentioned in each of them could be found
both before 1780 and after 1850. However, in the years under consideration
in this book, the interaction of the developments mentioned in these themes
produced a pattern of political and social instability, characteristic of the era
– that is why it was an age of revolution. The narrative of the book will try to
demonstrate this, being careful, along the way, to point out specific patterns
of development in individual countries, with a particular emphasis on the
similarities and differences between the peripheral powers, Great Britain
and Russia, on the one hand, and the other countries of continental Europe,
on the other.

The book begins with a snapshot of Europe in the 1780s, toward the end
of the old regime. This first chapter will concentrate on the contrast between
and the coexistence of older and newer forms of economy, society, government
and culture. The next three chapters will deal with the impact of the French
Revolution on Europe: the attempt of the revolutionaries to build a new
political, socioeconomic, legal and cultural order, and the reason that this
effort led to a brutal civil war; the way that prolonged, large-scale warfare
brought both the effort to build a new order and its potential for civil war to
all of Europe; finally, the way that under the authoritarian rule of the emperor
Napoleon Bonaparte a new, post-revolutionary order began to emerge, as far
as the emperor's preoccupation with military conquest (leading, in the end,
to his downfall) permitted.

The next two chapters will be more analytic and less narrative in nature.
Chapter 5 will be about social and economic developments in the years 1780–
1850. Starting from the general, continent-wide problem of a rapidly growing population, it will discuss changes in demography, the organization and
technology of production, and of social structure in response to them, and

[6]   suggest some characteristic national combinations of these responses. Chapter 6 will focus on public life in post-Napoleonic Europe, over the years 1815–50, considering characteristic patterns of international relations, the structure of the state, and the arenas, institutions and ideologies of politics, as well as some of the cultural forms in which they were expressed.

The last two chapters, dealing with political events of the years 1815–30 and 1830–51 respectively, will investigate the pattern of political stability and instability in a Europe torn between the memories of the upheavals of the era of the French Revolution and Napoleon, and the prospect of new political and social vistas. A major aspect of these chapters will be the assertion that neither the forces of order nor those of change were particularly effective, weak regimes and partial, ambiguous revolutions succeeding one another. A brief concluding chapter, surveys the changes occurring in Europe across the entire era, from 1780 to 1850, suggests some driving forces behind them, and takes a look at some questions for subsequent decades that would result from them. A select bibliography of English-language works rounds off the book.

Map 1   Europe in 1780

Iceland

Ireland

Great
Britain

Norway

Sweden

Finland

Denmark

Netherlands

RUSSIAN EMPIRE

Poland

Bavaria

AUSTRIAN CROWN LANDS

Hungary

Moldavia

Crimea

Wallachia

France

Switzerland

Venice

Bosnia

OTTOMAN EMPIRE

Portugal

Spain

Tuscany

Papal States

Sardinia

Morocco

Algeria

CHAPTER 1

EUROPE AT THE END OF THE OLD REGIME

Wherever we look in Europe in the 1780s, from the Atlantic to the Urals, from the Baltic to the Mediterranean, in society, the economy, cultural life, or politics and government, we see a continent in which older structures and institutions, formed over the previous two hundred and fifty years, faced newer, more recent developments, ones that would prove to be the precursors to the nineteenth century. This chapter surveys this double face of late-eighteenth-century Europe, comparing the nature of the old and the new, and ascertaining the relative size and influence of each. It concludes with some questions about the relationship between the forces of persistence and the tendencies toward change. Could the new emerge smoothly and continuously from the old, perhaps even engaging in a symbiosis with it? Or would the complete emergence of new ways of organizing, governing and thinking about society, economics and government require a sharp break with existing institutions?

A society of orders

The dominant mode of social organization in most European countries was the society of orders. Membership of the corporate groups making up this society was (theoretically, at least) fixed at birth, or through sacred action, such as a religious consecration. The groups and the individuals who belonged to them were explicitly unequal in their rights and obligations, but were arranged in a legally determined, religiously sanctioned, and patriarchally ordered hierarchy of status, affluence and power. The classical form of the hierarchy, still the official rule, for instance in France, distinguished a first order or estate, the clergy, a second, the nobility, and a third, the common people. Let us now look at European society in the old regime,

[10] seeing the way in which the actual patterns of power and affluence corresponded to the models of the society of orders.

In the original medieval pattern, the clergy were the very top of the society of orders, and to some extent, particularly in the Catholic countries of southern Europe, this was still the case. Catholic priests were exempt from many direct taxes; the church was a major owner of land and serfs – in some cases, such as the Electorate of Bavaria, in southeastern Germany, the largest such landlord. In central Europe, bishops and abbots could be simultaneously secular princes, running an actual government, as well as a diocese or monastery. The pope himself was the most notable such priest-ruler, and the Papal States covered a substantial portion of central Italy. In a society where, as we shall see, social distinction was largely based on rank fixed at birth, Catholic priests were an exception, but a kind of higher-order exception, since their status was based not on a natural distinction, but on a supernatural one, the sacred rite of consecration.

For all this exalted position, the place of the clergy was the single most striking example of how the neat tripartite division of society into three orders, dating from the middle ages, had, by the late phase of the old regime, been modified in many different ways across the continent. The Reformation, in reducing the sphere of the sacred, had ended the separate position of the clergy, who no longer formed an independent order in almost all the Protestant countries of central and northern Europe, with some exceptions in England and Sweden. There were similar developments in the Eastern Orthodox Church, so that in Russia too the clergy were no longer an independent order. Where this had occurred, the nobility stood at the top of the social pyramid.

However, even in the Catholic lands, the clergy's position as dominant order had been changed and transformed. Monarchs had been steadily undermining the clergy's prerogatives. The Catholic Church in France, for instance, did not pay direct taxes, but at regularly occurring assemblies of the clergy a 'don gratuit,' a 'voluntary gift' to the monarch was arranged as payment in lieu of such taxes, to ward off the possibility of the monarch imposing them. Nor were the Catholic clergy, for all their sacred status, entirely independent of the social order set at birth. The most prominent positions in the church, bishops, canons of cathedral chapters, and abbots and abbesses of major monasteries, were reserved for individuals from the nobility. Consecrated commoners had to be content with a more modest place in the ecclesiastical hierarchy, and the ordinary rural parish priest, for all his standing among his peasant parishioners, would have a hard time claiming precedence over a noble seigneur. Such an ordinary parish priest would probably be materially better off than most of his parishioners, but would still be living in quite modest circumstances.

All these considerations suggest that the nobility were the truly dominant order – whether still formally outranked by the clergy or not – and much of old regime Europe was arranged to guarantee their power, affluence and prestige. Nobles were exempt from many if not all forms of direct taxation; the choicest positions in government administration and the army officer corps were reserved for them. As just noted, the upper ranks of the Catholic clergy were an exclusively noble preserve, as was typically the case with the Anglican Church, although, admittedly, commoners had access to high positions in the Protestant churches of continental Europe and the Greek Orthodox churches. Not only were nobles the largest landowners in virtually all European countries, they generally possessed people as well as territories. In the eastern and central parts of the continent, peasants were serfs, required to perform unpaid labour for their noble landlords, while in the west rustics had to pay various forms of seigneurial dues. Finally, the nobility had precedence in public life: the right to wear a sword, to march at the head of parades and processions, to sit in a special pew at the front of the church, to stage elaborate hunts for game, to be physically closest to the monarch or his representatives – advantages not to be despised in a world that took such honorifics very seriously.

Of all features of the society of orders, rank as a nobleman was the one most strongly and exclusively fixed at birth and transmitted in hereditary fashion. Nobles thought in terms of 'quarters of nobility'. Four quarters meant four noble grandparents, eight, eight noble great-grandparents, and so on. In the Prince-Bishopric of Münster, in northwestern Germany, all prime government offices and high positions of the church were reserved for those nobles who could demonstrate thirty-two quarters of nobility. Most nobles in old regime Europe would have had a hard time demonstrating such extraordinarily blue blood. In France, for instance, there was a good deal more flexibility in entering the nobility than in most continental European countries. The government sold patents of nobility; certain government offices also granted nobility, either to the holder or his descendants. Consequently, a majority of recognized nobles could not even trace their noble ancestry back for a century, yet even under these circumstances, the official fiction prevailed that the king was not granting an individual nobility so much as recognizing his ostensibly inborn noble characteristics. Similar doctrines prevailed in Spain and Russia as well.

I say 'his' advisedly, because the society of orders was a patriarchal one, a regime ruled by adult male heads of household, in which a woman's place was primarily determined by her relationship to such a man: a father or other

[12] adult male guardian, or a husband. This patriarchal feature was emphasized in the Russian empire, another realm where high-ranking government service brought with it a patent of nobility. The courts ruled that a common-born wife of a man ennobled in state service was herself ennobled, but should her first husband die, and she remarry a commoner, her noble status could not be conferred on the new spouse. However, the patriarchal feature of this society extended beyond the determination of a woman's rank by her relationship to a man. The household headed by an adult male was the model according to which all social and political hierarchies were understood.

Despite all these shared characteristics, the nobility was, in many ways, a diverse group. One axis of difference was the relationship to the royal overlord. Some noblemen claimed an ancient lineage, distinct from any special connection to the monarch, the French *noblesse de race*, the German *Uradel*. In Spain, such old nobles proudly stated 'Being a *hildalgo* [a nobleman] is sufficient to say that one owes nothing to the king.'[1] Other nobles, whose nobility was often, though not always, of more recent vintage, were closely identified with service to the ruling monarch, the French *noblesse de robe*, the German *Dienstadel*. In Russia, until the 1760s, all nobles were, at least theoretically, in service to the ruler. In the German states, and the provinces of the Habsburg monarchy, the nobility were divided into two orders, the higher nobility, whose titles generally had not been granted by the ruling prince, and the lower, whose titles had.

Another axis of difference was between courtiers who were constantly in the presence of the king, and those living in on their country estates or town houses. The former, compelled to conform to rigid court etiquette, while simultaneously cultivating the arts of intrigue, might hope to win royal favour and receive rich pensions and profitable but largely ceremonial government offices. Some did so spectacularly. The Polignac family, favourites of Marie-Antoinette, wife of Louis XVI of France, are said to have accumulated over 2,500,000 livres due to royal favour, at a time when a prosperous provincial nobleman could live very pleasantly on 8,000 livres per year. However, such courtiers might also face disgrace and exile. In Russia, where court politics in the first two-thirds of the century were particularly rough, even torture and execution could await a nobleman who took the wrong side in factional struggles. Nobles living on their provincial estates faced neither the profits nor the dangers of life at court. However, they also tended to be cut off from the graces of court life, lacking a command of etiquette, dancing, or court-centred high culture, leading a boorish, uncultured existence; in Russia, many were even illiterate.

The single most important difference among the nobility was in regard to their wealth and power. At the top of the spectrum of the nobility stood the French princes of the blood, the close relatives of the royal family, or the Hungarian and Polish magnates, such as the Esterházys or the Radziwills, owners of tens of thousands of acres of land and almost as many serfs. Nicholaus Joseph Esterházy, known to contemporaries as 'the magnificent', proudly announced, 'There is nothing the [Holy Roman] emperor can do that I cannot.'[2] Most nobles were not in this league, owning just hundreds instead of thousands of acres of land, a fine country house or urban mansion rather than a colossal palace. They employed a small retinue of servants and retainers rather than a miniature army of them, having feudal or seigneurial rights over a village of peasants rather than a province full of serfs. There was also an impoverished nobility, that captured the attention of contemporaries and has impressed historians as well: the *hobereaux* of Brittany, or the 'sandalled nobles' of Hungary, who, degradingly, had to do their own farmwork on the little pieces of property they had left, wearing their swords as they ploughed or shovelled out manure. In the Polish–Lithuanian commonwealth, where poor nobles were unusually frequent, there were some who could not even afford a real sword, and so went around with a wooden imitation of one, as a symbol of their fiercely maintained place in the society of orders.

In most of western and central Europe, and in the Russian empire, where the nobility made up between one-half and one per cent of the population, such colourful sights were very much exceptions to a rule of affluence and influence. In Hungary, Poland and northern Spain, on the other hand, where the legally defined nobility included 5–10 per cent of the inhabitants, there were indeed many such individuals, whose legal position stood in crass contrast to the material reality of their lives. Yet the regionally significant presence of such impoverished nobles should not keep us from recognizing a basic fact about Europe in the 1780s: everywhere on the continent, from the economically most advanced areas of the British Isles to the most backward stretches of Russia or the Balkans, the nobility remained the dominant group, taking the lion's share of wealth, power and prestige, their firm hold on land and government favour guaranteeing their position.

The lowest offical rank in the society of orders, the third estate, was originally a residual category, all those who were neither clergy nor noblemen. However, by the late old regime, this group, generally something like 90–95 per cent of the population had become increasingly internally differentiated. More often than not, the burghers of the towns (in French, *bourgeois;* in German, *Bürger;* in Italian, *borghesi*) had arrogated to themselves the entire order

[14] of the common people and pushed the peasantry down to the bottom of the social hierarchy, although in a few exceptional cases, such as the Swedish kingdom and the principality of Württemberg, the peasants formed an order of their own.

The social existence of these burghers was corporate in nature; it was, in other words, determined by membership of groups defined by their charters of privilege. Guilds were perhaps the most important of such groups; their charters granted members the control over a craft or trade. At least in theory, guilds had the right to set prices and wages, and perhaps most importantly, to determine the life-course of members or potential members. Guilds determined who became an apprentice, learning the craft or business, and under what conditions. They regulated the conditions of employment for journeymen artisans, and who might become a master, able to practise a trade on his (I say 'his' advisedly) own account, and to employ labour and train apprentices. All these powers were used by the guildsmen to secure an adequate living for the guild members. The town or city itself was a municipal corporation, frequently composed of the guilds. Membership of this urban corporation granted burghers the right to reside in a town in the first place, and also to enjoy all that came with this residence: exemption from some taxes imposed on the peasants; often exemption from compulsory army service; use of the municipality's property, and its support in cases of illness or hard times.

Between 5 per cent and 30 per cent of the population were such burghers and their families, their proportion steadily increasing as one moved from eastern Europe, where population density was low, and towns were far and few between, to the more densely settled and urbanized western end of the continent, reaching its peak in the Netherlands – the only place in eighteenth-century Europe where over half the population lived in towns. The material circumstances of the burghers were even more varied than their representation in the population. Some, such as the members of the 'Six Corps', the guilds of Parisian wholesale merchants, or the first guild of the Russian merchants, in Moscow, were affluent and established. Others, say the shoemakers of a provincial German town, such as Koblenz or Wetzlar, to name two cities historians have studied in some detail, were deeply impoverished, and found their corporate existence helpful above all for the access to poor relief offered by membership of a guild, and of the municipality the guilds composed.

Burghers generally had the right to determine who could be a member of their corporate group and they exercised that right with extreme care. Being born to the status – that is, being the son of a burgher – was the best way to gain entrance; marrying the widow or daughter of one the next best alternative. (Women, of course, could not be burghers; their relationship with these corporate institutions was, once again, mediated via an adult male – father, guardian or husband.) Such restrictions were characteristic of the lives of burghers, whose social position was based on the exclusiveness guaranteed by their corporate charters: documents that limited those practising a trade to master craftsmen in the guild, or restricted inhabitants with a claim on a town's resources to members of the urban corporation. Burghers clung to these charter-based restrictions with great tenacity and militancy, including what might seem today like odd notions, such as the stubborn insistence of German master craftsmen that no young man born of an extra-marital union could ever be a member of their guilds. Exclusion of outsiders and immigrants, and a closely related fear of and hostility toward potential novelty and innovation was characteristic of the corporate world.

These burghers were far from the 'rising middle class', of old textbooks and professorial lectures that have not been recently updated. Although referred to by the same name as the nineteenth-century bourgeoisie, the old regime burghers were a quite different sort of group. In the nineteenth century, the designation *bourgeois, Bürger, borghesi,* would refer primarily to capitalist entrepreneurs who had at least some measure of interest in taking risks, introducing innovations, and aggressively making profits that members of such groups are supposed to have, according to the theories of economists and sociologists. Their old regime predecessors were primarily a source of stasis and inertia within a society of orders, not a fount of movement and change in a civil society of property owners. The movement from the old regime burgher to the nineteenth-century bourgeois was a long, slow process, one that we will trace in this book, but which was by no means concluded in 1850.

Burghers and their families were not the only group of townspeople in old regime Europe; in most cases, probably not even the largest group. Besides the privileged townspeople, with their corporate connections, there were the unprivileged ones, who belonged to no guild, and had to earn a living in a largely unregulated market. These folk enjoyed no claim on municipal institutions, and often had no firm right even to reside in the town, being required to pay extra taxes to be tolerated, or even subject to expulsion. Such unprivileged inhabitants were predominantly poor – irregularly employed unskilled labourers who, if men, carried, carted, pushed and shoved, or, if women, cleaned and mended. Journeymen artisans in large cities, such as Paris or Hamburg, who might never be able to open their own business and so would be lifelong wage-earners, joined their ranks, as did workers in the rare large manufacturing enterprises.

There were exceptions to this connection between poverty and lack of privilege. Wealthy Jewish bankers in, say, Berlin or Vienna, were just tolerated inhabitants, not all of whose own children were guaranteeed the right to remain in the city of their birth. The guilds of porters in many Italian cities, and the *porte-à-faix*, the dockers of the port of Marseilles, were examples of burghers, corporatively organized and privileged inhabitants, who were also unskilled labourers. Yet, overall, the unprivileged, the non-burghers in the towns, were disproportionately to be found in the ranks of the permanent wage-earners, the group that might be called, somewhat anachronistically, the proletariat.

The largest social group in late-eighteenth-century Europe was the peasantry, accounting for between one-half and over nine-tenths of the population in different countries. Their numbers varied in opposite proportions to those of the burghers: fewest in the western part of the continent, most in the east – some 96 per cent of the population of the Russian empire, according to the census of 1762. With the exception of the British Isles and scattered instances in the rest of the continent, farmers of the 1780s were not freeholders but possessed servile tenures. This means that if they owned the land they farmed – and many did not – they could only do so by paying seigneurial dues to, and/or by performing unpaid labour services for their masters: noble landlords, the church, and sometimes even the burghers of the towns. Their servile status went further, including such matters as the obligation to have their grain ground into flour only at the lord's mill; the requirement to allow their lords to hunt on their lands; to remain resident in their villages; or, even, not to get married without the lord's consent.

All forms of peasant servility could be found in different and locally extremely diverse forms everywhere on the European continent, but overall one could note that servile status grew more onerous and demands made by lords on peasants under their rule grew more extreme as one moved from west to east. The nadir of peasant life was in Russia, where rustics were forced to work at length – three and more days a week – for their lords; they could be sold to a new owner, either with their land attached, or without it, and so be forced to uproot and move to a new lord's properties and take up their life of toil anew. This condition, also found in parts of Poland and in the Balkans (then under Ottoman rule) was only marginally better than that of slaves in the eighteenth-century Americas. The main difference was that Russian serfs were usually – albeit, not always – sold with their families, while slaves, in changing owners, had no such guarantee.

These extreme circumstances were part of a broader division in peasant conditions that cut the continent into two parts, to the east and west of the river Elbe, roughly the same line as would divide Europe in the age of the Cold War. To the east of the Elbe, peasants generally had to perform labour services for their lords, and to ensure that they did so, were only allowed to leave their villages with their lords' permission. This combination of unpaid labour services and restrictions on free movement made up the condition we call serfdom. Exceptions to this rule of serfdom were found in mountainous or climatically unfavourable regions, where the nobility did not want the land. Thus, in old regime Scandinavia, the peasants of Finland and Norway, living on frigid and barren land, were free men; by contrast, the peasants of Denmark, which had a much more temperate climate and a flat and fertile topography, were subject to a severely servile regime. Swedish peasants, living in a country halfway between these extremes, enjoyed tenures halfway between them as well, although in the flatter and more fertile lands of southern Sweden, the extent of peasants' obligations to their lords was at its height.

Another group of free peasants lived in the lightly populated frontier regions of the east: in the Prussian province of East Prussia, among the Cossacks of the river Don, and in the Balkan military border districts of the Habsburg empire, for instance. As a reward for settling in these regions, and, frequently, for serving as border guards and the vanguard of advancing armies, these peasants were freed of most servile obligations. Admittedly, this liberation from serving noble landlords come at the cost, for the men among them, of having to perform a compulsory military service, often for their entire lives.

West of the Elbe, peasants typically paid dues of various kinds to their lords, were free to move about or marry, and could sell or pass on their property, albeit generally with their seigneur receiving a percentage. This system of land tenure was far from ideal, and peasants in western Europe were not slow to express their discontent with it. Yet their lot was much to be preferred to that of their counterparts east of the Elbe. Although there were many varying local circumstances, in general conditions of serfdom were a good deal more onerous in the east, took up more – usually much more – of a peasant family's resources and, all other things being equal, made farmers' lives more impoverished and wretched than in the western parts of the continent.

All other things were, of course, not always equal, and in the infinite diversity of conditions of rural life in eighteenth-century Europe the amount of property owned or worked also played a major role in determining the quality of life of a peasant family. Enough land, and crops grown on it, could even mitigate the more severe features of serfdom, by allowing the farmer to hire substitutes to perform his servile labour for him. Such prosperity, though,

[18] was very much the exception. Substantial farmers, who owned enough land to raise crops that could feed their families, be sold to pay taxes, seigneurial dues and/or labour services, and still have a surplus left over – in France, called the *coqs de village*, the village roosters, in Hessen, 'horse farmers', who possessed a team of these expensive animals to pull their ploughs – were the exception, making up at most 10 per cent and usually fewer of village inhabitants. Most peasant families in Europe at the end of the eighteenth century would be lucky to own or work enough land to provide for the basic necessities; a growing number – in more densely populated areas probably a majority – could not even manage that, and had to search for additional ways to earn even the most meagre living.

An increasing proportion of inhabitants of the countryside had little or no land at all. Some might be fortunate enough to rent a cottage and find employment, say as agricultural labourers for noble landlords or substantial peasants, but increasingly individuals and whole families were forced into a rootless wandering life, travelling over the countryside seeking work. Such migrant labourers were part of a miscellaneous rootless population, whose ranks included travelling pedlars and entertainers, beggars, army deserters, Gypsies, full- and part-time thieves (these categories were by no means mutually exclusive), and others on the move. Their numbers have been estimated at one European in ten, in more densely settled areas in the west of the continent, perhaps as many as one in seven. A few in their ranks, such as journeymen artisans who were moving around seeking work and perfecting their craft, might one day hope to climb back to a more respected place in the society of orders, but the vast majority of the travelling folk were at the bottom of the social hierarchy and treated with a mixture of hatred, contempt and fear.

This hierarchy of the old regime, combining wealth, power and prestige, and set at birth, was tangible and perceptible to contemporaries. It was widely understood and accepted as a fact of nature – and indeed it seemed to be so. Just as fathers ruled over their households, giving orders to the other members, beating those who were defiant or simply out of line, and caring for them paternally (albeit, without anyone to hold them to this), so the nobility treated the common people. Nobles were exalted; they towered over the rest of the population, as fathers did over their children. This was not just a figure of speech, but literally the case: the height of young noblemen at the end of their adolescence averaged about thirteen centimetres (five and a quarter inches) more than that of peasants, with young men from the burghers in between. In these circumstances, challenging the hierarchy of the society of orders or living outside of it was not at all an easy thing.

We might ask if there were any groups whose lives followed different principles, or who did not exemplify the combinations of rank set at birth, privilege, power and wealth, characteristic of the society of orders. The usual answer to such a question is to point to capitalists (the textbook 'rising middle class') – large merchants, bankers, or manufacturers – who combined wealth with entrepreneurial initiative, rather than with blue blood or status acquired at birth. There certainly were such people in Europe of the 1780s, particularly densely concentrated in the British Isles. On the continent itself, they were rather fewer and far between, clustered in the major port cities, such as Bordeaux, Amsterdam, Hamburg, Copenhagen or St Petersburg, and in the royal capitals (those last two, of course, both royal capitals and major port cities), attending to the extensive financial needs of monarchs and their governments. In this latter respect, such capitalists helped sustain rather than undermine the structures of power and hierarchy of the old regime. Outside these precincts, though, capitalist entrepreneurs were rare: guild burghers, with their hostility to innovation, interest in restriction and clinging to status assigned at birth, dominated both commerce and production.

Another group with an ambivalent status in the society of orders, probably more significant on the European continent than capitalist entrepreneurs, were members of the educated professions: attorneys, physicians, secondary school and university teachers, writers and freelance intellectuals. Some of these were quite outside the usual social hierarchy, the group called in Russia *nazochintsy*, people no longer belonging to their parents' social order, but not recognized as members of any other. In Sweden, these individuals made up an important part of the group called the *ofrälse ståndspersoner*, 'non-noble persons of quality', who were not members of any of the four orders – clergy, nobility, burghers and peasants – yet were also clearly not members of the impoverished, sub-corporate lowest classes. Such individuals were thickly clustered in capital cities, including the Grub Street freelance writers in London, or their Parisian counterparts, who eked out a living by their pens: a number of them would become revolutionary leaders after 1789.

However, many members of this group were closely integrated into the society of orders, even more so than the capitalist merchants and financiers. Lawyers wrote and administered that society's complex rules; teachers and professors articulated its basic doctrines and taught them to others. Additionally, many of these educated men were themselves nobles or clerics and, as such, part of the higher social orders. The French *noblesse de robe*, for instance, the legally trained nobility, who controlled the country's judicial ranks were a true pillar of the society of orders, often defending it against initiatives from the monarch's bureaucrats.

Yet there were a growing number of such educated men employed in royal bureaucracies, the church, or secondary and higher education, practising their professions on their own account, or earning a (usually precarious) living as freelance writers, who were sharp critics of the society of orders. They denounced its hierarchies determined at birth, its fixation on honour and prestige, its preference for restriction, and charters of privilege. Instead, they called for a new social order, that would be open to talented individuals, regardless of their birth, that would reward individual performance and ability, and use such criteria to judge everyone by the same standard. Voltaire, Adam Smith, and Immanuel Kant, one freelance author and two college professors, are three of the better-known examples, both to contemporaries and historians, of educated critics of the society of orders. Two lesser known ones are Vincent Gournay and Aleksandr Nikolaevich Radishchev. The former was a senior administrator in the French government's Division of Commerce, who coined the phrase *laissez faire*, and whose life's work, as an official of the French monarch, was directed to implementing these principles undermining the society of orders. The latter was a Russian nobleman sent abroad by the empress to study law, who returned to work for the government, becoming director of the customs office in St Petersburg. He became a public critic of absolutism; his 1790 book, *A Journey from St Petersburg to Moscow*, was the first written attack on serfdom and the society of orders in the Russian empire, and earned him a trip into Siberian exile.

The search for groups or individuals outside of and opposed to the society of orders thus yields ambiguous results. Some groups functioning within that society might include its strongest critics, as well as its most passionate defenders; others, working on different principles, might nonetheless help the society of orders to keep functioning. Perhaps we should reconfigure our search: rather than looking for individuals outside the society of orders, we might want to consider people within it behaving in ways that were incompatible with it. Certain kinds of sociable institutions provide a good example. Particularly in masonic lodges, but also in reading clubs and similar organizations, nobles and commoners, burghers and government officials, members of different Christian confessions and sometimes even Jews met and socialized on an equal level, jointly discussing and democratically deciding their group's affairs. Such an arrangement was subversive of the hierarchical principles of the society of orders, even if members of the groups were themselves often very much a part of that society and most of them were anything but subversives.

In another way, the power of money could distort the hierarchy of orders. In France, for instance, ownership of a seigneurie, a domain carrying with it dues from and powers over the peasants living in it, had, by the eighteenth century, been separated from membership in the nobility. Affluent commoners – Voltaire, to take the example of a prominent critic of the society of orders – could and did purchase a seigneurie, with all or most of the privileges associated with it, although unlike noble seigneurs they usually had to pay a special tax on their possession. By the 1780s, most French seigneurs may have been commoners. Such commoner landlords also existed in Sweden, and were another part of the group of 'non-noble persons of quality'. If masonic lodges and related institutions could be found everywhere in late-eighteenth-century Europe, this purchase by commoners of seigneuries was typical of the western part of the continent, one that was much less common and more fiercely resisted further east. Only nobles were legally allowed to own a *Rittergut* (literally, a 'knight's estate'), something like the Prussian version of a seigneurie – although by the end of the century, perhaps 15 per cent of these estates had passed into the hands of commoners who were not supposed to have them.

In sum, the society of orders was rather more porous in practice than it was in its rigid theory. Yet both the groups and individuals who were exceptions to its rules and the people who acted in contravention of its rules were just that, exceptions. Taking Europe as a whole, the society of orders, with its total social hierarchy seemingly a fact of nature, remained dominant in the 1780s. When we turn to economic, cultural and political arrangements, we will see how they reinforced this society and generally tended to thwart efforts to change it in peaceful fashion.

An economy of scarcity

Overall, the economic system prevalent in Europe at the end of the eighteenth century was not very effective. Productivity was low, and the efforts of tens of millions of peasants, artisans and labourers barely sufficed to provide the minimum of basic necessities in food, clothing and shelter. The poor quality of transport and communication, the inadequate organization of distribution, and the extremely primitive possibilities for the mobilization of capital made efforts to improve productivity difficult. While there were prosperous and growing portions of the economy, they tended (admittedly, with exceptions) to be segregated from the lives of a substantial majority of the

[22] population. For that reason, they lacked the capacity to act as leading sectors of a broader economic growth. In these circumstances of scarcity, it is hardly surprising that groups of the society of orders, would, as a matter of self defence, cling so tightly to their privileges and restrictions on other's actions, and embrace a hostility to innovation. Yet such attitudes and the legal institutions embodying them, became themselves hindrances to any efforts to improve production, finance, or distribution, thus creating a vicious cycle of scarcity/limitations and restrictions/more scarcity/more limitations and restrictions, perpetuating the existing, unsatisfactory state of affairs.

The economy's problems began with agriculture, the sector in which, as we noted in the previous section, a substantial majority of the population was employed. Systems of crop rotation then prevalent involved leaving between a third and a half of farm land fallow, not planted with any crop, so as to restore the natural fertility of the soil. With so much land out of production, even the very best of harvests could not feed a large number of people, or support a substantial non-farm population – which is why most Europeans were peasants. But to make matters worse, the yield on the land actually planted in crops was meagre, at most one-fifth to one-seventh of what it is today. A very large proportion of this sparse harvest was needed to feed the human population, leaving little over for extensive animal husbandry and thus hampering agriculture in a different way.

However, the difficulties of agriculture did not end with production, but were compounded by problems of distribution. Although there had been a substantial amount of road- and canal-building during the eighteenth century in such wealthier and better-administered European countries as England and France, elsewhere on the continent transport options were distinctly limited. As the intendant of Burgos, in central Spain, reported: 'The roads I have seen could not be worse; it only needs a few drops of rain and they are impassable; as for the inns, they are abysmal.'[3] Food products could only be moved by water, along rivers and by sea, limiting the chances for marketing and, consequently, impeding the spread of regional specialization, another potential source of improved agricultural productivity. Farmers in many parts of northern Europe continued to raise grapes for wine, even though it came out sour and bad-tasting; grain was grown in Mediterranean regions, whose hot and dry summers were ideal for grapes but poor for wheat, since there was no guarantee that a sufficient supply of grain could be brought in from outside.

The upshot of this situation was constant anxiety about the adequacy of the food supply. Everyone, from the monarch down to the most wretched beggar, looked apprehensively to the next harvest, fearing it would be insufficient and bring on a famine. Conspiracies to restrict the food supply – in France the celebrated 'pact of famine' – were widely believed to exist, even if they were largely in the realm of the imagination. Bread riots were frequent, representing the major problem for the preservation of public order. In these circumstances, ordinary people and the state authorities alike were reluctant to sanction a free trade in foodstuffs, acting to fix the wholesale prices of grain and the retail price of bread, closely regulating markets, and preventing the movement of grain out of the area where it was produced. Such remedies, by encouraging hoarding, illicit sales and localized shortages, gave credence to conspiracy theories and, more broadly, tended to exacerbate the problem they were supposed to solve.

In spite of all these difficulties, in the more affluent, western parts of the European continent, improvements in food production and especially in distribution and marketing had, by the second half of the eighteenth century, mitigated the worst effects of harvest failure. Shortfalls in grain supply no longer led to enormous numbers of deaths, either directly through starvation, or indirectly, via the spread of infectious disease, although they did mean the survival of growing numbers of chronically undernourished poor people. This slightly improved state of affairs was not to be found in the poorer, central and eastern regions of Europe. There, famine could still reign, and catastrophic harvests, such as those of 1771–72, when peasants in Bohemia were reduced to stripping the bark from trees and eating it, brought major increases in mortality in their wake.

Inefficient agriculture thus acted as a dead weight on the entire economic system in Europe, by claiming a very large proportion of the population to produce food, and by requiring a good deal of the income of consumers, leaving them with relatively little for other products. Demand for manufactured or craft goods, in other words, was weak, and this was the economic context for the corporate practices of the guilds in the society of orders. Sharply restricting the number of masters would enable each one to earn a living in a limited market; dismantling or even loosening the guilds' controls on access to the crafts would have threatened their members' livelihood.

The one unquestioned bright spot of the eighteenth-century economy was international, especially transatlantic trade. In the Atlantic maritime nations, this oceanic commerce grew at an impressive 4–5 per cent per year, easily five to ten times the rate of the economy as a whole. The 'wealth of the Indies' – by this time not so much the silver, gold and spices of Columbus's day, as sugar, cotton, coffee, tea, tobacco and indigo (purple dye) – enlivened the great port cities of London, Bristol, Bordeaux, Nantes, Cadiz, Amsterdam, or even Copenhagen and Hamburg. This commerce produced a spin-off effect, encouraging the development of sugar refining, shipbuilding or the manufacture of cotton textiles. Consumption of these tropical products increased and even began to reach the lower classes, once again, especially in the economically more advanced western parts of the continent and the British Isles. Commerce in the Mediterranean and Baltic Seas was at least partly an adjunct of this trade, Sweden and Russia (to take the Baltic example) selling furs, iron and forest products in return for tropical goods. Yet here as well, we need to note the limitations of this pattern: inland areas, and much of central and eastern Europe, far removed from this oceanic bounty, and unable, due to poor means of transport, to partake of it, gained little from the trade – to say nothing, of course, of the enslaved Africans who grew most of the items traded.

A quite different economic growth sector, where big profits were also to be made, was government finance. In so far as we can talk of an eighteenth-century capital market, it was centred on European monarchs' demand for cash in advance, to pay for their armed forces. Satisfying that demand, sometimes with the profitable addition of the contract to collect the taxes needed to repay the loan, was a lucrative enterprise – provided the ruler did not decide to default on his debts, leaving the bankers in the lurch. There is something odd that needs to be noted about this form of finance, namely its alienation from other forms of economic activity and indeed from the rest of the population. Royal financiers were notoriously of a different religion or nationality from the subjects of the monarch to whom they lent money: Swiss Protestants in France, Jews in much of central and eastern Europe. Maria Theresa, the Habsburg empress, who was more than a little anti-Semitic, was determined to rid her monarchy of its dependence on Jewish financiers, which she did for a while, only to find them replaced with foreign Protestants – a dubious victory for this deeply Roman Catholic ruler. This state of affairs might be seen as in some ways exemplary of the old regime economy, indicative of the separation between a market-oriented mercantile capitalism of international trade and government finance, that was relatively small and found at the geographic, social and religious margins of Europe, and a much larger heartland of an agrarian–artisan economy, characterized by (at best) slow growth, low productivity, a reluctance to innovate and a deep suspicion of the market.

As in the section on the society of orders, we can ask here if there were any exceptions to this rule, any examples of innovation and market-orientation coupled to basic production. In fact, we can point to two versions of this, both found to a fairly wide, if still limited extent in the 1780s, and both destined to spread and grow in importance over the following seventy years. The most basic involved the dominant sector of the economy, where most people were employed, and the most resources concentrated, namely agriculture.

As noted above, there were two chief sources of low agricultural productivity, the prevalence of fallow and the low yield of fields planted with grain. Eighteenth-century agricultural innovators ingeniously found a way to deal with both problems simultaneously, by planting the fallow with crops such as turnips, clover or vetch. These plants restored the nitrogen to the soil that grains took out of it, thus increasing its fertility, and also provided additional fodder for farm animals, whose manure improved the fertility of the soil still further. Around this central innovation, there followed a whole series of additional measures: planting new crops, such as potatoes or sugar-beet; drainage or irrigation projects to make use of land previously unsuitable for farming; redistributing strips of property (including the celebrated division of the village common lands) so as to make production more efficient; more systematic animal husbandry and the like. This complex of measures was highly effective, doubling and tripling the output of farm products. It was so great a change that historians have dubbed it the 'agricultural revolution'.

This jump in agricultural productivity it initiated, by enabling farmers to grow a lot more food, while simultaneously keeping a much larger number of animals, and hence to support a much larger non-farm population, was a necessary precondition to any further economic improvement. In the 1780s, these new forms of farming were limited to the British Isles and to Flanders. Elsewhere on the continent, they were found on scattered farms or noble estates, in trial situations, individual exceptions, with no impact on the general practice of agriculture. This state of affairs was not due to any lack of knowledge. British agronomists, such as Jethro Tull, or Arthur Young, had written at length on the new methods of cultivation, and their works were well known in Europe. A whole school of agricultural economists – the physiocrats – developed in France, who had taken the new ideas about agriculture and made them into the basis for elaborate social and economic theories. In Germany, a whole genre of pamphlet literature appeared, offering farmers helpful advice about the new methods, spread in the countryside by well-meaning government officials or Protestant pastors.

Yet all this effort yielded little beyond the realm of words, primarily because of the barriers that the system of servile tenures placed in the way of economic innovation. The new nitrogen-fixing crops were a labour-intensive affair – involving a good deal of weeding, for instance – as was caring for the growing numbers of farm animals they fed. Serfs, having quite

[26] enough to do, strongly resisted any extra burdens being placed on them – especially since noble charters of privilege delineating the serfs' obligations tended to be silent on turnips or vetch – or performed them badly. The various seigneurial dues that siphoned off the revenues peasants earned from selling their crops, also served to discourage innovation and more productive agriculture. Although the extent of this attitude has been exaggerated by historians, peasants themselves were reluctant to risk innovations, often lacking the money needed to invest in them, and fearing that the new-fangled methods would fail and leave them even more exposed to famine than they already were. As a consequence of all these hindrances, it would take decades and more for the new agriculture to penetrate throughout the European continent.

Innovations in the production of non-agricultural commodities were rather more common. The first example that comes to mind is the application of steam power to production – what is generally known as the industrial revolution. Yet here we have to distinguish between the invention of a device and its application. James Watt had certainly invented an efficient, powerful steam engine in 1769, but two decades later, Great Britain was the only country in the entire world where such engines were anything other than individual curiosities. Even there, they were used primarily to pump water out of mine shafts. Around 1800, the mining region of Cornwall had six times the horsepower in steam engines as did the great manufacturing centre of Manchester. The large-scale use of steam engines would only occur in Great Britain during the first half of the nineteenth century; on the continent, largely after 1850. Economic innovations before 1800 were centred less on new technologies of production than they were on new forms of the organization of production.

Innovating in organization meant evading the guilds, and their policies of limiting both the output and scope of enterprise, to ensure each master craftsman a living. Entrepreneurs determined to produce and sell on a larger scale had to overcome these restrictions and they found two ways to do so. One was simply to capture the guilds, turning them from an instrument by which master craftsmen controlled the production process to one in which merchant capitalists controlled the master craftsmen. Another possibility was to evade the guilds, by arranging to have work done in the countryside, where the town burghers' corporate charters of privilege were not valid. We can see both these strategies at work in textiles, the most important form of non-agricultural production, and the one where these innovations were most common.

Guild restrictions typically limited the number of looms a master weaver could have, and the output of cloth from each loom. Merchant capitalists could sometimes gain control of the guilds and break these limits, or arrange to have peasants produce for them, where the writ of the guilds did not run. In either case, the capitalists would sell or rent a loom to urban master weavers or to peasants (those whose property holdings did not suffice to support their family were particularly likely to take up the offer), and advance them, on credit, the raw materials to spin and weave into a finished product. When the work was done, the entrepreneur paid for it, and proceeded to market it immediately, or after handing it over to another craftsman for dyeing and finishing. In this way, a merchant, with no visible production facilities, just his counting house and perhaps a storeroom, could command the labour of hundreds or even thousands of nominally independent workers.

This system, nowadays referred to as outworking or proto-industry (older books call it cottage industry), had become extraordinarily common in late-eighteenth-century Europe. Centres of outworking included (and this list is far from being exhaustive) Flanders, Normandy, Brittany, Languedoc and Lyon in France; the Wupper valley, the lower Rhine, Saxony, Swabia and Silesia in Germany; Catalonia in Spain; the Zurich uplands in Switzerland, the Sambre Meuse region of the Austrian Netherlands (the future Belgium) and the Austrian provinces of Bohemia. Even in the economically not very well developed Russian empire, there were three rural regions where outworking was practised: textiles in the vicinity of Moscow, particularly silk-weaving in the Klyazma basin to the east of the city; cotton textiles in several districts of the neighbouring provinces of Vladimir and Kostroma; and metalworking in the province of Nizhnii Novgorod, where the cutlery produced in the village of Pavlovo made it known as the 'Russian Sheffield'. In Great Britain, outworking centres were omnipresent; some of the more dynamic and expanding ones were found in large cities, including London, Birmingham, Manchester, Sheffield, Leeds and Belfast, as well as in the countryside and smaller towns of Yorkshire, Lancashire, the Midlands, and portions of low-land Scotland and northeastern Ireland.

Outworking was particularly prevalent in the textile trades, where it had largely superseded the older guild system and was increasingly moving toward the use of imported raw materials, often connected with international trade, such as cotton and silk, although cloth made from indigenous raw materials, like wool, linen and even hemp, continued to have a considerable market share. Products of this system of outworking were sold in Europe and throughout the entire world; although most prevalent in textiles, it was used in a number of different crafts, for the manufacture of everything from razor blades to playing cards. If, overall, not yet as common as the corporatively

[28]   organized guild burghers, the number of outworkers was rising steadily. Outworking was, in sum, the most prevalent example of the new in the European economy of the 1780s, a form of production that united entrepreneurial initiative, market-orientation and production of basic commodities.

From the vantage point of the late nineteenth or twentieth centuries, the European economy of the 1780s appears pretty primitive, in many ways not all that distinct from the middle ages or perhaps even the Neolithic era. Most people were employed in agriculture; there was little in the way of powered machinery or the application of science to forms of production. This is certainly true, and we should be careful not to exaggerate the degree of change or innovation present at the end of the eighteenth century. The contrast between a profitable but marginal sector of transoceanic commerce and government finance on the one hand, and a much larger and not very productive agrarian–artisan economy on the other, remained the dominant form of organization of economic life. However, alternatives already existed, in both agriculture and industry (or, more precisely, proto-industry), ones that had achieved a certain degree of development and pointed the way toward the future.

A culture of confessionalism

If we think about culture in the broad terms of anthropologists, as a system of symbolic expression and interaction people use to make sense of the world in which they live, then we could say that in the decade of the 1780s religious confession was the dominant element in European cultural life. Whether in an individual's life-course from birth to death, in perceiving the passage of time, the changes in the weather and the seasons of the year, in grappling with the world of work and the acquisition and use of wealth, or in justifying social and political hierarchy, a religious confession provided the rites, the symbols, and the simple, popular, as well as the complex, learned explanations. Crucial agencies of cultural expression, such as the educational system and the print media were, if no longer exclusively religious in nature, still heavily dominated by a confessional orientation, especially as ordinary people came into contact with them.

In all these examples, the reader will note that I used the expression 'religious confession', rather than simply religion, and that for a very specific reason. It was not religion in general, or Christianity in particular, that dominated culture, but the specific Christian denominations or confessions: the

various Protestant churches, the Roman Catholic Church, the Eastern Orthodox churches (along with the much smaller groups of Jews and Moslems),
whose prominence in this respect was closely related to their distant and generally antagonistic attitude toward each other. Most Europeans of the late
eighteenth century were not simply devout or generically Christian, but fierce
adherents of their own particular church, whose doctrines and practices they
saw as the only appropriate guide to life, the sole road to eternal salvation.

Religious rites encompassed everyone's existence, from the cradle (baptism)
to the grave (burial), stopping for marriage on the way. Sunday was set aside
for church and attendance was almost universal. Prayers and Bible-reading
structured the household's day, at mealtimes and before going to bed. The
calendar year was also a liturgical year and religious rituals, such as blessing the
fields at planting times, or ringing the church bells to avert damage to the crops
during summer thunderstorms (a dubious practice, since the bell tower was
the highest point in the vicinity, and the bell-ringer was thus running the risk
of being struck by lightning), helped mark the seasons. Calendars or almanacs
were one of the few printed items ordinary people might have in their houses
and they were replete with pious sayings for each day of the year. Holidays
were religious holidays; care of the poor, who were, as we have noted, numerous, fell primarily to the churches; most – admittedly, not all – clubs and
societies were religious ones: religious brotherhoods among Catholics, Bible
study and prayer circles for Protestants, pious burial societies for Jews.

If ordinary people, and even many of the more affluent, owned a book of
any kind, then it would be a Bible, for Protestants, or a volume of lives of the
saints, for Catholics. This is hardly surprising, since education in Europe in
the late eighteenth century was pretty much a clerical monopoly. Where priests,
ministers or members of religious orders did not themselves offer the instruc-
tion, then they supervised the teachers who did so. Elementary education
was very patchy, with compulsory education laws a rarity (and generally not
well enforced in those countries where they were on the books) and schools
uncommon in the countryside. However, where such eduction existed, its
chief content was instilling religion: teaching children the catechism, religious
songs, prayers and Bible stories. Even more advanced schooling had a heavy
religious content. Indeed, the clergy were the educated class par excellence,
as was particulary noticeable in rural areas. In the intellectually most backward regions of eastern and southern Europe, say the Russian empire or the
southern Italian kingdom, the priest was generally the only literate person in
the village. Elsewhere, there would have been other literate villagers, but the
priest or pastor might well have been the only person who could read and

[30]   write with any facility and was thus indispensable in dealing with forms or written work required by the government. The Protestant pastors in the duchy of Baden in southwestern Germany, to take one example, supervised the work of the village council, the election of the village mayor, the hiring of the village midwife, the carrying out of a census, and the drawing up of lists of young men eligible for military service.

This influential cultural position of the clergy, considerably more important for it than its place or lack of it in the society of orders, only strengthened the authority of religion in Europe in the 1780s. The historian Michel Vovelle, who has studied with great acuity the decline of religious feeling in southern France during the eighteenth century, begins his work by noting that everyone went to church and fulfilled other basic Catholic religious obligations, such as the requirement to confess and receive communion at Easter each year. Vovelle points, instead, to the declining number of masses for their souls that people requested in their last wills and testaments. The fact that Vovelle had to go so far, to probe so deeply beneath the surface of conforming practice and belief in order to chart the decay of religious feelings is perhaps the best proof of the centrality of religion in the lives of most Europeans.

Churches of the time were very much established: protected, financed and endowed with legal powers by the government. Church courts watched over public morality, judging and condemning people for cursing, swearing, brawling, excessive drinking and the like. Sexual failings were, of course, a particular area of concentration for both these courts and the more general aspirations of the clergy to regulate public morality. Illegitimacy was scorned and harshly punished; unwed mothers might be publicly whipped. Even young women who persuaded the man responsible for their pregnancy to marry them could be punished by being married in the cemetery or having to wear wreaths of straw at their wedding. This concentration on women in such ceremonies of shaming testify to the patriarchal nature of religion, like everything else in the society of the old regime, but the very low illegitimacy rates in most of Europe and the still modest, albeit more substantial, extent of pre-marital pregnancy, suggests that the moral tenets proposed by the churches were not without their effect on the population.

Establishment of religion went a good deal further than fining drunkards or even whipping unwed mothers; here, in particular, we need to remember the dominant role of individual religious confessions. It was almost always the case that one church was established and supported by the government. States were supposed to be uni-confessional, in theory, if not always in practice. Members of other faiths were at best tolerated; more often denied the right to reside in the state; sometimes, even threatened with the death penalty for heresy. Tithes, that is, taxes (usually as a share of the harvest) levied on all non-exempt landowners – including those who did not belong to the established church, if such a position was legal – helped finance the established churches. The churches themselves owned large amounts of landed property: one-seventh of the Spanish province of Castile, about as much in the Austrian province of Bohemia, perhaps the same amount of the landed surface of France lay in the hands of the Catholic Church, for instance.

Establishment was a two-way street, with the established churches endorsing the social and political order that offered them a secure and powerful position. Monarchs ruled by divine right, and they could count on the established clergy reminding their parishioners of this fact, and calling on them to pray for their ruler. The reforming Habsburg emperor Joseph II even expected the clergy to communicate his reform laws and decrees to their parishioners as part of their sermons. Monarchs were religiously consecrated in their coronation ceremonies. At the coronation mass of the king of France, the newly anointed monarch took communion, receiving not just the wafer, as did all laypeople, but the wine as well, a distinction reserved in eighteenth-century Catholicism for consecrated members of the clergy, thus demonstrating the sacred character of the monarch. In Protestant countries, the ruler was the supreme bishop, the official head of the church; the Russian tsar held a similar position for his branch of the Orthodox Church.

The established churches also provided the main intellectual support for the society of orders. The domination of the nobility over the peasantry, the privileges of the burghers, the whole system of patriarchal hierarchy, was divinely inspired; good Christians, rather than rejecting such a system, should seek their place within it, and show subordination and loyalty to their natural superiors and benevolence and charity to those below them. Such a view of the world was perhaps more pronounced in Catholic or Orthodox countries than Protestant ones, but it was characteristic of all the Christian confessions.

Religious identity, as we noted at the beginning of this section, was a confessional one, and this applied to the connection between religion and authority as well. To be loyal to the king of England, the defender of the faith, was to be a good Protestant; subjects of the most Christian king of France had to be true sons and daughters of the Roman Catholic Church; the tsar's obedient subjects could only be Orthodox in their belief. Indeed, Russian army officers, in speeches seeking to inspire their troops, addressed them as 'Orthodox'. Diplomatic and political alignments of eighteenth-century Europe,

[32] to be sure, no longer entirely followed the confessional lines they had in the wars of religion of the previous two centuries: Protestant England and Holland, for instance, or Catholic France and Spain or Austria could be at war with each other. Yet the major war of the mid-eighteenth century, the Seven Years' War of 1756–63, pitted, among other alignments, Catholic France, Spain and Austria against Protestant England and Prussia. While monarchs, diplomats and government ministers may have pursued a foreign policy based on power politics and the rational calculations of the realm's self-interest, popular responses to this war – particularly among the inhabitants of the Protestant combatant states – still showed that confessional loyalties could continue to work in tandem with political ones.

After marking out in broad terms the general position of religion as a source of identity and guidance, we might note some more subtle differences among the Christian confessions. Perhaps the most significant was the different relationship between the sacred and the secular among Protestants, as compared to Catholics or to the Orthodox. For the latter, the two were more closely related. Corporate groups, such as guilds or municipal corporations, were religious brotherhoods, with their patron saints, on whose feast day the members would jointly attend church services. Village communities were parishes with their own patron saint; even social and drinking clubs were religious brotherhoods. Religion took on a semi-magical character, with the priest – himself a sacred and distinctly magical figure in the popular imagination – blessing the crops or the farm animals, to ensure their health and good growth, or leading the faithful on a procession around the fields to ensure divine blessing. Natural disasters such as earthquakes or plagues would be greeted with large, penitential processions, in the hope of gaining divine protection from such tragedies. The faithful went on pilgrimages to sacred shrines of saints or of the Virgin Mary in the hope of being cured of illnesses or infertility. At the great shrine of St Nicholas in Bari, in southern Italy, priests placed sacred bones in a silver bucket of water, and the faithful, who came from far and wide, could drink the water to cure sore eyes and an upset stomach. Visible tokens, such as rosaries, icons, medallions or scapulars (blessed cloths), symbolized this intervention of the sacred into the realm of everyday life and in popular practice (not necessarily endorsed by educated theologians) themselves took on a sacred character.

The Protestant world of the sacred was more closely tied to the church and linked more to written texts than to tokens or rites. For Protestants, guilds or municipal corporations, to say nothing of drinking clubs, were eminently secular institutions. They were at best sceptical of visible tokens of faith, or of public parades of piety; at worst, they regarded them as pagan, unchristian practices. Piety was channelled into church, where sermons instructing the faithful about biblical texts took precedence in services, and to the household, where reading the scriptures was stressed. Of course, the faithful had to know how to read in order to do this, so literacy rates tended to be higher in Protestant regions, peaking in the Scandinavian countries. In the eighteenth century, these lands were poor, and economically underdeveloped, but also places where the state church encouraged elementary education for religious reasons, so that a good three-quarters of the adult population could read and write. This generally more severe and abstract regime of piety was also more difficult to practise. Protestants were constantly tempted to make use of non-religious magic practices to guarantee, say, the flourishing of their crops, since their church refused to do it for them. Attendance at Sunday services, or observation of the precepts of sexual morality, although still at high levels, were generally somewhat less prevalent among Protestants in eighteenth-century Europe than among Catholics or Orthodox.

Another difference that one could point to is the relationship between church and state. As noted above, in both the Protestant and the Orthodox churches, the secular monarch was the head of the church, its supreme bishop, the ultimate source of its governance. These churches were thus very much state churches. Roman Catholics, as their name indicated, had a different arrangement, the pope in Rome having a position of leadership independent of any lay ruler. This was the theory, anyway, but in practice the late eighteenth century marked a low point of papal authority and a high water mark of Catholic monarchs' efforts to administer the church in their own country. Citing the doctrine of the 'Gallican liberties', French rulers claimed the right to name bishops, and approve or veto papal pronouncements within their kingdom. Calling themselves the Apostolic Kings of Hungary, the Holy Roman Emperors asserted a similar claims to authority over the Catholic Church in that kingdom, ostensibly derived from Saint Stephen. Spanish kings claimed their *patronato universal*, the right to appoint all clergymen in the kingdom, and by the 1750s had persuaded the pope to agree with their claim. One of the most remarkable and politically significant stories of nineteenth-century European history, that we will follow in subsequent chapters, is how this state of affairs changed, and the pope regained much of this lost authority in the church.

As this suggests, the powerful hold of confessional culture on Europeans of the late eighteenth century should not lead us to understand religious life then as proceeding in harmony and unison. Powerful doctrinal controversies punctuated much of the century: the great clash between the Jesuits and the

[34] Jansenists that reverberated through the first two thirds of the century in France; the bitter hostility between the 'Old Believers', those Russian Orthodox who rejected late-seventeenth-century liturgical reforms, and the majority that accepted them; the challenge to conventional forms of Protestant devotion by the Pietists in Germany and the Methodists in England, or the very similar sort of challenge to Jewish devotion raised by the Hasidim in Poland and Lithuania. Beyond these doctrinal controversies, we can note frequent quarrels between clergy and laity. The former might condemn popular religious practices of the latter (say specific prayers, processions or religious brotherhoods) as pagan in inspiration; the latter simply continued these condemned practices, or worse, stalked out of the church and headed for the taverns. The eminently sensible effort of Catholic priests to end the practice of ringing the church bells during thunderstorms generated bitter resistance among the faithful, who felt that their clerical shepherds were abandoning their offering of divine protection. In France in particular, historians have charted regional patterns of lay–clerical relationships, noting areas where they were relatively good and others where they were tense and strained: pattterns that would have significant future political and religious implications.

Yet all these disagreements occurred within the context of the culture of confessionalism, as it had developed out of the religious movements of the sixteenth century; they testify to its widespread acceptance. We might therefore ask if there was an explicit alternative to this dominant system of symbols, rites and interpretation of the world in late-eighteenth-century Europe. There was, and by the 1780s, the competing version of cultural interpretation probably posed a greater threat to the existing state of affairs than was the case with different forms of economic life or alternatives to the society of orders. The alternative mode of thought and interpretation was the intellectual movement that contemporaries named the Enlightenment. Without getting into elaborate issues of definition and interpretation that historians and scholars of literature have debated for decades, or dealing with the many differences of opinion within a large intellectual movement, we can simply suggest that the Enlightenment was defined by three basic dichotomies. Enlightened thinkers asserted the primacy of reason in human life over that of faith, and of empirical observation over divine revelation; they emphasized the natural equality and natural rights of human beings against schemes asserting the inherent superiority of one group of them, or particular charters of privilege; they saw talent, work, and their products as the basis of a social hierarchy, rather than distinctions of social order based on birth or sacred rites.

For the more militant minority of the Enlightened, the established confessions were largely a conglomerate of superstition, ignorance and bigotry.
Whether preventing the free process of scientific and intellectual inquiry;
overvaluing a life of religious contemplation and so hampering the economic
virtues of work and productivity; upholding a perverse hierarchy of orders;
or endorsing tyranny, oppression, confessional hatred, religious persecution
and war – the pernicious effects of established religion seemed self-evident.
In Voltaire's celebrated phrase, it would be necessary to '*écrasez l'infâme*', crush
the infamous thing – that is, Christianity. Probably a majority of adherents of
the Enlightenment were more moderate, endorsing their own confession and
seeing it as a potential ally for rather than enemy of critical inquiry, hoping to
practise a religion, as Immanuel Kant put it, 'within the bounds of reason
alone'. Yet even a more moderately Enlightened programme such as this implied large changes in the culture of confessionalism, as can be seen from the
efforts of many German and Scandinavian Protestant pastors in good faith to
reconcile their confession with their ideals of reason. By reducing the Bible
from divine revelation to a collection of morally edifying tales, and turning
Jesus Christ from the Son of God into a teacher of sensible behaviour, they
tended, unintentionally, to undermine much of Protestant piety from within.

By the 1780s, supporters of Enlightened ideas were turning up at a number
of the centres of power and influence in many European countries: in aca-
demies of science and literature, as university professors, among the monarchs'
close councillors and government ministers, even in the ranks of the upper
clergy. As we will see in the concluding section of this chapter, there were a
number of monarchs who proclaimed themselves disciples of the Enlightenment and shaped public policy in an Enlightened direction. Masonic lodges
and reading clubs, which, as noted above provided an alternative form of
social organization to the society of orders, were also arenas for the promotion
of Enlightened ideas among the group's members, who included noblemen,
high government officials, and affluent merchants and bankers.

In spite of these successes of adherents of the Enlightenment, defenders of
religious orthodoxy, typically those who also supported the society of orders, continued to be well represented among the powerful. Indeed, they even
mounted a counter-offensive in many places during the 1780s, so that supporters of the Enlightenment, while still influential, seemed to be losing some
ground. Additionally, while the influence of the Enlightenment was broad,
we might want to know whether it was deep, whether Enlightened intellectuals and elites were generals without an army, an island of rationalism and
anti-clericalism surrounded by a sea of popular piety. Certainly, that would

[36] seem to have been the case, in view of the almost universal church attendance, the strong popular attachment to practices and beliefs Enlightened thinkers regarded as superstitious or bigoted, and the lack of pro-Enlightenment literate and educated figures at the local level playing a role comparable to the one priests and pastors did for confessional orthodoxy. However, as noted above, popular religious life was not always harmonious; clashes between clergy and laity would sometimes provide a conduit, as it were, for the spread of Enlightened ideas in the population – in ways quite unexpected either by Enlightened thinkers, who also had no use for the popular practices the clergy condemned, or by the ordinary people who saw themselves as firmly practising their religion, even in opposition to the clergy.

Probably more so than in either society or the economy, alternative forms of cultural life were explicit and contrasting – not just to historians, but to contemporaries of the 1780s. The culture of confessionalism was powerful – both in the sense of being widely accepted and affirmed, and also in the sense of being enforced by the government – but it was also riven by internal conflicts and by the rise of what we might call an alternative culture, another way of interpreting the world, the Enlightenment. Clearly less powerful than the dominant culture, particularly less well anchored in general acceptance, and without the same access to the sources of governmental coercion, the Enlightenment was nonetheless a power in waiting, a shadow cabinet of practices and beliefs, whose adherents had no doubts about their own aspirations to cultural hegemony.

Absolutism and Estates; authoritarianism and anarchy

In the discussion of religion, the role of the state – the system of laws, the position of the ruling monarch, as well as the institutions of government – has been repeatedly emphasized. These considerations formed a backdrop for the accounts of the economy and the society of orders as well. It is now time to turn to the forms and actions of government, a topic of renewed interest among historians in recent years. Under the motto of 'bringing the state back in', they have emphasized the autonomous role of the government in economic, social, cultural and political developments.

Looking at the structure of government in Europe during the 1780s, we can observe two counterpoints. One was between absolutism, the drive of the monarch to rule his (or, occasionally, her) country without countervailing forces; and the claims of the Estates, the representatives of the society of orders, to a voice in governing the nation. The other was between authoritarianism, the demand of those officials representing the state to immediate and unconditional obedience, a demand enforced with a savage cruelty and violence, and the frequent powerlessness of these agents of the government, defeated by a system of administrative and legal diversity and abitrariness, that went under the heading of privilege, as well as by a lack of resources to accomplish their goals. I say counterpoints, since absolutism and the Estates as well as authoritarianism and anarchy, while sometimes in conflict, also complemented each other in practice. Linking each pair of the counterpoints was the overriding problem of fiscality, the extraction, via taxation, of resources from society to fund the government.

Ever since Louis XIV of France had announced that he was the state, most European monarchs had been engaged in efforts to extend their power over the making and execution of laws in all parts of their realms. It was not that such monarchs sought to undermine the hierarchy of the society of orders; indeed, in Russia, it was precisely the expansion of the monarch's power that first codified and guaranteed this hierarchy. Rather, the monarchs sought to increase their power and influence within the intellectual and legal boundaries of this society. This movement toward absolute rule, or absolutism, had generated the resistance of the Estates or Diets (that latter term typical of central and eastern Europe), the constituted representatives of the society of orders, and this clash between monarchs with claims to absolute rule and the Estates had generated much of the domestic political dynamics of European countries in the eighteenth century. To grasp the importance of this conflict, we need to understand the legitimation for, composition of and functions exercised by the Estates.

At first glance, the Estates might seem to resemble nineteenth- or twentieth-century legislatures, but they were in fact quite different. First of all, their members were not elected by all the eligible voters in a given geographic area, a constituency, but by order. The exact number of orders varied, but usually included the clergy, in Catholic countries, the nobility (sometimes there were two orders of nobility, higher and lower) and commoners, usually burghers of the towns. Peasants, the vast majority of the population, were either not represented at all, or thrown together with the burghers in a way that ensured that the latter would dominate the elections. There were few exceptions to this rule. One was in Sweden, where the peasants had their own representation in the *Riksdag*, the Swedish Estates. They were also represented in the Estates of the German principality of Württemberg, which was a peculiar place,

[38] since the principality's entire nobility had seceded from the prince's rule in the sixteenth century, during the political turmoil associated with the Reformation. In the assembled Estates, each delegate did not have a vote; rather, each order did. The delegates to each order voted and often debated separately, thus guaranteeing that the representatives of the nobility (and sometimes the clergy) had an equal or greater weight in decisions than those of the commoners, the vast majority of the population.

The powers of the Estates were enumerated in charters of privilege, that typically required the consent of the Estates to at least some forms of taxation and the promulgation of new laws – matters that absolutist monarchs regarded as their own, exclusive sphere, and hence the reason for conflict. However, such charters of privilege and the institution of the Estates as a whole were often provincial (and even very small realms tended to have more than one province), meaning that laws, taxes, and powers of the Estates were not uniform, but varied across the monarchy. Thus, in France the Estates of Brittany possessed different powers from those in Languedoc; in the possessions of the Habsburg emperor, the Diet of Bohemia had different powers from its counterparts in the Tyrol or in Hungary.

The upshot of this situation was that conflicts between Estates and monarchs produced very different outcomes across Europe. A classic example of the victory of the Estates would be the state of affairs in Poland, where the monarch could do little without the consent of the Sejm, the Polish Diet (which included representatives of the entire kingdom), and the Sejm itself could only act with unanimity. Any one of the noble deputies could veto any of its actions. Such circumstances guaranteed a weak monarchy, indeed. A classic contrast to Poland was the Russian empire, where the tsars or tsarinas (the two powerful Russian rulers in the last three quarters of the century were both women) had eliminated any form of corporate representative institutions and ruled like the autocrats they claimed to be. In still other countries – the kingdoms of France, Spain and Prussia come particularly to mind – the ruler had eliminated the Estates in some provinces, and could rule absolutely there, but in others the Estates continued to exist with their chartered powers and privileges intact.

The situation in France had a unique element, in that there was a second corporate body contending with the monarch for power and authority, the parlements, the high royal courts. Staffed by legally trained noblemen, these courts existed throughout the entire kingdom, and not just in certain provinces, as was the case with the Estates. Both courts of appeal and of first instance for serious civil and criminal questions, they also claimed the right to rule on the legality of royal decrees and measures. If they found them illegal, they could refuse to 'register' them, leaving them as invalid in the opinion of the courts, if not necessarily of the monarch.

The picture of a royal executive and a corporate legislature or judiciary contending for authority is incomplete and one-sided, since it neglects an important feature of the Estates. They were executive as well as legislative institutions, responsible, among other things, for tax collection, setting policy for dealing with the growing number of travelling poor, recruiting soldiers, issuing regulations to control the sensitive grain trade – in short, doing much of the work of executing the will of the would-be absolutist monarch. For this reason, the absolutist project was a problematic one, since in order to carry out his will the ruler was dependent on precisely the corporate bodies that opposed his absolutist pretensions. Monarch and Estates were opposed to each other and yet closely tied together. A similar situation existed in France with the parlements that possessed police functions in addition to their judicial ones: supervising the preservation of public order or the actions of the guilds and providing for the smooth running of markets, particularly the crucial grain trade, to name just a few.

Of course, rulers could and did try to build up their own bureaucracy to provide a framework of rule independent of the Estates, or, in France, the sovereign courts. This was a difficult task, both in terms of finding the people to do the work and the funds to pay for them. Mostly, what was accomplished was the creation of a structure of administration parallel to and sometimes rivalling, sometimes cooperating with that of the Estates. The practice, most common in France, but found elsewhere on the continent as well, of the 'venality of offices', that is, of selling positions in royal service, provided the government with money, but also saddled it with officials whose positions were their property and who could only be dismissed by taking their property from them. Even absolutist monarchs were reluctant to do this – if for no other reason than that such confiscation would discourage others from entering their service.

When we look at the whole apparatus of government in Europe in the last decades of the eighteenth century, we see a great discrepancy between monarchs' claims to absolute power and their abilities to exercise it. The monarch's officials were outnumbered by those employed by the Estates, by the lords in their seigneuries and by the corporate towns: according to the Austrian census of 1762 by a ratio of two to one. (This figure excludes the Hungarian kingdom, where royal officials were much fewer in number.) Overlapping and often conflicting jurisdictions made action difficult. How could the crucial grain trade be regulated, for instance, when, in France, the

[40] king's servants, the Estates and the parlements all claimed the right to do so and issued conflicting decrees and orders?

Compounding the problem of overlapping jurisdictions was the very modest presence of the monarch's officials at the grass roots. Except in a few large cities, police were, largely, non-existent, at best spread astonishingly thin. Preservation of public order, enforcement of the laws, collection of taxes, and other acts requiring official coercion, fell into the not terribly steady hands of the society of orders: the lords in their seigneuries, the burghers of the towns, or even the property-owning peasants of each village, whose willingness to cooperate with the royal authorities depended very much on whether their own interests were being served in doing so.

Arguably, anarchy might have been a better description of monarchical rule in Europe during the 1780s than absolutism. However, it was an anarchy tempered by cruelty and brutality. Precisely because the regular preservation of public order was difficult and the king's servants were so badly outnumbered, they found it necessary to respond to infractions of the law, committed by the lower classes, with savage repression. Beatings, whippings, and brandings were common punishments and particularly beleaguered and frustrated officials, such as tax collectors or customs agents, did not wait for the courts to sentence offenders but administered these chastisements themselves. To deal with major breaches of public order, the army would be called in; its use in policing and riot control work guaranteed that there would be a large number of deaths. In spite of efforts to limit its use, torture remained both part of judicial procedure and the penal system. The death penalty was used with abandon, not just for serious crimes such as murder or arson, but for a wide variety of lesser offences, including sedition, rioting and theft – sometimes even quite petty thefts. Executions were public spectacles, attracting a large and curious crowd to watch any officially ordered torture, to accompany the parade of the condemned to the scaffold, to see the dying man's or woman's (and while women were less likely than men to be executed, they were also victims of the dealth penalty) last moments on earth. In considering the widespread and frightening waves of violence unleashed by the French Revolution of 1789, we need to remember both the constant background of official violence and the way it developed out of the frustrations of authority.

We might sum up the nature of government in the old regime under three basic rubrics. One is the major significance of the diversity of conditions, based on chartered rights. There was no unified body of legislation, set of basic rights or even legal system applicable to all inhabitants of a monarchy: specific laws as well as the rights and privileges pertaining to them applied to each of the different orders; individual provinces had their own unique forms of representation, levels of taxation, even legal systems. As Voltaire said, a traveller going through France would change codes of law as often as he changed horses. Contemporaries summed up this diversity of conditions in the concept of privilege, from the Latin *priva leges*, private law – a law only applying to a certain group, rather than to everyone.

Privilege today implies illegitimate, special favour and historians have sometimes played off contemporary and eighteenth-century meanings of the word to assert that everyone under the old regime was privileged. This is certainly true, but, paraphrasing George Orwell, while everyone was privileged, some were more privileged than others. The private law applying to some groups gave them a greater share of wealth, power and prestige than others. In particular, nobles were more favoured than commoners, burghers of the towns than peasants, members of the established religion than those of another faith, inhabitants of some provinces, with lighter tax or customs burdens than those who lived in others, with a heavier weight of fiscality to bear. Note that the pleasures of privilege usually, if not always, coincided with position in the hierarchy of the society of orders.

The second rubric is the overlap of jurisdictions and powers. More than one state agency could and did claim the competence over a given subject. Judicial and legislative, legislative and executive functions were mixed and confused. You could be a judge in your own cause; indeed, seigneurial justice, where the lord was or appointed the policeman and the judge, and could simultaneously be one of the parties in any legal proceeding, was a characteristic feature of the old regime. Notions of impartial and even-handed government, or of public servants seeking to avoid conflicts of interest were, at best, very weakly developed; given the great significance of privilege in public life, of different rules and expectations for different groups, how could law or administration have been any different?

The third is the lack of distinction between public and private. Public offices could be purchased; bankers advanced money to the monarch who then granted them the authority to raise taxes in order to repay the loan. Similar arrangements existed for the collection of customs and excise taxes, or for state salt and tobacco monopolies. The place of the monarch him- or herself exemplifies this lack of distinction to perhaps the greatest extent. What was private, i.e. the ruler's personal possessions or expenditures and what was public, used or spent by the monarch in his or her position as head of state? There was, generally, no way to separate the two. In the patriarchal world of the old regime, the entire realm was, in some sense, the ruler's patrimony, just as a household belonged to the adult male who presided over it.

Were there exceptions to such a political order, as we have been able to trace in society, economy and cultural affairs? Here, the answer is less certain. To be sure, monarchs were not ubiquitous in late-eighteenth-century Europe. There were a few republican governments: city states, such as Frankfurt, Hamburg or Venice, and the Swiss cantons. (The eighteenth-century Netherlands and Poland are sometimes seen as republican governments, but the Polish commonwealth was an elective monarchy and the Netherlands had a hereditary prince, the Stadholder, from the House of Orange, who admittedly, did not always reign.) These were all small entities; having a republican, non-monarchical government over a larger, extended area was something just getting unsteadily under way at the very fringes of European civilization, in the former British colonies of North America. Few indeed would have suggested that such a form of government could be applied in a country like France, Spain, England, or the many German or Italian states.

As we will note in the final section to this chapter, reforming attempts to draw a line between public and private, or between legislative, executive and judicial functions had been attempted in a number of European countries from the 1750s onward, with only a modest degree of success. Attempts to end the rule of privilege had been even fewer; their success largely nil. Rather, what we could say is that the political system tended to oscillate between two of its principles: the realm as the monarch's patrimony, and his claim to administer it with the same power and religiously defined patriarchal care that a father would exert over this household, and the claims of privileged groups to the rights granted them in particular by their charters of privilege. Most political controversies were, in effect, clashes between adherents of the two principles.

Rules and exceptions

In the previous four sections we have enumerated some of the characteristic features of society, economy, cultural and political life in Europe during the 1780s, as well as the exceptions to these rules. There were certainly areas where one could find the exceptions to any one of the rules – regions or economic sectors in which proto-industry dominated; cities where mercantile elites set the tone for society rather than the nobility; realms in which proponents of the Enlightenment dominated the rulers' councils and supporters of the culture of confessionalism were on the defensive. However, the real question to ask is whether there was any one country where all the exceptions dominated, and so were more characteristic of the existing state of affairs than were the social, economic, political and cultural structures and institutions created in the two centuries after 1500.

The most plausible candidate for realm of the exceptions, a place that by the 1780s had left the old regime behind it, is Great Britain. Although this suggestion would have been just common sense for any nineteenth-century Whig, proud of his country's role as a beacon of progress, and endorsed by most modern historians of different political and methodological viewpoints, it has recently come under scholarly attack. A group of historians has, instead, been inclined to point out the ways in which the British Isles of the late eighteenth century were still very much an old regime. This is an assertion very well worth considering.

Great Britain's monarchs did claim to rule by divine right – a claim that found many intellectual supporters, although a fair number of opponents as well. There was an established church, supported by tithes paid by all landowners, including those not belonging to it. The landed nobility were unquestionably the most powerful and influential group and even held Scottish coal-miners as serfs. Towns were chartered and the members of their municipal corporations enjoyed special privileges as a result of this status. We might not think of the Houses of Parliament as Estates, but the members of the peerage and the bishops in the House of Lords did debate and vote separately from the Commons. Additionally, the lower house was elected by burgesses of the chartered towns and rural freeholders, that is, by privileged groups in each constituency, the circle of eligible voters differing widely and being determined, once again, by localized charters of privilege.

These elements of the old regime undeniably existed, and pointing them out does help us note the ways in which late-eighteenth-century Great Britain was like other European countries of the time and different from the United Kingom of the nineteenth and twentieth centuries. However, in the end, the more general characterization of Great Britain in the 1780s as a basically old regime society seems questionable. Rather, it is the old regime elements that were the exceptions; in particular, three crucial features separated the British Isles of the late eighteenth century from Europe of the old regime.

The first aspect is the extent of the exceptions to the general rules of society, economics and cultural life. While the same sort of exceptions existed in Great Britain as elsewhere in Europe, by the 1780s they had reached an extent not to be seen anywhere else. Outworking and more productive systems

[44]   of crop rotation, on the continent atypical, at best regionally significant forms of economic life, had become the dominant forms of economic activity in Great Britain. The profitable capitalism of overseas trade and state finance was closely integrated with these new forms of production, rather than being, as was more usual in continental Europe, isolated from the rest of the economy.

Integrally connected to the spread of such new forms of economic activity was the growth of a population outside the society of orders. Chartered towns with their medieval 'liberties' (chartered privileges) did exist, only, as was the case in London, corporate institutions, such as guilds, no longer had any power over the labour market and so enjoyed no more than ceremonial functions. Unchartered towns, such as the great manufacturing centres of Manchester and Birmingham, were quite lacking in burghers, corporate institutions or, as their name indicates, charters of privilege. Strongholds of economic innovation and market orientation, they were also the dynamic centres of population and economic growth. Also often closely connected to these centres of innovation was the large proportion of the British population that did not belong to the established church: such 'dissenting' Protestants (Catholics, admittedly, had a harder time of it) were still subject to various legal handicaps, but were both more numerous and on a greater footing of equality than non-members of established religions in the countries of the European continent.

A second point of difference lies in the agricultural sector, still the largest employer of the labour of the 12 million or so inhabitants of the British Isles in the 1780s, and the main motor of the economy. This was a realm of the free market, a place of hired labour and cash rental contracts, where seigneurial dues or coerced labour had vanished, and could not reappear. A little anecdote from the very margin of the European cultural world, the British colonies of North America in the year 1770, demonstrates this profound change in rural life. Sir William Johnson, an ambitious empire-builder in the British colony of New York, wanted the colonial governor to designate his landholdings in the wild territory of the Mohawk river valley as a 'manor', that is, a seigneurial estate. He was informed that feudal tenures had been abolished and the king himself no longer had the power to create such estates, so one of the monarch's colonial administrators certainly could not do so.

The third and final way in which Great Britain was unique can be seen in the organization and operation of the state. A growing royal bureaucracy, embodying absolutist ambitions and so coming into conflict with other administrations of the Estates, the lords and the chartered towns, so characteristic of much of the state of affairs on the European continent, was only a minor element of the political situation in the British Isles. Now, the British [45] royal government did create a very impressive bureaucratic structure in the eighteenth century and pay for it with an elaborate framework of taxation and public debt, but it was a bureaucracy directed outwards, towards the creation of an overseas empire and maintenance of a navy to defend it and a colonial army to garrison it.

The royal bureaucracy concerned with domestic matters was small, leaving much of the running of the kingdom's affairs to municipalities and large rural landowners. Administration also took place in a relatively uniform context. Provincial Estates, provincial legal systems, and provincial privileges, of the sort found in all large European countries (even in the Netherlands, a state and society that, in other respects, had strong similarities to Great Britain), did not exist in England. Admittedly, Scotland had its own legal system and a different established church, and eighteenth-century Ireland even had a separate parliament, so that the entire British Isles were not uniformly administered. Nonetheless, in Great Britain a relatively small royal bureaucracy went along with an unusual degree of administrative and legal uniformity.

This collaboration between a small royal bureaucracy and town corporations and rural landowners did mean that public order was not necessarily well preserved, as the 'Gordon riots' of 1780 testified. For five days, uncontrolled crowds ruled the streets of London, destroying Newgate gaol and liberating its prisoners, attacking Parliament and the stock exchange, and destroying town houses of the aristocracy and businesses and homes of manufacturers. Not just the army, but the artillery, was required to restore order. French observers noted these disorders as a consequence of the lack of an effective royal police force, and confidently predicted that such riots could never happen in a bureaucratically well-run city, like Paris. With hindsight, we can see that their judgement was not quite correct. The eighteenth-century British system did require the ability to live with disorder, on both a larger and smaller scale than was the case in the more bureaucratically organized regimes of the European continent, but it also avoided the social and political tensions that an expansion of a royal bureaucracy into provincially distinct and varied domestic affairs brought with it, whose disorderly consequences would become all too apparent in the subsequent decade.

In sum, the differences between the British Isles and the rest of the European continent at the end of the eighteenth century seem to have been greater than the similarities. This does not mean that Great Britain was as alien to the rest of Europe, as was, for instance, China: a distant realm, with only the loosest of commerical and intellectual contacts. Quite the opposite, Britain was

[46] deeply involved in the diplomatic and military relations of the European powers; Britons and continental Europeans lived in the same cultural world (albeit generally not one expressed in the same language); the great political events on the European continent would continue to have their major ramifications in the British Isles. Nonetheless, by the 1780s Great Britain had already reached a different place in its social, economic, cultural, and political structures. Historians often describe this state of affairs in terms of Britain being more advanced in, say, industrialization or popular political participation. Such a statement implies that there was a uniform path of development common to all European countries (or maybe to all countries) and that Britain was the first to move along it, with the continental European nations following along in due course. I find that such a unilinear conception of socioeconomic or political development obscures more than it clarifies. Great Britain in the 1780s was not so much further along a common European path of development as it was pursuing its own way, that would proceed over the subsequent decades on a diverging track, as we will see in subsequent chapters of this book.

The trials and tribulations of reform

Having sketched in some of the outlines of the normal state of affairs in old regime Europe, and the more prominent exceptions to it, we can conclude the chapter by considering efforts at reform. Of course, one might ask, as contemporaries certainly did, whether any major effort at reform was actually necessary. If the existing social and political system was working and its stability seemed assured, then those with power could just have left well enough alone. So let us begin by considering reasons and potential motivations for a programme of reform.

One possibility would have been the threat of the masses. Those at the bottom of the hierarchy of the society of orders, the serfs, labourers, and wandering poor, led lives of oppression and exploitation, and there was certainly the ever-present prospect of their breaking out into violent and organized rebellion. The society of orders was replete with social conflicts. Serfs refused to perform their labour services (thus provoking their lords to beat them) or deliberately performed them slowly and ineptly (thus provoking further beatings and further refusals); they took their lords to court or complained to the royal administration in decades-long controversies over seigneurial dues. In southern Spain, the claim of the noble Medinaceli family, that peasants on its [47] seigneurie had to use the family mills to produce olive oil from their olives, had been disputed by the peasants and fought out in court for one hundred and fifty years. In spite of the regulations of the guild system, journeymen artisans quarrelled with their masters and cursed them publicly or walked off the job and sought new employment. The expansion of the royal government met with similar forms of resistance, as the lower classes paid their taxes slowly and reluctantly, and patronized smugglers who offered duty-free commodities, or salt outside of the high fixed prices of the official monopoly.

Sometimes these forms of everyday resistance escalated into large-scale violent actions, such as the rebellion of the serfs of Bohemia against their feudal lords in 1775; the Pugachev uprising of 1773–75 in Russia, when Cossacks and frontier settlers rose on behalf of a pretender to the throne; or the great Horea rebellion in Transylvania of 1784, pitting largely Rumanian-speaking serfs against their mostly Hungarian-speaking lords. The 1780 Gordon riots in London showed that strong popular grievances against the government and the upper classes were present in the different socioeconomic and political order of Great Britain as well.

Although the use of troops was necessary, in the end all these uprisings were suppressed. There is no reason to think that such spectacular incidents of popular resistance to oppression were becoming more common as the eighteenth century wore on; if anything, they were less frequent than in the previous century, and the expansion of the royal bureaucracy, for all the conflicts and problems it brought with it, seemed to be doing a better job of preserving public order. Certainly, everyday forms of conflict between lord and serf, between tax-collector and taxpayer, between master and journeymen artisans, continued, and may even have increased in extent, but there is and was no reason to think that they posed a serious threat to the continuation of the society of orders or to the different agencies of the state.

Another argument that might have been made in favour of reform is that social and economic developments were combining to undermine the society of orders. New wealth, it could be asserted, accumulated by capitalists in transoceanic commerce, government finance, and early forms of manufacturing, stood outside of and subverted a hierarchy based on birth, noble status, and chartered privilege. Reforms would be needed to grant members of such social groups an influence on affairs of state and a social and legal position commensurate with their enhanced wealth.

This development is one that contemporaries observed, and they attributed the outbreak of the French Revolution to the inability to reform the

[48]   government and the social order in greater alignment with new capitalist wealth. Such a viewpoint was shared by people with very different political views, among them Antoine-Pierre Barnave, a militant leader of the early phase of the French Revolution, and Edmund Burke, the bitter British enemy of the revolutionary events. Ultimately, it would be taken up by Karl Marx and incorporated into his materialist theory of history, that would become an influential guide to understanding the developments of the European eighteenth century.

Now, there certainly was new wealth accumulating at least in western and parts of central Europe during the eighteenth century and the men (occasionally their widows or daughters, as well) who earned it did not belong to the nobility or the clergy, the designated upper ranks in the society of orders. However, the actual social weight of such capitalists was, overall, not so great as to require a revamping of the entire system. Furthermore, it is not clear that these new men and their new wealth were necessarily subverting the system of orders and privileges. French merchant-manufacturers, for instance, had taken over the weavers' guilds in Lyon and in the cities of Flanders, using them to their own capitalist ends. Bankers who financed the governments of the old regime were far from being its enemies. They were part of the system, and, if possible (religious differences did sometimes make it impossible), were likely to seek further entrée into it by purchasing patents of nobility. There were determined enemies of the society of orders present in the eighteenth century, but they were more likely to be found in the ranks of the monarchs' bureaucracies or among the freelance authors of the Enlightenment, than among the capitalists.

A powerful and probably decisive impetus for reform in the old regime did exist, the process of warfare. There had been a number of sharp confrontations among the Great, and not so great, Powers of Europe in the middle decades of the eighteenth century. These culminated in the Seven Years' War of 1756–63, which had been fought on battlefields throughout the continent, and in the portion of the war pertaining to the struggle between England and France, on a truly global scale. The massive conflict, ultimately exhausting all the parties involved, had required the raising of unprecedentedly large sums to pay for the troops in the field and revealed the limits of taxation where numerous 'private laws' allowed some of the monarchs' subjects, often the most affluent among them, to escape the burden of fiscality. It had also highlighted the inability of the existing economic system to create enough wealth that could be taxed to support armed ventures. The wars thus suggested the outlines of a reform programme: extension of the power of the king's bureaucracy to sweep away existing privileges that prevented the monarch from imposing taxes on all his or her subjects, and that were obstacles to the economic growth that could finance such taxes, and that might prevent the mobilization of the realm for war.

A particularly frightening example of what might happen if such a reform programme was not implemented was the fate of the Polish commonwealth. A seventeenth-century Great Power, a realm ruling over substantial parts of today's Ukraine, Belarus, Russia and Lithuania as well as the contemporary Polish republic, the elective Polish monarch in the eighteenth century was unable to establish any control over the country's nobility, and its representatives in the kingdom's Diet, and so had no power to raise taxes and fund an army. By contrast, the monarchs of neighbouring Prussia and Russia, in seventeenth-century power politics, rather in Poland's shadow, had great success during the eighteenth century in suppressing (in the case of Russia) or integrating (in the case of Prussia) noble-dominated, constituted bodies of the society of orders and developing substantial, tax-supported, standing armies. For such newly emergent powers, the weakened Polish state made a tempting target. In conjunction with the Habsburg monarchy, a Great Power in both the seventeenth and eighteenth centuries, Prussia and Russia divided up Poland in three separate partitions, beginning in 1772, ending the existence of an independent Polish state – with one brief exception – for over one hundred years.

If the competition of the powers was the driving impetus for reform, and the extension of the authority of the monarch's administrative bureaucracy the chief way reforms would be carried out, it was the Enlightenment that provided the intellectual rationale for the reforms as well as the cadres of administrators to execute them and the publicists who would justify them. Since the reforms involved efforts to implement monarchs' claims to absolute rule justified by Enlightened theories, historians generally call the reform movement 'Enlightened absolutism'. (Older textbooks refer to this in a blunter way as 'Enlightened despotism'.) In the years 1750–90, there were attempts made at such reforms in virtually every country of continental Europe, from Portugal to Russia. For our purposes, we can trace the process of reform and its outcome in three of the European powers: France, Austria, and Prussia. Each of these attempts to implement an Enlightened absolutism had unique priorities and emphases. They were carried out in different ways and met with diverse forms of opposition. In the end, though, it would be fair to say that all of them proved insufficient. Either they remained within the constraints of the society of orders, and so failed to provide the decisive changes needed to compete in Great Power warfare, or they attempted to go beyond those constraints and failed: a result that says a lot about the inflexibility of the political and socioeconomic structures in eighteenth-century continental Europe.

With some 25 million inhabitants (rather more than lived in the tsar's empire, including its non-European provinces), France was the most populous country in Europe, and, since the late seventeenth century, its leading military power. The shock of its decisive defeat in both the continental and the overseas theatres of the Seven Years' War gave proponents of drastic changes the upper hand in the king's councils, so in the fifteen years following the end of the war in 1763, France would experience an era of reform. The reforms were implemented in different and uncoordinated efforts, under two monarchs, Louis XV and his successor Louis XVI, and directed at different times by hostile and feuding senior officials of the crown, Terray, Maupeou, and Turgot, who had distinct and sometimes opposing priorities and preferences. Nonetheless, three general themes characterized the entire period: the attempt to end privileges, particularly the exemption of the nobility and the clergy from some forms of taxation; the abolition of restraints on trade and commerce, by eliminating controls on grain sales and abolishing the guilds; destroying opposition to royal power on the part of constituted bodies, such as the Provincial Estates and the parlements.

All these efforts failed and had to be revoked. Royal administrators could and did issue decrees freeing the grain trade, only to see the parlements and Provincial Estates issue their own proclamations reregulating it, and the police responsible to these bodies implementing their regulations rather than those of the royal government. Plans to end price controls on grain had been accompanied by a strengthening of the king's rural police and efforts to suppress begging and to incarcerate the wandering poor. This was no coincidence, since decontrol would mean that bread prices would rise, creating more poor people, before any increase in production and agricultural employment such decontrol might spur would bring lower prices and create more jobs. The government's plans for higher prices succeeded only too well. In the early 1770s, liberalization of the grain trade coincided with a run of bad harvests, producing a series of major bread riots across northern France, that have come to be known as the 'Flour War'. Troops were needed to restore order and drastic plans for a free market in farm produce came to an end.

Attempts to end fiscal privilege went along with attacks on the constituted bodies that supported them. Members of the unruly Provincial Estates in Brittany, an area of chronic difficulties for royal rule, were arrested. Losing patience with the parlements that consistently refused to register royal decrees, the government simply abolished all of them and sent the judges of these sovereign courts into internal exile. The constituted bodies struck back at the monarch with flaming manifestoes, denouncing such actions against them, and describing themselves as a bulwark of the nation and its liberties against royal despotism. These appeals circulated widely, spurring expressions of sympathy and street demonstrations in favour of enemies of the monarch. A substantial majority of the community of Enlightened writers, generally enemies of the constituted bodies and their defence of privilege, took their side on this occasion.

The attack on corporate bodies, whether the Estates, the parlements or the guilds, thus met with substantial resistance, but it was also, in an odd way, self-defeating. Ultimately, the purpose of all these efforts was to increase royal revenues, both by ending tax exemptions and by spurring on taxable economic activity. However, the abolished positions, whether a judgeship in a parlement or a membership in an urban guild were, in the laws of the old regime, individuals' property, and property, one might note, that was taxed by the government. Abolishing such corporate institutions meant offering compensation to their members for loss of property, in theory quite substantial sums, that would have had to come out of government revenues, thus counteracting the main reason for the reforms. Taking the more drastic step of refusing to pay compensation – in effect, confiscating property – would have moved beyond the bounds of reforming the system, and drastically shaken the confidence of the regime's financiers, who held similar kinds of property in government offices.

The combination of internal contradiction and external opposition defeated the project of Enlightened absolutism in France. By the end of the decade of the 1770s, all the abolished institutions and the privileges they preserved had been restored. The chronic fiscal problems of the royal government continued, only exacerbated by the French intervention on behalf of the American revolutionaries' struggle against British rule – a strategically successful move, but one that did not reverse the defeats suffered by the French in the Seven Years' War.

A similar story, albeit with a different slant, can be told about the reforms of Enlightened absolutism in Austria. Shaken by two defeats at the hand of its Prussian rival, a kingdom whose two to four million inhabitants (depending on the extent of its conquests) could support a larger army than the ten to twelve million subjects of the Habsburg emperor, efforts at administrative, military and fiscal reform had been in progress in Austria from the 1740s to the 1770s. However, these efforts developed in a new and more radical

[52] direction in 1780, on the death of the empress Maria Theresa – an absolutist, to be sure, but more bigoted than Enlightened – and the accession to supreme power of her son and previous co-regent, the emperor Joseph II. Joseph's moves toward administrative centralization and breaking the power of constituted bodies, such as the Provincial Diets, are reminiscent of the programme of Enlightened absolutism in France, but his interventions in the seigneurial system, the heart of the society of orders, and in the Catholic Church in his realm testify to his endorsement of the Enlightenment counter-culture and were unique among the European Great Powers before the French Revolution.

Building on proposals already carried out when he reigned with his mother to codify and limit the amount of labour services serfs of the provinces of Bohemia, Lower Austria and Styria owed their lords, Joseph went on to extend similar limitations to all the other provinces of the empire and then took the more drastic step of 'emancipating' the serfs, allowing them freedom to leave their lands or learn a trade. At the end of the 1780s, he promulgated his most extreme measure, abolishing the entire seigneurial system while simultaneously completely transforming the nature of direct taxation. After ordering the compilation of a cadaster, or register of landholdings, for the entire empire (a task that took six years), he used the records to declare that peasants holding land with servile tenures were now freeholders, who would keep 70 per cent of their annual revenue, and divide the rest up between taxes to the state and compensation to the nobility for their lost serf labour and seigneurial dues.

No less drastic were Joseph's religious reforms. Firmly accepting the Enlightenment tenets of the value of productive labour and the uselessness of religious contemplation, the emperor dissolved almost half the monasteries in his realm. He seized their considerable assets, using them to fund a system of public elementary education and to increase the number of parish priests (frequently former monks), who, in Enlightened fashion, were to instruct their parishioners in useful behaviour and read out to them the latest government decrees. A number of those decrees dealt with another favourite Enlightenment theme: the abolition of 'superstitious' and economically 'wasteful' religious practices and institutions, such as pilgrimages, processions, and religious brotherhoods. If such moves were not upsetting enough, the emperor struck a major blow at the culture of confessionalism. In two Patents of Toleration, he abolished many, if not all, of the limitations on religious practice, freedom of movement and eligibility for state service of the minority confessions in his realm: the Protestants, the Greek Orthodox, and even, to a lesser extent, the Jews. Abolishing the previously existing censorship of printed matter, he allowed ideas previously condemned on religious grounds to circulate in his realm.

Finally, Joseph moved vigorously to unify, integrate and centralize the [53] administration of the many diverse provinces of his realm. He introduced a universal criminal code, including such controversial measures as abolishing the crime of heresy. He hoped to engineer an exchange of territories, ceding the distant Austrian Netherlands (today's Belgium) in return for nearby Bavaria, thus geographically consolidating his realm. Provincial Estates were abolished or never called into session; their units of administration were dissolved and replaced with new government districts run by bureaucrats of the emperor's choice. Moving toward a unitary administrative structure, Joseph decreed that one language, German, would be the only one used in state administration.

Overall, this was a remarkable programme for deep-seated reform, propelled by the monarch's own intense capacity for work. In the decade of the 1770s, when Joseph had been co-regent with his mother Maria Theresa, the imperial chancellory issued an average of some one hundred new laws each year; the following decade, when he was the sole ruler, that number increased more than sixfold. This blizzard of new legislation, on crucial issues, had a powerful effect on contemporaries. Peasants eagerly anticipated their liberation from serfdom – perhaps a little too much. The Horea rebels in 1784, for instance, believed that in trying to massacre the nobility they were only doing what the emperor wanted. They were shocked when troops were sent to suppress their revolt, but, nonetheless, for decades after Joseph's death, the memory of the 'peasant's emperor' lived on among the monarchy's serfs, influencing political events as late as the revolution of 1848.

However, the very reason that made Joseph's reforms so pleasing to the peasants made them anathema to the nobility. Nobles and their representatives in the Estates tried to sabotage the surveying work for the new land register and suppress the emperor's decrees liberating the serfs. Resistance was particularly fierce in Hungary, with its large noble population. Word circulated that Joseph's reforms, from the liberation of the peasantry to the use of German in public administration in place of the previously employed Latin, were all a threat to the Hungarian nation. By the end of the 1780s, the Hungarian nobility were on the verge of armed insurrection against Joseph, their plans tacitly supported by the Austrians' Prussian rivals.

The emperor's religious policies proved more broadly unpopular. In a conflict between the ideas of the Enlightenment and the culture of confessionalism, most of his Catholic subjects, with the exception of a number of the emperor's officials, came down on the side of the dominant culture. The decrees abolishing religious holidays and institutions were widely ignored; the Edicts of Toleration, granting relief to the enemies of the true faith, were scorned by the very officials who were supposed to carry them out. As for the very modest measures the emperor took to improve the position of his Jewish subjects (often resisted by the Jews themselves, since Joseph demanded from them an end to the practice of a number of their religious traditions), they earned him the less than flattering sobriquet of the 'Jews' emperor'. Opposition to Joseph's religious policies peaked in the Austrian Netherlands, which were in a state of open rebellion by the end of the 1780s.

Compounding the emperor's difficulties was an unpopular and expensive war against the Turks in the Balkans. Increasingly, he was forced to suppress opposition, to reinstate censorship, to create a secret police to report to him on the increasingly hostile state of public opinion. On his deathbed in 1790, he gave in to the ever more widespread opposition, revoked his administrative reforms and suspended his abolition of the seigneurial system. The despairing epitaph he composed for himself, was a devastating commentary on his efforts: 'Here lies Joseph II, who failed in everything he undertook.'

Such a self-judgement was, in retrospect, too harsh. The Austrian era of reform was in some ways more successful than its French counterpart, for many of the changes Joseph instituted in religious organization – abolition of the monasteries, new schools, new parishes – remained after his demise, although most of the aspects of the toleration he extended to religious minorities and, in particular, his great reforms of the seigneurial system were revoked. However, both reforms showed the strength of the society of orders and its representatives in the Estates and other corporate bodies, and its ability to withstand the assault of an Enlightened monarchical absolutism, in part because these Estates were a necessary part of the state administration. In both France and Hungary, members of these corporate bodies issued an appeal to the 'nation', in their struggles against reforming monarchs, but the nation to which they appealed was the nation of the orders, with all their inequalities and chartered privileges, not the community of all the inhabitants of the realm.

In contrast to the fate of Joseph's Enlightened reforms was the success of those carried out in the kingdom of Prussia by its ruler Frederick II (ruled 1740–86), whom we usually know as Frederick the Great. Military considerations played a crucial role here as well, since the modest population of the Prussian kingdom was an order of magnitude less than those of the other Great Powers. Raising, financing and equipping a disproportionately large army from a thinly settled and not very affluent realm required a degree of bureaucratic efficiency not seen elsewhere in continental Europe. Building on the generally successful efforts of his predecessors to develop an efficient bureaucracy, and staff it with capable officials, Frederick required his state officials to have [55] completed a university course of studies in cameralism (a combination of law, public administration and economics) and even introduced a system of civil service examinations to sort out the most qualified candidates. Either completing previous efforts or working on his own, he eliminated or adjourned indefinitely the Estates in most provinces of his kingdom (so-called 'Estate committees', did continue to meet and audit the provincial government's books) and abolished the political powers of the municipal corporations, allowing his state administration to rule, collect taxes and draft soldiers without limitations.

Understanding the link between prosperity and tax revenues, Frederick systematically built up industry within his realm. Following a policy common to other old regime monarchies, but to an unusual extent, he encouraged, bullied and cajoled businessmen (often politically vulnerable ones, such as Jewish bankers) to start textile manufactures, placing buildings at their disposal for production, and arranging for a labour force, consisting of paupers incarcerated in workhouses, or of soldiers and their families, thus blurring the boundaries between factories, gaols, poorhouses and barracks. Such enterprises were generally offered government subsidies and monopolies within the realm.

To contemporaries, Friedrich's attitude toward religion, his rejection of the culture of confessionalism and embracing of Enlightenment ideals, were among the most striking features of his realm. In his realm, tolerance of Christian religious minorities (in Prussia, meaning primarily Catholics) was practised to a greater extent than anywhere else in Europe. Unlike Joseph II, the Prussian ruler was less favourable to the Jews, restricting philo-Semitism to symbolic gestures, such as receiving the Jewish philosopher Moses Mendelssohn at the royal residence. Beyond these measures, to ensure the service to his kingdom of subjects of different confessions, the monarch's open contempt for revealed religion, his patronage of Enlightened authors and his willingness to loosen or restrict censorship, made his capital city of Berlin into a centre of alternative cultural ideals in and beyond German-speaking Europe.

The contrast is clear between the success of Enlightened reform in Prussia, and its difficulties in France and Austria, and the results of the monarch's policies were apparent on the battlefields as well, since he was able to defeat the Austrian forces in two major wars and the French in one. However, Frederick obtained many of his successes largely by his unwillingness to tackle the central problem of the society of orders, and of economic production, agriculture and seigneurial relations. In particular, he did nothing to harm the position of the nobility in his realm, expressly reserving for them the leading positions in the armed forces and the state administration, and exempting their estates – with some provincial exceptions – from direct taxes. Far from curtailing seigneurial power, his administrative and military policies reinforced the seigneurial position of the Prussian noblemen, the Junkers, since they were responsible for carrying out government decrees at the local level and were also generally army officers with their serfs serving under them as common soldiers. This pattern of a reform effort aimed at increasing administrative efficiency and military might, endorsing or at least tolerating Enlightened ideas and using state resources to encourage economic development, while avoiding tackling any of the relations of hierarchy and oppression at the centre of the society of orders – serfdom in particular – was found in the reigns of a number of Frederick's contemporaries, including the tsarina Catherine the Great (ruled 1762–96) and the Spanish king Charles III (ruled 1759–88).

While in the short run more successful than the more drastic efforts in France or Austria, the long-term effect of such reforms remains in question. Frederick's reform programme certainly began to unravel. Although his armies had been victorious over a Franco–Austrian–Russian alliance in the Seven Years' War, much of the conflict had been fought on Prussian soil, leaving the country territorially intact but physically devastated and economically set back. To restore state finances, Frederick began dismantling his own model administrative structure and importing French entrepreneurs to whom he contracted out the collection of taxes. The industrial establishments he had built up, in contrast to the workings of proto-industry elsewhere in Europe, including in his own realm, provided poor-quality goods and only survived with heavy state subsidies and import prohibitions to prevent competition. After his death, the subsidies were discontinued and most of this industry disappeared.

In the reign of his weaker successor Frederick William II, adherents of Protestant religious orthodoxy, who had been forced from the centre of power during the tenure of the Enlightened monarch, made a strong reappearance. They gained the king's ear, reimposing censorship. In a symbolic but celebrated move, they humiliated the great Enlightened philosopher Immanuel Kant, by forcing him to sign a pledge, promising never to say or write anything against the doctrines of the state church. The Prussian state did retain the conquests it had made under Frederick the Great, and even gained new territories with the partition of Poland, but observers of the 1780s and 1790s were more than a little doubtful that the modestly populated state could retain its status as a Great Power. The fate of Sweden seemed a possible precedent, another smaller state that had been in the leading ranks in international affairs for several decades, but had been unable to retain that position.

This survey of reform efforts shows the difficulties inherent in trying to make gradual or piecemeal changes in the structures and institutions of the old regime. Ultimately, none of the reforms could change the bases of the society of orders, particularly the relationship between lord and peasant, with all its ramifications for agriculture, the basic element of the economy. They proved unable to overturn a system of privileges that weakened the possibilities of financing government expenditures; to create a unified and effective system of government administration; or to change a culture of confessionalism that provided a basis and legitimation for the existing state of affairs. The problems of the old regime, the ones that impelled the reform efforts in the first place, remained unresolved.

If we were to ask in which of the major European countries such a failure would have the greatest effects the answer would probably be France. The military burdens on state expenditures were greatest there, since France was the only 'amphibious' European state, the only one to try to maintain a major naval and land armed presence. It was a country in which the forces of the culture of confession and the counter-culture of the Enlightenment were both firmly established, with neither truly able to gain the upper hand. Both the royal administration and the constituted, chartered bodies representing the orders were well entrenched, each able to check the other's initiative but neither able to subordinate the other. Newer social groups and newer forms of social interaction, outside the society of orders, as well as new forms of economic activity were present to a greater extent than in any other continental European country, but had not yet obtained the dominant role they played in England. France was, in short, the place where existing forms of political activity had reached a dead end by the decade of the 1780s, and new forms would most need to be created.

Notes

1. Quoted in I.A.A. Thompson, 'The Nobility of Spain 1600–1800', in H.M. Scott (ed.), *The European Nobilities in the Seventeenth and Eighteenth Centuries*, 2 vols. (London and New York, 1995) vol. 1, p. 178.

2. Cited in Rebecca Gates-Coon, *The Landed Estates of the Esterházy Princes* (Baltimore and London, 1994), p. xiii.

3. Quoted in John Lynch, *Bourbon Spain 1700–1808* (Oxford, 1989), p. 225.

CHAPTER 2

A DECADE OF REVOLUTION: FRANCE, 1789–99

The significance of the French Revolution

The French Revolution of 1789 was one of those cosmic events that reshaped the history of Europe and, beyond it, of the entire world. We might compare it in scope and consequences with fundamental technological innovations, such as the invention of agriculture in the so-called 'Neolithic revolution', or the industrial revolution – both processes historians have named by analogy to the events of 1789. Other developments of parallel significance might be great religious movements, such as the founding of Christianity or Islam, or the Reformation. At the beginning of the twenty-first century, we can also see that the influence of the events of 1789 has worn well, outlasting competing revolutions, such as the Russian Revolution of 1917. Certainly, in the more limited time frame covered by this book, it would be fair to say that the French Revolution and the conflicts it brought forth set the stage for all subsequent political developments: redefining basic political concepts, formulating the fundamental issues of political life, originating the forms of political organization and representation, setting anew the scope of political participation, and, finally, via a quarter-century of warfare, violently imposing this new world on the entire European continent, in doing so changing international boundaries and the very nature of sovereign states. The effects of the revolution, however, went far beyond just the narrowly political, impinging on intellectual, social, economic, and cultural developments.

An event with such an enormous effect, and one produced with so much heated controversy and, we must note, with so much bloodshed, can only have been deeply divisive, pitting many varieties of adherents against an equally varied group of enemies. This polarizing effect of the French Revolution was strongly felt in the first half of the nineteenth century, and has by no means [59] vanished from the world. The extraordinarily tense debates among historians – generally a phlegmatic and detached group – on the occasion of the revolution's bicentenary in 1989 testify to its continuing ability to create discord and conflict, although happily on this occasion, in contrast to the wars of 1792–1815, or the revolutions of 1820, 1830 and 1848, no blood was actually spilled.

Thus we have a deeply significant event, complex in its structures, with manifold implications – and highly controversial to boot. One could discuss it for a lifetime, but in order to compress an account of it into the short space of one chapter, we will consider the revolution as an attempt to restructure in a fundamental way the political and social universe of the old regime. This attempt was unsuccessful in the short run, but in the longer term it would lead to a new order of things, that would characterize much of the nineteenth century – and a surprising amount of the twentieth. Beginning with the fiscal and governmental crisis of the old regime at the end of the 1780s, the account will show how, in the spring and summer of 1789 a crisis of the old regime became a revolution, a restructuring of the bases of social and political life. This occurred in different ways across the entire French kingdom, at all levels of the social hierarchy and in all possible realms of political decision-making.

The story will then move to the new order that the revolutionaries created in the two years after 1789, outlining some of its basic structures, and also showing its inherent instabilities. Basically, this restructuring occurred in the context of the social tensions, economic limitations and intellectual assumptions inherited from the society of the old regime, and produced not consensus but conflict – conflict over the exercise of public authority, over the nature of political participation, over the redefinition of the use of property, over the place of religion in a new public order – conflict that progressively sharpened until France was engulfed in a fierce civil war. The final portion of this chapter describes the search for the right variant on the revolutionary restructuring, one that would end the strife and create the bases for a political consensus. In the end, the search proved fruitless and the seemingly endless political conflicts were resolved by the creation of an authoritarian regime, but the many different solutions proposed in the years between 1792 and 1799 would become the starting points for different political traditions in the nineteenth century.

[60] The last crisis of the old regime

The mid-1780s saw the development of yet another fiscal crisis of the French monarchy, a chronic problem that had dogged it for a century. Like previous crises, this one was the result of military expenditures, in this case, the French intervention in the American War of Independence. The ultimate success of the North American colonials with French aid had been a major blow to the British empire, France's long-standing maritime and colonial rival, but had produced no material advantages for France that would have compensated for the war costs. These had been met primarily by borrowing, leaving a perennial budget deficit of some eighty million livres that persisted into peacetime, and had multiplied steadily as yearly deficits were covered with still more borrowing.

Louis XVI attempted to resolve this crisis by a series of measures similar to those attempted twenty years previously: introduction of new taxes, payable by all landowners, including the nobility, and the deregulation of the grain trade, to increase prices, output and productivity, thus creating more wealth to be taxed. The monarch and his advisers, the men who actually proposed the measures the king adopted, did attempt an innovation in comparison to these previous efforts. Instead of simply decreeing these reforms, and facing embittered opposition from the constituted bodies of the society of orders, they would engineer public consent by pretending to ask for advice about policy from individuals of the highest social rank. In 1786, the monarch summoned an 'Assembly of Notables', consisting of high-ranking nobles, senior members of the royal bureaucracy, and of the Provincial Estates and the sovereign courts. Its members were carefully chosen for their willingness to consent to the measures the king and his advisers had in mind.

The scheme misfired, because the Assembly refused to endorse the royal plans. Going ahead in spite of this, the government met the expected opposition to its decrees from the constituted bodies and acted as in the past: demanding that the parlements cooperate, and, on their refusal, dissolving the courts and sending their magistrates into external exile. The courts and the Provincial Estates issued flaming manifestoes, denouncing the royal government in the name of the nation, as they had in the controversies of the era of reform in the 1770s, and, as had also been the case back then, there were public demonstrations of support for them in Paris and provincial cities. A major riot in the city of Grenoble, in defence of the parlement of Dauphiné, led to clashes in the streets between civilians and soldiers. The town's inhabitants climbed onto their tiled roofs and began throwing them on the military – hence the name of the riots, the 'Day of the Tiles'.

France was once again experiencing a clash between the monarch, with his pretentions to absolutist rule, and the constituted bodies of the society of orders, the classic form of political conflict in the old regime. By 1788, it was clear that the monarch was emerging as the loser of this conflict. The government's finances were much worse than previously, with almost half the tax revenue going to fund debt service. Extensive borrowing was required to keep the royal government and armed forces in operation, thus piling up more debt and taking a still greater proportion of taxes to service it. At least the urban members of the Third Estate, from the monarch's bankers down to journeymen artisans and labourers, increasingly looked to the noble-dominated corporate bodies as representing them against a regime that seemed to be bent on little more than raising taxes. By 1788, Louis XVI was forced to agree to a major demand of the opposition emerging from the highest ranks of the society of orders. Consent to new taxation would require the summoning of the Estates General. Unlike the Estates of provinces such as Brittany or Languedoc, that had met regularly in the eighteenth century, this body representing the three orders – clergy, nobility and commoners – from the entire French kingdom had last met over one hundred and fifty years previously, in 1614.

Historians often refer to the events of the years 1786–88 as the 'pre-revolution', or the 'aristocratic revolution', yet such a nomenclature is misleading. The conclusion of the conflict of 1786–88, the king's summoning of the Estates General, after that body had been in abeyance for so many decades, seemed to mark a drastic shift in power within France, from the monarch and his bureaucratic administration built up in the course of the seventeenth and eighteenth centuries, to the constituted bodies of the society of orders, that had been both products and opponents of this development. Yet the conflict and its outcome were within the parameters of the social and political life of the old regime; they were precisely not a revolution, a change of these basic parameters. The year between the summoning of the Estates General in July 1788 and its meeting in June 1789 would see the transformation of the situation, from a clash within the political and social framework of the old regime, to a conflict over whether or not that framework should be retained or destroyed.

[62] From crisis of the old regime to revolutionary situation

It was the summoning of the Estates General, a legislative body that would, at the very least, have a role in the radical reshaping of taxation, that would be the vehicle for the transformation of the conflict. When these Estates had last met in 1614, their members, as was characteristic of such corporate legislatures, had debated and voted by order: all the deputies of the clergy had, jointly, one vote; all of the nobility one vote, and all of the commons one vote. Hence, precedent would imply that the representatives of the two highest orders, together less than 5 per cent of the entire population, could outvote the representatives of the common people, the Third Estate. An arrangement that was self-evident at the beginning of the seventeenth century was no longer so, after the growth in affluence and self-confidence of the the upper strata of the Third Estate and after the development of the counter-culture of the Enlightenment and the efforts at Enlightened governmental reform in France and other European countries.

A growing number of petitions, pamphlets and other forms of demands, from across the entire kingdom, loosely coordinated by the 'committee of thirty', a Paris-based group of reform-minded noblemen and professionals, demanded two basic changes in the voting procedure of the future Estates General. They called for the delegates to debate and vote together and for each delegate to have one vote, rather than the orders voting separately – 'voting by head', instead of 'voting by order'. Additionally, they demanded, along the lines of the situation in some of the provincial estates, that the delegates representing the Third Estate be twice as numerous as those representing either the nobility or the clergy, a demand quickly dubbed 'doubling the Third'.

Such demands met with the fierce resistance of the constituted bodies of the society of orders. The parlements unanimously condemned them, as did many of the noble-dominated Provincial Estates. All of a sudden, the locus of public debate shifted, from the familiar conflict of the old regime, the clash between absolutism and the society of orders, to a new and different issue: should the society of orders continue to be the basis for France's political organization? Members of the urban Third Estate who had previously cheered the parlements and demonstrated in the streets for them, turned against them. The nobility of the western province of Brittany, the heart and soul of corporate opposition to royal absolutism for decades, announced its intent to boycott the entire elections to the

Estates General, rather than submit to voting by head or a doubling of [63]
the Third.

Louis XVI, with the characteristic equivocation and vacillation that would prove disastrous for him over the next few years, agreed to the demand for doubling the Third, but was silent on the other issue, whether the delegates would vote by order or by head. With this question unresolved, the French turned in the first half of 1789 to electing delegates to the Estates General. The elections themselves were conducted, as might be expected in view of the old regime's reliance on local or provincial charters of privilege, according to a myriad of different rules and different regulations for each of the three orders. In general, though, these elections were indirect and multi-staged: voters gathered in initial assemblies and chose electors, who then travelled to a more central location to meet once again and choose the actual deputies. The franchise in the first two estates depended on membership in those privileged orders; for the Third Estate, generally adult male heads of household, with considerable local variations in the amount of property they held, had the vote: a substantial majority of them in the countryside, generally a minority in larger towns. Women could not usually vote, but since there was no universal rule restricting the franchise to men – as there were no universal rules about the franchise in any other way – in scattered instances, a few women could also participate in the process.

Perhaps the most interesting feature of the entire elections was the voters' and the electors' drawing up of *cahiers de doléance*, 'notebooks of grievances', lists of complaints and suggestions for improvements that were to serve as a guide to the deputies finally elected. These lists of grievances are revealing of the currents of opinion at the very end of the society of orders in France. As varied and individual as the conditions for the franchise, the grievances also often contained many issues of local or regional importance, relating, we might say today, to the promotion of special interests. Some general trends did emerge, though, showing the very different approaches of the different orders. The nobility and the clergy concentrated their fire on royal absolutism, denouncing the monarch's arbitrary rule. They called for the creation of a regular legislature, with authority to consent to taxation and state expenditures, as well as legal guarantees for such matters as freedom of expression or protection from abitary arrest. When it came to the question of their privileges, however, members of the first two orders saw relatively little in need of reform. By contrast, the grievances of the Third Estate, while also condemning absolutist rule, generally included sections roundly denouncing the prerogatives of the first two orders. The powerful grievances of the peasants, a

[64] substantial majority of the Third Estate, against the seigneurial system, however, tended to get edited out of the lists that were written down, since the
whole process of electing the commoners' deputies was controlled by educated
professionals, such as lawyers and notaries, middle-class landowners, or
merchants. These were groups with little sympathy for the French farmers'
problems and many were, themselves, owners of seigneuries. This gap between
city and country was, in its own way, as large as the one between the first two
Estates and the third, and would play a major role in the further course of the
revolution.

Overall, though, we should see the debates on grievances and the election
of the deputies to the Estates General as a process of politicization taking
place on an unprecedented scale. Much of the adult, male French population
had been drawn directly into the debate on the kingdom's future that had
begun among the elite. When the Estates General met in the royal capital of
Versailles, outside Paris, in May 1789, the question of whether it would vote
by orders, as in the old regime, or by head, that is, in a new and different – a
revolutionary – fashion had not yet been decided. Yet the elections to the
Estates General themselves, just by the enormous political participation they
generated, far beyond the narrowly circumscribed groups that previously had
a voice in deciding public policy, marked a decisive break with the old regime.

The opening ceremonies of the Estates General, a festive procession followed by church services, showed the proponents of a society of orders firmly
in charge. Deputies of the Third Estate were to dress entirely in black (leaving the more colourful clothing for the higher orders), march at the rear of
the procession and sit at the back of the church. The first business meetings
were, in this respect, no different: following a lengthy – and largely inaudible
– address to all the deputies together by the new, reform-oriented, comptrol-
ler general (the king's chief minister, in charge of government finances) Jacques
Necker, the three Estates were then sent to meet and debate separately. Such
a procedure strongly suggested that the king and his advisers were setting up
a vote by orders, in spite of the doubling of the Third.

The deputies for the Third Estate resolved to resist this direction. They
agreed that they would only act jointly with the deputies of the first two
Estates and would take no action separately, not even verifying their cre-
dentials, the initial step in parliamentary proceedings. However, the adherents of a society of orders made up a majority of the representatives of the
nobility and the clergy, and they refused to act jointly with the commoners.
After a six-week long stalemate, the deputies of the Third Estate took a
drastic – indeed, revolutionary – step. They proclaimed themselves a new

representative body, the National Assembly, and announced that taxes could [65] only be paid with the National Assembly's consent. Appalled by this challenge to his authority, the monarch sent soldiers several days later to drive the deputies from their meeting hall. They reassembled in an ad hoc venue, the royal tennis courts, and swore to meet wherever they had to and never to allow their assembly to be dissolved until it had given France a new constitution.

Let us underscore what was new about these acts, what represented a drastic break with the past, what made this the onset of a revolution. In the conflicts of the old regime, and not just in France, but in other parts of Europe as well, the corporate bodies of the society of orders had resisted the will of the absolutist monarch and proclaimed that they were acting on behalf of the nation. Their nation, though, was a nation of the society of orders, embodied in the representatives of the nobility, and sometimes the clergy. Commoners, the vast majority of the population, were either not conceived of as part of the nation, or were understood as, at best, a subordinate part, bound to obey the higher estates, who would act on their behalf. The declarations and oaths of the National Assembly proposed a profoundly different version of the nation, one composed of all the inhabitants of the territory of the realm, knowing no distinctions of birth and of order. As representatives of the Third Estate, that is, of 95 per cent of the entire French population, the deputies felt they had the right to speak for the nation in this new understanding of it.

Popular violence and the institutionalization of the revolution

It was one thing to have a new conception of the foundations of French public life, but quite another to make that conception the basis of state and society. The bold stand taken by the deputies of the Third Estate moved a minority of the noble and clerical deputies (admittedly, mostly those who were already sympathetic to the idea of the Estates General voting by head) to join them in their National Assembly, and even to persuade the king to back down and agree to the convocation of the entire Estates General in joint session. Yet the situation in Versailles remained tense and unresolved; the broader claims of the National Assembly, expressed in the oath of the tennis courts, were not yet recognized by the king or the deputies of the other two Estates. Equally unclear was the relationship between the events in the

[66] capital and those in the rest of the French kingdom, with its twenty-seven million inhabitants. Three violent mass movements, occurring in July 1789, would ensure the victory of the new forms of politics invented by the deputies of the National Assembly; they, in turn, would vigorously make use of these to institutionalize their innovations. At the end of this process, however, say by the fall of 1789, what contemporaries were already calling the 'old regime' would lie in ruins, but it was not replaced with a new one so much as with a series of unresolved issues that would generate still more conflict.

The most celebrated of the mass movements of July 1789, and the one most directly connected to the political situation in Versailles, was centred on Paris, the kingdom's largest city. Although Louis XVI had seemed to make concessions to the deputies of the Third Estate, under the influence of hardliners at court, including his brother, the count of Provence and his wife, the Austrian princess Marie-Antoinette, he had summoned a number of regiments from the frontiers to take up postitions in and around Versailles. It was difficult to avoid the impression that the purpose of these troops was to intimidate the deputies to the National Assembly or simply to send them home. The electors of the deputies of the Third Estate representing the city of Paris met in a body and called on the Parisians to arm themselves to defend the assembly from these threats against it.

They met with a tremendous response, not just from the well-to-do inhabitants, who had been the only ones able to vote for the Estates General, but from the small businessmen, craftsmen and labourers of the city as well. To understand their response, we need to realize that the harvest of 1788 had been extraordinarily poor and that bread prices in the spring and summer of 1789 were at their highest for eighty years. For the Parisian common people, who had believed, for decades, in the existence of a 'pact of famine', a sinister conspiracy of aristocrats and the clergy to hold grain off the market and raise the price of basic necessities, the need to spring to arms against sinister conspirators aiming at the Third Estate was only too clear. Tens of thousands of Parisians gathered together and scoured the city, searching for weapons. On 14 July 1789, they turned their attention to the fortress of the Bastille, stormed it, and seized it, after a running battle with its military garrison.

Although the insurgents were primarily interested in the fortress for the weapons they hoped to find stored there, the Bastille was also a famous symbol of absolutist rule, a place where people, seized by royal order without any legal charges brought against them, could be imprisoned indefinitely. Its capture by large masses of the common people of Paris was perceived immediately by contemporaries as a symbol of victory over tyranny, and it [67] remains known as such down to the present. More immediately, the half-hearted defence of the soldiers manning it and the increasingly open sympathies for the Parisian insurgents on the part of soldiers in the regiments summoned by the king, made it clear to the vacillating monarch that he lacked the means to intimidate the National Assembly. Louis XVI conceded to its demands, recognizing it as the instrument of the constitutional, legal and administrative reorganization of France, and ordered the reluctant deputies of the first two Estates to join its sessions, and abandon their adherence to the rules of the society of orders – which they did, if more than a little unwillingly.

The six hundred Parisian electors who had loosely coordinated the popular insurrection of mid-July also seized control of the municipal government in the kingdom's largest city from the previous corporate and royal administrators. This step was imitated throughout the kingdom in the second of the major mass movements of the summer of 1789, the 'municipal revolution'. Informed by correspondence with their elected deputies of the proceedings in Paris and Versailles, electors and other political activists of the Third Estate moved to oust corporatively elected municipal governments and direct representatives of absolutist rule. Such a transfer of authority occurred, at least partially, in twenty-six of the thirty largest cities in the kingdom, and many of the smaller ones as well, sometimes in relatively peaceful fashion, sometimes after tumultuous gatherings of the urban middle and lower classes and searches for weapons (often turned over willingly by soldiers sympathetic to the insurgents), and sometimes after bread riots or wider outbreaks of street fighting. The intertwined authority of the monarch and the constituted bodies of the society of orders thus collapsed, not just at the centre of the French state, in the royal capital and the kingdom's nearby largest city, but in urban areas throughout the realm.

Now 80 per cent of the French lived in rural areas in 1789, thus beyond the immediate effect of the municipal revolution. However, the third, the most widespread and perhaps the most significant of the three violent mass movements of the summer of 1789 took place in the countryside. It was the scene of the 'Great Fear', a mass panic resulting from the rumour that bands of brigands, or invading foreign troops, were marching through rural areas, destroying the grain crops before they could be harvested. Although the rumours were, of course, untrue, they had a basis in the very real fears of the countryfolk. There may not have been any actual brigands, but, as we saw in Chapter 1, there were growing numbers of the lowest classes of the French population, living without a fixed abode, moving around seeking work, begging or stealing to

[68]   stay alive. Foreign troops were sighted in border regions that had been in past decades the scenes of actual invasions, and tales of the destruction of the crops fitted all too well into the mood of a population deeply worried about the food supply as a result of the catastrophic harvest of the previous year.

The way in which the country people acted on these rumours shows the political background to the events. Often, it was said that the brigands, or even the foreign troops, were in the pay of clerical and especially noble conspirators, the enemies of the Third Estate. In many regions of France, peasants, generally led by the wealthiest and most influential farmers in the village, stormed the castles of the nobility, forced nobles and other seigneurs to renounce 'voluntarily' their feudal and seigneurial privileges, burned charters of these privileges and destroyed symbols of noble domination, such as the weather-vanes on the roofs of castles. From there, the peasants moved into a broader uprising, chopping wood in the forests, unrestrained by the owners of the woodlands or government regulations on forest use, and attacking tax collectors, customs agents, or officials of the state salt monopoly. Less well informed about the exact nature of the struggles in Versailles than the municipal revolutionaries, French peasants used their own awareness – vague and distorted thought it may have been – of the political conflicts in the capital to launch their own attacks on the local representatives of privilege and absolutism.

Making skilful and determined use of these mass movements, the former leaders of the Third Estate, now joined by the reform-minded deputies of the clergy and the nobility in the National Assembly, making up a group dubbed the 'patriots', acted swiftly to make the changes irreversible. In August 1789, they moved through the Assembly two great declarations that would have such an effect. The first emerged from the Assembly session on the night of 4 August, originally devoted to measures needed to be taken to restore law and order in the wake of the widespread violent mass movements. Patriot deputies, however, had prepared in advance motions to abolish seigneurial dues and end exemptions from taxation. Unexpectedly, these met with a sympathetic response from the deputies and the movement snowballed, as one motion after another was carried, abolishing all seigneurial privileges, the tithe, municipal and provincial exemptions on taxation, and the perquisites of the guilds. There were elements of cynicism in this conglomerate of motions, as noble deputies responded to clergymen calling for the abolition of seigneurial dues by moving the abolition of the tithe, the dues on crops that were the source of much of the clergy's income. Side by side with such calculations, however, was the feeling that the private laws, regulating distinctions based on birth and chartered rights had no place in a reformed French state and society. One [69] deputy summed it up: 'Let us abandon all distinctions; let us only regret that we have nothing else left to sacrifice; let us consider that henceforth the title of "Frenchman" will be distinction enough for every generous soul.'[1]

As the deputies themselves put it, they had in that session of early August 'abolished the feudal regime', eliminating the whole structure of privilege and replacing it with the idea of a nation composed of equal citizens. At the end of the month, they followed up this initiative by drawing up a blueprint of the new political, civic and social order they intended to create. This document, the 'Declaration of the Rights of Man and Citizen', formally approved by the National Assembly on 26 August, after a week-long debate, would preserve for the revolutionaries themselves, and for posterity, their notions about the world.

The seventeen articles of the declaration cover three basic aspects of public life: the source of the government's authority, the rights of citizens, and the forms of the application of the laws. On the first point, the declaration was crystal clear. Article three stated that sovereignty, the basis of legitimate rule, rested in the nation; all authority could only be exercised in its name. On the second point, the declaration enumerated a list of basic rights and offered examples of their application. These included what would become the classic civil liberties – freedom of speech, of the press, and of the exercise of religion – and a classic economic freedom, the right to the unrestricted ownership and disposition of private property. Freedom from arbitrary arrest and persecution rounded off this list of basic rights; individuals could only be detained for violations of the law and would be considered innocent until legally proven guilty. On the final point, the declaration stated in no uncertain terms that individuals were by nature equal and deserving of equal treatment under the law. All occupations and government offices would be open to anyone who had the ability to perform them. The declaration also enunciated the idea of a representative government: laws, especially those dealing with taxation and state expenditures, required the consent of elected representatives of those who paid the taxes. Securing the entire structure of rights, legal equality and representation, the document noted, was a government characterized by a division of powers between the executive, judicial and legislative branches.

This declaration was a concentrated rejection of both the society of orders and of absolutist government, indeed an outright condemnation of them as regimes of inequality, oppression and tyranny. It represented in a particularly decisive form much of the social and political thinking of the counter-culture of the Enlightenment as it had developed in the eighteenth century, and as

[70]   it had been represented in two classic political documents of that era, the American Declaration of Independence and the Bill of Rights in the U.S. Constitution. The resemblance between these documents and the Declararation of the Rights of Man and Citizen is no coincidence, considering that their prime drafter, Thomas Jefferson, was the American ambassador to France in 1789, and patriot deputies in the National Assembly who had drawn up the declaration consulted closely with him on its wording. Of these three documents, the Declaration of the Rights of Man has probably had the greatest influence on future events and has been the most emulated. It remains to this day a concise statement of the ideals of the French Revolution.

The declaration obtained its status as a classic, however, only as the result of decades of conflict arising from ambiguities and contradictions within it. Let us note three of them, that would shape and structure conflicts in the entire decade after 1789. First, there was a contradiction between the declaration's assertion that all sovereignty, all ultimate state power, resided in the nation, and its enumeration of basic rights, prerogatives of individuals, to be upheld against any form of government, prerogatives that were to be guaranteed by a governmental division of powers. If these two principles came into conflict, which had precedence – the power of the nation or the rights of the individual? Second, the declaration moved strongly in the direction of replacing the old regime definition of the nation as a hierarchically arranged society of orders, in which each group had its own, chartered privileges with the notion of the nation as composed of equal citizens. But who were these citizens? Did their ranks include women? What about African slaves in the French colonies? Such questions of the delineation of citizenship and political equality in terms of race and gender are of particular moment at the end of the twentieth century. Contemporaries of the 1790s did pose them, but they were more concerned with another issue, the place of adult, males (European, since there were few Africans living in France, and none of them slaves) within the ranks of the citizenry. Did all the rights of citizenship extend to all adult males, only to heads of household, only to taxpayers, or only to possessors of a certain amount of property? Finally, the declaration was remarkably silent about two of the most important institutions of the French old regime – the monarchy, and the established state religion, the Roman Catholic Church. Where did these two institutions, central to the old regime society of orders, but still widely endorsed, even venerated, in 1789, by the patriot deputies to the National Assembly and their supporters no less than by anyone else, fit into the new social and political landscape envisaged in the Declaration of the Rights of Man? All three of these considerations

may seem abstract or theoretical, but four major institutional developments [71]
in the turbulent summer of 1789 – the formation of a national guard, the
development of a periodical press, the creation of political clubs and the growth
of emigration and counter-revolution – guaranteed that these issues inherent
in the declaration would be expressed in and by organizations with a major
effect on public life.

All the mass movements of the summer of 1789 had included scenes of
mob violence that had escalated from attacking institutions and agencies, symbols and documents of oppression and privilege, or demanding the sale of
grain at fixed prices to open plundering and looting, or to ugly public lynchings. Just to take some examples from the kingdom's largest city, the commander of the garrison of the Bastille, the marquis de Launay, was seized by
the insurgents after he surrendered, dragged through the streets of Paris, killed
and his head paraded on a pike. A week later, similar public assassinations,
followed by processions of the decapitated heads, awaited the intendant,
or royal governor of Paris, Bertignier de Sauvigny, along with his father-
in-law, who were rumoured to be hoarding food. Now brutal executions
and the public display of criminals' corpses were typical of the old regime,
and the masses of lower-class Parisians, who carried them out, were following
the example of the former government, but the patriots were trying to abolish such cruelties in the spirit of Enlightened reform. How could they stop
these excesses, and protect persons and property, without, however, turning
to the officials, police and soldiers of the absolutist and corporate regime they
were trying to bring to an end?

They found an ingenious solution in the creation of a citizens' militia, the
National Guard. Such a force of patriotic volunteers, who would organize
their own military service and elect their own officers, was first suggested by
the committee of Parisian electors in the confrontations of July 1789; their
example was quickly imitated throughout the kingdom, in villages as well as
towns and cities. The flag of the Parisian National Guard, made by combining the red and blue municipal colours of Paris with the white of the royal
Bourbon family, produced the celebrated blue, red and white tricolour, that
would become the national flag and provide the basic pattern for such banners down to the present day. The first commandant of the Parisian guard,
the marquis de Lafayette, veteran of the American Revolution and one of the
leading reform-minded noblemen, would be a dominant – perhaps the dominant – figure during the early years of the revolution.

The connection between citizenship and bearing arms in the National Guard
would come to be characteristic of the revolution. In these circumstances, the

[72] guard's policies on membership would provide a key test of the limits of citizenship. The Parisian guard's requirement that its members provide their own uniforms and weapons was a sign that only the relatively affluent, who could afford to do so, would enjoy all the rights and perquisites of citizenship. Finally, the guard was an armed force under the control of its volunteer members, an important factor in a volatile political situation. In the summer of 1789, the National Guard was generally a force for the restoration and preservation of public order, arresting looters, pillagers or lynchers, preserving the property their members generally possessed. The activities of the citizen militia would not necessarily stay within such channels in the future.

The second main feature of the summer of 1789 was the emergence of an uncensored periodical press. The process of debate and deliberation in the elections of deputies to the Estates General had awakened a broad interest in public affairs, one only heightened by the dramatic events in Versailles and Paris in the weeks following the convening of the Estates. People wanted the latest news and they wanted it right away. The defeat of the existing governmental authorities in the confrontations of June and July led to the de facto abolition of the strict press censorship characteristic of the old regime, even before the Declaration of the Rights of Man had enshrined freedom of the press. No less than one hundred and forty periodicals were founded in Paris in 1789; although most proved ephemeral, thirty-four of them lasted longer than a year. Journalists quickly moved from simply reporting the National Assembly's proceedings verbatim (or as close as they could get, without any system of shorthand to take down the speeches) to offering their own opinions about public affairs, bringing the great issues of the day to the ever-widening circle of those interested in them. Different newspapers represented every shade of political opinion present in the National Assembly. The press also articulated extreme opinions, going well beyond what parliamentarians would assert, at least in public, from the ultra-royalist *Acts of the Apostles*, that called on its readers to hang all the deputies to the Assembly, to the *Friend of the People* of Jean-Paul Marat, whose bitter and vitriolic attacks on aristocratic and clerical conspirators did not spare the king, as the patriot deputies of 1789 and 1790 would. The unbridled press of the early phase of the revolution thus connected the parliamentary proceedings of the National Assembly with readers throughout the realm, simultaneously capitalized on and expanded public interest in politics, expanded the spectrum of possible political options and made sharper, more open and more blatant the existing differences between partisans of different policies.

The third major institution, begun a few months later than the first two, was the political club. It began as a caucus, or, more precisely, as an informal gathering of the deputies of the Third Estate from the province of Brittany. The nobles of that province, as we have seen, had been particularly hostile to the demands for adequate representation by the Third Estate, and to the whole idea of the dismantling of the society of orders. Consequently, the Third Estate deputies from Brittany, prominent among them an attorney from Arras, Maximilian Robespierre, had been particularly strong supporters of the patriot position in the National Assembly; increasingly, other patriot deputies came to the meetings of the Breton delegates. Crucial initiatives, such as the motions proposed on the night of 4 August, were planned there.

In the autumn of 1789, these deputies rented a hall in Paris (as we will see, the king and the National Assembly had moved to Paris in October 1789) and began holding their caucus meetings in public. Soon, non-deputies began attending, listening to and joining in the debates, and a private club was organized, whose members could attend and discuss public affairs. The hall where the deputies met had once been a convent of the Jesuits, or the Jacobins, as they were sometimes known, so the group was dubbed the 'Jacobin club'.

With remarkable speed, this political initiative spread throughout France. Working on the model of the masonic lodges and the reading societies, those institutions of the old regime that had gone beyond the social barriers of the society of orders, supporters of the ideas of the patriots in larger cities and smaller towns, formed similar clubs. Members could meet, read the latest issue of the Parisian newspapers, debate the subjects brought before the National Assembly, and take political actions, such as organizing petitions to the Assembly, holding open-air mass meetings, or even political demonstrations. Once again following masonic practice, many of these clubs recognized the Parisian Jacobin club as the leading society and formally affiliated themselves with it; others did not, but nonetheless looked to it for guidance. By 1793, there were nine hundred such political clubs in France, a number reflecting an exponential rate of growth, creating a nucleus of activists throughout the entire kingdom.

The final development we can point to in this period is the emigration. Once the victory of the patriots in the National Assembly became clear, a number of prominent noblemen, led by the king's youngest brother, the count of Artois, began leaving the country. Most of these émigrés gathered in the smaller German and Italian states on the borders of the kingdom, keeping in close touch with other firm adherents of the past regime still residing in France,

[74] and considered measures that could be taken to restore the society of orders and absolutist rule. Since the victory of the patriots had led to the legalization and institutionalization of the changes in government and society, such a return to the old regime could only be achieved in violent and coercive fashion – by the unleashing of a civil war. The very presence of the émigrés was a threat to the revolution, and a spur to its supporters to take drastic steps to ensure its survival; the fact that the émigrés had sympathizers inside the country, some even in the councils of the king, only increased their menace and made fears of conspiracy, already widely prevalent in French political culture, seem all too plausible.

Reforms and political polarization: 1789–91

The National Assembly sat for almost two years until June of 1791. In this period, its deputies strove to create new constitutional, administrative, legal, financial and socioeconomic institutions, replacing those of the old regime and embodying the ideals they had outlined in their two great initiatives of August 1789. If that was not enough, they also strove to deal with the imme-diate pressing problems of the realm, in particular with the crisis of govern-ment finances, that had led to the calling of the Estates General in the first place. It would have been little short of miraculous, had the deputies been able to draw up a detailed blueprint for a completely different political and social order, replacing the previously existing one and gain a wide consensus for it, while resolving the seemingly intractable difficulties of state finances – and doing it all in an atmosphere of broad and increasingly contentious politicization. Remarkably, there were a few moments, particularly in the summer of 1790, when it seemed this might be the case. However, both at the beginning of this period, in the autumn of 1789, and even more so at its end, in the first half of 1791, the work of the National Assembly evoked not broad consent, but polarization, as ever-growing numbers of Frenchmen – and women – were divided into the camps of those who wanted to push the revolution further, and those who wanted to revert to the pre-revolutionary state of affairs. In this section, we will look at the Assembly's work of reform and also at the forces of polarization, seeing how one of the key reforms turned into the greatest agent of polarization.

Administrative uniformity and abolition of provincial and local privilege were one major hallmark of the work of the National Assembly. The locally

infinitely varied system of royal and seigneurial justice was replaced with a [75]
unitary court system, under the control of the national government, that ran
from local justices of the peace up through layers of appeals to the central
court of cassation in Paris. France's provinces, with their unique sizes and
shapes and inhabitants' distinct rights and privileges were replaced with new
administrative districts, the departments – eighty-three of them, designed
around natural features of the landscape for maximum accessibility of the
government to the citizens. The city chosen as departmental capital was to be
no more than one day's horse ride from any point within the department.
Such departments form the basis of the French internal administration down
to the present day.

If the uniformity of the departments points to one way that the National
Assembly repudiated the old regime, by replacing provincial privilege with
uniform, equal administrative units, the emphasis on access in their design
points to another feature of the reform work, the repudiation of absolutism.
Government was to be brought near to the citizens and made responsible to
them. Important officials would no longer be appointed by the monarch or
the estates, and would certainly not be able to purchase their offices. Rather,
they would be elected, and the National Assembly set up a uniform system
for elections to municipal governments (major cities, like Paris, Marseilles or
Lyon, had neighbourhood administrations, the 'sections', in addition to their
municipal government), to the departmental administrations, and even for
the justices of the peace, the lowest level of the judiciary. Such elections were
duly carried out in the spring of 1790 and, like all those in the entire period
of the revolution, were public and open; they often involved lengthy journeys
from the voters' home towns or villages to a central location where the ballot
was held. The voting itself was cumbersome, since votes were cast publicly
and orally and election officials, who would certify the validity of the results,
had themselves to be elected, before any voting could actually take place.
The proceedings could easily last all day, or even longer. For that reason alone
– although there were many others – turnouts in elections held during the
revolution tended to be low, with less than one-half and usually less than
one-third of all eligible voters appearing at the polls. Still, the procedure shows
that the National Assembly took very seriously the idea of representative
government.

To uniformity and electability, we might add the preservation and redefinition of property as the third major theme in the reform work of the
National Assembly. All the seigneurial limitations on free transactions in
rural property were abolished during the night of 4 August. To be sure, the

[76] National Assembly did declare that the peasants would owe their former lords compensation for these privileges and demanded that the peasants go on paying their seigneurial dues until all the appropriate legislation had been enacted – an order that French farmers universally, and sometimes violently disobeyed. Following earlier reform precedents, the Assembly removed restrictions on the grain trade. Toward the very end of its session, in the spring of 1791, the Assembly removed all restrictions on crafts and manufacturing, abolishing the guilds that had been so important in the old regime, but also continuing the prohibitions on other groups, such as the brotherhoods of journeymen artisans, that had previously been illegal.

For the Assembly, 'property' (which had been declared sacred and inviolable in the Declaration of the Rights of Man) meant property that could be bought and sold on the free market, not the old regime version, where such economic activity had been hemmed in by chartered privileges and hereditary distinctions. Indeed, the possession of property became the way in which the National Assembly defined the terms of citizenship: it restricted the right to vote to adult males who paid a minimum property tax, between one-third and one-half of the entire adult male population of France. (Women were not given the right to vote, although in a number of instances they seem just to have gone ahead and done so.)

Crowning the whole edifice of reform was the constitution of 1791, reordering the whole French government. There was, as we have seen, a uniform national judicial system, and a vigorous local and regional self-government. The king was declared head of the executive branch of government, responsible for foreign policy, having the power to appoint the government ministers, and commander-in-chief of the armed forces. Facing him was a unicameral legislature, with ultimate law-making authority (the king could temporarily suspend laws voted by this body, but not permanently veto them). It was chosen, as noted above, by property-owning male voters, but eligibility to be a deputy required ownership of a much more substantial amount of property. By 1791, France was no longer an absolutist old regime monarchy, simultaneously collaborating and fighting with the constituted bodies of its society. It had become a constitutional monarchy, whose government was committed to a broad work of reform.

Much of this reform programme was relatively non-controversial. There were few regrets about the abolition of the parlements, the Provincial Estates, or seigneurial justice, and local interests lobbied deputies vigorously to have their town chosen as the departmental capital or as the seat of one of the new courts. The monarch, no longer an absolute ruler, but now a public official with a constitutionally guaranteed position, had seemingly been nicely [77] integrated into the government. The Assembly, by only allowing male tax-payers to vote, had created a distinction between 'passive citizens', who enjoyed the protection of the basic civil rights enumerated in the Declaration of the Rights of Man, but could not have a voice in public affairs, and 'active citizens', possessing a quite modest amount of property, who could. This would become a point of considerable disagreement in the near future, under the impact of political confrontations and economic crises, but was less of an issue in 1790. Indeed, the celebration of the first anniversary of the fall of the Bastille in July 1790, the so-called 'Festival of Federation', was a giant success for the new order in the making. National Guardsmen from all over France held a great parade in Paris, culminating in a massive assembly, where, led by the king in person, they took an oath of loyalty to the nation, before hundreds of thousands of spectators, followed by a festive high mass, celebrated by the patriot bishop of Autun. Armed (and generally property-owning) citizens, a federal state, everyone equal under the law and loyal to the nation, the incorporation of the church and the king in the new order – all the contradictions and ambiguities inherent in the Declaration of the Rights of Man and Citizen seemed to have been resolved.

Perhaps they had been – for a day. However, one crucial reform of the National Assembly guaranteed that such harmony and assent would be temporary and precarious. This reform was a result of tackling the big practical problem that had created the crisis in the first place, the government's lack of revenue. The turbulent events of the summer of 1789 had greatly intensified the state's financial difficulties, because much of the population, especially the inhabitants of the countryside, understood the great events of the day as meaning that they did not have to pay taxes. The Assembly attempted to deal with this situation by what might be called sympathetic magic, renaming taxes 'patriotic contributions', in the hope that the new name would make taxpayers more willing to pay up – a procedure which met with little success.

In several measures starting in the autumn of 1789, the deputies came up with a much more drastic solution to the kingdom's financial problems. They would seize all the lands belonging to the Catholic Church and sell them to pay off the government's debts. To be more exact, the government would issue bonds, called 'assignats', backed by church property, and redeemed after it was sold. Since the Assembly, on the night of 4 August, had already abolished the other main source of the church's income, the tithe, this step would leave the church completely without resources. Consequently, the

[78] government would be obliged to provide an income for the clergy, which the Assembly promised to do.

Having already taken that step, in the spring of 1790, the deputies took the next, truly decisive one. They decided to reorganize the administration of the Catholic Church in France along the lines of their reforms of government administration and the courts. The Civil Constitution of the Clergy, as they called their reform, would abolish the traditional dioceses, with their great differences in extent, religious customs, and privileges, dissolve many monasteries and nunneries and replace all these with new, uniform diocesan units, one for each department. Just as the administrators of the departments were to be elected by property owners, so the administrators of the dioceses, the bishops, were to be chosen in a similar way. And, just like all other government officials, the Catholic clergy would have to take an oath of loyalty to the nation, source of all sovereignty, according to the Declaration of the Rights of Man.

Steeped in the counter-culture of the Enlightenment, the patriot deputies who forced these measures through the National Assembly after tumultuous and embittered debate, understood their actions as ending unjustified privileges and reorganizing the state religion in a way that would do the most practical good. Seizing church property was a drastic step, but by abolishing the purchase of government offices or seigneurial rights, the Assembly had seized other kinds of old regime property as well. Since they did not include separation of church and state in their list of basic rights, the patriot deputies saw no reason not to reorganize religious administration as they had its judicial counterpart. There was precedent for this reorganization of the church in the actions of the absolutist kings of France, and Enlightened monarchs, such as Joseph II of Austria, had closed monasteries and rearranged ecclesiastical administration. However, both the election of the bishops and the requirement that the clergy take an oath to the nation went beyond even the efforts of Joseph II. For those deputies who maintained their loyalties to the culture of confessionalism, the Assembly's actions involved a profanation of God's own representatives on earth, an action that was sinful and little short of Satanic, and which they quickly attributed to pernicious enemies of the church, whether competing Christians, such as the Protestants, or deist groups, like the Freemasons.

The pope agreed with this and prohibited priests in France from taking the oath of loyalty to the nation. The upshot was a severe crisis of conscience, not just for Catholic priests, but for the 95 per cent (or thereabouts) of the inhabitants of France who were confessing Catholics. When the time came to take the oath, at the beginning of 1791, about half the clergy complied with [79] the government and half refused, although the proportions of 'jurors' (those who swore the oath) and 'non-jurors' (those who did not, also called 'refractory' priests), differed sharply in different parts of the country. The government moved to replace the non-jurors with new priests who would be loyal to it. The pious supporters of the non-jurors would rally in defence of their priests, insult, abuse and physically assault the jurors, whom they saw as traitors to the faith. Women were particularly active in defending their religion. Members of the Jacobin clubs, on the other hand, saw the non-jurors as counter-revolutionary conspirators and enemies of the nation. They mobilized sympathetic National Guardsmen from urban areas to march out to defend the juring priests and intimidate or arrest the non-jurors. In the first half of 1791, this conflict over religion spread throughout the length and breadth of France.

The conflict over the Civil Constitution of the Clergy was an enormously divisive issue, one in which fundamental passions ran high, and would soon erupt into murder and massacre. Its emergence demonstrates the powerful hold of the culture of confessionalism in eighteenth-century Europe, and the radicalism of the challenge to it by the counter-culture of the Enlightenment. The struggle over the church also, for the first time, created a mass basis for counter-revolution. Defence of the one true religion was a cause that could mobilize ordinary Frenchmen and women, especially in rural areas, in ways that other matters of the old regime – seigneurial privilege, the parlements, the Estates, the absolute rule of the monarch, the guilds – could not. The rapid spread of this religiously based counter-revolution throughout France convinced the patriots that it must have been the work of powerful conspirators trying to crush the revolution, and led them to redouble their efforts to enforce it. Indeed, in some sense the religious issue became the litmus test of politics in general, and not just in the 1790s. Historians who have investigated the matter have noted that the inhabitants of those regions of France where most of the clergy took the oath of loyalty to the nation, would be on the political left from the time of the revolution itself into the 1960s, while the regions where most priests were non-jurors, were areas generally favourable to the political right.

If the religious issue set the stage for the growth of political polarization, it was the actions of the king that became the focus of the competing, increasingly hostile forces. Continuing in his vacillating ways, Louis XVI had never been able to decide whether to go along with the initiatives of the patriots in the National Assembly, or to oppose them, but had tended in a half-hearted

[80] manner to pursue both policies at once. Cooperating with the patriots, indeed placing himself at the head of their movement, would have been a plausible strategy. Most of the patriots were convinced royalists, who wanted the king as their leader. The constitution they wrote left him, if no longer an absolute monarch, still with considerable powers, and he might well have been able to make use of them to exercise influence over the other branches of government. Already in the National Assembly the king had gained the confidential cooperation of one of its most popular figures, a prominent patriot leader, the count de Mirabeau, who found himself forced by personal financial difficulties to accept a secret subsidy from the monarch.

Standing in the way of such cooperation was the growing feeling that the royal family was in personal danger from the lower classes of Paris, while the patriot leaders were by no means afraid to make use of these Parisians for their own ends. At the beginning of October 1789, food prices increased once more, and rumours spread in Paris that members of the court were insulting the patriots and conspiring against the National Assembly. Several thousand women, in an angry mood, set out for Versailles from Paris – a twenty-mile hike – to demand bread from the king and punishment for the conspirators. Hastily calling out the National Guard, the marquis de Lafayette followed to protect the monarch from the angry crowd, and to carry out, not entirely unwillingly, their demand that he return with them to Paris. The National Assembly soon followed. The king felt himself a virtual prisoner, of the common people of Paris and of the patriot politicians, who were not above using them, but also not in control of their anger and suspicions.

The last straw for the king, though, as for millions of others in France, was the Civil Constitution of the Clergy. Personally deeply if naively devout, Louis XVI simply could not go along with a policy he understood as an attack on religion. Though never entirely breaking off his ties to some of the patriot leaders in late 1790 and early 1791, the king increasingly listened to the statements of the émigrés and the hard-line element at the court, especially the queen, whose reputation as the evil genius behind the scenes seems thoroughly deserved. Finally, he decided to break decisively with the revolution, with everything that had happened since the calling of the Estates General. Such a move would be impossible in Paris, with its National Guard and increasingly hostile and suspicious lower-class population.

Consequently, the king resolved to flee the city and head for the northeastern frontier. There, under the protection of loyal troops, and with the hoped-for support of his brother-in-law, the Holy Roman Emperor, he would combat the revolution. Leaving behind a decree condemning the Civil

Constitution of the Clergy and reinstating the parlements and other legal [81]
bodies of the old regime, the royal family fled Paris on the night of 20 June,
1791. Close to their goal, they were identified, spotted, halted at the town of
Varennes, and arrested by the National Guard. As they returned to Paris, thousands of people lined the roads, cursing, jeering and mocking them. The 'flight
to Varennes' brought to an end the hope that a new political order could be
created in cooperation with the king and the church, fundamental pillars of
the old one.

This flight to Varennes split the ranks of the patriots. On one side were
those, like the marquis de Lafayette, who were determined to retain a monarchy, in spite of the actual monarch's manifest opposition to their policy.
They persuaded the National Assembly to reinstate Louis as king, claiming
that he had been misled and kidnapped by conspirators in his entourage. This
group – we might call them the moderates – also wished to retain a franchise
based on property ownership.

Opposed to them were a more radical element, found in the Cordeliers
political club (a group founded by those who considered the Jacobins too
timid in fighting counter-revolution), and also among figures outside the
organized politics of legislatures and political clubs, such as the journalist
Jean-Paul Marat. The manifest hostility of the monarch to the revolution moved
them to call for a republic, and one that would be based on the democratic
principle of universal manhood suffrage. In July 1791, they staged a massive
demonstration to this end in Paris; the city's National Guard, acting under
Lafayette's command, opened fire on the demonstrators in the 'massacre of
the Champ de Mars'.

Moderates and radicals fought it out for influence in the Parisian Jacobin
club. The moderates seceded to form their own club, the Feuillants, and the
contest between moderates and radicals moved to a new stage: the struggle
for influence with the ever-growing number of affiliated societies throughout the kingdom. In the course of the second half of 1791, the radicals, led
by Maximilain Robespierre, were victorious and became more and more able
to lead the national network of political activists in the direction of supporting a democratic and republican regime. Both in alliance and in competition
with radical journalists such as Marat, they organized an ever more effective
following among the common people of the capital city.

By the fall of 1791, organized political life in France was falling into three
increasingly hostile groups, with very different attitudes toward the dramatic
changes of the two previous years. One such group was composed of those
who wished to see these changes reversed and revoked. Led by the émigrés

[82] and counting the scarcely concealed support of the royal family, their trump card and basis of popular support was the religious issue. Then there were those who wanted to bring the revolution to an end, to accept the abolition of the society of orders and the changes in the church, but to retain a monarch, and have participation in public life based on the possession of property. Finally, there were those organized in the Jacobin clubs who accepted the changes already made but wanted to move them further: towards a democratic republic. Each of these groups was vehemently hostile to the others. In these circumstances, the chances that the constitution drawn up by the National Assembly and put into effect in September 1791 would have a long life were slim indeed.

A further revolution: inflation, war and the republic

Two developments ensured that the rapidly escalating social and political tensions of autumn 1791 would explode into a further revolution and then a civil war: inflation and foreign war. The issuing of assignats to fund the budget deficit proved only a temporary stopgap: expenses continued to mount, taxes were still not being collected (the growing political turmoil did nothing to encourage their collection), and the sale of the church lands, itself obstructed by the controversy over the Civil Constitution of the Clergy (in areas loyal to the non-juring priests, purchasers of church lands faced threats, assaults, and even lynchings) proceeded too slowly to fund the notes. Consequently, the government was forced to issue still more assignats to fund its operations, and to insist that these notes be accepted as legal tender, creating a paper currency. Businessmen would only accept the notes at a discount on their face value, leading to a rise in prices. Farmers held back their crops rather than sell them for a depreciating currency, aggravating food shortages, caused by a run of bad harvests, and raising prices still further. The price level rose 20 per cent in 1791, and inflation accelerated steadily after that.

Growing concern about rising prices led to the emergence of an important social and political actor in France's large cities: the sans-culottes. The name means 'without culottes' (knee breeches), and it refers to those men (and, by extension, to their family members) who did some form of manual labour for a living, and so wore trousers, rather than more fashionable and delicate garb. Such individuals included master craftsmen with their own workshops, and small businessmen with their own shops, who could employ a fair number of workers and have a good amount of property, as well as journeymen artisans and unskilled workers or day labourers. Overall, one would have to place the sans-culottes in about the middle third of the urban social scale, below the great merchants and bankers, the professionals, or the substantial property owners, but above the itinerant labourers, beggars, and petty criminals of the very lowest groups in French society. Sans-culottes were both employers and employed, property owners and propertyless, but they were above all urban consumers, with a strong interest in seeing the price of basic commodities, especially bread, kept at a reasonable level, as inflation began to take hold.

Such a group came to the fore in every large French city of the day – Lyon, Marseilles, Toulouse, Bordeaux, or Strasbourg, for instance – but they were most energetic and active in Paris. Some sans-culottes could be found in the National Guard, the Jacobin clubs, and in the sections, the neighbourhood branches of large cities' municipal governments, although all those institutions were basically run by members of more educated and affluent social groups. But their greatest influence, as could already be seen in the fall of the Bastille in July 1789, or the march to Versailles in October of that year, was in their ability to group together and take action, whether at the behest of political activists trying to mobilize them, or on their own initiative. The return of the royal government to Paris in the autumn of 1789 meant that such mass gatherings would come to exercise a considerable influence on the centres of power in the revolution.

The second, and perhaps the most important factor in the movement from political polarization to further revolution and civil war was the involvement of France in foreign war. As we will see in more detail in the next chapter, the rapid and violent end of the society of orders in revolutionary France was beginning by 1791 to seem like a dismaying precedent to other European rulers. But it was the dynamics of French domestic politics that really led to the war. Thousands of émigrés had gathered in the smaller German states near the eastern French border, formed themselves into armed companies and were preparing an invasion of a country in increasing domestic turmoil, hoping to take advantage of allies within France itself.

The more militant patriots in the Legislative Assembly, the law-making body elected under the constitution of 1791, began pressing for war against the German states hosting the émigrés, and these states' protector, the Holy Roman Emperor. Led by a deputy from Bordeaux, Jacques-Pierre Brissot, and hence known as the Brissotins, these men hoped that a successful war would break the power of counter-revolutionaries, both in France and abroad,

[84] creating foreign governments sympathetic to revolutionary France and re-moving the foreign forces encouraging opposition to the revolution at home. Moderates also favoured war, expecting that a successful campaign, led by the marquis de Lafayette, would put them in a stronger position, and perhaps even allow the victorious general to use the army to intimidate his domestic political opponents. Finally, the king, still officially commander-in-chief of the armed forces, endorsed the war, even though it meant that army would be taking the field against the forces of the queen's family, whose protection he had hoped for in his failed flight to Varennes. The royal family, however, unlike the radical or moderate politicians, was hoping for a French defeat, so that the victorious Austrian armies could destroy the revolution and restore the old regime. The only major political figure to oppose the war was Maximilian Robespierre, who had emerged by this time as the de facto leader of the Jacobin clubs. He warned that the war would not be a quick easy tri-umph, and that it would not prove as simple as the Brissotins thought to export the French revolution to foreign countries.

Events quickly proved Robespierre right on all counts. The war began in early 1792 and things went wrong from the start. The king of Prussia, the Holy Roman Emperor's traditional rival, rather than staying neutral, or even supporting the French, joined in fighting against them. Soon the Brit-ish government, the king of Spain and most of the princes of the smaller German and Italian states had joined the war against France. While the motives of these powers in going to war against revolutionary France were mixed – their statesmen motivated in part by calculations of power politics and in part by ideological hostility to the revolution – the very creation of such an enormous, anti-French coalition, crossing previous lines of alli-ance and coalition, demonstrated that the domestic political and social policies of the new, revolutionary regime had also upset previous diplomatic alignments.

Even worse than having to fight all of Europe, was the fact that the French army was not in a position to do much fighting. Before 1789, one of the privileges of the French nobles had been that only they could be army officers. Like their fellow nobles, many of these officers joined the émigrés; others, still at their posts, had little desire to fight for a revolution-ary regime that had abolished their privileges. The enlisted men and NCOs had demanded the application of the revolution's principle of equality under the law to the armed forces, resulting in a number of mutinies and clashes between different army units in 1790 and 1791. The government did call for volunteers and mobilized units of the National Guard to reinforce the army for war, though the regular soldiers greeted their new comrades with undisguised hostility.

The initial battles, fought in today's Belgium and Holland, brought immediate defeats to the outnumbered, demoralized and badly led French troops. By the summer of 1792 Prussian and Austrian soldiers had penetrated into northeastern France. In the areas they occupied, they set about restoring the old regime, demanding payment of seigneurial dues, returning property to the church, and generally attempting to recreate pre-1789 conditions. The duke of Brunswick, supreme commander of these allied armies, issued a manifesto, announcing that the purpose of the war was to restore the legitimate authority of the king of France, and threatening the city of Paris with exemplary vengeance should the royal family be harmed in any way. In spite of the mixed motives for going to war, combining, on both sides, cynical, self-interested power politics and ideological commitment, the war was increasingly described by the leaders of the combatant powers as a political and ideological conflict, a war about the revolution.

For the radical leaders in the Legislative Assembly, but especially outside of it, in the Paris municipal government, and in the Jacobin clubs, the course of the war proved that their worst suspicions had come true. They asserted that counter-revolutionary traitors in the armed forces had led the armies to defeat, that the king, officially head of state and commander-in-chief of the armed forces was in treasonable correspondence with the enemy – as he actually was. The actions of the marquis de Lafayette reinforced their suspicions of the moderates: rather than leading his soldiers against the enemy, he tried to get them to march on Paris and destroy the power of the radicals there. When the troops refused, he deserted to the Austrians. If the war was to be won, and the revolution saved, then drastic measures would have to be taken. Georges Danton, a prominent member of the ultra-radical Cordeliers club, and deputy to the Legislative Assembly, made the point in a celebrated speech: 'Audacity, more audacity, still more audacity, and France will be saved.'

The leaders of the radicals began to prepare an insurrection. Calling on the sans-culottes of the city, and on the *fédérés*, 20,000 volunteer National Guardsmen from all the departments of France, who had gathered in Paris to join the army, they prepared a demonstration on 10 August. Demonstrators marched to the royal palace, fought with and defeated the king's bodyguards (massacring most of the survivors in the process), and declared the king deposed and France a republic. They forced the Legislative Assembly to announce its own dissolution and call for new elections – this time held under universal manhood suffrage – for a new parliament, a constitutional

[86] convention that would write a new basic document for a republican French government. The wartime crisis and the political alliance with the sans-culottes had made it possible for the leaders of the radical wing of French politics, those who wished to carry the revolution in the direction of a democratic republic, to carry out their programme. Elections were duly held – with only 20 per cent of eligible voters participating – and the Convention, the new parliament of the republican regime, gathered in Paris in September of 1792.

Foreign war and civil war

The Convention faced the same problems as had plagued its predecessor, only in sharper, more pronounced form. First, the war continued. To be sure, the Prussians and Austrians were defeated at Valmy in late September 1792, and retreated in disarray. The French forces then marched victoriously into the Low Countries and western Germany, but these successes proved temporary. Many of the volunteers of 1792, who had signed up for just one campaign, returned home, and the weakened armies of the republic were pushed back into France, with the enemy once again threatening Paris by the spring of 1793. General Dumouriez, commander of the French armies facing the Prussians and the Austrians, followed his predecessor Lafayette in deserting to the enemy. Worse yet, Spanish troops occupied parts of southwestern France and British naval forces seized the major Mediterranean port of Toulon.

The sans-culottes continued to act on their own initiative, bypassing the radical political leadership. In September 1792, with the Prussians nearing Paris, panic spread among the city's common people: they feared that with the National Guard at the front, the imprisoned counter-revolutionaries would rise up and slaughter the civilians behind the lines. Armed sans-culottes invaded the gaols and systematically massacred the prisoners: some of their victims were nobles and non-juring priests, technically counter-revolutionaries, although hardly a danger to anyone; most were thieves and prostitutes, the majority of the prisoners. The 'September massacres' were an ugly and embarrassing incident in the revolution; the charge of being a *Septembriseur*, a 'Septemberiser' would long dog the radical political activists.

Even more than ostensible royalist conspirators, the sans-culottes were angered by galloping inflation, heading from double- to triple-digit levels by 1793. They demanded controls on the prices of basic necessities; if farmers would not deliver their grain at fixed prices, then the government would have to coerce them. In the wake of this agitation, which reached a high point in the spring of 1793, politically active individuals, most prominently, a former priest turned revolutionary activist, named Jacques Roux, began championing the sans-culottes' demands. Although not a very effective force, Roux and his followers nonetheless raised the spectre of political leaders mobilizing the sans-culottes to overthrow the Convention, as the Jacobins had done to overthrow the monarchy.

The controversy between political leaders and activists who wished to carry the revolution further and those who wished to bring it to an end continued in the Convention. Those deputies who wanted radical measures sat together to the left of the presiding speaker, and hence became known as leftists; those opposing such drastic measures, sat, of course, on the right. This intellectual organization of politics on a left–right spectrum, that continues to shape the way we think about politics today, is thus a product of the Convention, and of the republican phase of the French Revolution.

Tensions quickly developed on the left between the followers of Brissot, the radicals of the previous Legislative Assembly (also sometimes known as Girondins, after the department of the Gironde, and its capital city of Bordeaux, from which many of the leaders of this faction came) and the Jacobins, led by Robespierre. In general, the Jacobins favoured stronger and more drastic measures to suppress counter-revolutionaries and to establish the republican regime; they were more willing to cooperate with the sans-culottes and make concessions to their ideas, particularly their insistence on interference in the free market to secure the grain supply. The issue that proved to be the sticking point between Girondins and Jacobins, though, was what to do with the deposed monarch.

A large majority of the deputies to the Convention had no problem with the idea of bringing the king to trial for treason. At his trial, Louis XVI and his lawyers took the stance of presenting him as a constitutional monarch, arguing that the constitution of 1791 had defined his person as inviolable, and thus not subject to such a trial. But royalist pamphleteers, writing from the safety of emigration, made the true old regime case: the king was the nation, the country was his patrimony. All his actions had to be devoted to the good of the nation, since he embodied it, and the convincing evidence presented that Louis had opposed the revolutionary movement since 1789, even to the extent of being in contact with the opposing armies in wartime, was proof that he was defending the nation against the revolutionary

[88]   usurpers. The deputies to the Convention, strong believers in equality before the law, were unwilling to accept either of these arguments concerning 'Citizen Louis Capet', as they now called the ex-monarch. Acting as a jury in the trial, they voted overwhelmingly to find him guilty.

The question that bitterly divided the Convention, however, was not Louis' guilt, but his sentence. Here the old regime concept of the monarch as sacred personage and embodiment of the nation clearly continued to exert an influence. The Girondins, in particular, wished to avert the execution of the ex-king found guilty of treason. They attempted to submit the Convention's judgement to a popular vote, to condemn Louis to imprisonment or exile, to delay the imposition of a death sentence – anything, really, to avert this measure, which they understood would mean a decisive break of the revolutionary regime with not just much of France, but all of Europe.

It was precisely this break that the Jacobins wanted, and they got their way. On the crucial roll call and debate on the penalty to be imposed on the king, in an unbroken session lasting thirty-six hours, his death was voted by a bare majority of deputies. On 21 January, 1793, the former king was taken to the scaffold and guillotined. He died calmly, encouraged by his confessor, understanding himself as a Christian martyr to the forces of evil, a view officially endorsed by the pope a few months later. The sans-culotte spectators at the execution, however, cheered the nation and the republic and sang the Marseillaise. Maximilian Robespierre, the most prominent proponent of Louis' execution, expressed succinctly how executing the former king had been a decisive sign in favour of a republican form of government: 'Formerly, when a king died at Versailles, the sign of his successors was immediately announced by the cry: *The king is dead, long live the king,* in order to make it understood that despotism was immortal! Now an entire people, moved by a sublime instinct cried, *Long live the Republic!* to teach the universe that tyranny died with the tyrant.'[2]

This dramatic deed brought the struggle for power between Girondins and Jacobins to a peak. Girondin deputies attempted to pass legislation to close down the radical newspapers and to prohibit the political clubs. The Jacobins responded by using the clubs and the Parisian municipal government to mobilize the sans-culottes. In a carefully planned demonstration in June 1793, armed sans-culottes stormed the Convention and demanded the expulsion or suspension of the Girondin leaders, a demand the Jacobin deputies were only too happy to fulfil.

The remaining deputies to the Convention were now free to take drastic measures in support of the revolution. They began with the war. In a celebrated proclamation of August 1793, they announced:

From this moment until that in which our enemies shall have been driven from the territory of the Republic, all Frenchmen are permanently requisitioned for service in the armies. The young men shall fight; the married men shall forge weapons and transport supplies; the women will make tents and clothes and will serve in the hospitals; the children will make up old linen into lint; the old men will have themselves carried into the public squares to rouse the courage of fighting men, to preach the unity of the Republic and the hatred of kings.[3]

The entire energies of the nation would be mobilized for war; in particular, as the decree notes, young men of military age were to be conscripted into the armed forces, the *levée en masse*, as it was called. The government was declared 'revolutionary until the peace', that is, a de facto wartime dictatorship of the Convention was set up, and the democratic and republican constitution was suspended.

The radicals dominating the Convention understood domestic opposition to their rule as treasonous activity in league with the foreign enemy; domestic opponents were to be intimidated, coerced, and, if necessary, destroyed. Bertrand Barère, a leading radical deputy, proclaimed that 'terror is the order of the day', and the republican regime set out to terrorize its enemies. Laws were passed creating 'committees of surveillance', throughout the country, whose members were to scrutinize the loyalty of their fellow citizens, awarding 'certificates of civic loyalty' to supporters of the national government, and warning or arresting its opponents. Members of the formerly privileged orders, ex-clergy or nobles came under particular suspicion. Special tribunals were created to try the enemies of the nation. The property of émigrés was confiscated and sold at auction.

The radical deputies did not – and could not – forget the sans-culottes who had put them in power. Somewhat reluctantly, since it went against their beliefs in the virtues of the free market economy, they introduced a 'Maximum', or, as we would say today, price controls. When farmers refused to sell their grain at these fixed prices, the Convention created 'revolutionary armies', sans-culotte militias, whose job it was to leave the large urban centres, go out into the countryside and seize foodstuffs.

Capping the structure of this wartime, revolutionary dictatorship was the Committee of Public Safety, a twelve-man executive body, elected each month from among the Convention's deputies, to implement the policies set by the Convention and coordinate the work of the government ministries. The leading figure in the Committee, although holding no special position or power within it was the veteran patriot and leader of the Parisian Jacobin club, Maximilian Robespierre. As the Committee set out to enforce the

[90] rule of the Convention, it found that in many parts of France, the elected municipal and departmental authorities were indifferent or openly hostile to its rule. Consequently, it selected deputies to the Convention to act as its agents, the 'representatives on mission'. Mostly sent out on their own, with no support or assistance, and armed only with their letters of appointment and a tricolour sash, the representatives had no choice but to turn to the unofficial supporters of the Convention, the members of the nationwide network of Jacobin clubs. The activist club members became the de facto government of the revolutionary dictatorship, sitting on the committees of surveillance and special tribunals, carrying out the orders of the representatives on mission, mobilizing the National Guard to fight the many internal enemies of the revolutionary regime.

Indeed, the more drastic the measures the regime took to fight its foreign and domestic enemies, the more enemies it created. In the larger cities of southern France, such as Lyon, Bordeaux and Marseilles, the struggle for power between the more moderate and the more radical element of the political activists, was, unlike that in the capital, won by the moderates. The news of the expulsion of the Girondin deputies from the Convention powerfully angered these moderates, and they responded by mobilizing their National Guards and launching an insurrection against the central government. The insurgents described themselves as 'Federalists', and denounced the way that the political activists of Paris had come to intimidate and dominate the legislature elected by citizens of the entire country. They wished to retain the structures of local and departmental self-government set up in the early years of the revolution, against the centralizing tendencies of the revolutionary dictatorship.

For all their hostility to the Convention, the Federalists were, mostly, supporters of the republican regime. The insurgents in western France were its open enemies; the uprisings there were the greatest internal threat the republican regime would face. These insurgencies arose from a combination of three factors, each of which demonstrated the most controversial features of the revolutionary project of replacing the society of orders with a new regime. First on the list was the religious issue: as a group, the inhabitants of western France were (and still are) deeply devout. They were vehemently hostile to the Civil Constitution of the Clergy; the overwhelming majority of the priests there refused to take the oath of loyalty to the nation. Verbal and physical attacks on juring priests, threats to purchasers of nationalized church property, violent clashes between the faithful and the patriotic National Guards dominated the years 1791 and 1792.

Other parts of France were equally devout but did not explode into such a
violent insurrection. Here we must look at another key issue of the revolution, the abolition of feudal tenures in agriculture, and the redefinition of the
nature of property. In most of France, the revolutionary legislatures who dealt
with this issue decided that the dues peasants paid their lords were feudal and
seigneurial and so, as a result of the decisions taken on the night of 4 August,
1789, were to be abolished, leaving farmers in sole possession of the land.
For the specific kind of land tenure typical in western France, however, the
legislature reached the opposite opinion: the nobles were the landowners and
the peasants were paying them rent, rather than feudal dues, so that no changes
in landownership were needed. The conditions of farmers in western France
were thus not in any way improved by the revolutionary legislation; for them,
the revolutionary regime was one that persecuted their church and offered
them nothing positive.

If the combination of these two factors created a negative and hostile
climate of opinion, the exigencies of war, in particular the institution of
conscription, provided the spark for the insurrection. Never particularly
enamoured of military service under the old regime, the inhabitants of western France now discovered that belonging to the nation meant that young
men would be forced to leave their homes and families and go to war for an
unloved government. From refusing to be conscripted to assaulting government authority was just a short step. Refractory priests and nobles quickly
stepped forward to lead these confrontations in the direction of a counter-
revolutionary insurrection. In the department of the Vendée, they organized
a 'Catholic and Royal Army', that sought to conquer first the major cities of
the region and then to march on Paris and overthrow the republic. To the
north of this department, the insurgents, known as the 'Chouans', resorted to
guerilla warfare, hiding in the dense hedgerows and thickets of the region
and ambushing supporters of the government. Both groups were in contact
with the émigrés, and hoped that they could get the British government to
intervene, landing weapons and troops on France's western coast.

The uprising in the west of France was about some of the most basic issues
of the revolution – the clash between the culture of confessionalism and the
counter-culture of the Enlightenment, the redefinition and redistribution of
agricultural property, the obligations of citizens to the nation, and the connection between foreign and domestic enemies. Here, more than anywhere
else, we can see how the attempt to replace the old regime with a new social
and political order led not to consensus but to conflict. It was a conflict
fought with a savage ferocity on both sides. Insurgents began by brutally and

[92] publicly massacring supporters of the republic, to the accompaniment of prayers and religious songs. Outnumbered supporters of the government battled desperately for their lives; on receiving reinforcements, they counter-attacked, systematically executing all their prisoners. The nature of guerilla warfare made it difficult to tell enemies of the government from non-involved civilians and even rural supporters of the regime, so that whole regions were devastated, their inhabitants killed or expelled.

The Reign of Terror and the republic of virtue

The period of the revolution running roughly from the autumn of 1793 to the summer of 1794 has come to be known as the Reign of Terror. It was, above all, a period of civil war and the government's attempt to systematically terrorize its opponents emerged from the increasingly drastic nature of the struggle and its close connection with the ever-growing foreign war being waged by the new republic. Historians' best estimate has been that there were about 35,000 victims of the Terror, half of whom died in jail, while the other half were dispatched by the guillotine, the new method of capital punishment introduced in the revolution – ironically, for humanitarian reasons – to replace the cruel practices of hanging and of drawing and quartering, by which the old regime had dealt with those condemned to death. Most of the victims of the Terror were people caught, weapon in hand, fighting against the government, so that the death toll was particularly high in those southern departments where the Federalist insurrection had taken place. These figures do not include the victims of the civil war in western France: they were much more numerous, perhaps as many as five times the number of those who died elsewhere during the Reign of Terror, albeit the victims of the civil war there were killed by fighters on both sides.

In comparison with the ideologically motivated mass murders of the twentieth century, or the slaughters carried out in ethnic, religious and tribal conflicts of recent decades, the number of deaths in the Reign of Terror seems relatively modest. As we will observe in Chapter 3, they were not out of line with similar political repressions carried out by other governments of the time against revolutionary movements. If the Reign of Terror continues to carry sinister connotations down to the present, though, it is perhaps because it occurred as part of a broader effort to remodel French society on a new basis, referred to by the phrase Robespierre coined, the 'republic of virtue'.

Even in the midst of foreign and civil war, the deputies to the Convention,
the representatives on mission and the activists of the Jacobin clubs went to
work, not just designing a republican form of government, but also creating a
fundamentally new cultural, social and political order that would be a final
and decisive break with the old regime. In some ways, this effort lasted less
than a year, broken off after the end of the most radical phase of the revolution in the summer of 1794; other aspects of it continued to be implemented,
ultimately unsuccessfully, for about a decade; still others, however, helped
shape nineteenth-century politics and have remained influential until the
present. We might see this effort as involving the creation of three new modes
of human existence: (1) a new culture that would replace the old regime
culture of confessionalism in all aspects of life; (2) a new realm of equality
in public life; (3) a new citizenship in which the nation and the republic
embodying its collective will would be the centre of loyalty and where individuals' lives would be reshaped to embody these new loyalties.

As a sign of the radical break they were making with the past, the revolutionaries changed the representation of the passage of time. Rather than
continue to count the years from the birth of Jesus Christ, they declared
22 September, 1792, to be Day 1, Year 1 of the French republic – thus representing the new regime as the beginning of a new era in human history.
The weeks were replaced with ten-day units, and the Christian Sunday was
replaced as a day of rest by the tenth-day festival, the *décadi*. Months themselves were renamed according to nature: the period of hottest weather in the
summer, became 'Thermidor', the month of heat; parts of May and June were
'Germinal', the time of the germination of the crops, and so on. This revolutionary calendar was unpopular: it reduced the number of days off work; it
obscured the religious holidays that previously marked the cycle of the year.
The majority of the population fiercely resisted efforts to impose it, so that it
was only used in official government business, and finally abandoned in 1806.

The revolutionary effort to restructure the understanding of space was more
successful. Before 1789, an endless variety of weights and measures was in
use in France, the result of irrational traditions, and, worse, sometimes based
on the person of the king – as in the length of the foot, originally taken from
the monarch's body. In place of these, the Convention created a simple, uniform, decimal system of weights and measures, whose basic unit of length
was derived from nature, one ten-millionth of the distance between the North
Pole and the equator. It was named the metre – and, unlike the revolutionary
calendar, it gradually won general acceptance and became the standard of
measurement for France and the rest of the world, with the strange exception

[94] of the United States, whose citizens cling to a system of weights and measures based on peculiar multiples of threes, twelves and sixteens. Along with the decimalization of weights and measures, the Convention decimalized the currency, creating a basic unit of one franc, subdivided into one hundred centimes.

Closely related to these innovations was a more generalized practice of renaming, replacing place and street names referring to kings or saints with ones referring to the nation or to ancient Roman and Greek heroes of republican virtue. True Jacobin patriots named their children Brutus, Cornelia or Franklin, after ancient and modern republicans, rather than baptizing them with the name of a saint. Republicans avoided the old regime forms of address, which involved distinctions between members of different orders and calling people lord or lady: everybody would address everyone else as 'citizen' or 'citizeness'.

All these practices revealed a desire to eliminate the culture of confessionalism and the republic of virtue was thoroughly inhospitable to Christianity, particularly to the Catholic Church. Jacobin activists broke into churches, smashed icons and sacred images, profaned hosts, performed public parodies of religious processions and generally showed their public contempt for Catholicism. Non-juring priests were, of course, enemies of the regime, and tended to act as they were regarded, often being found in the forefront of armed counter-revolution. However, the 'patriotic' constitutional clergy found little more sympathy. Under pressure from active Jacobins and representatives on mission, some 18,000 priests – perhaps one-sixth of all the Catholic clergy in France – publicly renounced their vocation and the religion they had claimed to profess. Many of them sealed this renunciation by getting married, and/or becoming revolutionary activists themselves.

The radicals were divided over what to put in place of Christianity. Some proposed public atheism, and the adoration of reason. The cathedral of Notre Dame in Paris was renamed and rededicated as a Temple of Reason; Jacobin clubs sponsored processions led by a young woman dressed as a 'goddess of reason'. In the end, though, a more cautious attitude, closely associated with Robespierre, prevailed and the republic began to sponsor a new, deist religion, involving the worship of a 'Supreme Being', and officially endorsing the immortality of the soul. This new religion was even more short-lived than the revolutionary calendar, not surviving the fall of Robespierre himself. The mere fact of its brief existence, though, is testimony to the desire of the radical republicans to make their regime a true and total break with the past.

The Jacobin regime resolved the doubts and hesitations about citizenship
apparent earlier in the revolution by forcefully declaring that all adult men
were citizens, possessing equal rights and duties under the law. In doing
so, however, the regime raised questions about both the ultimate extent of
citizenship and the nature of equality, questions whose ramifications would
remain important through 1850 and beyond. On two related, but previously
ambivalent points, the revolutionary regime was unequivocal. 'All adult
men' meant all adult men, without any restrictions for race or religion.
The Jacobin government abolished slavery in the French colonies (thereby
setting in motion a train of events that would lead to the creation of an
independent republic in Haiti) and announced that Jews would have full
citizenship rights.

When it came to women, the revolutionary movement was less certain.
One model of women's citizenship, or lack of it, was articulated in the Jacobin
clubs. After initial hesitations, women were allowed to attend the meetings,
although not to speak or vote at them. They could form their own, auxiliary
clubs, that would meet and discuss public issues, often following the reading
aloud of a newspaper, *La feuille villageoise*, that was designed to explain
politics to peasants, but ended up being read more by women. These auxiliary
clubs would help in planning revolutionary festivities and sew flags and
banners; their single members would pledge only to marry patriotic young
men.

Now none of this was insignificant, and, in fact, women's participation in
public festivals became ever more important as the Jacobin regime attempted
to replace the Catholic Church with its own revolutionary religion. Women
were generally seen as being especially loyal to the previously established
religion, so their being won over for the cultural policies of the revolutionary
government was a matter of considerable import. More broadly, the revolutionary regime wished to mobilize women for its ends: it called on them, as
we noted above, to support the war effort, to raise their children to be good
citizens of the republic, and to be vigilant, ever on the lookout for counter-
revolutionary conspirators. This last was something women could do
particularly well, since they were regularly in the marketplace purchasing
basic necessities for their families, and, ever since 1789, much of the fear of
counter-revolution had been connected to the food supply.

Women were thus called to work for the republic, both in the privacy of
their households and in public life as well – only not like men. Two crucial
aspects of citizenship, the right to bear arms and the right to vote, were
denied to women. Truth to tell, a large majority of women would not have

[96] expected to have these rights, although there was a smaller group, primarily Parisian intellectuals, who felt that citizenship rights belonged to men and women alike. The writer Olympe de Gouges, in her *Declaration of the Rights of Women* in 1791, made such a point. Another female activist, the actress Claire Lacombe, founded a women's political club, the 'Club of Revolutionary Republican Citizenesses', in the spring of 1793 to agitate among women on behalf of the Jacobins. The club and its members were among the supporters of the demonstrations against the Convention, that led to the purge of the Girondins, and apparently took part in the actual physical intimidation of the deputies.

However, the sight of women so politically active was unacceptable, both to the Jacobin leaders and the revolutionary municipal government of Paris. Additionally, the club's leaders had close ties to the political extremist, Jacques Roux, whom the Jacobins saw as a potential threat to their rule. The government encouraged the Parisian market women to threaten and beat up the proto-feminist activists, implying that their extreme demands were threatening the capital's food supply. Once the market women took action, the authorities then stepped in, closed the club and arrested its leaders.

In sum, the officials of the revolutionary regime, the political activists of the clubs, and most women themselves, while encouraging women to be active in specifically female ways – ways that centred on home and family, on subsistence, on supporting men in their actions – were sceptical of or downright hostile to women exercising equal citizenship with men. However, the very recruitment of women into some forms of public life, begun in the revolution, would by itself change women's political place. We will see how the sphere of women's activities expanded in the radical political movements and revolutions of the mid-nineteenth century, and the number of women involved in them increased, a development that began, however feebly, in the radical phase of the French Revolution.

The other crucial issue of citizenship that emerged in the Jacobin era was the question of whether political equality should imply some kind of social and economic equality. Now, the Jacobins were no communists. They passed a law making the advocacy of communism a capital offence, and instated the death penalty for proposing an 'agrarian law', the demand, dating from ancient Rome, that property be divided out equally. Most endorsed the ideas of Adam Smith and the physiocrats about free trade: 'the Maximum', or the large, state-run armaments workshops the government created in Paris, were measures forced on the radicals by the pressure of the sans-culottes and the exigencies of the war.

However, the Jacobins were also sceptical of unbridled capitalism. Their enemies, the Girondins, had found their prime base of support among the large mercantile and manufacturing capitalists in cities like Marseilles, Bordeaux and Lyon. Robespierre and a number of his close associates had a generalized suspicion of the 'rich', feeling that the single-minded pursuit of profit took people's minds away from the public-spiritedness needed by all citizens of the republic. Yet even here, the Jacobins were no levellers. Claude Javogues, the representative on mission who played a key role in suppressing the Federalist insurrection in Lyon, and was generally regarded, even by the other Jacobins, as an extremist and a wild man, asserted that the highest personal fortune that should be tolerated was 100,000 livres – a very substantial sum. Javogues believed that people owning such large amounts of property should use it productively, employing workers and creating wealth and useful products that would benefit all the citizens of the republic, but he would scarcely have disputed their right to own that property and make use of it in an efficient fashion, according to the laws of the market.

The Jacobins certainly envisaged a commonwealth in which all adult men would or could be owners of a certain amount of property, and in which that property would be more evenly distributed than in the old regime. They also believed in the free market and the possibility of making money and accumulating capital. It rarely occurred to them that there might be a contradiction between these two principles, that the application of the free market might decrease the proportion of adult men owning property. In so far as they reflected on this issue, they did so by engaging in an ideological sleight of hand, taking the term 'sans culottes' that had originally referred to a social and economic group and applying it to all supporters of their points of view. Even the well-to-do could be 'sans culottes' in the Jacobin regime, if they were republicans and patriots. A more self-conscious reflection on the relationship between the free market and the ability of adult men to own property would have to await the Jacobins' successors, the radicals of the first half of the nineteenth century.

Complementing or reinforcing the Jacobins' understanding of equality was their vision of the nation, and of the republic, its political manifestation. The nation was a community of citizens, a realm of fraternity, or, as we might say today, solidarity. It would guarantee the upbringing of its young people to be good citizens: the Convention developed plans for a nationwide system of primary education. It would help those unable to help themselves: the Convention decreed the creation of a 'Great Book of National Benevolence', a sort of guaranteed income programme for poor families and individuals

[98] unable to work. Both of these elaborate plans were financed by the inflationary issuing of assignats; when the French government returned to a better balanced budget and a sounder currency, in the second half of the 1790s, there was no money available for them and they remained just paper promises. Still, their very existence shows something of the idea associated with the nation.

Perhaps most of all, the Jacobins were concerned with ensuring that citizens would be loyal to the nation and that they would participate in the workings of the republic. They understood participation in particular in somewhat different terms than we might today. For them, political participation meant, above all, participation in public festivals, such festivals serving as a demonstration of loyalty to the nation. The representative on mission, or an activist of the Jacobin clubs, would gather the inhabitants of a village, plant a tree of liberty, lead them in singing revolutionary songs and conclude with cheers of 'Long live the nation!' – all this a preliminary to getting the young men who had been drafted to report to their units and go to the front. There were more elaborate and organized festivities in large cities as well; perhaps the most famous of these was the Festival of the Supreme Being, held in Paris in June 1794. It began with a ceremony in which images of atheism, egotism and discord were burned and the image of wisdom took their place. This was followed by an elaborate procession to the Champ de Mars, at which the literally hundreds of thousands of spectators sang hymns in honour of the deity and declared their hatred of tyrants and their loyalty to the nation.

Since the days of classical antiquity, European political theorists had agreed that a republican form of government could only be successful if its citizens were virtuous, public-spirited and morally upright, people who would place the common good before their own individual interests. These festivals were a form of political education, designed to reshape French men and women into good republican citizens. The goal of this political education was embodied in the republic's famous motto: 'liberty, equality, fraternity, or death'. 'Liberty' referred to the democratic republic, to a nation governing itself without a king to rule it. 'Equality' articulated the belief that all citizens were equal under the law. 'Fraternity', perhaps today the strangest of the revolutionary triad, was a reminder that citizens were brothers in the republic (note once again, women's subordinate status; their political role, as had been the case in the society of orders, was tied to their attachment to an adult male), as Christians were brothers in Christ. The last part of the motto was a reminder that the republic was an embattled regime, surrounded by foreign and domestic enemies – many, of course, of its own making – and that its

concept of citizenship was linked to an endorsement of the struggle against [99]
its enemies.

When this mystical belief in the nation and the republic embodying it, this idea that the new regime was a realm of individual regeneration, was practised in the midst of a savage civil war, then the more frightening side of the Reign of Terror appeared. To the embattled Jacobins, those French men and women who rejected the fraternity of the republic were outcasts, enemies and traitors, deserving nothing but death. When the armies of the central government reconquered Lyon from the Federalist insurgents, the Convention ordered the city to be renamed 'Ville Affranchie', 'liberated city'. The newly 'liberated' city was then to be largely destroyed and a monument placed in front of it, stating: 'Lyon made war on liberty; Lyon is no more'. This attitude was even more pronounced among the supporters of the republic fighting the civil war in western France. Prisoners were slaughtered on a large scale, most notoriously in the city of Nantes, where they were loaded, in chains, on barges, that were then sunk into the river Loire. After defeating one of the Vendéean armies, the republican troops took their prisoners:

> to the foot of the liberty tree which they had knocked down and which the soldiers had just replanted . . . The entire army was put under arms, and all those noble knights, all those faithful avengers of the crown and the Church . . . who were praying on their knees to spare their lives were guillotined, admist cries repeated a thousand times by our soldiers of 'Long live the Republic and its defenders!'[4]

We can see here, quite clearly, the idea of a republic as the regeneration of the nation, accomplished, in part, by the physical extirpation of its enemies, those who supported the previously existing regime.

The high point of the Jacobin regime and its end

The policies of the revolutionary regime brought it victory against its domestic and foreign enemies. By the end of 1793, the Federalist insurgents had been defeated and destroyed, as had been the counter-revolutionary army of the Vendée. (The guerilla warfare of the Chouans would prove more difficult to suppress.) French troops were victorious on all fronts against the foreign armies and by the spring of 1794 had repulsed the invaders and

[100]   carried the war beyond the frontiers. The government's leaders began to take steps to end the state of emergency.

The Revolutionary Armies were disbanded; many of the representatives on mission were recalled and the execution of the law on suspects and other terrorist legislation was taken out of the hands of the clubs or other ad hoc bodies and given to municipal councils, who would report regularly to the central government. Indeed, in the first half of 1794 the regime consistently downgraded the clubs, absorbing many of their most activist members into the newly created governmental apparatus. For the rest of the revolution, and, in many ways, until the 1820s, political radicalism would increasingly be associated with government employees and members of the armed forces. While not abolishing price controls, the government decided to add controls on wages to them, and set wage levels in Paris at a disquietingly low level. There is no mistaking the tendency toward bureaucratization, toward regularization of public business, toward an effort to tame the undisciplined sansculottes, even at the cost of losing their active sympathies.

Yet, at the same time as affairs seemed to be returning to normal and the state of emergency coming to an end, the government took measures to increase the Terror, so that this period is sometimes known as the 'Great Terror'. All revolutionary tribunal proceedings were centralized in Paris; arrests and executions in the capital itself rose sharply in June–July 1794; in June of that year a law was passed denying those accused of political crimes the right to a lawyer and pretty much abandoning the necessity to provide any evidence: merely being accused was proof of guilt. In addition, the Terror was applied, for the first time, not just to counter-revolutionaries, but to strong supporters of the republic.

Of all these victims of the Great Terror, the most spectacular was Georges Danton, the great revolutionary orator. Danton had always been a political radical, and, in fact, a long-term associate of Robespierre; his arrest and trial had been preceded by two eerie meetings with the paragon of virtue himself. The charges of treason brought against him were preposterous, and when he began to speak for himself at his trial, it quickly became evident that the court would believe him. Hastily, Robespierre had the Convention pass a law depriving Danton of the right to speak in his own defence (precursor to the later, broader legislation, in that respect) and saw to his quick condemnation and execution.

The trial of Danton demonstrated the danger of the Jacobin definition of the republic as a reign of virtue. Citizens, those entitled to have a voice in government, were those who were unselfish and public-spirited; others, who

represented not the public good but particular special interests, or 'factions',
as contemporaries said, were not citizens and had no rights – indeed, as potential enemies of the regime, they might expect to be arrested and executed.
Of course, the question then arose of just who was public-spirited; who knew
when he was acting on behalf of the nation and not for some insidious special
interest? Robespierre and his closest associates seemed to be asserting that
only they were public-spirited and anyone who opposed them or even disagreed with them was, by definition, a traitor.

For the deputies to the Convention, and the leading revolutionary activists in Paris, this attitude meant that anyone who disagreed with Robespierre,
or even might potentially disagree with him, was in danger of being arrested,
brought before a revolutionary tribunal, where the accused could not defend
themselves, and summarily executed. The case of Danton showed that this
could happen to, literally, anyone. As rumours mounted of a new wave of
arrests in June–July 1794, the deputies were moved to take action.

Robespierre was no Stalin or Hitler, no dictator with special powers. He
was just one deputy to the Convention, re-elected each month to the emergency executive, the Committee of Public Safety. He could be voted off the
committee, impeached and brought to trial under the very laws he had passed,
all by a majority vote of the Convention. And this was what happened to
Robespierre and his close associates on the ninth day of the month of
Thermidor in the Year Two of the French Republic – or, for those preferring
the old-fashioned calendar, on 27 July, in the Year of Our Lord, 1794.
Robespierre's supporters tried to rally the sans-culottes of Paris to his
defence, but the measures taken by the Jacobin government itself earlier
that year had disorganized and alienated its supporters among the common
people of Paris. Their attempted insurrection fizzled, and on the following
day the proponent of the republic of virtue was sent to the guillotine, along
with some eighty of his political allies and key supporters.

The Thermidoreans and the problem of ending the revolution

To contemporaries the meaning of the events of 9–10 Thermidor was
at first unclear. Were the deputies to the Convention intending to continue the Reign of Terror, only without Robespierre, or were they going to
initiate a basic change in government policy? By the autumn of 1794, the

[102]   Thermidoreans, as the dominant group in the Convention after the fall of
Robespierre is known, had dismantled the Terror. They began by stripping
the Committee of Public Safety of its role as an emergency executive. Then
they released tens of thousands of political suspects from gaol, and abolished
the Revolutionary Tribunal, the committees of surveillance, and the laws
depriving the accused in political trials of their rights. Municipal and departmental administration had their autonomy restored, and the role of representatives on mission was abolished. Prominent Terrorists were brought to
trial, such as Jean Baptiste Carrier, the representative on mission who had
been responsible for the mass drownings in Nantes, or Antoine Fouquier-
Tinville, the public prosecutor in the former Revolutionary Tribunal in Paris.
Their trials became widely publicized condemnations of the policies of the
Jacobin regime.

The Thermidoreans followed this repudiation of the Terror by attacking
the Jacobin clubs, which they held responsible for it. The clubs were first
denied the right to act collectively or correspond with each other, and later
prohibited. The Girondin deputies whom the Jacobins had expelled from the
Convention, and who had survived the Reign of Terror, were recalled early
in 1795. The Convention decreed the separation of church and state, and the
government cancelled the policy of persecuting the Catholic Church, permitting the resumption of religious services, at least so long as they occurred
indoors, in a church, and not out in public. The government negotiated a
truce with the leaders of the Chouans, the anti-republican guerillas of northwestern France. Other measures of the revolutionary government, particularly the Maximum, were abolished.

Finally, the Convention wrote yet another constitution. The republic was
now to be governed by a bicameral legislature and a five-man executive, the
Directory, that was separate from the legislature and one of whose members
would be replaced each year. While most (if not all) adult men would be eligible to vote, they would not vote directly for their representatives, but for
electors, who would in turn choose the deputies. To be an elector, however,
required a very strict property qualification: only some 30,000 adult men in
France possessed enough property to be eligible.

Contemporaries referred to these measures as a 'reaction' to the policies of
the Jacobins (the origins of the modern meaning of 'reactionary', as someone
who seeks to reverse left-wing or revolutionary policies), and so they were.
They involved, in effect, a different interpretation of the principles of the
Declaration of the Rights of Man. If the Jacobins had exalted the principle of
the sovereignty of the nation, and made it the basis of their regime, the

Thermidoreans subordinated it to the ideas of the division of powers, the [103] individual's basic civil rights, and a more federalized system of government. The Jacobins stressed equality under the law; the Thermidoreans the claims of the owners of property. The Jacobins felt that the destruction of absolutism and the society of orders, and their replacement with a new revolutionary regime would also require the suppression of the old regime culture of confessionalism; the Thermidoreans hoped that parts of that old culture could coexist with the republic of property-owners they were designing.

The Thermidoreans were returning to the project of the moderate politicians of 1790–91: bringing the revolution to an end, establishing a new government, and new social and economic arrangements that the French people could accept, rather than advocating a government of civil war that would terrorize its opponents into submission. The problem with these efforts was that the years between 1791 and 1795 had been filled with violence, with foreign and domestic war, economic turmoil, and resulting hatreds that did not subside and made a consensus solution impossible. Even before the new constitution went into practice, opponents of the new government attacked it from all sides.

For the sans-culottes of Paris, and, more generally for the lower middle and lower classes in France, the abolition of price controls was an economic disaster. The imposition of the Maximum had made farmers reluctant to plant, and an already modest sowing was diminished by the bad harvest of 1794. The harsh winter of 1795, one of the coldest in the century, when wolves roamed in the outskirts of Paris, made the subsistence catastrophe complete. Inflation galloped away; bread prices were eleven times higher than in 1790; mortality to famine and hunger reached new heights. Starving and despairing, crowds of thousands of sans-culottes, with women well represented among them – as was always the case when subsistence was at issue – invaded the Convention twice in the spring of 1795 (the insurrections of Prarial and Germinal, named after the months in the revolutionary calendar when they took place), attacking the deputies and murdering one of them. The crowds demanded 'bread and the constitution of 1793', i.e., a return to the Jacobin regime and to price controls; they received, instead, armed opposition on the part of the National Guard, whom the Thermidoreans had once more restricted to property owners. Their movement was easily defeated.

However, the call for a return to the Jacobin regime was feeble, compared to what the enemies of the Jacobins were doing. In Paris, bodies of young men – mostly lawyers, law clerks and draft-dodgers – systematically assaulted Jacobin and sans-culottes activists, invaded meetings of the clubs and the

[104]   sections, beat up the participants and drove them away. The Thermidorean government turned a blind eye to the actions of these young men; the name they chose for themselves, *muscadins* – scoundrels – showed their open repudiation of the former republic of virtue. However, the actions of the *muscadins* in the capital city paled before what was going on in the provinces, particularly in the southern part of the country.

There, bands of armed young men, composed in large part of draft-dodgers and deserters from the army, systematically murdered the local supporters of the Jacobins. The local authorities and the members of the National Guard scarcely hid their sympathies for the actions, and often facilitated them, by rounding up former Jacobins and placing them in gaol, where they would be particularly easy to murder on a large scale. Revenge and the Mediterranean tradition of vendetta played a large role in these slaughters, and the killers generally specialized in victimizing their neighbours, rather than murdering Terrorists from towns other than their own. However, the name of these actions, the 'White Terror', from the white flag, the banner of the Bourbon monarchs, shows the political context of such murders. Calling themselves the 'Companies of Jesus', and passing out cards with images of the Virgin Mary, the killers made clear their hostility not just to the Jacobins but to the entire republican regime. Blending opposition to the draft, a more generalized hatred of outsiders from a centralized government intervening in their town or village life, vague sentiments of counter-revolution and increasingly open highway robbery, such bands of young men undermined governmental authority in the southern part of the country for the rest of the 1790s. Taxes could not be collected; laws could not be enforced; conscripts would not report to their units; deserters would find refuge.

Finally, the Thermidoreans' attempt to reconcile the republic and the Catholic Church proved an unmitigated failure. No sooner were the actions of the refractory clergy legalized, than they began denouncing the republic as the realm of Satan and telling the faithful that all good Catholics needed to demand a return of the confiscated property of the church (in many parts of France, the purchasers of the church lands were duly assaulted and murdered), and a restoration of the monarchy, the tithe, and the seigneurial system. The Chouans in western France, shortly after signing their truce, resumed their guerilla activities, this time in conjunction with a landing of émigrés, supported by the British navy. In Paris itself, the royalists attempted an uprising, their street fighters led by the *muscadins*. Use of the army was required to suppress both these uprisings.

The Thermidoreans thus made the unpleasant discovery that there was no political consensus in France. Rather, the different, sharply opposing currents of public life that had existed since the beginning of the 1790s, continued – not just unabated, but with increasing, murderous passions. Abolishing the revolutionary dictatorship, restoring civil liberties and representative government merely allowed these opposing groups to fight each other on a more equal footing.

The Directory and the end of representative government

The government based on the constitution drawn up by the Convention, known after its executive as the Directory, lasted for four years, from the autumn of 1795 until December 1799. It was thus the longest-lived of all the regimes since 1789 (the National Assembly had ruled for two years; the constitutional monarchy for less than one; the Convention for three), but from its very beginnings it was a government buffeted by hostility from the left and the right and lacking any support in French society. The Directory's politics were, consequently, a seesaw: moving to the right in 1795 and 1796, until the power of the royalists reached the point of abolishing the republican regime; veering back to the left in 1797–98, and encouraging a revival of the Jacobins, until it seemed that a new Reign of Terror was about to begin in 1799; then veering to the right again, this time ending in the abolition of representative government altogether.

Behind this seesaw, we can note two consistent and related patterns of development in the Directory: the centralization, bureaucratization and consolidation of government administration, on the one hand, and the pursuit of foreign war, with the consequent promotion of the importance of the armed forces, on the other. The government ministries of war, foreign affairs, finance and police (in charge of domestic affairs), that had expanded greatly during the Reign of Terror, were reorganized; attempts were made to make their employees over into a professional civil service. 'National agents' were sent to oversee the work of the municipal and departmental governments. The assignats, which had lost almost all their value, were repudiated, thus resolving the long problem of government debt that had started the revolution. By reintroducing indirect taxes, the Directory attempted to put state finances on a sound basis. All of these efforts remained incomplete:

[106] government reorganization was never effective; the authority of the central government remained tenuous; and finances were never really secure. Nonetheless, the direction of the efforts was clear. Ultimately, there would be an executive that would not have to depend on a legislature, all too likely to be dominated by opponents of the government.

The Directory also continued the war with the European powers, begun in 1792. Once foreign troops had been driven out in 1794, all the fighting took place outside the borders of France – and would continue to do so, until 1814. Although there were reverses and setbacks, overall the war went well, and the victorious generals became national heroes. Under these circumstances, it was an ever-greater temptation to use the army for political purposes – a temptation that the Directors were unable to resist, and that they would ultimately use to bring their own regime to an end.

It is against this background of administrative centralization and foreign war that we can trace the political fluctuations of the Directory. The legislative elections of 1795 – held, like all the elections of the Revolution, with a cumbersome electoral system and a low turnout – were a victory for the royalists. In many parts of France, with the White Terror in full swing, republicans were too frightened to turn out to vote. Fearing this would happen, the Convention had rigged the results in advance by decreeing that two-thirds of the new legislators had to be chosen from the ranks of the Convention itself, thus preventing a total royalist victory and ensuring that the executive of the government, the Directory, would be loyal to the republic.

Nonetheless, the royalists went from strength to strength in 1795–96, gaining influence both within the legislature and outside of it. Veteran Jacobins in Paris became alarmed, and began to organize against the regime, openly in the 'Pantheon Club', a revived Jacobin club, and, in secret, with conspiratorial measures. The leader of this conspiracy, Gracchus Babeuf, has become famous in the history of socialism, since, in private, he advocated measures for the collective cultivation of farmland, and was hostile to large fortunes. More important than Babeuf's proto-communist ideas, which were not shared by most of his fellow-conspirators, and were not advocated consistently by Babeuf himself, was the way Babeuf and his 'Conspiracy of Equals' planned to seize power. Previously, radicals had mobilized the sans-culottes, the masses of the population of Paris, to seize power. By 1796, however, the sans-culottes were impoverished and apathetic, the political activists among them either arrested or working full time for the government. Instead of open political mobilization, the conspirators turned to a coup, to be carried out by members of a secretly organized group in conjunction with the help of friendly army units. This turn from open agitation to a secret society, and a conspiracy culminating in a military coup would characterize radical politics in Europe from the late 1790s until 1830 and beyond.

Babeuf's conspiracy was infiltrated by the police, and his planned coup a failure. He and several of his co-conspirators were tried and sent to the guillotine. However, his alarm about the progress of royalists was shared by the more moderate republicans of the Directory, especially when the royalists were victorious again in the elections of 1797, and followed up their victory with legislation designed to hamstring the republican executive, and with renewed preparations for an insurrection in Paris. Moving pro-republican troops into the capital, the Directors carried out a coup in September 1797 (known, after the date in the revolutionary calendar as the coup of 18 Fructidor, Year 5), arresting deputies, quashing the mandates of others, prohibiting oppositional newspapers. Large numbers of politically unreliable municipal administrators were dismissed from their posts.

The Directory then moved to the left. Reviving the tactics of the Jacobin regime, the Directors attempted to reinforce the culture of republicanism. The revolutionary calendar was to be strictly implemented; public festivals were ordered for every *décadi* and a whole new series of national holidays, complete with their festivals, was decreed. A new deist religion, theophilan-thropy, was given public support. Along with these tactics went a renewed offensive against the culture of confessionalism. Some 1,800 non-juring priests were rounded up and interned on islands off the coast; churches were auctioned off by the hundreds to the highest bidder.

In these circumstances, the former Jacobins were able to return to public life. Enjoying the benevolent neutrality of the government, they formed new political clubs, the 'Constitutional Circles'. There were several hundred of them across France, perhaps most influential in the southern city of Toulouse, where they controlled the municipal government. While some of these club members admitted that they had gone too far in 1793–94, and called on radicals to learn from the experiences of that era and moderate both their means and ends, others were unreconstructed Terrorists, who made no secret of their desire to repeat the policies of Robespierre's regime.

This prospect of the revival of the Terror was altogether too much for the Directory and the politicians supporting it, since their whole regime had been constructed on a repudiation of it. When the radicals made major gains in the elections of 1798, the government responded with a new coup in May of that year (22 Floréal, Year 6 of the revolutionary calendar), quashing the mandates of most of the leftist deputies, and closing down many of the

[108]   Constitutional Circles. This swing back to the right encouraged the royalists, in turn, and led to the final crisis of the Directorial regime.

The crisis began on the battlefield, as the war turned against the republic's forces – above all, because of the intervention of troops of the tsar. Fighting in Switzerland and Holland raised the spectre of a renewed invasion of France. At the same time, the Chouans in the northwest rose up in one last effort, and royalist conspirators launched an uprising in the southwestern part of the country. Both of these movements enjoyed initial success and threatened to capture major urban centres. It seemed like 1793 all over again, and the response of the radicals and of a vocal minority in the legislature was to call for a revival of Terrorist policies: a new declaration that the fatherland was in danger; a law taking former nobles and clergy hostage against counter-revolutionary movements; a forced loan levied on the rich to pay for the war effort.

This was the last straw for the Directors and a majority of them resolved to terminate the entire system of parliamentary government. To do this, they needed the army, and a popular general who would carry out their plans. Royalists, too, had toyed with the idea of restoring the monarch through a similar military coup, and the émigrés had even tried to bribe several of the republic's generals to this effect. Characteristically, the generals took their money but never acted. The Directors would be more successful in their search, settling on Napoleon Bonaparte. An effective military leader, whose triumphs had included recapturing the port of Toulon from the British in 1794, defeating the royalist insurgents in Paris the following year, victories over the Austrians in northern Italy, and, most recently, leading the militarily unsuccessful but spectacular French expedition to Egypt, Bonaparte was a popular and well-known figure. He was politically well connected through his wife Josephine de Beauharnais, whose family had close ties to leading politicians and through his brother Lucien, a parliamentary deputy. He had provided troops from his command for the coup of Fructidor, Year 5, and thus shown his loyalty to the directorial regime.

On the 18 Brumaire, Year 7 (9 November 1799), he was placed in charge of the Paris garrison. Troops under his command moved the legislators out of Paris, and on the following day intimidated them into placing power in the hands of three 'Consuls', Bonparate himself and two of the Directors. Any pretence of representative government, a pretence that had been growing steadily thinner across the history of the Directory, was now at an end.

The revolutionaries of 1789 had aimed to end absolutist rule, destroy the society of orders and promote political participation, secure individual rights and redefine private property, making it more secure. They succeeded in their negative goals, in their efforts to terminate the old regime, but attempting to implement their positive goals proved impossible in a country where the government had a chronic fiscal problem, whose inhabitants were obsessed – with good reason – by fears about the food supply, and where supporters of the culture of confessionalism and the counterculture of the Enlightenment faced each other across a yawning gap of suspicion and hostility. The attempt was not just impossible but deeply and bitterly divisive – leading to the launching of a foreign war, the outbreak of a bloody civil war, and to the resulting creation of bitter hatreds. It ensured that no regime even pretending to be based on the consent of the governed (one of the key principles with which the revolution began) could hope to maintain its existence. It would take an authoritarian regime to restore a relative stability to France and to begin sorting out the results of the revolution into new social and political order. The resulting state of affairs would not be universally accepted and would generate persistent conflicts in the first half of the nineteenth century – whose partisans generally took their positions from those first articulated between 1789 and 1799 – but it would never generate the same degree of discord and hatred as France experienced in the decade of revolution.

Notes

1. Quoted in Timothy Tackett, *Becoming a Revolutionary: The Deputies of the French National Assembly and the Emergence of a Revolutionary Culture (1789–1790)* (Princeton, 1996), p. 173.

2. Quoted in David Jordan, *The King's Trial: The French Revolution vs. Louis XVI* (Berkeley, 1979), p. 234.

3. Quoted in T.C.W. Blanning, *The French Revolutinary Wars 1787–1802* (London, 1996), pp. 100–1.

4. Quoted in Donald Sutherland, 'The Vendée', in Keith Baker (ed.), *The French Revolution and the Creation of Modern Political Culture*, 4 vols (London, 1987–1994), vol. 4, p. 103.

CHAPTER 3

THE FRENCH REVOLUTION AND EUROPE

Not just in France

The events of the summer of 1789 made it clear to people throughout the European continent that something extraordinary was occurring in France. The rapid succession of ever more drastic changes in the next four years, culminating in the proclamation of the republic and the execution of the king – both truly astonishing to contemporaries – only heightened that impression. As one might expect, intellectuals were particularly impressed, and the implications of the revolutionary events were passionately debated by British romantic poets, German students of philosophy, and Italian Enlightened authors. The statesmen and diplomats of the European powers, as well as members of the upper classes more generally interested in public affairs, followed closely developments in the continent's leading military power, and also reflected on the implications of the revolutionary reordering of France for domestic policy.

In some countries, Russia in particular, news of the French Revolution remained largely restricted to members of such elite groups throughout the 1790s. Elsewhere, whether via the gradual process of the circulation of information, or the more drastic and abrupt intervention of warfare, consideration of the implications of the French Revolution reached beyond the usual groups interested in politics during the old regime: the upper ranks of the society of orders, government officials, intellectuals and professionals, or affluent townspeople. Journeymen artisans in the north German city of Hamburg, tenant farmers of County Wexford in Ireland, agricultural labourers of Calabria, in southern Italy, soldiers in the Spanish army, to mention just a few examples from middle and lower ranks of European society, would all learn of and react to the French Revolution – often in drastic fashion – in the ten years following the fall of the Bastille.

The events in France were as polarizing as they were fascinating. Increasingly, those Europeans who were politically active had to take a position on the revolution, to support or to oppose it. More than that, the new way of thinking about politics introduced by the French revolutionaries exerted a powerful influence on the inhabitants of other countries, who tended to reinterpret their own social and political conflicts in terms of the French Revolution. In such circumstances, the idea of a recurrence of the revolution – of a similar sort of social and political upheaval ocurring in Great Britain, the German and Italian states, Hungary or Poland, for instance – became a central component of the political process, with some advocating it, others opposing it, still others imagining different ways of initiating the changes brought about by the revolution. Such a fixation on a potential repetition of 1789 or 1793 would remain central to political debate and political conflict in Europe until the middle of the nineteenth century.

Yet, ultimately, the idea of a recurrence of the revolution was a chimera, even in 1848, when it seemed, for a moment, as though 1789 was repeating itself Europe-wide. In part, the French Revolution could not be repeated, because other countries were not France, and translating French political language and political alignments to the very different social and economic landscapes of Poland, Hungary, Russia, Spain or southern Italy could only produce different results. In the 1790s, at least, there was another, more compelling reason for the failure of a revolution in France to spur similar uprisings in other countries, as would occur in 1830 and 1848. The war that began in 1792 and soon found revolutionary France in conflict with virtually all of Europe, quickly came to dominate internal domestic conflicts in most countries of the continent. Partisans of social, economic, cultural or political change – already reinterpreted in terms set down by the revolution in France – were forced by the pressures of warfare to become supporters of the French armies, their proposed revolution largely synonymous with occupation by foreign troops. The supporters of the status quo, on the other hand, could present their political views as opposition to invasion and foreign conquest.

In this chapter, we will outline the process of response to the revolution. Beginning with the initial evaluations, we will move on to the hardening and polarization of opinions that followed in 1792–93, in the wake of the outbreak of war and the declaration of the republic in France, and explain the terms of the debate on the revolution. Next to be considered is the warfare of the 1790s, the wars of the first and second coalitions, and the chapter will conclude by examining how the course of the warfare determined the domestic politics of different European countries.

[112] Initial impressions

The calling of the Estates General, its transformation into a National Assembly, the struggles of the summer of 1789 and the beginning of the great work of reform met with a strikingly positive response outside of France. Enlightened thinkers and statesmen saw these events as a justification of their own ideas and policies. The years 1789–90 were the last in the life of the reforming Holy Roman Emperor, Joseph II, and they were bitter ones for him, as widespread opposition forced him to retract most of his reforms. In these difficult times, the French Revolution was a small consolation, since he saw it as proof that his ideas would triumph in another country, if not in his own. Immanuel Kant, the last great philosopher of the Enlightenment, was a professor at the University of Königsberg, in the far eastern reaches of the Kingdom of Prussia. A long-term bachelor, and notoriously set in his domestic ways, Kant took a promenade every day, without fail, at 3.00 p.m., so promptly, that the good burghers of the town set their watches by his stroll. On the day that the news of the fall of the Bastille reached distant Königsberg, Kant was so overcome with excitement that he completely forgot to take his constitutional. More lively was the response to the fall of the Bastille in St Petersburg, where merchants from France, Denmark, England, the Netherlands, Germany and Russia itself embraced in the streets on hearing the news. The British poet William Wordsworth would later write about his own feelings at the great news coming from France: 'Bliss was it in that dawn to be alive/But to be young, was very heaven!'

On a different and more cynical level, the statesmen of the Great Powers welcomed the news from France, since it seemed to presage a period when Europe's most powerful nation would be preoccupied – whether in violent or peaceful fashion – with its internal affairs and for a time would be unable to take part in diplomatic and military confrontations. Great Britain would have a respite from the challenges of its naval and colonial rival. The three eastern powers, Prussia, Austria and Russia, who were deeply involved in wars against the Ottoman empire and, especially, in the partition of Poland among them, could continue, without having to worry about French interventions on their western flanks.

Somewhat more disturbing to the established order was the response of the continent's lower classes. Particularly on the French borders, although further off as well, there was a wave of refusals to pay taxes, peasant boycotts of feudal obligations and the like, in the wake of the unruly summer of 1789. In 1790, ten thousand peasants in the central German Electorate of Saxony

rose up against their feudal lords, sending hundreds of nobles fleeing to
the capital city of Dresden and major troop deployments were required to
repress the rising. Peasant insurgents explicitly mentioned the French
Revolution and its rustic uprisings of the previous year as an inspiration for
their actions.

Now the Saxon peasants were also stirred up by lay Protestant preachers
who told them that the French Revolution presaged the Second Coming of
Christ, suggesting that the rebellious countryfolk had only the vaguest idea
of exactly what was happening in France. Such vagueness was by no means a
speciality of the rural lower classes. In 1791, all the journeymen artisans in
Hamburg went on strike, and paraded through the city, calling out, 'Long
live the constitution.' This elision of constitution and revolution also demonstrates the point made by the Saxon peasants: the lower classes knew
that something was going on in France, that it related to their grievances
with the society of orders, but exactly what was going on and how it would
relate to them was not completely clear.

Although the stated motivations may have been novel, neither (relatively)
small-scale peasant uprisings nor unwillingness to pay taxes, nor demonstrations of journeymen artisans were anything unusual in the old regime.
Outside of France, the independent actions of the lower classes in the wake
of the great events of 1789 posed no serious threat to the absolutist regimes
or the society of orders. It was the internal dynamics of the revolution itself,
in the years 1792–93, that would transform it from an event whose effects
could be seen as positive, benign, or, at the very worst, mildly annoying, to a
powerful, looming threat to the continuation of the existing order everywhere
in Europe.

Hardening lines and polarizing attitudes

The Declaration of the Rights of Man asserted that the nation was the source
of all sovereignty, the will of the nation overriding any of the privileges
or chartered rights of the society of orders. Part of the internationally disruptive force of this idea was that the will of the French nation could override
privileges granted outside the French kingdom. The county of Avignon, in
southern France, was ruled by the pope, but the inhabitants' assertion that
they were part of the French nation – duly expressed in 1791 after a small-
scale but quite bloody civil war between partisans of French and of papal

rule – brought the county's annexation by France. A similar fate awaited the French-speaking inhabitants of Savoy, on the nation's southeast borders, ruled by the Italian Kingdom of Piedmont. France's eastern province of Alsace had been conquered from the Holy Roman Empire in the seventeenth century, but the French kings and the emperor had guaranteed the seigneurial rights of its feudal lords, many of them Germans living across the river Rhine. On the night of 4 August, 1789, the National Assembly, expressing the will of the sovereign nation, brought the feudal regime to an end in all of France, including Alsace, no matter who had previously guaranteed or exercised privileges there.

Such an exaltation of the sovereignty of the nation would be a threat to those states located on the French borders, in the Low Countries, western Germany, northwestern Italy, or Switzerland, whose inhabitants could be claimed as part of the French nation. This was difficult enough, but in November 1792, following the outbreak of war between France and a number of the European powers, the Convention declared that it would offer assistance to any and all peoples wishing to regain their liberty, thus creating the spectre of many national sovereignties that could disrupt the structure of government and society anywhere on the continent. The proclamation of the republic, the trial and execution of the king, and the institution of the Reign of Terror in 1792 and 1793 made it clear that the assertion of the sovereignty of the nation on the French model would take a particularly drastic course.

In such a situation, all those who stood between an intransigent, unyielding defence of the old regime on the one hand, and the creation of a revolutionary Jacobin republic, on the other – partisans of Enlightened absolutism, for instance, proponents of a constitutional monarchy, as was attempted in the early stages of the French Revolution, or as envisaged by the Whig opposition in Great Britain – were swept aside. They could not follow a moderate course and were forced to choose between one of the two extremes that were competing on the battlefield. The intellectual debate on the French Revolution that developed across Europe in the 1790s generally followed these lines of polarization.

In this debate, all the running was made by the counter-revolutionaries. Two in particular, Edmund Burke and Augustin Barruel, writing at the beginning and end of the 1790s, set the terms on the counter-revolutionary side, and were frequently seconded and imitated. In *Reflections on the Revolution in France* (first published in 1790), Burke launched a fierce attack on the work of the National Assembly by offering a justification for privileges and the society of orders. They were not, as the revolutionaries asserted, irrational survivals and oppressive burdens; they had a purpose, namely creating a structure of legitimacy that guaranteed all social and political order and all private property. If one revoked the nobility's claims to feudal dues, Burke noted acerbically, what justification remained for the peasants to pay rent to bourgeois landlords? The traditional provinces, with their long history and acquired retinue of privileges, were something people could identify with, and that identification helped to bring their loyalties to a higher level, that of the monarchy as a whole. Newly created departments, with geometrically drawn boundaries, would inspire no loyalty and so throw the whole structure of the state into chaos. By asserting that the monarch did not rule by divine right, but was merely the chief executive under a newly written constitution, by abolishing the estates and parlements and transforming beyond recognition the established church – all the institutions that people had obeyed, that provided the laws with their legitimacy – the revolution had removed all reasons for people to pay attention to any law at all. By destroying all historically based legitimate order, Burke concluded, the revolution was creating a state of anarchy, that could only end in the rule of force, in a military despotism.

Written at an early stage of the revolution, the *Reflections* seemed overly pessimistic, since in 1790 a new order was visibly in the making. What followed in the rest of the decade, however, showed that creating a new structure of social and political legitimacy was not so simple; the succession of violent, authoritarian and unstable regimes in revolutionary France, culminating, just as Burke had foreseen, in the rule of a general, gave the *Reflections* a great convincing force. It was translated into most European languages, and read with wide approval in the German states, in Switzerland, Italy, and even in Russia. In an ironic tribute to the power of the old regime's culture of confessionalism, the book was banned in Spain, the Inquisition feeling that anything written by a Protestant, even a savage blast at a godless revolutionary regime, was inappropriate for Catholic readers.

This incident, though, reveals a gap in Burke's work. He treated the revolutionaries as impractical and doctrinaire, as demagogues and incompetents, emphasizing what they were destroying, and not taking entirely seriously their positive aims and goals, or their facility in reaching them. In 1799, an émigré French priest, Augustin Barruel, wrote *Memoirs towards a History of Jacobinism*, that presented the aspirations of the French revolutionaries in a different light. Barruel had been a Jesuit, a member of a religious order that had been a particularly strong enemy of the counterculture of the Enlightenment, and whose suppression by the Pope in 1773 had been widely celebrated by Enlightened thinkers. Barruel presented precisely these thinkers as the forces behind the upheavals following 1789.

According to Barruel, the French Revolution was the result of an atheistic conspiracy to destroy Christianity – and, as an ex-Jesuit, when he talked about Christianity, he meant the Catholic Church. Gathering together in masonic lodges and other secret groups, such as the Society of the Illuminati (a German offshoot of the Masons, whose members, largely Enlightened government officials, had tried to press, systematically for political and socioeconomic reforms, even if their monarchical superiors had not encouraged them to do so). Enlightened intellectuals had pulled the strings behind the scenes in all the events of the revolution, with the intent of replacing a Christian social and political order with their godless one. Barruel's conspiracy theories are best described as paranoid fantasies, although with them he started a long and dubious tradition of interpreting political events as the results of secret machinations of the Masons or the Illuminati. Passing through such adherents as the Nazis, who were great believers in these kinds of conspiracies (adding the Jews to the Masons and the Illuminati in their list of conspirators) this intellectual tradition continues in certain circles until the present day. If Barruel's account of conspiracy is dubious, his assertion that the revolution was aimed at the old regime culture of confessionalism is not, and in emphasizing this, he brought to centre stage a crucial point about the revolution that Burke had touched upon, at best, very lightly. The revolution was an attempt to create a secular social and political order, not founded on the values of revealed religion – to devise, in effect, a new version of social and political legitimacy, something Burke had regarded as impossible. Controversies over such an effort would continue to play a central role in political life during the first half of the nineteenth century, and beyond.

The ideas expressed by Burke and Barruel were taken up, refined and modified by authors everywhere in Europe outside of France, and there were few who would oppose them. The Reign of Terror and the warfare accompanying it largely destroyed initial sympathies for the Revolution, among both intellectuals and the common people. Proponents of any form of social or political change, no matter how moderate, were likely to be branded 'Jacobins' – i.e., murderous, godless subversives – if they could be heard at all, since governments at war with France tightened already restrictive censorship. One example of the response to this new situation of an intellectual sympathizer with the revolution was the political doctrine expounded by Immanuel Kant in his late works. He asserted that it was a subject's duty to obey his monarch without question, just as any absolutist might want, although, if a revolution should somehow happen, then the subject was [117] obligated to act as a free citizen of the new regime.

The one voice clearly opposing this counter-revolutionary tide was the veteran cosmopolitan revolutionary, Thomas Paine. A native Briton but pro-pagandist for the American revolutionaries and supporter of their French counterparts (he was actually elected as a deputy to the Convention but his sympathies with the Girondins led to a jail sentence, from which he, unlike many prominent figures imprisoned at the time, escaped with his life), Paine responded to Burke in vigorous terms with *The Rights of Man* (1791–92). There, he directly attacked Burke's apotheosis of tradition. Starting from Burke's prejudices, such as his denunciation of the common people as the 'swinish multitude', his defence of the landed aristocracy, or the strange passages in the *Reflections* where Burke describes Marie Antoinette as almost a saint, Paine denounced the whole structure of tradition that Burke praised as an elaborate justification for past acts of oppression, robbery and tyranny. Abuses were not to be sanctioned merely because they had existed for a long time.

However, the question Burke posed about the basis of the legitimacy of a new regime was also one that Paine answered. In the second part of his book, he sketched in the outlines of a democratic and republican government, that would also provide for the welfare of the majority of the population, by low-ering taxes on basic items of consumption, introducing a progressive income tax, funding public education, and creating what we might today call social insurance programmes, such as family allowances, or state assistance for the elderly. Paine's book was popular in the British Isles, selling tens of thou-sands of copies. His version of a democratic regime, rather different from the Jacobins' republic of virtue, would prove to have a quite interesting political history in the nineteenth century. We should note, though, that his defence of the principles of the French Revolution appeared early in the decade; with the outbreak of war and the hardening of political lines, such a work could no longer be published. From 1793–94 onwards, the debate about the French Revolution was carried out primarily on the field of battle.

Revolutionary warfare

The war that began in 1792 would continue uninterrupted until 1815, except for a brief interlude of peace in 1802–3. There are several common features of this war that we need to keep in mind, as we consider the conflicts in the present chapter and in Chapter 4. First is the nature of the contending parties. Throughout the entire period, the French faced two main enemies: the Austrians on land and the British at sea. The two other Great Powers, Prussia and Russia, would come and go on different sides, as would most of the lesser European powers, such as the smaller German and Italian states, Holland, Spain, Portugal, Denmark or Sweden. In the end, it would take an alliance of virtually all those states to overcome the French armies, whose downfall, of course, was occasioned by Napoleon's disastrous invasion of Russia in 1812, but even here the French fate was only sealed by the Austrian decision to join the war against France in 1813.

This alignment of the powers was, in and of itself, not new. Since the days of Louis XIV in the last third of the seventeenth century, intra-European war had seen France facing Great Britain at sea and a coalition of Great Powers, usually enjoying British financial support, on land. However, the revolutionary era was also a period of revolution in warfare, so that the armies of the French republic were far more effective in combat than those of the Bourbon kings had ever been. Although aspects of the new forms of warfare can be traced back to the years before 1789 – new strategic doctrines, for instance, or improvements in artillery – it was above all the social and political changes introduced by the revolution that made this new kind of war possible.

To understand this change, we need to look briefly at the forms of land warfare under the old regime. Then, the infantry was drawn up on the battle-field in rows or lines – hence the phrase, 'line army'. Officers stood at the ends of the lines, with whips, sticks, swords and pistols, to ensure the troops remained in their rows. Infantry awaited the enemy's onset in massed rows, the ones in front firing, and then kneeling down to allow those behind them to shoot. They advanced in ordered rows, slowly and carefully, to ensure that the line remained intact. Successful old regime armies, such as those of Frederick the Great of Prussia, could manoeuvre in these formations quickly and efficiently, say by turning so they could march on the enemy at an oblique angle, without breaking the line.

This order of battle was appropriate to the society of orders, where the officers were from the nobility and the common soldiers were serfs or mercenaries. Soldiers did exactly as their noble superiors told them; indeed, Frederick the Great once explained that his ideal soldier would demonstrate *Kadavergehorsam*, the obedience of a corpse, and would show no intelligence or initiative at all. Endless drill ensured that soldiers would be able to manoeuvre efficiently, without having to consult their brains. The threatening presence of the officers would keep the infantry in line under fire; Frederick the Great asserted that he wanted soldiers who feared their officers more than the enemy.

The armies of the French Republic were composed of patriotic volunteers and newly drafted conscripts, who were thrown into battle with no time to engage in the elaborate drill required for the old regime armies of the line. Much of the old officer corps had joined the émigrés, and even if they had not, the new citizen soldiers would not have tolerated being treated like their subordinate predecessors. In the years 1792–94, the French armies were thus forced to develop a new style of warfare that would play to the strengths of the new kind of soldiers in its ranks, while minimizing the effects of the lack of an experienced corps of officers.

The republican troops did not fight in a line, but skirmished, breaking up into smaller groups to take advantage of the terrain and to fire, from cover, on the enemy, still standing neatly in rows. This form of tactics had already been proposed at the end of the old regime, but was first carried out effectively by the citizen soldiers of the republic's armies, who could be counted on to fight on their own initiative. When taking the offensive, the French forces charged in columns, presenting less of a target for enemy firepower, moving rapidly, cheering the republic, and brandishing their bayonets. They were led by their officers, no longer privileged members of the nobility, but, often, former comrades, drawn from their own ranks, who needed little training to master this relative simple method of attack. This style of warfare worked best with large numbers of troops, and the *levée en masse* of 1793 delivered them, creating an army of perhaps 750,000–800,000 men, guaranteeing the French forces a numerical superiority of almost 2:1 in important engagements.

Complementing these tactical innovations was a new strategic doctrine. Abandoning the old regime armies' slow pace of advance, required by the practice of bringing their food supplies with them, French forces turned to a war of rapid movement, as rapid as warfare in a pre-mechanized era could be. They would live off the country, seizing food, horses, clothing and other supplies in the territories they conquered. Militarily more effective, this decision was also a practical one, since the virtually bankrupt governments of the Convention and the Directory could not fund their armies adquately, in any event.

These new forms of strategy and tactics were decisive and would consistently bring the French victories in crucial battles. If the French were not always victorious, if the victories of 1792 turned into the defeats of 1793, if the triumphs of 1794–97 were, in part, reversed in 1798–99, if the wars lasted a long time – the war of the first coalition from 1792 to 1797, the war of the second coalition from 1798 to 1802 – this was because of two major factors. One was that the revolutionary armies' advances in strategy and tactics were not matched by corresponding progress in military organization. In the early years of the war, the French troops were ragged and untrained, their officers unsure of themselves, the new tactics still not completely thought out: the open, agressive style of fighting could as easily lead to disastrous routs as to resounding victories. By the later 1790s, the French troops were hardened veterans, but had substantially decreased in numbers, the 800,000-strong army of 1793 having dropped to under 300,000 troops by 1798, as a result of battlefield losses and, especially, widespread desertions. Unlike Frederick the Great's soldiers, the conscripts and volunteers of the republic's armies were not more afraid of their officers than of the enemy, and while their patriotic enthusiasm could win battles for them, it could also cool off and leave them with little incentive to stay in the field. The weak regime of the Directory was, as we have seen in the previous chapter, unable to deter deserters, and was reluctant to stir up any more opposition by introducing a regular system of conscription. No draftees were called up between 1793 and 1798, and ever fewer volunteers came forward, so that the decline in the strength of the republic's armies could not be stemmed. Under Napoleon's leadership, these organizational deficiencies would be remedied, and the French armies would be truly unstoppable, until their enemies began adopting the new forms of warfare that the revolutionary regime had pioneered.

The second main reason that the wars continued was the position of one of France's two main enemies, Great Britain, out of reach of the army. The French Revolution produced no innovations in naval warfare comparable to those on land, although Jeanbon St André, the member of the Committee of Public Safety in charge of the navy during the Reign of Terror, tried hard to introduce changes. Great Britain retained its maritime superiority throughout the entire period of warfare, from 1792 to 1815, keeping the French fleet bottled up in port, from which it was only occasionally able to escape to bring troops overseas, or to engage in disastrous naval encounters. The British were able to ferry troops, both their own and foreign, to crucial theatres of operation. Perhaps more importantly, they maintained their global commercial empire, and with it the financial resources to finance not just their own war effort, but, at least in part, that of their continental allies. If the Austrians were to take the field one more time, as they would do over and

again, in spite of repeated defeats, the prospect of British subsidies played an
important role in their decisions.

The war of the first coalition

The wars of the French Revolution are named according to the alliances of
different powers fighting France. In the war of the first coalition (1792–97),
the first three years were dominated by battles along the plains of northern
Europe and in the valley of the river Rhine. The initial advances of the allied
forces into northern France were stopped, as we noted in the previous
chapter, at Valmy, in September 1792. Their subsequent ponderous retreat,
aggravated by an outbreak of dysentery in their ranks that left Prussian
soldiers wandering, ill, in soiled clothing, begging for bread on the roadside,
allowed the French to advance victoriously that autumn. They defeated the
Austrians at Jemappes, and seized the Austrian Netherlands (the future
Belgium); further south, they advanced almost unopposed, to capture the
German cities of Trier and Mainz, cross the river Rhine and go on to occupy
Frankfurt.

The aggressive tactics that had worked so well in the autumn of 1792
turned against the French in early 1793. Fighting the Austrians in Neerwinden,
in Holland, French soldiers in open formation broke and ran, and the Austrians were able to drive the French out of the Low Countries and once
again march on Paris. At the same time, the Prussians were victorious in the
southern Rhineland, with Austrian assistance driving the French back into
Alsace. As noted in Chapter 2, the summer of 1793 marked the nadir of the
fortunes of the republic, with Prussian, Austrian and British troops occupying
a semicircle of northern French territory, from the Channel coast to Alsace, a
smaller Spanish army crossing the Pyrenees, the British navy occupying the
Mediterranean port of Toulon, and cooperating with domestic insurgents
against the government of the Convention.

If much of the military effort of the Convention's forces, raised in its
levée en masse, had to be directed towards these domestic insurgents, the
foreign enemies could obviously not be neglected. In the summer and autumn
of 1793, the republic's armies repulsed the Prussian and Austrian offensive in
Alsace, expelled the British besieging Dunkirk on the Channel coast, and,
at Wattignies (today in Belgium), defeated the Austrians. Following a pause

in the fighting during the winter, a renewed French offensive in the north led to the victory of Fleurus, in June 1794, bringing the Austrian Netherlands once more under French control, following which the French forces marched south and occupied the entire left (or west) bank of the Rhine; this area – the future Belgium, Luxemburg, and those parts of Germany to the west of the river Rhine – would remain under French control for the next twenty years. In a celebrated winter offensive, moving across the frozen canals, French forces conquered all of Holland. Meanwhile, in the Mediterranean region, French forces expelled the Spanish invaders and pushed into Spain, occupying portions of Catalonia, in the south, and the Basque provinces, to the north.

This was enough for the king of Prussia, who handily stabbed his allies in the back, leaving the coalition to negotiate with the French republic. In April 1795, France and Prussia agreed to the Peace of Basel, by which Prussia ceded its territories on the left bank of the Rhine, in return for which France agreed that Prussia could seek compensation elsewhere in northern Germany. France agreed not to send troops into northern Germany east of the river Rhine, a favourite spot for French interventions in the wars of the eighteenth century, and the two Powers turned that region into a 'zone of neutrality', a de facto Prussian protectorate.

Holland and Spain quickly joined the Prussians in making peace with France. The Netherlands did so while occupied by a French army and under the control of a pro-French government. This was not the case for Spain, where vigorous fighting was going on between French troops and the Spanish royal army, supported by enthusiastic volunteers. Rather, the Spanish government's stance was similar to that of Prussia. In return for modest colonial concessions, the government of the Directory withdrew its forces from Spain. The Spanish government then returned to its old regime policy of allying with France against Great Britain, in naval and colonial warfare. The reversion of the governments of both Spain and Prussia to a diplomacy of calculated self-interest and raison d'état, and their renunciation of the ideologically inspired counter-revolutionary enthusiasm with which they had entered the war, were a testimony to the successes of the French revolutionary armies.

This left Austria and Great Britain as the two Great Powers still in the war (Russia was reluctant to enter the war at all; an eventual decision to send troops was cancelled on the death of the Empress Catherine the Great in 1796). Several French attempts to defeat the Austrians by crossing the Rhine and marching southeast in 1795 and 1796 were unsuccessful, the invading armies being forced to retreat across the river. The decisive campaigns in this [123] second phase of the war of the first coalition came in Italy, where French troops under Napoleon Bonaparte – winning his first great victories – defeated the Austrians in the north in the spring of 1796, and continued victoriously south through most of the rest of the peninsula. In the spring of 1797, Napoleon led his forces through northeastern Italy into Austria, his vanguard coming within seventy-five miles of the capital, Vienna. This was enough for the Austrians, who agreed to an armistice in April and signed the peace of Campo Formio in the autumn. The treaty divided northern Italy between Austrian and French spheres of influence, with the French controlling the largest part. As the Prussians had done two years previously, the Austrians recognized the French annexation of the left bank of the Rhine and agreed that the German princes who had lost territory there should be compensated with areas to the east of the river.

The war of the first coalition was now over. Of all the powers allied against the French republic in 1793, only Great Britain remained at war, and peace negotiations – albeit inconclusive ones – were taking place between the British and French governments. The armies of the republic had won, on the battlefield, the debate over the French Revolution. Both on their own initiative and in cooperation with sympathizers in the conquered territory, they would try to bring the principles of the revolution to much of the continent, their efforts beginning in 1792 and reaching a highpoint of sorts after the victorious conclusion of the war of the first coalition in 1797–98. The story of revolutionary initiatives outside of France during the 1790s, to which we now turn, is thus indissolubly linked with the history of the revolutionary war.

Revolutions in the 1790s: domestic and imported

Shortly after the troops of General Custine occupied the German city of Mainz in the autumn of 1792, a political club was formed there, whose leaders asked to be recognized as an affiliate of the Parisian Jacobin club. These 'Mainz Jacobins', were five hundred strong, although, admittedly, their number included some soldiers of the occupying French army. There were businessmen and craftsmen of the city of Mainz among them, giving the group a membership not unlike that of provincial Jacobin clubs in France of the time, but the organization's leadership came from a group of Enlightened intellectuals, who had previously worked for the old regime government of the Prince-Archbishopric of Mainz. Their dominant figure was the prince-archbishop's librarian, Johann Georg Forster, one-time world traveller, proto-anthropologist, and correspondent of Kant. He was the very epitome of a reforming bureaucrat, a member of the social group that carried out the ideas of Enlightened Absolutist rulers, such as the prince-archbishop of Mainz. With the arrival of the republic's forces, Forster, and a fair number of Enlightened intellectuals and old regime government officials like him, would throw in their lot with the revolution coming from France.

The Mainz Jacobins, with the substantial assistance of General Custine's troops, set out to 'revolutionize' the countryside and small towns of the southern Rhineland, holding revolutionary ceremonies, destroying insignia of feudalism, and planting trees of liberty. They worked hard to gain converts to their cause, with some modest success in the towns of the region, but generally getting a much more reserved reception from the peasants. Even this reserved attitude began to turn toward open hostility as the occupying French troops, following the policy of living off the country, demanded large sums of money, food, horses, clothing and other supplies from the inhabitants, and, in outbreaks of anti-clerical zeal, smashed crucifixes and desecrated altars. Persevering nonetheless, the Mainz Jacobins brought together a group of activists from across the southern part of the left bank of the Rhine in Mainz in March 1793, for the meeting of a 'Rhenish–German National Convention', that was to debate the creation of a new, republican government. However, even as this Convention was meeting, the Prussian and Austrian troops were preparing their counter-attack. Retaking Mainz, they restored the old regime rule, clapped the local Jacobin leaders in irons and led them off to prison east of the river. Forster was later handed over to the French, in a sort of political exchange of prisoners and he died in Paris, politically disillusioned.

This episode of the Mainz Jacobins would be repeated over and again in much of western and southern Europe in the course of the 1790s; local and national differences notwithstanding, the basic story was the same. There were indigenous sympathizers with the radical and republican (we can say 'Jacobin' for short) ideas of the French Revolution in many parts of the continent, almost exclusively in urban areas, and very often these were one-time advocates of Enlightened political, economic and religious reforms. In this respect, they were not entirely different from the Jacobin activists in France itself. However, unlike the French Jacobins, these indigenous radicals of other

European countries were usually unable to gain popular support, and could [125] only come to power – in fact, could only act publicly – because of the presence of French troops. These soldiers were there, however, because of the success of their new revolutionary warfare, which included the strategic doctrine of rapid movement, made possible by living off the countryside. The exactions required would be sure to turn much of the local population – particularly the peasants, who, as always, suffered the most from the ravages of warfare – against the troops and the radicals they supported.

Thus the position of the German, Swiss, or Italian sympathizers with the French Revolution came to be completely dependent on the armies of the French republic. If the fortunes of war turned against them, then the radicals' cause was lost. Even if the French were victorious, the political destiny of the region was not in the hands of the indigenous radicals themselves, in spite of the governments they set up, but in that of either the French generals on the spot or the politicians of the Directory in Paris, who had to decide whether they wanted to incorporate the conquered territory into the French republic, allow it a quasi-indepedent existence as an 'allied' (or, we might say, less sympathetically, puppet) state, or just hold on to it, in the expectation of using it as a bargaining chip in a future peace settlement. In all of Europe, there were only two counries where indigenous radicals were able to act on their own accord in the 1790s – Poland and the British Isles, especially Ireland – and even in those lands, the ultimate fate of the revolutionary movements would depend on the fortunes of the revolutionary wars.

Outside of Poland and Ireland, indigenous radicalism was perhaps strongest in the Netherlands, a result of political conflicts of the 1780s. These had pitted, in typical old regime fashion, the constituted political bodies of the very loosely federated Dutch provinces, ministers of the established Reformed (Calvinist) Church, and burghers of the seaport towns against the rule of the prince of Orange, the stadtholder of the Netherlands. Although these conflicts were perhaps characteristically Dutch in that the rule of the prince was not very absolutist, and the urban, merchant oligarchy played an unusually prominent role in the Estates and old regime government, they were nonetheless quite severe, escalating to a minor civil war in the mid-1780s, and decided in favour of the prince by Prussian intervention in 1787. The leaders of the opposing faction, the 'patriots' as they called themselves, fled to France.

The outbreak of revolution offered them new chances and the approach of the republic's armies to the Netherlands in 1792 and again in 1794 moved the patriots' supporters to plan an insurrection against the prince's rule. The

[126] uprising was to coincide with a French offensive in October 1794, only the offensive never came off and the patriot insurgents were quickly arrested by the prince's troops, before they had a chance to rise up. Thus even in the relatively favourable circumstances prevailing in Holland, where there existed a sizeable body of supporters of revolution, and a not very popular ruler, whose rule had been imposed by foreign troops in the first place, the success of the revolutionary movement still depended on the French forces.

Their conquest of the country at the beginning of 1795 allowed the patriots to have their revolution and to proclaim the Batavian Republic. But 1795 was not just a revenge for 1787; the intervening French Revolution had fundamentally altered the terms of political debate. The patriots of the 1780s had been the supporters of the old regime institutions, particularly the cherished independence of the Dutch provinces; the Dutch Jacobins of the 1790s – largely, the same people as the patriots of the previous decade – wanted to create a unitary, centralist state, on the model of the Jacobin republic. The patriots had been strong supporters of the established church and Calvinist ministers some of their important supporters; the new Batavian Republic would disestablish Calvinism and grant equal rights to Catholics and Jews.

The symbols and institutions of the Batavian Republic would be borrowed from the French, from the tricolour flag, to the tree of liberty, to the National Guard, to the elaborate festivals endorsing public virtue, to the National Assembly, elected to create a constitution. (Actually, there were two National Assemblies elected after the voters, in a plebiscite, rejected the constitution written by the first.) There were moderate and radical politicians, whose political positions were strikingly similar to, and perhaps modelled on political tendencies in France during the second half of the 1790s. The executive was a Directory and it engaged in some of the same sorts of coups and political intrigues in 1797–98 as its Parisian namesake.

French influence on the Batavian Republic was far from just symbolic. The new government signed a peace treaty with France, requiring some small cessions of Dutch territory (mostly to round off the Austrian Netherlands and Luxemburg, that had been incorporated into the French republic), a very large war indemnity, and the obligation to host and supply an occupation force of ten thousand soldiers. Holland would join France in a military alliance, in particular, bringing its navy to bear against Great Britain. The French ambassador's residence became a focal point of politics in the Batavian Republic and important decisions were often cleared with him in advance, or just made in Paris, on his recommendations.

The newly proclaimed republic was a regime of foreign occupation [127] and, hence, higher taxes, circumstances that did nothing to enhance its popularity. Of course, the rule of the prince of Orange that had preceded it had also been a government imposed by a foreign power with an occupying army – one that had not left particularly good memories. For that reason alone, the government of the Batavian Republic enjoyed a certain amount of support. However, the basic problem of trying to bring about revolutionary change in the wake of an army of occupation would bedevil potential Jacobins everywhere on the continent. We can see this best in the years 1797–98, when the politicians of the Directory and French generals in occupied territory pushed for the formation of 'sister republics', on the Batavian model.

These years saw the abortive movement for a 'Cis-Rhenan' republic on the left bank of the Rhine, the creation of a Helvetic Republic on the territories of old regime Switzerland, and the founding in Italy of no less than six of these states: the Cispadane, Cisalpine, Ligurian, Luccan, Roman and Parthenopean Republics. The scenario was the same everywhere: the victorious arrival of French troops, the proclamation of the new republics, the planting of trees of liberty, the flying of tricolour flags, and the holding of elaborately staged political festivals, the creation of a National Guard, and the formation of 'constitutional circles', the most common name of French Jacobin clubs during the reign of the Directory.

Yet in spite of this distinctly imported character, the partisans of the republican regimes were indigenous. They were generally urban, educated and affluent; outside of France, few sans-culottes were to be found. In Switzerland, many republicans had been opponents of the narrow, oligarchical governments of the old regime mini-states, the cantons. The leading Italian Jacobins, on the other hand, were, like their predecessors five years earlier in Mainz, Enlightened intellectuals and government officials, who had carried out the reforming policies of the monarchs in the Kingdom of the Two Sicilies in the south, the Grand Duchy of Tuscany in the centre of the country, or the Duchy of Milan in the north, that had been under Austrian rule. Sympathizers and collaborators with the French troops occupying portions of Spain in 1795 came from a similar background. In the five years between the first attempt at an imported revolution, and the experiment with the sister republics, all those realms had renounced their Enlightened reforms, under the impact of the French Revolution, and left the authors who wrote in favour of them and the bureaucrats who carried them out, politically stranded. A surprising number of Catholic clergy sympathized with the revolutionary regimes, many of them Jansenists, partisans of a more austere and puritanical Catholicism. In southern Italy in particular, there were many noble Jacobins; members of the great baronial families, such as the prince of Montemiletto, were enthusiastic partisans of the Parthenopean Republic. Finally, there was the characteristic Mediterranean feature of vendetta, as was also practised in southern France: local struggles for power between different factions, based on competing wealthy and influential families. One of these factions, typically the losers, would turn to the new authorities, while its opponents would establish themselves as partisans of the old regime.

The narrow base of support such regimes enjoyed would only be reduced by the three chief ways that they impinged on the public: taxes and military requisitions, conscription, and anti-clericalism. No sooner had Napoleon's forces arrived in the Duchy of Milan, than he demanded twenty million francs in cash for his army, or about five years' tax revenues. Similar cash demands followed the French armies elsewhere in the Italian peninsula, along with the requisitions in kind for food, horses, and clothing, as the republic's forces followed their practice of living off the land. Initially on the whim of individual French generals, Italian art treasures were confiscated and sent back to Paris, to fill the republic's newly created art museums, but this soon became a systematic practice.

In one sense, the creation of the sister republics brought an end to this unsupervised looting, but, in another way, it merely organized and standardized the transfer of resources from the republics' allies to France. The Cisalpine Republic, for instance, whose territory was centred on the former Duchy of Milan, was required to support 25,000 French soldiers stationed there and raise an army of 22,000 men, under French command. Similar arrangments were made with the other sister republics. In other words, the inhabitants of these new regimes – especially the rural ones – would have to pay for the new state of affairs, not just in cash, but with young men as well. Conscription, as we have seen, had been deeply unpopular in France, where the revolutionary government, as a result of the political struggles of the years 1789–92, had obtained a substantial degree of support or at least assent in the population. In foreign countries, faced with military occupation and all its costs, and only supported by a thin group of largely upper-class individuals, compulsory recruitment to the armed forces was a recipe for provoking a counter-revolutionary insurrection, which would explode as soon as the military initiative in the war of the second coalition turned against the French occupiers.

From 1797 onwards (following the coup of 18 Fructidor, Year 5) the Directorial regime followed an increasingly anti-clerical policy and the sister republics, created under its auspices, moved in the same direction. Actually, French generals on the spot were, if anything, more likely to be inclined to suggest caution, advising the indigenous Jacobins to avoid antagonizing the religious feelings of the population. Napoleon Bonaparte, in particular, emphasized this advice, foreshadowing his later efforts to reconcile the revolutionary regime in France and the Catholic Church. The Italian radicals, in particular, whose rejection of the old regime culture of confessionalism and allegiance to the counter-culture of the Enlightenment was their single most prominent political characteristic, were generally not willing to listen to such sensible counsel. Instead, as happened in Rome, they publicly challenged the culture of confessionalism by burning cardinals' hats and the minutes of the Inquisition in front of an altar of liberty. Even had the radicals been reined in, it is hard to imagine how regimes that separated church and state, introduced equality of all confessions before the law (thus liberating Jews from their ghetto, a measure that particularly infuriated the pious), began to sell church property, and talked about allowing priests to marry, would have been able to make many converts among the supporters of the culture of confession, especially after French soldiers arrested the pope and deported him to France.

No sooner had the sister republics been established than miracles followed in their wake, crucifixes or images of the Virgin and the saints denouncing the regimes as the realm of Satan, and partisans of the Catholic Church – as in France itself, women were particularly prominent among them – demonstrating against the new governments. These sorts of actions, as one might imagine, were particularly prevalent in Italy, but they occurred in the mountainous regions of Switzerland as well, whose Catholic inhabitants resented everything about the Helvetic Republic: its anti-clericalism; its centralizing grip on their localities; its high taxes and its conscription.

Popular participation in the Spanish war against France in 1793 and Spanish resistance to French occupations of Spanish territory two years later was carried out in similar fashion, as a 'war of religion'. The decision of the Spanish government to make peace with France in 1795 and negotiate a withdrawal of French troops from the country prevented this religious war from turning into a full-blown crusade. In the changed political and military circumstances of the subsequent decade, however, when Spain would be occupied by French troops, such a war of religion against foreign occupiers would emerge to a previously unknown extent.

The sister republics themselves were not at all homogeneous, and they varied in the extent to which they had an independent existence. In both Holland and Switzerland, the new regimes could count on a substantial body of supporters – admittedly, only able to prevail over the substantial body of their opponents with French help. Even in Italy, where support for these regimes was pretty thin, distinctions can be noted. The Cisalpine Republic, for instance, existed for three years, and had a constitution written by an elected assembly. Its red–white–green tricolour would become the national flag of the modern Italian nation-state. By contrast, the Parthenopean Republic, comprising the territory on the Italian peninsula of the Kingdom of the Two Sicilies was proclaimed largely as an afterthought in 1799, following French victory over forces of the kingdom invading Rome. Uprisings against this southern Italian republic began almost immediately on the appearance of French troops, and the republican government in Naples never had anything resembling complete control of the capital city – to say nothing of the mainland provinces, or, especially, of the island of Sicily, where the deposed monarch, protected by the British fleet, took refuge. The extent of indigenous support, or lack of it, in the different sister republics would be revealed in 1799, when the war of the second coalition resumed and French occupiers were expelled.

Jacobins on their own: revolutionary movements in Poland and Great Britain

At opposite ends of Europe, in two very different countries, revolutionary movements in the 1790s posed a threat to the existing order on their own, without the perhaps dubious benefits of French armed assistance. Even in these relatively autonomous revolutionary movements, however, we can note the powerful influence of the French Revolution on their ideology and their forms of political expression, although it often involved adapting these political ideas to very different social circumstances. Partisans of these movements sought out French assistance and their ultimate fate was dependent on the course of the wars fought by republican and, later, Napoleonic France. Finally, the violent suppression of the insurrections in Poland and the British Isles would demonstrate a Reign of Terror in reverse, as the forces of order would shed blood to destroy potential revolution every bit as vigorously as the Jacobins had done to preserve it.

The political turmoil and military struggles in Poland during the first half [131] of the 1790s show how the ideas of the French Revolution could be taken up in a quite different environment and used by different social groups to quite different political purposes. If the 'pre-revolution' of 1788 in France began with an offensive of the constituted bodies of the society of orders against an absolutist monarch, Polish developments moved in exactly the opposite direction. The key question for the session of the Sejm, the Polish Diet, that began in 1788, was whether the virtually powerless monarch should gain the authority to create an executive power and, in particular, raise an army, to defend the state against its powerful absolutist neighbours, Austria, Prussia and Russia, who had already stripped it of a quarter of its territory. After 1789, the supporters of a strong executive began calling themselves the 'patriots' and referring favourably to the events in France. In May 1791, they acted, purging the Diet of the proponents of its unlimited power, creating a new constitution, while soldiers and civilians demonstrated in the streets of Warsaw, shouting 'Vivat Konstitucja!'

The demonstrators were only slightly more in touch with the French model than the Hamburg journeymen, who at the same time, were praising the 'constitution'. While the language may have been the same, the nature of political power and the demands for changes in it were quite different in France and Poland. The French patriots had been forced – at times, unwillingly enough – to act against the monarch in order to limit his power, while their Polish counterparts cooperated with the king to enhance his authority. The French National Assembly had destroyed the privileges of the nobility (and other groups as well) and brought the feudal regime to an end on the night of 4 August, 1789. In the Declaration of the Rights of Man, it had proclaimed the equality of all citizens under the law, and the sovereignty of the nation – actions that brought many of the noble members of the Second Estate into direct confrontation with the new regime. The Polish patriots, by contrast, were from the nobility, as were nearly all the political actors in Poland at the time. Their *Konstitucja* guaranteed continued noble privileges, granted the nobility a dominant role in the new legislature, and did absolutely nothing to emancipate the peasantry – over 90 per cent of the population – from the particularly rigid and oppressive condition of servitude to which the nobles had subjected them. The Polish 'nation,' whose sovereignty was now being asserted in revolutionary fashion, was the nation of the society of orders, composed primarily of the nobility – a larger group, in eastern than in western Europe, but still well under a tenth of the inhabitants of Poland. This transfer of the language of the French Revolution to a part of Europe with a very different social structure and its use by a quite different social group would continue to characterize revolutionary politics in Poland (to a certain extent also in Hungary) well into the nineteenth century.

In 1791–92, though, even the rhetoric of the French Revolution was too much for the Russian Empress Catherine, whose troops promptly intervened to restore the old regime, and did so after one year's war in the spring of 1793. Russia and Prussia then annexed over half the remaining Polish territory. From exile, and, within Poland, in secret societies, the Polish patriots, led by the veteran of the American War of Independence, Tadeusz Kosciuszko, launched a more radical uprising, and in March 1794, succeeded in seizing power in the main towns of Cracow, Vilna, and the capital, Warsaw. The new regime was more distinctly Jacobin, calling for a mass mobilization to free the nation from the invader, although, characteristically for the Polish situation, this revolutionary government had the sanction of the king. Its reign began with the 'sans-culottes', if one will, of these three cities attacking and murdering the Russian occupiers and their Polish collaborators.

Such a beginning could only guarantee a Russian riposte. The Poles hoped for fraternal revolutionary assistance from France. Replying to their requests on behalf of the Committee of Public Safety, Saint-Just, one of Robespierre's closest collaborators, informed the Poles that France would not offer 'the smallest morcel of gold' or any soldier's life, so long as Poland remained a noble-dominated monarchy. This might have been an assertion of republican virtue, or, more likely, a way of hiding the fact that the republic's armies, in early 1794 still battling their way across France's western borders, had no way of launching a campaign in eastern Europe, a thousand miles distant. Without allies against the Russians, the Poles succumbed after a six-month campaign. Entering Warsaw in November 1794, Russian soldiers killed something in the order of 25,000–30,000 people, in a counter-revolutionary Reign of Terror. Russia, Prussia and Austria then divided up the remaining Polish territory, bringing an end to the existence of an independent Poland, except for a brief interlude under Napoleon, until 1918.

If the French Revolution did little for Poland it can be argued, with some justification, that these Polish uprisings were the military salvation of the French Revolution. The Polish wars of 1792–94 prevented the Russians from intervening against France in western Europe, and diverted both Prussian troops and Prussian interests from the campaign in the west. They also encouraged the king of Prussia to make peace with the French republic, so that he might all the better digest his new Polish acquisitions. Even after the failure of their revolution, Polish insurgents would continue to link their cause with France. Polish refugees formed a legion that would fight with the forces of the French republic in Italy, and would later serve in Napoleon's army. Indeed, the modern Polish national anthem was composed by members of this latter group.

As noble revolutionaries who would do nothing beyond rhetorical gestures to help the serfs, the vast majority of the population, the Polish insurgents could not count on a vast array of support. Yet they still had more supporters and were able to act independently to a far greater extent than the west European Jacobins of the sister republics. That the Poles failed in their uprising while the Batavian, Helvetic or Cisalpine radicals succeeded in theirs, was a consequence of the war between revolutionary France and the other Great Powers, begun in 1792, that overshadowed all other factors in deciding the fate of revolutionary movements in Europe of the 1790s. Great Britain, the country with the strongest, most independent and most massive revolutionary movement outside of France in that decade, was also the Great Power that was the central element of the anti-French military coalition. In the British Isles, as well as on the continent, the fate of the movement for political change would ultimately be determined by the outcome of the war.

Throughout the 1780s, that is, well before the beginning of the French Revolution, there was a movement for reform in Great Britain, centring on political and religious issues. While reform movements in old regime continental Europe had generally been centred on the absolutist monarch and his state bureaucracy, the basic differences between political life in eighteenth-century Great Britain and the European continent had led to a different focus for reform. British reformers concentrated their interest on Parliament, demanding a broader and more democratic suffrage, and a reapportionment of constituencies, to bring representation in line with population changes, particularly for the rapidly growing manufacturing cities of northern England. The other main focus of the British reform movement, the demand for the lifting of the remaining forms of discrimination against Protestants who were not members of the Anglican state church – the 'Dissenters' – had greater similarities with events on the continent. Members of these Dissenting congregations had been at the centre of the movements for reform. As the Dissenters' theology had, in the course of the eighteenth century, moved in an increasingly rationalist direction, their campaigns could be understood as a British version of the counter-culture of the Enlightenment that was so important on the continent for both the reform movements of the old regime and the revolutionary ones of the 1790s.

The news of the great events of 1789 had been greeted enthusiastically by the British reformers, and their organizations, such as the London Revolution Society, had held celebrations in honour of the fall of the Bastille. The revolution of the London Revolution Society was not the French one of 1789, but the British 'Glorious Revolution' of 1688, and the British reformers, like their Enlightened absolutist counterparts in continental Europe, regarded the French Revolution as an affirmation of their own principles. The victory of the revolution in France spurred British reformers to greater efforts, in particular to the formation of political clubs – Revolution Societies, Constitution Societies, Societies of Friends of the People – especially in the manufacturing districts of northern England, whose representation in Parliament had been an important demand of the existing reform movement.

This effort began independently of the similar attempts of the French Jacobins, and actually predated them, so that in 1790 there was probably a larger and better organized network of political clubs in England than in France. Certainly, in the years 1790–92, there were repeated close contacts, by mail and in person, between British reformers and French Jacobins. However, the continued progress of the French Revolution, as against the stubborn refusal of the monarchy, the unreformed Parliament or the established church to consider any serious reforms, led to a subtle reversal in intellectual priorities. Increasingly, British reformers moved from seeing events in France as a triumph of their principles, to understanding them as a model for action in Britain. As the London Revolution Society wrote to the Jacobins of Vire in April 1791:

> Royal prerogatives, injurious to the public interest, a servile Peerage, a rapacious and intolerant clergy, and corrupt Representation are grievances under which we suffer. But as you, perhaps, have profited from the example of our Ancestors, so shall we from your late glorious and splendid actions.[1]

British reformers held banquets and sponsored parades on Bastille Day; they began to address each other as 'Citizen'. They followed closely the outbreak of war between France and the continental European powers in the spring of 1792, and celebrated the victories of French arms at Valmy and Jemappes in the autumn of that year, as triumphs for liberty. In the northern industrial town of Sheffield, 5,000–6,000 spectators watched the celebrations and cheered. Reformers in Scotland held a congress of their political clubs, which they designated, in reference to the revolutionary parliament meeting in France, as a 'Convention'. As had happened elsewhere in Europe,

existing political tendencies were being caught up in the intellectual sweep [135]
of the French Revolution – only in Great Britain, with its more open and
livelier political life, this was occurring on a much larger scale.

If British opponents of the existing order were taking on the linea-
ments of Jacobinism, its proponents were turning themselves into counter-
revolutionaries. 'Church and king' mobs, stirred up by Anglican ministers,
and tacitly tolerated by local magistrates, attacked the houses of leading
reformers, or the chapels of Dissenting congregations and burned them to
the ground. More peacefully, petitions to Parliament for political reform
were countered by others proclaiming their loyalty to the existing, if
unwritten, 'British constitution'. Members of the evangelical wing of the
established church distinguished themselves as energetic popular counter-
revolutionaries, adherence to the culture of confession emerging in England,
as in continental Europe, as a powerful counter-revolutionary force. Particularly prominent among these evangelicals was the author and pamphleteer
Hannah More, whose vigorous denunciations of revolutionary ideas as godless and subversive were widely distributed and read, providing the chief
popular competition to Thomas Paine's defence of the French Revolution. In
a process we have already noted in the countries of continental Europe, even
partisans of very modest reforms, such as the aristocratic Whig parliamentarians, who were no democrats, and not even Dissenters, were vigorously
denounced as Jacobins, or their stooges. Edmund Burke's *Reflections on the
Revolution in France* was written as the opening shot in this campaign, and
in the last years of his life, Burke's speeches and writings were designed
primarily to foster this political polarization.

With British entry into the war against France in the spring of 1793, the
position of the reformers became ever more precarious, since their political
views could now be interpreted as sympathy for a wartime enemy. The government cracked down on the movement, indicting its English and Scottish
leaders for treason. The Scots, tried under a judicial system that guaranteed
close cooperation between the prosecution and a powerful judge, were found
guilty and transported to Australia, but in England the jury had more independent power. The London jurors defied the authorities, and after a sensa-
tional trial, acquitted the accused. Tightening legal restrictions, by suspending
habeas corpus (thus allowing enemies of the government to be arrested and
detained without being charged or brought to trial), prohibiting public
meetings and extending the reach of sedition to include the public advocacy
of political reform, the authorities continued their campaign against the
'Jacobins'. In response, perhaps 100,000 Londoners demonstrated against

[136] the government in October 1795. Earlier that year, the residents of the capital city had attacked the king's carriage as George III went to attend the opening of Parliament, calling for peace and bread – showing that the social strains of the bad harvest of 1795 and of continued warfare, which had so plagued the government of the Directory in France, were also to be found in its main rival.

The continuing political polarization, however, had the same effect in Great Britain as in continental Europe. Political moderates, who looked to a peaceful reform of the system saw no way of achieving their goals and increasingly withdrew from active political life. The upper- and middle-class reformers – Whig nobles and gentry, Dissenting ministers and manufacturers, romantic poets – gave up on their open opposition. Into their place stepped more radical adherents of a republican form of government, people who really were Jacobins; their supporters were increasingly artisans or manufacturing outworkers, something like English sans-culottes. Barred from legal action, they turned to conspiratorial secret societies.

This form of action, and the political struggles of the second half of the 1790s, were strongest in Ireland. The renewed reform movements of the earlier part of the decade had been particularly pronounced there, especially among the Protestant Dissenters, living in the north of the island. The 'patriots', as the reformers were known, gained control of the popular militias, the Volunteers (originally formed against the threat of a Dutch or French invasion during the wars of the American Revolution), and turned them into a veritable National Guard: armed and active sympathizers with the French, holding, for instance, a massive parade in Belfast on Bastille Day, 1792.

The process of repression, polarization and radicalization of the reform movement following British entry into the war with France occurred in Ireland as well as in England, the patriots moving from calling for political and religious reforms to demanding independence and an Irish republic. In an unprecedented step, never to be repeated in a country plagued by centuries of sectarian conflict, the Protestant and Dissenting leaders of the patriots aggressively and successfully recruited followers among the Catholic population of the island, the numerically largest group, and the one suffering by far the greatest degree of religious, political and socioeconomic oppression. The revolutionary secret society they formed, the United Irishmen, counted some 300,000 members by 1796–97, a phenomenal number in an island with some 4.5 million inhabitants. (Irish living in England and Scotland seem to have played a central role in the revolutionary secret societies there as well.) Secret (and not so secret) military drilling at night, the hanging out of tricolour flags, crowds stopping postal coaches and demanding that the travellers give three cheers for the French Revolution – all these were signs of a populace on the verge of insurrection. As was the case with all European revolutionaries in the 1790s, the United Irishmen looked to republican France, and sent emissaries there to solicit military assistance. For a French government looking for a way to defeat its main Great Power rival, the possibility of an assault on its Achilles heel was very tempting.

The negotiations dragged on for months, since the United Irish emissaries wanted to wait for the landing of French forces before they would call on their followers to rise, while the French wanted the Irish to prove that their organization could actually stage an uprising, before they would commit troops to support it. In addition, the anti-clerical officials of the Directory had their doubts about the religious motives of the Irish insurgents, particularly the Catholic ones, whose attitudes seemed suspiciously similar to those of the counter-revolutionaries in western France. Finally, in December 1796, a French fleet, with Irish patriot leader Wolfe Tone aboard, evaded British blockaders and set out for Ireland. Scattered by bad weather (and incompetent seamanship), hampered from landing by unfavourable winds, the fleet spent two weeks off the Irish coast before returning to France. Throughout 1797, the United Irishmen lived in daily expectation of a new attempt.

They had good reason for these expectations. In the spring of 1797, there were widespread mutinies in the British fleet, temporarily depriving the island nation of its chief military arm and leaving it largely defenceless against foreign invasion. The exact motivations of the mutineers were controversial then and have remained so down to the present day. They are either seen as frustrated loyalists, insisting on their pro-monarchist sentiments, while vigorously protesting their low pay, wretched food and dangerously unhealthy accomodation, or as politically motivated insurgents, with close ties to British Jacobins. There is evidence to support both points of view, and probably sailors who embodied them, but whatever their motivations, Irish sailors played a conspicuously large role in the mutiny.

In what was perhaps the single most important event (or non-event) of the entire revolutionary and Napoleonic era of warfare, the French could not make use of this chance. Differences of opinion within the Directory about a military effort on the continent versus one on the British Isles and repeated problems with the French navy prevented a landing, while the mutiny continued. The Admiralty was able to regain control of the fleet and crush the mutiny and the British defeat of the fleet of France's Batavian allies in the autumn of 1797 brought an end to any serious prospects for an invasion of the British Isles.

While the Irish patriots were waiting, the British authorities were turning up their repression, sending troops and loyalist militias to search for weapons and arrest secret society leaders. The British made a special effort to play up the sectarian divisions, and separate Protestant from Catholic revolutionaries – with evident success. In 1798, the Directory, following the advice of its most successful general, Napoleon, decided that it should take naval action against Great Britain in the Mediterranean. Without the long-awaited French assistance, and with their secret organization under growing pressure from the British authorities, the United Irishmen finally launched their insurrection in May 1798. There was fighting in the north of Ireland, but the uprising was strongest in the southeast, particularly in County Wexford, where, rather to the suprise of both the insurgents and the authorities, the Catholic tenant farmers joined in vigorously, fiercely attacking their Protestant landlords.

British troops and civilian auxiliaries, armed by Protestant landowners, were able to suppress the uprising. Realizing too late what an opportunity it had missed, the Directory then sent a small naval force, that landed in northwestern Ireland in August. Thousands of Catholic labourers and tenants flocked to the French forces, exclaiming to the bemusement of the anti-clerical and republican soldiers that they had come to take arms for France and the Blessed Virgin. However, the French expeditionary force and its unarmed, irregular Irish allies were no match for the tens of thousands of British troops on the island.

There followed a savage repression. Captured insurgents were shot on the spot; other members of the United Irishmen were hanged without trial. Soldiers and armed civilians, organized into the Protestant 'Orange Order', a group designed to maintain British rule by inciting sectarian strife (a role it has played, with great effect, until the present) took their revenge particularly on Catholics, who were systematically killed, beaten, robbed and driven from their homes. Estimates of the number killed range from 30,000 to 100,000, of the same order of magnitude as the Reign of Terror in France, but in a country with just one-sixth of the French population.

There are four points that we can make about Poland and Great Britain, the centres of independent revolutionary movements in Europe during the 1790s. First, unlike the Jacobins of the sister republics, the revolutionaries of those countries did not have to contend with the handicap of a French army of occupation, alienating the indigenous population. Anti-war sentiments in England could be used to promote the revolution, rather than the counter-revolution, as was the case in much of continental Europe. The foreign occupiers, the Russians in Poland, and the British in Ireland, were arrayed against the revolutionaries, rather than on their side. However, the lack of French military assistance also doomed these revolutionary movements, a connection that is particularly evident in Ireland.

Secondly, the way that these revolutionaries adopted the language and political forms of the French Revolution – and unlike their counterparts in the sister republics, without the prompting of French troops – shows the powerful influence of the events of 1789–93 on political life in Europe. After that, people in all of Europe, not just in France, who thought about politics, thought about it in the terms set down in the turbulent period from the calling of the Estates General to the creation of a republic of virtue. These terms would provide the bases for political orientation in Europe, at least until the middle of the nineteenth century.

Thirdly, Poland and Ireland were unique in that it proved possible in those countries to forge a link between the old regime culture of confessionalism and the revolutionary movement, two phenomena that were elsewhere strongly at odds. To be sure, the Catholic clergy of the two countries, especially those from the higher ranks, steered clear of the revolutionary movements. The Polish bishops, largely in the pay of the Russians, were, with few exceptions, overtly hostile to the revolution, and the insurgent crowd in Warsaw in 1794 strung up two members of the episcopate, along with other Russian collaborators. The revolutionary leaders were generally anti-clerical in the Enlightenment tradition as well, but many of the ordinary participants were clearly motivated by strong opposition to religiously foreign – Russian Eastern Orthodox and British Anglican – rule. The very fact that the Polish insurrection began on Good Friday, and its leader Kosciuszko took an oath to the nation in the name of the Father and His martyred Son are a clear sign of this. Irish revolutionaries were also able to mobilize peasants against their landlords, the only place in Europe outside of France that social tensions in the countryside could be utilized politically by revolutionaries. Both these factors, the culture of confessionalism and peasant–landlord conflicts, would prove decisive for future revolutionary movements in Europe.

Finally, we can see in both Poland and Great Britain a pattern of political polarization and growing radicalism, similar to the one undergone in France between 1789 and 1793. There was a movement from a call for gradual reform to one for drastic changes, a transition from monarchism to republicanism. In Great Britain, very much as in France, a political opposition movement of nobles, landowners, merchants and professionals gave way to one with a stronger plebeian element, without, admittedly, the upper- and middle-class elements disappearing, or even entirely giving up their leading role.

[140] However, there was one crucial difference between the French case and the parallel ones in Britain and Poland. In France, the initial moderate forces had triumphed over the resistance of the old regime and created a political atmosphere in which it was easier for the advocates of more drastic measures to come forward, state their demands, organize themselves, and try to seize power. Once that had occurred in France, rulers everywhere in Europe were on their guard, and were unwilling to make any concessions to the moderates, lest they have similar results. Moderates themselves were sometimes less willing to press their claims, seeing what had happened in France after such claims had been granted. Consequently, the radical forces, everywhere in Europe, faced a fundamentally more difficult situation than their French counterparts. This made it impossible for them to seize or maintain power on their own, even with considerable popular support, as the Polish and British – especially Irish – examples explicitly demonstrate. In the end, the very success of the French Revolution meant that it could not be repeated; its export beyond France was only possible on the bayonets of the republic's armies. Once again, we need to return to the wars of the French Revolution, in particular the war of the second coalition (1798–1802), to ascertain the fate of the revolutionary changes unleashed by the French on the European continent.

The war of the second coalition

By late 1797, the only member of the first coalition still at war with France was Great Britain; the war of the second coalition grew out of the Directory's attempt to bring the war of the first coalition to a successful conclusion. Tackling Great Britain would involve a maritime effort and the superiority of the British fleet, especially after its defeat of France's Spanish allies in 1795 and Dutch ones in 1797, was all too apparent. Rejecting the idea of a French landing in Ireland, which, as suggested in the previous section, probably would have brought a favourable end to the war, the Directors endorsed a plan of Napoleon's for a Mediterranean offensive. Evading the blockading British once more in May 1798, a French expeditionary force seized Malta and the Ionian islands (off the Greek coast) and landed in Egypt.

From a military and diplomatic point of view, this was an extremely dubious move. A French occupation of Egypt would supposedly threaten India, the heart of Britain's overseas empire, but less time spent dreaming about the ancient conquests of Alexander the Great and more spent looking at a map, would have shown that the two countries were rather far apart. While the French forces under Napoleon easily disposed of the Turkish armies in Egypt at the Battle of the Pyramids, the British navy under the celebrated Admiral Horatio Nelson finally caught up with the French fleet at Aboukir Bay and sank it all, thus leaving the French expeditionary force stranded in the Middle East. Worse, the whole Mediterranean strategy antagonized the one Great Power that had hitherto done little in the war with France, namely Russia.

In the course of the eighteenth century, the Russian rulers had been expanding the power of their realm southwards toward the Crimea and the Caucasus; Russian fleets had operated in the Mediterranean, and it had come to be seen as an area of strategic importance. The French military presence in the area thus propelled the Russians into war, a decision made all the easier by the promise of large British subsidies to pay for the tsar's troops to go into action in western Europe. In these circumstances, the battered Austrians, also offered substantial financial support, were ready to resume combat, so by early 1799 the war of the second coalition was under way.

At first, the coalition's armies made all the running. Joint operations by Austrian and Russian armies inflicted repeated defeats on the overstretched and undermanned French forces in Italy. By June 1799, the French had been completely driven off the peninsula, except for a toehold they were able to retain in the port city of Genoa. Further offensives, once again by the Austrians and the Russians, drove the French out of those parts of Switzerland containing the Alpine passes leading to Italy. In August, a joint British and Russian expeditionary force landed in Holland and began a march on Amsterdam. These defeats of the French, coupled with counter-revolutionary uprisings in southwestern and western France (British subsidies and what we would today call covert operations, in conjunction with the French émigrés, played a role here, too), created, as noted in Chapter 2, a state of emergency in France. At least briefly, it seemed that the second coalition might succeed in destroying the republican regime, where the first had failed.

If the victories of the coalition's armies were a test of republican rule in France, they were an even greater test of the popularity of and support for the sister republics. The Italian republics failed this test completely. Everywhere the news of French defeats brought counter-revolutionary uprisings. Many of the same factors as had sparked the revolt of the Vendée in western France in 1793, could be seen in Italy six years later. In both cases, the republican regimes had brought conscription, higher taxes and an attack on religion, but no benefits to the rural population. In both western France and Italy, nobles and especially the Catholic clergy mobilized the peasants; in both cases, the defence of the culture of confessionalism against the anti-clericalism of the revolution was central to the uprising. The counter-revolutionary battle-cry in Tuscany was 'Viva Maria!'; in the north, the insurgents called themselves the 'Massa Cristiana' (Christian Masses); in the south, 'Santafede', or Holy Faith. Supporters of the godless republics who were unlucky enough to be caught, were slaughtered on the spot; in Siena, the insurgents celebrated the victory of their religion by seizing thirteen Jews and burning them at the stake.

The counter-revolutionary uprisings were at their most ferocious in southern Italy. Following the French conquest of the Kingdom of the Two Sicilies, and the proclamation of the Parthenopean Republic, Cardinal Fabrizio Ruffo, had fled with the Bourbon monarchs from their capital, Naples, to refuge in Sicily, under the protection of the British navy. In February 1799, he returned to the mainland, landing in the province of Calabria, and everywhere he appeared, counter-revolutionary uprisings followed. Since many of the supporters of the republic had been from the landowning nobility, the santafedists were only too pleased to stop paying feudal dues to them, loot their estates, seize their land – and extend these measures to noble landlords in general. The insurgents' marching song, 'Con trambuco et grancassa/Viva il re et la gente bassa!' (With trumpet and drum/Long live the king and the common people!), showed the ability of counter-revolutionaries to mobilize for their purposes the social conflicts in the countryside. This possibility of raising the rural masses against aristocratic revolutionaries would remain a distinct political spectre in many regions of large estates, as would a nobility in political opposition to the government throughout much of the Italian peninsula, Poland and Hungary, for instance until the middle of the nineteenth century.

This same combination of class hatred and counter-revolution was on display in the capital city, where the *lazzaroni*, the unskilled labourers of Naples, were strongly loyal to their deposed monarch, because of his charity, employment projects and subsidized grain prices, and equally fierce opponents of the short-lived republican regime. Indeed, Cardinal Ruffo himself, no enemy of either the nobility or of property, became dismayed by the anti-feudal hostilities, the looting and the widespread murder of political opponents his uprising had provoked. His pleas for gentle treatment of aristocratic republicans were rejected by the royal family and their British naval protector, Admiral Nelson, fresh from his victory over the French in Egypt. Rather, as the queen noted, the Naples republicans were to be treated just as the British treated the Irish: over one hundred of the leaders of the Parthenopean Republic were duly hanged.

Before leaving these counter-revolutionary uprisings in Italy, there is something we should note about the politics of their participants. They rose up in opposition to the republican form of government, and the destruction of trees of liberty was a symbolic action found everywhere in the Italian peninsula. They acted in defence of their faith, certainly, and in favour of their previous rulers, and unquestionably against the French. However, what was quite lacking from their movements – and this is also true of similar but smaller uprisings against the French in Belgium, Luxemburg or parts of Germany – was any sense of nationalism. Neither the leaders nor the rank and file of these uprisings called for a unified Italian state to replace the many old regime monarchies on the peninsula. Quite the opposite, the few Italians who thought in such terms were generally supporters of the sister republics and hoped that they might be a step in the direction of the nation state.

Much the same was the case, earlier in the decade, in the popular resistance in Spain to the French invasion. Both Catalonia and the Basque provinces, equipped with charters of privilege and a population resistant both to conscription of soldiers and taxes, had long been centres of opposition to centralizing absolutist rule in Spain. When their inhabitants joined the fight against French invaders, they did so in the name of their religion and their provincial homelands, not in the name of a centralizing and unitary nationalism. Although nationalist ideals and aspirations would eventually emerge in the course of opposition to French invasion and occupation (particularly in the late phases of Napoleon's empire), such ideas were a long time in coming, and remained strongly mixed in with old regime style loyalties to province, religion and chartered privileges.

The statesmen of the powers of the second coalition were generally delighted at the Italian uprisings and confidently expected a militarily decisive repetition of them further north. Here, they would be deeply disappointed, and it would become clear that the Helvetian and Batavian sister republics rested on rather firmer ground than their Italian counterparts. Rather than pouring out of their mountain strongholds, muskets in hand, to join the armies of the coalition, the Swiss were at best tepid and unenthusiastic about their Russian liberators. They quickly became visibly disenchanted, in view of the Russian soldiers' habit of taking everything that was not nailed down. In Holland, the longed-for uprising in favour of the prince of Orange was also nowhere to be seen, and the army of the Batavian Republic fought with the French troops, forcing the British and Russian invaders to leave the continent. While the Helvetian and Batavian Republics may have been less than wildly popular, the social and religious tensions that sparked the uprisings in

Italy were largely absent, and there was little strong desire to return to the old regime, with the assistance of the Cossacks.

The counter-revolution that did not take place helped to defeat the strategy of the second coalition. Strategic disagreements between the Russians and the Austrians allowed the French general Masséna to defeat the Russians decisively and drive them out of Switzerland. Thoroughly disenchanted with his allies, Tsar Paul, Catherine the Great's son and successor, left the war in 1800. In many ways, the military situation was back to where it had been in 1795: the French occupying the Low Countries and the left bank of the Rhine; Prussia and Russia neutral; Austria and England still at war with France.

Having seized power in France at the end of 1799 with the coup d'état of 18 Brumaire, Napeoleon realized that the first task in securing his rule would be to bring the war to a successful conclusion. He resolved to repeat his successes of 1796 in northern Italy, and after leading his troops in a celebrated march across the Alps, he decisively defeated the Austrians at the equally celebrated battle of Marengo, in June 1800. Also reminiscent of the campaigns of the mid-1790s, French troops under General Moreau crossed the Rhine and marched southeast toward Vienna. In 1795 and 1796, the French had been forced to retreat across the river Rhine, but in 1800 they were more successful, and culminated their campaign with a decisive victory over the Austrians at Hohenlinden, in December. The Austrians could no longer fight and had to sue for peace. The treaty of Lunéville, signed in December 1801, reiterated the settlement of Campo Formio four years previously: French annexation of Belgium, Luxemburg and the left bank of the Rhine was recognized; Holland, Switzerland and most of northern Italy would be French spheres of influence, under sister republics, while Austria would control part of northeastern Italy and receive other territorial compensation in Germany. In other words, the French had won, and their continental Great Power rival had been weakened, but not totally defeated.

With the Austrians out of the war, this once again left the British alone in the field. Unlike in 1797, war-weariness, both among the population at large and the ruling elite, was widespread, and the government showed little desire to go on fighting. Prime minister William Pitt, the symbol of the British war effort, and of the demand for total victory – that is, the continuation of the war until the old regime governments were restored everywhere on the continent – submitted his resignation. The destruction of the Danish fleet, the last major continental navy that might, in conjunction with the French, have been a challenge to British maritime supremacy, by the ubiquitous

Admiral Nelson in March 1801, made it possible for Britain to make peace as well. This was formally accomplished with the Treaty of Amiens, in March 1802. A few minor colonial acquisitions were all that the British could show for a decade of warfare, in contrast to France's considerable continental conquests.

In the end, war dominated the relationship between revolutionary France and the rest of Europe. It was war that led to the overthrow of the monarchy and the proclamation of the republic in France. Both republican governments, the Convention and the Directory, were wartime regimes, albeit of quite different nature. Increasingly, in the late 1790s, partisans of a republican form of government in France were found in the armed forces or in a civilian bureaucracy that was closely involved in the war effort. The survival of the republic in France depended on the outcome of the wars of the first two coalitions. The republic survived its foreign enemies, but was overthrown by its most successful general.

The tendency for disputing political groups everywhere in Europe to take over the language and the political forms of the French Revolution was accelerated by the revolutionary wars, as was the process of political polarization, forcing politics into a confrontation between intransigent supporters of revolution and republicanism, and equally rigid supporters of the old regime. Victories on the battlefield enabled the political, socioeconomic and cultural innovations of the revolution to spread far beyond the French borders, while also burdening these innovations with the deep and heavy costs of a severe foreign occupation and guaranteeing that indigenous revolutionary movements would be unable to repeat the sequence of events in France. The French Revolution was also a revolution in warfare, bringing the social egalitarianism and nationalism of the revolutionaries to bear – decisively – on the field of battle. War thus placed its stamp on the French Revolution, and the ultimate conclusion to be drawn from the events of the 1790s, that revolution leads to war, was one shared by all Europeans, statesmen and peasants alike. When they thought of revolution in the first half of the nineteenth century, revolutionary war was never far from their minds.

Note

1. Cited in Albert Goodwin, *The Friends of Liberty: The English Democratic Movement in the Age of the French Revolution* (Cambridge, MA, 1979), p. 129.

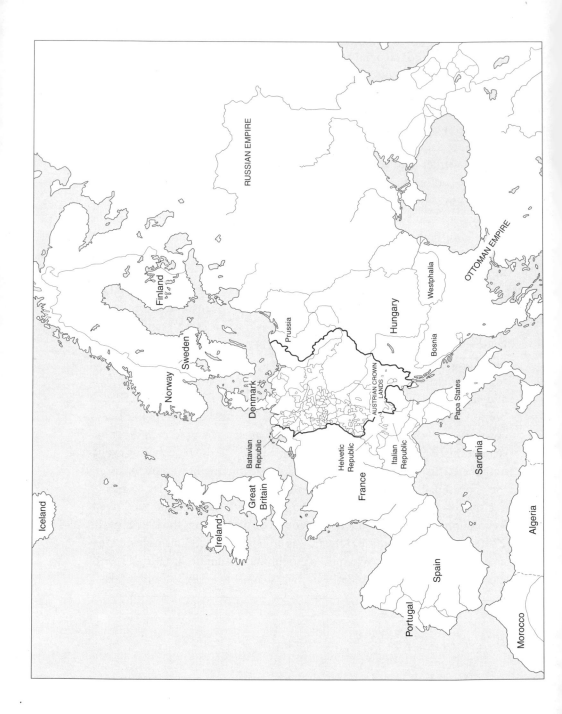

Iceland

Ireland

Great
Britain

Norway

Sweden

Finland

RUSSIAN EMPIRE

Denmark

Batavian
Republic

Prussia

Helvetic
Republic

France

AUSTRIAN CROWN
LANDS

Italian
Republic

Hungary

Westphalia

Bosnia

OTTOMAN EMPIRE

Papa States

Sardinia

Portugal

Spain

Algeria

Morocco

CHAPTER 4

NAPOLEON'S EUROPE

Napoleon and the French Revolution

The coup of December 1799 that ended the Directorial regime left the extent of the changes begun ten years before deeply and precariously unclear. Republic or monarchy; centralized or federalized state; rule of property, or rule of all adult men; priority for the sovereignty of the nation, or priority for individual rights; reconciliation with the new regime of the church and the nobility, previous rulers of the society of orders, or continued hostility to them – these were all questions that remained open. The different answers to them proposed by the previous regimes between 1789 and 1799, had all proved unsatisfactory. Without an answer to these questions, there could be no functioning legal system, no preservation of public order, no stable currency, and consequently no regulated circumstances in which agriculture, manufacturing and commerce could flourish – and hence, no social stability and, ultimately, no political stability, either. France would continue to be in that unstable, intermediary zone, emerging when the society of orders and the absolutist monarchy had been overthrown, but no successor to them could be derived that might gain the assent of a large portion of the population.

By 1799, however, both the successes of the republic's armies, and the setbacks they had recently suffered, had made the question of the creation of a post-revolutionary order one whose importance extended well beyond the borders of France. Where would the border lie between the French sphere of influence, in which the new regime would be established, and those regions where the old order had maintained itself against the pressures of the revolution? How would these two portions of Europe relate to each other? These two groups of questions – the nature of the post-revolutionary settlement, and the extent of its acceptance in Europe – were interrelated.

[148]   The nature of the settlement would depend, in part, on the extent of the French sphere of influence, which, in turn, would be the result of the creation of a stable regime that could effectively support and control the armies which created this sphere of influence in the first place.

Under Napoleon, all these issues, still so open and difficult when he seized power, would be resolved. The legal and administrative system developed under his aegis would settle many of the outstanding questions posed in the 1790s, and remain a permanent feature of French government after his rule came to an end. His astonishing conquests would bring most of the European continent under French control and extend, to a greater or lesser degree, his understanding and implementation of the changes brought about by the French Revolution from Brussels to Warsaw, from Hamburg to Naples. Outside the borders of France, many of these changes would prove to be less durable, not outlasting the military defeats of the years 1812–15. Others, however, such as the Napoleonic Law Codes, the secularization and sale of church property, or the prefectural administrative system, would remain in much of western and southern Europe. Even where the Napoleonic regime would be just a transitory episode, the changes it left behind could not be reversed; the end of Napoleon's rule after 1812 generally did not mean a reversion to the old regime, but the creation of a social and political system, in which some of the changes instituted by the French Revolution would coexist with other changes wrought in opposition to it.

In the light of these accomplishments, it would be reasonable to say that the influence the French Revolution exerted on nineteenth-century Europe was, more than anything else, Napoleonic in form. Such a significant connection to that titanic event made Napoleon, in the eyes of his contemporaries, and for succeeding generations of the first two-thirds of the nineteenth century, a figure that towered above all others. Although this is a controversial point among historians, I would say that such a judgement is well founded. Napoleon Bonaparte's role in institutionalizing, in making permanent, the changes initiated by the French Revolution, and spreading them so widely throughout the continent, made him the single most influential individual in Europe during the age of revolution. This chapter will thus focus on the link between Napoleon and the revolution. It will start with Napoleon the conquerer, showing how his great military victories of 1805–7 gave him a continentwide hegemonic position that the republican regime of the previous decade had never been able to achieve. From Napoleon the conquerer the chapter will proceed to Napoleon the adminstrator, outlining the new legal and administrative system he devised, showing how crucial decisions he took resolved issues that had remained bitterly divisive after a decade of [149] revolution. The next aspect to be considered is Napoleon as reorganizer of Europe, describing how his conquests led to the definitive end of many aspects of the old regime in much of the continent, and initiated a new state system in its place. Connected to this section will be a look at those areas on the margins of Europe that were outside the Napoleonic orbit. Even there, the influence of the Napoleonic regime could be felt. These accounts of Napoleon as conqueror, administrator and reorganizer lead logically to a consideration of the nature of the Napoleonic system – of its relation to the different tendencies in the French Revolution, of its strengths and weaknesses, of the nature of its supporters and its opponents.

The chapter concludes with the downfall of the Napoleonic regime. Beginning with a consideration of the different forms of resistance to Napoleon's rule, and their spread to different areas of the continent, it moves on to the economic crisis in the years after 1809 and the fateful decision to invade Russia in 1812, resulting in the creation of a continentwide military coalition that would destroy the Napoleonic system. The final victories of the allied powers in 1814–15 would bring to an end the entire period of the French Revolution, that, as we saw in the previous chapter, was so intimately connected to the warfare it incited. This would be an appropriate place to step back and consider the entire revolutionary and Napoleonic era, the whole quarter-century from 1789 to 1815, to see how we can characterize the changes it brought about and the unfinished questions it left for subsequent decades.

The conqueror

As noted in the previous chapter, Napoleon's great victory over the Austrians at Marengo in 1801 brought the war of the second coalition to an end. The continental powers were ready for at least a temporary period of peace, and, indeed, did not go to war with each other for four more years. However, France and Great Britain retained a deep mutual suspicion, with the governments of both countries refusing to carry out completely the provisions of the Treaty of Amiens. After a series of minor incidents, the war resumed in 1803. The French had the initial advantage, since Britain was unable to secure any major land power as an ally, but, once again, they faced the problem of how to deal with English maritime supremacy.

In the brief interlude of peace, Napoleon had attempted to lay the foundations for a naval war in the West Indies, a classic zone of Franco–British confrontation in the eighteenth century. However, a French expeditionary force sent to recapture the rebellious colony of Santo Domingo, now the independent republic of Haiti, and to reimpose slavery on its black inhabitants, was undermined by tropical disease and then decisively defeated by the Haitians, who had no desire to become slaves again. In 1803, Napoleon renounced his West Indian ambitions, and instead sold the Louisiana Territory (previously acquired from Spain) to the United States, thus turning the North American republic into a continental power.

Napoleon decided, instead, on a two-pronged strategy against Great Britain. First, he gathered his troops in Boulogne, on the English Channel, and began systematically to reorganize his army for a landing in England. The threat of an invasion was a serious one. The British government mobilized half a million men – perhaps one-third of the adult males of military age in England and Scotland – into volunteer militias, and patriotic cartoons and ballads proclaimed that these indomitable Britons would make short work of the foreign invaders. Fortunately for the British, they did not have to put their boast to the test, for the largely unarmed volunteers would have been no match for the well-trained and equipped French veterans. However, they were spared this encounter, since, as had been the case in 1797–98, the French had the problem of getting their troops across the English Channel.

The dilemma five years later was actually worse, for repeated naval defeats of the French and their allies meant that they were no longer in a position to confront the Royal Navy openly. Instead, a plan of evasion was implemented. Admiral Villeneuve was to take the remnants of the French navy west, in May 1805, leading the blockading British to think he was heading for a campaign in the West Indies. Once they were across the Atlantic, following him, he was to return to Europe and escort the invasion force across the Channel. It was a desperate strategy, and proved a failure, since the British caught Villeneuve's fleet on its return to Europe, and blockaded it in Spain. His attempt to emerge from the harbour of Cadiz led to the sea battle of Trafalgar in October 1805, at which Admiral Nelson was once again victorious, destroying the remains of the French navy, along with its Spanish allies, while suffering a romantic and oft-dramatized death in the combat.

The first prong of the French strategy had thus been a failure, but the second prong was what we would today call economic warfare. By sending troops to occupy port cities in Italy and northern Europe, Napoleon attempted to disrupt British exports to the continent. Although primarily directed against

England, these moves seemed increasingly menacing to Austria and Russia, who in 1805 joined England in war, creating the third anti-French coalition. In a remarkable campaign, Napoleon marched his reorganized forces, now named the 'Grande Armée' (the Great Army), southeast from the English Channel, towards Austria. Reaching the river Danube in southern Germany in just six weeks, he decisively defeated the main Austrian army at Ulm in October, and occupied Vienna. In December, he took on a joint Austrian and Russian force at Austerlitz in Moravia (today's Czech Republic) and destroyed it. The tsar pulled his remaining troops out of the war, and the Austrians were forced to sue for peace; the resulting Treaty of Pressburg, as we will see in more detail below, eliminated the Austrian position in Italy and turned most of Germany into a French protectorate.

With this decisive defeat of Austria, the Prussians, who had spent the previous ten years being neutral, courted by both the French and the coalitions of Powers opposing them, found that this agreeable strategy had collapsed, leaving them isolated against Napoleon's overwhelming strength. After six months of vacillation, and conflicting advice from his leading statesmen, the king decided to attack the French armies, engaging in what the Germans call 'Flucht nach vorne', fleeing by advancing. To be sure, Prussian diplomats had reached an agreement with the tsar, but Russian armies, engaged in a war with the Ottoman empire, were not available when Prussia marched against the French. The British refused any subsidy or other forms of assistance.

The Prussian army of Frederick the Great had been the best fighting force of the old regime, and it was an army fighting in Frederick the Great's style, and commanded by his officers (literally — half the Prussian generals were over the age of sixty), that took the field against the Grande Armée, which had raised to an unprecedented height of military art the principles of revolutionary warfare. In the battle of Jena and Auerstädt in October 1806, the Prussians' neat geometric formations were riddled by infantry and artillery fire, their lines destroyed by charging columns. Napoleon's overwhelming victory was a textbook demonstration of the changes in warfare introduced by the French Revolution. The French occupied Berlin, and the monarch, his government officials, and the remnants of his armed forces retreated to the province of East Prussia, the northeasternmost portion of his kingdom, bordering the tsar's empire, in the hope that Russian intervention might save Prussia.

The tsar did indeed intervene, and after several fierce battles between Russian and French troops in East Prussia during the first half of 1807, which were French victories, but not decisive ones, Napoleon and Tsar Alexander signed the Treaty of Tilsit, marking the end of the war of the third coalition. The two-year-long campaign, from mid-1805 to mid-1807, had been the apotheosis of Napoleon as general and conquerer. His Grande Armée had marched perhaps 2,500 miles, and fought five great battles, destroying the armies of two Great Powers and defeating those of a third, a record of conquest not seen since the days of classical antiquity. French hegemony in continental Europe was now virtually unlimited. Prussia met its worst fate, being reduced to a second-rate German power, along the lines of Bavaria, while the tsar's troops retired behind Russia's borders.

Britain was left alone against the French, secure against invasion, but open to economic pressure. In the Berlin decrees of December 1806, Napoleon intensified his economic warfare by implementing what he called the 'Continental System', an embargo of British goods on the entire European continent. With all of Europe now either incorporated into France, or under French influence, and with the last remaining independent Great Power, Russia, agreeing at Tilsit to join this boycott, British prospects looked bleak. Certainly, Napoleon was free to reorganize Europe as he wished.

The administrator

It is a mark of Napoleon's abilities, that while he was planning and executing these military conquests, he was also reorganizing French government and settling the open questions left by the revolution. We can point to four interlocking groups of actions taken in the first half of the decade of the 1800s: (1) the creation of agencies of an effective centralized administration and the education of a cadre of administrators to run them; (2) the renewal of state finances; (3) the reconciliation with the clergy and nobility; (4) the shaping of an authoritarian regime.

The Directorial regime in the second half of the 1790s had rejected the centralizing policies of its Jacobin predecessors, only to find that its efforts at reinvigorating local and departmental self-government provided open enemies of the republic with power and influence, prevented taxes from being collected, or soldiers from being recruited, and, especially in southern France, created a climate of chaos and lawlessness. With four crucial innovations, Napoleon reversed this course and put in place a relatively effective, centralized administration. First, there was the gendarmerie, the state-controlled paramilitary police force employed primarily in the countryside. Created in 1791, it was strengthened and reinforced in Napoleon's regime, with a group of at least five gendarmes stationed in every canton (administrative unit below the departmental level). This small but ubiquitous presence made the gendarmerie an effective instrument for the suppression of brigandage and highway robbery, for the apprehension of draft dodgers and deserters and for the enforcement of the collection of taxes.

Second was the institution of a new senior government official, the prefect, to head departmental administration. Appointed by the central government in Paris, and accountable exclusively to it, the prefect was in charge of all aspects of administration in the department. These included the state's two big demands on the population – for taxes and conscripts – as well as the services it provided: road-building, secondary education, encouragement of industry and agriculture, the gathering of statistics on the population and the economy (a new and important task for administration) and the preservation of public order. Additionally, the prefect was expected to submit regular reports on the state of public opinion, giving the authorities in Paris at least some idea of what the population thought of the regime. The prefect supervised town and village government as well, whose officials were either appointed outright, or whose election needed to be confirmed by the central government.

We can certainly point to institutional predecessors of the prefect, previous agents of a centralized, national administration. The monarchs of the old regime had their intendants, royal provincial governors, and the Directory had appointed departmental agents, to implement its will outside of Paris. However, both these previous government administrators faced opposition: the intendants from the parlements, Provincial Estates, and other constituted bodies of the society of orders; the departmental agents from the elected municipal and departmental governments, all too often dominated by enemies of the regime. The revolutionaries of 1789 had destroyed the parlements and other such institutions of the old regime, in favour of a single national sovereignty. However, they were both undecided and in conflict over the question of whether such a sovereignty should be exercised in federalized or centralized form. Napoleon's innovation in favour of the latter set French government on its centralist course, which it would maintain until the very last decades of the twentieth century.

Such a centralized administration required its agents, its professional civil servants, both on the spot, like the prefects, and at the ministries in Paris. Napoleon's educational policy, his third innovation, set out to create a cadre of trained experts for the state. The emperor could build on one of the major innovations of the revolution, the founding in 1794 of the École Polytechnique in Paris, a state-run institute that trained civil and military engineers, a key group for Napoleon's rule. In 1802, Napoleon reorganized the system of secondary education. The new schools, the lycées, were a state-run monopoly, whose curriculum was centred on mathematics and Latin, subjects that would prepare their pupils for advanced study in engineering and the law, two key subjects needed for imperial administrators. Their (exclusively male) pupils would wear uniforms and experience a sort of military discipline, thus demonstrating the close links between civilian and military administration in the Napoleonic world. The educational edifice was completed in 1808 by the founding of the university, not a college or university in the modern sense (or even in the sense understood by contemporaries in Italy, Germany or Russia), but a centralized state bureaucracy supervising all educational institutions, from primary schools, through the lycées to the faculties of law and medicine, to the specialized institutions of higher learning, such as the École Polytechnique, for engineers, and the newly founded École Normale Superieure (1810), that trained teachers for the system.

This system granted a low priority to two aspects of education. One was the university as centre of scholarship and teaching in the arts and sciences. Faculties of letters and sciences did exist, but in comparison to the law and medical faculties they were understaffed, underfinanced, and of little significance. Nor was primary schooling a major emphasis in the Napoleonic regime. While primary schooling was planned to be universal (for boys at least), in practice there was little or no funding provided for such schools. The destruction of the church-run primary schools of the old regime and the lack of any serious replacement led to a decline in basic literacy in Napoleonic Europe.

The creation of an elite of technically and legally trained administrators, flourished quite in contrast to primary education. A younger generation, growing up after the revolutionary decade of the 1790s, went through the educational system and was brought into government administration as 'auditors of the empire'. These youthful cadres would become crucial figures in maintaining Napoleonic rule as it spread throughout the European continent.

The fourth innovation had been developed in 1798, at the end of the Directory, but it was refined and perfected in the Napoleonic regime. This was the yearly draft call, one day per year on which all young men of the appropriate age (usually twenty) reported to the seat of cantonal administration for a physical examination and then drew a number in the conscription lottery. Those receiving a low number would be drafted for a seven-year term in the armed forces, while the others would not be called up. This system, when successfully implemented – and in most of France, it worked surprisingly well until the bitter end in 1814 – provided a steady stream of recruits for the armed forces. It came complete with a loophole: someone conscripted could hire a substitute to serve in his place. A flourishing market in such substitutes soon developed, although the prices charged generally meant that only affluent families could afford to purchase their sons' way out of the army.

To run such a bureaucracy required money, but it also offered the possibility of obtaining it. A crucial prerequisite was the foundation in 1800 of a central bank, the Bank of France, and, along with it, the creation of a currency on the gold standard, abandoning the inflationary experiments with paper money in the 1790s. Under the Napoleonic government administration, the revolutionary abolition of privilege could be brought to bear in fiscal matters, as all landowners were obligated to pay taxes and the government had the bureaucratic apparatus to collect them. To ensure that the property tax, a major source of state revenue, was fairly assessed, the government set to work drawing up a cadaster, or land register. This was a gigantic undertaking, that involved surveying landed property in the entire country and estimating the economic return to be obtained from it. Napoleon also reinstated a number of indirect taxes on foodstuffs and other items of basic necessity – not a popular move, but one that helped to keep the government's books in balance. As a result of the abolition of privilege and the development of a relatively efficient government tax-collection agency, Napoleon was able to maintain a much larger standing army than the Bourbon monarchs of the old regime. He was able to do so with far less fiscal strain despite the fact that the army was engaged in almost continuous warfare.

Perhaps the single most important decision on domestic affairs in Napoleon's regime was the accommodation with the Catholic Church. Once the clergy's position as one of the privileged orders in the old regime had been abolished, and the intimate connection between the Catholic Church and the French monarchy destroyed, no satisfactory way had been found to reconcile the church and the new regimes. Neither national reorganization of the church in the Civil Constitution of the Clergy, nor its attempted suppression, during the Reign of Terror and in the later stages of the Directory, nor the separation of church and state, promoted by the Thermidoreans and the early Directory, had been successful, popular, or inspiring of wide acceptance. Quite the opposite, the confrontation with the old regime culture of confessionalism had been a source of conflict, indeed of hatred, murder and civil war, the chief

[156] animating factor of counter-revolution. Napoleon's solution was to seek a Concordat, a negotiated agreement between the French state and the Vatican, regularizing the position of the church in France. The election in 1800 of a new Pope, Pius VII, provided him with a helpful negotiating partner. As bishop of Imola in the late 1790s, the future pope had tried to come to terms with the Cisalpine Republic, and he asserted, quite in contrast to hard-liners within the church, that the Catholic religion was compatible with different forms of government, including those arising from the revolution.

The Concordat, signed in 1801, did not recognize Catholicism as a privileged or state religion, but did assert, truthfully enough, that it was the religion 'of the great majority of Frenchmen'. After years of persecution, the clergy and the faithful would be free to practise their religion, both in church and in public, with religious festivals and processions. The sale of church property would not be revoked, but the French government undertook to pay a salary to the clergy. The registration of vital events – births, marriages and deaths – would continue to be a government monopoly, but the faithful were free to hold religious ceremonies of marriage, baptism and burial, if they wished. Diocesan and departmental boundaries would coincide, and the appointment of bishops and even parish priests required the approval of the government. The agreement was a compromise, in which both sides made concessions: the government renounced its anti-clericalism and efforts to promote alternatives to Catholicism, and agreed to pay for the church; the church, in turn, renounced both its former privileges and its property, and, at least tacitly, agreed to support the government and stop promoting and endorsing counter-revolution.

Although both sides gave ground, the church probably conceded more. Napoleon, personally an Enlightenment rationalist, but also a cynic, who believed that Christianity was necessary to get the common people to obey the law and keep their hands off the property of the rich, got what he wanted: priests who would preach obedience to the laws and the payment of taxes, while advising young men to accept their draft calls. The non-juring clergy, weary of their decade-long struggle with the revolutionary regime, were generally willing to make this concession, so that they could once again live in peace and guide the faithful, although, in their heart of hearts, most of them would have preferred a return of the Bourbon monarchs of the old regime to the rule of the conqueror brought forth by the revolution.

The church's reluctant acceptance of Napoleon's rule was shared by the other privileged order of the old regime, the nobility. Issuing an amnesty to the émigrés, Napoleon invited most of them – not, of course, the relatives of the late Louis XVI and claimants to the throne – to return to France and 'rally', as he put it, to his rule. In the first years of the nineteenth century, many of the émigrés did return to France, where they found their former privileges gone, and much of their property seized and sold. Relatively few actively rallied, joining the new bureaucracy as prefects, or serving as officers in the armed forces, but more did so passively, obeying the Napoleonic regime and not seeking to overthrow it, quite in contrast to its revolutionary predecessors.

This whole rapprochement with the former pillars of the society of orders was eased by the non-revolutionary appearance Napoleon gave to his rule. Already 'First Consul' after 18 Brumaire, Napoleon proclaimed himself First Consul for life in 1802 and Emperor two years later, faithfully following the precedents of ancient Rome in the titles he adopted. He even had the pope come to Paris for his coronation ceremony. (Characteristically, though, when the moment came for the pope to place the crown on his head, he snatched it from the Supreme Pontiff, and placed it on himself.) The creation of a 'Legion of Honour', was followed up by the re-establishment of a nobility, and an imperial court. France would no longer be a republic, even if its new monarchical head of state could hardly claim royal blue blood.

The imperial regime was not one that brooked much opposition. While there was a two-house legislature, both houses were figurehead bodies, without any political power. Newspapers were censored and their numbers greatly reduced, at the end, to just twelve for all of France. Political clubs, of course, already prohibited several times during the 1790s, were not tolerated in any way. Prefects kept a careful eye on public opinion. Under the direction of the minister of police, Joseph Fouché – a veteran of the Reign of Terror who adroitly managed to serve every single succeeding regime in France for the subsequent quarter-century – a political police kept potential opposition under close surveillance. Jacobin adherents of a democratic republic, partisans of the old royal house, or those who were content with an emperor, but wished to see him rule in more constitutional fashion, with a legislature that was more than just a fig leaf for absolutism, were tolerated, in more stable periods, provided they undertook no action against the government. In moments of crisis, they were likely to be arrested and detained.

Napoleon's rule was unquestionably absolutist, and there is a tendency among historians to see his empire as the last and most perfect example of eighteenth-century Enlightened absolutism. Although this comparison is tempting, I would have to say that it is basically false. For all the monarchical trappings, and the authoritarian rule, Napoleon's government was not a product of the old regime, as were the Enlightened absolutists, but of the French

[158] Revolution that had overthrown it. Napoleon may have given himself an imperial title, but the decree in which he did so proclaimed that the government of the French republic was being confided to an emperor – thus declaring his realm a result of the revolution. For all the reconciliation to be effected with the former leading elements of the society of orders, it was on the revolution's terms of equality. The Napoleonic nobility enjoyed imposing-sounding titles, such as secret-police chief Fouché's, Duke of Otranto, but had no privileges, enjoyed no feudal or seigneurial rights, and were subject to the same laws and paid taxes like everyone else. (Admittedly, Napoleon did allow his nobles to create entailed estates, which was a reversion to old regime practice.) Access to the nobility was not by birth, but by imperial appointment, generally offered for distinguished service in the armed forces or the state administration – and such posts were not limited to a narrowly defined group, but were, as the revolutionaries of 1789 wanted it, careers 'open to the talents'. The Catholic Church was supported by the Napoleonic state, but citizenship rights were not tied to professing its faith, as Protestants and Jews enjoyed equality under the law.

Napoleon's government thus retained the decisive break with the society of orders carried out in 1789, which old regime Enlightened absolutists had either been unable or unwilling to do. In a different way, we could also say that Napoleon's government was not exactly an absolutist regime, as absolutism was practised in the eighteenth century. In one crucial respect Napoleon's regime – in fact, the emperor personally, who took a great interest in this project – advanced the rule of law, by creating three new legal codes. These Napoleonic Codes of civil, commercial and criminal law were a lasting monument to Napoleonic rule, being in many parts of Europe the basis of the legal system down to the present. (The English-speaking countries, with their common law tradition, generally have a different history, except for the American state of Louisiana, peculiar in this respect as in many others, where the Napoleonic Code is the basis of civil law.) They also demonstrate Napoleon's attitude toward the French Revolution, his endorsement – for all the gestures toward the old regime, and all his doubts about Jacobin ideas of republicanism and democracy – of the revolution's basic innovations.

We can see this attitude most clearly in the most successful of the three codes, the code of civil law. It primarily regulated the use of property (articles concerning property outnumbered articles concerning people in the code by three to one) and it enshrined the results of the night of 4 August by insisting that a piece of property can only have one owner – unlike the seigneurial system, where both lord and peasant had differing claims to the same piece of land – who could dispose of this property as he or she pleased. Distinctions [159] of birth and order in the use of property were abolished.

Perhaps not all distinctions of birth were abolished, for the civil code did not treat women fairly. It enshrined the husband as head of household and gave him control over his wife's property; it permitted fathers to discriminate to some extent among their heirs in disposing of property – a clause that in practice was unfavourable to daughters. A notorious article prohibited paternity suits. In contrast to legislation passed during the rule of the Jacobins, that established a fairly simple system of divorce, and one that treated men and women equally, the civil code made divorce more difficult and its provision on adultery was outrageously inequitable. A wife's adultery was grounds for divorce, but a husband's was only if he brought his mistress to live with him at home. Even in this unequal treatment of women, the Napoleonic Code may have been a regression in contrast to the most radical phase of the French Revolution, but not to the practice of the old regime, where divorce was prohibited altogether, and differing legal practices of inheritance sometimes allowed fathers to designate a sole heir and disinherit their daughters, for all practical purposes. Studies of inheritance patterns have shown that after the revolution and the new Napoleonic Code women were more likely to receive a larger and more equitable share of the paternal estate than in the old regime.

Much the same can be said of the criminal code. The presumption of innocence and the right of habeas corpus, both enshrined in the Declaration of the Rights of Man, were not taken up in Napoleon's criminal code, as we might expect from a regime with a strong authoritarian streak and an unchecked police force. However, torture of prisoners, so prevalent in the old regime, remained prohibited, and jury trials for felony offences – another victory of the revolution over absolutist rule – remained in practice. Admittedly, they were suspended in a number of departments, where the authorities feared that jurors would be unsympathetic to, for instance, the prosecution of draft dodgers.

There is a consistent principle underlying all these aspects of Napoleon's rule, one the emperor himself was aware of, in vague form. It involved taking apart the complex of ideas brought forth in the turbulent summer of 1789, and separating out those that had the potential for broad support, leading to the creation of a viable new political and socioeconomic order, from those that had, in practice, been unable to bring about a consensus, but had led to strife, violence and civil war. In the former group Napoleon would have placed the abolition of privilege, and the construction of a uniform, universally applicable, legal and administrative system; the destruction of feudalism,

[160]   and the creation of an inalienable individual right to the use and disposal of private property. Belonging to the latter would have been the idea of representative government, particularly one with a broad, democratic franchise; any policies designed to lead to social equality or to an equalization of incomes among social groups; and the idea of abolishing the old regime culture of confessionalism and replacing it with a new, rationalist religion – whether a cult of reason or one of the nation – to serve as a basis for political loyalties.

The reorganizer of Europe

It was a characteristic of Napoleon's rule that his roles as conqueror, administrator, and heir to the revolution converged beyond the borders of France. From the end of the war of the second coalition, and, at an accelerated pace and in an expanded area after his great victories in 1805–6, Napoleon attempted to export to much of the European continent the principles of his government and the post-revolutionary social and economic order he sanctioned in France. In order to carry out such a thorough transformation in the interior of the different European states, he would have to transform them externally, in their relations to each other and to France. These diplomatic changes were also designed for their own sake, to forge instruments of a French military and diplomatic hegemony, but many aspects of this diplomatic transformation, like the political and socioeconomic changes it brought in its wake, would remain even after Napoleon's defeat and the end of French hegemony on the continent.

Napoleon's efforts would build on the Directory's project of creating a system of sister republics, although he would reconstruct these governments along the lines of the regime he had created in France. While these Napoleonic states were to be found everywhere in Europe, from the Kingdom of Holland to the Grand Duchy of Warsaw, their disruption of the existing order, and shaping of a potential new one, was probably greatest, and had the most consequences for the future, in Italy and Germany.

The Directory's Cisalpine Republic, renamed the Italian Republic after the French reconquest in 1801, became, in 1805, a year after the end of the republic in France, the Kingdom of Italy, with Napoleon as its monarch. Following the defeat of the Austrians in the war of the third coalition, their former sphere of influence in northern Italy fell to this kingdom, and the southern Italian Kingdom of the Two Sicilies was once again conquered by the French (the island of Sicily, under the protection of the British fleet, became once again a refuge for the Bourbon monarchs as it had been in 1799), renamed the Kingdom of Naples, and given to Napoleon's brother, Joseph, to rule. Later in the decade, the remaining independent Italian realms, in particular the Papal States, were annexed to France. Thus, by 1810, the varied duchies, monarchies and independent city states of pre-1789 Italy had been reduced to three realms, all under direct or indirect French rule.

Still more drastic were the changes introduced by Napoleon in Germany. To understand their impact, we need to look at the German state system of the old regime, which was, by today's standards (and even to many contemporaries), a peculiar one. Before 1789, Germany, or much of it, was an empire, the 'Holy Roman Empire of the German Nation', as it was officially known. However, the emperor, in spite of his imposing title, and the ability to trace his office back to Charlemagne, had little authority, compared with the more prosaic kings of say, France, England, or Spain. Rather, his realm was composed of a wilderness of autonomous principalities – both secular and religious – duchies, free cities, and the like (between 300 and 1,800, depending on how you count them), whose rulers, represented in a feudal legislature, the Imperial Diet or Reichstag, claimed all the specific and particular contractual privileges of the society of orders. In spite of these complicated legal obligations to their nominal sovereign, although also in part because of them, the pre-1789 German rulers were largely independent of the emperor in international affairs; indeed, one of those legally subordinate princes, the king of Prussia, was the emperor's chief military and diplomatic rival. The power of the Holy Roman Emperor was thus not in his position, but in his role as one of the empire's princes, the head of the House of Habsburg, the ruler of the Austrian lands, and his position, outside the empire, as king of Hungary. (To make things even more complicated, the imperial title was not hereditary, but elective – chosen by a group of German princes. Since the fifteenth century, however, they had, with just one exception in 1740–45, elected a Habsburg prince as Holy Roman Emperor.)

The Empire thus did not count for much in international affairs. It was, however, a power within the individual German states, as a guarantor of the chartered privileges of the constituted bodies of the society of orders in these states. If a German prince developed absolutist ambitions, as many rulers in the eighteenth century did, the constituted bodies of the society of orders could and did appeal to the Emperor and the Imperial Diet for protection from these practices. It took a strong and militarily successful prince, such as the king of Prussia, to ignore the institutions of the Empire and create an effective absolutist rule. In the conflict between rulers and the constituted bodies of the society of orders, so typcal of the eighteenth century, the structure of the Empire ensured that the monarchs would have a hard time getting their way, either in the Empire itself, or within its many constituent states.

Since the Empire was good at preventing rulers from acting decisively, it was not a very effective organization for waging war, especially against a government determined to fight a new kind of all-out warfare, as was the case with revolutionary France in the 1790s. While the Imperial Diet did declare war against France, legally committing all the princes of the Empire to the conflict, the Prussians dropped out of the war in 1795, and a number of the rulers of the smaller states in the Empire did so as well, some even joining in alliance with the French. The Emperor ended up fighting the revolutionary armies in his capacity as ruler of the Habsburg realms, his role as nominal sovereign of Germany leading mostly to additional political commitments but no corresponding additional military support. With the French conquest and annexation of imperial territory on the west bank of the river Rhine, officially recognized by the Empire in the peace of Lunéville in 1801 (although accepted de facto, for a good five years previously), the entire system collapsed.

The peace treaty included a clause compensating those German princes who had lost to the French all or parts of their realms on the west bank of the river Rhine, with territory to the east. These arrangements, legally carried out in the 'Main Recess' of the Imperial Diet of 1803, amounted to a process by which the larger of the princes of the Empire – the rulers of Prussia, Baden, Bavaria, Württemberg or Hessen, for instance – would seize the territory of the smaller princes, the city-states, and the principalities ruled by the church. In the war of the third coalition, many of these newly expanded German states, particularly Bavaria, but Baden and Württemberg as well, fought with the French against the Austrians.

Austria's defeat in 1805 sealed the fate of the Empire. The Holy Roman Emperor, Francis II, who had already given himself a new title, Francis I, Emperor of Austria in 1804, now abdicated as Holy Roman Emperor and declared the Holy Roman Empire dissolved – from a fear, not wholly unjustified, that Napoleon would get the German princes to break with their centuries-long tradition and elect him as the Holy Roman Emperor. (Napoleon was certainly a much more plausible figure as heir to Charlemagne than Francis ever could have been.) Following his defeat of Prussia the following year, Napoleon now extended the reconstruction of the German system begun by the princes of the Empire themselves, albeit with French encouragement. Prussia, which had distinguished itself by the greed and avidity with which it swallowed up its share of the smallest states allotted to it in 1803, was now cut out of this arrangement. [163]

The rulers of the medium-sized states, who had been Napoleon's allies, were rewarded with still more territory. Equally important, with the abolition of the Holy Roman Empire, these princes could now call themselves fully fledged sovereigns, and take strides toward an absolutist rule, or at least one unchecked by the constituted bodies of the society of orders, as had been the case in the eighteenth century. In addition, Napoleon created two new German states, the Kingdom of Westphalia and the Grand Duchy of Berg. These would be 'model states', in which all the changes of the French Revolution, as modified and codified by Napoleon, would be carried out, demonstrating to the Germans the virtues of the new political and socioeconomic system. To ensure that these states really were models of the French reforms, many of their government ministers came straight from Paris; the king of Westphalia was Napoleon's brother, Jérôme. These model states and Napoleon's other German allies were grouped together into a 'Confederation of the Rhine', a new league of states, all tied to France by military alliance.

Although German affairs never quite reached the administrative simplicity they had in Italy, the institutional complexity of the Holy Roman Empire had given way to a tripartite arrangement. The westernmost part of the Empire, the area on the left bank of the river Rhine, had been incorporated into France; Napoleon's allies, the new 'model states', and a few remaining German principalities, some thirty in all, were part of the Confederation of the Rhine. Finally – and this part is the most different from Italy – the two Great Powers, Prussia and Austria, remained outside the system of French hegemony. They were not part of the Confederation of the Rhine and so not part of a French military alliance system. Nor were they not bound, as most of the states in that confederation were, to introduce some version of the revolutionary and Napoleonic reforms. However, as a consequence of their defeats in the war of the third coalition, they had lost a good deal of territory, faced heavy war indemnities, and French occupying forces. Defeated and weakened, they were hardly Great Powers any more – especially Prussia – but they were not destroyed or transformed into satellites or reliable allies of France.

Outside of Germany and Italy, the changes wrought by Napoleon were more in the nature of modifying and refining the political system developed by the Directory than creating a whole new state of affairs. In 1805, the Batavian Republic, the first of the 'sister republics', became the Kingdom of the Netherlands, with Napoleon's brother Louis on the throne. Two years previously, another sister republic, the Helvetic Republic, with its centralized rule, was abolished, and a revived version of the federal Swiss Confederation re-established, with Napoleon as its 'protector'. These steps involved a renunciation of the Jacobin and republican policies of the more radical phase of the revolution and the politics of the Directory. They were measures of political pacification and reconciliation with the former supporters of the old regime, similar to those carried out by Napoleon in France. More stable governments in the Netherlands and Switzerland would, Napoleon hoped, make it easier to raise troops there to support his military position, and both the Kingdom of Holland and the Swiss Confederation were tied to France by treaties of military alliance.

Finally, in 1807, following the defeat of Prussia, Napoleon revived an independent Polish state, the Grand Duchy of Warsaw, out of territory that had been seized by Prussia in the third partition of Poland. Unlike the Italian states, the Confederation of the Rhine, the Kingdom of Holland or the Swiss Confederation, this Napoleonic creation did not lie on or close to the borders of the French empire, even at its greatest extent. It ought to be understood as a sort of eastern vanguard of the Napoleonic system, a potential military threat to Prussia, should its government think of resuming hostilites, and to Russia as well, if the tsar decided to break the Peace of Tilsit. This Polish mini-state owed its existence to Napoleon and would prove to be his most faithful and militarily most heavily committed ally.

Thus Napoleon surrounded his empire with a ring of allies and satellites. These states would provide soldiers to reinforce the Grande Armée, in case of a conflict with Russia, or an effort by defeated Austria or Prussia to revive their military fortunes. They would also support Napoleon's economic warfare against England, joining – often reluctantly, and under duress – in his embargo. (In a rather different vein, they would allow the emperor, as a good Corsican, to support his close relatives on a quite lavish scale.) However, these diplomatic arrangements were just one part of the story of Napoleon's Europe; equally important, and proving to have a far more long-lasting effect, were the political and socioeconomic reforms introduced in these states, both after French prodding, and on the initiative of the ruling groups within them.

There were four major areas of reform that were planned and executed to a greater or lesser extent. Central to all of these was an attack on the institutions and legal arrangements of the society of orders. Its particularity and chartered privileges would be replaced with a uniform system of government and administration; special, private rights would be abolished and replaced with a body of citizens equal under one law. One group of reforms concerned [165] government administration. The constituted bodies of the society of orders – Estates, municipal governments – would be abolished, and replaced with a unitary, centralized state administration, controlled by the monarch in the capital city and executed by a state bureaucracy, modelled on the Napoleonic system of prefects and departments. If there was to be any check on this central government, it would come from a constitution and elected legislature. The second reform was the legal and juridical pendant to its administrative counterpart: the abolition of the special position of the different orders, or of the privilege of religious confessions, and introduction of legal equality for all citizens, including, of course, an equal subjection to taxation. Ideally, this new legal order would be institutionalized by the introduction of the Napoleonic Code.

The third and fourth group of reforms was directed at the nobility and the Catholic Church, two pillars of the society of the old regime. Napoleonic governments proposed to suppress the feudal and seigneurial system in agriculture, and allow the unrestricted sale, purchase and mortgaging of agricultural property and the free employment of agricultural labour. They would create, on the French model, a new land register to record the new property arrangements and to ensure that they were fairly taxed. Finally, they undertook the 'secularization' of the property of the Catholic Church. In other words, they seized the church's property and sold it off to the highest bidder, in the process closing down many of the monasteries and abbeys that had been supported by this property, and sending the regular clergy and female religious inhabiting these institutions out into the cold, or, at best, off on their own with very modest pensions.

Once again, we can see here the Napoleonic version of the French Revolution, distinctly downplaying democratic forms of government, or individual civil liberties, and emphasizing the equality of citizens in a legal system administered by an authoritarian bureaucracy. However, in France, Napoleon was working with a country that had already experienced a decade of revolution, including some very drastic measures under the republican regimes. The Napoleonic satellite states were starting from a quite different background, either the old regime society of orders, or the chaotic sister republics, whose brief and insecure rule had often been interrupted by the French defeats and triumph of counter-revolution in 1799. Although the extent of both the planning and the implementation of the reforms differed enormously in the very different states of Napoleon's Europe, in general their effects were less drastic and far-reaching than in France, leaving more of the old regime in place.

The creation of a centralized administration, with its potential for collecting taxes and conscripting soldiers and the destruction of the constituted bodies of the society of orders, that might have opposed such plans, went ahead at the most rapid pace and to the greatest extent. Even the victory of counter-revolution in 1814–15 would not roll back these changes, at least in western and southern Europe. In contrast to the new administrative system which made a centralized government more powerful and effective, the constitutional and legislative plans that would have checked the power of the rulers installed by Napoleon or working in alliance with him, remained largely on the drawing board until the end of Napoleonic hegemony.

The introduction of equality under the law fell somewhere between the rapid establishment of administrative centralization and the very slow and gradual progress of constitutional and legislative plans. Equality of taxation came quickly, and particularly in Germany, where the Holy Roman Empire had guaranteed a particularly thick and legally elaborate layer of noble privilege, the Napoleonic regimes meant that many nobles would have to pay direct taxes for the first time. The abolition of other, legal privileges for the nobility went more slowly, and even haltingly. This was the case in the Kingdom of Naples, where both indigenous administrators and those imported from France were strongly determined to break noble power; the guilds and municipal governments encompassed by them put up a constant opposition to the abolition of their privileges. While the idea of legal equality for both Christian confessions generally proved possible to implement, extending this equality to Jews was a step that few governments were willing to take without hesitation. In Germany, only the officials of the Kingdom of Westphalia, one of Napoleon's model states, were willing to do so; elsewhere, all sorts of requirements were set up for Jews to fulfil (such as changing their religious customs or their primarily commercial occupations), or legal equality was only offered 'gradually', beginning right away with the obligations, such as paying taxes and serving in the army, while leaving the equal protection of the laws for later.

While the Napoleonic Code was introduced in the Swiss Confederation, Holland and the Italian peninsula, to remain the basis of the legal system even after 1815, this would prove not to be the case in central Europe. German-speaking jurists, coming from a very different legal culture, one stressing the significance of custom, and the particular, chartered rights of the society of orders, either misunderstood the idea of the Napoleonic Codes or deeply mistrusted it, when they did understand it. They resisted strongly its implementation in the states of the Confederation of the Rhine, so that the Code only went into effect in those portions of Germany on the left bank of the [167] river Rhine, that had been annexed to France.

Progress in the introduction of the Napoleonic Code rather paralleled the progress in the abolition of feudal and seigneurial tenures, perhaps not surprisingly, since the Civil Code was designed, among other things, precisely to regulate the abolition of these old regime forms of agricultural property. Once again, such tenures were largely destroyed in Switzerland, the Low Countries, northern Italy (where they were already on the way out, even before 1789) and in those portions of Germany annexed to France. In most of the rest of Napoleonic central, eastern and southern Europe, on the other hand, liberation of the peasants from the burdens of their lords and liberation of agricultural property from restrictions on its free marketability proceeded much more slowly. Outright serfdom – the personal unfreedom of peasants, the requirement they do forced labour for their lords, and their inability to leave their plots of land – was, to be sure, abolished, but, as we noted in the first chapter of this book, such serfdom was rare in western and central Europe, even under the old regime. It was common in the eastern part of Europe, in Poland, the Prussian monarchy, the realms of the Habsburg emperor and those of the tsar. But it was precisely those regions that were not part of the Napoleonic system, and in the one small area that was, the Grand Duchy of Warsaw, the government, run by and dependent on the nobility, made no serious attempt to do anything to improve the lot of the serfs.

Other forms of seigneurial privileges, particularly the dues peasants paid their lords, noble hunting rights, or control over woodlands or milling, to name some of the more common ones, were not to be abolished outright; instead, the nobles were to receive compensation. Typically, the peasants were expected to make a single payment of twenty to twenty-five times the average yearly dues, after which they would be relieved of these feudal burdens and own their property outright. Of course, the peasants generally did not have that sort of money and there were no purveyors of credit to lend it to them. Consequently, most of these seigneurial obligations remained unredeemed.

This idea of a redemption of seigneurial obligations had been the plan of the National Assembly in France, the way that the bold statements about the abolition of privilege made on the night of 4 August, 1789 had been legally implemented. However, in the growing radicalism of the French Revolution, and the lessening grip of a government on its way to incipient civil war, the peasants had simply refused to pay these redemption fees; the Convention, recognizing the situation, had cancelled redemption payments, and no one had ever dared to call for them to be resumed. The situation was very different in Napoleonic Europe, where reforms began with the idea of creating a strong state, able to enforce its laws, where there had been no radical, Jacobin phase of political life, and where the nobles, jurists, and bureaucrats of the old regime continued to have an influence in the new governments.

Additionally, Napoleon himself created circumstances militating against his own desire to bring seigneurialism to an end. These were the so-called dotations, lands in the Napoleonic states outside of France that had previously belonged to the Catholic Church, or the deposed ruling monarchs, that Napoleon turned over to his leading generals and administrators, as a personal reward – and a very generous one – to bind them all the more firmly to his rule. Such dotations were very considerable in extent. They accounted for one-fifth of all the land in the Grand Duchy of Warsaw; in the Kingdom of Westphalia, the income from these dotations amounted to one-quarter of the state's entire tax revenues. A large part of the value of these dotations was in the seigneurial rights that went with them; any uncompensated abolition of feudalism would greatly diminish their value. Consequently, Napoleon's own generals and government ministers became the leading opponents of Napoleonic policies of ending seigneurial relations in agriculture.

If the Napoleonic regimes changed agricultural property relations only slowly and reluctantly, the same cannot be said for their policies towards the property of the Catholic Church. Working both from the precedents of Enlightened absolutists, such as Joseph II of Austria, and the revolutionary Civil Constitution of the Clergy, the rulers of the Napoleonic kingdoms were relentless in their pursuit of church property. State officials appeared at the gates of monasteries, backed up by a detachment of soldiers, made an inventory of all the possessions, from agricultural land to sacred images, turned the monks or nuns out and converted the buildings into barracks or government offices. Much of the property was then auctioned off to the highest bidder.

This 'secularization', as the action was known, that took place on a massive scale in Napoleon's Europe during the first decade of the nineteenth century, was the latest act in the long conflict between the culture of confessionalism and the counter-culture of the Enlightenment. The supporters and administrators of the Napoleonic regimes generally had Enlightened attitudes about religion, particularly about the Catholic Church, and saw the dissolution of the 'useless' monasteries, and the return of their property from the 'dead hand' of institutional religious ownership, to productive individuals, as a major victory for their attitudes toward society. Going along with this secularization were limitations on religious holidays (Napoleon

cut them down to four – Christmas, Easter, Corpus Christi and Assumption, [169]
which was also declared to be the feast day of a very dubious Saint Napoleon)
and on pilgrimages and religious processions, many of which were associated with the monasteries that had been dissolved.

Even if not carried out to quite so great an extent as in France (parish lands
were generally not sold), the sale of church lands produced a considerable
transfer of property. Historians who have studied this property transfer generally agree that possessions were auctioned off in large lots, meaning that
the purchasers were generally well-to-do – a surprising number of nobles,
but also affluent commoners, merchants, financiers and rentiers living in towns.
In some spectacular examples, such as the German city of Aachen, capitalists
actually turned urban monasteries into textile factories, but most of the church's
property was agricultural land. In Italy, the sales of church land seem to have
ended there, producing a new group of middle-class landowners, to go along
with the older, landed nobility, while farmers themselves were largely shut
out, peasants only owning substantial amounts of farmland in the infertile,
mountainous areas. By contrast, in France itself, and in much of Germany, the
original purchasers often took the land and subdivided it, and then resold it
in smaller parcels to farmers, substantially expanding the group of peasant
proprietors, now individuals who owned their land free and clear of feudal or
seigneurial obligations.

A still different case is provided by the Kingdom of Bavaria, where
the church had been the largest feudal landlord in the old regime. The
secularization of the church's land was particularly rigorous and thorough
there, but the transfer of property now made the state the largest feudal
landlord. Badly in need of money to finance its army raised to fight with
Napoleon's forces, the kingdom's officials were loath to sell all this land, or
to take any measures to abolish seigneurial dues, which were now providing
a substantial portion of government revenues. Just as with the dotations in
the Grand Duchy of Warsaw or the Kingdom of Westphalia, the secularization
of the church lands in the Kingdom of Bavaria retarded the reform of agricultural property relations.

Regardless of what happened to the land once it had been seized, the
fact of its seizure was a gigantic blow to the Catholic Church. Even though
it no longer had to face the prohibitions of the radical phase of the French
Revolution, the difficulties suffered by the church in Napoleonic Europe
were great enough. Monasteries were abolished and their property seized,
as well as a good deal of other church property meeting the same fate; the
tithe, previous support of the church, was abolished; many religious practices

were prohibited; the ecclesiastical principalities of the Holy Roman Empire were abolished; pastoral care (previously tied to both the monasteries and to the ecclesiastical principalities) was badly disrupted; whole dioceses were dissolved, and no sucessors were named for deceased bishops – or even deceased parish priests. The years between 1800 and 1815 were a disaster for the church on a scale not seen since the Reformation. As with the Reformation, in some areas – particularly in some regions of France, but in other parts of western and southern Europe as well – the church never recovered from these blows. Substantial portions of the population – admittedly, more men than women, more town-dwellers than countryfolk – either severed all their ties with Catholicism, or rejected it as an overarching guide to how they should lead their lives, as it had been during the old regime.

Yet, it would be fair to say, these disasters were also a blessing in disguise, and the positive – and unintended – effects of the secularization ultimately outweighed its negative, harmful ones. By removing the church from its role as feudal landlord, by destroying the ecclesiastical principalities, whose clerical administrators had typically been the younger sons of the nobility, the Napoleonic regimes forced the church to concentrate on pastoral care. The destruction of the church's privileges, and its close connections to the ruling groups of the society of orders forced it to rely more closely on the faithful common people. Facing a hostile or, at best, secular state, the clergy would have to draw together, and form a compact, hierarchical body, united under papal leadership. The remarkable revival of the Catholic Church in nineteenth-century Europe, whose beginnings we will trace in subsequent chapters of this book, was a direct consequence of the defeats it suffered in the Napoleonic era.

For the Protestants and Jews of Napoleonic Europe (most Orthodox Christians lived to the east of the furthest reaches of Napoleon's influence), the Napoleonic era brought rather fewer changes. During the Reformation, the state had already seized the church property and run the church in Protestant areas, so that the Napoleonic regimes merely introduced some organizational changes into an already existing system of church government. Jews had little in the way of supra-local religious organization; Napoleon and, following in his wake, the other states under his indirect rule or influence, introduced such organizations. It would not be unfair to say that any possible negative influences for these groups were more than outweighed by the abolition of special confessional preferences: these allowed Protestants and, to a lesser extent, Jews to settle in predominantly Catholic areas, previously closed to them, and take up business opportunities there. While Catholics enjoyed similar

freedoms in formerly exclusively Protestant regions, they were generally less [171]
given to such entrepreneurial initiatives. In sum, the assault on the culture
of confessionalism, and the structure of privilege associated with it in
Napoleonic Europe weighed more heavily on Catholics than on Europeans
of other confessions.

Successes and failures; supporters and opponents; nature and character

It might seem questionable to talk about the structure and development of
Napoleon's Europe, given that it lasted at most ten years, from the end of the
war of the second coalition in 1802, until the invasion of Russia in 1812.
Other aspects of the regime date only from the Peace of Tilsit in 1807, or
even from the reorganization of the empire of 1809–10. Yet this brief period
of rule was itself a culmination of developments since 1789, and would have
reverberations lasting well into the nineteenth century. In that sense, Napoleon's regime is embedded in the quarter-century-long history of the French
Revolution and its effects on Europe, so that a consideration of the strengths
and weaknesses of the Napoleonic system, of its supporters and opponents,
and an attempt to characterize its basic nature, from a longer-term perspective seem in order here.

Napoleonic government had many of the same problems as the Directory
and the sister republics, but it also possessed strengths that its unstable predecessors lacked. In particular, the years 1802–12 were a period of relative
peace and stability for the Napoleonic imperium. A new administrative system restored public order, eliminated or at least greatly reduced brigandage
and robbery, rebuilt roads and bridges, or constructed new ones. The war of
the third coalition was fought well outside the territory of the empire, or even
of its allies, so that the burdens of revolutionary warfare, the constant requisi-
tioning of money, food, clothing, and horses, were diverted outwards to
enemy populations.

The three big stumbling blocks of the Directory and the sister republics –
taxes, conscription and anti-clericalism – remained under Napoleon. If the
Concordat had eased the burdens of church–state relations in France, it did
not apply elsewhere in Napoleonic Europe, and could not prevent relations
between the emperor and the pope, and with him, most of the Catholic Church,
from worsening after 1809. Additionally, the well-organized, centralized

bureaucracy of Napoleon's empire and his satellites and allies proved more effective at carrying out these three major intrusions into people's lives than the chaotic administration of the earlier governments. Indeed, after 1808, the violent uprisings against Napoleonic rule in Spain, in central and especially southern Italy, and in the Tyrol (the Alpine region on the border between today's Italy and Austria) would centre on these three issues. Yet, if more efficient and in some ways more oppressive than its predecessors, Napoleon's administration was also smoother, less arbitrary, and sometimes even more given to observing consistent legal norms. In many parts of the empire, the virtues of the administration outweighed its defects; it is certainly remarkable that most of the realm kept functioning even after the disastrous defeats of the Grande Armée in 1812, and continued to function until the allied forces marched into Paris in 1814.

The relative stability also marked an era of prosperity. The first decade of the nineteenth century, quite in contrast to the last decade of the eighteenth, was a period of good harvests and lower grain prices. Restored public order, the lessened burdens of war, a sound currency and (fairly) stable government finances created a favourable economic environment, especially when combined with the reforms of the French Revolution that had ended many of the restrictions on the free market economy, both in agriculture and manufacturing. Sceptics have cast doubt on the idea that the abolition of the feudal and seigneurial regime in France made a significant difference to agricultural production, pointing out that farm output (as best as we can tell from very scanty, fragmentary, and not terribly reliable statistics) under Napoleon does not seem to have exceeded that of the 1780s. If this is true, French farmers were nonetheless more productive, since they were working with a noticeably smaller labour force, given that Napoleon's standing army was two to three times that of the Bourbon monarch, and its recruits were drawn, above all, from the ranks of young peasants. Probably a similar verdict could be rendered on farming in western Germany, the Low Countries or northern Italy. Indeed, it might be seen as a judgement on the revolution itself. The energies it liberated by abolishing the oppressions and restrictions of the society of orders were channelled above all into warfare, rather than into improving productivity and standards of living.

This ambivalent judgement is less relevant to the manufacturing sector of the French economy, whose output, in the first decade of the nineteenth century, may have been as much as 50 per cent higher than at the end of the old regime. To be sure, there was not much technological advance; steam power, on the forward march in Great Britain at this time, remained largely unknown on the continent, and production was primarily in the form of outworking. Other parts of continental Europe, in particular Belgium and the German lands on the left bank of the Rhine (officially annexed to France after 1802), the Kingdom of Saxony, and even the province of Bohemia in repeatedly defeated Austria, saw similar upsurges in manufacturing output, particularly textiles. Napoleon's Continental System, by eliminating British competition, spurred on the progress of manufactures; while many establishments could not meet the British challenge after the return of peace in 1815, others remained and would form the vanguard of economic development in the first half of the nineteenth century.

The prosperity of manufacturing in Napoleonic Europe stands out, however, against the decline, indeed the outright ruin, of the leading growth sector in the economy of the old regime – maritime commerce. With their exports cut off by British blockade, and imports prohibited by the embargo of the Continental System, the great port cities lost much of their economic activity. France's major Atlantic port, Bordeaux, saw its population decline by a third from the level of the 1780s; grass, quite literally, grew in its streets. Bordeaux's fate was shared, to a greater or lesser extent by other maritime centres in Napoleon's Europe, from Marseilles to Amsterdam to Hamburg.

Overall, the Napoleonic period saw a turning inward of economic development in continental Europe. The first decade of the nineteenth century marked the beginnings of what might be called an inland industrialization, in which administrative and technological innovations in manufacturing would be cut off from their connection to overseas commerce. This disjunction would make economic growth more difficult on the continent than in Great Britain, where overseas trade and industrial production, growth sectors of the eighteenth- and nineteenth-century economies respectively, would move hand in hand.

These economic and administrative developments suggest something of the contours of potential support and opposition to Napoleonic rule. Farmers and their families – a majority of the population, let us remember – do not seem to have been producing significantly more food, and were facing additional burdens in the form of higher and more efficiently collected taxes, and the well-organized conscription of young men. As compensation, however, the regime promised them liberation from feudal and seigneurial burdens, and the possibility of owning their own property outright. Where those measures had been carried out completely by the Jacobins in the 1790s – pre-1789 France and the territories annexed by 1802 – Napoleon could reap the credit and gain popularity for his regime. In much of Italy and the states of the Confederation of the Rhine, on the other hand, where abolition of seigneurial burdens required redemption payments, or where the sale of nationalized church properties brought no benefits to farmers, then the peasants were tormented by the possibilities of emancipation and property ownership held out to them, yet tantalizingly out of reach. All that remained was frustration, discontent with the burdens of conscription and taxation, often hostility to anti-clerical policies and a growing distance from or hostility to the regime.

For craftsmen and urban wage workers, the years of Napoleon's rule, until 1810 at least, were a period of full employment and low food prices. The emperor reaped the benefits of this; he was tremendously popular among the sans-culottes of Paris, and made it a regular practice to enter the capital city through the neighbourhoods that had been one-time strongholds of the Jacobins. Manufacturers, as a group, were no less pleased with the emperor. Inhabitants of coastal regions were less happy with a regime that had cut off their chief means of earning a living. They were forced to turn to smuggling, which became a big business for the inhabitants of coastal regions and inland waterways. In the Rhine harbour city of Cologne, for instance, the town's leading bankers and merchants employed bands of smugglers; there were even insurance companies who wrote policies to cover them against the seizure of their smuggled goods by the authorities. Such practices brought the inhabitants of these regions into chronic conflict with police and customs agents and hence with the Napoleonic regime.

It would not be unfair to say that many of the bases of support and opposition to Napoleon's empire and his allies and satellite states reflected the patterns already developed in the 1790s, in the Directory and the sister republics, albeit on a larger scale, and with the Napoleonic regime – better organized, more stable, a little more cautious in dealing with the culture of confessionalism, more able to keep the burdens of warfare away from its own population – in a rather more favourable position than its predecessors. Napoleon was also more favourably placed with regard to the question of organized political opposition. As we noted in the previous chapter, the Directorial regime was in a chronically precarious position, facing organized opposition from both royalists and Jacobins, unable to gain the support of much of the population or even to have its measures obeyed. There were similar internal conflicts among the partisans of the sister republics, but these were regimes whose own further existence was very much open to question.

Things were quite different under Napoleon. Political opposition, so fierce and destabilizing in the previous decade, was very muted. One-time Jacobins were less than happy about seeing the abolition of the republic and Napoleon's proclaiming himself emperor, but there was little they could do about it. The sans-culottes of Paris, weary of political activism and repeated defeats, won over by low bread prices and regular employment, were strong supporters of the emperor. Increasingly, as noted in previous chapters, political radicals were found in the army or the government administration. Napoleon sent the most pro-republican regiments to Haiti in 1802, thus (literally) killing off the possibility of any opposition to his future imperial rule.

Particularly in Italy, a few veteran radicals tried to form secret societies and revolutionary conspiracies against Napoleonic rule, but such efforts had as little success as they had support. Ultimately, former Jacobins were faced with the choice of either serving Napoleon or retiring from public life. The actions of two former members of the Committee of Public Safety during the Reign of Terror illustrate these choices. Lazare Carnot, who had organized the revolutionary armies in the trying days of 1793–94, was, ten years later, a member of the Tribunate, one of the two houses of Napoleon's legislature. He spoke out in favour of the republic, and against Napoleon's becoming a monarch. Napoleon did not take any reprisals against the one person to oppose his plans publicly, but he did abolish the Tribunate, a few years later, taking away a platform for even nominal opposition to his rule. Jeanbon St-André, who had been in charge of naval affairs during the Reign of Terror, on the other hand, agreed to join Napoleon's service, becoming prefect in Mainz, working long and hard – and not without some success – to gain the loyalties of the inhabitants of this border department, on the left bank of the river Rhine, for the imperial regime. Looking on a broader scale, it was probably the case that former Jacobins in France, especially those with experience in national political life, such as former members of the Convention, were more likely to keep their distance from Napoleon's rule, seeing it as a direct affront to their democratic and republican sympathies. In the allied and satellite states, on the other hand, and everywhere, at the local level, Jacobins of the 1790s rallied to the emperor, and served in his administration.

The open counter-revolutionaries, the proponents of a return to the rule of the pre-1789 dynasty in France, were at first delighted by Napoleon's seizure of power. They hoped that the circumstances of the seventeenth-century English Revolution would repeat themselves, when, after a decade of unstable and changing republican regimes, General Monk had seized power and restored the monarchy. Bonaparte was no Monk, and he let members of the royal family know, in no uncertain terms, that his offer to the old regime nobility to rally to his rule, did not extend to them. His repeated military victories made it clear that his regime, unlike that of the Directory, was firmly established. Not just that, but the military power of the French empire meant that other European nations would not continue, as they had in the 1790s, to patronize the émigrés. When Louis XVI's brother, the count de Provence, heir to the throne following the execution of Louis XVI and the death of his son in prison, wished to issue a manifesto reasserting his claims in 1804, following Napoleon's proclamation of himself as emperor, no European country was willing to allow it. The émigré would-be monarch was forced to hire a ship and sail out into international waters of the Baltic Sea, to find a venue in which he could make his statement.

This action alone was enough to show how dim the prospects were for the former royal family. Supporters of the Bourbons either rallied to the new government, or, more commonly, tacitly tolerated it, retiring, like the ex-Jacobins, to private life. The story was much the same with the princes in Germany or Italy who had been deposed by the Napoleonic regimes. No one was willing to take up arms for them; many of their government officials took service with Napoleonic creations, such as the Kingdoms of Westphalia or Naples, while others, once again, found withdrawal into private life the best way to cope with the new world that Napoleon had created out of the chaotic legacy of the French Revolution in the 1790s.

One last oppositional group ought to be mentioned, composed of individuals who approved of many aspects of Napoleon's rule: the abolition of the privileges of the society of orders, the well-organized and efficient administration, the preservation of public order, the creation of a social and political system built on the ownership of private property. They opposed, though, the authoritarian features of his regime, and called for an independent legislature, a free press, a respect for the rule of law, and a willingness to govern on constitutional lines. This point of view was, in effect, a kind of internal opposition, calling on the Napoleonic regime to act according to the political principles it officially endorsed, instead of violating them in authoritarian fashion.

Perhaps for this reason, Napoleon was particularly hostile to such critics of his rule. Benjamin Constant, a French novelist and literary critic who broached these ideas from the Tribunate, was expelled from it by Napoleon in 1803. Germaine de Staël, another author presenting such ideas, was forced to flee France and live in exile in Germany. However, other personal circumstances of these two critics of Napoleonic rule are suggestive of some of the historical contours of their opposition. Madame de Staël was the daughter of Jacques Necker, Louis XVI's reforming comptroller-general in 1789. Many other individuals, not just in France, but in Italy, Spain and Germany as well, with ties to old regime Enlightened reformers and sympathizers with the early, monarchical phase of the French Revolution, shared de Staël's criticisms of Napoleon's ruthlessness and militarism. If Madame de Staël's personal biography connects this strand of criticism of Napoleon with the past, then Constant's life shows its connections with the future. After Napoleon's fall in 1814–15 and the return of the Bourbons, Constant would continue to articulate publicly the ideas of equality under the law, the Franchise for owners of property, and a constitutional regime, respecting civil liberties and involving a divison of powers between the different branches of government. In doing so, he would become one of the founders of the doctrines of nineteenth-century liberalism – once again, not just in France, but in many other European countries as well.

Yet for all the future implications of this kind of criticism, its practical effects were nil – and the same can be said for all the other varieties of political opposition to Napoleonic rule. The emperor had placed himself on his throne with his great military victories; with a combination of concession and repression, of actual institutionalization of the revolution and seeming return to some of the practices of the old regime, he had secured himself there, placating much popular discontent, and reducing the rest of it to a manageable level. Only a military defeat of his armies would allow oppositional tendencies to express themselves effectively, and, ultimately, to profit from the destruction of his regime.

Characterizing Napoleon's rule

In the many different ways that contemporaries, Europeans of subsequent generations, and historians have sought to understand and characterize Napoleon, there are three that might stand out. Perhaps the most obvious is the idea of the conqueror, a figure on the same level as the heroes of classical antiquity, such as Alexander the Great and Julius Caesar, or the medieval emperor Charlemagne. Many aspects of Napoleon's career, particularly the victories in the war of the third coalition, justified such a comparison, and the emperor himself did nothing to discourage it. One need only think of the famous painting by David, that shows Napoleon leading French troops across the Alps in 1801, in the footsteps of Hannibal and Charlemagne. There is no denying the truth of this image, although its propagation

[178]   probably reached a high point after Napoleon's fall in 1814–15, and, even more, after his death in 1821. In many ways, it was a nostalgic picture, appealing to the French, who had lost their hegemony over Europe, and to a younger generation, whose members had not themselves experienced the carnage of the Napoleonic battlefield, or to veterans, who chose not to remember it.

The twentieth century has not been kind to this picture of the conqueror; if anything, some historians have reversed it, and described Napoleon as a precursor to Hitler. In foreign policy terms, this comparison might have some legitimacy: both men commanded armies whose military innovations contributed to the conquest of most of Europe; British naval power prevented both from making these conquests final; an invasion of Russia brought them both down. But on other levels, the comparison between the two is dubious, at best. Napoleon was not a racist and plans for the racially justified murder, enslavement or expulsion of millions of human beings were no part of his ideas or actions. While Napoleon's rule was authoritarian, it was not fundamentally beyond the political parameters of his day; it was not the leap to a new level of totalitarian dictatorship that Hitler's was.

One famous example of Napoleon's lawlessness was his order in 1804 to kidnap the duke d'Enghien (an obscure member of the former French royal family, living in Germany), bring him to Paris and have him executed. (Napoleon thought, wrongly, that a – real – royalist plot to assassinate him, would be followed by naming the duke as king of France.) Contemporaries were appalled; Napoleon's foreign minister, Talleyrand, coined the celebrated remark that the action was worse than a crime, it was a mistake. However, we might compare the unjustified murder of one possible enemy of Napoleon's regime with Hitler's systematic murder or imprisonment in concentration camps of hundreds of thousands of his enemies, to get an idea of the differences between the two rulers.

Understanding Napoleon's rule as, above all, a period of conquest, drawing a parallel between him and other great conquerors, whether of the ancient world, or of the twentieth century, thus misses many other aspects of his rule. One image, known to contemporaries, and very important in the first half of the nineteenth century, although rather faded today, is that of Napoleon as symbol of the changes brought by the French Revolution – here again, not just in France, but across Europe. The emperor symbolized the end of feudalism, as peasants in the Rhineland were still telling folklorists in the twentieth century: the bonfires they set on Midsummer's Eve comemorated Napoleon who had driven away the lords and given them the land. The Polish

Plate 1.
A peasant carrying a prelate
and a noble on his back, late
eighteenth century

Plate 2.
A Fountain of Regeneration is erected on the ruins of the Bastille, 1793

Plate 3.
Irish rebels destroying
property, 1798

Plate 4.
Napoleon I at his
coronation, 1804

Plate 5.
The Great Hall of The United Service Club, 1840

Plate 6.
Yorkshire tailors dressing cloth, early nineteenth century

Plate7.
A scene from Peterloo, 1819

Plate 8.
Monseigneur Affre, archbishop of Paris, is fatally wounded at the barricade, 1848

national anthem, that asserts that Poland will once again emerge as an independent state, because 'Napoleon has taught us to be victorious', presents another aspect of this same characterization. Needless to say, it was the French Revolution that had destroyed the old regime; Napoleon's own initiatives in this direction, in Italy, the Confederation of the Rhine, or the Grand Duchy of Warsaw, if anything hampered this process. Still, it was under Napoleon that the results of the previous, chaotic revolutionary decade were institutionalized, that a somewhat more stable environment was created, in which the benefits of the end of feudalism and of the abolition of the privileges of the society of orders could be enjoyed.

It is this view that points to a third way of understanding the Napoleonic world, one that contemporaries also perceived. We could call this the creation of French hegemony in Europe by means of induced social and political revolution. A carefully controlled version of the changes produced in France in turbulent fashion during the 1790s would be introduced into the territories annexed to the French empire, the Napoleonic satellite states, and the kingdoms allied with France. These changes would lead to the abolition of the society of orders, and of the old forms of government by an absolutist monarch and his Estates; in their place would be a new social and political elite, owing its position to the changes brought about by the Napoleonic governments, and so favourable to them and to their military and diplomatic alliance with France. The broader beneficial effects of these changes would produce a population of loyal subject/citizens – 'administratees' was the offically preferred phrase – that would guarantee the permanence of these regimes. Napoleon himself emphasized these points in a letter to his brother Jérôme, as he headed for Kassel, to take up his crown as ruler of the newly created Napoleonic satellite state, the Kingdom of Westphalia:

> The happiness of your subjects is important to me, not only for the influence it can have on your glory and mine, but also from the point of view of the general system of Europe. Do not listen to those who say that your subjects, accustomed to servitude will receive the benefits you give them with ingratitude . . . your throne can only be truly founded on the confidence and love of the population. What the peoples of Germany impatiently desire is that individuals who do not belong to the nobility, yet are capable and talented, have an equal right to your consideration for employment, that all kinds of servitude and any intermediary bodies between the sovereign and the common people be completely abolished . . . This manner of ruling will be a more powerful barrier against Prussia than the Elbe river, than fortifications, than the protection of France. What people would want to return to the abitrary Prussian government when they have enjoyed the

benefits of a wise and liberal administration? The peoples of Germany, those of France, of Italy, of Spain desire equality and wish for liberal ideas.[1]

The entire programme is there: the abolition of feudalism and the introduction of equality under the law, the creation of a new elite, leading to a popular, if authoritarian, regime, secure against potential enemies and firmly tied to the French empire.

This programme, however, never had the lasting recognition of Great Britain and Russia, the two Great Powers outside of his system, and the Napoleonic governments remained in a permanent state of warfare. The 'wise and liberal administration' the emperor advised his brother to install had constantly to be put aside for military reasons, and was sabotaged by Napoleon's own system of dotations, designed to secure the loyalty and allegiance of the generals and administrators he needed for his military projects. In most of Europe outside of France, never more than an outline – a projected code of law, a new administrative system, a proposed redefinition of agricultural property relations – Napoleon's system was overthrown by his foreign enemies.

Perhaps, though, precisely because it remained an outline, a project, the Napoleonic system would also be a guide to future political aspirations, an alternative to the society of orders. The new elite the system was designed to create had a name in Napoleonic administration, the 'notables'. These were the locally most affluent and influential men, their wealth and influence sometimes stemming from manufacturing or commercial enterprises, usually, though, from the ownership of agricultural land. Some came from the nobility, those who had been especially privileged under the old regime; others would have been commoners in the society of orders. The exact mix of nobles to commoners varied from place to place in Napoleonic Europe, but the point was that the former distinctions of birth and order no longer mattered: their position was shaped primarily by the ownership of property, open to anyone who could acquire it.

The notables' influence, as the definition suggests, was local. In the authoritarian Napoleonic system, broader decisions about policy affecting an entire realm were taken by the state bureaucracy. These technically trained experts were, like the notables, a mixture of nobles and commoners, in different proportions in different Napoleonic states, but also, like the notables, a group that was no longer part of the society of orders. The notables and the bureaucracy were the core of a post-revolutionary society, defined by abolition of feudalism and privilege, equality under the law, priority for property and property owners, and a centralized bureaucratic administration.

The preservation of such a post-revolutionary society, its full implementation in contrast to the still existing society of orders, and the institutionalization of the political representation of at least its most influential members,
would be the key questions for the political agenda in Europe during the
first half of the nineteenth century. The Napoleonic system was thus a proposal for constructing a new social and political order from the wreckage
that the French Revolution and the warfare associated with it had left of
the old regime. The ultimate impact of this system, though, would come
not during its existence – always provisional and overshadowed by military necessities – but after its end, when it would set the stage for future
developments.

Outside the Napoleonic orbit

On the northern, southeastern and western margins of Europe, there were
states beyond the immediate reach (or sometimes just the immediate interest)
of Napoleonic power. Their socioeconomic and political developments, in
the decades of the 1790s and 1800s were, at least in part, independent of
direct French influence, although they were affected by the intellectual ramifications of the French Revolution, and the wars of the three coalitions.
Three groups of such states could be mentioned: (1) the three northern monarchies: Denmark, Sweden and Russia; (2) the lands of southeastern Europe,
under the nominal rule of the Ottoman emperor; (3) the British Isles, resolute
centre of hostility to Napoleon's aspirations. The differences and the similarities in developments between these states and those under Napoleonic domination make for an interesting contrast.

Politically, the three northern kingdoms remained in the revolutionary
and Napoleonic era what they had been throughout much of the eighteenth
century. All had the characteristic old regime pattern of different provinces
possessing privileges and forms of representative institutions. Denmark (then
including Iceland, Norway and the Duchies of Schleswig and Holstein, most
of which are today in Germany) was an absolutist regime, whose monarchs
had succeeded in eliminating all but the most feeble remnants of the constituted bodies of the society of orders. By contrast, government in Sweden (then
including Finland, and a small piece of Pomerania, at the far northeastern
edge of today's Germany) was characterized by a clash between monarchs
with pretentions to absolutist rule and the kingdom's Estates, the *Riksdag*,

[182] which included – quite unlike most Protestant countries – the clergy as a
separate order, and had an order of free peasants as well. Russia was an empire in which the absolutist rule of the tsar was tempered by court intrigue
and the possibility that the all-powerful ruler might be murdered by noble
conspirators and officers of the regiments of the royal bodyguards.

Historians can trace many echoes of the revolutionary and Napoleonic era
in the north, from the Copenhagen guild of wholesale merchants meeting in
1793 to toast the republic and sing the Marseillaise, to the Russian peasant
uprisings against serfdom in 1797, to the massive riots in Stockholm in 1810.
None of these were a threat to the existing regimes; and the unavailability of
French armies ensured that the partisans of radical change would not get their
way. However, the actions of these regimes nonetheless reflected the impact
of the revolutionary and Napoleonic era.

Agrarian reforms, begun in Denmark in 1788, were vigorously implemented in the 1790s and 1800s. Serfdom – which had been widespread
and severe in Denmark and the Duchies, although not in Norway – was
abolished. Peasants were free to move and get married; compulsory labour
services were commuted to cash payments and favourable terms were arranged
for peasants to purchase from their lords all their seigneurial obligations.
The absolutist government brushed aside the protests of the nobility and
continued its agrarian reform programme, with measures encouraging the
consolidation of farms into one block of property and the introduction of
new agricultural techniques. The Danish agrarian reforms were among the
most successful in Europe, turning a servile peasantry into a class of agricultural freeholders. There is a striking contrast between the great success of
these reforms, and the failures of similarly drastic efforts on the part of
pre-revolutionary Enlightened rulers, such as Joseph II of Austria.

By contrast, the main changes in Sweden were of a political nature. From
the 1770s onward, the Swedish monarch had gained the upper hand in his
battles with the *Riksdag*, and, while not abolishing the Estates, had tried to
call them into session as rarely as possible. Following the Swedish defeat in
war with Denmark and Russia in 1809, however, Gustav IV was forced to
summon the Estates, who proceeded to reassert their influence. Quite a number
of the delegates seriously considered a plan to abolish the whole scheme of
representation by order and go over to a bicameral legislature, with a suffrage based on property qualifications. It was a striking reflection of the influence of the new political ideas, even if, in the end, the plans were dropped,
and Sweden, in fact, became one of the last countries in Europe to give up its
Estates, retaining them until 1866.

The Russian Tsar Paul, who succeeded his mother Catherine the Great on her death in 1796, would only reign for five years before he was murdered in a palace coup, and power placed in the hands of his son, Alexander I. As in the case of his eighteenth-century predecessors, it was not his policies as such (although he made a few, largely empty, gestures in the direction of easing the serfs' burdens) that occasioned his fate, so much as his personal eccentricity and viciousness. His erratic foreign policy, whereby he went from a leading figure in the second anti-French coalition, to a convinced opponent of Britain, who was sending an army of Cossacks off to conquer India via Afghanistan, did not inspire trust. Nor did his renunciation of the pledges of previous rulers not to use corporal punishment against the nobility – and in fact having noble army officers whipped and beaten – add to his popularity with the realm's elites. Perceiving enemies at every turn (with his behaviour, he was busy creating them) he had over 12,000 people arrested, including seven field marshals, 333 generals and 2,261 army officers. These measures to avoid a coup only brought it on, and the plotters sealed their success by strangling the emperor in his bedchamber.

Alexander I, who had been party to the plot to murder his father, proved mentally more stable, and also more open to the political influences of the new era. His reign (1801–25) was characterized by a series of plans for social and political reform, clearly reflecting the influence of the revolutionary and Napoleonic changes, and devised by the monarch and his close advisers, such as his de facto prime minister from 1807 to 1811, Mikhail Speransky. However, also characteristic of Alexander's rule was that all the plans for a constitution, an elected legislature, or the liberation of the serfs, remained completely on paper. In the end, the tsar was not prepared to give up either his position as an absolute ruler, or the Russian version of the society of orders, which was guaranteed by and organized through the monarch. Alexander did introduce a number of smaller reforms: a reorganized bureaucracy centred on functional government ministries (ideas propounded by both Enlightened absolutists and the French revolutionaries and Napoleon) that improved the efficiency of the state apparatus. The tsar encouraged public education, but even with his efforts, schooling in his empire remained at extremely modest levels, just some 70,000 pupils in all levels of education in the first decade of the nineteenth century, a derisory number in an empire of 40 million inhabitants.

Although it was not until Napoleon's invasion of Russia in 1812 that the warfare of the era really rolled over the lands of far northern Europe, the dynamics of the confrontation between revolutionary France and Great Britain, in particular, nonetheless affected the region. All the countries there were quite interested in Baltic maritime commerce, and reacted with hostility to nations that tried to restrict it. Until Napoleon's introduction of the Continental System, this meant primarily Great Britain, and regardless of the northern kingdoms' attitude toward the land warfare of the first three coalitions, they opposed the British blockade of continental Europe. However, their navies were generally no match for the British, and Admiral Nelson's destruction of the Danish fleet in 1801, and the Royal Navy's bombardment of Copenhagen in 1807 (an act of blatant terrorism, which burned down a substantial portion of the city) made this point all too clear. By contrast, Napoleon's efforts to prohibit trade with Great Britain were only half-heartedly enforced in the north, and, increasingly, vigorously resisted. When Russia de facto opted out of the embargo in 1810, its government placed itself on a course of open conflict with the emperor, a move that played no small role in Napoleon's ultimate decision to go to war two years later.

In the diplomatic alignments of land warfare, Sweden had been consistently on the side of Napoleon's opponents, while Denmark had been a French ally. Russia had veered between neutrality, active opposition to France, and, after Napoleon's victories in 1806, a temporary alliance with him. However, in regard to the power politics of the Baltic, these broader connections were largely a pretext for territorial and dynastic aspirations left over from the seventeenth and eighteenth centuries. Sweden, having been defeated by Russia in the Great Northern War which lasted for two decades at the beginning of the eighteenth century, sought to regain its one-time predominance in the Baltic. This was a dubious course of affairs, involving a kingdom of some 2–3 million inhabitants going to war against an empire with ten to fifteen times the population. Russia, on the other hand, sought to round off its Baltic triumphs with the conquest of Finland. In a more equal confrontation, the Swedish monarchs hoped to seize Norway from Denmark, and the Danish rulers entertained thoughts of regaining territory lost to Sweden at the beginning of the seventeenth century.

None of these aspirations had been achieved in the several wars of the eighteenth century, but in 1807–9, Sweden went to war with both Denmark and Russia. Ostensibly arising from the war of the third coalition, when Sweden mobilized in support of Prussia in 1806, the warfare was really a continuation of older Baltic struggles, especially with Russian intervention on the side of Denmark. Swedish forces were defeated and Sweden was forced to cede Finland to the tsar. In taking this new territory, Alexander I showed his more reformist side, allowing his new Finnish possession a great degree of autonomy, and refusing to impose serfdom on the free peasantry of the far north. Indeed, the tsar's reforming plans, stillborn in the core of his realm, often emerged on its periphery. In Russia's Baltic provinces (today's Latvia, Lithuania and Estonia), for instance, serfdom was abolished in the first decade of the nineteenth century. When Russia came into possession of a big chunk of Poland after 1815, a similar effort at reforms on the periphery of the empire would be tried, with unfortunate results.

The Swedish *Riksdag*, called in the wake of military defeat, not only reasserted its control over the monarch, it elected a successor to the childless Gustav IV. Ultimately, the choice of the Estates fell on an extremely implausible individual, the field marshal of Napoleon's northern army, Jean-Baptiste Bernadotte. A common soldier under Louis XVI, Bernadotte had owed his rise in the military hierarchy to the revolutionary abolition of noble privileges. He had been a supporter of the Jacobins, who is said to have had 'death to the king' tattooed on his chest. A most unlikely monarch, Bernadotte nonetheless accepted the nomination, with his emperor's blessings, converted to Lutheranism, and took the appropriately Swedish name of Karl-Johan XIV. His election seemed to be evidence of the expansion of Napoleonic power in the Baltic region, although, as Swedish regent, Bernadotte would pursue a diplomatic policy that would confound his erstwhile imperial patron. The very fact of his election, though, which would have been beyond anyone's wildest dreams before 1789, showed how much things had changed in Europe in the two intervening decades.

Looking more generally at these northern kingdoms during the last decade of the eighteenth and the first of the nineteenth centuries, we see basically a continuation of old regime aspirations, structures and conflicts. Yet, increasingly, they were reconceived in the light of the new state of affairs brought about by the French Revolution, and the triumphs of Napoleon's armies – even when these armies did not directly impinge on the states in question. This effect of casting previously existing events in a new light would also be felt, if perhaps more feebly, in the Balkans on the southeastern margins of Europe.

Most of the Balkan region was then under the control of the Ottoman Empire, and the first decade of the nineteenth century saw the beginnings of a movement for independence from Turkish rule, that would continue for the next hundred years, culminating in the Balkan Wars of 1912–13. This was a movement, however, that in many ways owed little to the French Revolution, but had its own quite distinct origins. Successive defeats at the hands of the Russians and Austrians during the eighteenth century had considerably weakened Ottoman domination in the Balkans. The so-called

[186] Danubian Principalities of Moldovia and Wallachia (today's Moldova and parts of Rumania) were already under the control of indigenous Christian princes, who were feudal vassals of the sultans, and the Turkish rulers attempted to reinforce their shaken rule in Greece and Serbia by redistributing governmental authority away from Islamic feudal nobility to the indigenous, Christian population. Militias were formed among them, and tax collectors chosen from the ranks of the influential men in the villages – those who owned large herds of livestock, the dominant pursuit in this economically extremely underdeveloped region.

The Serbian uprising of 1804, the start of the Balkan independence movement, developed out of an effort to retain this state of affairs, threatened by officers of the Turkish army who were disloyal to the sultan, and wanted to carve out their own little imperium in the pashalik of Serbia, one of the sultan's Balkan provinces (just a small part of today's Serbia). It was precisely the recently appointed officials and influential villagers who sponsored the uprising and, at first, the insurgents actually proclaimed their loyalty to the rule of the Sultan. The insurgents, however, attacked (massacred, actually) not just the disloyal administrators but the *sipahi*, the Moslem feudal land-lords, and Moslem townspeople as well. Proclaiming the abolition of feudal-ism and the return of land to the peasants, as well as total independence from Turkish rule, the insurrection's leader, the cattle dealer Karadjorde Petrović (who, in the Austro-Turkish War of 1788–92, had been a volunteer in the Austrian army), soon emerged as the prince/leader of an independent Serbian state, with claims on additional Ottoman provinces. As such, he was in conflict not just with dissident military units, but with the entire Ottoman empire.

This conflict certainly would seem to have some resonance with the social upheavals and reform plans of the French Revolution and the Napoleonic era, but the motivating force of the uprising came not from the new ideas of the revolutionary era, but from the old regime culture of confessionalism. Orthodox priests and monks were central to rallying support for the upris-ing, as we can see from the oration of the Archpriest Atansaije, one of Karadjorde's advisers: 'The holy altars of God which decked Serbia like flowers under our tsars and kings [in the middle ages] are today stables of Turkish horses . . . brothers, in the name of God, the Creator and our Savior, let us rise up in arms!'[2] The new Serbian government met in monasteries; its armies went into battle accompanied by Orthodox banners and relics. When its forces seized Belgrade, they forced captured Turkish officials to convert to Christi-anity. The Turkish forces, in turn, defined the insurrection as a conflict of

confessions, proclaiming a *jihad*, or holy war, against the Christians, and
seizing, torturing and executing as many priests and monks as they could get
their hands on. The ultimate plans of the insurrection's leaders also showed
little of the revolutionary interest in abolishing the society of orders. As Turkish
forces were temporarily driven out, and the insurgents established themselves,
a number of their military leaders, the *vojvodas*, set themselves up as feudal
lords and began trying to collect for their own benefit the feudal dues formerly owed to the Moslem seigneurs.

Whatever the plans of the insurgents, in the long run it was unlikely that
their little province of 400,000 inhabitants could triumph over the entire
Ottoman empire, even given that realm's grave political and military weaknesses. The Serbian government could only survive with the support of one
of the Great Powers, and it cast around for allies. A plausible revolutionary
choice would have been the French, and in the years after 1805 Napoleon's
armies, in the course of the wars with Austria, had, in fact been in the vicinity
of Serbia, in today's Slovenia and Croatia. The emperor, however, having
failed in his Egyptian adventure to overthrow Ottoman rule, had decided to
support the Turkish state – a traditional French ally – as a further safeguard
against Russia. Appeals to the government of the Austrian empire, which
contained a sizeable Serbian population, and had, in past decades, been at
war with the Turks, went largely unheeded. Taking on Napoleon was more
than enough for the Austrians; they needed no additional enemies.

This left the Russians, fellow Orthodox, chronically at war with the Turks.
Alexander I did toy with the Serbian insurgents, sending military experts to
organize their armies, some supplies, and a number of diplomats, who engaged in intrigues with members of the Serbian government. The Russian
war against the Turks, while not fought in Serbia, nonetheless provided some
relief to the Serbs, as Turkish troops had to be redeployed to fight the tsar's
forces. However, Russian commitment to a war against the Turks depended
on the tsar's other military ventures, weakening during the military confrontations with France and Sweden in 1807–9, and ending altogether at the time
of Napoleon's invasion in 1812. The tsar and sultan made peace, and by 1813
Turkish forces had regained control of the insurgent province.

Thus the chief influence of the French Revolutionary era on the Serbian
uprising was the diplomatic and military constellation in the Balkans developing out of the Napoleonic Wars. However, there was a lesser, ideologically
more direct connection as well. News of the uprising spread rapidly among
the Greek Orthodox population under Turkish rule throughout the Balkans.
Volunteers and enthusiasts joined the struggle. Among the better-educated

[188] Greek-speaking mercantile community, who did not live in Greece itself, but in major commercial centres from Vienna to Odessa, there were a number of activists who, familiar with the ideas of the Enlightenment and the French Revolution, saw the Serbian uprising as a war of national liberation, and began to imagine a similar war in the Greek provinces of the empire. Their organizational efforts, which would enjoy tacit Russian support (a counter-revolutionary Great Power supporting potential insurgents for reasons of power politics), would come to insurrectionary fruition two decades later in the 1820s, during a quite different phase of European history.

Unlike far northern or southeastern Europe, the events of 1789 had made a major impact on Great Britain. By 1800, though, the substantial, indigenous, radical-reformist and revolutionary movements of the 1790s, inspired by the events in France, had been crushed by the government. The virtually continuous warfare against Napoleon in the following decade and a half did not give them much of a chance to re-emerge. As the island empire found itself by 1807 virtually alone in its struggle against Napoleon, even moderate opposition to the government took on the appearance of treason. A coalition 'ministry of all the talents', devoted to prosecuting the war, included representatives of the previously Francophile Whig opposition. In so far as any opposition could be articulated, it took the form of a demand for an end to the war. However, Napoleon's repeated conquests and evident lack of willingness to compromise made the advocacy of a peace policy a dubious cause.

Nevertheless, beneath the surface of the beleaguered nation, with a government supported by widespread patriotic enthusiasm, new conflicts were gathering strength. The Napoleonic Wars were a period of rapid social and economic change in the British Isles, wartime demand for textiles and iron spurring on industrialization. Growing opposition, particularly on the part of handloom weavers, to the introduction of machinery, took the form of both peaceful petitions to Parliament, and night-time raids on factories, in the course of which machinery was destroyed. The machine-breakers claimed to be led by a General Ludd, and so were known as 'Luddites'. Adding these new social strains to older grievances about taxation weighing heavily on the lower classes, inequality of parliamentary representation, and discriminatory treatment of Protestant Dissenters created an explosive mixture, largely held down by wartime repression and patriotism. With the end of the wartime era, this tensions would break out into the open, making the British Isles the centre of political mass movements and drastic oppositional challenges to the government in the years after 1815.

The end of the Napoleonic order in Europe [189]

The crucial role of the long period of warfare stressed in the previous section concerning developments on the fringes of Europe is all the more true in the centre of the continent, dominated by Napoleon's armies. If the French revolutionary regimes and their Napoleonic successors were ultimately war-time creations and shaped by the necessity of virtually constant warfare, their downfall was military as well. The never-ending war with England would drive Napoleon into further measures on the European continent that would lead to more war, placing an ever-greater strain on the system, multiplying its enemies and increasing its unpopularity, and tempting the emperor to aim at yet another military victory to reinvigorate his rule. We can trace this spiral of self-defeating military effort from the Iberian peninsula in 1808 to Germany in 1809, via the economic crisis of the years after 1810, to the final, fatal decision to invade Russia in 1812.

The Spanish war

The Spanish crisis of 1808 was the first test of Napoleon's rule, following his astonishing military victories of the three previous years, and it would never be resolved, dogging the emperor until the end of his realm. 'The Spanish labyrinth', title of a famous book on the Spanish Civil War of 1936 would also apply nicely to Spain in the Napoleonic era, and there are at least four different ways we can understand the events there. They formed part of the continuing warfare between France and Great Britain; they were an example of popular, Catholic, rural counter-revolution, like the insurgents of the Vendée in France during the mid-1790s, or the Sanfedisti of Calabria in 1799; they involved a new, counter-revolutionary version of nationalism; they also saw the development of a new form of political liberalism, indeed the coining of the very name. Let us try, in brief, to follow these four threads through the Spanish labyrinth of the early nineteenth century.

Except for the warmer weather, one might be inclined to compare Spain's position between 1792 and 1807 with that of the northern kingdoms. Like Russia, Spain switched sides in the war, a member of the anti-French coalition until 1795, and then a French ally. However, Spain got the worst of both its military engagements. Opposing France led to the invasion of revolutionary forces and their partial occupation of the country in 1794–95. Joining with France meant primarily supporting its naval effort against Great

[190] Britain, which ended in the Spanish fleet being sunk by the Royal Navy. In domestic affairs, one might want to compare Spain in this era with Russia. The ruling monarch Charles IV, and his chief minister Manuel Godoy, had a programme of socioeconomic and political reform, including the sale of the property of the Catholic Church, that they were, however, very reluctant to implement. Also reminiscent of events in Russia, Charles's son Ferdinand was party to a group of noblemen who opposed the king's policies and were not disinclined to overthrow him. We might say that Charles and his supporters were more favourable to a reform programme, and to Enlightened and anti-clerical ideas, while Ferdinand and his were more inclined to retain the institutions of the old regime, and to support an intransigent Catholicism, but – as was the case in Russia – such broader intellectual currents were largely submerged in personal rivalries and desire for power.

These court rivalries interacted with the larger currents of the Napoleonic Wars in 1807, when French troops passed through the territory of their Spanish ally to invade Portugal. This was a move in Napoleon's economic warfare against Great Britain, since the port of Lisbon had become the main centre of evasion of the embargo on British goods. Taking advantage of the presence of French troops, both the monarch and his son appealed to Napoleon for help. The emperor summoned them to France, where he revealed his frustration with his incompetent allies, whose inconsistent government was not helping with the embargo against England, by deposing the Spanish Bourbon royal family and declaring his brother Joseph, named king of Naples just the year before, king of Spain. (Joseph was replaced on the throne of southern Italy by Joachim Murat, one of Napoleon's generals, and also his brother-in-law.) The 100,000 French troops in the country, as part of the campaign against Portugal, would suffice to ensure that the emperor's wishes were carried out.

Such Napoleonic reshufflings of thrones had been accepted, or at least tolerated in Italy and Germany, but Spain was a different matter. Rebellions broke out across the entire country, at first spontaneous, but soon acquiring the leadership of clergy, nobles and government officials, organized into provincial juntas, and loosely and ineffectively coordinated by a supreme national junta. There were now two Spanish governments, Joseph's monarchy, and the juntas, at war with each other, a war that would last until 1813. When the two sides met in open battle, the forces of the juntas were almost invariably defeated by the French armies supporting Joseph, and the territory the juntas controlled had been reduced, by 1810–11, to a few coastal and mountain redoubts. Yet all the victories never gave the

Napoleonic regime control over the country. There were two main reasons [191] for this state of affairs.

First was the role of Great Britain. The Royal Navy defended coastal towns for the juntas, and shuttled their members around the country. A British expeditionary force landed in Portugal, defeated the French occupiers, and turned the entire country into a kind of garrison state, devoted to war on the Iberian peninsula. Ultimately these British troops and their Portuguese auxiliaries, under General Arthur Wellington (the future victor of the Battle of Waterloo), would drive the French out of Spain, but for years they kept large French forces tied down in combat with them, preventing them from being used to pacify the country.

Second were the activities of peasant irregulars, what we would today call guerillas or partisans. The French had had a brief foretaste of their action during the occupation in 1794–95, but now these forces were unfolded to their fullest extent. Urged on by the numerous and influential Catholic clergy, who condemned Napoleon's rule as the instrument of Satan, peasants made life impossible for the officials of the Napoleonic government, and attacked and ambushed French troops. Angered and frustrated, the soldiers responded with brutal counter-insurgency measures, typically involving reprisals against civilians, just bringing more people into the war. This form of insurgency was simultaneously nationalist, popular, but also counter-revolutionary, an effective counterpoint to the revolutionary warfare pioneered by the French republic in the 1790s, and one that would be implemented on a Europe-wide scale, leading to Napoleon's demise.

Indeed, the unending warfare there contributed to it, since Napoleon was forced to commit 300,000 troops to the country, to fight the regular British and Portuguese armies, and the Spanish guerilla insurgents. This was a very large number, almost as many as the emperor would send from France to invade Russia in 1812. Before the Russian invasion, this very considerable expenditure of men and money in Spain was difficult but perhaps tolerable for the Napoleonic empire, but after the emperor overextended himself in the east, the lack of these troops at a crucial moment would contribute to his disaster.

Politically, the situation in Spain by c. 1810 seemed similar to that in southern Italy in 1799: a minority of Enlightened and anti-clerical individuals, typically from the educated upper classes supporting French rule (the *afrancescados*, they were called in Spain), while the lower classes, particularly the rural population, with the encouragement of the clergy and the nobility, fought on behalf of church, king and the old regime. However, the story in Spain becomes a little more complicated than that. Since both Charles and

[192]   Ferdinand, the quarrelling representatives of the old ruling dynasty, had been forced by Napoleon to abdicate, and were prisoners in France, the provincial juntas had no central government they could oppose to the Napoleonic regime. Under British protection, they convoked a Cortes, or national parliament in 1812.

Elected with a broad franchise, albeit under wartime conditions, with no regular representation from those parts of Spain controlled by the Napoleonic government, this Cortes was divided. A minority of delegates, the 'serviles', wished to retain the old regime, and proclaim the authority of the church and the Bourbon dynasty. A majority of delegates to the Cortes took the opposite stance, claiming sovereignty in the name of the Spanish nation, and drew up a constitution, with a division of powers between different branches of government, basic civil liberties, equality under the law and guarantees for property. While this constitution retained Catholicism as the established and only legal religion, it did abolish the Inquisition. The majority of delegates who proposed such a course of action were known as the 'liberals', giving a name to a major political movement of nineteenth-century Europe. Their basic ideas were very similar to those of the *afrancescados*, who served Napoleon, but they hoped to implement them in opposition to French hegemony, rather than in support of it.

The Spanish liberals were the political spokesmen of an insurrectionary movement, whose participants fought for their religion, their monarch and against foreign bureaucrats, taxes and conscription, as well as the domestic collaborators with these foreign occupiers, whose ideas were very similar to those of the liberals. In the long run, the liberals' position was not viable, and the defeat of the Napoleonic kingdom in Spain would lead to the return of the absolutist Bourbon monarchs, the Inquisition in tow, rather than to a liberal, constitutional regime. Still, the idea of an indigenous, autonomous political movement – one not connected to French aspirations for diplomatic and military hegemony – calling for an end to the practices of the old regime, was an interesting innovation, one that we can observe elsewhere in the later years of Napoleonic Europe.

The Austrian war of 1809

To meet the military challenges on the Iberian peninsula, Napoleon took personal command of the French armies there in 1808, and summoned reinforcements from troops stationed in central Europe. For the 'war party', in the Austrian empire, led by the minister of foreign affairs, Count Stadion, and the Habsburgs' best general, Archduke Karl, this provided a good opportunity to strike at the French. Not only that, but events in Spain showed how such a war could be conducted to maximum effect, namely by calling for a nationalist uprising against the foreign occupiers. Well armed with propaganda to this end, supported with British subsidies (albeit modest ones), Austrian forces invaded France's ally, Bavaria, in April 1809. However, things did not go the way the Austrians had hoped.

The patriotic appeals to turn the war against Napoleon into a national uprising fell on deaf ears. Worse, they frightened the German princes of the Confederation of the Rhine, Napoleon's allies, who saw themselves as the victims of such a national revolt, and supported Napoleon with 100,000 soldiers. The Austrians also underestimated the efficiency of Napoleon's military administration, which enabled him to raise new troops with his draft calls and transfer, with remarkable speed, his best soldiers from Spain to southeastern Germany. By May 1809, the French were in Vienna, and although Napoleon, due to unusual tactical blunders, lost the battle of Aspern shortly thereafter, in July his victory at Wagram (both battle sites near Vienna) forced the Austrians to sue for peace. The peace treaty stripped the Austrian empire of more territory, and required a large indemnity and a limit on its armed forces. The leaders of the war party retired in disgrace, and the new minister of foreign affairs, Prince Metternich, set Austria on a policy of close cooperation with the seemingly invincible Napoleon.

The hoped-for national uprisings in Germany did not take place, but the Austrians' offensive did lead, rather more unexpectedly, to uprisings from the Alps through the Italian peninsula, down to its southern tip in the Kingdom of Naples. Characteristic of all of them was the insurgents' attachment to the Catholic Church and the old regime rulers, coupled with their resentment of the taxation, conscription and anti-clericalism of the Napoleonic governments. The strongest uprisings were at the northern and southern ends of this chain.

To the north, in the Tyrol, the Alpine area between Bavaria, Austria and Italy, the insurgents, led by the innkeeper Andreas Hofer, were particularly incensed by the anti-clericalism of Bavarian rule and desired to return to their previous status as subjects of the House of Habsburg. Adroitly employing guerilla warfare in the mountainous regions, the insurgents, tacitly supported by the Austrians, were able to defeat Bavarian soldiers sent against them, but proved no match for higher-quality French troops, who defeated them and executed their leader in 1810. Hofer would be a great martyr for nineteenth-century German nationalists, but their own ideas – anti-clerical,

[194] anti-particularist, and often anti-Austrian – were far from those of the figure they idolized.

To the south were uprisings in Calabria, the territory of the sanfedisti of 1799. The insurgents rising against the Kingdom of Naples did so for many of the same motives that had encouraged them to rise ten years before against the Parthenopean Republic, and, as had also been the case ten years previously, they received aid and assistance from British naval units operating from the island of Sicily. Unlike the sanfedisti, these insurgents were unable to sweep away the government of the Kingdom of Naples, but could reduce its control over its territory to a minority of urban centres, and force it to commit thousands of troops to a fruitless counter-insurgency campaign, equally vicious and brutal as the one in Spain, and with no greater success than the French enjoyed there.

In the end, Napoleon had mastered the first crisis of his expanded empire. The major military threat from the Austrians had been defeated, as had most of the popular insurgencies. To be sure, guerilla warfare continued at the southern tip of Napoleonic Europe, in Spain (Napoleon never returned there to command his armies in person) and Calabria, adroitly supported by the undefeated British, and caused a continuous drain on the empire's resources, but not at a level that threatened its continued existence. Nonetheless, the events of 1808–10 had suggested some of the ways that the empire was vulnerable, and shown the potential for a popular, anti-French and counter-revolutionary nationalism that might threaten its existence further.

Prussia and its reform movement

The statesmen of the two defeated and subordinated German Great Powers, Prussia and Austria, took quite different paths in trying to find a place for their states in a Europe dominated by Napoleon. Austrians looked primarily for military and diplomatic solutions, whether war with the emperor, or alliance with him. In Prussia, on the other hand, the leading figures in the government, the armed forces and intellectual life sought an internal solution, a way to reform their state to meet the challenges of the era of the French Revolution.

One arena of reform was the armed forces. The battles of Jena and Auerstädt had shown definitively that the dynamic order of battle first devised by the revolutionary armies was superior to the rigid line tactics of the old regime, in which the Prussians had excelled. Consequently, a whole group of military reformers began retraining the Prussian army after its defeat, introducing the idea of skirmishing and advancing in columns. They prepared for a draft, so that all Prussian subjects would serve in the armed forces. However, as the French Revolution itself had shown, new tactics for a draft army required new soldiers, ones who could be motivated to fight on their own initiative. New soldiers meant new citizens, and new citizens meant a new social and political order.

After the defeats at Jena and Auerstädt, the military governor of Berlin had issued a notorious bulletin: 'The king has lost a battle; the first civic duty is to remain calm'. Subjects remaining calm, passively obeying the orders of the absolutist monarch and his bureaucrats was precisely what the Prussian reformers did not want, and they set out to turn the subjects of their monarch into active citizens of the state. Under the reforming chancellors (heads of the Prussian government), Karl Freiherr vom Stein in 1808, and Karl August, prince von Hardenberg after 1810, reformers sought to mobilize the population politically. Stein introduced an elected government to Prussia's municipalities, hoping to end both old regime guild rule and domination of civic life by absolutist bureaucrats. Hardenberg experimented with a legislature, an 'interim national representative body', he called it, to gain the support of public opinion for the government's plans.

Such an active citizenry, the reformers understood, could not be found in the society of orders, and they took steps to bring that society to an end. In a celebrated edict of 1808, Stein abolished serfdom in Prussia, allowing the previously bound peasantry freedom of movement, and thus liberation from the rule of their landlords. He was dismissed as chancellor before he could deal with the next question, namely what to do about the labour services the serfs owed their lords. Stein's successor, Hardenberg, found an ingenious solution to this problem. Rejecting the revolutionary idea of abolishing such feudal obligations without compensation, Hardenberg also avoided the policy of the Napoleonic satellite states, of demanding cash payment to redeem them. Instead, he and his bureaucratic co-workers devised a policy by which the former serfs would cede to the lords some of their land to redeem their feudal obligations. Land, in contrast to cash, was something the peasants possessed, so that the Prussian policy for ending feudal and seigneurial relations in agriculture would work much more successfully than the path chosen by the German states under Napoleon's influence.

Hardenberg also took aim at four additional areas of privilege in the Prussian version of the society of orders. He declared the guilds to be non-compulsory: they would continue to exist, but individuals in both town and country, could practise a trade without becoming members. Knight's estates (Prussian seigneuries), previously the exclusive preserve of the nobility, could now be purchased by commoners as well. The Prussian tradition of allowing commoners as well as nobles to be senior government officials, and to make access to state office dependent on a civil service examination was well established. Hardenberg reinforced it, by introducing a new, uniform system of state-controlled secondary education, and reforming the universities, to produce a standard career path for aspiring civil servants. Finally, and most dramatically, Hardenberg declared an end to most measures discriminating against Prussia's Jewish subjects, who would now be free to live where they pleased, marry without needing government consent, practise whatever occupation they wished, and serve in the armed forces. This final reform was one that almost all the states of Napoleonic Germany had refused to introduce.

The reformers in the state bureaucracy and the armed forces worked in tacit cooperation – albeit one that was not always entirely smooth or free of rancour – with a group of academics and freelance intellectuals who sought to deal with the broader meaning of Prussia's defeat by France. Their conclusion was that the French were fighting for a national cause, which motivated them and made them feel superior to their opponents, while Prussia's subjects were not, so that a successful response to Napoleon's domination of Germany would be the creation of a German nationalism. The versions this nationalism took ranged widely, from the philosopher Johann Gottlieb Fichte's lectures on the moral superiority of the German nation, to the writer Ernst Moritz Arndt's praise of the German middle ages (which led to the fad of educated young men running around in 'medieval' costumes), to Friedrich Ludwig Jahn's formation of gymnastics societies, in which young men would practise a quasi-military drill, and strengthen their bodies, to prepare for a war against the national enemy. From a contemporary standpoint, these nationalists might seem both silly – the preposterous medieval costumes, or French officers in the garrison occupying Berlin, listening, with amusement, to Fichte's lectures on Germany's superiority – and sinister, since the Nazis acknowledged them as their predecessors and embraced the hatred of France that they preached. At the time, the nationalists were a relatively small group, largely from the educated middle class, but the ideas they propounded would have an ever-greater influence on the politics of the nineteenth century.

There are three observations we can make about this whole Prussian reform movement. First, it stands in sharp contrast to the policies of the

Austrian government. While taking some modest and partial steps toward [197] military reform, Austrian officials made no attempt to involve their monarch's subjects in civic life, or to end the society of orders. The main measure of reorganization of the monarchy was the declaration of a state bankruptcy, which did free the regime from the burden of the debts it contracted to fight the wars against Napoleon, but also ensured that its finances and currency would never again, during the entire first two-thirds of the nineteenth century, emerge on a sound footing. This contrast between a more flexible Prussia, able to adapt to new developments and a more rigid Austria, unable or unwilling to do so, would also characterize German affairs in the nineteenth century.

Second, the reform movement did nothing to resolve Prussia's diplomatic and military dilemma. The French occupation after 1807 and the enormous war indemnity exacted in the Treaty of Tilsit threatened the very future of the state; if Prussia was able to avoid the Austrian solution of a government bank-ruptcy, it was only by the narrowest of margins. While the overall thrust of the reform movement was towards a military reckoning with Napoleon, sup-ported by a nationalist insurgency, when the opportunity came in 1809, the government was far from ready, and so made no attempt to join in the war. Particularly under the chancellorship of Hardenberg, begun the following year, Prussian policy, like that of the Austrians, turned to appeasing Napo-leon and finding a way, however reluctantly, to ally with him.

Finally, the plans of the Prussian reform seem in many ways similar to those of the liberals in the Spanish Cortes of 1812. Both groups sought a gradual end to absolutism and the society of orders, but in opposition to Napoleonic rule, rather than in cooperation with it. Like their Spanish coun-terparts, though, the Prussian reformers were a relatively small educated group in the government, facing a society that was not always excited about their plans. In Prussia, guildsmen protested vigorously about the abolition of their monopoly on practising a craft; members of the nobility raged furiously against the state's plans to end their feudal privileges, to the point that Chancellor Hardenberg had two particularly obstreperous noble opponents imprisoned in a fortress. Town burghers even petitioned the authorities to abolish their municipal self-government and rule over them in absolutist fashion once again! Just as was the case in Spain, it was very unclear how the plans of the re-formers for an anti-French, anti-revolutionary, German nationalist move-ment would affect their efforts to carry out reforms. Hence, the Prussian reform movement, certainly the most coordinated, well-planned and extens-ive, independent, autonomous response to the Napoleonic domination of Europe, left an ambiguous legacy for the future.

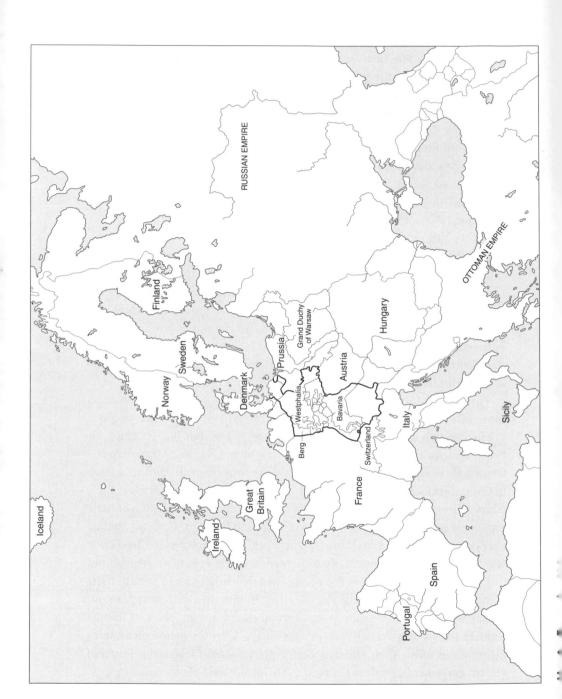

Iceland

RUSSIAN EMPIRE

OTTOMAN EMPIRE

Finland

Norway   Sweden

Denmark

Prussia

Grand Duchy
of Warsaw

Austria

Hungary

Westphalia

Bavaria

Berg

Switzerland

Italy

Sicily

Great
Britain

Ireland

France

Spain

Portugal

Crisis and reorganization of Napoleon's empire, 1809–12

The challenges and threats of 1808–9 prompted the emperor to expand his rule still further and change its nature. First, he tried to shore up his economic warfare with England by gaining greater control of the coastline. Defeated Austria was forced to cede to France its Illyrian provinces (roughly, today's Croatia) and their coastline on the Adriatic; Napoleon then annexed the entire North Sea coast from Holland to Hamburg, making it part of France. For good measure, he brought the Papal States of central Italy into the empire, thus bringing the last of Italy's Mediterranean ports under his control.

Napoleon also moved to secure his personal rule. Since his marriage with Josephine de Beauharnais had not resulted in any offspring, he divorced her and married Marie-Louise, daughter of the Austrian emperor. Her father's consent to this alliance reflected the Austrians' post-1809 policy of conciliating the French in any way possible. The couple's son, born in 1810, represented the beginning of a Bonaparte dynasty, a distinctly old regime form of legitimacy, quite different from the revolutionary forms Napoleon had previously employed. The last Austrian princess to occupy a French throne had been Marie-Antoinette, so that the marriage itself suggested a greater reversion to pre-revolutionary forms in his rule. Other aspects of this late phase of Napoleon's reign, such as returning to the hated practice of tax farming, by which independent contractors would advance tax revenues to the government, and then collect the taxes themselves – usually taking more than they were supposed to – also demonstrate a step back to the era before 1789.

Napoleon did not intend to re-establish the old regime completely, as his policies toward the Catholic Church showed. Following the annexation of the Papal States, French soldiers arrested and detained the pope, eventually sending him into forced residence in France. Several thousand protesting priests in the former Papal States were also arrested. The fragile agreement between the Catholic Church and the post-revolutionary state embodied in the Concordat seemed about ready to collapse, and a confrontation between church and state, reminiscent of the revolutionary era, lay on the horizon.

The most difficult of all the challenges the emperor had to face in these years was an economic one, caused by the very bad harvests of 1810 and

[200]   1811. The prosperity that had been such a major feature of most of his rule vanished; industrial unemployment grew, and the popularity of his regime – meticulously tracked by his prefects – dwindled. Coastal regions, already cut off from their usual occupations by the embargo against England, were particularly hard hit by the rises in the prices of basic necessities. Indeed, Napoleon's own creations such as his brother Louis, king of Holland, and his former field marshal Bernadotte, as regent of Sweden, rejected the embargo, as did his difficult and problematic ally, Tsar Alexander I. Napoleon responded by annexing Holland to the French empire, thus dethroning his own brother, but Sweden and Russia were too far away for him to take any immediate action.

Now the economic difficulties of these years were by no means limited to France, or to continental Europe. Great Britain suffered considerably from them as well, and the British government also faced considerable domestic discontent due to high food prices, combined with artisans' resentment against the introduction of industrial machinery that threatened their jobs and standards of living. Indeed, in 1812 more British troops were stationed in the unruly manufacturing regions of northeastern England, suppressing the Luddite disturbances, than were under Lord Wellington's command in Spain, fighting the French. In many ways, we could see the difficulties of these years as a sign of a general, continent-wide, exhaustion from two decades of unprecedentedly extensive warfare.

Still, in the end, the British government was better able to master its domestic discontent, resolve its economic and financial difficulties, and continue its war against Napoleon – taking on, in 1812, an additional war against the United States. By contrast, the emperor felt his system, if not collapsing, at least in a certain degree of difficulties. Problems included: the need for incessant military efforts against ever-more hostile insurgents in Spain and southern and central Italy; attempting, with insufficient personnel to police an ever larger stretch of coastline; hard times robbing him of much of his popularity among former supporters and increasing the antagonism of his opponents; a growing conflict with the Catholic Church; his Russian ally openly breaking with him. All this was happening while he was trying to establish his dynastic rule over an enormous territory, that, given the primitive state of transport and communication, was just too large to administer in the detailed, intrusive fashion for which his bureaucracy was designed. The temptation to resolve all these difficulties by another glorious military victory gradually became irresistible.

The invasion of Russia and the downfall of Napoleon   [201]

The tsar's abandonment of the Continental System gave Napoleon the occasion he was seeking. By striking a blow against the tsar on land, Napoleon thought he would advance his war on England, and so reduce the pressures on his empire. Of course, the problems Napoleon was seeking to resolve were those of governing his unwieldy, overextended and increasingly unpopular realm, and invading Russia would not really help to solve them. In practice, the invasion destroyed the empire it was supposed to reinforce.

The Grande Armée Napoleon put together and stationed in the Kingdom of Prussia for his invasion, that would begin in the summer of 1812, numbered 650,000 men, an unprecedented size for a military unit designed for one campaign. Perhaps half the troops in this army were French; the others came from Napoleon's allied and satellite states, and from Austria and Prussia, both of whose governments, under heavy French pressure, had agreed to send an army corps for this campaign. Ironically, the one power that refused to join Napoleon was Sweden, a kingdom governed by a former French field marshal. Bernadotte not only broke with his emperor, he broke with the century-long Swedish policy of seeking a war of revenge against Russia.

Even without the Swedes, the army was enormous and its very size meant that it could not adopt the principles of speed and living off the land, that had been the keys to success in revolutionary and Napoleonic warfare. There were too many troops to live off the land in Russia, which, as a relatively poor area, could not have supported even a much smaller invading force. Consequently, the Grande Armée's advance included a distinctly old regime system of supply wagons, slowing down the soldiers' progress and hampering their flexibility.

Russian strategy played on this difficulty, the tsar's generals falling back, rather than engaging the invaders, burning and destroying all the territory they left, so that the Grande Armée would occupy a devastated region. One of Napoleon's officers described the increasingly nightmarish aspect of the invasion:

> ... frequent forced marches along abominable roads, either smothered in sand or knee-deep in mud ... under skies alternately unbearably hot or pouring forth freezing rain ... many regiments had no more than three days' supply of rations, which because of the total devastation of the countryside, could never be

adequately replenished . . . our drink consisted of . . . brackish liquid scooped from stinking wells and putrid ponds . . . the army, and in particular the infantry, was being ravaged by a variety of diseases, chief among them dysentery, ague and typhus . . . Inexorably, the whole vast host seemed to be moving ponderously to disaster . . .[3]

When the forces did finally meet, at the battles of Smolensk and Borodino, the Russians advanced on the invaders in old regime fashion, in tightly formed rows, and were brought down by infantry and artillery fire. But because the Russian armies were so large, the soldiers were able to keep on coming, inflicting equally large casualties on Napoleon's troops. By September, Napoleon's forces had occupied Moscow, but the Russians had evacuated the city and set it on fire, so the already weakened Grande Armée found itself in possession of a ghost town.

Capturing the largest city in Russia had accomplished nothing, and the army was too weakened, its supply lines too overextended to advance further. In October 1812, Napoleon gave the order to retreat. Russian peasants, rather like their counterparts in Spain, fought a guerilla war for their monarch and his religion, against invaders whom the Orthodox priests described as 'a legion of devils, commanded by the anti-Christ'. They killed sick and wounded enemy soldiers, and ambushed couriers, stragglers and supply units. The ever-more badly supplied Grande Armée faced the rigours of an early and harsh Russian winter. By the time it reached the Prussian border, fewer than 100,000 soldiers were left. The emperor hastened back to Paris, to organize the new army his officials were already raising.

Here, Napoleon's bureaucracy showed what it was capable of, because recruits were quickly drafted, mustered and sent to the front. By the spring of 1813, the emperor was back in Germany with a new army, albeit one consisting primarily of raw and untrained draftees, reinforced by more seasoned troops withdrawn from Spain. But in the interval the Prussian contingent of Napoleon's invasion force, under General Yorck, one of the military reformers, had, with Russian support, changed sides. General Yorck called out the Provincial Estates of East Prussia, and they proclaimed a German national uprising against Napoleon. Nervously and more than a little reluctantly, the Prussian king and his chancellor, Hardenberg, joined in the call, and resolved on a new war against Napoleon. Inspired nationalist volunteers from many parts of central and eastern Germany – in the end, at least 100,000 of them – joined the king's ranks, along with the draftees conscripted as a result of the Prussian military reforms.

Thus the campaign of the spring and summer of 1813 pitted nationalist armies using the new tactics of the French Revolution against each other. Napoleon's forces won initial victories, that were followed by a truce for negotiations, which proved fruitless. Austrian chancellor Metternich, who had carefully remained neutral until he saw how the war would develop, now joined in the anti-Napoleonic coalition, that was, once again, financed with large British subsidies. At the 'battle of the nations', near Leipzig, in October 1813, over one million soldiers were in action, the largest military engagement ever fought until then. Larger ones would only come a century later, during the First World War.

The French were defeated and forced to retreat eastward toward the river Rhine; the smaller German states that had previously been Napoleon's loyal allies now switched sides. British and Spanish forces drove the French out of Spain and advanced over the Pyrenees into France. In the Baltic, Sweden now declared war on France, although its regent carefully kept its troops out of the fighting against French soldiers, concentrating instead on France's Danish ally, in order to seize Norway from it. By 1814, French troops had been pushed back across the pre-1789 borders and at the end of March of that year Russian, Prussia and Austrian soldiers entered Paris. Napoleon still wanted to fight on, but his own generals and senior administrators had had enough, and the emperor was forced to abdicate. The long forgotten count of Provence, Louis XVI's brother, became king of France and the former emperor was sent into exile, to rule the little island of Elba off the coast of northern Italy.

The era of the French Revolution should have come to an end at that point, but it did not. Impatient with his miniature kingdom after dominating all of Europe, Napoleon escaped from Elba in March 1815 and returned to France. The process by which he seized power once again, and his brief reign, the so-called 'Hundred Days', are really part of the history of the post-1815 era, the period of the Restoration, and we will discuss them in Chapter Seven, which deals with the years 1815–30. For now, suffice it to say that the allied powers who had just defeated Napoleon had no intention of letting him regain his power. At the Battle of Waterloo, fought in Belgium in June 1815, British and Prussian troops defeated the French and forced Napoleon to abdicate once more. This time, the ex-emperor was exiled more securely to the distant Atlantic island of St Helena. The era of the French Revolution now really was over, once and for all.

[204] Thinking about the era of the French Revolution

While the era of the French Revolution may have ended in 1815, the debate about the meaning, significance and consequences of that quarter-century began immediately and has continued, in one form or another down to the present day. At first, contemporaries pondered the meaning of the events they had personally experienced, then subsequent generations thought about the world the revolutionary era had created; finally, the debate became increasingly a matter for professional historians. For much of the twentieth century, the Marxist interpretation has provided perhaps the single most important way to understand the Revolution. Based on observations made by contemporaries, including the counter-revolutionary Edmund Burke, and Antoine Barnave, one of the leading Patriot deputies in the National Assembly, the interpretation was first developed by Karl Marx and Friedrich Engels, born in 1818 and 1820, respectively, and thus members of the post-revolutionary generation. It was elaborated by historians working between about 1920 and 1970.

In the Marxist version, the old regime was, basically, a feudal social and economic order, politically dominated by an aristocratic ruling class, that owed its power to its ownership of estates with seigneurial rights. During the revolution, this aristocratic ruling class was overthrown and replaced with a new dominant group, the capitalist bourgeoisie, bankers, merchants and manufacturers, who had been growing in strength and influence before 1789, but whose interests had been constantly controverted by the government of the old regime. This bourgeoisie then shaped a capitalist and industrial society and economy, defeating challenges from the sans-culottes, and the most radical of the Jacobins, who were already thinking about overthrowing this capitalist regime and putting a socialist one in its place. Napoleon, in this interpretation, stabilized the new bourgeois, capitalist society and introduced throughout Europe many of the changes it had brought in France. Even after the military defeat of Napoleon, most of these changes remained in place.

This interpretation has been under increasingly severe criticism since the 1950s, and the scholarly appraisals issued during the bicentenary of the French Revolution in 1989 made it clear that the critics have carried the day. They have noted that the dichotomy between an agricultural and feudal France, with an aristocratic ruling class before 1789, and a capitalist–industrial one, with bourgeois rulers afterwards, is altogether too simple and empirically incorrect. Commoners could and did own seigneuries in the old regime, giving them 'feudal' rights that were thus not an exclusive preserve of the aristocracy. In 1815, France remained a predominantly agricultural country, with most of its wealth in land, and still with most of its wealthy landowners, including a very large and affluent group of pre-1789 nobles. Far from encouraging capitalism in France, the revolution disrupted it, through its inflationary policies and constant warfare. Indeed, one of the main eighteenth-century capitalist growth sectors, overseas commerce, was destroyed as a result of the revolution and the naval war with England. In short, many of the social and economic developments attributed to the revolution were the result of longer-term changes occurring gradually over decades, and the revolution's role in them was negligible or even outright counter to what the Marxist interpretation suggests it should have been.

Critics have been equally harsh on the Marxist interpretation of the politics of the revolution itself. Capitalists, as a group, were hardly enemies of the old regime, and often found their interests quite well respected by the existing governmental institutions. Many of the patriot leaders of the early revolution were from the aristocracy, and while the radical politicians of the republic may have been of commoner backgrounds, they were more likely to have been professional men – lawyers, authors, even doctors – than capitalist entrepreneurs. Both Jacobins and sans-culottes were strong defenders of private property and had no interest in socialism.

There is no denying the strength of these criticisms, even if they may at times have been a bit exaggerated. (The surge in manufacturing activity during the Napoleonic era, for instance, does suggest that a crude and primitive form of industrial capitalism was on the increase after 1800, both in France and elsewhere in continental Europe.) However, after dismantling the Marxist interpretation, the critics have had a hard time finding another one to put in its place. Perhaps the most popular in recent years has been the cultural/linguistic interpretation, which describes the revolution as above all a revolution in language, the invention of a new way to talk and think about politics. There is no doubt that the revolutionaries did invent a new way to talk about politics – and society, economics, space, time, foreign affairs, gender relations and a number of other things as well – but they went rather beyond just talking about these things. In implementing their new discourse, in acting on it, they faced material realities, embedded in social and economic structures, so that the changes of the revolution simply cannot be reduced to linguistic ones.

In this sense, the idea that the French Revolution involved the violent introduction of a new social order on the European continent is a sound one, and the history of at least the first half of the nineteenth century is hard to understand without it. However, the traditional (or 'orthodox') Marxist version, that identifies specific social classes as the prime mover seems inadequate, because it is often not clear if these social classes acted as the doctrine says they should have, or whether they even existed at all. Moreover, the link between the revolution and capitalist industrialization, central to the Marxist theory, seems questionable, if for no other reason than that the terrific economic disruptions caused by the revolution and the wars that resulted from it presented many handicaps for economic development, outweighing any advantages to it that might have stemmed from the restructuring of property ownership and property relationships.

Before 1789, the countries of continental Europe had been examples of a society of orders, a hierarchical social arrangement with access to property, power and influence primarily a result of categories set at birth, and where privilege, private laws, granted specific, chartered rights to individual orders, social groups or inhabitants of particular provinces or of certain towns. (Arguably, this society of orders had already been at least partially dismantled in Great Britain.) The French Revolution destroyed this state of affairs, and by the Napoleonic era we can see a different order emerging, a civil society of property owners. There, individuals were equal under the law, and this law guaranteed, above all, the rights of owners of property to use and dispose of their property as they pleased. Such a new regime of property might have a favourable effect on economic development, or it might not; the extent of such property ownership might vary from country to country, as might the previous social identity of property owners – nobles or commoners under the old regime – but in all these different and varying circumstances were products of the changes wrought by the revolution in France, and as brought by armed force, to much of the rest of continental Europe.

When we look at Europe in 1815, we can see this movement from the society of orders to a civil society of property owners as the key to future political developments. First was the extent of the actual transformation. In France, the Low Countries, Italy, Spain and the westernmost part of Germany – the western part of the continent – only minor remnants of the society of orders remained; the new form of social organization was triumphant. In most of central and northern Europe, on the other hand, the transformation had only begun, or had stopped halfway, leaving elements of both kinds of society in place. Further to the east, in the Austrian empire, Russia, and the remaining realms of eastern Europe (still under the domination of the Turkish sultan), the society of orders had not been challenged at all; its abolition was a task for the future.

Second was the nature of this new social order. In particular, by 1815, it [207] was not yet clear how farmers, by far the single largest group of Europeans, would fit into this society of property-owners. Although crucial to both revolution and counter-revolution, inhabitants of the countryside had been, above all, the recipients of outside initiatives during the years 1789–1815, and had responded to them; their active participation in the new social order would be crucial for its future development.

Two other major issues had emerged as a result of this social transformation. One was the question of how such a new society was to be governed. Between 1789 and 1815, all sorts of different regimes had been tried out, in France and countries under its influence, from a constitutional monarchy, to a democratic republic, to a property-owners' republic, to an authoritarian empire, but, ultimately, none had lasted. The second was how to integrate certain institutions of the old regime into the new society, particularly the Christian churches, and especially the Catholic Church. Efforts to abolish them had been singularly unsuccessful, and had led to bloody civil wars. The power of the culture of confessionalism was such, and its hold on so many Europeans so strong, that a successful version of the post-revolutionary order would have to find a way to come to terms with the institutions that embodied it.

In the rest of this book, we will trace the fortunes of the new world created by the French Revolution, see the social and economic changes wrought within it, and observe the political struggles over the open questions it left for the future.

Notes

1. Quoted in Helmut Berding, *Napoleonische Herrschafts- und Gesellschaftspolitik in Frankreich* (Göttingen, 1973), pp. 116–17.

2. Cited in Michael B. Petrovich, 'The Role of the Serbian Orthodox Church in the First Serbian Uprising 1804–1813', in Wayne C. Vucinich (ed.) *The First Serbian Uprising 1804–1813* (Boulder CO, 1982), p. 268.

3. Quoted in Janet Hartley, *Alexander I*, (London and New York, 1994), p. 113.

CHAPTER 5

SOCIAL AND ECONOMIC CHANGE, 1780–1850

The chapters on the French Revolution and the Napoleonic era have shown us history at high speed: drastic changes in government, in legal systems, in property relations, in international boundaries, in ways of thinking about society and politics – all compressed into a relatively few years. No less drastic were the means by which changes were brought about: revolution, civil wars, large-scale warfare between the Great Powers. Now we will turn to another history, proceeding at a decelerated pace, where changes occurred gradually over decades, and their impact is measured in the demographic abstractions of birth- or death-rates, in the dry figures of the gross national product or real wages, in such unspectacular developments as the transformation of crop rotation systems, the building of canals and paved highways, or small producers' declining direct access to the market.

To be sure, even this history in the slow lane produced its share of dramatic events; for the period under consideration, we could find them in the use of steam engines for industrial production, the building of railways, or, less optimistically, in the Irish potato famine. We must be careful not to be misled by these events, though. Considering all economic sectors, the entire seven decades and the whole European world, it is the slow and gradual pace of social and economic change that predominated. Indeed, in many parts of the continent, particularly, although not exclusively, on its eastern and southern margins, even slow and gradual change was less common than stasis, than little or no change at all. Still, even slow and partial change, when occurring over a long enough period of time, produces a major effect. The dynamics of the age of revolution, the era under consideration in this book, were a result of the combination of the accelerated history of politics in the years after 1789, and the decelerated history of society and economy over a course of decades.

The lash of Parson Malthus

In 1797, Thomas Malthus, an English country parson, published *An Essay on the Principle of Population*, an uncommonly influential book, that both reflected the conflicts and dilemmas of the time in which it appeared, and also helped to shape – or, perhaps, to distort – future actions. Even if its main thesis was ultimately incorrect, the book is nonetheless useful to us, for it provides a way to thematize the main lines of social and economic development. Malthus asserted that, generally, animals could reproduce themselves more rapidly than vegetables, or, specifically, that the natural increase in the human population tended to outstrip the growth in the food supply. In his economic model, favourable conditions for the lower classes, such as high wages and low food prices, would lead them to marry young and have many children. The resulting growth in the number of mouths to feed would inevitably be greater than the increase in the amount of food to feed them, so that a rise in mortality via famine and disease would bring the population back to, or below, the level from which it started.

Malthus's vision was a dismal one, in which no long-term improvement in ordinary people's standard of living is possible, since any short-term favourable trends are invariably eaten up by excessive reproduction and looming death. The implications of his work, and that of others following him in this theory, is the main reason that his British contemporaries referred to economics as the 'dismal science'. In later years, Malthus changed his mind a little, to allow for the possiblity of 'preventive checks'. These were not what we today call Malthusian methods, that is, birth control, which he, as a clergyman, regarded as sinful and unnatural. Rather, he advocated what might be seen as collective cold showers, a willingness on the part of the lower classes to curb their sexual urges and resulting reproduction by marrying at a later age and accepting the possibility of life-long celibacy. While better than famine, this was still a pretty dismal prospect.

Malthus's work needs to be seen in the context of the political agitation of the British radicals in the wake of the French Revolution. He was a defender of the existing order and his book was designed to prove that the changes demanded by these opponents of the regime could never lead to any improvement in the lives of the ordinary people for whom the British Jacobins claimed to speak. However, the work was also a product of the social and economic circumstances of the 1790s, a decade of bad harvests, high food prices and declining popular standards of living in the British Isles and in most parts of Europe. Such events could easily be interpreted as

[210]   precisely the beginning of the catastrophe resulting from overpopulation that Malthus predicted.

When we look back at the previous seven hundred or so years of European history, Malthus's predictions do take on a certain plausibility. Periods of rising population, in the thirteenth and early fourteenth, as well as the sixteenth and early seventeenth centuries, had been followed by periods of disease, famine and population decline, in the later fourteenth and fifteenth, the later seventeenth and early eighteenth centuries. As contemporaries were dimly aware, and modern historians have ascertained rather more firmly, population, in both the British Isles and continental Europe, had been on the rise since around 1750. This increase would continue at an accelerated pace in the nineteenth century. But the disaster Malthus predicted never occurred; while the population of Europe doubled between 1800 and 1900, going from about 200 million to 400 million (there are different figures, depending on just how one draws Europe's boundaries), standards of living rose to an unprecedented extent. Indeed, at the beginning of the twenty-first century, all predictions of Malthus and his followers that a rising population – and not only in Europe, but pretty much anywhere in the world – would outstrip the food supply and lead to a demographic catastrophe have not come true.

There is, of course, no guarantee that they will not come true at some future date, but, from the middle of the eighteenth century until the present, the production of food and of all other basic necessities, far from lagging behind population growth, has exceeded it. In Europe during the years 1780–1850, however, production outstripped population by only a narrow margin. The need to reorganize production and distribution, and to allocate and re-allocate labour and capital to keep up with a growing population – speaking metaphorically, the lash of Parson Malthus – was the main impetus for social and economic developments. More than that, the social changes produced by the reorganization needed to increase production resulted in chronic conflicts and popular discontent, that helped make this period an age of revolutions.

This process of economic change induced by population pressure, leading to social transformation and social conflict, will provide the structure for this chapter. Starting with a brief account of population growth, we will go on to consider the two main variants of economic developments that enabled Europeans to deal with their growing numbers. The chapter will then discuss both the changes in social structure and the nature of the social tensions arising from these economic developments. In the last segment, we will look at some overall trends, trying to chart changes in social structure and gender

relations, considering which groups benefited and which did not, and seeing [211]
how the changes previously outlined were distributed in space and time.
We will conclude by looking at some national variations in these overall
movements, considering the different ways that general, Europewide trends
appeared in specific countries.

Growing numbers and responses to them

Table 5.1 offers some estimates of the growth of population in several European countries over the one hundred years between the middle of the eighteenth and nineteenth centuries. Although the figures for the earlier period
are not terribly reliable, and there are many individual differences, the overall
pattern is one of a steadily increasing rate of population growth: from 1750
to 1800, averaging about 0.5 per cent per year; in the first half of the nineteenth century, doubling to 1.0 per cent. The carnage of the Napoleonic era
had slowed down these rates in some countries, but with the return of peace
in 1815, the population rise resumed. In the German states, for instance,

Table 5.1   Population of selected European countries, 1750–1850

	Population, in millions			Yearly population growth (%)	
	1750	1800	1850	1750–1800	1800–1850
England	6.1	9.2	17.9	0.82	1.34
Germany	17.0	24.5	34.4	0.73	0.68
Scandinavian countries	3.6	5.0	7.9	0.66	0.92
France	21.7	27.0	35.8	0.44	0.57
Italy	15.3	17.8	24.0	0.30	0.60
Europe, without Russia	101.8	132	213	0.54	0.98

Sources: Taken from John Goodman and Katrina Honeyman, *Gainful Pursuits: The Making of Industrial Europe 1699–1914* (London, 1988), p. 23; and David Grigg, *Population Growth and Agrarian Change: An Historical Perspective* (Cambridge, 1980), p. 60.

[212] population declined between the beginning of the nineteenth century and the peace settlement, but between 1815 and 1850 rose at an accelerated pace, of 1.3 per cent per year. Although today we might consider such increases modest in comparison to the 2–4 per cent yearly rates of population growth reached in a number of African and Asian countries in the second half of the twentieth century, to contemporaries, the increase in their numbers was daunting enough, especially as it represented a rate at least twice as fast as the average of the years 1600–1750.

Historians, demographers and physicians have argued for some time about what caused these changes. Basically, there are two points of view, based on the two ways that population can increase – more people being born, or fewer dying. The fertility proponents, as we might call the first group, suggest that in this period birth rates were increasing, because a greater proportion of the adult population was getting married (or having extramarital relations leading to conception) and, especially, was marrying or having extramarital relations at a younger age – all developments that would increase the number of births. The mortality proponents, on the other hand, suggest that more extensive and reliable food supplies were increasing nutrition and thus boosting immune defence systems to resist disease. They propose, too, that improvements in public health, such as inoculation for smallpox or the disappearance of the bubonic plague (which does not seem to have had anything to do with human actions, but was a result of the natural decline of the population of the black rat, which carries the plague), were leading to lower death rates. Increases in the number of physicians as a cause of declining mortality have generally been ruled out, since doctors' treatments in those days were more likely to kill their patients than cure them.

Adherents of both groups have made their points with great ingenuity and persuasive power; unfortunately, the available statistics are so scanty, crude and unreliable, that neither side has been able to offer decisive evidence. It is probably true that both fertility and mortality changes played a role in the increasing rate of population growth, although it may be that the relative importance of each of these demographic movements varied from one country to another and probably in different regions within individual countries as well. Suffice it to say that populations were growing, and generally at an ever-increasing rate, whatever the causes of this population growth may have been.

Looking at the situation in the broadest possible way, we can discern two different paths to the increased production needed for this growing population. One we might describe as setting out in a new direction. In agriculture,

it meant, above all, changing the crop-rotation system by planting nitrogen-
fixing crops that restored the fertility of the soil, allowing an end to the
necessity of keeping at least one-third of the farmland fallow. Outside of
agriculture, taking this path meant changing the basis of production from
relatively limited organic resources, often only obtainable in competition with
food production, to inorganic ones, that did not suffer from such limitations.
This development involved a system of substitutions: in place of human power,
fuelled by grain (or by meat from grain-eating animals), being used to drive
spinning wheels and looms, were coal-powered steam engines that ran mule
jennies and mechanical looms; in place of walking or being pulled or towed
by animals, people would ride in steam-powered boats and trains. In the old
regime economy, iron ore was turned into pig iron, wrought iron, or steel
by being heated with charcoal (burnt wood); now, coke (burnt coal) would
be used in its place. Wood had been the favoured material for heating and
construction; coal and iron would replace it.

The second path involved perfecting the productive system of the old
regime: taking the basic agricultural, craft and manufacturing techniques
prevalent in the eighteenth century and devising ways to organize them more
completely and efficiently. Examples of such a development would include a
growing specialization of agriculture, in which farmers in different regions
devoted an ever-greater portion of their effort to crops best suited to the local
soil and climate, or the introduction of New World crops, such as potatoes
and maize, into an existing system of crop-rotation without changing the
proportion of land kept fallow. The expansion of outworking and proto-
industry and their extension to crafts where they had not previously been
practised would probably be the best example of this way of increasing
production outside of agriculture.

We need to make three specific observations about these two paths of
economic response to population growth in Europe over the years 1780–
1850. Above all, we should note that the second path, the perfection of the
productive system of the old regime, with its gradual and modest increases in
output, was the predominant response; in most economic sectors and most
regions it was the only one. The first path, with its drastic changes and major
technological innovations, was far more visible, both to contemporaries and
to later observers. In particular, the substitution of inorganic for organic
materials and sources of energy in non-agricultural production – what we
generally call the 'industrial revolution' – seemed to be the story of economic
and social developments in the period. The term 'industrial revolution' is far
too well established ever to be rooted out, but the idea it expresses, a sudden,

[214]   drastic and all-encompassing change in economic life, a technological and industrial storming of the Bastille, is a very dubious way to understand the history of the era.

For industrialization was far from all-encompassing. At the end of the period we are considering, use of steam engines was limited to transport, textiles, and mining and metallurgy. Construction, wood products, leather goods, clothing, paper wares, food products – the list of branches where organic raw materials and sources of energy prevailed is long, and could easily be extended. In manufacturing itself, the use of mechanical power was concentrated in a small number of regions, with large stretches of most nations untouched by this new path of economic development. Of all European nations, it was only in England (in some ways, perhaps Belgium, as well), and there primarily in the last twenty years of the period 1780–1850, that these islands of industrialization swelled to the point where their influence on the entire economy, in terms of investment, employment, and the movement of the gross domestic product, outweighed that of the surrounding terrain as yet untouched by steam power. This surrounding terrain, we must emphasize, was not itself static and unchanged; rather, it was subject to the more gradual developments of the first path of economic development, the perfection of old regime techniques.

The second general point that can be brought up here is the crucial importance of the growth and liberation of market forces for both paths of economic development. Agricultural specialization, where some farmers limit their planting of subsistence crops, or renounce it altogether, is only possible with a functional and flexible market in food products. Similarly, the doubling and tripling of grain output that new systems of crop rotation brought, only made sense if there were a market for all the grain produced. Investment in canals and railways required mobilizing large amounts of capital, and a capital market to make this mobilization possible. Both the expansion of outworking and the introduction of factory production would require a flexible labour market – certainly one more flexible than guilds would allow, and probably more flexible than workers in these occupations would have preferred. Either perfecting the productive techniques of the old regime, or introducing new forms of production thus required a threefold advance in markets: physical improvements in transport and communication – canals, navigable rivers, paved roads, and, ultimately railways – institutional innovations in mobilizing capital and providing finance, and legal transformations in the treatment of obstacles to the market, such as the guild system or seigneurialism and collective usage rights in agriculture.

Finally, we need to understand that these two paths of economic development, while conceptually distinct, tended to overlap in practice. Planting sugar beet, for instance, could be both an example of agricultural specialization, involving the growing of a market-oriented, non-subsistence crop, but also part of a new crop rotation eliminating land left fallow. Regional specialization in agricultural products, a continuation of old regime practices, worked best when the specialized products could be brought to market via the railway, a fundamentally new means of transport, dependent on inorganic sources of power. Mechanized textile production generally developed from outworking, and the two could be combined. Textile outworkers in one country might face the competition of machine-spun or machine-woven textiles in another.

Let us now look at economic developments and their social consequences by sector, starting with agriculture and moving on to non-agricultural production in crafts and industry. In each sector, we will observe the two paths of economic development, and see how they sometimes crossed and sometimes led in separate directions.

Farming and farmers

To start, we might describe the 'classic' plan for the transformation of agricultural production. It involves three components. First is the planting of fallow lands with nitrogen-fixing crops, such as turnips, clover or vetch. These restore the fertility of the soil for grain crops, and also feed more animals than fallow land could. More animals mean more manure, that is, more fertilizer (chemical fertilizers were only used in the last third of the nineteenth century), and hence more grain. Since animals can now be fed crops, without taking away anything from human consumption (in fact, while increasing the amount of grain that can be grown for people to eat), there is no longer any need for village commons where animals would graze. The second component is thus to divide up the common lands and put them to other purposes. Finally, use of these and any other new farming techniques needs to be left to the individual farmer, and not subject to village approval or other forms of collective cultivation. Individual fields are thus to be enclosed, surrounded by fences or hedges; to facilitate this, landowners can exchange parcels of their land with each other, to create larger, contiguous holdings, easier to farm.

[216]   In and of themselves, none of these techniques was new or innovative; they had been known, and sporadically practised, since the Middle Ages. However, their use on a broad scale only began in England during the seventeenth century. Throughout the eighteenth, they spread from the fertile lowlands into the more remote and mountainous parts of the country, and elsewhere in the British Isles. By 1800, the average return to seed for wheat in England – that is, the number of grains of wheat harvested for each grain planted – was running about 10:1; a similar figure for continental European countries would be in the order of 4:1 to 5.5:1. Progress in output continued and probably accelerated in England during the first half of the nineteenth century, with returns to seed rising by at least one-third between 1800 and 1850. (Just for comparison, today's farmers in western Europe and North America using the most mechanized and technological methods produce returns on seed of about 25–30:1.)

Before 1800, this new kind of agriculture had been practised in continental Europe almost exclusively in Flanders – the Flemish-speaking areas of northern France, and the future Belgium – as well as neighbouring parts of the Netherlands. In the first half of the nineteenth century, aspects of its practice – in particular, the elimination of the fallow and the planting of nitrogen-fixing crops, as well as the division of common lands – gradually spread from this area into the flatlands of northern Europe: along the northern coast of France, in the Rhine valley, in Saxony, in much of Denmark and on the plains of southern Sweden. However, in enormous stretches of southern, central and eastern Europe, these innovations had little appeal. As one might expect, the new practices were not much tried in mountainous, drought-ridden or otherwise infertile regions, but it was not only there that older practices persisted. Even in areas that might have seemed ideal for them, such as the Beauce, the fertile plains southeast of Paris, where larger farmers grew cereal grains for the avid consumer markets of the capital city, three-field crop rotation, with its extensive fallow ground, continued until the last third of the nineteenth century.

This limited regional introduction of techniques for fundamentally changing agricultural productivity is reflected in the national figures. Returns to seed on wheat in France or Germany, starting from a figure about half that of Great Britain in 1800, probably increased by 10, or at most 20 per cent (estimates differ and are generally based on very sketchy figures, anyway) over the next fifty years. If about one-third of the agricultural land in France was fallow in 1800, a little over a quarter was still without crops by the middle of the century, showing that the regional introduction of new agricultural techniques had only a modest effect on the country as a whole.

Rather, increases in farm output, which were generally considerable, outstripping population growth, if not always by a large degree, came from other sources. One was the cultivation of previously unused lands, in the older forms of agriculture, without introducing any new crops or forms of crop rotation. This was particularly important in the eastern portions of Europe, in eastern Germany, Hungary, or Russia, regions that were still relatively lightly populated in the eighteenth century, and where farmland was available. (France, c. 1770, counted around 45 inhabitants per square kilometre, Poland, 19.1, and the Russian empire a mere 5.5.) The increase in the amount of cultivated land in the German states, concentrated in the more lightly populated eastern regions, against the more densely inhabited western ones, may have been as high as 20 per cent in the first half of the nineteenth century. There was a similar practice in Spain, where wheat was planted on previously uncultivated but marginal land in the lightly populated, arid high plateaus in the centre of the country. Between 1800 and 1860, the amount of land planted in wheat increased by three-fourths, while the yield to seed declined by almost 10 per cent. While such large increases were not possible in more densely populated portions of Europe, since the available land simply was not there, a good deal of effort was put into draining swamps and marshes, thus allowing more land to come under the plough.

Another major source of agricultural output was the cultivation of two crops brought to Europe from the New World, potatoes and maize, both of which produced considerably more food per acre than did grains. Following a slow start in the early to mid-eighteenth century, cultivation of the potato spread rapidly after about 1780. It was the classic food of the poor, and the prevalence of potato cultivation in Ireland, eastern Germany, Bohemia, or western France, all regions with a major concentration of landless or impoverished peasants, speaks for itself. Maize grows poorly in the cool, damp climate of northern Europe; it was cultivated in the southern part of the continent: in southwestern France, central Italy, and, above all, in the Danubian principalities of Moldavia and Wallachia, then part of the Ottoman empire, the core of the future Rumania.

The output of specialized, non-subsistence crops or the raising of animals and their products for sale in the market was also growing in this period: grapes for wine or brandy, mulberry trees for silk, and olives for oil, in southern Europe; sugar beet, hops, or flax for linen, in the north; dairy products in the Alpine regions. It was precisely the planting of such crops that differentiated the more prosperous areas of northern and central Italy during the first half of the nineteenth century, from the poorer regions in the south. Grain

[218] yields were equally mediocre in all parts of the Italian peninsula, but the ability to diversify and produce different crops in addition to grain, to supplement an older, inefficient system of crop rotation for subsistence farming with more market-oriented products, was the chief marker of economic progress in the agricultural sector. Going from the southwestern to the northeastern edge of Europe, we find a similar development in the Russian empire, where the major agricultural innovation in this period, occurring primarily in its latter decades, was the planting of sugar beet on an increasingly large scale. Seven refineries sufficed to process the empire's output of beet sugar in 1825, but by 1860, 448 were required.

This second path of supplementation and limited change, of modest increases in agricultural output, had a number of fundamental limitations. Planting New World crops was an effective way to increase the basic food supply. The movement towards a potato monoculture, though – the direction in which the poor were going in a number of regions, most prominently in Ireland – brought with it the danger of a catastrophe, should this one specific crop, on which so many people were dependent, fail – as would happen in the mid-1840s. Maize, on the other hand, was a crop that exhausted the nitrogen in the soil to a much greater extent than grains such as wheat, rye or oats. Replacing the fallow in a crop-rotation system with maize, as was a perverse but common practice in Tuscany, in central Italy, would, in the long run, only multiply problems for the food supply.

Growing speciality crops for the market was a fine idea, and certainly a much more efficient use of natural resources, than planting subsistence crops in areas less well suited for them. What, however, were the farmers who planted grapes, flax, or mulberry trees, to eat? Such specialization could only work if there were other regions that successfully specialized in basic foodstuffs – as we have seen, this was not entirely the case in continental Europe – and if the transport system was far enough advanced to bring the speciality crops to market, and also to move grains from areas where they were produced in surplus to other regions where they were needed.

Particularly in France, the Low Countries, Scandinavia and central Europe, the transport system was being steadily improved, as roads were built, canals dug, and rivers made navigable. By contrast, rather less was accomplished in Spain or Russia, and there may even have been a decline in the quality of the transport system in the first half of the nineteenth century. However, even when transport was improved, this process had certain limitations. In particular, perishable crops – spring vegetables, for instance, or cheap wine – could not reach the market fast enough. While the system could generally move grain around (if it was available) fairly well, in years of bad harvests, when larger amounts of food had to be moved, it tended to get overloaded. A technological innovation was developed in the 1820s that would fundamentally remove these obstacles, namely the railways, which would make marketing easier and encourage specialization enormously.

Contemporaries were aware of this, and followed the progress of rail transport closely. As soon as railways began to be constructed in Great Britain at the end of the 1820s, plans were made in continental Europe to imitate them. Both from an engineering and a financial point of view – for building railways consumed colossal amounts of capital – this proved more easily said or planned than done. Before 1840, Great Britain was the only country in Europe with anything like a rail network; several thousand miles of railway line were built on the continent during the 1840s, and the physical potential for an expanded market in agricultural goods began to take shape, but the network was still far from complete, and proved unable to cope with the economic shocks of the middle of that decade.

In sum, the slower, second path of agricultural development, although perhaps sufficient, was a circuitous route containing a number of serious obstacles. One might wonder why the first path of fundamental innovation was not adopted more widely and rapidly. Legal and social structures helped preserve old regime practices, and this was one important reason. In addition, the path to agricultural innovation led through a fundamental social reorganization, that was more than a little problematic to many of the inhabitants of the countryside.

The new agriculture was labour-intensive: root crops require prolonged weeding and increasing the number of farm animals meant greater efforts in their care. In areas where serfdom was practised – and even after the end of the revolutionary and Napoleonic era it remained in force in the eastern portions of Germany and of the Austrian empire, as well as in most of the European lands of the sultan and the tsar – serfs were highly reluctant to perform these additional tasks, and could generally point out that their lords' rights to such feudal obligations were silent on turnips or vetch. Particularly in portions of the Austrian empire, a growing number of noble landlords began to wonder whether serfdom was really worthwhile if it prevented the adoption of such promising, new agricultural practices. The example of the eastern provinces of the Prussian monarchy suggested the possiblities of a new system. There, the reforms adopted in the early part of the nineteenth century gradually led, by the 1830s, to a situation in which noble landlords no longer had the right to uncompensated serf labour, but had, instead, more

[220] land and a large population of landless labourers or smallholders needing to do paid farm labour to make ends meet.

Yet even in the central and western portions of the continent, where serfdom no longer existed, old regime obstacles remained. In particular, 'servitudes', or usage rights persisted – the right of inhabitants of the village to use other people's land – for instance, to collect some wood from forest property, or to pasture animals on land belonging to others after crops had been harvested, or when the land was fallow. At several points during the French Revolution and the Napoleonic era, the French government, along with those in its dependent states, had considered a fundamental reform in or outright abolition of such impediments to the unlimited rights of private property and a free market in land, but had never carried them out.

In the years between 1815 and 1850, not much changed in that respect. To be sure, a number of governments made an effort to abolish usage rights in forest lands, both in large-scale legal projects, such as the French Forest Code of 1827, or the Austrian forest ordinances of 1839, and in smaller measures adopted in many other states. However, peasants fiercely resisted this new policy, insisting on their right to gather leaves and branches, cut wood and pasture their animals in forest land, ignoring the law, openly and on an increasingly large scale, and sometimes violently resisting agents of the state. 'Only fear can safeguard the woods,' was how the Prussian state officials in the province of Westphalia put it, and official coercion and peasant resistance on forest usage were characteristic of the first half of the nineteenth century in most of Europe.

This one example shows the broader problem of servitudes: rather than understanding them as obstacles to a more rational, productive and profitable agriculture, peasants generally regarded them as expedients they would need to survive in economically difficult times. The results of the general abolition of such customs and the division of the common lands in Great Britain shows that the peasants' fears were not entirely unjustified. The loss of these usage rights deprived smallholders in the United Kingdom of an important possibility of pasturing their animals, and, ultimately of being able to support themselves on the plots of land they owned or rented.

By the beginning of the nineteenth century, landownership in Great Britain had taken on a distinctive pattern. Almost 70 per cent was in the hands of the aristocracy or the gentry. These gentlemen proprietors generally did not direct the exploitation of their estates themselves, but rented their lands out to tenant farmers, capitalist agricultural entrepreneurs, who vigorously pursued the most advanced farming techniques. They, in turn, worked the land

by employing propertyless or virtually propertyless agricultural labourers, [221]
whose numbers seem to have been increasing as their wages were falling, and
their seasonal unemployment becoming an ever greater problem.

In fact, when we look at those portions of continental northern Europe
where the new farming techniques were introduced, we see a similar state of
affairs. Large landowners renting their estates out to tenant farmers were a
substantial presence, although on the continent there was often also a large
group of substantial peasant farmers, as well. But the agricultural labourers and
the smallholders who made ends meet by working part-time as agricultural
labourers, were a large portion of the rural population, if perhaps not quite so
large as in Great Britain. Now this very unequal division of land and a countryside characterized by large landowners and/or substantial farmers on the
one hand, and agricultural labourers on the other, was not unique to areas of
the new, advanced agriculture. There were plenty of regions – in most of
Italy, in central and southern Spain, in large stretches of eastern Europe –
where large landowners presided over a very backward and inefficient agriculture. But the very same social reorganization that made the rapid introduction of modern agricultural techniques possible – the end of usage rights
and the division of the commons – also created a most inegalitarian social
structure. Under these circumstances, it is no surprise that smallholding peasants in most of Europe would be less than enthusiastic about wholeheartedly
adopting revolutionary agricultural innovations, or that, if they were going to
try something new, they would do so in a partial and cautious way, along the
lines of the first path to agricultural improvement that we have sketched out.

Our survey of the two paths to the increase in agricultural products to meet
population growth thus leads to not entirely optimistic results. The first path,
with its transformation of the system of crop rotation, and its abolition of
usage rights, was very successful in terms of output. This kind of agriculture,
as late as 1850 practised primarily in the British Isles and in the flat lands of
northern Europe, was a definitive answer to the pessimistic speculations
of Parson Malthus, showing that the increase in food output could outstrip
population growth. It did not just support more people, but different kinds
of people: people who no longer had to work on the land, but could pursue
crafts or industrial occupations; other farmers who could turn their attention to specialized non-subsistence crops. However, this growth in output
required a legal and cultural revolution: the abolition of both serfdom and
usage rights, and a determined movement from a collective, villagewide
approach to cultivation to an determinately individualized one. It also came
at a considerable social cost: a polarization of rural society into a large group

[222]   of wage-earners on the one hand, who possessed no property, or not enough to support their families, and a smaller group of landowners, capitalist tenant farmers and substantial peasants on the other – the exact mix of these groups varying from country to country.

The second, gradual, path was more compatible with a broader distribution of property ownership in the countryside, although it could occur in a very inegalitarian environment as well. Not involving a frontal attack on the existing forms of agriculture, it was easier to adopt, and it spread widely in continental Europe during the first half of the nineteenth century. However, it was, overall, less effective: growth in output was precariously close to the increase in the population; reliance on New World crops for basic subsistence brought with it the dangers of any monoculture, namely a very specific crop failure; it required a degree of marketing that was, especially in years of poor harvest, rather beyond the existing transport systems. It would be fair to say that in the years 1780–1850 both paths of agricultural improvement were problematic and stress-filled for society; the economic environment at that time offered few unequivocally good choices.

Crafts and manufactures

It is here that the differences between the two paths to increased output were most visible and apparent. Steam engines, multi-storied factories, with giant yet precise hammers in the engineering trades, and rows of mule-jennies or power looms in textiles, all set in an industrial landscape of rows of smoking chimneys, with speeding trains, charging ahead at a life-threatening thirty miles per hour – contemporaries were powerfully impressed by these images, and they continue to shape our notion of an industrial revolution. No less striking to contemporaries were the human beings inhabiting this industrial age: living in the wretched slums of fast-growing manufacturing cities, labouring to the ceaseless rhythm of steam-powered machinery, descending into the depths of coal-mines to wrestle in their narrow galleries with the coal seams, and bring to the surface the raw material that made possible the entire era. To characterize this new and unprecedented social group, people of the first half of the nineteenth century revived and gave new meaning to an old word, first employed in ancient Rome: the proletariat.

Now, these images were not just a literary invention or a generalization from a handful of individual, isolated cases. They reflected a very tangible reality in Great Britain during the decades following 1800. Its deepest embodiment, the industrial city of Manchester, had become, as early as the 1820s, almost a site of pilgrimage for educated Europeans, who attempted to read in its social and economic life the future of their own lands – whether in emulation, or perhaps more frequently, as something to be avoided. However, just as in agriculture, we must emphasize the importance of the less dramatic second path of increased output. According to the 1831 English census, only about 10 per cent of the labour force was engaged in industrial or crafts production for a supra-local market; over three times as many made or sold goods that were marketed locally. Of those producing for large markets, most probably did not work in factories, in large, steam-powered workshops. Indeed, the number of handloom weavers in England peaked during the 1820s at about a quarter-million, and gradually declined over the next thirty years. By contrast, in continental Europe, the number of handloom weavers increased – and often substantially – in the first half of the nineteenth century.

Thus, when we consider the urban lower classes and the manufacturing sector of the economy in this period, we need to remember that shoemakers, tailors, weavers and cabinetmakers – to name the most common crafts – substantially outnumbered coal-miners, machinists [engineers] or power-loom operators, and that this state of affairs, certainly the case in 1780, remained so in 1850. Often as not, contemporaries used terms like 'proletariat' or 'working class', to refer, more generically, to the entire group of journeymen artisans, urban day labourers, struggling master craftsmen and manufacturing outworkers, and not just to the new groups of the industrialized sectors of the economy. Our discussion must thus consider both the smaller, but far more dynamic and increasingly influential steam-powered sector and its labour force, and the slower-moving, yet also changing – if in more subtle ways – artisanal sector, to gain a complete picture of social and economic change in the period under consideration.

The classic arena of the early industrial revolution was the textile industry, in particular the manufacture of cotton textiles. Before 1850, more steam power was employed there than in any other industrial sector. The central technological innovation was Samuel Crompton's 'mule-jenny' of 1780, a machine, or engine ('jenny' for short) that combined two earlier forms of spinning machines, and so was named after a farm animal that was the offspring of two different species. Both of its predecessors were ten to twelve times as productive as spinning wheels; the mule not only combined them but was easily adapted to steam power. Between 1780 and 1820, its triumphant progress marked the process of industrialization in Great Britain. A further innovation

[224]   of the 1830s, the 'self-acting', or, as we would say today, automated mule-jenny, made the device easier to operate and so increased still further the productivity of mechanized cotton spinning.

Mechanizing weaving proved technologically more difficult, and a satisfactory power loom was only invented several decades after the mule-jenny. Consequently, the initial result of the expansion of mechanized cotton spinning was to increase handloom weaving; the number of weavers peaked, as we noted above, in the 1820s. Then, however, mechanized cotton spinning began to spread rapidly, the number of power looms in use in British cotton textiles almost doubling, from 55,000 in 1829, to over 100,000 in 1833. This was a powerful blow to the handloom weavers, whose situation was already very hard-pressed; by the middle of the century, there were few left.

The same basic pattern was repeated in the manufacture of other fibres, such as woollens and silk. Woollens were tougher than cotton, though, and silk, finer; the mechanization of both methods of production started later, and it would not be until after 1850 that steam-powered weaving mills would replace outworking handloom weavers in these branches of the textile industry. A similar process occurred in the cotton manufacture of continental European countries. The very first steam-powered spinning mills were installed in Alsace during the Napoleonic era, thus 25–30 years later than in England. Mechanized, steam-powered cotton spinning only became the dominant form of manufacture in France, Belgium, Spain and the German states between 1830 and 1850. The same expansion of handloom weaving that had occurred in Great Britain several decades earlier took place on the continent during that period. The number of cotton handloom weavers in the Düsseldorf district of the Prussian monarchy, one of the continental centres of the early introduction of mechanized spinning, doubled, from 6,000 in the early 1820s, to 12,000, some 30 years later. In contrast to Great Britain, cotton handloom weaving in continental European countries only gave way to mechanized production in the second half of the nineteenth century – and this statement is even more true of other textile branches, such as woollens or silk.

The interaction between mechanized and artisanal methods of textile production should caution us against seeing the introduction of steam power in textiles as a drastic break with the past. Textile mills were generally located in areas that had previously been centres of proto-industrial outworking; the entrepreneurs who founded the first factories were themselves typically from families that had been in the textile business, as wholesalers and/or as employers of outworkers. Rather the same was true of the labour force as of employers: early industrial textile workers were frequently from families of outworkers. Although the industrial workplace was very different from its cottage predecessor, some of the organization of employment had a certain similarity. Outworking had been a family affair, with a sex- and age-based division of labour: the father as weaver, the mother as spinner, the children helping them out. There an element of the same family workplace survived in early textile mills, with adult spinners – sometimes men, sometimes women – having children, very often their own, or those of relatives, as their helpers.

This process of the transformation of proto-industrial regions into industrial ones in the development of industrialized textile manufacture was not smooth or automatic. Indeed, much of the story of this period is the extent to which some proto-industrial regions developed into industrial ones, or at least put down the foundations for such development, while others did not, and became deindustrialized, or at least began to do so. Southwestern England, the West Riding of Yorkshire and Lancashire had all been centres of textile outworking in the eighteenth centry, but while the latter two developed into remarkable centres of industrialization, drawing the attention (literally) of the entire world, and selling textiles to it, the former area did not make the transition, and became predominantly agricultural, with very modest amounts of industrial development. Normandy, in northern France, and Languedoc, in the south, had been major outworking centres before the French Revolution; by the middle of the nineteenth century, the former area was well on its way to mechanized industry, while the latter's textile production was still not mechanized and, at best stagnant, soon to head into rapid decline and total extinction.

Such examples can be multiplied across much of Europe. The reason for one region's success and another's failure are complex and highly varied, including differences in labour costs, ability to reach markets, or to find new ones, presence or lack of entrepreneurial aggressiveness and willingness to innovate. One particular branch of the textile industry, the manufacture of linen products, had a particularly hard time with the transition. Linen-spinning and weaving was the oldest branch of textile production in Europe, with some forms of outworking having begun in the middle ages. It tended also to be the least well organized from a capitalist point of view. However, the even deeper problem with linen was that it was inferior to cotton for most purposes, and generally more expensive to boot, so that the crucial period of transition from outwork to industry occurred in the context of a shrinking market for linen goods. The linen-weaver's lot – in northern Ireland, Flanders, Westphalia or Silesia, to name a few centres of linen outworking – was not to be envied. The economic crisis of the 1840s was particularly severe in

[226] regions of linen outworking, characterized by despair, starvation, sometimes futile riots and protests, and, increasingly, flight in the form of massive emigration to North America.

If the mechanization of textiles was a process of gradual transition from outworking to factory industry, the mechanization of metallurgy was more of break with previous practice, a development that come closest to an industrial revolution. It involved a decisive change in the source of a crucial raw material, from organic to inorganic. The pre-industrial practice of converting iron ore into pig iron, a basic intermediary product, and from there into wrought iron or steel, involved heating the iron ore with charcoal, burnt wood; in the industrial version, the iron ore was heated with coke, burnt coal. This technological innovation changed the location of the iron industry, from hilly forested regions, filled with wood, to coalfields. It altered the scope of the process as well, from forges that could, at best, produce ten tons of pig iron per week, to blast furnaces that produced nine to ten times as much. Finally, and decisively, it transformed the scale of output in the industry. Before industrialization, the total amount of iron forged from ore depended on the availability of wood, a slow-growing and increasingly scarce organic raw material. After industrialization, it could utilize a mineral present in virtually unlimited quantities. Even today, after one hundred and fifty to two hundred years of increasingly extensive coal mining in Europe, there is no coal shortage; rather, the main economic question is how to reduce the amount of coal mined to avoid an unsold and unsalable surplus.

In the years 1780–1850, this process of drastic transformation in metallurgy combined with an enormous expansion of coal mining was played out in full in Great Britain. Around 1750, iron manufacture had been scattered through forested areas in central England. Output was modest, since there was simply not enough wood in this densely populated country to feed the forges, and at least half of British consumption of iron was imported. This imported iron came from the major powers of eighteenth-century ironworking, the economically backward but lightly populated and heavily forested countries, Sweden and Russia. The combination of more intensive coal mining and the perfection of blast furnace technology in the years 1760–80, making it possible to use coke to reduce iron ore, completely changed the situation.

British iron- and steelmaking were centralized in three locations, each with abundant coal supplies: South Wales, the Black Country of the West Midlands and the northeast. While the Black Country had been a centre of various kinds of proto-industrial outworking in metals, the other areas had not; eighteenth-century observers had even suggested that much of Wales was socially and economically closer to Peru than to any part of Europe. These newer regions proved to be centres of an extraordinarily productive industry. Increasing amounts of coal made it possible to forge ever-greater quantities of iron and steel. These, in turn, could be the raw material for steam engines, that enabled coal mines to be sunk ever deeper (the engines pumping water out of the subsurface areas), ever richer coal seams to be mined and ever more iron forged. The Napoleonic Wars, increasing the demand for iron in military products, while making imports more difficult, greatly facilitated this process. Coal and ferrous metals output soared; by 1800, Great Britain was a net exporter of iron. However, the industrialization of iron production was not just a wartime event. Output grew steadily after the return to peacetime conditions in 1815. From the late 1820s onward, a new major demand source emerged in the railways. Iron was the raw material for both the rails and the trains, and railways, in turn, facilitated and greatly cheapened the overland transport of heavy wares, such as coal and steel, opening new markets and making possible further economies of production. By 1850, coal and pig iron production in the United Kingdom was at least twice that of the continental European countries combined.

Thus, we can see in Great Britain during the entire period a feedback process between the iron industry and the rest of the economy. Modernization of iron and steel technology, in particular the use of coking coal, liberated output from the slow growth of the wood supply. New steel products, such as steam engines and railways, then provided a market for this expanded output, but their use, in turn, made it possible to produce more coal and iron, whose use could then be spread over the entire economy, as steam engines, for instance, expanded textile production, and railways made possible the extensive marketing of farm crops, and further agricultural specialization. The wealth thus created produced more demand for iron and steel products.

With the partial exception of Belgium, no continental European country adopted the new methods of iron and steel production before 1850, continuing, instead, to use older charcoal forges. Consequently, on the continent, both the supply side advantages of using coke in place of charcoal, and the demand side incentive from the expanded use of iron and steel products were either non-existent or present at a much lower level. These circumstances were reflected in the much more modest pace of growth in the manufacture of iron and steel. The most remarkable example of this was in the Russian empire. The world's chief producer and exporter of iron in the eighteenth century, when wood supply had counted more for iron manufacture than technological innovation or the feedback between iron, coal, steam power and railways,

[228] the tsar's realm had fallen to eighth place by 1850. Iron manufacture was concentrated in forested areas of the Ural mountains, on the border between Europe and Asia, so that Russian iron faced high transport costs in its journey to its primary export market in Great Britain. Until the late eighteenth century, this was nonetheless a profitable business, since Britain's economy demanded more iron than British iron-masters could produce, for there were just not enough forests in the United Kingdom to provide all the charcoal needed to reduce iron ore. Once British iron-masters switched to coking coal instead of charcoal, this production bottleneck was eliminated and Russian imports were no longer competitive.

In contrast, there was no special demand for iron in Russia, and production in the Urals, still using charcoal forges, began to run out of wood for charcoal. Output was stagnant for many decades, only in the 1830s passing its peak of around 1800. It ultimately doubled between 1780 and 1850, but that left Russian iron production in the middle of the nineteenth century at a mere one-tenth of British levels. All the factors on the supply and demand side that fuelled the expansion of the British iron industry – from coking coal, to railways, to steam engines, to a growing domestic market – were lacking in Russia. If the new forms of iron manufacture had largely passed the tsar's empire by (a similar pattern of lack of development existed in Sweden, the other major eighteenth-century iron producer), we can trace a steady, if modest growth in the manufacture of pig iron in France and Prussia (Prussia accounting for the lion's share of both iron and coal output in the German states), with French output growing to more than double that of Russia by mid-century, and Prussia just about catching up with the Russians. Most of that growth of output, however, was primarily in charcoal-forged iron, a development with little future, since the production of iron in that way used up wood faster than forests could grow it, as the Russian example demonstrated. The revolutionary transformation of iron and steel manufacture, occurring in close combination with the expansion of coal mining, railway building and use of steam power, would only occur on the continent in the decades after 1850.

As noted at the beginning of the chapter, textiles, metallurgy and coal mining were the productive sectors in which industrialization occurred in this period. While more common in textiles, industrialization was, in some ways, also less of a drastic change there, since it evolved from proto-industrial outworking in the same regions, and with similar employers and labour forces. By contrast, industrialization was a drastic change in metallurgy and coal mining, but its effect was limited to a single country. If the French Revolution spilled over the French borders into all of Europe within [229] a few years of 1789, the 'industrial revolution' remained a more circumscribed affair, its transformational effects above all regional in nature.

Indeed, a main characteristic of industrialization was the way that it developed regionally. Consider this description, by a perceptive French observer, of the workings of the Lancashire textile industry in the middle of the 1840s:

> Manchester, like a diligent spider, is placed in the centre of the web, and sends forth roads and railways towards its auxiliaries, formerly villages, but now towns, which serve as outposts to the grand centre of industry . . . An order sent from Liverpool in the morning is discussed by the merchants in the Manchester Exchange at noon, and in the evening is distributed amongst the manufacturers in the environs. In less than eight days cotton spun at Manchester, Bolton, Oldham or Ashton, is woven in the sheds of Burnley, Stalybridge or Stockport, dyed and printed at Blackburn, Chorley or Preston and finally measured and packed at Manchester.[1]

Add to this hub of industry in Lancashire, the textile districts of the West Riding of Yorkshire, the mining and metallurgical regions of the West Midlands, South Wales and northeast England, and we have more or less summed up the areas touched by industrialization in England in the first half of the nineteenth century.

The lesser progress of industrialization on the European continent implied that there were fewer such regions, and we can, in fact, really only point to three. Characteristic of all three of them was that they crossed national borders, and the web of marketing and financial and labour relations described for Lancashire crossed these borders as well. One such region extended from northern France through the Liège/Hainault district in Belgium into western Germany. Including textile manufacture as well as mining and metallurgy, and, in fact, largely following the coal seams that run through the area, this industrial region encompassed most of Belgium, so that pre-1850 Belgium was not so much a uniquely industrialized country, as a small one, much of whose territory was taken up by continental Europe's major node of industrial development. The other two industrial centres were primarily in textiles and also crossed national lines: one was in the upper Rhine valley, and included Alsace in France, and neighbouring regions, around Basel and Zürich in Switzerland, as well as some towns across the river Rhine in southwestern Germany. Finally, furthest to the east, there was a vigorous centre of textile manufacturing in southwestern Saxony and in neighbouring areas of the Austrian province of Bohemia, in today's Czech Republic.

[230]   Large capital cities, such as London, Paris, Berlin and Vienna, if owing their economic importance primarily to their governmental, commercial and financial functions, also contained a certain amount of industry, typically in metallurgy and the construction of machinery. Outside of the industrial districts and the capital cities, stationary steam engines and large manufacturing establishments were few and far between – in Barcelona, for instance, where the industrialized manufacture of cotton textiles was just getting underway in the 1830s and 1840s. The map of industrialization in Europe, including the British Isles, before 1850, would show a few black patches in a vast sea of non-industrialized white.

If we now turn to craft production in this large, non-industrialized territory, and to the many individuals who continued to work at the crafts in the industrial regions themselves we can note the main trends in the years 1780–1850: expansion of the number of artisans; growth in the proportion of artisans who were wage-earners, that is, journeymen and apprentices; and an increase and intensification in the practice of outworking. In some ways, these trends overlapped; in other respects, they might seem to contradict each other, but when fully considered, they result in a comprehensive and not entirely optimistic picture. Let us consider each of these trends in turn.

Numbers of craftsmen were growing throughout this period, at least as far as we can tell from the very primitive census figures and government statistics, and their share of the labour force was increasing as well. Even in rapidly industrializing England, this seems to have been the case until around 1830; in the two subsequent decades, though, the balance was reversed, with employment in large-scale production (admittedly, including outworking as well as factory work) growing at about 4 per cent annually, as against just 2 per cent for employment in retail trades and locally oriented craft production. In continental European countries, on the other hand, the proportion of artisans and outworkers in the labour force continued to grow. In Prussia, a state with relatively good statistics, craftsmen – not including outworkers, such as handloom weavers – made up 4 per cent of the population (one should at least double this figure to arrive at the proportion of craftsmen in the labour force) in 1816, and 6 per cent in 1849.

This was a primitive, but not totally ineffective response to the question posed by Malthus: an increasing population needs more clothing, which more tailors sew for them, with the growth in agricultural productivity sufficing to feed the tailors and give them the energy to go on sewing clothing. However, both the productivity of the tailors and their standard of living were related to the two other trends that we have noted above. The tailor sewing clothes was rather more likely to be doing so at the behest of a master, than on his [231] (or, for ladies' clothing, sometimes her) own account. Those same Prussian statistics cited in the previous paragraph show that in 1816 for every nine master craftsmen, there were about five journeymen and apprentices; at the middle of the nineteenth century, there were five journeymen and apprentices for only seven master craftsmen. Masters, those with their own business, working for their own account, still outnumbered craftsmen working for a wage, but numbers in the more dependent group were growing.

This was a development that seems to have been common to most countries, at least as far as contemporary statistics go. We cannot attribute it to some form of mechanization, which meant that one needed more capital to set oneself up in business, for the crafts were not industrialized at all in this period. The trend seems to have been strongest in those parts of central, northern and eastern Europe, where the guild system had not been abolished in the Napoleonic era, and there it was the understandable reaction of master craftsmen, trying to defend their standard of living by refusing to allow more competitors into their craft. However, even in areas without guilds we can see this development, and it is above all the result of a growing population, and, particularly, a growing number of craftsmen. As more and more young men (and, in the needle trades, women) entered the crafts, they started, as all craftsmen did, as apprentices and journeymen, as wage-earners. Thus, just the growth in the number of craftsmen alone, without any major structural changes in the crafts, would be enough to change the relative numbers of craftspeople working on their own account, and those working for a wage.

An important structural change also occurred during this period, the third of the three major developments in the crafts: the spread and intensification of outwork. In some cases, this was simply a continuation of trends from the old regime. The steady expansion of the number of handloom silk weavers in Lyon and its vicinity, for instance, that had begun in the eighteenth century, continued well into the nineteenth. From the beginning of the nineteenth century, the merchants who controlled the city's silk manufacture began to place more and more of their work with handloom weavers living in the countryside, outside of Lyon itself. A quarter of all silk weavers lived outside the Lyon city limits in around 1830; by 1850, one-half did. This process was also a continuation of older trends, moving outwork away from more expensive urban labour to cheaper rural counterparts. Much the same thing happened in Krefeld, the centre of German silk manufacturing, where the number of handloom weavers grew, but weaving was increasingly shifted to surrounding rural areas, or in England, where the silk merchants provided less work

[232] for the long-established Spitalfields hand-weaving community in London, preferring instead cheaper rural weavers in the north of England.

All these silk manufactures were classic examples of proto-industry, of decentralized craft production for a Europe-wide or world market. A newer development, one that seems to have picked up steam after c. 1800–1820, was the introduction of outworking in trades such as tailoring, shoemaking or cabinetmaking, whose wares were sold in a more local market. This was certainly the case in large capital cities, like Paris, London, Vienna or Berlin. What contemporaries called in France '*confection*', and in England the 'sweated trades', became increasingly influential in tailoring: master tailors, sometimes working alone, sometimes employing help, sewed orders received from clothing merchants, sold them their goods and, more often than not, were in debt to them. It was these merchants who were in contact with the customers, and who increasingly dominated the trade, pushing the nominally independent masters to work ever harder to earn the same or less. Although this way of organizing craft production has been best studied in large capital cities, it seems to have been prevalent in smaller provincial ones as well, increasingly determining the nature of craft work.

This expansion of outworking certainly increased the productivity of artisans, although largely by making them work harder for less money. The third variation on changes in craft production involved introducing a division of labour into outworking. Rather than giving the raw materials to one artisan to shape into a finished product, the merchant would go through several, each of whom would perform one part of the productive operation. In the Birmingham metal trades, an individual item could go through no less than fifty different hands, before it was completed. Rather less elaborate was the practice in shoemaking, where one 'master' shoemaker might cut the sole, another make the uppers, a third sew them together. There was not much left of a craftsman's master status in such circumstances; merchants directing the production process might try and play this up, by getting women or children, who customarily received lower wages, to do these snippets of craft work in place of adult men.

Changes in the crafts between 1780 and 1850 were, in contrast to the industrializing sector of the economy, centred around the organization of production, not the technology of production. Bit by bit, merchant capitalists gained greater control over crafts, extending their influence from trades with world- or Europe-wide markets, to those working for a more local clientele; slowly, they reorganized production in the direction of a greater division of labour and a more pronounced orientation toward market criteria.

Guild practices, where they still existed, and guild habits, where they did not,   [233]
slowly gave ground to capitalist ones. Historians sometimes describe this as a
process of 'proletarianization', of once-independent craftsmen being turned
into wage-workers. Yet such a description is misleading, if we think of the
proletariat in terms of the industrial workforce. Unlike at least some industrial workers, outworking weavers, tailors or cabinetmakers could be – and
often were – themselves employers, paying wages to journeymen or apprentices. Most unlike factory workers, outworkers continued to be masters, working on their own account, owning their own tools and having their own
workshop – even if that workshop was nothing more than part of a wretched
one-room attic or basement apartment. What does seem to have been happening to a majority of artisans in this period, whether to the growing proportion of them who were journeymen and apprentices, or to the increasing
number of masters working for and in debt to merchant capitalists, was that
they were losing any direct relationship with their customers and clients. Their
access to the market for their products, or their services was increasingly in
the hands of others. This reorganization of the crafts increased productivity
and efficiency, providing greater output for a growing population, but the
craftsmen themselves saw primarily the negatives, their growing dependence
on capitalist merchant contractors. From the artisans' point of view, these
were, as the furniture makers of Berlin put it, 'usurious middlemen, who have
shoved themselves in between the public and the producers'.

Long-term trends (1): Structural change

In the previous chapter, we discussed how the drastic events of the French
Revolution and the Napoleonic era had brought to an end the old regime
society of orders in much of continental Europe. Landed property had been
redistributed and, even more importantly, redefined; privileges had been
abolished, to a greater or lesser extent; two new elite groups had begun to
come into existence: the notables, the locally most influential men, and the
officials of a centralized state bureaucracy. Here, we will consider the effects
of the more gradual changes we have outlined in this chapter: the pressure of
population growth, and the two paths of economic change, looking to see
how they changed social structure and gender relations. Then, we will study
how these changes occurred over time, charting the course of economic
development and trying to ascertain who profited from these changes over
the long run.

[234]   Outside of England and Holland, most Europeans lived in the countryside in 1780 and by 1850, even though population had doubled in the interval, rural and urban populations had increased at about the same pace, so the proportion of people living in the countryside had changed little. With twice as many people living in rural areas in 1850 as in 1780, there was less cultivatable land per person. The average size of rural landholdings thus declined, although this decline in the average size could conceal two quite different developments: one in which a small number of estate owners and/or large peasant farmers confronted a growing population of propertyless labourers, and one in which most farm families had some property, only all of them had consistently less.

Yet, it seems that as we go from 1780 to 1850 farmers learned to get more out of less, to make better use of the shrinking amount of land available to them. The landless poor could work for substantial farmers and estate owners, especially when that latter group began to make use of more labour-intensive and productive systems of crop rotation. Cultivating New World crops and specialized, market-oriented products enabled peasant small-holders to get more out of their modest-sized plots of land. Proto-industrial outwork, whenever it was available, offered additional opportunities. In most of Europe, such outwork was increasing in extent and being concentrated in rural areas. There are important exceptions, though, to this general rule. After the 1820s, rural outwork in Great Britain was in decline, and everywhere in Europe the linen trades were in trouble, and so, in some regions, provided less support for the landless and small landowning population.

One additional possibility became increasingly available in the years after 1820, and that was migration. The peak periods of overseas migration would be at later dates than those covered in this book: the decade of the 1850s, and the years 1880–1914, but overseas migration to North America steadily increased between 1820 and 1850, particularly from Great Britain and central Europe. Some 400,000 Germans would come to the United States in the 1840s. In France, by contrast, a country with almost no overseas migration, inhabitants of the poorest rural areas, such as the mountainous Limousin, in the central part of the country, began systematically supplementing the meagre living they drew from their infertile soil and harsh climate by moving, temporarily, within the country. Ever-larger numbers of men from the mountain villages lived in Paris, from spring to autumn, working in construction, while their womenfolk remained behind to cultivate the soil. The Limousin mason became a well-known figure in the capital, dominating the craft. This yearly cycle was increasingly organized, with some village masons setting up as subcontractors, arranging to bring in a whole gang of workers – chosen from friends, relatives and neighbours – to work for Parisian construction contractors. Marseilles, the major city in southern France, received a similar seasonal inflow of construction workers from northern Italy.

All of these ways to supplement the earnings from a plot of land – rural wage-labour, new crops, outworking, temporary or permanent migration – tended to reduce the ranks of the very lowest classes of rural society, the home less wandering poor, who had been so common in the old regime, and had provided the social backdrop to the Great Fear at the beginning of the French Revolution. Rural beggars and homeless wanderers had by no means disappeared by the middle of the nineteenth century, particularly in the poorer regions of eastern and southern Europe, and their numbers would swell everywhere, in years of bad harvests, with high food prices and economic recessions, but overall they were a gradually shrinking social group.

The net result of social changes in this entire period is thus an ambivalent one. The number of large and medium-sized farmers, who could support a family from their lands was probably decreasing, while the number of smallholders and the totally landless was on the rise. Yet supplemental possibilities for earning a living were increasing as well, making it more possible, rather than less, for peasant families to support themselves with their own labour – if, perhaps, a more intense and increased labour, and one that included some not entirely legal appropriation of products from the forest – and slightly less likely to have to beg for a living. Still, the growing pace of emigration was an indication that the net effect of all the changes in rural society, from the very different forms of the abolition of feudalism, and the redistribution of property that accompanied it, through the institution of new methods of farming and new crops, with their potential for property redistribution, through the expansion of outwork, was to leave a growing proportion of the rural lower classes unable to earn a living in the countryside.

Another way to sum up the changes in rural Europe between 1780 and 1850 would be to say that those years saw the growing progress of market relations. Earning a living by non-market activity – raising and consuming one's own crops, coercively expropriating those crops or the labour needed to raise them in a feudal or seigneurial system, begging for food – was giving way to the mediation of the market in rural life, from raising crops for sale rather than subsistence, to cultivating these crops with hired labour, to working for wages, in many different ways, to supplement one's own harvest. The pace of this expansion of the market in rural Europe should not be exaggerated, particularly in regard to labour relations. Serfdom remained the rule in

[236]   the Russian empire and the Danubian Principalities of Moldavia and Wallachia throughout the entire period under consideration in this book, and was only abolished in the 1860s. In the Habsburg Monarchy, both outright serfdom and other seigneurial structures remained in place until the revolution of 1848. Even in the western portion of the continent, seigneurialism was not fully abolished in Spain until the 1830s. Yet even in those realms of coerced labour or unfree property relations, commercialized, market-oriented agriculture was increasing in extent, and hired farm labour was increasingly employed in addition to coercive servile labour.

This progress of the market characterized urban society as well, both in its dramatically changing industrial sector, and in the slower-paced world of the crafts. Such a development was certainly apparent in cities that were the centres of the industrial revolution – particularly pronounced in Manchester or Preston in cotton textiles, Bradford in woollens, for instance – and found to a lesser degree in the industrial centres of northern France, Alsace, the Rhineland and Saxony. At the top of the social pyramid were the industrialists – factory owners, every fibre of whose being was devoted to producing and marketing at a profit. The workers they employed were, in the revealing phrase that came into common useage in England at this time, 'hands'. They were there to produce, and produce at a profit; if they could not do so, or if the market, in one of its periodic downturns made it impossible for them to do so, they would be dismissed without a second thought. Yet these capitalists drove themselves no less hard than they did their workers. As one author in Bradford observed, the industrialists were 'a race of moles that burrowed in the earth and needed not the sunshine of amusement: a generation that was forever hungering and thirsting, scraping and saving – on weekdays saving money, and on Sundays striving and hoping in the very insanity of avarice to save even their own joyless, worthless, miserable souls'.[2]

Particularly in England, these industrialists were the core of a larger group of entrepreneurial capitalists, that included bankers, wholesalers and brokers, a whole elite division of labour in the business of financing, producing and marketing factory products. Affiliated and working with them were members of the professional middle class, particularly in the legal professions, who intermarried with the capitalists and attended to their legal needs. In continental Europe, by contrast, this elaborate division of labour had, with a few regional exceptions, generally not yet proceeded quite that far. Manufacturers did much of their own wholesaling, and financed their enterprises with retained profits or money from their families. Banking and financial services were more likely to remain centred on the needs of the state, as they had been

in the old regime; professionals were also more closely tied to the state, living [237]
more in an occupational world of their own, that had fewer contacts with
specifically industrial enterprise. In fact, the growth of a newer capitalism in
Great Britain could even help to extend the life of the older, state-centred
financial capitalism on the continent. The Rothschild brothers, the leading continental financiers of the first half of the nineteenth century, whose
banking activities spanned state boundaries, made their enormous fortunes
as middlemen between English investors, looking for a place to put their
money, and continental monarchs who sought loans to finance their
governments.

At the bottom of this industrial social pyramid were the factory workers
themselves, whose lives differed in three crucial respects from those of
other wage-earners of the era, such as journeymen artisans, proto-industrial
outworkers, or casual day labourers. First, they worked their twelve- or
fourteen-hour days to the rhythm of the machines, standing in front of the
untiring mule-jennies and power looms. Their production-obsessed employers would hire foremen and supervisors to ensure that they did not slack
off, but kept up with these mechanical pace-setters. Other wage-earners
might work equally long hours, but at a pace that was more under their
control, both because they provided the motive power and because their
supervision was generally not as tight.

Second, factory workers were dependent on their wage for their living,
and would have nothing in the foreseeable future but further wage labour.
Rural outworkers might have a plot of land to supplement their earnings; the
factory workers of Stockport, Lille or Chemnitz could count on no such assistance. Illness or unemployment during business-cycle downturns would
mean the poorhouse, and that at a time when social policy was often moving
in the direction of treating the poor in a noticeably harsher way. Journeymen
artisans also faced the dangers of illness or unemployment, but they could
still aspire to becoming masters one day, although it was becoming more
difficult to do so, and the independence of the master craftsman, given the
growth of outworking, was becoming ever more illusory. Still, the chances of
one day having their own workshop were infinitely better than those of a
factory worker becoming an industrialist.

Finally, the social distance between the capitalist elites and their 'hands'
was very large and pronounced. The two groups lived in separate worlds,
with little or no personal interaction. The work they performed was fundamentally different in nature, with no experiences in common: the factory
owners, cotton brokers or their bankers and lawyers did not stand in front of

[238] a self-acting mule-jenny, in a stiflingly hot and very damp factory building (both heat and humidity were needed to ensure that the fabric was spun and woven properly) all day long; the workers did not engage in marketing, plan or finance business expansion, or set production quotas. In the crafts, masters could and did work alongside their journeymen in the workshop; even those craft masters who might have a large enough enterprise to be able to devote themselves to organizing and directing the business, had, at one point in the past, done the physical labour themselves.

It was not that factory workers were particularly badly paid. A minority among them, particularly the skilled metal-workers, were probably the most affluent of all wage-earners. Even unskilled textile hands were making more than many of the badly put-upon handloom weavers. Nor was their job security unusually bad. Unemployment related to the business cycle was a danger that other labouring groups, such as dockers and porters or construction workers, also faced. Rather, what these three characteristics distinguishing the condition of the industrial work force from that of other non-agricultural wage labourers had in common was the way that industrial workers' lives were determined by the labour market, and the way that both their labour and the conditions under which they sold in it the market were determined by their employers, by members of a fundamentally different social group.

As we might expect, the changes in the social world of the crafts were noticeably more subtle than those experienced in industry. Still, the steady advance of market forces and market-orientation had its effects in the crafts as well, above all by the combination of the shrinking proportion of masters and the growth in outworking. What careful local studies of the crafts have shown is that these two trends, that might at first seem contradictory, actually complemented each other. The ranks of master craftsmen tended to become polarized: a minority, who employed all the journeymen and ran their own businesses on their own account; a larger group, who could not afford any hired help – in and of itself a recipe for poverty – but were also most likely to be outworkers, and under the thumb of merchant capitalists.

In this sense, the crafts were also divided by the expansion of the market, as was mechanized industry. However, the division in the crafts was not between those who sold their labour and those who bought it, those who organized, planned and financed production, and those who physically carried it out, as it was between those who had direct access to the market – namely, that minority of masters who employed the journeymen and ran their own small businesses independently – and those who did not have this access:

the growing ranks of both journeymen and masters working for merchant capitalists. This distinction was a more subtle one than the wide gap between factory masters and their 'hands' characteristic of industrial enterprises; it was also a division across which there was more social movement, albeit in both directions. Journeymen could become independent masters, or even vary between working for someone else and working on their own account. Masters working for and in debt to merchant contractors could run successful businesses, a pattern most common in the construction trades. But successful masters could also fall into debt, and into the grip of moneylenders, losing their direct and independent access to the market.

If the growth in market relations over the years 1780–1850 led to changes in social structure and in relations between different classes, it seems appropriate to ask if it also led to changes in gender relations, and in the social positions of men and women as well. In some ways it did, although the pattern of these changes was more gradual, more comparable in extent to what was happening in the crafts than to developments of industrialization. Most Europeans, both men and women, were employed in agriculture, and the path toward a greater market-orientation in agriculture may well have required greater efforts by women. Nitrogen-fixing root crops required extensive weeding and cultivation, both typically women's work on the farm. Market-oriented speciality crops, such as mulberry trees, grown to feed silkworms, were another area of women's activity.

The historian David Sabean, who has studied in depth the southwest German village of Neckarhausen, a place where energetic farmers introduced a whole series of agricultural innovations in the years 1780–1850, to get the most out of their small plots of land, that grew ever smaller from generation to generation, has found that the increase in women's labour strained marital relations. Divorces, previously almost unknown, increased about tenfold; exhausted farm wives berated their husbands as drunks and wastrels, unable to support a family, and the latter responded by beating their wives in an – often drunken – rage. If this was a typical example of what happened as a result of increasing market relations in agriculture, then they were clearly harder on women than men.

Still, as Sabean notes, women did not take up all the slack in the peasants' struggle to earn a living; the men in the village he studied took increasingly to spending large portions of the year away from home as construction labourers, rather like the French peasants of the Limousin. In southern England, not an area of small peasant farming like southwestern Germany, but one of large, landed estates, rented out to capitalist tenant farmers, and worked

[240] by landless agricultural labourers, the introduction of the new techniques of agriculture had a very different effect: rather than intensifying women's labour, they led to women's unemployment, with paid field work increasingly performed by men. Such very different results from similar forms of agricultural innovation should caution us against making any unequivocal judgements about how they affected men's and women's labour. Since the old regime and the post-revolutionary social and legal orders were distinctly patriarchial ones, these changes in agriculture began in societies where women were in a weaker position than men, and so were more likely to have a greater portion of the burdens of the rural population's struggle to survive loaded onto them.

One development particularly common in rural areas of Europe between 1780 and 1850, but not unknown in cities as well, the increase in illegitimate births, shows the particular difficulties that women faced in this era. Pre-marital sexual relations and pregnant brides, although condemned by both Christian churches, were by no means unknown in the old regime, if more common among Protestants than Catholics. The disruptions of organized religion during the French Revolution and the Napoleonic era at least temporarily weakened clerical opposition to this practice. To a young man from the pre-industrial lower classes, marrying a pregnant girlfriend meant committing himself to supporting a family, something that was usually accomplished by owning his own farm or craft workshop. But, as we have seen, the number of young men who could not do this, who were landless labourers, or could anticipate inheriting a plot of land too small to support a family, or faced a long future as a journeyman, was on the rise. Their response to the pregnancy of their female companion was to leave town, or to disavow the child, leaving the young woman in the lurch.

To contemporaries, probably the most noticeable change in gender relations was in the mechanized textile industry. Adult men were few and far between in the labour force of textile mills, with women and children generally accounting for between 50 and 80 per cent of those employed. This state of affairs stood in striking contrast to that in textile outworking, which directly preceded industrialization, and coexisted with it for several decades. There, the main breadwinner, the handloom weaver, was typically an adult male; as factory production expanded and, in England, at least, handloom weaving contracted, adult men found that they were earning less than women and children: a result that all involved found distinctly perverse.

We can note that such a picture is not quite so clear cut as it might seem at first glance. Sometimes, as happened in parts of northern France, women did

handloom weaving, and in some branches of the textile industry, particularly [241]
the mechanized cotton spinning of Lancashire, men monopolized the best-
paid factory jobs. Before 1850, handloom weaving in most of continental
Europe was increasing rather than declining, so that a craft dominated by
adult men could coexist with an industry where they were overshadowed
by women and children. Still, for all these cautions and adjustments, the
decline of adult male labour in the textile industry, and the increasing
salience of women in it was the single largest change in gender relations in
this period.

  In other areas of industry, crafts and non-agricultural employment, more
generally, there were rather fewer changes in the sex composition of the labour force. Women had not had much of a role in pre-industrial metalworking, and they were far and few between in early ironworks or machine shops.
There had been a considerable number of women and children employed in
coal mining, and as mining expanded in Great Britain, this portion of the
labour force grew with it, until it became a public scandal. This was not primarily due to the fact that mining was dangerous and heavy labour, since
both women and children did physically exhausting work in agriculture, without anyone getting too upset. It was the prurient images of men and women,
adults and children, working together underground, often scantily clad as a
result of the sub-surface heat, that sparked an ultimately successful reform
movement among the church-going middle class, to make coal mining an
occupation reserved for grown men.

  Outside the industrial sector, women's employment opportunities were
generally limited, and remained so throughout the period: dressmaking, street
vending, domestic service and related tasks (such as laundering) and, of course,
prostitution. This last was generally not a full-time occupation, but an occasional response of young, single working women, when they were unemployed, or unable to make ends meet on their generally meagre wages. In
urban areas, outside of factory towns, female and male employment profiles
in 1850 would have been strikingly similar to those of 1780.

  Some historians have suggested that there was a major shift in gender
relations among the commerical and professional middle class in this era.
Their argument is that women took a substantial part in family businesses
(and almost all businesses were family businesses) in the eighteenth century,
but that in the first half of the nineteenth, there was a growing separation
of male and female worlds, with women being increasingly relegated to private life, to home and family, while men monopolized the public realm, in
business, civic affairs, voluntary associations and politics. It is certainly true

that the ideal of women in the home and men in public life spread widely among middle-class families in Europe during the first half of the nineteenth century (and even, to some extent, among the aristocracy, too), but it is much less clear how much actual social practice itself changed. In the eighteenth century, women did not practise professions, and they would only have an independent role in business as a widow, or, more rarely, as the unmarried daughter and heir of a businessman. Even then, their influence in family businesses was more behind the scenes, related to the wealth they would bring into marriage through a dowry. It may have been the case that in the first half of the nineteenth century widows became less likely to run a business after their husband's death, but the general pattern of their publicly deferring to an adult male relative did not change.

The broader argument that women retreated into private roles and men developed public ones in the decades around 1800 seems even more questionable. It is true that the movement from a society of orders to a civil society of property owners, that was the result of the French Revolution, and that was well under way in England before 1789, did open possibilities for participation in public life for a greater number of men, above all from the property-owning and professional middle class. However, the patriarchal society of orders was no arena of women's influence on public affairs, except perhaps for a few highly placed and hardly typical aristocrats, such as Marie Antoinette. In fact, the post-old regime society of the first half of the nineteenth century would offer women from the middle classes many more opportunities for organized participation in public life. These were in nurturing, 'womanly', roles to be sure, such as organized charity and church work, and in associations for the care of the sick and of small children, or for the training of servants, and, except during revolutions or other periods of political crisis, they generally did not directly impinge on politics and government, but they were certainly not ones that confined women to the household.

In the end, the ever-greater progress of market relations in the years 1780 to 1850 did not greatly change gender roles or relations between the sexes. Certainly, opposing claims made by historians that the capitalist market economy either dramatically liberated women or drastically worsened their situation both seem distinctly exaggerated. Both the old regime society of orders and the post-revolutionary civil society of property owners were patriarchal social arrangements, if perhaps patriarchal in different ways. Since women started from an inferior and less powerful position in both societies, they had a harder time averting the burdens and obtaining the benefits of social change, as compared to men in their respective social classes.

Long-term trends (2): Change over time [243]

Tables 5.2 and 5.3 give a very approximate idea of the pace of industrial development and of progress in the utilization of steam power in Europe during the first half of the nineteenth century. The very earliest available comparative figures, from the years 1820–30, show Great Britain already well ahead of other European countries in key measures of industrial production; in fact, generally above levels they would reach by the middle of the

Table 5.2   Industrial production in selected European Countries, 1820–50

Country	Pig iron output (000 metric tons)				Cotton spindles (000)	
	c.1820	c. 1830	c. 1840	c.1850	c. 1830	c.1850
Great Britain	374	688	1,419	2,285	10,000	20,977
Belgium	?	90	95	145	200	400
France	198	266	348	406	2,500	4,500
German states	85	110	190	210	626	900

Source: B.R. Mitchell, *European Historical Statistics 1750–1970* (New York, 1975), pp. 391–92, 434–35.

Table 5.3   The progress of steam power in Europe, 1830–50

Country	Rail lines (kilometres)			Steam engines (000 horsepower)	
	c.1830	c.1840	c.1850	c.1840	c.1850
Great Britain	157	2,390	9,797	620	1,290
Belgium	—	334	854	40	70
France	31	410	2,915	90	370
German states	—	469	5,586	40	260

Source: W.R. Mitchell, *European Historical Statistics* (New York, 1975), pp. 581–2; David Landes, *The Unbound Prometheus: Technological Change and Industrial Development in Western Europe from 1750 to the Present* (Cambridge, 1972), p. 221.

[244]   nineteenth century. In other words, the process of industrialization was well under way in certain regions of the British Isles by the 1820s; it would accelerate from then until 1850, with the British lead over its closest continental competitors steadily increasing. The sevenfold increase in pig iron produced in England's coke-fired blast furnaces between 1820 and 1850 is particularly impressive, in comparison to the way that production in the charcoal forges in use in France and the German states, starting from a much lower level in 1820, could only manage to double. This development was a dramatic demonstration of the superiority of production processes using inorganic raw materials over those using organic ones.

Although clearly overshadowed by England, continental European countries did experience a certain amount of industrial development in the first half of the nineteenth century. The 2.5 million cotton spindles in use in France as early as 1830 is suggestive of this. Their number grew to 4.5 million by 1850, and by the later date they were mostly steam-driven, rather than run by water, human, or animal power as they would have been in the earlier period. The Liège-Hainault region of Belgium was the one area in Europe where coal-fired blast furnaces had come into common use; the 145,000 tons of pig iron produced there in 1850 were three-quarters of what was manufactured in the German states, although they had eight times Belgium's population.

If we look closely at Table 5.3, we can see a certain quickening of the pace of mechanization in the 1840s. That decade saw the first steps taken toward the construction of a rail network on the continent; use of steam engines increased substantially. Rail construction would stimulate demand for iron and steel, increasing the pace of the adoption of coke-fired blast furnaces; it would open new possibilities for marketing of agricultural products as well, increasing opportunities for specialization and improving farmers' income, thereby raising demand for industrial and craft products, and thus giving a boost to the entire economy. All these good things would happen, at least in western and central Europe – but in the quarter-century after 1850. At the very end of the period covered in this book, they were tantalizing possibilities, visible on the horizon, but not yet the reality that they had become in England.

Thus, the whole pattern of economic development in Europe over the years 1780–1850 is an extraordinarily complicated story: old slogans, like the 'industrial revolution', simply will not suffice to explain it. Two themes that do seem common across the continent and the entire time period are the growth of population and the extension of market relations and market-orientation in production and distribution. Yet these two common themes were exemplified in an extraordinarily diverse way in different regions, economic sectors and countries. While population growth was considerable just about everywhere, the spread of market relations was regionally quite differentiated: greatest in the British Isles, and considerable in the northwestern and central portions of continental Europe, but weaker in the eastern and southern edges of the continent. As we survey this broad, diverse and sometimes contradictory field of developments, we would find it even harder to answer a very frequently posed question: who profited from all these changes and who was harmed by them?

Historians' answers to these questions have varied considerably – so much so, that scholars generally talk about them as part of the 'standards of living controversy'. The usual way the issue is addressed is via a computation of real wages, that is, a comparison of money wages against the cost of living, to ascertain whether wage-earners' purchasing power was increasing or decreasing. Such an approach, however, has a number of weaknesses. Even today, with the existence of elaborate government statistical services as well as private economics institutes, with much more extensive and detailed information available, the exact calculation of real wages remains controversial. Surviving figures on wages and prices from the late eighteenth and early nineteenth centuries are few and far between, often unreliable and very probably unrepresentative, so that calculations based on this data are no better than the data itself.

Even if we could develop a degree of certainty about the available material – and historians and economists have truly been ingenious in searching out figures and finding ways to check their reliability – additional problems remain. Wage figures are generally based on adult men, working full-time. They take no account of the very real problem of unemployment, and they generally do not include wages earned by women and children, although their income could be an important part of a poor family's resources. Also, not everyone was paid in cash: especially in agriculture, but in crafts and industry too, workers received – or took, without asking permission – wages in kind. A majority of the lower-class population was not completely dependent on wages, but combined wage income with subsistence or market crops that they grew on small plots of land. In view of all these difficulties, some historians have tried to use alternative measures for the standard of living, such as looking at the height of army recruits, to see if they were getting smaller or taller over time, or trying to discern trends in the consumption of basic consumer commodities. These procedures have their own sources of inaccuracy and unclear relationship to the actual standard of living as well.

[246]   Under these circumstances, I will not draw a neat graph, with a line going up or down to indicate the changes in the standard of living, and a scale giving a precise index figure. Rather, I will suggest that in the years 1780–1850 there were two quite different mechanisms that determined which groups profited from and which groups were damaged by social and economic change. One, I would call the old regime system. In the relatively static and hierarchical world of the society of orders, wage rates, or the prices paid for the goods and services of master artisans, tended to remain the same over longer periods of time, or at least to change less than the price of grain. Movements in the price of this basic commodity would determine standards of living across a broad sector of the population. If grain prices rose, standards of living fell for those who purchased grain – urban craftsmen and labourers, proto-industrial outworkers, and those smaller farmers whose plots of land did not suffice to feed their familes – and rose for those who sold grain, dealt in grain, or owned the land on which grain was produced: noble estate owners, urban commoners who owned and rented out farmland, merchants, millers, and substantial, property-owning (or renting) farmers. When grain prices fell, the results were reversed: the first group, generally the lower-class majority of society, did better, the second, the more affluent element of the old regime, lost some of their wealth.

Even after the French Revolution and the Napoleonic era put an end to the society of orders in parts of Europe, or at least curtailed and modified it substantially, its mental habits remained, and can be traced down to the middle of the nineteenth century. We can thus use the course of grain prices as a way to provide a first approximation of the development of standards of living. In this context, the years between 1750 and 1800 were ones that showed the full effect of Parson Malthus's more dire predictions. Population rose, but grain output generally did not keep pace. Food prices increased, and those who had grain to sell, or owned land on which it was grown did well; those who had to purchase it were steadily worse off, a pattern that seems almost universal, in continental Europe and the British Isles.

The first decade of the nineteenth century saw a reversal of the pattern, a period of good harvests and lower prices. This was a period of extended warfare, and with so many young men under arms, and out of the labour market, labourers' and journeymen's wages, quite exceptionally for the period, tended to go up. Of course, the economic strains of warfare, from higher taxes, through declines in trade, to the toll in human lives, both on the battlefield and through the spread of epidemics, rather dampened the positive effects of price trends for the lower classes. Most of the decade after 1810 saw a renewed increase in prices, peaking in 1816–17, the year of major crop failures, the last full-scale subsistence crisis, a time when widespread lack of sufficient food raised the spectre of starvation.

We could interpret this, as contemporaries often did, as a continuation of the pre-1800 trend, with the first decade of the nineteenth century just marking a pause in a relentless increase in food prices. However, the years 1817–28 suggested something quite different: a drastic decline in grain prices, between 40 per cent and 70 per cent in different regions, bringing them down to levels of the years 1740–70. Recovery from the quarter-century of warfare, favourable weather, and the increased use of new agricultural techniques combined to throw large quantities of grain on the market, providing relief for the sorely pressed lower classes, and distress for those who had profited from higher food prices. Hundreds of noble landowners in eastern Germany went bankrupt in the 1820s, and saw their ancestral estates sold off at auction. These circumstances did not last forever: from the late 1820s, until the middle of the century, grain prices fluctuated erratically but overall rose in continental Europe (although not in England) by 25–35 per cent.

Judging by this old regime mechanism alone, we could conclude that popular standards of living declined steadily in the eighteenth century, recovered, albeit with considerable fluctuations, in the first quarter of the nineteenth, and then declined again in the second quarter of that century. However, we now need to note a second economic mechanism that was gradually coming into play in the decades after 1800. In this case, what we see is greater changes in wages, as well as in the prices of non-subsistence commodities, such as speciality crops raised by small farmers. Increased productivity, a result of industrialization and growing specialization and market-orientation, offered the possibility of rising incomes for the lower classes; unemployment in business-cycle downturns ('crises' or 'panics' as contemporaries said; 'recessions', we would call them today), or competition from more advanced technology, as some outworkers faced, could have the opposite effect. Advances in industry, large-scale commerce and finance, gradually created an elite group whose wealth was not related to land ownership or farm prices.

Sometimes these two economic mechanisms that determined standards of living could counteract one another. This happened in the postwar years after 1817, as grain prices fell, benefiting working people's standards of living, but manufacturing output went into a recession, and ex-soldiers returned to the labour market, increasing unemployment, driving down wages, and reducing standards of living. The two mechanisms could reinforce

[248]   each other positively, as happened in the late 1830s, when industrial production increased, railway construction began, and grain prices stayed relatively
stable; they could reinforce each other negatively, as in the crisis years 1845–
47, when crop failures produced high grain prices, and a recession raised
levels of unemployment.

Until the 1820s, the old regime mechanism determined standards of
living, that rose or fell primarily with grain prices. In that decade, newer
determinants came to the fore, related to productivity and the business
cycle – most intensely, as one might expect, in Great Britain, to a lesser
degree in continental Europe. Highlighting the difference between the British Isles and the continental countries was the fact that grain prices themselves largely stagnated in the former between the late 1820s and the middle
of the nineteenth century, but showed an upward trend in the latter.

If we were to sum up all these developments, it would be to note that the
years 1780–1850 were difficult ones for Europe's lower classes. Grain prices
rose throughout most of the era; periods of falling prices, on the other hand –
particularly the first and third decades of the nineteenth century – were times
of economic difficulties for other reasons, such as wars and recessions. A rural
population growing faster than the amount of land available to till meant that
a progressively smaller proportion of countryfolk – most Europeans, let us
remember – were in a position to take advantage of rising grain prices. It is
certainly the case that the new economic mechanisms relating to increases in
productivity came into play in the years 1830–50; they (along with other
developments, such as increasing emigration to North America) helped cush-
ion, if not reverse, the impact of rising grain prices in continental Europe, and
probably led to a persistent, if not uninterrupted, rise in standards of living
for many (although not all) of the poorer inhabitants of the British Isles. This
background of decline, or at best stagnation and uncertain improvement
in popular standards of living was a source of continuous social and political tension; it was a key reason why the years 1780–1850 were the age of
revolutionary Europe. Unambiguous, persistent and continued gains in the
standard of living, and the potential for social and political stability emerging from them, would have to wait for the decades after the middle of the
nineteenth century.

If economic and demographic developments made the period between
1780 and 1850 a difficult one for the lower classes, they presented problems
for the affluent as well. Elites whose fortunes were tied to grain and the land
on which it was grown may well have been the most successful of any group

over the entire period, assuming they could avoid losing their property in the upheavals of the revolutionary and Napoleonic eras, but the sharp price breaks in two of the first three decades of the nineteenth century were major threats to their position. Reshaping and reorganizing industrial and crafts production – erecting steam-powered textile mills, building rail networks, creating outworking empires and financing all these developments – offered merchants, industrialists and bankers the possiblity of accumulating wealth in hitherto unknown ways, and at a pace that astonished their contemporaries. Colder appraisals in retrospect note that these new capitalist groups as a whole still took second place in wealth to large landowners, or to bankers who continued the old regime practice of financing state debts.

In addition, new ways of accumulating wealth brought new ways of losing it. Starting in the aftermath of the Napoleonic Wars, a new and disturbing development made itself apparent: the economic crisis of overproduction. Unlike the old regime, when economic downturns developed because of warfare or a bad harvest, both leading to a shortage of basic necessities, these difficulties occurred because there were too many manufactured goods. They lay around unsold, bringing the manufacturers who had produced them and the merchants who distributed them into bankruptcy, and often provoking a chain reaction of business failures, as one capitalist who could not pay his debts caused another to fail to meet his obligations, and so on. These business cycle downturns would be repeated regularly in the first half of the century, for the last time in our period in 1847, periodically thinning out the ranks of the newly successful capitalist entrepreneurs – to say nothing of the effect on workers of the unemployment prevalent at such times.

In sum, the period 1780–1850 was one of repeated and varied economic innovation. Driven by the need to produce more to feed, house and clothe a rapidly growing population, people in all the European countries, men and women, aristocrats and capitalists, artisans, peasants and labourers developed a variety of new and innovative ways to produce more, to distribute this production more widely, and to carry out the whole process more efficiently. However, these innovations themselves could only succeed by disrupting previously existing practices, and by upsetting familiar ways of life. Although, in the end, the demands of providing for a growing population were generally met, the disruptions following in the wake of the innovations could be threatening, impoverishing, and conducive to a climate of uncertainty and insecurity.

[250] Three national variations on a theme

Up to this point, the account has stressed general trends, common to all of Europe. In so far as variations have been discussed, they have been regional in nature. Industrialization or agricultural innovation certainly did take place in regions, both those that were only one part of a country and those that crossed national boundaries. However, if social and economic changes largely occurred on regional lines, these regions themselves made up differing extents of individual European states, the consequences of socioeconomic change for social policy and for politics were played out within the borders of different European states, and the policies individual governments adopted could have their own effects on the further path of social and economic development. Hence in this final section, we will look at three national variations on a theme, that we might call the British way, the French way, and the German way. Each will describe how specific versions of the changes outlined previously in the chapter affected the populations of different European countries.

Much of this chapter has been devoted to noting the spread of market relations in Europe after 1780. But in Great Britain, these market relations were already widespread at the beginning of the period under consideration: a specialized, market-oriented agriculture, with capitalist tenant farmers using the most productive agricultural techniques and employing wage labour; outworking in its most complex and diverse forms, in a wide variety of manufactures; a water-based transport system that supported a market-orientation, decades before railways or steamships were technological possibilities; good financial and retailing networks, that faciliatated production for and sales in the market. This highly developed market system, with its many possibilities for the lower classes to earn a living by their wage labour, encouraged early and frequent marriage, leading to a rapid population growth.

This was Parson Malthus's starting point, and he was convinced that the system had reached the limits of its flexibility; further population growth could only have disastrous consequences. He was probably right; the market-oriented, but pre-industrial British economic system, as it existed in the late eighteenth century, had probably gone as far as its underlying technology would permit. Thus, much of the story of the subsequent seven decades was the movement from this very efficient, market-oriented production system, based largely on human or animal power and organic resources, to a new production system, working with steam power and inorganic resources – in other words, the process of industrialization. We might see the decades from the 1780s to the 1820s as the period of transition from one market-oriented production system to another, and then from the 1820s until mid-century as the age of the consolidation and expansion of the new, industrial economy. The process was intense, concentrated and proceeded at a rapid pace – and it had to, since the driving force of population increase accelerated relentlessly throughout the period.

The initial phase of the transition was the most difficult. It was unclear if the growth of output could outpace that of the population; indeed, economic growth rates may actually have declined from those of the preceding, pre-industrial decades; real wages were mostly in decline; and there were persistent fears that all the increase in production would be soaked up by large landowners, whose rents seemed to be rising faster than anything else. The decline in farm prices, the rapid growth in industrial output and the construction of a rail network, all starting in the 1820s, gradually laid such fears to rest. As the transition phase came to an end, the wealth created by new industrial enterprise began to trickle down to the lower classes. Standards of living rose, and English prosperity slowly became a source of wonder and model for emulation. The classic expression was the phrase coined by visitors to the great International Exposition in London in 1851. Seeing the vast mass of British industrial goods on display, they concluded that Great Britain was the 'workshop of the world'.

However, the beneficial effects of industrial prosperity were limited by one final characteristic of the British way that we can note: the thorough and utter ruthlessness, with which the values of the market and the orientation of all aspects of society toward the market were implemented. It would not be unfair to say that such an unleashing of the free market contributed to a rapid pace of economic growth – one which was much needed, given the increases in population – but this market-orientation could become, at times, an obsession, and one with pernicious consequences for those who were in an unfavourable position in the marketplace. Two celebrated, or perhaps notorious examples of this orientation, are the New Poor Law of 1834, and the great potato famine in Ireland.

Until 1834, poor relief in Great Britain had been locally implemented and quite varied. One important version, known as the Speenhamland system, after the original locality of its implementation, had tried to guarantee a minimum income to poor households; either by direct grants, if there was no one capable of working for wages, or by supplementing wage-earners' earnings, if they were insufficient. From the point of view of the unlimited free market, this system had the effect of encouraging people not to work, if they were

[252]   only marginally capable of it, and of unfairly subsidizing employers who paid low wages. Local property owners, who were taxed to pay for poor relief, had obvious reasons to oppose the system as well.

Adherents of the free market gaining their way in Parliament, the old system was replaced with a new, nationally implemented one, in which no grants would be provided to households. Recipients of poor relief would be forced to leave their homes and live in barracks-like workhouses, informally known as 'Poor Law Bastilles', where personal property would be confiscated, families would be broken up and the sexes housed separately, with food, clothing and housing reduced to the barest minimum. The workhouses were designed to be so unattractive that people would be reluctant to use them, and would prefer, instead to find work on their own initiative. But for two of the major groups of the poor – agricultural labourers with little to do, outside the peak seasons of farming, or industrial workers laid off during a recession – unemployment was not a matter of lack of desire for work, but a question of no jobs being available. The New Poor Law was merely a gratuitously cruel form of degradation for them, one that did little to resolve the problem of their poverty.

The story of Ireland is an even more dramatic example of the problematic features of an unlimited attachment to the free market. Most of the land there was in the hands of English noble absentee landlords, who rented it out to larger tenants, who might farm it themselves or rent it out to sub-tenants. At the bottom of this social scale, a substantial majority of the population was made up of a group of impoverished sub-tenants and day labourers, who only had relatively small parcels of land at their disposal. Agriculture as practised in Ireland in this period was quite modern and efficient, only the new techniques of crop-raising were used to produce grain for sale in the market (or to feed livestock, itself then sold in the market), to pay the rents of absentee landlords. In particular, the lowest classes lived from a New World crop, the potato, that would produce a very considerable harvest even from a small patch of land.

The system worked well enough, until the mid-1840s, when a plant disease struck, the potato blight, that rotted the crops in the fields. Most of the population simply did not have enough to eat. Other possibilities for earning a living were few: the once widespread proto-industry had been centred in linen-working, that was in severe decline; larger farmers, employers of agricultural labour, were themselves hard-pressed to pay their rents, and could not afford to take on more labourers. The British government was reluctant to provide emergency aid, since that might lead Irish labourers to avoid working their hardest to provide food for their families. In the famine era, the second half of the 1840s, 'excess mortality' – deaths above the rate that had been prevalent in the previous decades – totalled about one million, people who died of hunger and disease. This was an enormous death toll, in the order of the total casualties of the Napoleonic Wars.

The largely unfettered market, that provided few obstacles to the progress of social and economic transformation characteristic of the British Isles during the years 1780–1850, made it possible to master the problems of a rising population. This very same orientation to the market also meant that the disruptive and impoverishing effects of the radical changes occurring would be allowed to take their course – in Ireland, their terrible and fatal course – with little attempt to mitigate these consequences. When we look at France, Europe's second most important economic power in this era, albeit one that in both absolute and per capita production figures was well behind Great Britain, we find a rather different orientation.

As Table 5.1 showed, the rate of population increase in France was rather less than that of most European countries, a disparity particularly noticeable in the first half of the nineteenth century, when the population grew at a pace only about 60 per cent of the continental average. Such a low rate of population growth was not the result of high death rates; if anything, mortality in France, particularly infant mortality, was on the low side, by contemporary standards. Nor was it the result of fewer marriages, since the marriage rate was increasing in this period. Finally, we cannot attribute it to emigration, since the French were then, and have remained to the present day, notoriously uninterested in leaving their native country. Rather, the low population growth rate reflects the increasingly widespread practice of birth control – something unique to the French in this era, although systematic efforts to limit births may have been sporadically attempted by some social groups, and perhaps inhabitants of some regions, such as central Italy. Using the simple, technologically very undemanding, if not completely perfect method of withdrawal, a growing number of French families limited themselves to two or three, rather than six or eight children.

By decreasing population pressure, the French made it possible to slow the pace of social and economic transformation. Farmland could remain fallow; common land was undivided and could continue to be used by all the village's inhabitants. Small farmers, secure in their property after the revolution, had abolished seigneurialism and could continue to maintain a modest economic independence, or experiment, slowly, with adding new, market-oriented crops, without abandoning their subsistence agriculture. Outworking

[254]   could continue and even expand in extent. Makers of social policy, whether Catholic and conservative or free-thinking and free market in orientation, almost universally regarded the English New Poor Law as cruel and inhuman.

Secularization of church property during the revolutionary era had reduced the number of potential sources for poor relief, leaving it mostly in the hands of municipalities, with occasional assistance from private organizations and societies. Policies were not standardized, although there was a general trend, encouraged by the national government, in the direction of providing assistance to poor families with dependent children. Starting in the 1830s, this policy had been expanded to include help for single mothers. The main goal of these efforts, pursued with some success, was to reduce or eliminate the old regime institution of foundling hospitals, where unwed mothers in particular could leave their unwanted children, to an uncertain, although frequently fatal destiny. Periods of food shortages could still produce broader problems of poverty, and when the potato crop failed in France, as it did in Ireland during the mid-1840s, the government took measures to ensure that mass starvation did not occur, by prohibiting exports of grain and potatoes, and subsidizing imports from Russia or North America.

We might go so far as to say that there emerged a society-wide consensus against pushing the pace of social and economic change. It was not a solution to be rejected out of hand. While the average rate of increase in the gross domestic product in Great Britain during the nineteenth century was probably about twice what it was in France, when we take population into account, and estimate the per capita growth rates, the British lead shrinks considerably, to something like 1.3 per cent per person per year, as against 1.1 per cent in France. Economic output increased more slowly in France, but there were fewer people among whom it needed to be shared.

This description might make France in the first half of the nineteenth century seem almost idyllic. It was not, of course, and we should take into account two important aspects of the period, that might modify this account. First, it was only after the middle of the nineteenth century that the practice of birth control reached the extent where population growth in France dropped to very low levels; before 1850, while less than in other European countries, it was still considerable. The classic Malthusian problem of a growing population pressing on limited resources had been mitigated but not solved. Output still had to grow, or standards of living would decline, as they may well have done for wage-earners.

Second, France was a country where economic development was regionally sharply differentiated. The northern and northeastern part of France were

regions where the pace of transformation was rapid, with industrialization in
Normandy, Flanders and Alsace, new forms of crop rotation in many farming
areas of the north and some industry and ever more complex patterns of
outworking in the large urban centres of Paris and Lyons. Social results of
this transformation were apparent there as well: a rural society, in which large
landowners and well-off peasants confronted a group of landless labourers; a
prosperous industrial and mercantile bourgeoisie faced an increasing industrial working class, and a very large group of outworkers and journeymen
artisans, who would never have their own business and work on their own
account. The economic results of these changes should not be despised
either. With a quickening of the pace in the 1840s, as Tables 5.2 and 5.3
show, France maintained and even expanded its position as the leading
industrial power on the European continent. The German states were ahead
in the construction of a rail network, but as contemporaries noted, the
French rail network, although smaller, was of considerably higher quality:
double-tracked, with broad curves, against the more cheaply and quickly
built German system, that was single-tracked, with sharp curves limiting
speed and cargo capacity.

By contrast, central and southern France were regions characterized by a
slower pace of social and economic change. There, older, less efficient crop
rotations persisted; smallholding farmers were more prevalent, mixed in with
sharecroppers and agricultural labourers (sometimes these different roles were
played by the same person); there was little industry and outworking was
noticeably less innovative. We might call this part of the country backward,
and all the indicators of prosperity, from per-capita income, to the average
height of draftees, show it ranked below the more dynamic regions to its
north, or we might observe rural experiments with market-oriented crops,
and the bustling port city of Marseilles and suggest that a willingness to accept a somewhat slower pace of growth and lower standard of living, although
perhaps a more equitably distributed one, went alongside a receptiveness to
more modest and gradual forms of economic innovation.

Ultimately, we might go so far as to suggest that France in the late eighteenth and first half of the nineteenth century was almost two different countries. The northern and northeastern part belonged to the same world of
rapid socioeconomic change that one found in Belgium, western Germany
and Great Britain; it was in impressive company, but could keep up the pace.
The central and southern regions, on the other hand, belonged to a Mediterranean area of slow population and economic growth. But compared to Italy
or Spain, even the less dynamic portions of France seemed quite impressive,

[256]   both for the extent of economic growth, and for the way that such growth reached very large, poorer social groups such as smallholding farmers. In that sense, the composite portrait we have drawn of France is the summation of two quite different regional experiences, each respectable in its own way.

It would not be too unfair to suggest that social and economic developments in Spain and the Italian states in this period bore a family resemblance to the French model, albeit with a greater tendency toward stagnation and lack of innovation. Both countries (if one may use the expression 'country' for the different and distinctly disunited states of the Italian peninsula in this period) showed lower rates of population growth than were the case in the lands of northern, central and eastern Europe, albeit somewhat faster than in France. They were also both divided into regions of more substantial economic innovation, and those of of stagnation and continued routine. In Italy, there was a clear north–south divide, with the northern provinces of Lombardy and Venetia, then under the rule of the Austrian empire, areas of a growing proto-industry (specializing in silk production), and of a growth in agricultural specialization. However, in contrast to France, where the use of steam engines in industry, and the building of a rail network had begun in the 1830s and 1840s, these developments in the Italian north would have to wait for the decades after mid-century. While the employment of new systems of crop rotation was only sporadic in even the economically advanced regions of northern France, it was still little practised in Italy.

Also as in northern France, the agriculturally productive portions of these northern Italian districts – such as the fertile fields in the valley of the river Po, where rice was cultivated on a very large scale – were areas in which a small number of large landowners confronted a very large body of landless rural labourers. The seizure and sale of church property and the abolition of feudalism and seigneurialism in the Napoleonic era had largely rebounded to the advantage of large proprietors and the vast majority of the rural population had gained little from it. Peasant smallholders, owning and working their own land, were primarily to be found on mountainous and infertile soil.

As one moved south in the Italian peninsula, the extent of agricultural innovation and proto-industrial outwork steadily declined. In the far south, and on the island of Sicily, returns to seed for grain do not seem to have been markedly different in the first half of the nineteenth century from what they were in the days of the Roman empire. There were areas where land use followed patterns in the Balkans, based primarily on the herding of sheep and cattle. In the Italian south, great inequalities in landownership prevailed, with the upheavals of the Napoleonic era having thrown up a new class of large landowners of common background, alongside the noble proprietors who [257] had been there since the days of the society of orders. As in the south of France, the rural lower classes of southern Italy were a mixture of smallholders, share-croppers, and agricultural labourers, with the same individual often filling a number of different social roles. The warm, Mediterranean climate of the area offered the possibility of agricultural innovation, for specialization in non-subsistence crops such as olives, lemons and oranges, but the lack of trans-port and connections to potential markets discouraged such innovations, which would have to wait for the latter decades of the nineteenth century.

Spain saw a similar contrast between innovative and stagnant regions of the country, although the innovative regions were smaller and the stagnant ones more prevalent, and the clear north–south distinction in France and Italy lacking. Above all Catalonia, on the Mediterranean coast, was the centre of economic innovation in Spain, with cotton textile production centred in Bar-celona, where, from the 1830s onward, older networks of proto-industry were increasingly coexisting with steam-powered factories. Farmers in the coastal districts of Catalonia and neighbouring Valencia were also experimenting with those market-oriented, non-subsistence Mediterranean crops, still quite lacking in southern industry. In northern Spain, in the Asturias and the Basque country, there were good reserves of both coal and iron ore, but iron produc-tion there continued to use the old, inefficient technology of charcoal forges until the middle of the nineteenth century.

Lack of navigable rivers, a poor road network (the already poor roads of the old regime deteriorated in the bitter fighting of the Napoleonic era) and the fact that railway building started late ensured that economically stag-nant regions would outnumber innovative ones in Spain. Conditions of rural property-holding varied substantially: overall (there were many individual regional exceptions), the centre and south were areas of large landed estates and numerous agricultural labourers, while in the north and on the At-lantic coast there were more smallholders, and the abolition of seigneurial-ism did little to change these patterns. However, throughout these regions, there were few agricultural innovations in this period: the growth of grain on marginal, previously unused land was the major change, one that was successful in the short run, but over the long haul would produce barren, infertile landscapes where wheat had once been grown.

Poverty remained common in these Mediterranean regions, although the presence of such widespread poverty was nothing new in the late eighteenth and early nineteenth centuries. Responses to poverty continued to operate through established channels, centring on Catholic alms-giving. Since the

[258] secularization of church property in Spain and Italy was carried out both later and less completely than in France, the Catholic Church there still possessed institutional resources to help the poor, supplemented by the donations of pious individuals. In Italy in particular, foundling hospitals remained a characteristic feature of society, and continued to receive new-borns, not just from single women, but from married ones as well, who could not provide for another mouth to feed.

The experience of the German states suggests a still different pattern, one that was replicated to a greater or lesser extent in northern and eastern Europe. Unlike in France, or, to some extent in Mediterranean Europe, population pressure was unrelenting in Germany. Population growth rates were already considerable in the second half of the eighteenth century; once the losses of the Napoleonic era were made good, they accelerated rapidly in the decades after 1815. However, the introduction of industrialization, that enabled Great Britain to master its even more rapid rate of population growth, did not occur in central Europe before 1850. Even the 1840s saw only relatively modest increases in industrial output and in the use of steam power.

Population pressure was thus very strong in Germany, and the pace of agricultural transformation needed to keep up with it was correspondingly quick: by the middle of the century, only about 15 per cent of farmland in central Europe was left fallow, as against 25 per cent in France. There was thus enough food to go round, but it was less clear if the mass of the population would have enough income to purchase it. As a growing population filled the slots of an economy technologically still largely run along old regime lines, artisanal trades became, as contemporaries said, 'overcrowded', with too many masters chasing too few customers, and even more journeymen journeying around frantically, looking for jobs with masters who lacked the income to employ them. Such craftsmen were easy prey for outworking merchants, whose growing grip on the trades only worsened the artisans' plight. Much the same was the case in agriculture, as the succession of generation meant that farms were divided into ever-smaller plots. Perhaps the limit was reached in the village of Rineck in Baden, where the plots had become so small that the villagers made a living by stealing potatoes from the fields of neighbouring villages. In regions of impartible inheritance in northern Germany, where only one son received the family farm, such division into miniature holdings was averted, but the proportion of cottagers and landless labourers increased to a daunting extent, and even the employment opportunities provided by the new forms of crop rotation did not suffice to support them. Outworking, the classic means of support for the rural lower classes, showed a mixed picture. In some branches and areas, cotton and silk textiles, or metalworking, in particular, it was on the rise; in others, above all linen textiles, it was, by the 1830s, well on the way towards extinction.

The continued prevalence of seigneurial dues in Germany east of the river Rhine, and the existence of serfdom in some of the eastern provinces of the Prussian monarchy and in the Austrian empire (admittedly, most of the German-speaking peasants of the empire were not serfs, while the Hungarian-, Rumanian-, Ukrainian-, Polish- and Croatian-speaking peasants usually were) only exacerbated the social tensions brought on by a rising population crashing against an economic and technological structure that lacked the ability to find gainful employment for them all. The existence of guilds in most German states outside of the Prussian kingdom, also created additional social stresses. Frustrated journeymen were persistently denied the chance to become masters and could journey around for decades. In the states of southern Germany in particular, state officials, strongly influenced by the ideas of Malthus, made a concentrated effort to curtail the working-class population. To be eligible to get married, couples had to conform to residence and property requirements that young working people generally could not fulfil. The upshot was that in Bavaria, where such legislation was enforced most strictly, during the years 1820–50, one baby in five was illegitimate.

This outlook also influenced the means of support for the poor in the German states. Poor relief was generally a municipal responsibility, with town and village governments providing a wide variety of forms of support – sometimes via the churches, and sometimes directly. In larger cities, physicians were increasingly involved in poor relief, and their diagnoses (actually, quite sensible, given the state of medical knowledge and practice) that the poor needed more food to improve their health, only increased the costs of supporting the poor. Cost-cutting measures, such as workhouses, in the style of the New Poor Law were not found; rather, home relief of various sorts was the rule. Consequently, local governments did their best to avoid having more poor to support, by denying marriage licences and residence permits to anyone they deemed likely to become a recipient of poor relief. In other words, the main element of poor relief was trying to get someone else to take care of the poor. By the 1830s and 1840s, it was increasingly clear that such a system did not work well, and contemporaries talked ever more about 'pauperism', a growing widespread impoverishment, that was overwhelming the abilities of municipal governments to counteract it.

Also a German characteristic, although similar if less extensive developments existed in the Austrian empire and the Italian states (less so in France),

[260] was the way in which the difficulties in finding gainful employment reached the educated middle class. A growing number of young men were enjoying a secondary school and university education, but without the close connections, found in England, between a growing industrial sector and the professions, job opportunities were scarce. Neither state service nor private practice sufficed for these growing numbers of educated young men, and contemporaries began talking darkly of an 'academic proletariat', few in number, of course, when compared with the labouring classes, and certainly possessing better prospects than they did, but a striking feature of the times as well.

In zones of intense proto-industrial, and in the 1840s, early industrial development, such as the Rhineland, Saxony and, perhaps, parts of Silesia, there were at least some employment opportunities for the lower classes, albeit often at very minimal wages. The boom in railway construction during that decade offered jobs to unskilled day labourers. Historians have often noted these initial developments and frequently attributed them to the beneficial actions of the German states, whose actions in subsidizing industrial enterprises, transferring technology and technical knowledge from abroad, arranging industrial financing, sponsoring the construction of railways, and imposing protective tariffs, are said to have created a counter-model to the British version of a market-driven industrialization.

More recent scholars have cast a rather more sceptical eye on such state initiatives. Often they involved subsidizing outdated and backward technologies, such as hand-spinning and hand-weaving of linens, or charcoal forges for making iron. State tax, tariff, monetary and fiscal policy hampered the financing of industrialization, at least as much as they assisted it. Leading Prussian officials in charge of aiding industrialization, such as Peter Beuth, head of the business and industry division in the ministry of finance, or Christian Rother, director of the *Seehandlung*, a sort of state-run investment company, were both appalled by the steam-powered factories of industrial Lancashire and the proletariat working in them. The 'industrialization' they envisaged was rural, decentralized, and largely without inorganic sources of power, much closer to outworking than to the actual industrialization just beginning in the 1840s, and that would take off in the subsequent three decades.

If the role of the state in sponsoring industrialization in Germany was not all that an earlier account has suggested, the influence of industry on employment and on the whole economy in Germany before 1850 was distinctly limited. Considerably more important was emigration. German journeymen artisans, condemned to travel around seemingly endlessly, swarmed across the borders of other countries, working in Switzerland, Belgium, England and France. In the 1840s, 50,000 or one-twentieth of all the inhabitants of Paris were Germans, mostly journeymen artisans looking for work in the capital city of the country that had the largest economy in continental Europe. A further, more permanent, emigration to North America, as we noted above, grew ever more prevalent in that decade, and seemed to many like the best way out of poverty. Certainly the government officials of the Grand Duchy of Baden thought so. They resolved the problem of the impoverished inhabitants of Rineck stealing potatoes from neighbouring villages by paying for the passage of everyone in Rineck to the United States.

Given the rapid population increase and the lack of opportunities for gainful employment, summed up in the contemporary diagnosis of 'pauperization', one has to wonder about the possibility of mid-nineteenth Germany suffering an economic catastrophe of Irish dimensions. The potato blight of 1845 – 46 did produce a modest rise in mortality in the German states, and manifest hard times, but a combination of factors kept the worst from happening. Opportunities for earning a living in outworking were better in Germany (and the crisis was worst in those areas where linen-weaving was collapsing); distribution of farmland was more equitable than in Ireland; emigration had already helped take some of the poor out of the country. Finally, the power of free-market ideology was less. German governments' interventions in the market may not have done much to spur on industrialization, but by limiting food exports, subsidizing imports, selling grain from military stores at reduced prices, and remitting tax collection on the poorest inhabitants they prevented a major disaster. It was a close thing, though, and the much more massive emigration of the 1850s – about 1.1 million – testifies to the extent of the economic problems in the first half of the century.

This combination of rapidly growing population with a lack of industrialization was also typical of the Scandinavian countries in this period, and they experienced social and economic difficulties of a similar nature to those of the German states in this period. Much the same can be said about the countries of eastern Europe – the eastern portions of the Austrian empire, the Russian empire, and the Serbian and Danubian Principalities (the future kingdoms of Serbia and Romania), then under Turkish sovereignty. These were heavily rural areas, with very modest urban populations (only 9 per cent of the inhabitants of Russia's fifty European provinces lived in cities and towns in 1838), and little manufacturing or proto-industry. Most of what did exist, such as Russian iron manufacture, was technologically backward and showed little in the way of innovation or expansion. Admittedly, some

[262] mechanized textile manufacturing did begin to develop in parts of Russia during the 1840s.

Poverty was very considerable, but the basic response to it was the alms-giving of pious and charitable individuals. The eighteenth-century Enlightened tsarina Catherine the Great had secularized much of the property of the Orthodox Church in Russia, so the sort of institutional religious support of the poor still prevalent in Catholic countries of the western Mediterranean was little in evidence. Tsar Alexander I, as part of his sporadic programme for reform, had encouraged the creation of private charitable societies – in part organized, however, by state officials, and in part supported by government funds – that would experiment with more organized forms of assistance to the poor, found in western and central Europe, whether in the form of institutions such as orphanages and workhouses, or of home relief for poor families. These experiments remained just that, and as the tsar's interest in organized philanthropy waned, the experiments became ever more marginal.

In those eastern reaches of the continent, the population was not quite so dense, and even with a backward agriculture, where the new techniques of crop rotation or the planting of speciality crops were less prevalent (although not unknown, as can be seen in the growth of sugar beet cultivation in Russia, or of maize-growing in the Danubian Principalities), and where serfdom continued to exist throughout the first half of the nineteenth century, there was more land to support a growing population. This was particularly true in the Russian empire, that had become the single most populous of the European states by the early nineteenth century. In the more temperate regions of the empire, such as its Ukrainian and White Russian provinces, the amount of land sowed in grain increased by 50 per cent between 1800 and 1850. Much of the uncultivated land in Russia was too frozen to be of much use, but in the areas conquered from their Islamic rulers in the course of the eighteenth century, in the southwest of the empire, and along the river Volga, there was a good deal of available, fertile land. Population there grew rapidly, in a kind of internal emigration, in part sponsored by the tsars and the great nobles who transferred their serfs to these new territories. Overseas emigration from eastern Europe would have to wait until the end of the nineteenth century, after several more decades of population increase.

In the end, whether in the German states, or anywhere else in Europe, we have to come back to the strain of population increase in the years between 1780 and 1850. Just by itself, it put intense stress on existing social and economic structures – and that without any of the exacerbating factors of the revolutionary and Napoleonic Wars, the injustices of serfdom, or the extreme

rigours of an unchecked laissez-faire capitalism. Economic and technolo-
gical innovations, large and small, drastic and gradual, in agriculture, industry, the crafts, transport, marketing and finance, kept basic resources ahead of the increase in population, and at least pointed to, perhaps to a modest extent actually led to, circumstances in which the number of people and their level of affluence could increase together. Yet these solutions created their own social and economic strains as well, sometimes depriving many in the lower classes of the income needed to purchase their share of the growing mass of consumer goods. Without some additional ways to ease the burden – whether birth control, farming previously unused land, or emigration – the problems would probably have been too great and some of Parson Malthus's more dire predictions might well have come true.

Notes

1. Cited in M.J. Daunton, *Progress and Poverty: An Economic and Social History of Britain 1700–1850* (Oxford, 1995), p. 141.

2. Cited in Theodore Koditschek, *Class Formation and Urban-Industrial Society: Bradford, 1750–1850* (Cambridge, 1990).

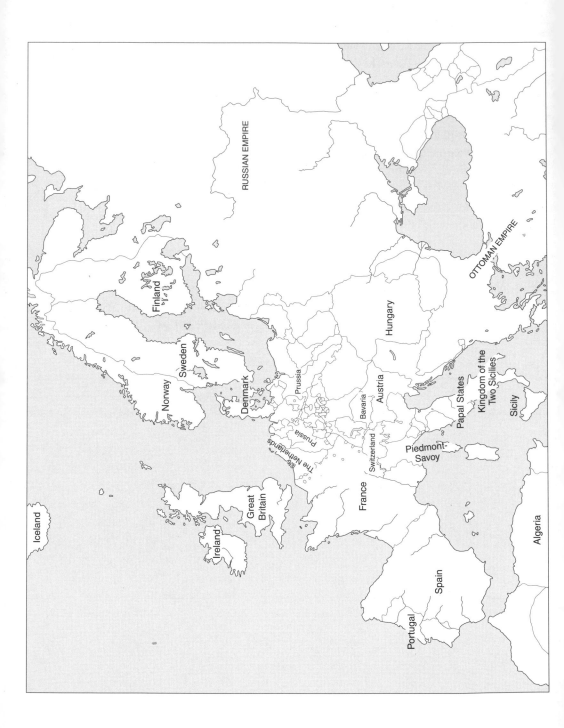

CHAPTER 6

THE SHAPES OF PUBLIC LIFE, 1815–50

The quarter-century of the French Revolution and Napoleonic rule, with its Europe-wide political and social upheaval, its insurrections, wars and civil wars, and its fundamental reforms developed, carried out in both drastic and gradual fashion, but also thwarted or revoked, marked a fundamental break with the social, political and cultural world of the old regime. Admittedly, we can trace continuities across the revolutionary divide, see new trends emerging even before 1789, and note areas, such as the economy, where the chaotic circumstances prevalent during much of the two and a half decades after the calling of the Estates General, had produced more disruption of these previous trends than far-reaching innovations. Still, it is hard to avoid the impression that the fundamental, irreversible changes taking place after 1789 outweighed the elements of continuity. Many contemporaries certainly were aware in 1815 of the gulf that separated them from the world of the 1780s; even those who denied these changes, or, more commonly, loudly proclaimed a desire to roll them back, found themselves acting in ways that demonstrated their acceptance of a new state of affairs.

Yet this new state of affairs was less a fixed social and political order than a framework for contention, in which different groups could present claims for their version of an appropriate social and political order and dispute with others, both peacefully and violently, about what that order should be. In this chapter, we will investigate this new framework, ascertaining its parameters, and noting the possibilities for contention and change within them. We will begin with the system of international relations, the world of interaction between the European states. From there, we will consider the individual states, and their relationship with their subjects. The focus then shifts from states to non-governmental organizations, as we investigate the structures of civil society. The last part of the chapter will be devoted to the motivating ideas of political action: both the three main political tendencies, and also

[266] some broader cultural trends that underlay all of them and offered models of action cutting across their boundaries.

The system of international relations

At first glance, the result of twenty-five years of almost continuous warfare might have seemed virtually nil, with relations among the European states in 1815 little different from how they had been in 1789. The Great Powers on the eve of the French Revolution – Great Britain, Russia, France, Austria, and Prussia – were still the Great Powers of the Congress of Vienna, that met in 1814–15 to devise a new international settlement after the defeat of Napoleon. In fact, if anything, the role of the Great Powers had been enhanced, since lesser powers, such as Sweden or Spain, that had still played an independent, if generally subordinate part in old regime warfare and diplomacy, were now quite excluded from such a role. Among the five Great Powers, the 'Pentarchy', as contemporaries referred to them, Russia and Austria had expanded modestly, with both gaining more territory from the partitions of Poland, and the latter enlarging its rule in northern Italy. Prussia, the smallest in population of the Great Powers, remained so, although it had gained considerable population and land in both the east, after the partitions of Poland, and in the west, when the Congress of Vienna awarded it two provinces on and near the river Rhine. Defeated France did lose its enormous Napoleonic empire but suffered no dismemberment or annexations, remaining within its territorial limits of 1790.

Yet such a surface view of continuity misses four broader and more significant changes that made the system of international relations developed at the Congress of Vienna fundamentally different from the world of the old regime, differences that would remain until the Crimean War of 1854–56 brought this system of international relations to an end. These four changes are in the role of overseas possessions and colonial rivalries in European politics; the power and influence of the tsarist empire in the European state system; the place of the smaller and medium-sized states, particularly those in Germany and Italy, in the system of international affairs; and the place of warfare and the threat of warfare in the European state system.

For almost three hundred years, throughout most of the period from the sixteenth to the eighteenth century, the colonial rivalries and overseas wars of the Atlantic maritime countries were inextricably intermingled with the continental struggles of the Great Powers. After 1815, this era of colonial competition came to an end, not to be revived until the last quarter of the nineteenth century. The French colonial empire had been reduced to a few islands in the West Indies; the Spanish empire in South America was largely dismantled by rebellious settlers. Lesser powers, such as Portugal and Holland, retained some colonies, but it was only the two major victorious Great Powers of the Napoleonic era, Great Britain and Russia, that maintained extensive extra-European possessions and military and diplomatic interests. The overseas British empire was particularly strong in the Indian subcontinent and Australia, while the southward expansion of the realm of the tsar into the Caucasus brought Russia such dubious acquisitions as Chechnya.

To be sure, as the Russians moved south, and the British north from India, the two powers threatened to meet somewhere in the mountains of Afghanistan. Much diplomatic effort went into that potential meeting or confrontation, the 'Great Game', as it later came to be called, particularly beloved of the authors of thrillers and historians of diplomacy. However, the pleasures of this great game were ones of anticipation only; it was never actually played, and the potential confrontation between the British and Russian empires remained in the realm of what might have been.

More significant for continental diplomacy was the enhanced and strengthened position of Russia. While eighteenth-century Russia had been a steadily expanding and ever more influential power, the sphere of its actions had been primarily on the eastern fringes of Europe: in the Baltic, Poland, the Balkans and the Crimea. The brief occupation of Berlin by Russian troops during the Seven Years' War had marked the very height of the westward extension of the tsar's power. The dispatch of Russian troops to Italy, Holland and Switzerland in the war of the second coalition of 1799 was an early indicator of a changing state of affairs; the active participation of the tsar's army in the final anti-Napoleonic coalition of 1813–14, which culminated with the Cossacks leading their horses to drink in the river Seine, sealed the new state of affairs. Russia would now have a say in diplomatic arrangements and potential military confrontations in the centre and west of Europe, as well as in the eastern regions of the continent.

In parallel with the rise of Russia were territorial rearrangements among the smaller states of the continent. In the east, Poland had vanished in the 1790s, swallowed up by the three partitioning powers: Austria, Prussia and Russia. The brief Napoleonic revival of a Polish state, the Grand Duchy of Warsaw, was only possible after these powers had been defeated. With their renewed victory in 1813–15, independent Poland vanished again. Changes

[268]   were less in the Iberian peninsula or in Scandinavia – although Norway was transferred from Danish to Swedish sovereignty, an event of significance primarily to the 900,000 Norwegians. The major developments were in Germany and Italy. There, many of the boundary changes of the Napoleonic era proved irreversible. The myriad of petty principalities that had made up the Holy Roman Empire were gone forever, as was the empire itself and the medium-sized German states, such as Bavaria, Württemberg or Hanover, that had gained both territory and sovereignty in the Napoleonic era, retained the better part of their gains. If there were perhaps three hundred political units in Germany in 1789, there were only thirty-nine in 1815. Napoleon's Italian creations, on the other hand, did not survive his fall, but neither were the ancient Italian city-states, such as Genoa or Venice, revived after the end of Napoleonic rule, so that the trend toward medium-sized political units existed in more modest form on the Italian peninsula as well.

The statesmen in Vienna perceived the need to provide some sort of broader international entity encompassing the German territories. They created a league of states, the German Confederation, that roughly followed the boundaries of the old Holy Roman Empire – albeit modified for post-1789 concepts of sovereignty, since the German Confederation, unlike the old regime empire, did not include the French territories of Alsace and Lorraine, or the one-time Austrian Netherlands, that had been made part of the Dutch kingdom. The Confederation was openly dominated by Austria and Prussia, the two Great Powers keeping a sharp eye on the international relations of the other German states, not offering them the opportunity to align themselves with France, as many had done both before and after 1789. In periods of political turmoil, these Great Powers monitored the domestic affairs of the other German states as well, ensuring that political changes in them did not get out of hand – a system of repression that worked reasonably well until 1848, when the domestic situation got out of hand in Prussia and Austria, making it impossible for them to act.

There was no such formal diplomatic arrangement on the Italian peninsula. Rather, the role played by the German Confederation was taken there by the Austrian empire. The northeastern provinces of Lombardy and Venetia, the wealthiest and economically most advanced portion of Italy – in the revolutionary era, the core of the Cisalpine Republic and later Kingdom of Italy – were directly under Austrian rule. Most of the other states were Austrian satellites, whose monarchs and their ministers looked to Austria for direction, and were, ultimately, dependent on Austrian soldiers for maintaining their regimes. The only exception was the small northwestern Kingdom of

Piedmont-Savoy, that strove to follow an independent course in foreign [269] affairs. The Italian states had exchanged the revolutionary hegemony of the French for the post-revolutionary hegemony of the Austrians.

A peculiarity of Austrian hegemony was that one of the Italian states that were de facto Austrian protectorates was ruled by the pope. In a period when the Vatican would be rapidly regaining authority within the church it had lost in the nineteenth century, in the context of a reshaping and potential re invigoration of Catholic religious life, the supreme ruler of the Roman Catholic Church was dependent for the existence of his political rule (the so-called temporal power of the pope), and, indeed, for his physical security, on the Austrian government. While the Austrians would not be so intrusive and meddlesome in papal affairs as Napoleon had been, nonetheless their diplomatic and military influence on the Italian peninsula would both shape and set limits to the development of the Catholic Church in the first half of the nineteenth century.

Both Italy and Germany were thus organized to reduce French influence, and this points to the third major difference between the international relations of the years 1815–50 and the periods before then. Fear of France, to be more precise, fear of a newly revolutionary France repeating its previous conquests, structured the system of diplomatic relations, set up at the Congress of Vienna. Territories in western Germany went to Prussia in 1815, to place a Great Power athwart a potential military line of advance. Outside of Prussian territory in western Germany, fortresses of the German Confederation, in Mainz and Landau, were garrisoned by Prussian and Austrian soldiers. Austria was firmly ensconced in transalpine, northern Italy, the terrain of Napoleon's first great conquests. Even the one-time Austrian Netherlands were given to Holland to keep them out of French hands.

The architects of the system of international relations devised in Vienna, particularly the Austrian chancellor Prince Metternich, did not desire a return to the circumstances of the old regime, when the different Great Powers jockeyed for position, changed alliances, and went to war, in the interests of their dynastic and territorial aggrandizement. Rather, they wished to keep the Powers fixed on the threat of renewed revolution, and the potential for a revival of the French advances of the 1790s and the Napoleonic era. Additionally, such a system might mitigate the increase in Russian power, by tying the tsar's government into a common counter-revolutionary endeavour, and preventing it from developing hegemonic aspirations of its own. In view of the potential threat from France, the other Powers were encouraged to settle their disputes short of war – which they did, until the Crimean War,

[270]   which spelled the end of the diplomatic system developed at the Congress, the termination of Russia's enhanced role among the Great Powers, and the initiation of a new period of warfare, albeit on a different basis than in the eighteenth century.

If this structure of containment, to borrow a phrase from the age of the Cold War, did work until the 1850s, it was not just because of its diplomatic alignments. The quarter-century of warfare had left the Great Powers exhausted, and heavily in debt. Austria was in the worst situation: it had had to declare a state bankruptcy, and its currency and government finances were never really put on a sound footing until the last third of the nineteenth century, but all the Powers found their means sharply limited. War was just too expensive, and even the mobilizations that accompanied the war scares of 1830 and 1840 were a substantial drain on the state budgets. Very much in contrast to the eighteenth century, that had seen one major war after another, climaxing in the altogether new intensity of warfare after 1789, the Great Powers of Europe were at peace with each other between 1815 and 1850. Even their wars against the smaller powers or their colonial ventures were few and far between. This reluctance to go to war was probably greatest in the immediate aftermath of the Napoleonic Wars; with the passage of time, military conflict became more thinkable, and almost broke out in the course of the revolutions of 1848. But while the mid-nineteenth century revolutions saw civil wars and smaller international conflicts, the feared clash between revolutionary and counter-revolutionary Great Powers never occurred, even when a major wave of revolution once again encompassed most of Europe.

The nature of the state

As explained in the first chapter, one of the main elements of most European states in the old regime had been the interplay – a relationship of both conflict and cooperation – between an absolutist monarch and his officials, on the one hand, and constituted bodies of the society of orders, on the other. After 1815, this whole, long, multi-sided ambivalent relationship, that had developed for centuries, was basically at an end. In the states of western Europe, the unitary, uniform, centralized, bureaucratic administrative system devised in the French Revolution had triumphed. Great Britain and Russia, which had already had forms of centralized administration – albeit extremely different ones – in the old regime, continued to maintain them. To be sure,

Estates, and provincial Diets did exist in some of the Scandinavian countries, in the provinces of the Prussian kingdom and the Austrian empire, and in 'Congress Poland', the largest portion of the former Polish kingdom that had been awarded to the tsar by the Congress of Vienna.

However, in a basic change from the old regime, these constituted bodies were not rivals of an absolutist bureaucracy, that kept for itself basic tasks, such as tax collection, law enforcement, conscription, devising new legislation, or setting economic policy, but were designed to complement and enhance its rule. The Diet of Congress Poland, for instance, would become a forum in which the nobility that had formerly dominated the Polish kingdom (and often vehemently opposed their monarch having the slightest power) could cooperate with their new, Russian ruler. Such a new conception of the role of the Estates reached a high or perhaps low point in the Prussian kingdom, where the monarch's bureaucrats envisaged the Provincial Estates taking up matters such as the administration of insane asylums or the provision of compulsory fire insurance for home owners, thus liberating government officials from the annoyance of having to deal with them and instead leaving them free to set policy and make laws on important issues. In all of post-1815 Europe, it was only in Hungary that the corporate institutions of the society of orders played the role of state administrator and opponent of absolutism in anything like the way they had done under the old regime. Even there, as we shall see below, this older role was gradually being transmuted into a newer one, involving different conflicts, more characteristic of the nineteenth century.

If, after 1815, the governments of most European countries were thus rid of a problem that had plagued them before 1789, they continued to face another difficulty of governance familiar from the old regime – that of trying to impose order on an anarchic society, with relatively few resources at hand. The difficulties of this task were compounded by three new characteristics of the state in the post-1815 era: the development of new arenas of governmental action, the integration of new subject populations, and the new questions of the legitimacy of their rule, a legacy of the era of the French Revolution. The combination of new and old difficulties would be a constant source of conflict.

Just as in the old regime, governments of most European countries remained fundamentally understaffed. They also suffered from chronic budget problems as a result of the weight of debts contracted during the revolutionary and Napoleonic warfare, and the uneven economic performance of the first half of the nineteenth century. Consequently, they did not have the money to hire new state servants. The frugality of the Kingdom of Prussia was notorious in

[272] this respect. Since the eighteenth century, it had required young men with law degrees who aspired to careers in the upper levels of both the executive and judicial branches of the state bureaucracy to serve an unpaid administrative apprenticeship. After 1815, the government gradually extended the term of the apprenticeship from two–three to five–ten years, thus getting additional upper-level civil servants without having to pay for them.

Such savings at the upper levels of government administration may have been a Prussian peculiarity, but there can be no doubt that state officials were few and far between at the local level in post-1815 Europe. As late as the 1840s, there was only one gendarme (rural, paramilitary state policeman) for every 3,000 inhabitants of the French countryside, while in Prussia there was one gendarme for every 7,000 inhabitants. Urban areas were only marginally better policed. France and Prussia were two of the better and more elaborately administered states in continental Europe; state officials were by no means so frequent in, say, the states of southern Italy, or in the Austrian empire. The one really well-policed state in Europe was Great Britain. With one constable for every five hundred inhabitants of Ireland, the disaffected Irish were kept well under control. Reforms in 1839 created effective and numerous police in major English cities, as well.

Under these circumstances, the chronic problems of governing, of enforcing the state's authority, that had plagued European states in the old regime, continued well into the nineteenth century. Collecting taxes and customs duties, or preserving law and order continued to be problematic tasks. The chronic banditry in southern Italy was notorious to the point where guidebooks took care to warn affluent travellers about it, and circumstances were similar in mountainous regions of Spain. Smuggling and contraventions of the forest law also flourished in such relatively well-administered and policed states as France and Prussia, and the authorities had great difficulty getting it under control. Riots and mass demonstrations presented a particular problem for state officials, since gatherings of hundreds or thousands of individuals were well beyond what the feeble police could hope to prevent, or even keep in check. Faced with such situations – which were very common in the years between 1815 and 1850 – state officials could either concede to the rioters, try to rally private citizens or subjects to their aid, or turn to the one effective means of coercion available, the use of the army. Employing soldiers for crowd control work usually just angered the crowds, escalating the confrontation and leading to larger-scale riots with substantial casualties.

In some ways the whole situation was exacerbated by a change in attitudes toward crime and punishment, between the old regime and the post-revolutionary circumstances of the nineteenth century. The widespread use of torture and capital punishment declined sharply; even whipping and other forms of physical chastisement became less common. In their place was a commitment to punishment by imprisonment, with the intent of rehabilitating offenders, rather than stigmatizing them. A group of scholars, following the work of the eccentric French philosopher/historian Michel Foucault, have argued that such a commitment to remaking an individual's morality and transforming his or her personality was really much crueller than the old regime practice of physically marking criminals as sinners by whipping, branding, torturing or drawing and quartering them. One need not agree with such a provocative and exaggerated assertion to understand that a policy of punishment by imprisonment introduced additional difficulties for law and order in the administrative work required to imprison and then to release convicted criminals, to say nothing of the additional claims on the state's resources required by a growing number of prisons and prison inmates.

A change in attitudes toward punishment was not the only difference between the old regime and the first half of the nineteenth century, that made state action chronically difficult. As a result of the changes wrought by and in opposition to the French Revolution, states in Europe found themselves active in a far greater variety of areas than had been the case before 1789. A prime example was conscription, which was universal in continental Europe after 1815. Young men all too often showed strikingly little desire to serve, and the yearly draft call and visit of the recruitment staff, complete with a registrar, brandishing a list of all those eligible and physicians to examine them, was met by young men running off into the forests or the hills to avoid their grasp. Of course, merely compiling such a list of young men implied a bureaucracy able to count and sort out the population, and to register vital events, yet another task taken on by the state. Such an interest in statistics grew into a broader commitment to acquire, evaluate and sometimes even publish data, particularly about the economy. Collecting figures on foreign and domestic trade, on employment and output, on the use of steam engines or handlooms required more government activity, as well as the cooperation of a suspicious population, that might not be inclined to understand the difference between census-takers, tax-collectors, and the conscription registrar.

Even in areas where the central government played no direct role, it supervised local authorities and developed legal frameworks in which they had to act. This was the case with – to name three important arenas of action that directly affected large portions of the population – rules governing the use of forest land, elementary education, and poor relief. All of these areas involved

[274] a certain degree of coercion – from requiring parents to send their children to school, to limiting the cutting of trees and requiring that particular species be planted, to placing impoverished families in workhouses – and all generated a good deal of ill will, that sometimes turned into demonstrations and riots, once again requiring state action.

Hard enough as all this was, the issue of the legitimacy of governmental rule made actions by the authorities even more difficult. As a result of the territorial rearrangements of the revolutionary and Napoleonic era, followed by those of the Congress of Vienna, a growing portion of the inhabitants of central and southern Europe found themselves living under different rulers than they had been previously – frequently under a rapid succession of different rulers. Previous attachments, generated by living under the same dynasty for generations, had vanished. When rulers changed at such a rapid pace, why obey yet another one? Such a strained relationship between a monarch and his new subjects was at its most tense when the two belonged to different religious confessions. The Catholics of the Rhineland and Westphalia, Prussia's acquisitions in western Germany at the Congress of Vienna, were not particularly happy about their new Protestant monarch and his equally Protestant bureaucrats and officers. Catholics of the former Austrian Netherlands, ruled by the Protestant king of Holland, Catholics of the one-time Polish kingdom under the sceptre of the Orthodox tsar, or Protestants of northern Bavaria, ruled since the Napoleonic era (and its changes sanctioned by the Treaty of Vienna) by the Catholic Wittelsbach dynasty, were other examples of such a new and difficult situation.

The political heritage of the French Revolution contributed yet another factor to this potential crisis of legitimacy. If nothing else, the experience of the quarter-century of dramatic political change had suggested that monarchs could only rule with some form of consent by their subjects, that the latter required some kind of representation. Since the constituted bodies of the society of orders, the old regime form of representation, had either been abolished or reduced to an agency of absolutist rule, the expectation of some form of parliamentary representation and a charter or constitution to guarantee it, was widespread. The conflict over the creation of a charter or constitution, and over the exercise of powers of the different branches of government, when such a document existed, was chronic in Europe between the end of the Napoleonic era in 1815, and the outbreak of the revolution of 1848. Admittedly, interest in constitutional questions was primarily to be found among the urban, better-educated and more affluent population, a distinct minority everywhere, and, in the eastern and southern reaches of Europe, quite a small group. Peasants did not know or care much about charters or the balance of powers, and the urban lower classes – with exceptions in Great Britain, and the larger French cities – were generally not terribly interested.

However, as noted above, the lower classes did experience a whole range of conflicts with the state: over taxes, conscription, smuggling, use of the forests, workplace issues and many other everyday matters. While generally not understanding sophisticated theories of constitutionalism and representative government, they nonetheless had a keen sense of legitimacy, and were likely to reject the claims to obedience of monarchs and their officials if they lacked long-term ties of dynastic and confessional loyalty. If circumstances arose in which educated and popular demands for legitimacy in government were brought together, then the upshot would be a major crisis of the regime, and the potential for a new revolution. In the years around 1820, 1830 and 1848, such a juncture of these different demands would occur, to a greater or lesser extent, and in quite different countries each time, producing the three periods of revolution and near-revolution, characteristic of the whole era from 1815 to 1850.

In many ways, the changes in the nature of the state in Europe between 1780 and 1850 are not all that dissimilar to the changes in the nature of the economy, discussed in the previous chapter. Just as in the economy, there was a broad movement towards the increasing influence of the market and market relations, we can note a similar broad movement in government towards a unitary state, free of the old regime dualism between absolutist monarch and constituted bodies of the society of orders. But also just as most economic change was gradual, involving the improvement of production and marketing techniques first developed in the old regime, so the governments of most European countries continued to wrestle with old regime problems, in particular the inability of a seriously understaffed government bureaucracy and police force to enforce the law and maintain orderly conditions. Finally, just as the economic situation throughout Europe generally remained precarious in this era, as production and distribution just kept a little ahead of the growth in population, with different kinds of economic crises periodically making this evident, so the legitimacy of the state remained precarious as well, with recurring bouts of revolution and near-revolution a testimony to that state of affairs.

In fact, we can connect these similar developments in the economy and the state to suggest something of the nature of the years 1815–50. They were a time when governments were making greater demands on their subjects, claiming more of their obedience, their time, and their physical and economic

[276] resources. Such demands had developed primarily during the era of the French Revolution and the continent-wide warfare it brought about. However, after the return to peace in 1815, things did not revert to pre-1789 conditions; rather, the new and intrusive demands of the government on the population continued. They continued at a time when, as a result of economic restructuring, most ordinary people had fewer physical and economic resources, or thought that they did. Finally, this was a period when previous conceptions of political legitimacy had been shattered by the upheavals of the French Revolution, and widely accepted new ones had not yet been put in place. Consequently, claims of the state were likely to be more fiercely resisted. All of these factors working together would make the period between the Congress of Vienna and the middle of the nineteenth century an era of political movement, of domestic insecurity and instability. Such political movement would require ways for people to organize and associate, to mobilize themselves for action. This is the next topic of the chapter.

The structures of civil society

Civil society is a concept developed in the Enlightenment, particularly by Scottish philosophers and economists, such as Adam Ferguson and Adam Smith. In the first half of the nineteenth century, it was an idea that reached continental Europe, providing a key concept for figures such as the German philospher G.W.F. Hegel. Although rather fading from view after 1850, it was revived in the 1970s and 1980s by eastern European dissidents, as a way to express their criticism of the late phase of communist rule, and from there has come back into increasingly common use in western Europe and North America. It is particularly helpful for understanding the potential for various forms of political action in Europe between 1815 and 1850.

The eighteenth- and nineteenth-century theorists of civil society took as their starting point the end of the corporate society of orders. Membership of corporate groups, such as guilds or the three orders, had been compulsory in the old regime, generally patriarchal and hereditary in nature – and certainly legally required, although, paradoxically, these corporate groups were constantly feuding with the royal authority of the absolutist state. Corporate groups both cemented distinctions of inequality between each other and among their members and also prescribed much of their members' behaviour – just think of the way that guilds tried to regulate output, members of the nobility were prohibited from engaging in many commercial and industrial occupations, or commoners, in some countries, from owning noble estates. This state of affairs was already dissolving in eighteenth-century Great Britain and was forcibly destroyed in most of western, and some of southern and central Europe by the French Revolution and its aftermath.

In place of the corporate society of the old regime, there was now a clear distinction between the state that made the laws, on the one hand, and the public realm of the economy and society where individuals acted freely and of their own accord, within the framework that the laws provided for them. Civil society was that realm of voluntary action, free from the restrictions of the society of orders. Sometimes, the concept was used primarily to consider the economy, the area of the increasingly free market; at other times, and this is how it will be used here, it was to delineate the space for social and political action. Civil society was where individuals communicated with each other, expressing and debating their ideas, and then went on to form organizations and associations, voluntarily joining together to implement their ideas. There were three pillars of civil society, three foundations for its structure of debate, organization and action: the periodical press, voluntary associations, and public meetings.

In many ways, the press was the weakest and shakiest of these three pillars. Print-runs were modest; individual issues quite short; and their appearance was infrequent. Small-town newspapers, appearing once a week, might manage a few hundred copies; those appearing in larger urban areas might have three to six editions per week, with a press run of 3,000 to 5,000. The very largest, such as the Parisian daily *Le Siècle*, with a press run of 20,000, the *Northern Star*, the weekly national newspaper of the Chartists, the British radicals of the 1830s and 1840s, with as many as 40,000 copies, were very much the exception.

There were major technological obstacles in the way of expansion. Type had to be set by hand, and this would limit considerably the length of the newspaper, twenty pages being about the maximum possible for a daily. Printing was also usually done by hand, minimizing the possible press run. Introduced in Great Britain during the 1830s, the steam press would eliminate this bottleneck, but, like most other industrial technologies, it was just beginning to reach continental Europe during the 1840s. Political barriers to the spread of newspapers, though, were far higher than technological ones.

In most of continental Europe, from the beginning of the 1820s to the outbreak of revolution in 1848, the press was subject to prior censorship. That is, the state authorities had to approve, in advance, all newspaper copy.

[278] Even printing a censored journal often required a government licence, and such licences were granted sparingly. In Great Britain, and those continental European states with better established constitutional governments, such as France, the Low Countries, or Switzerland, newspapers were not subject to prior censorship, but they faced other state-made obstacles to their circulation: a stiff tax on each copy, creating, for instance, the British 'stamped press', newspapers with a tax stamp, set at such a high level that few people could afford to purchase them. There were licensing requirements, and strict libel laws, rigidly enforced, so that even in regimes with legally or constitutionally established freedom of the press, the press was not really all that free.

Besides technological and legal bottlenecks, the periodical press was also restricted by cultural ones. Overall, only a minority of adults in Europe were literate, and many of those who could read and write were uncomfortable with doing it on a regular basis. Newspaper reading was skewed toward those with the time, money and education for such a pastime: the reading public, who made up 'public opinion', was heavily male, urban, and middle and upper class.

With all these limitations, one might wonder why the periodical press was significant in any way at all. The basic answer is that there was a way around each of the limitations mentioned above. Press runs were small and publications infrequent, but each copy of a newspaper went through many hands. It was not just individuals who subscribed to newspapers, but groups, such as clubs or societies, and businesses, like bars and cafés, spreading the considerable cost of one copy across a wider range of individuals, and encouraging group readership of the press, with individual articles read out loud, to accompanying comments and debate.

Censorship was a more serious problem, but journalists and editors found ways to smuggle their opinions past the censor, in guarded or Aesopian language. If nothing else, they would print their issues with white spaces, where the censor had cut out articles – a practice promptly prohibited. Ostensibly non-political periodicals, such as the religious press, economic or scientific and medical journals, often discussed political themes, that, had they appeared in daily newspapers, would have been subject to more rigid censorship. Journalists could set up shop just across the border, and defy the censor. Inhabitants of Prussia's Rhineland province could and did read newspapers printed in Luxemburg; enterprising publishers in Leipzig did a big business printing works prohibited in the neighbouring Austrian empire and then smuggling them over the border. In general, the censors were less concerned with news from other countries, so that a regular perusal of a foreign newspaper would legally provide information that could not be found in a domestic one.

While the literate may been a minority in Europe before the middle of the nineteenth century, their numbers were expanding. The years between 1815 and 1850 saw a distinct increase in elementary education in much of western and central Europe. It was, admittedly, not of the highest quality, with class-rooms of seventy and more pupils, taught by poorly trained teachers. In a money-saving British innovation, the younger children were 'taught' by the older ones, who were very loosely supervised by an adult. The curriculum was heavily weighted toward religion – songs, Bible stories, and the catech-ism – while basic reading and writing skills did not get the attention they deserved. Still, this educational effort was not without some effect, and, by the 1840s, as many as 90 per cent of the adults in Scandinavia could read and write; perhaps 75 per cent in the British Isles and the German states, and 60 per cent in France or Belgium. Literacy rates in southern and eastern Europe, at between 5 and 30 per cent of the adult population were much lower, and everywhere more men could read than women, but there was clearly an upward trend, so that the potential audience for the press was becoming steadily larger, and socially more diverse. The development of a workers' press in France and the British Isles during the 1830s, periodicals written for, and sometimes even by, manual labourers, is testimony to the growing potential for interest in public affairs.

Such changes were least pronounced in rural areas; even individual copies of newspapers remained few and far between there, limited primarily to the priest or pastor, or perhaps the unusually intellectual schoolteacher or enter-prising innkeeper. Still, other forms of printed matter, particularly broadsheets, circulated in the countryside. One-page fliers, with a little text and lots of pictures, sold by wandering pedlars, usually known under their French name of colporteurs, offered rustics some view of important current events, such as wars or revolutions – mixed in, admittedly, with accounts of two-headed calves, axe murders, and other popular but lurid details. They were a poor substitute for the press, but they did exist.

If we consider the periodical press between the Congress of Vienna and the outbreak of the revolutions of 1848, in comparison to earlier and later periods, we are more likely to be struck by its limitations. While the press was both more widespread and informative than the crude news sheets of the old regime, the energy and diversity of the press during the early days of the French Revolution was not present; nor were the enormous press runs, in the hundreds of thousands, of the state-subsidized newspapers during the Jacobin republic. The second half of the nineteenth century, particularly its last quarter, a period of much more advanced communications and printing technology, a

[280]   much less restrictive legal environment, improved education, and more widespread affluence, was, in comparison, a golden age of the press. Newspapers were everywhere; most adult men read one daily; and press runs of the leading dailies could go from six to even seven figures. In the developing civil society of European countries during the first half of the nineteenth century, newspapers had a more modest and limited, if nonetheless important and steadily increasing role.

Of the three pillars of civil society, voluntary associations were by far the largest and sturdiest; their significance in this period is hard to overestimate. The simplest way to demonstrate this is to survey the different kinds of associations that existed, along with their membership and the tasks they performed. From there, we can consider the distinct place of voluntary associations in Europe in the years 1815–50, as compared to both previous and later periods.

One basic form of association was the social club, whose members met regularly in rented rooms, or, if they were particularly well off, in a building they owned, to eat, drink, converse, play billiards, read newspapers, and, generally, just socialize. Such groups were almost always the domain of the notables, the locally most influential men. 'Public opinion', basically, the attitudes of the notables, was shaped in and by such groups, through conversation and newspaper reading. Business deals were arranged, policies for municipal government formulated, larger issues of the day discussed. Particularly in periods of increasing politicization, say in the 1830s and 1840s, these groups might split along political lines, with different social clubs for adherents of different political positions. The notables were the locally most influential *men*, and membership of such groups was exclusively male. However, these associations would regularly hold festive dinners or dances, with a mixed-sex company, such proceedings also being the main forum of the marriage market for young people from the notables' families.

Segregation by social class was in some ways stricter than by sex. Men who were not among the most affluent or influential would not be accepted as members of these social clubs, and could not have afforded the membership dues, in any event. However, they did not usually found their own: ordinary people and almost all inhabitants of rural areas socialized informally in taverns, and at fairs and festivals. These provided plenty of chances for socializing, both exclusively among men, and between the sexes, but offered fewer opportunities to form a public opinion, or to prepare for common action. There was one interesting exception to this rule, in parts of southern France, an area of particularly dense and concentrated settlement, where even farmers lived

in proto-urban villages with several thousand inhabitants. There, 'chambrées',
social clubs for craftsmen, shopkeepers and peasants became increasingly
common. To be sure, probably more drinking (generally of cruder, cheaper
and stronger alcohol than among the elite) went on in them than among the
'circles', the social clubs of the French notables, and less reading of newspapers or discussion of politics. Nonetheless, in this one exceptional case, the
lower and middle classes were able to make use of a form of voluntary association very prevalent among their social superiors.

A variation on the social club was a society devoted to cultural or intellectual ends: to the support of the arts, the promotion of local history, or the
understanding of developments in the sciences. Sometimes social clubs did
these as well; other associations were devoted to all these ends at once, as was
the case with the 'Museum Societies', common in early nineteenth-century
Germany: not societies devoted to museums, but clubs where the muses, the
classical deities of the arts and sciences, held sway. Like social clubs, membership of these culturally oriented societies was generally confined to the
notables, but was typically open to women, and women would be invited to
attend the cultural activities of otherwise all-male social clubs.

Even in these sorts of groups, men made up the majority of the members.
There was one form of elite-oriented voluntary association that was a predominantly or exclusively female realm: charitable societies, devoted to helping the poor, the sick, new mothers, or infants and children. Such organizations
were one of the few ways that women of the upper classes could meet and act
publicly. However, since such groups were often, although not always, religious in nature, and enjoyed church sponsorship, women had to share the
organization, planning and initiative with male members of the clergy. Probably such groups, and women's more general participation in public life were
most extensive in Great Britain. It was certainly there that women's participation in groups devoted to charitable and virtuous purposes came to have the
most influence on public policy, above all in the many organizations devoted
to the abolition of the slave trade, a movement with strong church support
and prominent female participation.

If these groups devoted to sociable, intellectual, cultural and charitable
purposes were a domain of the notables, there was another, very widespread
kind of voluntary association that was characteristic of the urban lower and
middle classes, the mutual benefit or friendly society. This involved a group
of individuals who would pay regular dues and receive, in return, the money
for a funeral on their decease and, sometimes, funds for consulting a physi-
cian, and purchasing medicine – in a few cases, even some money to make up

[282] for lost income – when they were ill. The group might even provide more immediate solidarity, with members tending sick comrades, or, especially, joining in their funeral procession.

These groups were everywhere in urban Europe during the first half of the nineteenth century. As early as 1803, there were almost 10,000 such organizations in Great Britain, with 700,000 members; although comparable figures are not available for other countries, there can be little doubt that, by the middle of the nineteenth century, membership reached into the millions, across the entire continent. Sometimes these societies were confessional in nature – among Catholics a religious brotherhood under the patronage of a saint; among Protestants and Jews, a Bible-study or prayer group. Other such associations were formally or informally limited to members of specific crafts, testifying to their links with the master artisans' guilds and the journeymen artisans' brotherhoods of the old regime. Still others were neighbourhood-based, or accepted any reasonably healthy person who would pay dues. While membership was most common for men, women could join as well. Craftsmen and unskilled labourers were the most typical members, but people from the lower middle class, such as clerks, shopkeepers, even lower-level civil servants, might also join, or form societies of their own.

Such organizations provided a modest amount of assistance at difficult times, when there was no income coming in, due to natural causes. Might they, or similar groups, have offered help during other kinds of hard times, such as periods of unemployment, or even provided a way to improve working people's earnings? Such a change or expansion in function would involve crossing the boundary from mutual benefit society to trade union, a move that was simultaneously a step from public activities, carried out in accordance with the laws, to clandestine, illegal action. In all of continental Europe, unions and industrial actions, such as strikes, were strictly prohibited in the first half of the nineteenth century, with a brief exception, during the revolution of 1848.

Consequently, much of this potential working-class organization was hidden or camouflaged; we only know about it when it burst into the open, as happened in France in 1833, a year of upsurge in strike activity, with about seventy such labour conflicts. Officers of an otherwise legal mutual benefit society, open to journeymen in a particular craft might be arrested, for making demands – say for better pay – on the employers in their trade. As this last example suggests, the lines between legal and illegal activity, between mutual benefit funds that the authorities and the upper classes endorsed, and labour conflict, that they did not, were very blurred.

In particular, it is hard to tell unions of the years 1815–50 from the jour- neymen's brotherhoods of the old regime. The latter were illegal organizations that had helped journeymen artisans travel around the country, largely by seeking out arrangements with friendly innkeepers, and supported them in their quarrels with the masters who employed them, although all their activities were within the context of the society of orders, in which journeymen might hope to become masters themselves, one day. Such groups continued to exist in the first half of the nineteenth century, still illegal, still helping journeymen travel around the country, still sometimes intervening in their quarrels with masters, and still practising their old regime rituals. In France, these groups, known as 'compagnonnages', were divided into three rival societies, whose members would wear distinctive clothing and, on meeting members of rival groups would engage in bloody brawls, leaving the losers with cracked skulls.

Yet these organizations were also gradually changing: while still helping their members travel around the country, some members of the compagnonnages dropped their internecine feuds to concentrate on opposing the masters. They would accept married men as members, an impossible idea in the corporate world of the old regime, where marriage was supposed to coincide with becoming a master and setting up one's own business. If the members preferred to keep up their brawling, then dissidents would secede to form their own organizations devoted to these more modern ends. In this way, slowly and irregularly, in a process at least partially hidden from view, because it was all illegal, journeymen's societies moved from being organizations on the fringes of the society of orders to groups within the newly formed civil society. When legal circumstances changed, as they did during the revolution of 1848, these organizations could and did emerge into the open.

In Great Britain, such a transition was both further advanced and more evident, above all because unions were legalized in 1824–25. Even before then, many of the mutual benefit societies were, illegally, engaging in trade union-like activities. There was even an effort, in 1819, to unite workers of all the different London crafts into an organization called the 'Philanthropic Hercules', whose name alone points to the close connection between mutual benefit societies and nascent unionism. Legalization brought with it a burst of activity, including unions in craft trades, such as the carpenters and joiners (formed in 1827) and in new industrial enterprises, like the cotton spinners (formed in 1831). There was even the Grand National Consolidated Union, in 1834, that was to be a nationwide organization for workers in every trade and industry. Its connections with radical politics, however, brought the

[284] authorities down on it, and it collapsed. British unions remained largely craft-based, although well organized and nationwide in scope, with perhaps 100,000 members in the early 1840s. In all respects – number of members, supra-regional extent, and degree of organization – this was far beyond anything on the continent, and demonstrates the pioneering role of Great Britain in the creation of the institutions of civil society.

This pioneering role can also be observed in other kinds of association devoted to the furtherance of economic special interests, formed by members of other social classes. The classic example of this kind of association, both to contemporaries and to historians, was the Anti-Corn Law League, the British group of the 1830s and 1840s that launched and sustained a massive, nationwide campaign for the repeal of the Corn Laws, the tariffs on imported grains. It would be hard to point to similar groups in continental European countries; only with the revolution of 1848, can we see even the beginnings of nationwide organizations devoted to economic special interests.

Somewhere in between economic special interest groups, clubs for social and cultural purposes, and even trade unions, lay associations for social reform. Once again, this was primarily a British speciality, and organizations devoted to the abolition of the slave trade, improvement of public education, to reforms in sanitation and public health, to improvement of conditions in the industrial workplace, were ubiquitous in the UK. There were a few similar groups in continental European countries. In the 1820s, such associations had briefly flourished in Russia, under the patronage of Tsar Alexander I, but when he lost interest in them, they went into rapid decline, only accelerated by the general hostility toward all organizations shown by Alexander's successor Nicholas I. Toward the middle of the century, as interest in the 'social question' mounted, we can see another wave of founding of social reform associations, such as the ponderously named 'Central Association for the Welfare of the Working Classes', in the Kingdom of Prussia, that was created in 1844. About the same time, a number of organizations devoted to child welfare, focusing on the children of the urban poor, began appearing in France and the Italian states.

The leading role of the British Isles in the formation of these institutions of civil society deserves some comment. In part, it reflects social and economic developments. Transport and commerce were much better developed in the United Kingdom than in continental Europe; the extensive networks of railways, canals, and turnpikes, already quite elaborate in the 1830s, and on a truly national scale in the following decade, enhanced by telegraphs, facilitated the creation of organizations and associations with a national scope.

The regional webs of economic ties connected with industrialization also facilitated the interchange of ideas, individuals and organizations. Yet this can hardly be the whole story: locally oriented voluntary associations were more common in Great Britain than on the European continent, and even in the early decades of the nineteenth century, before the industrial revolution transformed communications and transport, voluntary associations of all kinds were far more prevalent in the British Isles than in continental European countries.

Another crucial difference lay in the legal and constitutional structures that shaped the activities and goals of voluntary associations and, more broadly, the nature of the emerging civil society. The hand of the state lay much heavier on voluntary associations in continental Europe than it did in the British Isles. While broad legal restrictions on the formation or activities of associations did not exist in Great Britain (although even there, laws would be passed prohibiting explicitly political associations, if the country's rulers saw their politics as sufficiently subversive), in the rigidly absolutist regimes of Russia and Austria, such organizations were prohibited outright, or only allowed in exceptional cases, often with explicit royal patronage, and on a very local level. Even in countries with charters and legislatures, typical of much of western and central Europe, especially after 1830, forming associations generally required some sort of government approval, that was granted with greater or lesser willingness, depending on the individual countries and their current political circumstances, as well as on the membership, goals, and nature of the association.

The most sensitive kind of association, and the last one to be considered in our survey, was the one devoted to explicitly political ends. Here, once again, the United Kingdom was, in many ways, in the vanguard of organized activity. Within Great Britain, the development and activity of political associations was most pronounced in Ireland, centred around the Dublin barrister Daniel O'Connell. The Catholic Association he founded in 1824 to campaign for the abolition of British legislation discriminating against Catholics (among other things, not allowing them to sit in Parliament or hold most government offices), distinguished itself by developing a mass membership. By lowering dues, the 'Catholic rent', as O'Connell called it, to as little as a penny per month, and using the parochial structure of the Catholic Church to collect them, the Association gained a six-figure membership and a quite sizeable income, that O'Connell and its other leaders could use for their political campaigns. Having reached his goal, with the law on Catholic Emancipation, passed by the British Parliament in 1829, O'Connell would attempt to repeat his success, on a wider scale, a decade later, with the Repeal Association,

[286] devoted to repealing the union of Ireland and England, and creating, in effect, a politically autonomous Ireland. Ultimately suppressed by the British government, and never achieving its aim, the Repeal Association nonetheless represented an unprecedented step in mass political activity.

Just as Jacobin radicalism of the 1790s had been stronger and more widespread in Ireland than in any other part of the British Isles, so O'Connell's were the largest and best-organized examples of mass political associations in the British Isles in the second quarter of the nineteenth century. (Also as had been the case in the 1790s, Irish emigrants were very active in English radical political associations in the 1830s and 1840s.) Certainly, the largest political association in England and Scotland during this period was the Chartists, the supporters of a 'People's Charter', a democratic constitution. While Chartists were to be found in over a thousand towns and villages, their organizational structure was less well developed than was the case with Daniel O'Connell's groups. The Chartists were more a federation of local associations, loosely tied together by a small cadre of prominent national leaders, and could never achieve either the level of financing or the coordinated and relatively well-directed policies of their Irish counterparts.

There is something that we should note about all these groups. Neither the Chartists nor the Irish political associations were political parties. In contrast both with the Jacobin clubs of the French Revolution, and with parties as they would develop in the second half of the nineteenth and the twentieth centuries, these groups had little or no contact with parliamentarians or with the process of electing them. Rather, they were extra-parliamentary associations, devoted to bringing down, or, at least, totally reforming, the existing political system. Those operating within the system – the politicians and parliamentarians – did not have these sorts of mass association. They were united in parliamentary caucuses and were connected to their constituents primarily through informal contacts with the notables. We can see in the life of Daniel O'Connell this contrast between mass associations working outside and against the parliamentary system, and politicians, parliamentarians and their notable friends within it. In the 1830s, when he was not leading a mass political association, he was deeply involved in parliamentary politics, trying to unite the Irish MPs in the Parliament at Westminster into an effective political bloc.

However, while the mass associations of British politics and the parliamentarians of British politics were two separate, distinct – and often mutually hostile – groups, Parliament and parliamentarians were nonetheless the object of mass associations, the focus of their political activity: these groups directed extra-parliamentary actions in order to pressure Parliament into

changing the law. It is precisely the existence and recognized and institutionalized power of a legislative body that provided the framework for British
political associations, even when these associations were made up of individuals excluding from sitting in or voting for Members of Parliament.

In continental Europe, the sorts of political association found in the British Isles, with mass membership and a nationwide scope were unknown for
most of the period under consideration. At most, one might see loose ties
between parliamentary deputies and local notables, endorsed by a portion of
the periodical press, as was true of French liberals opposing the conservative
regime in the second half of the 1820s. However, even these relatively limited sorts of political association were relatively uncommon, for they required
both a parliament – not found in much of Europe – and a relatively tolerant
attitude on the part of the government authorities toward such associations,
which was even less common.

Instead, organized political life in continental Europe in the years 1815–
48 took two major forms: the crypto-political association and the secret society. The first were groups devoted to aims that were not necessarily directly
political, but nonetheless had important political ramifications. Examples of
such groups would include the phil-Hellenic societies, organizations that
offered support to the Greeks fighting for their independence from the Ottoman empire in the 1820s, or the so-called 'free congregations', Unitarian
churches that were common in Germany during the 1840s. In the first case,
the sympathizers with the Greek insurgents made little secret of the fact that
their sympathies extended to changes in the political life of their own countries; in the second case, advocating different religious doctrines in countries
with an established state church invariably involved an interest in changing
the political system, as well as the religious one so closely tied up with it.

While crypto-political groups generally tried to act within the law, although
often meeting with the hostility of the authorities, and their frequent prohibitions, secret societies were both overtly political and equally overtly illegal:
groups organized for the purpose of arranging the violent overthrow of the
existing political system. The largest and perhaps most famous of these groups
was 'Young Italy', the secret society organized in the early 1830s by Giuseppe
Mazzini, beginning what would be a four-decades-long career as a republican revolutionary. His group may have had as many as 50,000 clandestine
members throughout the Italian peninsula. Of course, a clandestine group
with so many members would not stay clandestine very long, and illegal
secret societies generally ran into a contradiction between their aims and their
means: to be effective at opposing repressive, usually absolutist regimes, they

[288] needed a large membership, but a large membership invariably included police informers, allowing the authorities to uncover and break up the secret, conspiratorial organization.

The golden age of secret societies was the decades of the 1820s and 1830s; they flourished particularly in Spain, Italy, and, to a lesser extent, France. Indeed, we might note a certain geographical distinction, with crypto-political associations more common in central and northern Europe, and secret societies in the southern and western parts of the continent, although there were certainly secret societies in Germany – or even England – and crypto-political associations in Italy. An example of such a group was the Congress of Italian Scientists, whose members met yearly to discuss scientific issues, but whose scholarly proceedings usually included concealed or implicit demands for changes in the governments of the Italian states, and an end to Austrian rule in the northern portion of the peninsula. What is certainly the case is that before the revolution of 1848, political associations in continental Europe simply could not compare in scope, membership, or activities with their counterparts in Great Britain. This would change, and change drastically during the 1848 revolution. With the heavy hand of the state gone, political mass associations would emerge throughout the continent, on a scope and scale not seen since the days of the Jacobin clubs during the French Revolution.

All these considerations might lead us to understand the years 1815–50 as a heroic age of voluntary associations. In constrast to the old regime society of orders, with its many compulsory and corporate groups, and an only occasional presence of voluntary associations, such as masonic lodges or reading clubs, the post-1815 age was a period in which the idea and the practice of associating on a voluntary basis for a wide variety of common ends spread widely and broadly, shaping the nascent civil society of property owners. Admittedly, there were some limitations on the triumphant march of clubs and societies: they remained uncommon in rural areas, and in eastern Europe; governments exercised tight control over their actions and were quick to engage in prohibitions. Organizations were mostly local in scope; supra-regional initiatives were difficult to create and maintain; their efficiency was limited. Paid professional staffs and well-developed organizational structure – making groups more effective, if, admittedly, more bureaucratic – would have to wait for the second half of the century. It was legally difficult to found explicitly political groups, and even where such groups existed, their relation to the political process was often unclear or irregular. Yet even with these limitations, the groups were widespread, and when there were favourable political circumstances, as was often the case in Great Britain, and in continental Europe during the revolution of 1848, explicitly politicized forms of voluntary association truly came into their own.

Voluntary associations were crucial to the construction of the third pillar of civil society, the public meeting: an organized and orderly gathering, open to a broad range of participants, for the purpose of discussing and acting upon matters of public concern. Such meetings might lead to the founding of an association, or, perhaps more commonly, might be organized by a voluntary association. The range of topics that might be discussed at a public meeting were many and various: from forming a ladies' association to provide charitable assistance to the infant children of poor mothers, to a discussion of the interest of inhabitants of a city in having a planned railway line come through their town, to calls for legislation on particular economic issues, such as, for instance, protective tariffs, to the demand that the existing regime be completely transformed or face being overthrown. The circumstances of such meetings were equally varied: inside or outdoors, with a small group in attendance, or a crowd of tens of thousands; with sedate and measured debate, or passionate and violent speeches; thoroughly within the bounds of the law, or quasi-insurrectionary in nature.

Once more, Great Britain shows the greatest development of this aspect of civil society. There were countless, smaller, localized public meetings, a typical example of which would be those held in the manufacturing city of Birmingham in the course of 1825 to found an 'Infant School Society', that would sponsor education for the children of the working class. After a founding meeting, the organization held several additional public meetings to present its plans, ask for funds, and mobilize the ladies of the city's middle and upper classes to participate. The British Isles also saw public meetings at their most massive. Daniel O'Connell's two associations specialized in holding very large public gatherings, where tens, sometimes even hundreds of thousands were in attendance. The groups synchronized meetings, holding them on the same day and the same topic in many different parts of the country. Such gatherings reached extraordinary large portions of the population; about half the entire population of Ireland is said to have attended public meetings of the Repeal Association.

At such meetings, the participants heard 'The Liberator' denounce British rule in such fierce terms, and issue scarcely veiled threats of potential insurrections – although O'Connell himself was always firmly committed to nonviolent and legal tactics – that the authorities finally prohibited what was to be the largest of his meetings in Clontarf in 1843 and brought him to trial on charges of conspiring to overthrow the government. The Chartists, the

[290]   Anti-Corn Law League, and other oppositional groups, held mass meetings on a similar scale.

There were, occasionally, similar mass gatherings on the European continent, such as the 'National Festival of the Germans', held in 1832 on the grounds of a ruined castle, in the village of Hambach, in the extreme southwestern tip of Germany. The 30,000 participants (or at least those standing near the podium) heard speakers denounce the existing German governments, call for the institution of basic liberties, such as freedom of the press, and the creation of a unified German nation-state. Yet the upshot of the meeting suggests something of the difference between continental Europe and Great Britain. The authorities of the Kingdom of Bavaria, on whose territory the meeting took place, arrested its organizers and prohibited the 'Press and Fatherland Association' that had sponsored it. Members of this group, reorganizing themselves as a secret society, launched an abortive revolutionary insurrection in the city of Frankfurt, the following year.

In general, mass meetings closely connected with political opposition that were sometimes (if not always, as Daniel O'Connell's experiences show) tolerated in Great Britain, were not permitted in continental European countries. If they occurred, it was usually in a period of revolution, such as the Hambach festival, which was the last manifestation of the revolution of 1830, or were precursors to a revolution. This was the case with the 'banquet campaign' of 1846–47 – oppositional mass meetings, loosely disguised for legal purposes as banquets – launched by the opposition to the French monarchy, that led directly to the revolution of 1848, the overthrow of the monarchy and the proclamation of a republic. In the course of the 1848 revolution, public meetings of all sorts would become virtually daily occurrences, at least in urban areas, and would even take place in the countryside.

In other words, these sorts of meetings occurred in continental Europe during periods when the government was no longer entirely in control of public order. When the authorities were in control, they were suspicious of public meetings, would not tolerate those with explicitly political ends and were generally wary even of meetings with politically more innocuous agendas. Certainly, meetings of any kind held out of doors, with a large crowd in attendance, were instant objects of suspicion.

In looking at the press, voluntary associations and public meetings, these pillars of the emerging civil society in Europe during the first half of the nineteenth century, we can point to three main factors influencing their growth and development. One was economic and technological: the availability or lack of mechanized printing technology, for instance, or the development of

networks of communication, transport and economic exchange, that facilit- [291]
ated the expansion and spread of voluntary associations. A second involved
social structure and associated intellectual attitudes: the stronger the remnants
of the society of orders and the ways of thinking about it, the weaker the
institutions of civil society. A vigorous urban middle class, both professional
and entrepreneurial, was central to all three forms of civil society; urban lower
classes emerging from the mental universe of the old regime and coming to
grips with a capitalist society were important as well, as we can see best in the
remarkable spread of mutual benefit societies, somewhat less in trade unions.
Finally, the nature of the law was of great importance: legal or constitutional
guarantees of freedom of the press, freedom of association and of assembly,
or their lack; the existence and power of a legislative body that could act as
the focus for and object of many different kinds of debate, organization and
action. In all these respects, the British Isles were well ahead of continental
Europe (as had been the case in the eighteenth century, as well), and on the
continent itself, we can see the development of civil society becoming progressively more rudimentary as we go from west to east and north to south.
In comparison to circumstances in the second half of the nineteenth century,
civil society remained only modestly developed. Still, overall and everywhere,
the years between 1815 and 1850 were a period in which all three of the
pillars of civil society were built steadily higher and placed on ever-firmer
foundations.

The ideologies of political action

If the French Revolution of 1789 marked the beginning of the modern patterns of political life, in particular the emergence of a left–right spectrum on
which political views could be placed, the years 1815–50 saw the elabora-
tion and completion of this development. In the first half of the nineteenth
century, the terms 'conservatism', 'liberalism' and 'radicalism' came into
common use as the way to describe the three main divisions of the political
spectrum. The consolidation of these three positions involved a process of
reflection upon the course of the French Revolution and an effort to draw
lessons from it for the future. As we consider the content of these positions
we need to keep in mind the context in which they emerged. Although the
division of the political spectrum into conservatives on the right, radicals on
the left, and liberals somewhere in the middle (sometimes closer to the left,

[292]   sometimes to the right) continues to shape the way we understand politics today, the meanings of conservatism, liberalism, or radicalism in the first half of the nineteenth century were very different from what they are at the beginning of the twenty-first.

Conservatism

On the right were the conservatives, the group that rejected the French Revolution. Indeed, the deeply traumatic experience of the revolution and its Napoleonic aftermath had united members of very different and previously often mutually hostile groups – bureaucrats and nobles; supporters of absolutism and of the powers of the Estates; the religiously orthodox, the heterodox, and even some adherents of the Enlightenment; Protestants, Catholics and eastern Orthodox – in a common political standpoint. The events of the years 1789–1815 had, for conservatives, laid bare the folly of the revolutionaries, and shown the vacuity of some of their key assumptions: that new political and socioeconomic orders could be created by reasoned debate, that there existed universal human rights, that governments should be moulded to protect and preserve these rights, and that human beings were equal in their possession of these rights. To these universalist and rationalist ideas, conservatives counterposed the triad of legitimacy, hierarchy and patriarchy.

More narrowly understood, legitimacy was the policy developed at the Congress of Vienna and articulated by the Austrian chancellor Prince Metternich, Europe's main conservative statesman between 1815 and 1848. It represented a guarantee of the continued rule of existing sovereigns, and opposition to any change in their rule, be it by revolution, or by military conquest related to revolution. But in the broader sense, legitimacy implied for conservatives an emphasis on tradition and continuity. States and societies were living, organic entities, that had grown over time in a process of long-term accretion; revolutions, and other drastic interruptions in this process, would only lead to disaster. Each country had a different history and its unique traditions could not be encompassed in a universalizing document, such as the Declaration of the Rights of Man. The prominent Russian conservative intellectual, Nikolai Karamzin, author of a best-selling (by Russian standards anyway) multi-volume *History of the Russian State*, that analysed its historical traditions, and powerfully advocated their continuation in the present, strongly opposed the musings of Tsar Alexander I about granting a constitution for Russia, declaring in 1818, 'Russia is not England . . . autocracy is its soul'.[1]

Conservative dislike of the Declaration of the Rights of Man did not stop [293] at the rationalist, Enlightened and universalizing principles of the document; its assumption of a basic human equality was equally abhorrent to them. In early nineteenth-century conservative thought, human society was constituted by a series of hierarchies: monarchs over their subjects; nobles over commoners; lords over serfs; masters over journeymen; paternal heads of household over their dependents. Those on the lower level of such hierarchies owed their superiors loyalty and obedience; those set above them had the duty to care for them and also to correct them, if they acted falsely. Such chastisement could be physical in nature, and conservatives would distinguish themselves by their support for corporal punishment, and their general belief in the need for obedience and order. Joseph de Maistre, the Franco-Italian conservative political theorist, a particularly influential figure in the 1820s, once asserted that the hangman was the foundation of all society.

The conservative hierarchy, it might be noted, bore more than a passing resemblance to a patriarchal family. And, indeed, conservative theorists often understood the family as a model for society and government. Karl Ludwig von Haller, the Swiss conservative, who invented the phrase 'the Restoration', to describe his political ideals (a phrase which has become the name for the 1815–30 era), envisaged society as a conglomerate of families, with authority going to the adult male heads of household. At the top was the monarch, whose relation to his country was that of a paterfamilias to his household. Conservatives could often, if not always, describe their social hierarchies in patriarchal terms: the lord as father to his serfs, the master craftsman as father to his apprentices and journeymen.

All three characteristics of legitimacy, hierarchy, and patriarchy had, for conservatives, a common foundation: they were divinely blessed. Legitimate monarchs, they asserted, ruled by the grace of God; a union of 'throne and altar', the close alliance of monarch and established church, was a crucial conservative principle. The established church would bless the absolutist monarch, who, in turn, would rule on behalf of the church. As Don Carlos, the conservative pretender to the Spanish throne explained, absolutist rule was necessary, for the 'glory of God and the prosperity and splendour of his Sacred Religion'.[2]

Such divine grace was by no means limited to political rule: in conservative thought, lords commanded serfs as fathers did their families, by divine privilege. Conservatives understood the social and political order they endorsed as a being a direct consequence of Christian, revealed religion, as a repository of divinely inspired truth. If one's own views are those of the Lord,

[294] then opposing ones are unacceptable and inquitous; there could be no room for tolerance, or freedom of opinion. Faced with the alternative of choosing between Christ or Barabbas, the Spanish conservative Donoso Cortès sneered, liberals would form a committee.

Such views made conservatives of the first half of the nineteenth century particularly strong opponents of constitutional monarchies – to say nothing of republican regimes, that conservatives were likely to see as the spawn of Satan – whose creation, or preservation was one of the major political issues of the era. As the Prussian king, Frederick William IV, a prominent if, at times rather eccentric conservative, announced shortly after coming to the throne in 1840, he would never approve a constitution, never let 'a piece of paper', come between him and his people. Prussia's historic traditions could not be subsumed in an abstract legal document like a constitution, and its conservative ruler was no more inclined to rule his land with a consitution than a father would rule his family with one.

Conservatives generally favoured the retention of guilds, serfdom, and other aspects of the corporate society of orders. These were, after all, the products of historical development and long tradition; the inequalities inherent in them were divinely sanctioned; and they represented – or could be claimed to represent – a patriarchal form of social organization. Conservatives viewed with suspicion, and often alarm, the growth of the institutions of civil society. For the very same reason, conservatives tended to be distinctly critical of the growing trend toward freer markets. They regarded the general laws that economists claimed ruled the market with the same scepticism they had toward other universalizing doctrines. Market relationships were not patriarchal in nature and they were certainly not divinely sanctioned, as a glance at the New Testament would make clear. Characteristically, conservatives denounced 'political economy', the name contemporaries give to pro-free market economic doctrines and called, in revealing phrases, for their replacement by a 'moral economy', or a 'Christian political economy'. Indeed, some conservatives made a career out of denouncing capitalism and industrialization, coming to anticipate later attacks on it of communists and socialists. The so-called 'Tory radicals' in Great Britain carried these sentiments into practical politics, with their calls for labour-protection legislation and bitter attacks on the distinctly non-patriarchal (and not very Christian) New Poor Law of 1834. At the beginning of the twenty-first century, when 'conservative' generally refers to someone who is, above all, an advocate of unlimited free markets, it requires a real effort of will to realize that the original conservatives generally held quite different social and economic views.

If the ideas of legitimacy, hierarchy and patriarchy united conservatives, there were three areas where differences – perhaps best seen as differences of emphasis – in their interpretation could divide them. One such area was the nature of legitimate authority. While rejecting the political principles of the French Revolution, early nineteenth-century conservatives were unsure about which aspect of old regime government to emphasize – the absolutist monarch or the Estates. The Prussian king Frederick William III (ruled, 1797–1840), for instance, basically wished to rule via his state bureaucracy, like an old regime Enlightened absolutist, only without any Enlightened ideas or policies. By contrast, his son Frederick William IV, like many other conservatives, distrusted the state bureaucracy, seeing it – not entirely incorrectly – both as riddled with officials of liberal sympathies and also contradictory to conservative principles. Did fathers rule their households with a tenured civil service? Was administrative efficiency a tenet of revealed religion? A similar tension developed in France after 1815, as conservatives in the restored Bourbon monarchy disputed among themselves about whether to use for their own purposes the centralized administrative bureaucracy created by the revolution and Napoleon, or to destroy it and return to a France of provinces and Provincial Estates.

Because corporate bodies were largely subordinated to absolutist monarchs after 1815, rather than being at their throats, as was sometimes the case in the old regime, the tensions between these two versions of conservatism remained relatively muted. The other two differences of emphasis tended to be sharper. One concerned the proper attitude toward the heritage of the French Revolution. Should conservatives insist on rolling it back completely, on returning to the world as it was before 1789? This was an extreme position, and its advocates in France were known as the 'ultras'. Others, and here the figure of Austrian chancellor Metternich is paradigmatic, realized that such an effort would itself be disruptive of order and discipline, and likely to lead to new revolutions. For such more pragmatic conservatives, the main political task lay in limiting the influence of and trying to shape in a conservative direction the effects of the institutions left behind by the French Revolution, the dynamics of the free market, and the nascent civil society.

A third and final difference of emphasis was on the altar side of throne and altar. Since conservatives believed strongly in legitimacy, tradition and divine sanction and opposed sharp breaks and disruptions in the social fabric, there developed in conservative thought a strong tendency to see the Reformation as the initial break in Europe's social and political fabric, the point at which sinful humans rebelled against the divine plan, and everything went

[296]   downhill toward the Reign of Terror. Conservatives from Catholic countries naturally adopted such an argument; indeed, it was first developed in France in the first decade of the nineteenth century. (Most Russian conservatives, generally strong proponents of Orthodoxy, tended to condemn all western versions of Christianity, whether Catholic or Protestant, as subversive.) However, a surprising number of Protestants found it hard to resist. Karl-Ludwig von Haller decided that the Reformation was 'the most complete picture and predecessor of today's political revolution', so he found it necessary, as a conservative, to convert to Catholicism, He was joined by a number of prominent Protestant German conservatives, including Friedrich Karl von Savigny, the most important conservative legal scholar, and Friedrich Gentz, the leading conservative political theorist and Metternich's close advisor, all of whom found the argument that the Reformation was the root of all revolutionary evil, impossible to resist. Other Protestant conservatives, including Prussia's king Frederick William IV, toyed with the idea of converting, but never did.

However, other Protestant conservatives rejected this idea and clung to their country's confession. Supporting the privileged position of the Anglican Church was one of the main preoccupations of conservatives in Great Britain and their defeat with Parliament's passage of Catholic Emancipation in 1829 was the sign for the end of four decades of almost uninterrupted Tory rule. Russia's Tsar Alexander I, Napoleon's great enemy, gathered around himself a whole circle of conservative thinkers from different European countries and Protestant, Catholic and Eastern Orthodox backgrounds, who found ways to tie their right-wing political conceptions to all of their religions. After 1815, this tsar tried to sponsor a 'Holy Alliance', a union of European monarchs from different Christian confessions, to oppose godless revolution. Characteristically, the tsar's efforts primarily brought a vigorous reaction from dignitaries of the Orthodox Church, objecting, among other things to the ecumenical distribution of Bibles by Alexander's supporters. The Orthodox clergy vigorously pressed their case, and by the end of Alexander's reign in 1825, had largely rolled back the ecumenical version of conservatism and replaced it with a more narrowly Orthodox one.

It is hard to avoid seeing the general thrust of conservatism in the years 1815–50 as defensive, as directed against the political changes set loose by the French Revolution, against the progress of the market and of the institutions of civil society, in favour of preserving all that remained of the pre-1789 society of orders. Supporters of conservatism would be found among the proponents of the post-revolutionary status quo: a central and eastern European aristocracy anxious to keep its remaining privileges; high state officials;

at times, master craftsmen who clung to the remnants of the guilds. Theirs [297] was a difficult task, and in the years 1815–48, as both the market and civil society made steady progress, and the heritage of the French Revolution was ever more developed, conservative politics seemed in steady decline. However, nineteenth-century conservatives were also the party of God, and they could find adherents among the pious and devout from all walks of life, particularly, although by no means exclusively, among the rural population. This potential support among the faithful would prove to be conservatives' political ace in the hole, one that would stand them in good stead, after the revolutionary events of 1830 and 1848 seemed to have confirmed their worst fears.

Liberalism

If conservatism was defined by its rejection of the French Revolution, liberalism in the first half of the nineteenth century was characterized by a cautious assent to the revolution, especially its early, moderate and monarchical phase of 1789–90, that, additionally, seemed to resemble the political world of Great Britain after the Glorious Revolution of 1688 – another potential model for liberals. Against the conservative affirmation of legitimacy, hierarchy and patriarchy, liberals counterposed ideals of individualism, equality and property. Public life was, for liberals, an arena in which self-reliant individuals, enjoying a guaranteed equality of rights, interacted voluntarily, within the bounds set by the law – a law designed by property owners, that would guarantee individuals' acquisition and retention of property.

Liberals saw government as emerging from the process of rational debate and deliberation, exercised by self-reliant individuals. Basic legal rights enabling such a process to be carried out, such as freedom of speech, the press, association and assembly were fundamental to liberal conceptions of government. However, the exercise of these rights in order to govern required self-reliance and independence. Women, by their biological nature and their role in the process of reproduction, dependent on men, had to be excluded from this process, as were men who did not own enough property to support themselves or their familes. For being without sufficient property meant earning a wage by working for someone else, and so being dependent on him.

Like conservatives, liberals thus wished to see government in the hands of a minority of the population. However, unlike rightists, liberals did not see this minority as determined at birth (at least for men) or by a place in the hierarchy of the society of orders. Potentially, all adult men, exercising their

[298] self-reliance, could garner enough property to gain their independence and role in government. François Guizot was one of the leading figures of the liberal post-1830 regime in France. When critics denounced the regime's rigid property qualification for voting, that restricted the franchise to about 5 per cent of adult men, Guizot replied, 'Enrichissez-vous!' (Get rich, and you too can participate in public life.)

Liberals strongly opposed any social and legal inequalities that might be placed in the way of a self-reliant individual's buying, selling and disposing of property in the attempt to get rich. Serfdom, and any other limitations on the free disposition of land and labour in the countryside, guilds and other restrictions on the free choice of occupation, residence or marriage, were inappropriate and needed to be abolished. Adult men would thus be free to exercise their self-reliance, although women and children would not. Liberals' conception of family life was strongly patriarchal. In contrast to conservatives, however, whose similarly patriarchal conception of family life was a model for broader social and political relations, liberals restricted patriarchy to within the family, and saw public life, in which adult, male heads of households interacted, as run on very different principles.

Liberals took very seriously this model of a society of families, headed by legally equal, self-reliant adult male heads of household. The post-1832 liberal governments in Great Britain showed how this principle could be carried to truly extreme ends. The New Poor Law of 1834 ensured a humiliating fate for those adult men who were not self-reliant, and for women and children who had no self-reliant adult man to support them. An even more determined application of this liberal principle can be seen in the response of the British government to the terrible potato famine in Ireland, over the years 1845–49. Rather than infringe on the self-reliance and independence of the Irish, by giving them food, the authorities allowed about one million of them to starve to death.

At the beginning of the twenty-first century, when 'liberalism' is often associated with social welfare programmes, it requires a certain intellectual effort to understand that nineteenth-century liberalism was quite different – orientated toward free markets and individual efforts and self-reliance, rather more like today's conservatives. Liberals of the early nineteenth century believed in equality of rights and formal equality of opportunity. A classic liberal slogan of the era was the phrase originally associated with Napoleon, 'the career open to the talents'. Occupations, in other words (and this slogan referred particularly to employment with the government), should not be restricted by criteria of heredity or order, but should be available to anyone who was competent and qualified. Of course, such an equality of opportunity was purely formal: people from poor backgrounds were much less likely to have a chance to receive an advanced education or to accumulate property than those from affluent ones. The transition from a nineteenth-century free market liberalism to a twentieth-century social welfare liberalism began to occur around 1900, when this consideration became more important to liberal thinkers and liberal politicians, who slowly began to consider social welfare programmes and other ways to make such a formal equality of opportunity a more real one.

While conservatives sought a union of throne and altar, and insisted that their political opinions were divinely sanctioned, liberals generally sought to detach religion from public life, by calling for the equality of citizens of all confessions before the law. Particularly in the Catholic countries of southern Europe, liberals were strongly anti-clerical, although rather less so in the Protestant lands of the northern part of the continent. Everywhere, though, liberals looked to education as the intellectual and spiritual basis of their programme, as conservatives did to revealed religion. Education, particularly elementary education for children of the lower and middle classes, would help to instil liberal principles in the population, destroying traditional ideas of hierarchy or dependence.

Liberals generally saw the ideal state for their social vision in a constitutional monarchy, so much so that in much of the period under consideration, liberals in continental Europe were known as 'constitutionalists' or 'constitutional monarchists'. A constitution would guarantee the basic rights that liberals saw as essential for the process of open political debate and decision-making, as well as the existence of an elected legislature, with decision-making authority. However, the ideal liberal government was a constitutional *monarchy*, in which an hereditary, royal executive power would be opposed to the legislature. These two branches of government, each with an independent source of power, would counterbalance each other, and thus lessen the strength and effectiveness of government, an idea known in the English-speaking world as the doctrines of 'separation of powers' and governmental 'checks and balances'. Similar ideas, under different names, were common in continental Europe.

Such a government, in which the executive and legislative branches checked each other, would be unable to oppress the population and take away its rights and property. Liberals, drawing on the experience of the French Revolution, contrasted this situation with two forms of unipolar government: a monarchical absolutism, where there was nothing to check the power of a potentially despotic executive, and a Jacobin, republican regime, where an elected legislature

[300]   held all powers, including the appointment of members of the executive. In this situation, as the events of 1792–95 seemed to indicate, there was no check on the power of the majority of legislators. Since the first alternative was one potentially favoured by conservatives, and the second, by radicals, liberals could and did define themselves as men of the middle, the '*juste milieu*', as Guizot said, the partisans of liberty and property against differing forms of extremist despotism.

As with conservatives, agreement among liberals on basic points of political doctrine could go along with differences in emphasis on specific issues. While liberals might agree that public affairs should be reserved for independent, adult men, there was a fair amount of difference about how to interpret independence. In practice, this difference of opinion had to do with the franchise. Some liberals demanded a stiff property qualification, leaving just a small fraction of adult men eligible to vote; others wished to lower the property limits, and, at a time when the owning of small amounts of landed property was still quite widespread, have, in effect, a more democratic franchise.

More difficult for liberals was the relationship between the vision of a society of self-reliant adult men and the belief in a free market in land, labour, and capital. What would happen if the result of the unhindered operation of the free market was to reduce, steadily, the number of adult men who were independent, property owners? This was not just a theoretical question, but one that seemed to be increasingly the case as the result of socioeconomic developments in the decades after 1780. Some liberals in southern Germany began to argue against a free labour market, demanding a retention of the guilds, so as to prevent a drastic increase in the number of adult men who were not economically independent. The liberals of the Grand Duchy of Tuscany, in central Italy, wanted to see the region's primarily agricultural and crafts economy preserved, arguing that industrialization on the British model only led to an ever-growing mass of propertyless proletarians. Although regionally dominant, adherents of such attitudes were probably a minority among liberals in all of Europe. However, coupling the free market with the idea of a society of property owners meant accepting an increasingly plutocratic vision of society and government, a tendency that definitely grew stronger among liberals, between the early and the middle decades of the nineteenth century.

A final difference that could be mentioned concerned the idea of free trade. It was a hallmark of the liberal movement in Great Britain, and the Anti-Corn Law League, with its strident demand for the abolition of tariffs on imported grain, was, for contemporaries, the very quintessence of British liberalism. In continental Europe on othe other hand, the idea of free trade received a more sceptical hearing. The main protagonist of this sceptical opinion, whose ideas were broadly followed on the continent (and, in more recent years, in East Asia) was the German economist Friedrich List. List argued that free trade was fine, if conducted between countries of equal levels of economic development. When, however, a technologically and economically more advanced country, such as Great Britain, traded freely with other lands, then this free trade would tend to reinforce the more backward status of Britain's trading partners. List called for tariffs to protect countries' nascent industrial enterprises, until they could reach the level of the more advanced lands and then be in a position to trade freely with them. For many liberals, particularly in central and eastern Europe, who saw industrialization and economic development as necessary steps to bring to an end the old regime society of orders, and to institute a regime of civic equality, this argument was a convincing one.

The same developments of the years 1815–50 that conservatives found dismaying – the spread of the market, the growth of the institutions of civil society, the reinforcement of the constitutionalist political principles associated with the French Revolution – were encouraging to liberals. Nonetheless, for much of the period (the exact times differing in different countries), political power was in the hands of men of conservative ideas, and the government and legal system ran along conservative lines. Thus, the first half of the nineteenth century might also be called the oppositional or heroic phase of liberalism, when liberals used the institutions of the emerging civil society to try to bring about changes in the government.

The many associations and societies formed in this era were often centres of liberal ideas and liberal sentiments. It was, above all, the notables who were members of such groups and liberalism was, primarily, a movement of the notables, of the property-owning and educated middle class, including in the latter category many civil servants, thus confirming conservatives' worst fears about them. In southern Europe, and in Russia, there were a suprising number of army officers among the liberal ranks. During this oppositional and heroic phase of liberalism, the liberal opposition to absolutist rule and to the society of orders, and the anti-clerical hostility to established religion, attracted support and interest from beyond the ranks of the notables: from smaller property owners, women, and the lower classes. Liberals were ambivalent about this support: it certainly helped them in their struggles against conservative or absolutist regimes; yet it also involved the political participation of individuals who were not self-reliant, who could not be counted on to have the right ideas about the preservation of property and the expansion of the free

[302]   market, and who were thus not appropriate for the process of governing as liberals understood it.

Ideally, most liberals would have preferred that the existing conservative or absolutist rulers gracefully abdicate, or accept the liberals' political principles. This liberal vision of a peaceful political transition, not involving violence among the lower classes – whose consequences, as the events of 1789 showed, could be very problematic – was actually accomplished in Great Britain, with the passage of the Great Reform Bill, in 1832. A similar triumph evaded liberals of the major countries on the European continent; to ensure the victory of their political principles they would have to take their chances with revolutionary violence – as they did in 1820, 1830 and 1848. The results were mixed, but, overall, they showed that the liberals' reservations were well justified: a political doctrine calling for the rule of the notables, the locally most influential men, was not well adapted to a revolution, a situation of mass political participation.

Radicalism

Turning to radicalism, the most left-wing of the three main political tendencies of the first half of the nineteenth century, we find the group that endorsed unreservedly the most militant of the doctrines of the French Revolution. If the conservatives were the party of God, and the liberals the adherents of the rule of the notables, then the radicals were the supporters of liberty, equality and fraternity. We might also counterpose to the conservatives' legitimacy, hierarchy and patriarchy, and the liberals' individualism, equality and property, radicals' dedication to popular sovereignty, republicanism, and solidarity.

For radicals, legitimate political power was not constituted by tradition, divine sanction or the need to preserve property, but by the will of the people. A legitimate government would, therefore, be one that provided basic civil rights, freedom of the press, speech, association and assembly, for these were the ways in which the people's will could be expressed. However, such a government would also have to have the people's sanction, as expressed, democratically, in universal manhood suffrage. This insistence on democracy was a characteristic element of radicalism in Europe in the first half of the nineteenth century.

For radicals, such popular sovereignty was antithetical to the idea of hereditary monarchy. Radicals were thus republicans – a daring and fundamentally contrarian stance in post-1815 Europe, where the preservation of legitimate monarchical authority formed the very basis of the international order and the only non-monarchical governments, the Swiss cantons, and the German city-states of Frankfurt, Hamburg, Bremen, and Lübeck, ruled over small areas and exercised a very modest sovereignty. By contrast, the envisioned radical republic would be a strong state, with just one focus of sovereignty and political action, a democratically elected legislative and/or executive authority. At best, radicals might accept a figurehead monarch, who was a nominal head of state, but had only ceremonial duties, while political power was concentrated in a democratically elected parliament. Yet even that was asking a lot, for most radicals of the post-1815 era preserved the Jacobin tradition of visceral hatred of kings and their retinue of aristocratic supporters.

It goes without saying that radicals of the first half of the nineteenth century believed strongly in equality under the law, and opposed serfdom and other such remnants of the society of orders. Like supporters of other political positions, they had a basically patriarchal vision of the family, and, with few and rare exceptions, did not believe that women should have the vote or play an autonomous role in public life. There was a tendency among radicals, however, to endow women's domestic labours with political importance. As mothers, women would have to raise their children to be good citizens of a republican and democratic state. Republican households, some radicals continued, could not be petty monarchies; the paterfamilias should view his wife as comrade and adviser, rather than as his serf.

Radicals of the first half of the nineteenth century generally went beyond the idea of equality (at least for adult men) before the law, to advocate a government that would incorporate some form of social solidarity, that would, in some way, act to improve the conditions of the lower classes. Exactly what these measures would be, or how they were carried out, was generally not entirely clear, and the social and economic programme of radicals in Europe was usually vague. This is very much in contrast to twentieth-century radicalism, which has largely been defined by its social and economic programme. In the first half of the nineteenth century, radicalism was, above all, political, concerned with changing the nature of the government.

Particularly after about 1830, though, as the pace of social and economic change accelerated, and the 'social question', the issue of the effect of such change on the urban lower classes, became more salient, radicals devoted more time and effort to social and economic affairs. Even then, they often continued to cast the issue in primarily political terms, asserting that a change in, say, taxation, or an end to wasteful corruption, or a drastic pruning of the size of 'the standing army of soldiers and officials', to quote one popular phrase

[304] from the revolution of 1848, might be the solution to the problem. When radicals took up explicitly social and economic programmes, they were extraordinarily varied, ranging from a belief in the free market, along the lines of contemporary liberals, to an interest in producers' cooperatives, to calls for an alliance of producers – capitalists and workers – against parasitic aristocrats and landowners, or another alliance of producers – in this case, employers and workers – against parasitic moneylenders and financiers, or ideas of nationalization and economic planning, derived from the nascent socialist movement. Common to all of these very different and sometimes mutually contradictory concerns was the belief that only a democratic government, a regime of popular sovereignty, preferably a republican one, could take the necessary steps toward a programme of social reform. In a slow process, still just getting under way at the middle of the nineteenth century, radicals were moving from being 'republicans' to 'red republicans', from 'democrats' to 'social democrats', radicals for whom the social question was a matter of major importance.

To complete our survey of radical political doctrine, we need to note two more of its features. One was anti-clericalism: like the liberals, but much more so, radicals were powerful opponents of established religion. Particularly in the Catholic countries of Mediterranean Europe, this anti-clericalism was downright anti-Christian, and radicals would regularly curse and sneer at the clergy, make fun of public religious rituals, such as processions, or even throw rocks at the participants. There was some of this outspoken anti-clericalism in Protestant countries as well, but radicals there often adapted Christianity toward their ends, invoking a rationalist, republican or socialist Jesus, who preached a gospel of liberty, equality, and fraternity. It was a unique feature of the English-speaking world (there were similar developments in Scandinavia, although generally later in the nineteenth century) that radicalism and revealed religion could be reconciled, and even there, devout Protestant radicals would not be members of the Anglican state church, but of dissenting Methodist or Baptist congregations.

This attitude toward Christianity was just one of a number of ways that the radicalism of the first half of the nineteenth century appeared as the successor to the Jacobinism of the French Revolution. Some radicals saw themselves as continuing this Jacobinism, largely unchanged: sporting the Phrygian cap, praising Robespierre, cheering the guillotine. Others, however, understood their politics as an improvement on or updating of the radicalism of the 1790s. Giuseppe Mazzini, for instance, influential as a radical theorist and political leader throughout Europe, and not just in his native Italy, argued that the radicalism of the 1790s had been individualist in nature, and centred [305] in France, while the radicalism of the nineteenth century that he advocated involved association, and would be centred in Italy.

Radicalism was very much an outlaw movement in Europe during the first half of the nineteenth century: sometimes tolerated in Great Britain, at times partially tolerated in France, Spain, Switzerland and the Low Countries, but basically illegal in central and eastern Europe. In these circumstances, the characteristic form of radical political organization was the secret society. While such groups were occasionally formed by supporters of liberal and, on rare occasions, even conservative ideas, it was radicals who made up the vast majority of such associations and their members, in this respect continuing a trend begun with Babeuf and his 'Society of Equals', in the second half of the 1790s.

In some ways more than the other two main political movements, radicalism changed its nature over the years 1815–50. From the end of the Napoleonic empire to the revolution of 1830, the period of conservative dominance in Europe, radicals and liberals were both in opposition to the existing regimes and not always easy to tell apart. Radical mass movements did develop in the British Isles during these years, but on the continent, radicalism was confined to small groups of conspirators, many of whom were former or even current soldiers and government officials, continuing a trend begun in the later years of the French Revolution. Indeed, in continental Europe, radicalism was closely associated with aging veterans of the revolutionary period, or members of their immediate families, containing a strong element of reminiscence or nostalgia.

The 1830 revolutions and the more peaceful reform movements in Great Britain both brought liberals to power in much of western Europe and also began to make the distinctions between liberals and radicals a good deal more apparent. Hostilities between them, covered up in the years of conservative domination, began to emerge. These years also saw something of a generational transition, as younger people, with no memory of the decade 1789–99, gradually came to the fore among radical activists. Rather than being characterized by elderly revolutionaries' nostalgia for the great days of 1793–94, post-1830 radicalism became associated with youthfulness, with visions of the future. It is no coincidence that Mazzini named his secret society 'Young Italy', and that he explicitly looked to young men as the vanguard of his planned revolution in the Italian peninsula. In terms of social composition as well, younger men from the urban lower class, particularly journeymen artisans, became increasingly active in radical secret societies. This change matched the growing interest of radical leaders in the 'social question'.

By the 1840s, radicalism was, potentially, in continental Europe what it had become in Great Britain: a political mass movement. Making the transition from a movement organized around secret societies to one acting openly and seeking the broadest possible support was a tricky business. In particular, radicals had little or no experience in dealing with farmers, a majority – often a substantial one – of the population in continental Europe. Much of the history of the revolution of 1848 would involve radicals' efforts, with varying degrees of success, to meet this challenge, to turn a movement for popular sovereignty into a popular movement, to make the striving for democracy democratic.

The cultural dreams of totality

Although contemporaries in the first half of the nineteenth century increasingly thought of politics in terms of a spectrum reaching from right to left, and this still provides the best way for us to approach the politics of the period, such an understanding then – as well as at later times – is incomplete. There were political movements whose founders and adherents understood themselves as moving into another dimension, transcending the world of left and right. Important cultural movements also affected all political tendencies of the years 1815–50, giving them a distinct cast, that they did not have in the era of the French Revolution, and would not have in the second half of the nineteenth century. Common to all these developments was the search for totality, the desire to create (some contemporaries would have said to recreate) a unity of meaning and purpose in response to the perception of unsettling political and socioeconomic change. There are four major examples of this search for totality in this period that we might wish to consider: romanticism, ultramontanism, nationalism, and socialism or communism, the latter including feminism, which was closely associated with it.

Romanticism

Historians, art historians, literary critics, and musicologists have often debated the nature of romanticism and its relation to other cultural movements. For our purposes, romanticism is best understood as a cultural style, certainly, perhaps primarily, found in the arts, but apparent in other forms of intellectual activity and in public life as well. It developed in contrast to its predecessor, classicism, and we can see the relationship between the two in terms of a

series of dichotomies. Classicism emphasized elegance, restraint and proportion; in romanticism, authenticity, desire, and dynamism had priority. Classicism was about universals and the universally valid; romanticism was about the
individual; in classicism, a detached attitude was cultivated; romanticism was
all about passions and ineffable longings and, more generally, the expression
of strong emotions. Classicism favoured the human-shaped environment,
romanticism the individual's communion with wild and untamed nature.
Classicism looked to the pagan world of classical antiquity for intellectual and
aesthetic models; romanticism to the Christian world of the Middle Ages.

While the transition from classicism to romanticism as the dominant cultural style came in the decades around 1800, the exact timing and extent of
the change differed considerably from country to country, and from one art-
istic or intellectual field to another. Among the arts, romanticism dominated
in music. Virtually all the major composers in the first half of the nineteenth
century – and well on into its second half – composed dramatic-sounding,
striking works, with strong tonal contrasts. Particularly in music, however,
although in other fields of the arts as well, the romantic and classical cultural
styles could overlap. Mozart, for instance, was the great classical composer,
while Beethoven was the epitome of a romantic one, but the late music of
Mozart and the early music of Beethoven sound strikingly similar.

The visual arts were another area where the romantic style was predominant, and artists such as the German Caspar David Friedrich or the English-
man Joseph Turner turned out powerful landscapes with wild, mountain, forest
or ocean scenes, often dominated by mysterious, cloudy skies. Individual
human figures in them, dwarfed by wild nature, gazed into the unknown and
infinite distance. Architecture was also affected by romanticism; churches,
particularly, but secular public buildings as well, were built as imitations of
Romanesque churches or Gothic cathedrals. Here, however, the classical style
was not quite so completely eliminated, and structures built on the models
of classical antiquity, such as the British Museum or St Isaac's Cathedral in
St Petersburg, remained present on the urban scene. Some aspects of interior
design, such as the Biedermeier style, prevalent among the German middle
class roughly in the years 1825–50, were characterized by simplicity and
elegance in the classical tradition.

Romanticism was certainly the dominant trend in literature throughout the
first half of the nineteenth century, whether in the form of the German author
Hölderlin dedicating himself to the mysterious powers of the night, the Russian
Alexander Pushkin writing poems based on medieval folk tales, or the English
poet William Blake seeing the world in a grain of sand. Romantic authors

[308]   often seemed larger than life, because they lived the passions they exalted in their writing, leaving their spouses or claiming someone else's when their heart allowed them no other choice, dying tragically in duels, or descending into insanity, as a conclusion to their life's work. However, the dominance of the romantic style in literature was not quite so complete as it was in music or the plastic arts.

In part, this was because classicism never entirely lost its adherents: the Olympian figure of German letters in the era of romanticism continued to be the classicist poet, essayist and novelist Johann Wolfgang von Goethe. In addition, the hegemony of literary romanticism was challenged from the 1820s onward by a new style, that of realism, with its project of faithfully (one might say photographically) and often cynically, representing human life, rather than exemplifying either classic or romantic ideals. If realism would only become the dominant literary style in the second half of the nineteenth century, authors such as Stendhal or Charles Dickens were already writing that way before 1850, and literary figures sometimes identified with late romanticism, such as Sir Walter Scott, or the Italian novelist Alessandro Manzoni, often had a strong realist bent in their writing.

Much the same was true of the relative roles of the romantic and classicist styles in what we might today call the humanities and the social sciences, then largely a branch of literature. The brothers Jacob and Wilhelm Grimm, important founders of the scholarly discipline of philology, or, as we might say today, historical linguistics, did their work by collecting folk tales, stylistically crude but authentic expressions of the genuine folk. Other romantics, such as the German poet Clemens von Brentano or the Norwegians Peter Christian Asbjørnsen, Jorgen Engebretsen Moe, or Magnus Landstad, made similar collections of folk tales and ballads. Post-Kantian German philosophers, such as Fichte and especially Schelling, articulated the quasi-mystical unity of the individual and the universal; historians, such as the Frenchmen Jules Michelet and Alphonse de Lamartine, described a past stirring with passion and longing. Yet here as well, classicist models survived: very much like Goethe, the Olympian figure among German philosophers in this romantic era was the very classicist G.W.F. Hegel. In contrast, the historian Leopold von Ranke, who began his work in the 1830s, expressed the distinctly realist notion that the study of history should be, above all, about providing the most exact possible representation of past events, a representation based on the intensive study of archival documents.

For all these exceptions and counter-trends, we can nonetheless see romanticism as the dominant cultural style in Europe during the first half of the

nineteenth century. When this cultural style was applied to politics, it involved [309]
bringing individual longing and desire into a unified whole with commitments to public life. Individuals were not to be stoic and deny their inclina-
tions, as was the case in the political models of the eighteenth century, including
the notions of citizenship in the French Revolution. Rather, they were to live
and feel their commitments; the political doctrines they believed in, the policies they followed, were to stem from their passions. This was a style of politics that was compatible with many different points on the political spectrum.

Romanticism could certainly be conservative, glorying in the corporate
world of the middle ages, in the powerfully felt personal ties of loyalty
between lord and vassal, between master and journeyman, pointing out the
great beauties and soul-moving passions of the Catholic Church. Governmental bureaucracy or constitutions granting basic civil rights, romantic conservatives would assert, could stir no such passions. Such a viewpoint was
particularly common among German conservatives, such as Friedrich Schlegel,
Adam Müller and Joseph Görres. The French author, François-René de
Chateaubriand, the man who invented the term 'conservatism' to describe
this wing of the political spectrum, also exemplifed this attitude, in his *Genius
of Christianity* of 1802. His eulogy of medieval Catholicism as an embodiment
of emotionally stirring poetic inspiration is a quintessential early expression
of romantic ideals.

However, romanticism was also prevalent on the left. The radical and
romantic French historians, writing in the 1830s and 1840s, Jules Michelet
and Alphonse de Lamartine, published wildly popular histories of the French
Revolution of 1789, as great, soul-stirring struggles of the people, in which
both the masses and their leaders wrestled with their passions, as much as
with the old regime or the counter-revolutionary Great Powers. Eugène
Delacroix's painting celebrating the French Revolution of 1830, *Liberty Leading
the People on the Barricades*, in which an allegorical figure of liberty, in the form
of a bare-breasted woman carrying the tricolour flag, leads insurgents from
the common people and the upper classes (acting in passionately felt social
unity) toward victory, over the corpses of those who have fallen heroically in
the struggle, exemplifies perfectly romanticism in the service of the basically
moderate liberal ideals of the 1830 revolution. Such a romantic attitude was
particularly popular on the left in southern and eastern Europe: Polish, Hungarian or Italian radicalism of the years 1830–50 is almost inconceivable
without it.

Perhaps the best example of the political malleability of romanticism was
the attitudes of the British romantic poets. William Wordsworth, Samuel

[310]   Coleridge and Robert Southey began as sympathizers with the turbulent, stirring events of the French Revolution. The first two became disillusioned and withdrew into an emotionally intense, if apolitical, communion with nature, while Southey turned into an unabashed Tory. William Blake, on the other hand, remained a sympathizer with the left all his life, in his poetry even identifying classicism with the conservative and counter-revolutionary politics he despised. George Gordon, Lord Byron, went to Greece in 1823, to fight with the Greek revolutionaries against Turkish oppression, and lost his life there.

It is easy to be cynical about political romanticism, to see the conservative, romantic glorification of the middle ages as a veil hiding the brutality of serf-dom, the economic rigidity of the guild system, and the bigotry of discrimina-tion against the Jews. Romantic histories of the French Revolution might appear as a justification of the Jacobins' practice of political murder; the political twists and turns of the British romantic poets as the self-indulgence of the literati. Certainly, surviving figures from the age of classicism, such as Prince Metternich, were appalled by the politics of romanticism; a post-1850 generation, practising the new cultural style of realism, would look back with bemusement on the preceding era, and its search for an emotionalized total-ity. (As the reader might guess, this author is also no particular fan of the romantic cultural style.) Still, this cultural style was the dominant one in Europe during the first half of the nineteenth century; some of the major political developments, particularly nationalism, religious revivals, and the revolutions of 1830 and 1848, expressed themselves in a language saturated with the concepts of romanticism.

Ultramontanism

Ultramontanism comes from a Latin phrase meaning 'beyond the mountains', and when one travels beyond the Alps into Italy, one comes to Rome, home of the pope. In a narrower sense, ultramontanism was the religious, cultural and political movement among Catholics to restore the primacy of the pope in the Catholic Church, particularly through the use of religious orders designed to be agents of papal influence, such as the Jesuits and the Re-demptorists. However, ultramontanism as a religious movement, and often a religious mass movement, went well beyond this. Papal power was to be restored, for the purpose of counteracting all the changes in religion – and, increasingly, in society and politics as well – resulting from the Enlightenment, the French Revolution, and the capitalist market economy. In their place, ultramontanists hoped to create a new order, unified in its devotion to the [311] Catholic faith.

Such a new order would emerge from the revival and renewal of the Catholic religion itself, begun in the first decade of the nineteenth century in Italy under Napoleonic rule, and spreading through the rest of Catholic Europe in the first half of the nineteenth century. The initial instrument of renewal was 'popular missions', religious revivals in which members of an order such as the Redemptorists would come to a town, erect a giant cross, and begin preaching fire and brimstone sermons, bringing their audience to an emotional frenzy, plunging them into deep despair over their sinful condition, and raising them to jubilation at the hope of their salvation. The missionaries would go on to bring back features of an emotionalized faith, that had been condemned by Enlightened Catholics: veneration of the Virgin and the Sacred Heart, using the rosary, taking part in religious processions and pilgrimages. They encouraged a belief in miracles, and admiration for stigmatics – devout believers (generally young women) who developed the wounds of Christ's crucifixion on their bodies – was a characteristic feature of ultramontanism. More generally, emotionalized, anti-rationalist devotions, practices and beliefs became key elements of ultramontanist Catholicism.

Expanding from this religious core, ultramontanists looked for a government that would break with the absolutist tradition of the state running the affairs of the Catholic Church, but would instead allow, even endorse this renewal and revival of the Catholic religion. Such a government, both privileging the ultramontanist programme for the church and allowing it to develop, would receive the endorsement of the ultramontanist clergy and their lay followers. A revived and renewed Catholicism would provide a basis for social renewal as well. Ultramontanists vigorously attacked the social question; they condemned godless capitalism and looked for answers in church-sponsored organized charity and economic and social reforms enacted by a government with the church's blessing.

All things considered, ultramontanism, whether as an increase in papal authority, or as the cultivation of both a new religious sensibility, and a revival of older pious practices was on the increase in the first half of the nineteenth century. Its spiritual and doctrinal rivals, whether the austere and puritanical Jansenist Catholicism of the old regime, or the rationalist Catholicism of the Enlightenment, had been dealt a major blow by the French Revolution. Many of the adherents of those views had been drawn into the secularized and anti-clerical world of revolutionary and Napoleonic politics, and had left the church altogether; the remaining supporters of such ideas

[312] had been discredited by the close connections between them and the revolutionary cataclysm. The seigneurial and political privileges bishops, monks and even ordinary parish priests had once enjoyed, that provided them with a legal, economic and doctrinal independence vis-à-vis the Roman curia, had been destroyed by the destruction of ecclesiastical privileges and the sale of church property. If the clergy wanted to preserve any independence or autonomy against the claims of the post-revolutionary European states, then there was no choice but to rely on the pope.

The revolutionaries had also wiped out many of the old regime sources of Catholic lay piety, such as the religious brotherhoods. Hence, the clergy would have to be central to any effort to preserve or revive the religious sentiments of Catholic laypeople, shaken or at least challenged in the revolutionary and Napoleonic era. The popular religious rituals encouraged by ultramontanism, would be the way to do it. The close connections of ultramontanism to the dominant cultural trends of romanticism would help the church gain or regain the loyalty and support of intellectuals, and sophisticated members of the upper classes: women in particular, who were often active lay supporters of ultramontanist priests, but men as well.

Political developments of the years 1815–50 generally favoured the progress of ultramontanism. Ultramontanist theology was close to conservatism. The political and social order endorsed by a revived and renewed Catholicism was often understood as a medieval revival (note here the connection with romantic ideas), with the institution of a society of orders, headed by a devout monarch, absolutist but definitely not Enlightened, who would leave education and public morality in the hands of the church and would crush liberal notions of freedom of religion and equality of confessions before the law. Conservatives in the Catholic countries of western and southern Europe had strong sympathies for ultramontanism. The Franco-Italian conservative theorist, Joseph de Maistre, whom we have previously met endorsing the executioner as the basis of society, also wrote a work asserting that a truly Christian social order would be one in which the pope would be the ultimate political ruler. The popes of the post-1815 era, particularly Leo XIII (elected 1823) and Gregory XVI (elected 1831) were strong, even politically militant supporters of extreme conservative ideas, certainly in the Papal States they ruled, but throughout Italy and most of Europe, as well.

However, ultramontanism was not an exclusively conservative doctrine. In Ireland, Poland, and many of the German states, where Catholics lived under non-Catholic rulers, who were generally suspicious of an independent, active Catholic Church, and unwilling to allow the ultramontanists to activate their programme of religious renewal, to say nothing of their broader plans, ultramontanism had a different political import. In these circumstances, the question arose of whether supporters of ultramontanism could not make common cause with liberal opponents of conservative regimes. Something like this did happen, to a certain extent, in Great Britain, where Catholic Irish nationalists, whose popular support was closely related to their endorsement by an increasingly ultramontanist clergy, would be the political allies of English liberals for most of the nineteenth century. In continental Europe, however, all such efforts ultimately proved unsuccessful: liberals could not overcome their secular, anti-clerical and sometimes Protestant orientation; ultramontane Catholics could not find a way to cooperate with political movements outside their totalizing view of the world. Ultramontanists would continue to oppose Protestant rulers, as well as Catholic ones who maintained the absolutist tradition of state domination over the church, as was the case in the Austrian empire during the first half of the nineteenth century (ultramontanists were equally hostile to Catholic priests who supported such states, or who advocated rationalist and Enlightened ideas, and support of these two often went together), but this opposition would involve a competition with liberalism rather than a cooperation with it.

The most famous instance of this failed connection was the French priest and political author, Felicité de Lammenais. After 1815 both a prominent ultra and ultramontanist, the events of the revolution of 1830, particularly the uprising of Catholic Poles against their tsarist oppressor, caused him to change his mind. In his newspaper, *L'Avenir* (The Future) and his 1834 book, *Paroles d'un Croyant* (Slogans of a Believer), he asserted that the renewal of Catholicism needed to be undertaken in conjunction with the developing institutions of civil society, and the liberal and democratic political movements endorsing them, rather than in opposition to them, through conservative politics and a glorification of the middle ages. Lammenais's writings were condemned by papal encyclical, and his works placed on the Index of prohibited books. He broke with the church and ended up cooperating closely with the Freemasons, the anti-clerical arch-enemies of ultramontanism.

Among Protestants, we can see some similar developments in the first half of the nineteenth century, particularly the idea of a religious revival, involving an individual's direct, personal, emotionalized relationship to God. This movement of revivalism, known among Protestants in a number of different countries as 'the awakening', stemmed from eighteenth-century tradition of criticism of doctrinal orthodoxy. In the years after 1815, the fronts changed: orthodoxy and its critics fused in the awakening, to oppose Enlightened and

[314] rationalist ideas. Rather like the Catholic ultramontanists, awakened Protestants sought to suffuse state and society with their religious principles. However, both a generalized religious scepticism and an explicit support of
Enlightened ideas were more common among Protestants than Catholics, limiting the influence of the awakened. Protestant religious doctrine, with its
greater separation of the sacred and the secular, also ensured that a totalizing
vision comparable to that of the ultramontanists did not emerge.

Both ultramontanist Catholics and awakened Protestants were immensely
conscious of their own confession and sceptical of – and often downright
hostile to – the other. In this respect, they were both successors of the old
regime culture of confessionalism. However, both these movements were revivals, designed to strengthen and reshape (among other ways by the adoption
of a romantic sensibility) a confessional culture that had experienced the French
Revolution, and its project of a non-religious public life. Key advocates of
these nineteenth-century religious movements felt self-consciously beleaguered, fighting against the further progress of developments that had begun
in 1789. It is not that their efforts were condemned to failure. Quite the opposite, Catholic ultramontanists in particular, and Protestant revivalists as well,
of the first half of the nineteenth century, enjoyed considerable success in
reviving, reinvigorating, reworking, and sometimes even expanding popular
religious loyalties of the old regime – with particularly great effect among
women. Religious loyalties and forms of self-identity continued to play a central
role in political life. With the expansion of political life accompanying the
rise of civil society, such loyalties and identities became, in some ways, even
more important to politics then they had been in the old regime. However,
the very existence of these movements of religious revival and renewal testified to the fact that the self-evident character of the old regime culture of
confessionalism had come to an end. The organized Christian religions would,
in the first half of the nineteenth century battle against a secularly organized
public life, and, ultimately, in the decades after 1850, come to terms with
their place within it, rather than setting the intellectual parameters for it, as
had been typically the case before 1789.

Nationalism

The first half of the nineteenth century also saw the rise of a very different
vision of totality, one that, in some ways, was in competition with religious
visions, and could be seen as a replacement for them. This was nationalism,
and, rather like ultramontanism, nationalism and the nationalist political

programme had both a narrow and a more extended, emotionally charged, [315] and totalizing meaning. The narrower meaning asserted that nations, groups of people bound together by a common language, culture and historical experience, should form the basis for political life. State boundaries, in other words, should follow national lines, defining nation-states, a phrase making its appearance in this period. Nations should have the opportunity to form their own states, a doctrine that would be dubbed, at the end of the nineteenth century, 'national self-determination'.

Even this narrower meaning of nationhood was politically explosive. If the Europe of 1815 were to be a Europe of nation-states, then Ireland would have to be independent of Great Britain; the seven Italian states merged into one; the thirty-nine German states also merged; the tsar's empire broken up, particularly by the secession of its Polish territories, and, most drastically, the Austrian empire divided into its component national groups – and the lands where they lived include all or part of today's Austria, Hungary, Czech and Slovak Republics, Poland, Ukraine, Romania, Serbia, Slovenia, Croatia and Italy – even assuming contemporaries could have agreed on the boundaries of the different nations, or even on which nations some groups belonged to, which they could not. Such a nationalist realignment would have had as disruptive an effect on the European state-system as all the wars of the French Revolution and Napoleon.

However, nationalism meant more, and it was this broader meaning that actualized the potential threat to the existing state of affairs contained in the narrower implication. In this broader sense, the nation was to be the object of everyone's highest loyalty and devotion. All religions, social classes, regions, dynasties were to be subsumed under the nation. As August Hoffmann von Fallersleben's *Deutschlandlied* (written in 1840) proclaims, 'Deutschland, Deutschland über alles/Über alles in der Welt' – Germany, Germany, above everything/Above everything in the world. For truly convinced nationalists, the nation stood above all mundane considerations; it was transcendent, an object of almost religious devotion, indeed, often a substitute for such devotion.

Nationalism of the first half of the nineteenth century was thus very much in the romantic tradition of a powerful emotional longing for individual connection with a greater totality, in this case, the nation. Such an emotional response, however, had a very real social context in the institutions of an emerging civil society. In a sense, nationalism was the feeling of participation in these institutions, the feeling of unity with other participants while taking part in a mass meeting of Daniel O'Connell's Repeal Association, or the 1832 National Festival of the Germans in Hambach; the feeling that emerged from

[316] attending a public lecture or theatrical performance in which the Rumanian or
Czech language was used for the first time. Nationalist feelings emerged from
working closely with other conspirators in a secret society. Newspapers,
offering reports from everywhere a common language was spoken, helped to
build this feeling. In Germany, between 1815 and 1850 there developed the
three organizations that became the bearers of nationalist ideas, not just in
the German-speaking world, but in much of continental Europe: the choral,
gymnastics and sharpshooting societies. Nationalism was cultivated in such
groups, in the experience of choral singing; in the unison movements practised in gymnastics societies (in contrast to the floor exercises or apparatus
work of today's gymnastics); in the sharpshooters marching behind a flag –
and, of course, in being part of the crowd witnessing these spectacles.

Just as these institutions of civil society tended to be primarily a matter for
the educated and, to a lesser degree, the urban population, so nationalism was,
in this period, an experience of these groups. Nationalists themselves often
extolled, in romantic fashion, the organic unity of all members of the nation;
they saw their nation, once again in romantic fashion, with its language, cul-
tures and traditions, emerging from the peasantry, whose lives embodied the
unity of a nation and its territory, its soil. Peasants, however, were strikingly
uninterested in nationalism: little involved in the emerging institutions of civil
society, their political loyalties remained parochial, tied to their village, and
hostile to 'foreigners' – that is, anyone outside their village. If they thought
about loyalties on a wider scale, these were typically dynastic or religious
in nature. Nationalism appealed to the rural population if religious loyalties,
as in Ireland, or large-scale political experiences, such as, in France, the 1789
revolution, and particularly the Napoleonic era, could be brought to bear.
One of the great stories of the nineteenth century, just a relatively small part
of which will be followed in this book, is the spread of nationalism, the way
that the ideas and the emotions attached to it, moved from a relatively small
circle of educated young men to encompass the entire population. The revolution of 1848 in particular would drive this process forward, but it was still
only getting underway in the middle of the nineteenth century.

The fierce emotions of nationalism were politically ambivalent, in a number
of different ways. Passionate loyalty to one's nation could be combined with
an equally passionate hostility towards another. German nationalists, whose
formative political experiences were the wars against Napoleon in 1813–14,
could be wildly Francophobe. As Ernst Moritz Arndt, one of their leaders
asserted, 'I hate all the French, without exception, in the name of God and
my nation. . . .' 'Throw out the Germans', was a major slogan of the Italian

nationalists, referring to the German-speaking Austrian officials, who ruled [317]
the northern provinces of Lombardy and Venetia.

This hostile and bellicose context for nationalism would, in the long run, be the dominant one. Yet, particularly in the first half of the nineteenth century, nationalism could also involve a call for reconciliation and cooperation among nations rather than conflict between them, such as Giuseppe Mazzini's celebrated plan for a European map redrawn on national lines, to emerge from the cooperation of different nationalist movements. In pursuit of this vision, Mazzini strove to federate the radical secret societies of different national groups into a 'Young Europe'. Speakers at the National Festival of the Germans at Hambach in 1832 included French and Polish nationalists, who called for the cooperation of different nationalities in Europe. The cause of Polish nationalism was a particularly popular one, supported by virtually all other nationalist movements in Europe – including, one should note, many German and even Russian nationalists, who in subsequent decades would come to have a very different relationship to Polish nationalism.

In terms of the political spectrum, nationalism in the years 1815–50 was primarily oppositional, usually espoused by those to the left of centre, among radicals and in the liberal opposition. In the radical concept of popular sovereignty, the people were constituted as a nation; liberal plans for constitutional monarchy were generally for the government of a nation-state. Following in the footsteps of the French Revolution, radicals of the years 1815–50 usually envisaged their seizure of power as intimately connected with a nationalist war against conservative powers. Much of the emotional impetus and potential for popular support among these oppositional movements came from their endorsement of nationalism.

Conversely, conservatives were usually strong opponents of nationalism. Forming nation-states in Italy and in central Europe seemed impossible without destroying the fundamental conservative principle of legitimacy, the rule of existing princes. Prince Metternich, whose desire to preserve legitimate rulers, peace among the European Powers and the position of the distinctly multinational Austrian empire, went along with his classicist cultural style, and strong distaste for romantic expressions of nationalism, never made any secret of his hatred and contempt for nationalism. Other conservatives, proponents of throne and altar, observed – and quite accurately – that nationalism was a form of idolatry, a worship of the nation that would replace Christianity or subordinate it to the nation.

There was, though, an intellectual counter-current among conservatives, particularly those impressed by romantic ideas, suggesting that nationalist

[318] loyalties and nationalist hatreds could be coopted, and tied to the existing monarchies. Sergei Uvarov, minister of education under Tsar Nicholas I, propagated the idea of the combination of 'quintessentially Russian', as he said, principles of orthodoxy, autocracy, and nationality. Such a plan to combine absolutism and the Eastern Orthodox religion, two bases of the tsar's rule since the old regime, with the newer idea of a Russian nation, implied a campaign of oppression directed against the many non-Orthodox, non-Russian subjects of the Russian emperor: Ukrainians, Poles, Jews, the Baltic peoples, the Islamic inhabitants of the Crimea and the Caucasus. Gradually replacing old regime concepts of tsarist rule in the nineteenth century, and acquiring a name, 'official nationality', in the 1870s, it was still a nascent alternative to oppositional forms of nationalism in the first half of the nineteenth century.

In some ways, the most active and effective promoter of conservative nationalism before 1850 was Frederick William IV, the romantic conservative king of Prussia. He wanted to encourage a German nationalism that would glorify the middle ages, the society of orders and the many different German princes, while condemning liberal or democratic ideals and the emergent civil society as foreign and subversive, as French and revolutionary, and hence to be despised by German nationalists. In a characteristic gesture, he sponsored the completion of the construction of Cologne's cathedral, a great medieval monument begun in the fourteenth century, but never finished. Handily, the cathedral was located in a city on the river Rhine, in an area that had been part of France between 1794 and 1813, and, as a result of the wars against Napoleon, become part of the Prussian kingdom, thus allowing the king to emphasize the unity of medieval nostalgia, counter-revolution, and an anti-French German nationalism.

Frederick William's attitudes were far from meeting with universal approval among other conservative rulers. Metternich, for instance, considered his plans to be a dangerous playing with revolutionary fire, and thought the Prussian monarch mentally unbalanced, which he probably was. Unlike the situation in the later nineteenth and twentieth centuries, when nationalism was a conservative force employed to great effect by those wishing to uphold the status quo, before 1850 it was generally to be found in the more discontent, the potentially revolutionary elements of society and politics. Whether on the left or the right, though, nationalism in the first half of the nineteenth century was an extraordinarily powerful example of the longing for totality, seeking a new intellectual, political and emotional unity, in a period when previously existing socioeconomic and political structures were dissolving.

Socialism, communism, feminism [319]

Socialism or communism (contemporaries used the terms interchangeably) developed after about 1830, thus somewhat later than the other political and cultural movements considered in this section. Nonetheless, socialism was also characterized by a search for totality, one that centred on the rapidly expanding market economy. Each of the three intellectual founding fathers of socialism, the French authors Henri de Saint-Simon and Charles Fourier, and the English industrialist Robert Owen, attacked the idea of private property and its free disposition, characteristic of the market economy, but each emphasized a different aspect of the market in their critiques.

Saint-Simon was the advocate of economic planning, of creating a total system of order and progress. He understood this as necessary in an economy characterized by advances in science and technology, an era of industrialists and industrialization – phrases that he invented. Fourier, by contrast, had little interest in industry and technology; his concern was with the distinction between toil and leisure, work and pleasure. In his socialist future, people would live in communes called phalanasteries where these distinctions would be abolished and productive labour would be pleasurable. Robert Owen was primarily concerned with the labour process, with the relationship between the owners of industrial enterprises who gave the orders, and their propertyless workers, who carried them out. He envisaged a realm of co-operatives, in which industrial enterprises would be owned and governed by the men and women who worked in them.

Interestingly, all three of these doctrines involved a feminist aspect; abolishing private property seemed to go hand in hand with abolishing women's inferior position in society. In one way or another, the thinkers – or in the case of Saint-Simon, his disciples, after the master's death – asserted that the capitalist system oppressed women. It forced them into marriage as a property transaction, rather than as an affair of the heart and the emotions. (Once again, note the romantic idea of the unfettered expression of emotion.) It burdened them with the all the labour of housework and raising children; it imposed on them a sexual double standard, requiring their chastity and monogamy, while allowing men much more freedom. With the abolition of private property, socialists asserted, relations between men and women would be characterized by intense, mutual, emotional involvement and voluntary commitment; collective and cooperative labour would lessen the burdens of child-rearing and housework. Women and their labour would gain a dignity equal to that of men. This was an attractive view and women by the thousands,

[320]   and perhaps tens of thousands, particularly in Great Britain and France developed a strong interest in socialism.

As was the case with other political movements of the 1830s and 1840s, this feminism was quite different from the version which emerged in the late twentieth century. Women's work outside the home and equality of men and women before the law were not central issues for the socialists. (A very few did advocate the practice of birth control, but that was not a central issue, either.) Female suffrage was generally not a cause they espoused. Indeed, it is important to understand that in this respect, as in most others, early socialism or communism was not a political movement at all.

This is particularly hard to comprehend today, because in the twentieth century, communism has been associated with the extreme left of the political spectrum. Socialists of the 1830s and 1840s, however, frequently understood themselves as a movement going beyond the left–right distinctions of the political spectrum. They were, ideally, not interested in republics or monarchies, in democratic or limited suffrage, in plotting revolutions or campaigning for parliamentary office. The point of socialism was that change would occur peacefully, voluntarily, and in a non-political fashion. The thousands of followers of Robert Owen, or of Étienne Cabet, the leading socialist in France and, more generally, in continental Europe during the 1840s, tended to reject any cooperation with contemporary radicals – who, we need to remember, saw political change as their primary task, even in resolving the social question. Socialists saw no need for conspiracies, barricade fighting or a reign of terror. Peaceful demonstrations of the value of the socialist way of life would convince everyone of the value of such a system. The classic – and admittedly rather pathological – example of this attitude was how Charles Fourier arranged to be at home around noon every day for twenty years, so that he would not miss meeting the millionaire he was sure would come to offer him the financial backing to create one of his phalansteries. Robert Owen voluntarily turned his textile factory into a worker-owned and managed cooperative, to illustrate the value of his ideas. Followers of Owen, Fourier or Saint-Simon repeatedly attempted to found communes, often emigrating to conveniently vacant territories of North America, to do so.

Still, for all their pretensions to be beyond left and right, socialists and their followers generally moved within a left-wing milieu, and found greater interest in their ideas among radicals than adherents of the centre and right of the political spectrum, who tended to lump the socialists in along with godless or propertyless subversives. With the increasing interest in the social question, radicals began picking up some of the ideas of the socialists and incorporating them into their worldview. Auguste Blanqui, leader of the [321] extreme French radicals during the years 1830–50, an inveterate conspirator and founder of secret societies, who spent most of his career in gaol, after his conspiracies failed and his societies were broken up by the police, coined the phrase 'dictatorship of the proletariat', to describe the revolutionary government he would form. Louis Blanc, another prominent French leftist talked of how a democratic and republican government would introduce the 'organization of labour', and create 'national workshops', phrases redolent with socialist ideals.

Although relatively obscure figures in their day, the individuals who developed the most influential combination of radicalism and socialism were the German intellectuals Karl Marx and Friedrich Engels. Both spent a good deal of time abroad in the 1840s, Marx in exile in France for his political activities, Engels in England on business (he was from a family of textile manufacturers), meeting both radicals and socialists, and people trying to combine the two doctrines. In their *Communist Manifesto* of 1847, written for the Communist League, a secret society of radical German artisans living in England, France, Switzerland and Belgium, Marx and Engels proposed the most rigorous merger of the two ideas. They described a radical revolution of the nineteenth century, that would initiate a revolutionary regime, much like the Jacobin republic of the 1790s. But just as Mazzini's nineteenth-century revolution would be an improvement on the French Revolution of 1789, so Marx and Engels' revolution would be as well, because their radical regime would take the necessary steps to initiate a communist society. Dreams of a new social totality are not immediately apparent in the *Manifesto*, since Marx and Engels had grown weary of the drawing up of elaborate schemes for a communist society without any practical way of achieving it, a practice they condemned as 'utopian'.

Still, when we read their call to action carefully, we can see elements of the socialist and feminist vision of totality within it. Communism, the authors of the *Manifesto* assert, would involve the abolition of marriage, to 'do away with the status of women as mere instruments of production'. The communist society would be one in which 'the free development of each is the condition for the free development of all'. Putting these aspirations into practice proved difficult. Marx and Engels both played a very active role in the revolution of 1848, but primarily as radicals, aiming at sharp changes in government: the introduction of a republic in Germany, and a revolutionary war like that of France in the 1790s. Their efforts to create radical/communist politics were strikingly unsuccessful; the urban lower classes of Cologne, where they were

[322] based, seemed much more interested in the idea of communism as peaceful and largely non-political change.

Although their particular version of communist doctrines was certainly not typical of the era, the aspirations of Marx and Engels are nonetheless in line with some of the broader tendencies in public life during the years 1815–50. This was an era in which the old regime with its absolutist yet ineffective governments, its society of orders, its economy, with large sectors poorly integrated into the market, was coming to an end. In its place there were increasing claims of European states on their subjects, increasing demands of an expanding market on producers and consumers, and expanding institutions of civil society that – at least potentially – offered a forum for debate and an arena for action, in dealing with the problems caused by political and socioeconomic changes, or the lack of these changes. Reflections on the experiences of the era of the revolutionary and Napoleonic era helped guide the debate and offered potential models for action.

At least, this is the way the situation looks in retrospect. For contemporaries, the outlines of an emerging socioeconomic or political order were less clear, or, if they were clear, seemed most unwelcome. The popularity, across the political spectrum, of cultural visions of totality testifies to the relatively low level of attractiveness of an emergent bureaucratic state, market economy, and civil society of property owners, even among their proponents and supporters. In their political and socioeconomic practice, Europeans of the years 1815–50 increasingly adapted to the emergent new surroundings, but the cultural visions inspiring them were often of something altogether different. This gap between practice and ideal was a characteristic feature of the first half of the nineteenth century, not seen in earlier or later periods.

Notes

1. Cited in Janet Hartley, *Alexander I* (London and New York, 1994), p. 168.
2. Quoted in Raymond Carr, *Spain 1808–1975*, 2nd edn. (Oxford, 1982), p. 185.

CHAPTER 7

IN THE SHADOW OF THE PAST,
1815–32

An age of epigones

In 1830, Marie Henri Beyle, best known by his pen-name, Stendhal, published his novel, *The Red and the Black*. Its protagonist, Julien Sorel, a young man of modest but not impoverished background, dreams of the great days of the French Revolution and the Napoleonic era, of a life as revolutionary leader, or, even better, as a conquering general in Napoleon's armies. But war and revolution seem out of the question in France of the 1820s, ruled by the restored Bourbon monarchs, and politically dominated by the conservatives. Nobles and affluent, non-noble landowners – the leading figures in the post-revolutionary civil society of property owners – hold the levers of power, leaving no place for an ambitious youth of the lower middle class. Julien takes out his frustrations in two, rather oddly juxtaposed directions. He enters a seminary and prepares to become a priest – an ultramontanist one – seeing a pro-papal career in the Catholic clergy as the one route to power and influence in the pious and conservative political atmosphere. However, he also becomes a bedroom athlete, getting his revenge on the wealthy and powerful men who block his ascent in the world by seducing their wives and daughters.

Julien soon finds himself moving in a world of political intrigue, dominated by conservative extremists and religious manipulators, by ultras and ultramontantists. These men, while holding the reins of power, are obsessed with the fear of a repetition of the French Revolution, the Reign of Terror and the Napoleonic Wars; they devise one scheme after another to return France to the way it was before 1789, or, more precisely, to the way they imagine it to have been. Their fears, Stendhal tells us, are not unjustified; common people – peasants, masons – make brief appearances in the novel, hoping for a return of Napoleon, a figure who exemplifies for them the whole

[324] revolutionary era. Julien becomes a trusted agent of the reactionary conspirators, but in doing so must pay for the fulfilment of his ambitions for power and glory by renouncing his political ideals. Such a situation can have no good end, and in a scene anticipated in the very earliest pages of the book, he attempts to kill a former mistress, is tried, convicted and, refusing all avenues of legal appeal, or pleas to the court for mercy, executed.

The Red and the Black was not a big literary success when it appeared, since its author had broken with the dominant romantic cultural style, and written a novel in the realist mode that would only become popular after the middle of the century. Combining shrewd psychological insight, cynical evaluations of the social hierarchy, politics, government and the church, with (for the time) frank portrayals of sexuality, Stendhal produced a work that is now a literary classic but was shunned by contemporary critics and the reading public, who wanted something more uplifting and emotionally stirring. However, precisely the harsh and realistic portrayals of the day that made The Red and the Black unpalatable to contemporaries, turn it into a useful guide to the era of the Restoration, the years between the Congress of Vienna in 1814–15, and the revolutionary and reform movements of the early 1830s.

The story the Red and the Black tells is of an age of epigones, of people living in the shadow of the past. The repetition of the events of 1789–1815 is simultaneously a hope, a fear, and an obsession; whether seeking to emulate them or avert them, no one can avoid their impact. Yet, at the same time, the protagonists are all aware that they are living in a lesser world, one of shrunken aspirations and diminished capacities, in comparison to the giants of the revolutionary and Napoleonic eras. In this airless environment, dominated by great deeds of the relatively recent past, by older men with long memories, there is no place for ambitious members of a younger generation, such as Julien Sorel.

Stendhal's own personal life mirrored his fiction: a former officer in Napoleon's army, he had a minor position in the French foreign service and was convinced that his liberal and pro-Napoleonic sympathies (which frequently went together in France of the 1820s) were preventing him from establishing a successful career. Ironically, this portrait of a world of epigones, of frustrated hopes for change – hopes that are a melange of personal ambition, militarism, chauvinism, nostalgia, and opposition to a stifling but not totally repressive social and political order – appeared a few months after the French revolution of 1830 had put an end to the world it had cynically yet incisively portrayed. Nonetheless, its description of a world that is post-revolutionary, but whose politically active figures are unable to conceive of the future [325] except in terms of the events and antagonisms of the revolutionary past, provides a key to understanding the entire era.

The Restoration that began with a revolution

In the pithy phrase of the Swiss conservative Karl-Ludwig von Haller, that gave a name to the entire era 1815–30, the aspiration of European statesmen was a restoration of the continent to its pre-1789 condition. The diplomats of the Congress of Vienna, at their deliberations in 1814–15 were bombarded with supplications to do precisely that: to restore all the baroque social, political and diplomatic circumstances of the Holy Roman Empire, for instance. The tsar dreamed of a 'Holy Alliance', a divinely sponsored league of Christian statesmen who would bond together to bring the godless results of the previous quarter-century to an end. Such romantic excess irritated and frightened Austria's chancellor, Prince Metternich, who had a more modest goal: to restore pre-1789 circumstances only to the extent where they were compatible with political stability. The events of 1815 in France, at the very beginning of the Restoration, would show that Metternich was right. The Restoration order was extremely fragile, constantly threatened by a renewed outbreak of revolution.

The first example of political convulsion in the era following the French Revolution was unleashed by the most important figure of that era, Napoleon Bonaparte. Escaping from his exile on the island of Elba and returning to France with a small group of followers at the beginning of March 1815, he entered Paris in triumph three weeks later. His rule lasted just three months, the celebrated 'hundred days', and was ended by the allies' defeat of his army at Waterloo in mid-June 1815, which brought Louis XVIII back to the French throne. These military confrontations were the very last phase of the revolutionary and Napoleonic Wars; the domestic aspects of the 'hundred days', however, already belong to the subsequent era. Three of these aspects, in particular, indicated the shape of things to come.

First, was the total collapse of the Restoration monarchy. Napoleon did have about one thousand followers with him on reaching France, but that hardly counts as an invasion force. The state officials, police, and armed forces of the restored Bourbon monarch offered no opposition to him of any sort.

[326]   Marshal Ney, one of Napoleon's leading generals, who, like so many of his top followers had abandoned the emperor following his military defeats in 1814 to take service with the restored Bourbons, was ordered by Louis XVIII to arrest Napoleon; instead, Ney returned to the emperor's service, a double betrayal for which he would face a firing squad after Waterloo. His behaviour during the 'hundred days' was typical of the French army as a whole. This lack of support was a lesson Louis XVIII would not forget. On returning from exile in London to take up his rule once again in the summer of 1815, he left his entire private fortune behind, safely deposited with English bankers – not precisely a vote of confidence in the solidity of the restored monarchy.

Second, the wave of support for Napoleon had many of the characteristics of a revolution – a revolution made on the model of 1789 to defend the accomplishments of 1789. Peasants of the Rhone valley, under the impact of the widespread rumours that seigneurial dues were to be reinstated and the church's lands restored to it, rose up in favour of Napoleon, as the man who would preserve their free landownership. In Lyon, France's second city, crowds of silk weavers greeted the emperor with cries of 'Down with the priests! Death to the royalists!'[1] Napoleon himself played to these sentiments, declaring that he had returned to prevent France from falling back into its enslaved, pre-1789 condition. He repudiated his own authoritarian past, pledging to rule with the consent of a bicameral legislature and a public opinion whose open expression was to be protected by a guarantee of civil liberties. The formulation of these promises in a constitutional document, the *Acte additionel*, won Napoleon the support of a number of his previous liberal critics, most prominently the author and political theorist Benjamin Constant.

Finally, there developed an organized political mass movement in support of the emperor's rule, the *fédérés*, or confederates. The *fédérés* were begun by the 'young men', the law students and shop and office clerks of the western city of Rennes. Fearful of a recurrence of the counter-revolutionary insurrections that had marked western France during the 1790s, they proposed to work together to support the emperor's new liberal government, and to defeat any domestic violence directed against his regime, thus securing the rear for the troops fighting foreign enemies at the front. This idea of organized support for the government spread throughout France. With the tacit, if sometimes reluctant backing, of Napoleon's officials, hundreds of thousands of *fédérés* were organized.

The name of the group was a conscious reference to the early stages of the French Revolution, to the 'festival of the federation' of 1790. Activists among the *fédérés* included one-time constitutional monarchists, ex-Girondins, a number of former Jacobins, regicides and terrorists, as well as Napoleonic loyalists, all cooperating – at least publicly – in support of the emperor's proposed, liberal regime. However, as the identity of the originators of the scheme showed, *fédérés* were not just revolutionary or Napoleonic veterans, but members of a new generation, who had not personally experienced the struggles of the 1790s, but had grown up under Napoleonic rule, and, as law students, were preparing to take an active part in it. After Napoleon's defeat at Waterloo and the return of the Bourbons, they would continue, both in public activities and in secret conspiracies, to act on behalf of the principles they had publicly articulated during the hundred days.

These three aspects of the hundred days demonstrate the difficulties of the Restoration, primarily in France, but in at least some respects, in all of Europe. Any serious effort to restore pre-1789 socioeconomic conditions would meet with determined resistance from portions of the population who were hostile to the society of orders and felt a strong attachment to the revolution's creation of a civil society of property owners. There existed, as well, a political opposition, in which elements of revolutionary moderates and Jacobins – liberals and radicals, to use the new political vocabulary of the post-1815 era – were joined together, in the name of Napoleon, to oppose conservative rule. While many of the opposition's activists were veterans of the previous era, the ideals of the revolution had reproduced themselves, as it were, spread to a new generation that had not experienced the events of 1789–99 (at least not as adults), but had grown up during the initial years of the nineteenth century. In this sense, the era of Napoleonic rule was the seedbed of liberal and radical movements during the Restoration. Outside of France, it might well be the case that the political principles of the revolution were spread to a wider extent during the authoritarian reign of Napoleon, than in the revolutionary decade of 1789–99 itself.

These circumstances taken together conspired to make the Restoration order politically quite unstable. An excess of conservative policies, or economic difficulties stemming from either high food prices or a business cycle downturn, might suffice to bring together oppositional activists and popular discontent, to try to repeat the events of 1789. The political history of the Restoration era can be understood as one of Europe-wide cycles of confrontation between conservative rulers and a mixed liberal–radical opposition. The first cycle ran from 1816 to the early 1820s, and featured a double combat: among members of the government over the precise nature of the

[328] post-revolutionary order, in particular over the extent of liberal elements within it, and between governments and an at least quasi-revolutionary opposition. The cycle ended with the elimination of potentially liberal elements from most governments in Europe, and the defeat of the oppositional, potentially revolutionary forces, with one admittedly curious exception.

Much of the 1820s was a decade of conservative dominance, a period of frustration and despair for Stendhal and his fictional creation, Julien Sorel. Conservative regimes seemed firmly established, and the main issue of a very limited political life was the distinction between moderate conservatives who were cautious about the extent of a policy of restoration and ultras who openly wanted to return to pre-1789 conditions. The late 1820s, however, saw the re-emergence of a considerably more powerful and effectively organized oppositional movement. The subsequent revolutions of 1830, and the more peaceful reform movement of 1828–32 in the British Isles brought the continent-wide domination of conservative regimes, and hence the era of the Restoration to an end. The subsequent two decades would see political life moving in new directions.

The first cycle: conflicts and clashes after 1816

No sooner had Napoleon been defeated at Waterloo, the rule of Louis XVIII restored again, and the concluding documents of the Congress of Vienna signed, thus bringing to a final end the period of revolutionary and Napoleonic warfare, than opposition to the newly created political order began. In this section, we will first look at the political turbulence of the years after 1816 country by country: in Great Britain, where the movement of opposition was probably at its most massive and influential; in the countries of Mediterranean Europe, where secret societies were most central to the course of events; in the German states, where the conflict was less between government and opposition, and more among members of the government over the exact nature of the post-Restoration political order; and, finally, at movements on the margins of Europe, in Greece and in Russia. To conclude, we will consider the events of the era as a whole and note the Europe-wide general trends expressed in them, as well as the differences in specific nations, and the reasons that the conservative forces of the Restoration were generally able to prevail.

Opposition movements in Great Britain [329]

As was noted in Chapter Three, the revolutionary movement in the British Isles during the 1790s was the strongest in all of Europe outside of France. A combination of severe repression, including, in Ireland, the massive use of armed force, with the mobilization of patriotic and nationalist feelings during the two decades of warfare between England and revolutionary and Napoleonic France had led to the defeat of the revolutionary initiative. Yet the sources of discontent that had produced movements for reform and later revolution – the discrimination against Catholics and Dissenting Protestants; the drastic misapportionment of parliamentary seats and the limited if erratic franchise; the many instances of favouritism for large landowners and courtiers – had not gone away. Nor had many of the activists of the 1790s. In the first fifteen years of the nineteenth century, they had had to be more discreet, to avoid being seen as giving aid and comfort to the wartime enemy, confining their activities to a few strongholds of radicalism, such as metropolitan London, and to occasional parliamentary elections, or calls for an end to the war. These wartime constraints on political activity vanished with the victory of the allies over Napoleon.

The war years produced additional sources of discontent, in particular the demands of an enormous military effort on state finance. The return to peacetime conditions merely emphasized the long-term nature of the burdens imposed by two decades of war. In 1817–18, over 90 per cent of government revenue went on debt servicing and payment of veterans' pensions. In addition, the wartime years saw the initial introduction on a large scale of steam-powered textile machinery, and violent opposition to this new technology, on the part of the Luddite handloom weavers and other textile artisans, whose livelihoods were threatened by it.

Peace produced its own discontents. Some 300,000 demobilized sailors and soldiers flooded the labour market, increasing unemployment and driving down wages. The wartime boost for industry – textiles for uniforms, iron for guns – vanished, and business activity declined. In view of the technological advances and productivity of British agriculture, the bitterly cold and very wet weather of 1816 did not lead to outright famine, as it did in continental Europe, but it did drive food prices up to very high levels. Discontent about food was sharpened by the passage of the Corn Laws in 1815, which imposed a tariff on imported grain. Openly designed to make working people pay more for their food, so that farmers could receive more for their crops and turn this money over to noble and gentry landlords in the form of higher rent, the passage of the bill provoked days of rioting in London and other cities; it seemed visible evidence of the truth of reformers' denunciations of the political system as inequitable and corrupt.

In these circumstances, both veterans of previous opposition efforts and novice activists began campaigns that combined the long-standing issues of the political opposition with newer questions from the wartime and postwar era. These campaigns were characterized by the extensive use of the institutions of civil society. One veteran of reform efforts of the 1790s – actually, he had been active since the 1770s – was Major John Cartwright, who began creating voluntary associations, the Hampden Clubs, to press for political reform. Starting even before the end of the Napoleonic Wars, and intensifying his efforts after 1815, Cartwright paid particular attention in his organizing efforts to the industrial areas of northern England, where there had been widespread discontent, as was apparent in the campaigns of the Luddites. Cartwright's own views wavered between liberal demands for a uniform national franchise based on paying direct taxes and the democratic demand for universal national suffrage. A former army officer and an estate owner, he was far from a revolutionary firebrand, and his hopes were always directed toward a union of liberal and radical elements, led by members of the upper classes such as himself.

However, he was willing to organize mass support among the aggrieved manufacturing lower classes. Other, similar organizations – Political Protestants, Political Unions – followed, and a network of these groups emerged in metropolitan London and the manufacturing districts of northern England. The question, though, was what such groups were to do to enforce their demands, and here another radical leader – a younger man without any political experience in the 1790s – the gentleman farmer Henry Hunt, offered a solution from another one of the institutions of civil society, namely the public meeting. Hunt suggested that such associations hold public mass meetings, demanding political reform. A gifted public speaker, as his nickname 'Orator Hunt' indicates, Hunt held such meetings, with tens of thousands of participants in the strongholds of the oppositional political associations. The demand for reforms – for a democratic franchise and a reapportionment of parliamentary seats, for an end to corruption and favouritism, for lower taxes and the repeal of the Corn Laws – would be given weight by being proclaimed before an enormous, enthusiastic crowd.

Hunt would appear at these meetings, the 'mass platform', as he called them, decked out in a Phrygian cap, a direct reference to Jacobin radicalism, one that was eagerly taken up by his followers. His rhetoric on the platform played with the threat of revolution: reiteration of peaceful intent, and commitment to non-violence, calls on the government to adopt peacefully the demands of the mass movement, but a warning not to stand in its way or try to repress it, actions that would have violent, revolutionary consequences. The government, however, called his bluff: repressive legislation, including the 'Six Acts' of 1819 effectively suspended civil liberties, abolishing freedom of association and assembly, and allowing the authorities to intern political suspects without trial. The associations were dissolved and their leaders arrested. Efforts to hold unauthorized mass meetings were brutally suppressed: the use in 1819 of the yeomanry (a militia of property owners) against an unauthorized mass meeting of reformers from Manchester and the surrounding area on St Peter's Field, resulted in a least ten deaths. The ironic designation of that effort as 'Peterloo', a domestic Waterloo and triumph of counter-revolution, not over French soldiers, but over peaceful participants trampled to death by the yeomanry's horses, would gain public sympathy among middle-class liberals, but not alter the conservative regime's repressive policies.

Some members of this oppositional movement did respond as Orator Hunt had threatened, with attempted revolution, in the form of abortive risings in London and manufacturing regions of the north, in 1817 and 1820. These attempts, in which police spies were heavily involved as *agents provocateurs*, were more pathetic than threatening. As had been the case with the British Jacobins of the 1790s, without an initial revolution, supported by moderate elements, the conservative government remained firmly in place, and the radical opposition was unable to overturn it.

The oppositional movement of this period had one final fling, the so-called Queen Caroline agitation of 1820–21. The estranged wife of the new monarch, George IV, returned to England in 1820, to claim her share of the throne, and radical activists took up her cause. Supporters of the king and queen traded charges of adultery and immorality (both were quite active in this arena); mass meetings were held in support of the queen, and there was an enormous outpouring of largely illegal broadsides and pamphlets in her favour. Activists thus successfully defied the government's repressive legislation, and by taking up the cause of a woman wronged by her husband – who, as king, headed the entire corrupt and repressive government reformers opposed – the opposition gained support it had never previously had: among soldiers, and especially among women, from otherwise reticent and publicly unassertive middle-class provincial ladies to otherwise apolitical London prostitutes. But the cause of the queen was far from involving any change in the socioeconomic or political order, and when she accepted a cash settlement,

[332] and died shortly thereafter, the movement in her favour ended, and the entire wave of postwar opposition in Great Britain came to an end.

Soldiers, secret societies, and revolutions in Latin Europe

The political struggles of the years between 1815 and the early 1820s in the countries of Latin Europe, the Italian states, Spain, Portugal, and France, involved a conflict between often quite extreme partisans of a restoration and supporters of the achievements of the revolutionary era. Quite in contrast to Great Britain, where adherents of reform or revolution were on the offensive after 1815, in Latin Europe it was the reactionaries, those who wanted to restore some or all of pre-1789 circumstances, who took the political initiative. The actions of their opponents, the supporters of the ideas and ideals of the French Revolution, whether open and legal, or conspiratorial and illegal, were primarily defensive in nature.

The end of French predominance in the Iberian and Italian peninsulas had meant a return to absolutist rule. Ferdinand VII, the restored Spanish monarch, began his reign by revoking the constitution of 1812, that his own supporters, the Spanish insurgents against Napoleon, had devised. For good measure, he reinstated the Inquisition as well. Such a symbolic reassertion of one of the most extreme institutions of the old regime culture of confessionalism was a declaration that the post-1815 absolutist regimes would hardly be Enlightened ones. To be sure, while the restorationist regimes of Latin Europe were both absolutist and ultramontanist, they generally did not attempt to roll back the social and economic changes of the revolutionary era, by reinstalling a society of orders or attempting to reverse the sale of church property. The one exception to this relative moderation was in the Papal States, where Pius VII, returning from his Napoleonic captivity in France, tried to reinstate the whole old regime in his reign, complete with returning the church's property and shutting up the Jews of Rome in their ghetto.

In such circumstances, there was no room for any legal opposition to conservative rule; unlike in England, there could be no public use of the institutions of civil society to engage in political action. Rather, opponents of the Restoration gathered in secret societies, the best known of which were the Carbonari of southern Italy. The name means 'charcoal burners', and it refers to rural inhabitants who earned a living by selling the charcoal they made by burning felled trees. It was a clandestine activity, practised in secret (and often illegally, since the trees they were felling and burning were on property that did not belong to them), in the depths of the forest. Members of this society, bound by elaborate oaths of loyalty and secrecy, would be equally clandestine.

Now the Carbonari had first been formed before 1815 by opponents of Napoleonic rule, but their members quickly transferred their hostility to the equally authoritarian Restoration era successors to the Napoleonic regimes. They were largely an elite group, with a membership made up of substantial landowners, professionals, students, and a considerable number of soldiers and even state officials. In short, the Carbonari's members came from the leading ranks of the post-revolutionary civil society of property owners. Their political plans for the future were vague, ranging from constitutional monarchism to republicanism, with a mixture of supporters of the Napoleonic regimes – this latter group particularly strong in southern Italy, where the reign of Joachim Murat, one of Napoleon's generals, had left behind a surprising number of partisans. Uniting all these different – and generally not well-articulated – points of view was a fierce anti-clericalism, that provided much of the impetus for opposition to the Restoration era governments in this part of Europe.

The situation in France was somewhat different. Here, the returning Louis XVIII had agreed to a constitutional form of rule. To be sure, he made out that the Charter, as the constitutional document was officially known, was a gift of his – a voluntary abridgement of his royal, sovereign powers, rather than being a constitution emanating from a sovereign nation, an idea abhorrent to the former émigré, who had fled France in 1789 after the initial successes of the National Assembly in establishing this new notion of sovereignty. Such philosophical principles aside, the Charter functioned as a constitution, guaranteeing basic civil liberties, providing for a bicameral legislature with a lower house elected by a property franchise (and a stiff one, with just 3 per cent of adult men eligible to vote), and a strong, independent monarch, who appointed government ministers and had a veto over legislation. The conservative monarch had, in effect, agreed to govern on the basis of modestly liberal principles.

However, while it would be wrong to see the Charter as a façade, it is also true that the 'ultras', the counter-revolutionary extremists in the government and among the conservative politicians in France, were committed to evading it, hollowing it out, or simply destroying it. They had their moment in 1815, after Napoleon's defeat at Waterloo, and his second abdication. In the wake of the return of Louis XVIII – historians talk of the 'Second Restoration' – the ultras tolerated and even encouraged counter-revolutionary violence, the 'White Terror'. Particularly in the old strongholds of counter-revolution

[334] in southern France, supporters of Napoleon, former Jacobins, 'confederates' of 1815, even Protestants (who, in southern France, tended to be well represented among all three) were lynched by devout and monarchist mobs. In the elections held for the Chamber of Deputies (the lower house of the French parliament under the Charter) under these circumstances, opponents of the ultras were understandably reluctant to vote, or to vote against them, and the resulting parliament, the 'Chambre Introuvable', or 'Incredible Chamber' was too conservative even for Louis XVIII and his ministers. Thus, the ultras demonstrated that through extra-legal coercion they could undermine constitutional principles of government without formally doing anything against them.

Since the Restoration era government in France had a double face, legal and extra-legal, constitutional and unconstitutional, opposition to it had an equally ambivalent nature. Formally, civil liberties existed, and the opposition could publish newspapers, such as *Le Constitutionel*, or *La Mercure*, the journal of Benjamin Constant, the liberal opponent of both Napoleon and the Restoration government. With the return of more ordered and legal circumstances after 1816, and the ebbing of the White Terror, members of the opposition could stand for the Chamber of Deputies and organize election campaigns. However, the government could also act to circumscribe the opposition's freedom of action, by introducing legislation limiting freedom of the press, rewriting the election laws to guarantee conservative victories, or employing the authorities to pressure voters (voting was public and oral) to support the government.

Thus, there was an illegal wing of the opposition too, in the form of secret societies, the most important of which was the *Charbonnerie*, the French version of the Carbonari. With a membership not all that different from that of the Carbonari, these secret societies were committed to the overthrow of the government, and actively conspired in that direction. It is important to realize that the leaders of the legal and the illegal opposition – such as the marquis de Lafayette, decades before, the dominant figure among the moderates in the early phase of the French Revolution – were the same people. Thus, both the government and the opposition in Restoration France had an instrumentalist attitude toward the Charter, supposedly the basic document of government, and the foundation of a legal, political life. When it was in their interest, they loudly proclaimed their loyalty to it, but were simultaneously active in evading or subverting it.

As in the Italian and Iberian peninsulas, the opposition to the Restoration regime in France included a mixture of constitutional monarchists, republicans, and Bonapartists, that is, partisans of a renewed Napoleonic rule.

Many had been confederates in 1815. Their anti-clerical opposition to ultramontanism and their desire to retain the legal institutions, and social and economic structures resulting from the French Revolution were the same as well. However, a strong sense of nationalism, connected with memories of the military glories of the Napoleonic era also animated them. After defeating Napoleon again, the victorious allied powers imposed somewhat harsher peace terms on France than they had in 1814, including the payment of a substantial war indemnity and the occupation of portions of France by Austrian, Prussian and Russian troops, until the indemnity was paid.

Foreign occupation was a grievance that rankled, especially as many of the occupying soldiers, and their commanding officers, took the occasion to take their revenge on the French for their depredations during their occupation just a few years previously. The French government, already facing a considerable debt from the Napoleonic Wars, but no longer able to loot foreign countries to solve its financial problems, was intent on paying off the war indemnity quickly, and ridding itself of the occupying soldiers (achieving this by 1820 was a major success for the regime). Rejecting demands of the ultras for a state bankruptcy, the government rigorously cut expenses, reducing substantially the size of the armed forces, and retiring thousands of officers on half-pay. These half-pay retirees were a particularly fertile source of support for the political opposition, in both its legal and illegal aspects.

The clash between Restoration regimes in Latin Europe and their opposition came to a head around 1820, at about the same time as in England. This clash was most dramatic where the governments were most authoritarian, in the Iberian and Italian states. When Ferdinand VII ordered army units to depart for South America, to reconquer Spain's former colonies, the troops gathered in the Atlantic port city of Cadiz, rather than going aboard ship, mutinied in January 1820. Their officers, influenced by secret society members, announced a *pronunciamento*, a military coup, and began to march on Madrid. The monarch hastily gave in to them, appointed liberal ministers, and announced that he would reinstate the constitution of 1812. In the summer of 1820, there were similar military coups, whose officers acted in concert with members of secret societies, in Portugal, and in the Kingdom of the Two Sicilies in southern Italy, resulting in the creation of liberal, constitutional monarchies. In March 1821, it was the turn of the Kingdom of Piedmont Savoy, in northwestern Italy, the coup once again involving close cooperation between army officers and secret society members.

[336]   These successes for the opposition made a major impression in France, intensifying and sharpening the clash between the government and the opposition. In yearly elections (one-fifth of the deputies of the Chamber were to be replaced each year), the opposition had made steady progress, and the government became increasingly concerned. Now with revolutions on France's southeastern and southwestern borders, the situation seemed critical, and the government turned to repressive measures within the Charter: a new press law to stifle opposition newspapers; a new elections law that would make it easier for state administrators to intimidate voters and would also improve the chances of conservative candidates. The opposition responded with a greater emphasis on illegal activity and made plans for a joint action between discontented army units and secret society members as had occurred in Spain and Italy.

The attempted military coups in France proved abortive. A number of those involved were arrested, tried and condemned. Four conspirators, all NCOs, were executed, making these 'four sergeants' martyrs of the opposition's cause. Yet the government, still controlled by more moderate conservatives and not by the ultras, was reluctant to engage in a massive crackdown on the illegal opposition, for fear of sparking further resistance. None of the prominent leaders of the secret societies, whose participation in these plots was widely known, were arrested or tried. The marquis de Lafayette did feel it prudent to leave the country and go on an extended speaking tour in the United States.

The successful defence of the conservative regime in France against revolutionary conspiracy would prove crucial to the fate of the revolutions in southern Europe. Tensions quickly emerged in these countries between *exaltados* and *moderados* as the tendencies were called in Spain, that is, between radicals and liberals. Spanish radicals organized political clubs, on the model of the Jacobins in the capital, Madrid, and the larger port cities. Often in conjunction with sympathetic army officers, club members mobilized the urban lower classes to demonstrate against the moderate government ministers. In rural areas of northern Spain, the clergy began calling on the peasants to rise against the government, now controlled, the priests asserted, by godless Freemasons. As had been the case with Louis XVI, Ferdinand VII tacitly endorsed and encouraged these movements, ostensibly directed against the constitutional government that he himself headed. These events demonstrate how influential the model of 1789–94 would be for revolutions in the first half of the nineteenth century, the way that political actors understood events in terms of the French Revolution of 1789 and its consequences.

By 1822, Spain seemed headed, as France had been in 1793, for a major [337]
civil war; similar, if not quite so violent tensions were apparent in the revolutions in Italy. However, the fate of these revolutions was not to be decided
internally. Rather, the Austrian chancellor Metternich, who perceived them
as both a threat to his own country's position as a Great Power, and to the
conservative international order he had designed after the fall of Napoleon,
was determined to end them by outside military force. At the congresses of
Troppau and Laibach in 1821 and 1822, he received the diplomatic backing
of Prussia and Russia for his plans. Austrian troops marched into Italy and
restored the absolutist rule of the two monarchs, that had been challenged by
the 1820 revolution. A similar intervention in the Iberian peninsula proved
diplomatically trickier, since Tsar Alexander I was eager to employ Russian
troops for it, thus expanding his realm's influence in the service of a counter-
revolution desired by the Great Powers. Metternich was able to finesse this
wish, and, instead, in 1823 a French army crossed the Pyrenees, overthrew
the Spanish government, and reinstated absolutism; British forces would perform a similar intervention in Portugal (always regarded in London as part of
a British sphere of influence) later in the decade. These military interventions
brought the revolutionary challenge to the Restoration in Latin Europe to an
end, and restored unrestricted conservative rule – absolutist in Spain, Portugal and Italy, still nominally constitutional in France, but with the ultras in an
increasingly influential position.

Reform and reaction in central Europe

Events in the states of central Europe followed a still different path from
those in the British Isles or in the Mediterranean countries, with regard both
to political issues and alignments, and to the uses made of the institutions of
civil society for political purposes. The strong continuity in political issues
one can observe in Great Britain from the 1790s (or even earlier) until the
1820s, did not exist in the German states; the quarter-century of warfare and
political upheaval had changed circumstances beyond all recognition. But
the clash between partisans of a restoration and defenders of the revolution,
so characteristic of the Latin countries, was also not the main political theme
in central Europe.

There were politically active figures, such as the former Prussian reformer,
the Freiherr vom Stein, who wanted to return to the baroque, pre-1789 world
of the Holy Roman Empire. Such individuals, however, were isolated and
there was more than a little of the eccentric and the crank in them. The great

[338] territorial rearrangements of the Napoleonic era, themselves rearranged at the Congress of Vienna, had increased the power of the German princes and their state bureaucracies far too greatly for them to think seriously of giving up these benefits. At the other end of the political spectrum, open supporters of the principles of the French Revolution and of the Napoleonic regimes were few and far between; the wave of nationalism that had encompassed the educated and much of the urban population in the years of liberation from French hegemony, 1813–15, made public advocacy of such principles at the very least politically inexpedient.

Consequently, the major political issue in the states of central Europe during the years 1815–20 was the new organization of political life. There were two main aspects of this issue. The first concerned the individual states of central Europe. What sort of government would the German states emerging from the period of Napoleonic rule have? Would they be constitutional or absolutist regimes? Would legal equality or corporate privilege characterize them? The second aspect was the relationship of the central European states to each other. With the end of the Holy Roman Empire, would the now sovereign states treat each other like foreign powers, or would there be some more intimate sort of arrangement between them?

The constitutional question was played out on several levels. A constitution for the Prussian kingdom would mark a break with the Napoleonic era. In 1813, King Frederick William III proclaimed to his subjects that after the liberation of the monarchy's territory from foreign rule, he would grant them a constitution as a reward for their loyalty to the royal house. By contrast, in the states of southern Germany, in Bavaria, Baden, Württemberg and the Hessens (there were four of them), the creation of a constitution represented a continuity in policy with the Napoleonic period. The same princes and their ministers governed these states after 1815 as before. By joining the alliance against Napoleon in 1813, they retained all or most of the territory they had gained in their alliance with him. Essentially the same motives governed their rulers' actions: the search for institutions that would enable them to incorporate the inhabitants of these newly won territories into their states.

Underlying the question of a constitution was the chronic problem that plagued all of postwar Europe, state finances. As we have seen above, government taxation and spending policies in England and France weighed heavily on the politics of the day; the countries of central Europe, suffering no less from the heavy fiscal burdens of the Napoleonic era, faced similar difficulties. The Prussian king's promise of granting a constitution was accompanied by a subsequent promise not to take out new state loans or to raise taxes or introduce new forms of taxation without the consent of a future elected legislature with constitutionally defined powers. The proposed constitutions of the states of south Germany would provide an additional layer of government institutions to guarantee the state debt and to encourage financiers to lend the hard-pressed governments still more funds.

In all these respects, the Austrian empire was an exception. Under Metternich's guidance, Emperor Francis rejected any possibility of constitutional government; the coexistence of an absolutist monarchy with provincial estates, still organized along the lines of the society of orders, would continue after 1815 as before. Rather than constitutions and legislatures to guarantee the state debt, the monarchy resorted to proclaiming bankruptcy and instituting the use of a paper currency, largely unbacked by reserves of precious metals. This was a risky financial procedure for the day, and one that was only made possible by withholding from the public any information about government finances, with the exception of a few privileged bankers, who charged dearly for their secret knowledge of the monarchy's fiscal vulnerability. Not content with retaining absolutist government in Austria, Metternich employed diplomatic pressure on the other central European states, to push their governments away from a constitutional path.

This pressure notwithstanding, there were advocates of constitutional, absolutist and corporate forms of rule in the bureaucracies of the different central European states. Until the early 1820s, at least, proponents of any of these forms of government could claim official sanction. On the other focus of political life, though, the nature of the relationship between these states, distinctions between officially sponsored and unofficial positions were quite clear. Germany's monarchs and their government officials guarded jealously their newly won sovereignty; any closer cooperation than the very loose ties of the German Confederation was most unwelcome to them. The opposite position, the call for a unified German nation-state, or even for closer, national cooperation of the different central European states was an extra-governmental affair, part of the 'national movement', a characteristic feature of Germany in the first two-thirds of the nineteenth century.

The national movement in the years 1815–20 was largely made up of young men, many university students and many veterans of the wars of 1813–15 against Napoleon. Unlike oppositional political movements in Great Britain or the Latin countries, this national movement is difficult to place on the political spectrum. Some aspects of it clearly belonged on the left: social egalitarianism, in particular, and a strong suspicion of ruling elites – monarchs,

[340] aristocrats and bureaucrats – who stifled the aspirations of the nation and held themselves above it. Proponents of this viewpoint were generally in favour of civil liberties, freedom of the press, association and assembly, in particular.

However, other aspects of this movement could be attributed to the right. Supporters of the national movement glorified the 'German' middle ages and condemned the French revolutionary ideal of equal citizenship as a degrading, foreign notion, that no good nationalist could consider. Their very vaguely envisaged German national state would be neither a republic nor a constitutional monarchy, but some sort of idealized medieval kingdom, complete with corporate social distinctions, and a strong rejection of the Jews, for whom there was no place in a 'Christian' German state. It is a characteristic feature of the politics of the national movement that its supporters could oppose the aristocracy yet glorify the society of orders, reject the old regime culture of confessionalism, but insist on the Christian basis of the state.

This national movement was a good example of the cultural ideals of romanticism politically unleashed. Its members were loosely united in two different voluntary associations, the *Bursenschaften* or student fraternities, and the gymnastics societies. Both demonstrated the romantic politics of personalized, emotional commitment. The *Bursenschaften*, founded by veterans of the Napoleonic Wars returning to their studies, were a break with the old regime tradition of German student organizations, that had been dominated by young men from the aristocracy, organized on a regional and confessional basis, and largely devoted to drinking and chasing after prostitutes. In contrast, the new fraternities would be open to all Germans (at least all Christian Germans) and their members would devote themselves to cultivating chastity, piety, and loyalty to the nation. Much the same link between nationalism and personal self-transformation existed in the gymnastics societies, whose members felt that their paramilitary exercises would lead them to a chaste and virtuous lifestyle and a quasi-religious devotion to the nation.

The way that these political controversies were played out also demonstrates a version of civil society in central Europe that differed both from the turbulent mass politics of the British Isles in this period, and also from the conspiratorial politics of the Mediterranean countries. Political debate in the five years after 1815 was relatively open, and the major questions of the day were discussed freely and extensively in a periodical press and a substantial pamphlet literature. As the states of southern Germany introduced constitutions and elected legislatures, these elections became an opportunity for the notables to gather and discuss public affairs.

However, we can note one distinct German peculiarity about these nascent institutions of civil society: they were strongly dominated by servants of the state. Differing positions were publicly articulated primarily by government officials; such officials were, by far, the single largest social group among the deputies elected to the legislatures of the German states. The debate within the bureaucracies of the German states about forms of government and the debate outside the government, in the realm of public opinion, was largely carried on by the same people. There were few organized political associations, and even fewer efforts to exert pressure on the government by way of public meetings, appeals or petitions. Characteristically, such events, and, indeed, an active political life that extended beyond the ranks of government officials, were most common in the Rhineland, the extreme western portion of Germany, that had been part of the French republic and Napoleonic empire for almost twenty years, and where the institutions of civil society and the ideals of the revolution, at least as expounded in the Napoleonic era, had taken hold among a large portion of the population.

The young men of the national movement, as university students, were themselves largely aspiring state officials, since working for the government was the typical career track for a university graduate in central Europe. They did have their associations, their student fraternities and gymnastics societies; a few of their members veered off into illegal conspiracy, and the realm of the secret societies. However, their ranks were relatively small in number, a few thousand at most, noticeably fewer than the participants in English mass meetings, and probably fewer than the members of secret societies in western and southern Europe.

Far from being conspiratorial, though, their activities were a variation on the theme of the mass meeting, namely the public festival. The most famous of them was the Wartburg Festival of 1817, in the course of which hundreds of fraternity members marched by torchlight to a castle in the hills of Saxony, where Martin Luther had lived, when he translated the Bible into German. There, they burned symbols of oppression: books by conservative political theorists, the final act of the Congress of Vienna, a wig (symbol of the bureaucracy of the old regime), and sticks used by officials, noblemen and army officers to beat their subordinates. As much expressions of deep, personal feelings in the romantic mode as political actions, these were perhaps designed, in the manner of the English mass platform, to impress the authorities – although they lacked both the weight of participation of their counterparts occurring at the same time in Great Britain, as well as a clear set of demands formulated at such meetings.

[342]   What the national movement did provide, however, was a convenient pretext for the supporters of absolutism in the German states to gain the upper hand over their bureaucratic opponents. In 1819, a war veteran and student fraternity member, Karl Sand, assassinated the playwright August von Kotzebue. Kotzebue was in the service of the tsar, and widely suspected of spying on the activities of members of the national movement for him; he was also the author of a number of widely popular but kitschy plays, which the upright fraternity member felt condoned immoral behaviour, such as divorce. This deed, in and of itself inconsequential, had a tremendous public impact, and it provided the opportunity Prince Metternich had been seeking. Proclaiming Sand the vanguard of a revolutionary terrorist conspiracy, he induced representatives of the German Confederation to agree to the so-called Karlsbad Decrees. A sort of German version of the British Six Acts, these decrees required the Confederation's member states to institute a strict censorship of the press and dismiss 'subversive' teachers from the universities. Fraternities and gymnastics societies were prohibited of course; nervous officials even cancelled physical education classes in secondary schools, out of fear that they might be seen as subversive.

Under the impact of these events, the long-running bureaucratic struggle in Prussia between the proponents of a constitution and supporters of absolutist rule was decided in favour of the latter. Thus, Prussia and Austria, the two Great Powers of the German Confederation adopted the conservative, authoritarian course. The rulers of most of the smaller south German states, on the other hand, granted constitutions between 1815 and 1820, containing elected legislatures with the power to approve government expenditures and taxation. Such legislatures provided, theoretically at least, a forum for public life in which representatives of all the subjects of these states could participate. However, it was a very limited public life indeed, in view of the requirements of the Confederation for press censorship, and the rigid prohibitions on the formation of political associations.

The movements of opposition and for political change in the states of central Europe had been weaker and more ambivalent in their goals than their counterparts in the western part of the continent or in the British Isles. Their fate, though, was very much the same. In the years 1819–23, the authorities in different European states suppressed oppositional movements, generally, as they did so, taking measures to limit still further basic civil rights and the possibility of open debate on matters of public concern. The era of political ferment that characterized the five years following the end of the Napoleonic Wars was now at an end.

On the margins of Europe: conspiracy and revolt in Russia and Greece

In the three waves of revolution in Europe during the first half of the nineteenth century, 1820, 1830 and 1848, the 1820 wave was by far the feeblest, least widespread and produced the fewest political or social changes. It was also the most far-flung, including political movements on the extreme eastern edge of Europe, in Russia and Greece. Political unrest in both these countries displayed many of the features found in more centrally located parts of Europe, in particular the close connections between army officers and members of secret societies. However, social, economic and political structures in these countries differed greatly from those in the rest of Europe, so that the same institutions of conspiracy and rebellion, when transplanted to new environments, would produce rather different results.

One might want to compare politics in post-1815 Russia with those in the states of central Europe, in that it was primarily government officials who formulated different political alternatives, and these alternatives largely involved a choice between absolutist and constitutional government. Nevertheless, that said, the differences seem stronger than the similarities. If in central Europe the state officials directed or led the institutions of an emerging civil society, such institutions were essentially unknown in Russia. There was neither a press with a wide circulation (under 10 per cent of the population was literate), nor public political debate, nor gymnastics societies and student fraternities – indeed, little in the way of higher education or an educated middle class. There was certainly no elected legislature of any sort, or even a representative body of the society of orders, in the form of Estates or a Diet, except in the tsar's Polish possessions. Within the very limited circle of those aware of and interested in politics, absolutist ideas, generally held in conjunction with a devotion to Orthodox Christianity, had a far more dominant position.

In these circumstances, it is perhaps no suprise that secret societies became the main alternative to the tsar's autocratic rule. First founded in 1816, by army officers recently returned from campaigns against Napoleon in western Europe, such societies spread over the following years, forming, dissolving and re-forming, splitting and reuniting. Their membership, as was typical of secret societies in Restoration Europe, was drawn from the military and the civil service, although the Russian groups were almost exclusively from their very highest ranks. Characteristic of this state of affairs was the identity of two of the main conspiratorial leaders, Nikolas Turgenev, a high official in the Ministry of Finance, and Captain Nikita Muraviev, from one of Russia's

[344] leading families of government officials. A number of his close relatives would gain notoriety as particularly brutal and oppressive servants of the tsar. The secret societies' activities were not particularly secret, and liberal, constitutionalist members of the officer corps and the civilian state service were often aware of them, even if not themselves members.

Also as elsewhere in Europe, the political goals of the Russian conspirators were vague and mixed; some aimed for a constitutional monarchy, others for a republic. Their social and economic plans were equally vague, although they do seem to have agreed that serfdom needed to be abolished, and a society based on the possession of property be created, characteristic features of European early liberalism. The major political thinker of the conspirators – at least the one who put his ideas down on paper – was Paul Pestel, a German officer in the tsar's service. Pestel was a favorite of Tsar Alexander I for his great abilities as a military organizer and troop commander; he was, ironically, the most fervent Russian nationalist among the conspirators. Pestel thought in terms of a post-revolutionary dictatorship. Latter-day historians have tried to make him into an ominous precursor of Lenin or Stalin, but Pestel himself expressed, as might be expected from an oppositional activist in Restoration Europe, great admiration for Napoleon. The authoritarian but reforming policy identified with Napoleon seems to have inspired Pestel and other conspirators.

The Russian conspirators were a very small group, nothing like their French, Italian, or Spanish counterparts. Some actually placed their hopes in the tsar, and Alexander I on several occasions gave hints that he was thinking about granting a constitution for his entire realm. The events of 1820 elsewhere in Europe excited the secret society members, but frightened the tsar, who finally abandoned the reform plans he had been playing with for almost two decades. Consequently, the conspirators' chance came in December 1825, with the unexpected death of Alexander I. Exploiting confusion over which of the two brothers of the childless tsar was to succeed to the throne, and acting within the eighteenth-century Russian tradition of palace coups (which was how Alexander I came to the throne in the first place), the high army officers in the ranks of the conspirators called out several units of the St Petersburg garrison, with the intent of seizing members of the royal family and the central organs of government. Their coup failed, the five thousand or so soldiers they had convinced to go along with them, lined up, uncertainly, in formation in one of St Petersburg's main squares, in bitter sub-zero weather for hours, until loyal troops dispersed them and brought the conspiracy to an end. Four conspirators were executed; over one hundred were sent in exile to Siberia.

The Russian secret societies had failed, not least because they had no popular support of any kind; the conspirators had not even dared to tell the troops
they were planning to use for the coup of their real plans. Their Greek
counterparts, however, alone of all the conspirators in Restoration Europe,
were able to gain popular support – albeit of a somewhat peculiar kind, and,
with the considerable assistance of the Great Powers, suceed in carrying out
a revolution.

The Greek revolution and modern Greek nationalism, as noted in the
chapter on Napoleonic Europe, began among the communities of Greek-
speaking merchants, intellectuals and bureaucrats, who were scattered throughout southeastern Europe in the Ottoman, Russian and Austrian empires. They
began to aspire to the 'rebirth', as they put it, of the Greek nation, a nation
they saw in terms of the Enlightenment's idealization of classical antiquity.
Characteristic of this nationalist movement was a desire to return to the
language of ancient Greece, and an anti-clerical contempt for the Orthodox
Church, the shaper of Greek culture as it actually existed at the time. The first
secret society attempting to put these nationalist ideas into practice, the *Philiki
Etairia* (Friendly Society) was founded by members of such a Greek-speaking
community in the Russian city of Odessa in 1814.

Mainland Greece of the time was a very different, economically very primitive place. Pastoralism, that is, rearing flocks of sheep and goats, was one of
the main economic activities, carried out by inhabitants of mountain villages
who brought their flocks down into the sparsely populated lowlands during
the cold winter months. (There were parallel forms of economic activity in
southern Spain and Italy, but there they were one of several forms of earning
a living, as against the dominant one, in Greece.) This was a situation ripe for
banditry, and bandits were present in large numbers. The feeble Ottoman
government of Greece could do little to preserve order, so in a move similar
to the one it had carried out in Serbia in the 1790s, it deputized village chieftains and owners of large herds (themselves often ex-bandits) to head armed
militias to fight the bandits. Such mountain shepherds/warriors/thieves knew
little of the glories of ancient Athens or of the idea of Greek nationalism,
but they were armed and dangerous, and did not have much enthusiasm for
paying taxes or submitting to governmental authority.

A conflict between the Ottoman central government and its governor in
Greece, the Albanian Muslim Ali Pasha, not so dissimilar to the one that had
set off the Serbian uprising of 1804, seemed to offer the conspirators their
chance, and they led an invasion force into Greece in early 1821. This force
was quickly defeated by Turkish army units, but their proclamation of an

[346] uprising found favour with many of the highland chieftains, who promptly joined the rebellion, as it seemed to offer unprecedented opportunities for looting and pillaging. This might merely have been another in a long series of episodes of disorder on the margins of the gradually collapsing Ottoman empire, had the sultans' agents not reacted with excessive brutality. They promptly hanged the Orthodox patriarch in Constantinople, even though the leading Greek clergyman had not supported the revolt – quite the opposite, as a devout conservative, he had called on his co-religionists to be faithful subjects of their legitimate, if Muslim, ruler. Turkish forces ruthlessly massacred a large portion of the inhabitants of the Ionian island of Chios, an event that was very unpopular in most European countries.

The victorious conservatives of post-1820 Europe, who were themselves usually pious Christians and so no friends of the Muslims, found this form of legitimate government too much. While the war continued between the insurgents and Turkish forces (with the bandit chieftains fighting on both sides), the Great Powers gradually moved in the direction of intervention on the side of the insurgents. Even Metternich made this case an exception from his usual policy of support for legitimate monarchs. In 1827, British, French and Russian naval units destroyed the Turkish fleet, which had brought troops from Egypt to suppress the uprising. The following year, Russia declared war on the Ottoman empire, the latest in a series of expansionist moves to the south, that would extend from the eighteenth century until the 1870s. The sultan's government was forced to recognize Greek independence, and, as part of the arrangement, also to recognize an autonomous Serbian prince, still very vaguely under Turkish suzerainty. While the Serbs had their own indigenous ruler, Miloš Obrenović (one of whose major deeds was the execution of Karadjordje, the leader of the 1804 uprising), the Greeks had no ruler of their own, so the Great Powers then chose a European monarch for the newly independent country, Otto, the younger son of the king of Bavaria. Demobilizing the shepherd-insurgents proved difficult, and banditry, insurrection and chronic disorder would characterize the Greek kingdom for most of the nineteenth century.

An unsuccessful wave of revolutions

The peculiar success of the Greek revolutionaries offers a counterpoint against which the failures of the other insurgents and conspirators of the years around 1820 can be judged. Unlike their Greek counterparts, most would-be revolutionaries of the early Restoration era found little popular support. There were a fair number of riots and disturbances in the years between 1815 and 1820 – bread riots in much of Europe during the famine years 1816–17, for instance – but, perhaps with some exceptions in Spain during 1821–23, activists were unable to politicize such discontent over the high cost of basic necessities in the direction of political change, as had proved possible in France during the years 1789–93. Rather, political life in continental Europe remained the province of a small group – centred on soldiers and state officials, with some satellite groups of the urban middle class, such as the notables in France and university students in central Europe, revolving around them. A good deal of the impetus for politics developed out of issues of particular concern to these groups, that in turn were a consequence of the Napoleonic era: the problem of paying the debts contracted in the decades of warfare; the need to demobilize the armed forces and reduce state employment in order to cut the budget; or, in a quite different vein, the efforts of the king of Spain to reconquer his rebellious South American colonies.

This was a playing field tilted in favour of the existing governments: political and fiscal exhaustion after decades of turbulence and warfare; little popular interest in politics. What is surprising in these circumstances is not that the revolutionary wave of 1820 was so feeble and ultimately defeated as that it accomplished so much: overthrowing Restoration regimes in Spain, Portugal, Naples and Piedmont-Savoy, seriously threatening the rule of Louis XVIII of France, and sending political shock waves throughout central and eastern Europe. Such considerable effects from very modest causes reveal the other side of the coin: not just the weakness and lack of support of movements for reform or revolution, but the feebleness of the forces of order, the lack of power and authority of the governments of particularly the smaller countries of Restoration Europe.

The political and socioeconomic transformations of the revolutionary and Napoleonic eras had destroyed the bases of governmental legitimacy in the old regime. Seriously restoring these seemed an implausible alternative, but developing a new, post-revolutionary basis of legitimacy proved equally difficult. The post-Napoleonic governments inherited the Napoleonic regimes' desire to interfere in people's lives, via conscription, taxation, and a wide variety of state regulations. To be sure, the toll of young men's lives taken in decades of warfare was gone, but peace seemed to have brought relatively little in the way of relief from the burden of taxation.

In these circumstances of weak governments and weak oppositions, the decisive factor was the fact of outside military intervention. Europe's monarchs and their government ministers demonstrated their international

[348] solidarity in combating the insurrections. No Great Power was upset by re-volution, so, under Metternich's careful guidance, French and Austrian armed forces could bring revolutionary movements in southern Europe to an end; Austrian and Prussian diplomatic pressure could limit the extent of reform-ing, constitutionally oriented policies in many of the smaller German states. Only in Greece, where a combination of peculiar circumstances produced an intervention of the Great Powers, particularly the Russians, on the side of a revolution that had gained its own very distinct form of popular support, could a revolutionary movement ultimately overthrow an existing government, although it took a decade to do so.

The above remarks only partially apply to Great Britain. While postwar demobilization and the continuing fiscal burdens of wartime were certainly crucial to the political confrontations in the British Isles during the years 1816–20, politics there attracted a much greater degree of interest and political par-ticipation. Both the opposition and the government it confronted were stronger and more active than in continental Europe. The forces of reform and poten-tial revolution in England did remain regionally limited, unable to gain much support outside of metropolitan London and the industrial regions in the north of the country. Ireland, in particular, remained quiet – unlike in the 1790s – and the same conservative government that had thrown off a revolutionary challenge in that decade was able to do so again, twenty-five years later. How-ever, both the more open and more participatory character of politics in the British Isles, and the greater use of the institutions of civil society there were signposts in the direction of future events in continental Europe as well, as the revolutions of 1830 would demonstrate.

The revolutions of 1830 and the end of the Restoration

From the early 1820s until about 1828, the post-revolutionary era of conservative rule reached its high point. The organized, determined opposi-tion of the years around 1820, and its very last flare-up in the rising of the Decembrists in 1825, had been crushed. There were some liberal represent-atives in the parliaments of Britain and France, but they were always an outvoted minority. The very margins of legal opposition were occupied by the Phil-Hellenes, organized sympathizers with the Greek struggle for independence, who, at least in private, were likely to draw parallels between

oppressive Turkish rule and that of their own governments. Ultimately, [349]
Metternich would crack down on these groups as well. The mid-1820s was
a period of low grain prices, a blow for substantial farmers and large estate
owners, but a blessing for the lower classes. Industrial and manufacturing
activity, particularly in Great Britain, but to a lesser extent in the western
regions of continental Europe, enjoyed good years, so that relative prosperity
rendered people from very different social groups content with the existing
state of political affairs. Stendhal's *The Red and the Black*, the quintessential
literary testimony of the Restoration, is set in this period of political calm,
conservative rule and prosperity – a stifling time for ambitious young men,
yearning for the prospects of military glory that the revolution and the
Napoleonic era had provided.

Actually, even as Stendhal was writing his novel, the situation was changing. Economic conditions deteriorated toward the end of the decade, as five
years in succession of poor harvests, from 1828 to 1832, produced not famine or dearth, but a condition of chronic economic stress, particularly for those
without resources. The diversion of purchasing power to ever more expensive foodstuffs lessened demand for manufactured and craft goods, weakening the entire economy. Political offensives of the ultras, who began trying to
push a much more aggressively Restorationist political programme in the second half of the decade, prompted organized opposition that would prove a
good deal more successful than a decade earlier, both in devising a political
strategy, and in mobilizing popular support. The upshot would be the revolutions of 1830, and the English reform movement of that period, that would
bring the era of the Restoration to an end.

Leading up to a revolution

The big difference between the revolutions of 1830 (those of 1848 as well)
and their predecessors in 1820, was that the wave of revolution encompassed
France, still the most powerful and affluent of the Great Powers of continental Europe, and the site of the original revolution of 1789, a revolution that
continued to be an obsession for politically active Europeans. A new revolution in France would invariably have continent-wide ramifications. Most,
although not all, of the pre-history of the 1830 revolution was French.
Rather as in 1820, these events were primarily a defensive move against the
efforts of the ultras.

Louis XVIII died in 1825, and was succeeded by his younger brother,
Charles X. In 1789, as the Count of Artois, this youngest brother of Louis

[350] XVI had been one of the leaders of the hard-liners at the royal court, who had advocated dissolving the Estates General and crushing all opposition by military force. After the triumph of the National Assembly, he had become one of the first of the émigrés. Reaching the throne at the age of 67, he quickly demonstrated that his hard-line views had not softened with the years.

His coronation in the cathedral in Rheims set the signal for his reign. The elderly monarch kneeled, while the archbishop consecrated him with a flask of holy oil – used before 1789 for coronations, destroyed by the godless revolutionaries, and now miraculously recovered. Thousands of doves, symbols of the Holy Ghost, were released inside the cathedral, and the newly crowned monarch then laid his consecrated hands on sufferers from scrofula (tubercular lesions of the skin), to cure them with his sacred, royal touch. Understood as a return to the faith and tradition of the pre-revolutionary era, the coronation was a spectacle that testified to the influence of romantic aspirations and the romantics' idealized picture of the middle ages.

It also testified to the influence on the new monarch of the ultras, and their way of thinking. A number of additional steps quickly followed. The government proposed, and the conservative majority in the Chamber of Deputies, the lower house of parliament, approved, a law declaring the death penalty for sacrilege, for the theft or destruction of consecrated communion wafers (the Host), or vessels containing them. Nobody was ever executed, or even condemned for the violation of this law, but its very promulgation was a symbol of the governments' determination to restore the old regime's culture of confessionalism. The rumour quickly spread that all appointments to high government offices had to be approved by the Jesuits, and when members of the Parisian National Guard shouted 'Down with the Jesuits!' at an 1827 review, the king ordered the guard disbanded.

Having shown his royal favour to the old regime First Estate, the new monarch went on to the second, proposing government appropriations to compensate noblemen whose property had been confiscated during the revolutionary era. This 'billion [francs] for the émigrés', as the measure quickly became known, only aroused fears among peasants and middle-class property owners about their own lands, without greatly benefiting the old nobility, since the total amount was only a drop in the bucket of their losses during the revolutionary era. The coronation, the law on sacrilege, the indemnity for the émigrés were all typical of Charles X's politics: largely symbolic actions that put him in the worst possible light with a good section of the politically active public, without actually accomplishing much of practical use for the restorationist aims of the ultras.

In fact, these actions served above all to revive the liberal opposition. Un- [351]
like ten years previously, the liberal leaders of the late 1820s were very careful not to toy with secret societies and planned insurrections, but to present
themselves to the public as the defenders of the Charter and of a legal, constitutional order that was being threatened by the conspiracies of the ultras and
ultramontanists. Oppositional politicians created a national political organization, with the eminently liberal name 'Heaven Helps Those Who Help
Themselves'. Led by Paris-based deputies and writers, this group had contacts with like-minded notables in the provinces. Together, they organized
quite effectively a campaign emphasizing their anti-clericalism, and playing
up the threat of an ultra-led return to the old regime in the general elections
of 1827. An unprecedentedly large number of deputies elected in that year
supported the liberal opposition, the most since 1815. The stage was thus set
for a confrontation between the monarch and his conservative government
ministers, increasingly influenced by the ultras, the extremist wing of the conservatives on the one hand, and a liberal opposition, that was the strongest
force in parliament, on the other.

The late 1820s saw a similar stirring of political opposition elsewhere
in western Europe, in which the institutions of civil society were used to
oppose conservative regimes. This was the period of Daniel O'Connell's
campaign for Catholic Emancipation in Ireland. A similar clash was developing in the Kingdom of the Netherlands, where the (Protestant) king was
insisting on making changes in the Catholic Church within his monarchy,
bringing it further under royal control. In those portions of the kingdom
that had been assigned to it by the Congress of Vienna in 1815, and lacked
any long-term dynastic loyalty to the Dutch royal house – the territories that
had been the Austrian Netherlands before 1789 and would be Belgium after
1830 – opposition to these efforts featured an unusual cooperation between
ultramontanist and otherwise conservative Catholics, and otherwise anti-
clerical liberals. Together, they organized a very widespread petition campaign against the monarch's measures, collecting hundreds of thousands of
signatures. There were similar movements against conservative rule in a number
of the Swiss cantons.

What turned these still hesitant and scattered political initiatives into the
revolutionary wave of 1830 was the attitude of the king of France. In 1829,
Charles X appointed a government ministry consisting entirely of ultras. Its
prime minister, the prince of Polignac, had no particular governmental experience but was the son of one of Marie-Antoinette's close confidantes. This
latest example of symbolic but impractical policies was only emphasized by

[352] Polignac's major foreign policy initiative. Hoping to gain public support by re-emphasizing France's position as a Great Power (without, however, alienating the conservative Great Powers, Austria, Prussia and Russia), Polignac revived one of the most dubious aspects of Napoleon's foreign policy, the extension of French influence in North Africa, by sending an army to conquer Algeria at the beginning of 1830. This new colonial possession would prove, in the long run, a dubious acquisition for France. Its conquest had little effect on public opinion and ensured that the monarch's best troops were out of the country when they would be most sorely needed.

In the spring of 1830, on the reconvening of the parliament, a majority of deputies demanded that the king dismiss Polignac and his fellow ultras, and appoint a government ministry more to their liking. The king, seeing this – and not incorrectly – as a challenge to his royal prerogatives, and to his position under the Charter, instead dissolved parliament and called new elections. State officials were ordered to ensure that only reliable candidates were elected; the Catholic clergy, from archbishops down to parish priests, threw themselves into the government's election campaign, telling the faithful that the choice between the government and opposition was one between God and Satan. Satan, however, in the form of the increasingly well-organized opposition, wielding its press and its election committees, triumphed; a substantial majority of the deputies chosen were the candidates of the liberal opposition. The king then announced that he was dissolving parliament once more, imposing censorship on the press, and decreeing a new franchise law, that would reduce to a very small number the ranks of eligible voters and allow the government still more influence on the elections.

In taking these steps, Charles appeared to be violating the Charter, thus playing into the hands of the opposition, that had insisted it was upholding the laws and the constitution. Precisely this recourse to a strict legality facilitated the transition to revolution. Appeals in the Parisian press led to street demonstrations; the demonstrators flew the tricolour flag of the revolutionary and Napoleonic era, and began denouncing the king and cheering for the republic and for Napoleon. The police, a very modest force, were unable to control the demonstrators and the government then sent in the army. Demonstrators began building barricades, blocking the streets with paving stones, overturned carriages, and any other large objects they could find, to impede the troops' passage. Such pitched battles between insurgents and soldiers had been rare in the French Revolution of 1789; by contrast, these battles and the barricades built by the insurgents, would be typical of the mid-nineteenth century revolutions of 1830 and 1848.

The street fighting lasted from 27 to 29 July 1830, the 'three glorious [353] days', as they would come to be known. The days were so glorious because the soldiers, not very enthusiastic about fighting in the first place, grew ever more reluctant: several divisions went over to the insurgents; others refused to rejoin the fighting. The king was forced to flee the capital, first to western France, and then to England. A group of oppositional deputies, meeting in the city hall, took control of the situation. They summoned one of the surviving heroes of 1789, and a prominent liberal activist of the Restoration, the marquis de Lafayette, from his estate on the outskirts of Paris. He appeared on the balcony of the city hall with the deputies' choice for the new monarch, Louis-Philippe, duke of Orléans.

The Orléans family, close relatives of the Bourbons, had been, since the days of the Estates-General, sympathetic to the new political ideals. Louis-Philippe's father had even been a deputy to the Convention, the Jacobins' republican parliament. Under the appropriately republican name of Philippe-Egalité, he had voted for the execution of Louis XVI, although this gesture had not stopped the Jacobins from guillotining him shortly thereafter. His son had endorsed the liberal opposition during the Restoration and was quick to accept the former oppositionists' offer of the throne. His coronation symbolically demonstrated the difference from Charles X. Louis-Philippe came to the Chamber of Deputies, and, surrounded by the parliamentarians, took an oath to preserve and defend the Charter. He thus demonstrated that he would be a constitutional monarchist, and that his regime would be guided by liberal principles.

The French revolution of 1830 was not just a Parisian event, and it was not limited to the three glorious days. As in 1789, the changes in the government sparked a wave of popular protest, with demonstrations of unemployed workers and craftsmen, attacks on tax-collectors and particularly bitter conflicts over the use of the forest. As in 1789, there was a 'municipal revolution' in 1830 as well. Following anti-regime demonstrations, local opposition leaders, often former 1815 confederates or Napoleonic army officers retired on half pay, triumphantly seized control of city halls and prefect's offices throughout the country. Also as in 1789, National Guards were created everywhere, both to reinforce the new regime and to restore order after popular disturbances.

Thus, in many ways events in the summer of 1830 were a replay of those of 1789. However, this second time around, there was less improvisation. Everybody knew the forms a revolution was supposed to take, from flying the tricolour to arming the national guard. There were also some differences

[354] in 1830. While grain prices were high, they had not reached the outrageous levels of 1789, so subsistence riots, so crucial to events then, were a rarity. 1830 saw a wave of attacks on churches, the Catholic clergy – several archbishop's palaces were stormed – and on symbols of the Restoration era church, such as the large stone crosses the Jesuits erected when they held their missions. Such events had been a rarity in 1789; it was only later on in the original revolution that anti-clericalism had come to be associated with the revolutionary forces, a tradition that was strongly expressed in 1830.

From France throughout Europe

The single largest difference between 1789 and 1830 was that the latter revolution quickly stimulated imitations in many parts of Europe. Just the news of the triumph of revolution in Paris was enough to embolden already active oppositional forces, to bring the more cautious out of their reserve, and to embolden conspirators and secret society members. In the Netherlands, the joint liberal–Catholic opposition to the policies of the Dutch king intensified; street demonstrations in Brussels at the end of August 1830 turned into clashes between demonstrators and royal troops. Barricades were built, and the soldiers were defeated by the insurgents in two separate episodes of street fighting, in August and September. Similar episodes followed in a number of other cities in the post-1815 Dutch territories, and by November there was a provisional government of the newly independent Belgium.

A similar process of demonstrations followed by street fighting occurred in the autumn of 1830 in central Europe. Throughout the autumn, there were demonstrations, armed clashes and mini-civil wars in a number of the Swiss cantons. Individual cantonal governments were overthrown, and inhabitants of some cantons seceded to form new ones, both of these movements involving the creation of more liberal cantonal constitutions, but the movement did not reach the 'national' level. The Swiss Confederation remained a loose league of independent cantons, and revolutionized, or 'regenerated' as contemporaries said, and non-revolutionized cantons faced each other in a state of tension and hostility, sometimes involving smaller armed clashes, for the following seventeen years.

September 1830 saw the revolutionary scenario of demonstrations followed by the building of barricades and street fighting, in several of the medium-sized German states. The events were most spectacular in Brunswick, where the insurgents seized and burnt the ducal palace, and the authoritarian monarch abdicated in favour of a more liberal relative. They were, however, most significant in Saxony, one of the economically most advanced of the German states, where commerce flourished in the city of Leipzig, a major centre of trade between western and eastern Europe, where agriculture was fast modernizing, and where textile outworking was widespread in the western portions of the kingdom, and the first mechanized cotton mills were being built. Even though the king of Saxony had been one of Napoleon's closest allies, Saxony had preserved, throughout the Napoleonic era, its Estates, and the entire panoply of the society of orders, including guilds and an extensive seigneurial system in agriculture.

Demonstrations in Leipzig and in the capital city of Dresden at the beginning of September led to clashes with troops and the formation of a middle-class militia, along the lines of a National Guard. While middle-class politicians and journalists demanded a constitution, journeymen artisans in Leipzig attacked and destroyed the city's brothels, and peasants assaulted their lords and burned their charters of seigneurial privilege. The king agreed to grant a constitution, including a legislature, elected by a property franchise, and to abolish feudal and seigneurial relations in rural areas, albeit with compensation for the nobility, but on terms that made the peasants' task of paying this compensation a relatively modest burden.

In those southern German states that already possessed a constitution, Baden, Bavaria and Württemberg, the news of the revolution in Paris reinvigorated the liberal opposition that had been largely passive during the 1820s. Parliamentary elections held in these states in 1830 or 1831 saw liberal victories, that went furthest in Baden, where the newly elected legislature proceeded to enact a law abolishing censorship and instituting freedom of the press. This movement of reform and revolution in central Europe, however, never reached the two Great Powers of the German Confederation, Austria and Prussia. Although there were individual instances of riots and disorders in these realms, their governments neither altered their conservative course voluntarily nor were put under serious pressure to do so.

The 1830 wave of revolution reached the Italian peninsula at the beginning of 1831, where a mixture of conspiratorial actions by secret societies and street demonstrations in central Italy produced a series of short-lived revolutionary regimes. The most serious of these was in the northern part of the Papal States, centred around the city of Bologna, where insurgents threw off the rule of the pope, created a provisional government, and prepared to march on Rome itself. The affected governments – besides the Papal States, the tiny duchies of Parma and Modena – were essentially helpless against these movements. Their salvation required armed Austrian intervention, an event that

[356] would re-emphasize the fact that most of the Italian states were de facto satellites of the Habsburg monarchy. Indeed, a good deal of the agitation, public demands, conspiratorial manoeuvres and street demonstrations involved in the Italian revolution of 1830 had centred on nationalist hostility to the dominant role of a foreign power in Italian affairs, a theme that would be renewed, with much greater vigour in the revolutions of 1848.

The most dramatic of the events of 1830 took place in Congress Poland, the largest portion of the old regime Polish kingdom, that the Congress of Vienna had awarded to the tsar. Secret societies, whose members were mostly younger officers in the Polish divisions of the tsar's armies, some of whom had previously had contacts with their Russian counterparts, in the course of their conspiracies in the first half of the 1820s, decided that the three glorious days in Paris were the signal for action in Warsaw. Their planned coup would not have gone any further than the one carried out by their Russian counterparts five years previously, had not the lower classes of Warsaw joined the insurrection, built barricades, and driven the Russian authorities out of the city. Quickly, a revolutionary government was formed for Congress Poland.

This government would face the prospect of Russian military intervention to reconquer the insurgent province. The Polish troops of the tsar who had gone over to the revolution would be considerably outnumbered by the rest of the tsar's army, so the revolutionary government sought to raise support among the population. There was a good deal of sympathy for the insurgents in Warsaw, but most inhabitants of Congress Poland were peasants, who were to be armed with scythes beaten straight and attached to sticks. This was a dubious option for the peasants, even more so because they were serfs and the leaders of the revoutionary government calling for them to march into battle so armed were their feudal overlords. The peasants announced that they would first massacre the nobility, and then fight the foreign invaders. This difficult relationship between noble revolutionaries and hostile serfs would bedevil Polish nationalism and Polish attempts at revolution throughout the first half of the nineteenth century.

Even without this popular support, the Polish troops did put up a stubborn resistance and it took a campaign running from February to October 1831 for the tsar's generals to reconquer the insurgent province. It is not impossible that the troubles in Poland prevented Alexander I's deeply reactionary successor, Nicholas I, from carrying out his threat of an armed intervention in western Europe against the Belgian and possibly even the French revolutions. The concessions and quasi-autonomous status, including the Diet, granted in 1815 were revoked; the tsar's Polish subjects would be governed [357] in the same bureaucratic and absolutist fashion as almost all the others. Thousands of Polish revolutionaries fled westward, through the German states into France. Everywhere they went, they received a hero's welcome; the Polish national cause would thenceforth be one taken up by radicals and nationalists, and even many liberals, from all European countries. Brandishing their slogan, 'For your freedom and ours', exiled Polish revolutionaries would return the favour; they would fight alongside insurgents in a number of different countries during future revolutions.

Nonetheless, the events in Poland do reveal something about the nature of the 1830 revolution. In contrast to 1820, opposition political leaders from the middle and upper classes from Paris to Brussels, to Bologna, to Warsaw, were able to make common cause with the urban lower classes, whose previously passive attitude toward the Restoration governments had been shattered by high prices, and the recession that followed in their wake. The rural population, in many parts of Europe, was agitated as well, and acted against seigneurial burdens or restrictions on the use of the forests. These disturbances right across the social spectrum proved enough to overturn the government in France and spark imitations in much of the rest of the continent. However, the three eastern Great Powers, Prussia, Austria and Russia, were little touched by these events. There were certainly riots of the urban and rural lower classes, but civil society and a political opposition that could make use of its institutions were not sufficiently well developed for the events in Paris to touch off revolutions there. The action of these Great Powers would ensure that the 1830 revolutions did not spread to the entire continent, as the Russian reconquest of its Polish possessions most decisively demonstrated. It would only be in 1848, when an even larger and more dramatic uprising in Paris touched off similar results in Berlin and Vienna that a continent-wide revolutionary movement would occur.

More peaceful reform in Great Britain

In one way, though, the revolutions of 1830 had wider ramifications than any of their precursors or successors. The Europe-wide movement for political change not only reached Great Britain – as had happened in the 1790s and in 1820, and would again in 1848 – but it also produced an effect. While occurring through the existing, legal channels of government, and not involving a break in political systems, the passage of the Great Reform Bill of 1832 was nonetheless the result of years of mass movements, violent and

[358]   peaceful, organized and spontaneous, closely synchronized with the events in continental Europe. The challenge to the existing conservative regime that developed in the United Kingdom during the mid- to late-1820s and eventually culminated in a new liberal government, with a reformed electoral system was the British variant on the political changes in western Europe during this period.

In some ways, it was Great Britain – or, more precisely, Ireland – that led the way out of the political passivity and quiescence that had characterized Europe after the conservative victories in the crisis years around 1820. As noted in the previous chapter, Daniel O'Connell's campaign for Catholic Emancipation in the years 1824–28 marked an unprecedented mobilization of the institutions of civil society, including voluntary associations and mass meetings. The campaign culminated in O'Connell's victory at a parliamentary by-election in 1828.

O'Connell's very candidacy was a conscious provocation. Catholics – that is, most people who lived in Ireland – were barred by law from being seated in the Parliament at Westminister. Previously, supporters of Catholic Emancipation, including O'Connell himself, had concentrated on electing sympathetic Protestants from Irish constitutencies; now, he would challenge the entire system, and raise the possiblity of another insurrection or civil war in Ireland, should he not be admitted to his seat.

The conservative British government, under the Duke of Wellington, hero of the Napoleonic Wars, and a strongly right-wing figure, was not willing to take that risk. It proposed, instead, to repeal most political restrictions on Catholic subjects. Gathering parliamentary support from the Whig opposition, and the more moderate of the Tories, against the opposition of the 'Protestant' wing of the ruling conservatives, or the 'ultras', as they were also known, the proposal became law in 1829. For good measure, existing, lesser restrictions on Dissenters, Protestants who were not members of the Anglican state church, were also repealed.

This measure served, unintentionally, as a wake-up call to supporters of political reform in England and Scotland. They quickly imitated O'Connell's actions, forming 'political unions', voluntary associations in support of reform, in a number of cities, these groups quickly gaining 10,000–20,000 members. Such groups, rather like the opposition in continental Europe during the 1820s, had a politically mixed complexion: supporters of universal manhood suffrage, such as Henry Hunt, the veteran of the mass movements of a decade earlier, mixed with liberals, such as the philosopher James Mill, who aimed at a franchise for property owners, and a reapportionment of parliamentary seats. Ironically, these demands for reform were seconded by [359] the ultras, who felt that their calls for the retention of privileges for Protestants would be better received in a larger political audience. They founded their own associations, the 'Brunswick clubs', and held their own mass meetings and sent in their own political petitions.

The outbreak of revolution in continental Europe only heightened the mood of expectation in the reform movement, and the summer of 1830 would prove to be a tense and strained one in Great Britain as well. It was the time of the 'Swing riots', a series of uprisings by agricultural labourers in southern England, who for decades had suffered a gradually declining standard of living. Their situation was made more acute by high food prices from the period of bad harvests beginning in 1828, and brought to a fever pitch by the introduction of threshing machines, which threatened to increase post-harvest unemployment. Rioters smashed the threshing machines and burned down the farms where they were used. They demanded higher wages and more generous poor relief. Rather like the Luddites of 1812, they claimed to be commanded by a mysterious 'Captain Swing', hence the description of these movements as the 'Swing riots'.

In and of themselves, the Swing riots were not expressly political. Nor were they a fatal threat to public order, as had been the three glorious days, occurring in Paris at almost the same time. Deputized, armed property owners, backed up by small numbers of regular troops, suppressed the riots; ringleaders were executed or transported to penal colonies in Australia. Still, the riots showed, in drastic fashion, the extent of disaffection in the countryside. Increasing demands of the rioters for lower taxes, or an end to the tithes paid to the Anglican Church (generally suggested to them by farmers, who noted that with their expenses decreased they could afford to pay higher wages) demonstrated the possibility that even the most unpolitical discontent could be politicized.

The general elections of August 1830 were an occasion for express politicization. Held on the death of the monarch George IV, and the accession of his successor William IV, the campaigns at these elections centred on demands for parliamentary reform, raised by the political unions. Supporters of reform won a modest victory, and the new monarch, who was not the hidebound authoritarian conservative his predecessor had been, decided to offer the Whigs, the long-term political opposition, whose members generally possessed some version of liberal sympathies, the opportunity to form the government. It was the first Whig government (with a brief exception in 1807) since the 1780s.

[360]   The new prime minister, Lord Grey, promptly began work on a proposal for parliamentary reform. In 1831–32, the issue was at the centre of attention, both in Parliament and among the general public. The political unions held mass meetings, with tens of thousands of participants. Three thousand separate petitions in favour of reform were sent to Parliament. There were major riots in Derby, Bristol and Nottingham. Particularly at the peak of the agitation, in May 1832, when the House of Lords rejected the government's proposal and it resigned, the political situation seemed to be veering out of control. Middle-class and politically moderate activists such as James Mill called on the property owners to withdraw all their money from the banks and destabilize the financial system. Members of the political unions started armed drilling and toying with the idea of an insurrection. This was, however, the point at which the situation in Great Britain diverged fundamentally from that on the continent. Rather than continuing a politics of symbolic obstruction as Charles X had done in Paris, William IV rejected the option of an ultra government led by the duke of Wellington. He returned Grey to office and the threat of the government creating enough new peers to force the legislation through the House of Lords compelled the aristocracy to give way and vote for the measure.

The Great Reform Bill, as the measure was called, can be seen as a prime example of early nineteenth-century liberalism. It rejected the existing electoral system, with its wide variety from one constituency to the next in the numbers of people represented and the extent of the franchise. The law replaced these traditional arrangements, the result of local charters of privilege. Gone were the freemen, scot and lot, burgage, Corporation and potwalloper franchises; in their place was a uniform rule: adult men, who owned or rented a dwelling assessed at £10 for tax purposes (additionally, in the countryside, tenants of farm property worth £50), had the right to vote. While in individual constituencies, the number of eligible voters could either increase or decline, given the almost infinite variation in the pre-reformed franchise, overall, the number of eligible voters increased by some 50 per cent, to the point where every seventh adult male could vote. Constituencies were reapportioned: medieval towns, with few or no inhabitants were merged into larger districts, while major industrial centres, such as Manchester, previously unrepresented, now elected their own MPs. Finally, an electoral register was introduced: a standard list of eligible voters in each constituency, which could be easily derived from the tax rolls. In the unreformed political system, given the infinite diversity and complexity of the rules for the franchise, no one was ever completely sure who had the right to vote.

The Reform Bill thus demolished the conservative notion of politics as [361] traditionally and divinely sanctioned specific and particular privilege. Instead, it incorporated the liberal idea of a civil society of property owners, living under legally uniform rules. Indeed, contemporaries consciously made this distinction, supplementing the traditional political distinctions of Tory and Whig with conservative and liberal. However, the Reform Bill was directed just as much against radical and democratic political notions, as against conservative ones. The advocates of the bill made clear that it would not bring about universal manhood suffrage. Rather, only substantial property owners would have the vote, those who could be counted on to be respectable and self-reliant, 'those middle classes, who are also the genuine depositories of sober, rational, intelligent and honest English feelings', as Lord Brougham described them.[2]

This was certainly a sentiment that the French or Belgian liberals could share, and that the regimes they created in revolutionary fashion in 1830 were also designed to embody. However, the fact that such regimes were created in revolutionary fashion, involving a combination of violence, aggressive popular participation, and a break with legality, opened up the possibility of a revolution going further, beyond the principles of liberalism, as happened in France between 1790 and 1793. The British political crisis of 1828–32 included most of these elements. There was violence in the Swing riots and in Bristol and other cities; the political unions involved considerable mass popular participation, and, at least in May 1832, there was the potential of breaking with legality. But unlike the continental revolutions, in Great Britain these different aspects of the crisis remained disconnected. At the crucial moments, with Catholic Emancipation in 1829 and the passage of the Reform Bill three years later, the conservative forces decided not to risk a confrontation along the lines of 1789 or 1830, and in doing so ensured that the peaceful reform in Great Britain would remain within the limits of the civil society of property owners.

Toward new vistas

The revolutions and related political movements of the years around 1830 marked the end of the era of the Restoration. Attempts to recreate the social and political world of the old regime, or even, as in England, to defend still existing old regime principles, had been decisively defeated. This defeat was, admittedly, a partial one, including only the northern portions of western Europe. In Italy, most of the German states, and the Austrian and Russian

[362] empires, the dominant political elements of the Restoration were able to maintain themselves, preserving authoritarian rule and even remnants of the society of orders. However, the existence of liberal regimes elsewhere in Europe was a constant challenge to these conservative governments. They provided an example of possible change, a model for attempts at reform. Oppositionists of all sorts from all these countries could gather in the centres of new government – in Zürich, Brussels, London, or, especially Paris, that became the mecca of liberals and radicals, of oppositional journalists, students, or conspirators from the entire continent.

Thus, the creation of liberal regimes opened up the constricted and stifling political world of the Restoration, which had reached its peak in the 1820s. However, these liberal regimes involved the opening up of political options in a different way. Their future was uncertain, in the light of the precedent of the French Revolution, the basis for contemporaries' understanding of politics. The new liberal governments would allow the classic freedoms of the press, association and assembly. Political life would be more openly expressed; it would deepen and diversify. In such circumstances, could the liberal regimes establish a legitimate and recognized rule, or would the period of uncertainty and instability connected with their coming to power, lead, as it had, after 1789, to a process of radicalization and political polarization? What form would such a radicalism take, as it contended for power? Would the initial successes of revolution in 1830 quickly lead, as had been the case in 1789, to a renewal of warfare between revolutionary and counter-revolutionary powers? The revolutions in Belgium, Italy and Poland certainly seemed to open the prospect for interventions and Great Power confrontations.

In 1830–32, the concluding years of the period of crisis and instability that began in 1828, no one knew the answers to such questions. What was clear, though, was that the stifling prospect of a dreary and oppressive future, that had so dismayed Julien Sorel, had disappeared. New vistas had opened up in political life, and the events of the subsequent two decades would rush on in their direction.

Notes

1. Quoted in R.S. Alexander, *Bonapartism and the Revolutionary Tradition in France: The Fédérés of 1815* (Cambridge and New York, 1991), p. 2.

2. Quoted in D.G. Wright, *Radicalism and Reform: The Working-Class Experience 1780–1880* (London, 1988), p. 88.

CHAPTER 8

OLD CERTAINTIES AND NEW VISTAS, 1830–51

Picking up the pace

The two decades following 1830 saw a quickening of the pace of economic and social developments, and a broadening of their effects when compared to the years of the Restoration. Economic innovations, such as the use of steam engines in manufacturing, the creation of new networks of transport and communication, the introduction of new forms of organization and marketing of craft production, or the utilization of new agricultural techniques, all proceeded more rapidly and were found in more European countries than had been the case in the previous fifteen years. Parallel to these economic innovations and often interacting with them was the process of the development of the institutions of civil society. There were more newspapers, organizations and mass meetings, with ever-greater readership, membership and participation. They dealt with an ever-greater range of issues, appeared in more regions of more countries, and were tied together in ever more complex networks.

In these circumstances, it is hardly surprising that political life expanded in extent and complexity as well. A greater range of political options was available than had been the case during the Restoration; there were more avenues for political participation and a growing number of individuals who took advantage of the opportunity to participate. While politics continued to be shaped by the experience of the French Revolution of 1789, the principles of the revolution were increasingly employed in a forward-looking direction, as a way to create new forms of public life, rather than, as had been the case between 1815 and 1830, to bring back previously existing ones. This new orientation for politics both coincided with and was accelerated by a generational change in political actors. After 1830, the generation that had experienced the revolutionary and Napoleonic eras as adults gradually faded

[364] from the political stage; a newer, younger generation, born after 1800, came to the fore, throwing off the weight of the years 1789–1815, that had burdened their predecessors so heavily.

Like all generalizations, these statements need a few qualifiers. Both the extent and the pace of socioeconomic and political changes varied. They were greatest and most rapid in Great Britain (indeed, beginning earlier there than elsewhere); still considerable in the western and central reaches of the continent; less in far northern Europe; sharply less in the Iberian peninsula, southern Italy and in southeastern Europe; modest indeed in the tsar's empire. The course and speed of change was not unilinear or continuous. There would be setbacks – years of crop failure, such as 1845–47; periods of political repression, in the middle of the 1830s – when older patterns seemed to return. Political participation, in particular, did not develop steadily, but lurched forward in discontinuous leaps: the high points of Chartist agitation in 1839 and 1842 in Great Britain, or, especially, in the Europe-wide revolutions of 1848. In fact, as we consider the entire two decades following 1830, we can see four roughly delineated periods of political development.

The first encompassed the early years of the 1830s, dominated by the excitement over the mass movements of the 1830 revolution and the reform process in England. This was a period when changes were under way. Many options seemed open, and it was not clear just how far the rejection of the conservative principles of the Restoration would go. It quickly became apparent, however, that things would not go much further than they already had. The liberal regimes that had come to power in the early 1830s would not yield to more radical ones, and those portions of central and eastern Europe where the 1830 revolutions had not broken out or had been suppressed would not be able to make up this deficit. Thus, most of the 1830s fell in the second of these four periods: a time of reaction and repression – not on a par with the Restoration, certainly, but also not to be compared to the turbulent years at the beginning of the decade. Starting at the end of the 1830s, we can make out a new period of growing discontent, and rising political opposition. This third of the four periods in the years 1830–51 began first and peaked earliest in Great Britain, particularly in 1839 and 1842, the high points of the Chartist movement. By contrast, in continental Europe, the opposition movement only really got going in the early 1840s, and reached its peak in the economic and political crisis years, 1845–47. The last of the four periods was the years of revolution and reaction, 1848–51. While the Chartist movement in Great Britain had one last stab in 1848, it was already clearly past its

peak by then; the action was in the widespread wave of revolution on the
European continent. The initial successes of these revolutions, the growing
political polarization and confrontation that developed within them, and their
ultimate suppression, marked the end of the two-decade period following
the July revolution of 1830, but also the end of the entire age of revolution in
Europe that had begun in 1789.

Containing the 1830 revolution

While the three glorious days of July 1830 terminated the Restoration era,
not just in France, but across all of Europe, the future they opened up was at
first unclear. The events in Paris had led to the replacement of a conservative
monarch with a more liberal one, but three uncertainties remained after
Louis-Philippe ascended to the throne. Would the example of revolution
that brought him to power spread throughout Europe? Would his moderate
liberal regime remain in power, or be replaced by a more radical one, as had
previously happened between 1789 and 1792? And, as had happened then,
would a revolution in France be the precursor to a major European war
between revolutionary and counter-revolutionary countries? These three
questions were interrelated: both the spread of revolution and its radicalization, as the events after 1789 had shown, were closely connected to warfare.

At first, it seemed that revolution would lead to war, and the spread of
revolution would offer the occasion for such a war to begin. The new government in France declared itself no longer bound by the treaties of 1815;
the governments of Prussia, Austria and Russia mobilized their armies. The
revolutions in Belgium, central Italy and Poland made ideal causes for a war.
However, no war broke out; quite the opposite, the new liberal regime in
France tacitly cooperated with its conservative counterparts in eastern Europe
– the 'three northern courts', as they were called – to avoid it.

An international conference, meeting in London, recognized the independence of Belgium and its separation from any existing military alliances. This
was the famous 'Belgian neutrality', that would, in 1914, provide the pretext
for Great Britain to enter the First World War. When the king of Holland
refused to recognize this decision, and sent his army to reoccupy his insurgent
provinces, French troops intervened to expel the Dutch soldiers. The new
Belgian monarch was a Dutch prince, not a French one, as the French had

[366] hoped, but he married one of Louis-Philippe's daughters. None of the northern courts had moved to stop the French, and the government of Louis-Philippe returned the compliment by not intervening when Russian troops crushed the Polish insurrection and Austrian troops restored the rule of the Pope in central Italy.

The 1830 revolutions thus did not result in war between revolutionary and counter-revolutionary regimes, but in the tacit partition of the continent, into a western part, dominated by the liberal Great Powers, France and England, and a central, southern and eastern portion, dominated by the three conservative Powers, Austria, Prussia and Russia. We can see in this partition the hand of Metternich, and his policy of flexible conservatism. Rather than attempting to preserve the Restoration settlement in all of Europe by war, and thus perhaps sparking a new wave of revolution, he preferred to concede a portion of the continent to liberal regimes to preserve conservative rule in the rest of it.

The Spanish civil war of 1833–40 would demonstrate how this partition worked in practice. The war began as a dynastic confrontation, not unlike the one in the first decade of the nineteenth century, that led to Napoleon's disastrous intervention. The question this time was about the appropriate successor to Ferdinand VII, who had no male heir: his daughter, Isabella, or his younger brother, Don Carlos. Ferdinand's death in 1833, with his daughter just two years old, and the appointment of Isabella's mother, the Italian princess Maria Cristina, as regent, brought the issue, which had previously turned primarily on the interpretation of obscure points of dynastic law, into a military confrontation between the partisans of Don Carlos and those of Isabella.

The alignment of these clashing dynastic interests with different political groupings, that had become considerably more active in Spain following the 1830 revolutions, particularly in neighbouring France, changed the nature of the confrontation. Radicals and moderates in the army and in the politically active civilian population, often ex-activists of the 1820 revolution, rallied to the cause of the regent. Conservatives, especially in the unusually devout northern regions of the country, became the partisans of Don Carlos. (Indeed, the name 'Carlists', would spread beyond Spain and become widely used for supporters of the extreme right in southern Europe for several decades.) While the supporters of Isabella and her mother, the regent, controlled most of the country, the Carlists created their own government in the north, and the ensuing civil war between opposing dynastic claimants became a political struggle between revolution and counter-revolution. The war attracted Europe-wide attention, and politically motivated volunteers from across the continent joined the armies on both sides.

The central government, whose civilian leadership was increasingly a de [367] facto coalition of liberals and radicals, in the course of pursuing the civil war, seized and sold church property, abolished entailed estates, and brought seigneurialism to an end. These measures had first been proposed with the constitution of 1812, and again with the revival of that constitution in the 1820 revolution, but had once again been abolished by previous counter-revolutions. This time the results were permanent, because the government's forces would eventually triumph over the Carlists, in seven-year combat, marked by major lost opportunities on both sides. Conflicts between the victorious liberal and radical elements followed in the wake of the military suppression of the Carlists, and the political situation only settled down, temporarily, in 1844, following a military coup and the promulgation of a liberal constitution, similar to that of the July Monarchy.

This civil war began what one might call the decoupling of Spanish politics from that of the rest of Europe. Beginning in 1834, after the revolutionary tide of 1830 had ebbed everywhere else, it reached its maximum intensity in the late 1830s, a time of political quiescence in the rest of the European continent. The 1848 revolution, that would stir up all of Europe, on the other hand, quite passed Spain by. A new cycle of revolution, military coups, and civil war would begin there in 1854, when the rest of Europe lay in the post-revolutionary grip of the era of reaction. It is precisely this uniquely Spanish aspect of the civil war of 1834–40 that reveals its broader European significance.

Quite in contrast to the previous revolution and civil war in Spain, in 1820–23, or the revolutions in the Italian states of 1820 and 1830, the civil war and its outcome had their origins, above all, in the domestic situation: there was, in other words, no outside intervention. The reactionary eastern Great Powers, the Russians in particular, had considered intervention, but they were held off by the informal division of the continent following the 1830 revolution. The grandiloquently named 'Quadruple Alliance', linking the liberal Spanish government and its counterpart in Portugal (which was undergoing a similar dynastic controversy turning into a politically charged civil war, at about the same time that Spain was) with the western liberal powers, England and France, in opposition to any outside intervention, made the risks of such an intervention too high. Metternich, in particular, was unwilling to consider one.

The influence of the liberal western powers did not extend to the Italian peninsula, or to central and eastern Europe. Prussia and Austria used the institutions of the German Confederation to act against liberal currents in the

[368] other German states, that had emerged in the wake of the 1830 revolutions. They obtained, for instance, a decision of the Confederate Diet forcing the Grand Duchy of Baden to abolish its recently established freedom of the press, on the grounds that such a freedom violated the fundamental rules of the Confederation, laid down in 1815.

This cementing of the Restoration era status quo in the states of Italy, Germany and eastern Europe would provoke permanent unrest, particularly in view of the creation and establishment of liberal regimes in the western portion of the continent and in the British Isles, a result reinforced by the progress of the civil war in Spain. We can see this attitude during the early 1830s, in the response to the Prussian and Austrian assault on liberal legislation in the constitutional states of southern Germany. Liberal activists in Bavaria established a 'Press and Fatherland Association', to oppose the authoritarian offensive. Their group, with thousands of members, showed the political potential of the institutions of civil society. It made use of another of these institutions, the mass meeting, sponsoring political festivals across southwestern Germany in 1832. The largest of these, the Hambach National Festival, held in the Palatinate, the Bavarian possession in the extreme southwestern corner of Germany, in May of that year, had 30,000 participants. Besides the black–red–gold national flag, Phrygian caps appeared, reminders of the two decades when the area had been under French republican and Napoleonic rule. Speakers strongly but vaguely denounced the conservative German governments; Polish and French radicals appeared on the platform along with their German counterparts, in a solidarity characteristic of early nationalist movements. The Bavarian authorities, caught off guard, quickly responded by prohibiting the group, arresting its leaders, and sending half the kingdom's entire army into its southwestern province to convince the inhabitants not to demonstrate their radical sympathies.

If the continuation of conservative regimes in central Europe was an occasion for determined political opposition, the newly created liberal governments in the west of the continent themselves quickly disillusioned a substantial proportion of their one-time supporters, who had brought them to power in the first place. The overthrow of the Bourbon monarchy in France and the passage of the Reform Bill in England had been the result of a tacit coalition of liberal – constitutionalist, politically moderate – and radical – democratic and republican – elements. It soon became clear that the newly established governments were dominated by the former groups.

The liberal British government that passed the Great Reform Act in 1832 was the same one that devised the New Poor Law of 1834, creating a centralized, standardized, as well as harsh and degrading treatment of those [369] in need of assistance. A standardized and stiff property franchise for municipal elections was introduced in 1835, replacing many local variations, and excluding most adult men from participation. The new liberal government would be, as liberals wished, a regime of property owners. While the British government had repealed most measures discriminating against Irish Catholics, the liberal governments of the 1830s were determined to see that they did not exercise their rights in any way that might threaten British rule: habeas corpus was suspended in Ireland, and the power of the exclusively Protestant justices of the peace reinforced.

Radical disappointment with the new liberal regime was, if anything, even greater in France. Suffrage was extended after the 1830 revolution – but only from 3 per cent of adult men, to 5 per cent. For radicals, who believed strongly in universal manhood suffrage, and even for those liberals who had a generous notion of how many property owners should have the vote, this openly plutocratic voting regime was a serious affront. Radicals of the first half of the nineteenth century, as the reader will recall, were a militaristic group, looking for a war against the reactionary Great Powers and a solidarity of revolutionary nationalist movements. Louis Philippe's government, however, let the Russians destroy the Polish revolution and the Austrians intervene in Italy, without doing much more than making some mild diplomatic protests. It did help hold off intervention of the reactionary powers in Spain, but refused to intervene itself on the side of the government against the Carlists, as radicals wished. All these actions were an affront, both to the older revolutionary and Napoleonic tradition, and to the newer, nineteenth-century, radical cause of an independent Poland.

Adding insult to injury, the trial of the former ministers of Charles X, whose counter-revolutionary machinations had led to the July revolution in the first place, ended with suspiciously light sentences. There were demonstrations and riots in Paris when the verdict was announced. The funeral of General Lamarque, one of the republican leaders (as had been the case since the 1790s, many prominent republicans of the early 1830s were army officers) in June 1832, led to demonstrations and the building of barricades. The government had to call in the army, to assist the National Guard, and in the ensuing street fighting, some eight hundred people were killed before order was restored. Letting off the conservative counter-revolutionaries easily and shooting down republicans in the street – this was how radicals came to see (perhaps somewhat unfairly) the liberal order of the July monarchy.

[370] Conspiracy, insurrection and repression

Legal and open opposition, both to continued conservative rule in central, eastern and southern Europe, and to liberal rule in the west of the continent, had been met with repression and military force. The middle years of the 1830s were a second high point of secret societies, as radical activists tried to establish conspiratorial networks that could be used to overthrow regimes that they could not oppose legally. A good example of this transition from legal to illegal opposition is provided by some younger – mostly student – and more hot-headed members of the German Press and Fatherland Association. Following its prohibition in 1832, they reorganized themselves as a secret society, and attempted to launch an insurrection in Frankfurt, capital of the German Confederation, the following year. A similar path can be traced in France, where the more radical members of the Heaven Helps Those Who Help Themselves association, the organization of opposition to the government of Charles X, regrouped as a conspiratorial, republican, Society of the Rights of Man. The secret cells of the group were named after Robespierre and other heroes of the Jacobin republic of the 1790s.

The largest of the radical secret societies in the 1830s was Giuseppe Mazzini's Young Italy. Founded in Marseille by Mazzini, it recruited its original cadres among refugees from the central Italian revolution of 1830, who had fled to safety in liberal France. It quickly organized tens of thousands of adherents in the Italian peninsula, who were prepared to rise up when the exiles launched an armed incursion. Such an uprising, Mazzini hoped, would lead to a nationalist war against the Austrian occupiers of northern Italy and the creation, from this warfare, of a united Italian republic.

However, Young Italy's incursion/uprising of 1834 was a failure, as was the effort of the youthful German radicals in 1833, or the planned uprisings of the French republican secret society members in 1834 and 1839. Further efforts of secret society members in 1846, in Austrian Poland and in southern Italy, proved equally unavailing. The basic problem with secret societies was that their needs for secrecy, for conspiratorial organization, and for widespread support, so as to make their insurrection, contradicted each other. Secret societies with very large memberships, such as Mazzini's Young Italy, simply could not remain secret from the police. Indeed, the 1834 uprising the group sponsored was forced upon it, when police uncovered the organization and Mazzini felt that he had to move or see his group disbanded. By contrast, smaller and more tightly knit secret societies, such as the Society of the Seasons founded by Auguste Blanqui, the French revolutionary, who was one of the first to bring communist ideas into his radical organization, could [371] remain hidden from the police. When they took action, though, as happened when Blanqui called his one thousand followers into the streets of Paris in 1839, they were too few to pose a serious challenge to the authorities, and could be easily suppressed.

In the end, the legal and illegal opposition of the early and mid-1830s was met, in both conservative and liberal states, with renewed repression. Under Metternich's guidance, the German Confederation reiterated its opposition to basic civil liberties and created a central office for political police work, to track down dissidents in all the German states. In the Papal States of central Italy, the government organized its conservative supporters into paramilitary leagues, the 'centurions', handed out weapons to them, and let them slaughter their opponents, in an action that was half vendetta and half White Terror. However, repression, if perhaps not on quite so drastic a scale, took place in the liberal states as well, whether growing police measures in Ireland, or the passage of legislation in France requiring government permission for the formation of associations, and prohibiting attacks in the press on the royal family or the public advocacy of the republic. By the mid-1830s, these repressive measures brought the period of political movement and possibility that had been so characteristic of the beginning of the decade to an end.

The challenge of the Chartists

The radical journalist Bronterre O'Brien, who named the newspaper he edited *The Poor Man's Guardian*, would later describe, quite succinctly, the disappointment that leftists in Great Britain felt about the outcome of the Great Reform Act:

> What was the first act of the Reformed Parliament? The Coercion Bill for Ireland. What was the last act of the first session? The New Poor Law for England. Why did that base Parliament pass both these acts? To place the labouring classes of both countries at the feet of the rich assassins, who rob, brutalize and enslave the population of both.[1]

Such a condemnation delineated the difference between the liberal view of a civil society of property owners, and the radical vision of a democratic polity. Liberals might maintain that only substantial property owners possessed the independence and insight to vote appropriately for parliamentary

[372] representatives, who could then govern the country in the common interest. From the viewpoint of the disenfranchised, the propertyless or almost propertyless labourers, craftsmen and the new and growing group of industrial workers, this purported common interest seemed more like the particular interests of those who had property. Also as O'Brien's passage indicates, this was not just a theoretical concern, but in view of the Poor Law, or the coercive legislation on Ireland, one with implications for working people's everyday lives.

In the mid-1830s, this viewpoint was widespread among political activists who had gained experience in the agitation over the Great Reform Bill at the beginning of the decade. They formed or re-formed associations, such as the London Working Men's Association, or the Birmingham Political Union that made universal manhood suffrage – a voice in government for the propertyless – a central concern of their activities. In 1837, a committee of six working-class activists, and six radical Members of Parliament met to draft a programme, the People's Charter. Its six points were exclusively political in nature. Their central demand was universal manhood suffrage, along with some related points, such as the secret ballot, so that the propertyless could exercise their franchise independently of the pressure of property owners, or paying Members of Parliament, so the propertyless could afford to hold such an office. Over the next five years, the demands raised by the Chartists, the supporters of the People's Charter, would be central to political life in Great Britain, and would represent the first widespread offensive against the liberal regimes that had come to power at the beginning of the 1830s.

The Chartist movement made full use of all the institutions of civil society. Its main national newspaper, *The Northern Star*, had a press run of 40,000 at its peak, a remarkable figure for the era. The newspaper printed the speeches and tactical and strategic proposals of the leaders of the movement, but it also reported at length on the activities of the ordinary members, creating the sense among its readers of belonging to a nationwide political movement. Countless local newspapers, admittedly often small and short-lived ventures, contributed to the effort. Public mass meetings were a key feature of Chartism, and the movement brought forth a whole array of political agitators, who were riveting public speakers, including its dominant figure, the Irish gentleman attorney Feargus O'Connor.

Most important, perhaps, was the voluntary association. The National Charter Association, that sought to unite and centralize all individual groups involved in the movement, counted 400 affiliated societies, with 50,000 members, but that was just a fraction of the individuals and associations involved. These groups made possible a reform movement, by organizing public meetings, parades and demonstrations, or sponsoring petition drives, but they also met regularly so that their members could socialize or educate themselves. Their support for the People's Charter overlapped with other causes, such as opposition to the New Poor Law (a particularly powerful issue in northern England), hostility to slavery, support for a shorter working day, or the founding of producers' and consumers' cooperatives. Membership of Chartist groups and other organizations, such as mutual benefit societies or trade unions, overlapped, and it was not always easy to tell them apart.

A particular feature of Chartism was that it offered women an unusually expansive opportunity to participate in public life. There were at least 150 'Female Chartist Associations', whose members would support the Chartist campaigns. Women came in large numbers to the Chartist mass meetings and public demonstrations; some even participated in riots and clashes with the police and the army. They spoke in their own female groups, and even sometimes before a mixed-sex audience. Admittedly, a good deal of women's Chartist activities, very much in the tradition of women's activity in the Jacobin clubs during the French revolution, and, as would later be the case in continental Europe during the revolution of 1848, was of an auxiliary nature: sewing banners and decorations, preparing festive and social occasions, or gathering contributions to support the families of political prisoners.

Women justified their political actions in these terms as well. Only a small number of women active in the Chartist movement called for female suffrage; most just supported the demand for universal male suffrage. Chartist women explained that they had left the female sphere of home and family because a government run by property owners had reduced them and their families to want and misery. They denounced the oppressive legislation that, they asserted, had placed the lower classes in poverty and forced married women to leave their homes for the workplace, thus neglecting their families. A parliament elected by all adult men, including an appropriate number of representatives of the propertyless, would ensure that such conditions no longer obtained.

Like other radical political movements in Great Britain since the 1790s, the Chartists faced the problem of how to obtain their goals in the face of a hostile government. The members of the various Chartist associations geared up to present mass petitions to Parliament: the petition of 1839 had over one million signatures; that of 1842 over three million. Only a small minority of MPs voted in favour of even receiving and debating the petitions; a

[374] substantial majority of both liberal and conservative Members of Parliament preferred simply to ignore them. This was less than surprising, and Chartist leaders had to consider how to proceed further. They reached back into the history of radical movements for potential strategies.

The petitions were backed up with threatening mass meetings, at which speakers made allusions to the need for the people to use force to gain their rights, along the lines of what Daniel O'Connell had done in Ireland fifteen years earlier. However, the government was not impressed; it merely made plans to use the newly created police force, backed up by the army, to restore order. The Chartist leaders twice called a 'Convention' – a national gathering of delegates of Chartist Associations – as their British Jacobin counterparts had done in the 1790s. The delegates debated what could be done further. Some, the 'physical force' Chartists (as opposed to the non-violent, 'moral force' Chartists), thought the time had come for violent, insurrectionary action. Chartists drilled and gathered arms, actions which led to the arrest of some prominent leaders. An insurrection did break out in Wales in the autumn of 1839, the 'Newport rising', in which an armed, night-time march of several thousand Chartists (largely coalminers) on the town of Newport was defeated by the combination of bad weather and a small army garrison. There were links with potential insurgents in a number of industrial cities in northern England, although, as had been the case in past potential insurrections, the connections involved government agents.

Already in 1839, and, more pronouncedly three years later, some Chartists proposed a quite different strategy, what they called a 'national holiday' or a 'sacred month', what we would today call a general strike. Working people would leave their jobs en masse, provoking a government intervention and a more generalized insurrection. In the summer of 1842, the year of a severe business cycle downturn – a depression really, in which unemployment was widespread and severe wage cuts for both factory workers and outworking artisans the order of the day – this option seemed more attractive. Large-scale work stoppages in Manchester and other northern industrial cities – known as the 'plug riots', because factory workers pulled the plugs on steam boilers to stop the machinery from working – were mixed in with demands for the Charter. However, once more, the government ultimately remained in control, again arresting Chartist leaders. While not entirely disappearing, the movement gradually faded after that, although it would put in one more large appearance in the revolutionary year 1848.

Historians have long understood Chartism as a precursor to the organized socialist and labour movement of the early twentieth century, and seen it as a response of factory workers to the Industrial Revolution. In more recent scholarship, a somewhat different view has emerged, that emphasizes instead the connections of Chartism with earlier episodes of radical movements in Great Britain: the British and Irish Jacobins of the 1790s, the mass movements after the Napoleonic Wars, Daniel O'Connell's campaign for Catholic Emancipation in Ireland, and the campaigns for the Great Reform Bill. Like all these predecessors, Chartism centred on the demand for political reforms that would break the power of an unfair and unrepresentative Parliament, dominated by the parasitic and unproductive classes, and enable democratically elected legislators to deal with the pressing problems of the productive citizens. Chartist connections with these past movements were close. Local leaders and activists had generally gained their initial political experience in them. Orator Hunt, the recently deceased leader of the mass movements of the post-1815 period, was a major political hero in the Chartist pantheon, and Chartists used political symbols, like Hunt's white hat, or the Phrygian cap of the Jacobins of the 1790s, in their meetings and demonstrations. Daniel O'Connell, the leader of the movement for Catholic Emancipation was one of the six MPs who had helped formulate the People's Charter; Feargus O'Connor, the major Chartist leader, began his political career as one of O'Connell's parliamentary lieutenants. O'Connell, however, quickly broke with the Chartist movement, taking many of his Irish supporters with him, which would prove to be a major weakness for the Chartists.

Also like its predecessors, the strongholds of Chartism were in London and the industrial or proto-industrial centres of England or Scotland; it was a movement that attracted little support from the agricultural population. As far as can be told, most active Chartists were not factory workers but craftsmen and outworkers – with the fast-declining and increasingly desperate handloom weavers making up a large portion of the members, once again, like earlier radical political movements. Unlike the case in later labour parties, trade unions frequently kept their distance from Chartism, looking to build their organization and negotiate higher wages from employers, rather than placing their eggs in the basket of parliamentary reform. While individual supporters of Owenism, the socialist movement in Great Britain during the 1830s and 1840s, endorsed the People's Charter, the Owenite movement itself and its leader and chief theorist Robert Owen, denounced Chartism. For Owen, as was the case with most early socialists, political solutions were useless in confronting social problems; a 'new moral world', a spiritual revolution among property owners and the propertyless, was the only way to resolve the problems of the day.

[376]   Chartism looks different when placed in this context – more a last example of the radicalism of the age of revolution, the years between 1789 and 1850, than a precursor of future socialist and labour movements. This view also explains the weaknesses of Chartism. Unlike the Reform agitation of the years around 1830, it was unable to draw on middle-class support (and largely lacked the Irish connection of the Reform agitation as well), and faced a problem common to earlier radical movements of the 1790s and the post-1815 period: how to force change on an unwilling government, that could count on a broad backing from liberals and conservatives, from the middle and upper classes, and the tacit support of a politically largely indifferent agricultural population. The resulting veering between two equally unsatisfactory tactics, peaceful petitions and mass meetings on the one hand, and insurrectionary preparations on the other – between 'moral force' and 'physical force', as the Chartists said – was common to earlier movements as well.

However, one must not overdraw this portrait. As the plug riots showed, there were factory workers in industrial towns like Manchester and Oldham who supported the Chartists, and some trade unionists were also involved in the movement. The Chartists were a political movement and did not have an economic or social programme; the ideas of their supporters, as was generally the case with radicals in Europe during the first half of the nineteenth century, ranged over a wide variety of positions, from endorsing the free market, to experimenting with producers' cooperatives, to proposing to resettle city dwellers and industrial workers on small plots of land in the countryside. The strategy of a 'national holiday' or 'sacred month', however, the idea of beginning a confrontation with a general strike, suggests the growing conceptual significance of wage labour in the Chartists' understanding of the world. The importance of the 1842 depression – a business cycle downturn, not a crisis year of bad harvests and high food prices – for trying to implement this strategy shows the influence of a new, increasingly industrialized social order. While the Chartists may have drawn a distinction between the productive and unproductive classes, as their radical predecessors did, they increasingly included capitalist merchants and factory owners among the unproductive, along with the earlier landowners, state officials and clergy of the established church, while identifying the productive classes with the working classes, admittedly a group including craftsmen and outworkers, as well as factory proletarians. Thus we might say that Chartism was more a culmination of past developments than a precursor of future ones, but it also showed a number of newer, forward-looking features within its broader continuity with the past.

Also unlike past radical movements, the Chartists were acting in a more highly developed civil society, and in a political system with a reformed Parliament and conservative and liberal political parties more capable of taking action. The Chartists' belief that a still unrepresentative Parliament could not resolve issues of interest to the unrepresented and propertyless population would prove not to be true. In the second half of the 1840s, Parliament, following a long campaign of the Anti-Corn Law League (a mass campaign of the liberal middle class, whose scope might be compared to Chartism) abolished the Corn Laws and thus brought down the price of food. The Ten-Hours Bill of 1847, limiting the length of the working day, was another example of legislative action for social reform.

One final dissimilarity between Chartism and past British radical movements was the lack of synchronization between events in Great Britain and on the European continent. The English, Scottish and Irish Jacobins of the 1790s were part – indeed, a major part – of a Europe-wide political movement. The reform agitation of the years 1816–20 was also the leading edge of a postwar political movement that extended into continental Europe. The passage of the Reform Bill and the continental revolutions of 1830 were closely connected. However, the high point of the Chartist movement in the years 1839 and 1842 was a low point of oppositional political activity in continental Europe. By contrast, the declining years of Chartism after 1842 marked a period of increasing political tensions and the onset of a major European revolution. In 1848, when virtually all of continental Europe would be shaken by revolution, the Chartists would revive somewhat in England, but could hardly match their earlier efforts, much less the struggles taking place on the European continent.

Heading for a revolution: continental Europe in the 1840s

In the course of the 1840s, the tacit post-1830 partition of the continent between a conservatively ruled east and south, and a moderately liberal west began to unravel. Both the conservative regimes, where much of the political and intellectual structures of the Restoration era remained after the 1830 revolution, as well as their cautiously liberal counterparts, came under attack. There were two main causes that lay behind this development. First was a change in the general economic situation. The difficult years 1828–32 gave

[378]   way, later in the 1830s, to a more prosperous period, characterized by lower food prices (although still higher than in the early 1820s), the expansion of commerce and outwork, and the very earliest beginnings of industrialization in continental Europe. While these commercial and industrial developments continued into the 1840s, and were accompanied by the beginning of the building of a rail network, the situation in agriculture – still the dominant sector of the economy – became less favourable. Harvests were poor; the price level rose; particularly bad harvests in 1843, that created near-famine conditions in parts of Europe, were followed by the major subsistence crisis of 1845–47, the very last peacetime, continent-wide famine. This economic crisis tended to destabilize existing governments.

The second main cause was the further development of civil society. The steady spread of associations and the press during the 1830s and 1840s brought ever-larger segments of the population into consideration of and participation in public life. Now, governments tried to direct this development away from potentially subversive channels by requiring official consent for forming voluntary associations or holding public meetings, by censoring the press or limiting its circulation. However, these efforts did not have their desired effect. Political associations might be prohibited, but it was impossible to prevent members of associations for civic improvement, or adult education, of choral societies, religious groups, scholarly associations or theatrical societies, from discussing public affairs at their gatherings. The press might be censored, but people could still gather in cafés and taverns to read newspapers and discuss what was not printed in them. Festivals and parades could and did take on a political content, in spite of all the insistence on the part of the authorities that they should not do so.

The upshot of both these developments was that events of diplomacy, the royal courts and high politics were increasingly politicized, the subject of public discussion. Examples of such a politicization would include the so-called 'Rhine Crisis' of 1840, which briefly brought forth the danger of a general European war; the coming to the throne of a new monarch, Frederick William IV, in Prussia that year, or the election of the bishop of Imola as Pope Pius IX in 1846. The very substantial public reaction to each of these events, well beyond the usual circles of the powerful and the well educated, demonstrated the growth of a politicized public opinion, that would be difficult to reconcile with the post-1830 structures of government.

There are, as usual, two qualifications that need to be noted about these developments. First, there is the familiar west–east spectrum. Generally, the political public was larger, encompassing a greater portion of the population, and the activities of civil society more pronounced the further west one proceeded in Europe. Admittedly, this distinction is not a perfect one: the political public was remarkably large in Hungary – and not just by eastern European standards – while in far southwestern Europe, in southern Italy and the Iberian peninsula, it was a considerably smaller part of the population than in France, the Low Countries or Switzerland. For all these distinctions within continental Europe, the contrast between Great Britain and the continent remains very stark. Before the revolution of 1848, there was nothing in continental Europe to compare with the campaigns in Great Britain of the Chartists, and Anti-Corn Law League, or Daniel O'Connell's movement for political autonomy in Ireland (the 'repeal' campaign). Second, and closely related to the first, these developments were very largely found in urban areas. They could include portions of the urban lower classes, particularly artisans, but the farming population – a majority of the inhabitants of most western European countries, and a substantial majority in eastern Europe – was generally excluded from this process of politicization. Let us now examine this process more closely, starting with sketches of its unique features in France, the Italian states, the German states, and the Austrian empire. Then, we will consider the crisis years 1845–47, and the creation of a pre-revolutionary situation, leading up to the events of the spring of 1848.

France

The July Monarchy, as its name indicates, had come to power in the revolution of July 1830, and the liberalism characteristic of the regime had originally been an oppositional doctrine; the politicians who espoused it in the 1820s had done so in semi-revolutionary fashion. By the 1840s, though, these days of liberalism as a doctrine on the left side of the political spectrum – still very much a live notion elsewhere in Europe – were largely at an end in France. The dominant figure in the French government during that decade, François Guizot, a liberal oppositionist of the 1820s, pursued a cautious, establishment version of liberal policies. These included support for elementary education, via a law requiring each municipality to have a free public school for boys (Guizot was not opposed to educating girls; they just had a lower priority), and for economic development, through protective tariffs to encourage industry and government planning for a nationwide rail network, and financial help for the entrepreneurs who started to build it. This close cooperation with big business was reflected in the high property requirement for voting, that enfranchised just 5 per cent of adult men. Guizot renounced,

[380]   on the other hand, the more militant, left-wing side of liberalism, that had been apparent in the 1830 revolution, and continued to be visible for the following decade. He abandoned anti-clericalism and strove for good relations with the Catholic Church; rather than an aggressive foreign policy aimed at the Treaty of Vienna and the domination of conservative powers in much of Europe, he looked to peaceful cooperation with them, and even toward an alliance with the Austria of Prince Metternich, the leading statesmen of the Restoration.

The July Monarchy remained a liberal regime, with constitutional guarantees of basic rights, in spite of legislation in the 1830s that had restricted these rights. There existed an unusually wide spectrum of oppositional groups, but they had trouble working out a political strategy. On the left, the republicans, following the failure of their armed uprisings in the 1830s, were much more cautious. Grouped around the editorial staff of the Parisian newspapers, *La Réforme*, and *Le National*, their following was concentrated in Paris itself, and a few larger provincial cities, such as Toulouse. Their leaders criticized the government's unwillingness to confront conservative and counter-revolutionary powers in its foreign policy, its accommodation with organized religion, its undemocratic franchise. Open advocacy of a republic was illegal, and tacit republicans, on the left, were grouped with supporters of the existing ruling dynasty, who wished to see a more democratic regime under an Orléans monarch.

Such leftists were quite unsure of their economic and social policy. Some opposed the government's protectionism and, following the example of the British Anti-Corn Law League (that seemed quite impressive in France), were in favour of free trade and the free market. Others, in the Jacobin tradition, considered a society of small property owners. The third and smallest group, most evident among those former secret society conspirators who had evaded being arrested, had vague ideas about socialism. All could agree to expose scandals in the regime and denounce it for its corruption – whose existence was perhaps not too suprising, given the efforts at encouraging economic development.

France, in the 1840s, did have a substantial and growing labour movement and a very large socialist movement as well. Craftsmen, above all, made illegal use of their mutual benefit societies as trade unions, and launched frequent strikes, which were illegal, too. Sympathetic intellectuals collaborated with such craftsmen, and the decade saw the flourishing of a labour press in France, where ordinary workers expressed their ideas in print. Both the intellectuals and the workers who collaborated in this labour press often had socialist sympathies, but most French socialists, like their Owenite counterparts in England, were generally suspicious of left-wing politics, of conspiracies, insurrections, and a new Jacobin regime. In the fashion of the early socialist movement, they looked to individual moral regeneration, often expressed in a Christian language, as the way to a new, cooperative regime. Thus, the socialist/labour movement and the radical political opposition largely went their separate and different ways

However, since 1830, the French government had faced opposition not just from the left, but from the right, from the 'legitimists', as the French conservatives were called, the partisans of the legitimate Bourbon monarchy that had been overthrown in July of that year. Since conservative thought, as it developed into a body of doctrine during the Restoration era, was based on the notion of divinely sanctioned legitimate government, conservatism had been a doctrine of those in power. For conservatives, being in opposition was a new and bewildering experience. French conservatives followed a variety of different tactics.

One possibility, favoured by the nobility and the devout inhabitants of western France, was to refuse to recognize the new regime. A few tried to imitate the actions of the Chouans, the counter-revolutionaries of the 1790s, but the stronger and more effective government forty years later, operating on a terrain of greater socioeconomic and legal stability, made short work of their uprising in favour of the Bourbons in 1832. After that, such conservatives just withdrew from politics and waited for divine judgement on the godless government of Louis-Philippe. Another option, favoured by conservatives in southern France, was to use the institutions of the liberal regime to oppose it, to criticize government policies, often not too differently from the left-wing opposition, and to run conservative candidates for parliament, frequently making political deals with leftists in doing so. Strict conservatives, including the Bourbon pretender, condemned this approach as unprincipled. Finally, a number of conservatives rallied to the regime in the 1840s. They could live with Guizot's very moderate brand of liberalism, and saw supporting it as a lesser evil, compared to the option of a republic or a socialist regime.

There was one more, uniquely French, political option: Bonapartism, the return to power of a member of the Napoleonic dynasty. Both the emperor himself and his son, who lived his whole life as a quasi-prisoner in Vienna and died at a young age, were gone by the early 1830s. Louis-Napoleon, the son of Napoleon's brother Joseph, took up the dynastic cause and proclaimed himself Napoleon III. He twice attempted to come to power as his uncle had

[382] in the 'hundred days', by landing in France with a few followers and winning over the armed forces. Both efforts, in 1836 and 1840, were dismal failures. Although there was plenty of sympathy for Napoleonic rule in the French army, and, in fact, virtually everywhere in French society (most of the participants in the 1830 uprising, for instance, had thought in terms of a return of Napoleon rather than an Orléans monarchy), Louis-Napoleon seemed unable to exploit it. Yet the amorphous character of Bonapartist sympathies would prove to be a strength as well as a weakness. For support of a Napoleonic regime cut across political lines: one could be virtually anywhere on the political spectrum, from the left to the right and be enthusiastic about a new Bonpartist emperor. Louis-Napoleon himself was careful to play on this ambiguity, finding ways to make himself appealing to socialists and conservatives, simultaneously.

The actual difficulties and potential promise of Bonapartism are in some ways characteristic of the French political scene in the 1840s. In terms of the existing system, Guizot's status quo liberalism seemed fully in control. The notables, the locally most influential men, clearly liked his government, and the opposition could make little headway by going through legal channels, as was revealed, most convincingly, in the general elections of 1846, when more pro-governmental deputies were elected than at any point in the previous thirty years. Yet there was a growing amount of discontent with the rule of the July Monarchy – a discontent that would be sharpened by the economic crisis well under way as these 1846 elections were held. If any or all of the opposition groups were to oppose the regime successfully, they would have to find ways to do so outside the formal, legal channels of the system.

Italy

For all the difficulties of the opposition in France, the circumstances they faced would have seemed ideal to their Italian counterparts. None of the Italian states had any form of constitutional government in the 1840s, and they lacked both parliamentary representation and any guarantees of civil liberties. Still, as the decade progressed, a liberal political opposition developed, and found avenues for self-expression. Typical were ostensibly unpolitical meetings, such as the yearly Congress of Italian Scientists, that brought together scholars from across the entire peninsula, officially, to discuss scientific advances, but also to advocate, in barely concealed fashion, liberal reforms.

The fact that the congress participants came from all the Italian states is particularly relevant, since one of the main aspirations of the liberal opposition was the nationalist union of all the Italian monarchies into one state. Giuseppe Mazzini's radical supporters had tried to do this via an insurrection in the 1830s; the more moderate Italian liberals of the subsequent decade looked to other means: cultural connections, such as the Congress of Italian Scientists, economic ties, including railway building and the creation of a customs union of the Italian states. Still, all these efforts would leave unresolved the problem of the wealthy and populous northern provinces of Venetia and Lombardy, that were part of the Austrian empire. Gradual and peaceful means would not undermine Austrian rule – stronger measures would be needed.

However, almost all the nominally independent Italian states were de facto satellites of the Austrian empire, whose existence as the interventions in 1820 and 1830 had shown, was heavily dependent on the armed forces of the Habsburg Monarchy. Their conservative rulers, particularly the monarchs and government ministers of the southern Kingdom of the Two Sicilies, the most populous of the Italian states, made no attempt to hide the situation, but quite openly proclaimed the Restoration era principle of legitimacy, by which their absolutist rule was to be upheld, if necessary, through the intervention of the conservative Great Powers. Only the small northwestern Kingdom of Piedmont-Savoy renounced this legitimist patronage of Austria, but its diplomatic and military weight was modest, and its conservative government reluctant to oppose the principle of legitimacy. Then, in 1846, the arch-reactionary Pope Gregory XVI died; his successor, the bishop of Imola, who took the title of Pius IX, was reputed to be a man of liberal sympathies. Indeed, he took some initial cautious steps to reform the extremely reactionary government of the Papal States and even to encourage an Italian customs union, one of the liberals' nationalist goals. The new pope quickly became a hero of the liberal opposition and cries of 'Viva Pio Nono!' echoed throughout the peninsula. The link between liberal and nationalist aspirations, on the one hand, and the Roman Catholic culture of confessionalism, reinvigorated in ultramontanist fashion on the other, seemed unstoppable.

Italian radicals, in view of their strong anti-clericalism, were more than a little sceptical. Giuseppe Mazzini himself, struggling to reconstruct his Young Italy in exile, after the insurrectionary fiasco of the 1830s, still felt that liberal gradualism would lead to nothing, that a revolution and war of liberation against the Austrians would be the only way to achieve the goal of national unity. However, the radicals had no way of achieving their goals. An attempted

[384] incursion and secret society insurrection in Sicily in 1846 were even bigger failures than their predecessors of 1834. With little else to do, radicals in Italy increasingly lined up behind the liberal opposition and its new programme of gradualism, and support for a seemingly sympathetic pope.

Politics and public life in Italy were generally fixed around the linked questions of national unification and liberation of the northern provinces from Austrian rule, pitting nationalists, who also called for liberal or radical governments, against pro-Austrian conservatives, who endorsed the political status quo. The issues of the social question, the spread of socialist ideas (except among a very few intellectuals), and the growth of a labour movement, that were typical of France and England in the 1840s, were not found in the Italian peninsula. Nervous property owners in Italy often talked of their fear of communism, but by that they meant such things as the poor peasants of the south seizing forest land and chopping down wood without permission, or the riots and turbulent demands of the guilds of porters, important features of economic life in large Italian cities. Social and economic questions remained largely unthematized in political culture and public life.

The German states

Public life in the thirty-nine German states sprawled across the centre of Europe presented a very mixed and diverse picture during the 1840s. The political arenas differed sharply between those German states, especially in the south, that had constitutions and elected legislatures, and the two Great Powers, Austria and Prussia, where absolutist rule continued unchecked. While the spectrum of political views was similar in composition and complexity to that of western Europe, its transfer to the different social and especially political environment of central Europe meant that advocating the same sort of ideas could take on a different meaning in this different environment. Finally, national unification was every bit as central to German politics as it was to Italian, but the call for national unity in a country with two major Christian confessions and two potentially hostile Great Powers proved to be more a source of discord than of cohesion.

In the parliamentary states of southern Germany, the 1840s were a decade of increasing politicization. At each election, the voters returned a growing number of liberal deputies who opposed the conservative policies of their countries' monarchs and government ministers. These statewide contests reverberated at the local level, pitting elected, liberal municipal governments (which enjoyed an unusual degree of autonomy as compared with other continental European states) against state bureaucrats. Increasingly, the oppositional deputies found themselves to be popular figures – 'heroes of the Chamber [of Deputies]' or 'men of the people', as they came to be known. Such parliamentary agitation spilling over into a broader public would be a major training ground for political leadership in the revolution of 1848.

In comparison to France, though, this political life was rather more restrained. Newspapers, in particular, continued to be subject to prior censorship, and political associations were harder to form. However, public life in the constitutional states of Germany was far freer and more open than in the absolutist Great Powers, where there were no parliamentary institutions to act as a focus for public opinion and no constitutional guarantees of basic rights, and where an authoritarian (if, at times, well-meaning) bureaucracy attempted to monopolize political decision-making.

Particularly in the Kingdom of Prussia, but throughout Germany, the 1840s were the golden age of crypto-political assocations. Above all, there were the three classic groups – the choral societies, the gymnastic societies, and the sharpshooters' associations – whose nationalism was generally connected with liberal and even radical political opposition. Other groups, such as carnival (German Mardi Gras) societies, were also a breeding ground of political opposition. These carnival societies would savagely caricature and mock ruling monarchs and their policies in their pre-Lenten festivities, and then tell outraged government officials that it was all in fun, and should not be taken seriously. Another important crypto-political group were the free congregations, composed of Unitarians who had seceded from the state-sponsored and government-controlled Protestant and Catholic Churches. Just advocating a rationalist religion, that took issue with the Bible and church dogmas, was oppositional enough; but members of these free congregations generally had oppositional views on a wide range of issues, ranging from national unity, to constitutional government, to the emancipation of women. (They were generally in favour of it, unlike the official churches, which strongly opposed it.) Like the parliamentary 'heroes of the Chamber', the leaders of these crypto-political associations would play major roles in the revolution of 1848.

The prominent role of the free congregations in political dissent during the 1840s points to the disproportionate significance of confessional identities in German public life. Germans continued to be Protestants and Catholics, religiously orthodox and free-thinking, even when they were dealing with issues that went well beyond those of the old regime culture of confessionalism. National unity is a good example. While nationalists believed

[386]   that a united nation should encompass all Germans, regardless of their religious confession, Protestant nationalists just naturally assumed that the predominantly Protestant Prussian kingdom would play a leading role in a future German nation-state, while Catholic nationalists expected the strongly Catholic Austrian empire to do that. Such confessional perspectives cut across the left–right political spectrum and made it more difficult for adherents of any political tendency to gather support for their ideas.

Unlike the case in France, liberalism remained an oppositional political movement in 1840s Germany. Liberals continued to press for the creation of constitutional government in the absolutist states and for the expansion of parliamentary power and civil liberties in those states that already had constitutions. Besides reforming the individual German states, liberals aspired to their federation into a united nation-state. In contrast to their Italian counterparts, German liberals already had a model for national unity, in existing institutions, such as the German Confederation, or the All-German Customs Union of 1834. Following in the gradualist perspective of liberalism, they wished to work within these institutions, say by creating an elected parliament for the German Confederation, to meet in conjunction with the already existing confederate Diet, a gathering of diplomats from the individual states.

Liberals hoped to obtain the cooperation of the governments of the individual states in their plans. This meant, particularly, the governments of the two Great Powers, that dominated the German Confederation. The death in 1840, of the elderly and rigid absolutist Prussian monarch Frederick William III, and the advent of his much younger, more personable and articulate successor Frederick William IV, seemed to be just what liberals were waiting for. However, while the new monarch rejected the bureaucratic absolutism of his predecessor, it was in favour of a romantic, medievally minded conservatism, rather than a liberal viewpoint. Frederick William IV dreamed of the middle ages, of the Holy Roman Empire and the corporate institutions of the pre-1789 era, and announced that he would never endorse a constitution, since he would never permit a piece of paper to come between him and his people. Trapped between the bureaucratic conservatism of a Metternich in Austria, and the romantic conservatism of Prussia's king, German liberals were frustrated in their efforts at political change in collaboration with their governments.

In view of the dominance of conservative governments, radicals and liberals remained hard to tell apart in 1840s Germany, rather like the situation in France two decades previously. Radicals in Germany shared many of the same goals as their liberal counterparts: constitutions and parliamentary governments in the individual states; a united nation-state. On social and economic questions, radicals were more likely to be sceptical of laissez-faire than liberals, more attuned to the ideal of a society of small property owners. They advocated government action to 'redress the disproportion between capital and labour' and to secure 'freedom, affluence and education for all' – these being two popular slogans of Badenese radical leader Friedrich Hecker. However, by no means all German liberals were especially fond of the free market. Like their liberal counterparts, German radicals were more likely to be Protestants than Catholics, closer to free-thinking and Unitarianism than to religious orthodoxy.

As the 1840s continued and political life developed further, in spite of all attempts on the part of the governments to prevent this from happening, radicalism gradually developed separate contours. Above all, the two political tendencies began moving apart on questions of ways and means. Radicals lost patience with liberal attempts to cooperate in reform programmes with state authorities, who showed little interest in cooperation. They began to consider forms of political mass mobilization, thinking about how to coerce unwilling governmental authorities, rather than trying to gain their approval. The radical ideal of a democratic form of government amplified these tactical differences between liberals and radicals: popular sovereignty, the rule of the people, would have to be obtained by popular action.

The 1840s were a period of declining popular standards of living in central Europe and people from all different political points of view avidly debated the social question, offering remedies for the growing 'pauperization', as contemporaries said, of ever-greater portions of the population. The solutions proposed were equally varied, ranging from the endorsement of the free market to the strengthening of the guild system, from shrinking government to increasing the sphere of its action. Prominent among those who dealt with this question were the socialists, 'true socialists', as they called themselves. They adopted from their French and English counterparts many of their critiques of liberalism, capitalism, and a civil society of property owners. In central Europe, however, unlike the case in the western portions of the continent, these institutions socialist criticized had generally not established themselves against absolutist governments and the old regime corporate institutions, but many 'true socialists' had trouble understanding this point. Marx and Engels certainly did, and in their *Communist Manifesto* they vehemently denounced most German socialists for failing to understand that their socialist ideals could not be realized under the existing undemocratic and authoritarian German governments.

[388]   There was also a labour movement developing among Germans in the 1840s, only this German labour movement developed outside Germany. Tens, perhaps hundreds of thousands of journeymen artisans, unable to find work in central Europe, moved to western cities such as Zurich, Brussels, London or Paris. There, they came into contact with existing socialist and labour movements, and gradually formed their own organizations. The *Communist Manifesto* was written for the Communist League, one such group of German artisans living abroad.

The growth of these different currents of political opposition, and the wealth of organizational forms they took, put Germany's ruling conservatives increasingly on the defensive. Authoritarian policies were losing their effect, and conservatives were unsure of how to attempt to mobilize a popular following. Implicitly, they had a trump card in the form of the orthodox clergy and the religiously devout from all different social classes, but tensions between Protestants and Catholics made it more difficult to mobilize religious and related dynastic loyalties for political purposes. Exceptional incidents, such as the great pilgrimage to the Seamless Robe of Trier in 1844, when Protestant, Prussian government officials and ultramontanist Catholic priests cooperated in sponsoring a major demonstration of a romantic religion, whose politically pacifying effects were personally applauded by Austria's Prince Metternich, were just that – exceptional. More usually, Prussians and Austrians, ultramontanist Catholics and neo-orthodox Protestants were opposed to each other, and sometimes even more inclined to cooperate with free-thinking liberals than with members of an opposing confession. Much like their Italian counterparts, conservative adherents of the status quo in Germany were hard-pressed by the late 1840s to stop the forces of change.

The Austrian empire

In the realm of the Habsburgs, the political trends in the neighbouring German and Italian states were echoed, but rather more feebly. Particularly in the heavily rural, eastern portions of the empire, where illiteracy was the rule rather than the exception, and the institutions of civil society were little developed, there were few avenues for politicization and not many people who were open to being politicized. In these circumstances, the efforts of a Restoration era bureaucracy, still clinging to power, to suppress the emergence of public opinion were likely to have more success than elsewhere. In the larger cities and the provincial capitals, such as Vienna, Prague, Graz, Milan, Venice, Budapest, Cracow, Zagreb and Lemberg, a political life did develop, largely via crypto-political associations, like the Juridical-Political Reading Club in Vienna. However, the interested public was small and different political tendencies remained vague and hard to separate: liberals, radicals, and even old-fashioned conservatives, who longed for a strengthening of the Provincial Diets, could all be found in an unspecified opposition to the ruling absolutist bureaucracy. The absolutist bureaucracy itself was not too well directed, since it lacked an absolutist monarch to lead it. Ferdinand I, who came to the throne in 1835, was mentally retarded; his political abilities were summed up in a widely quoted statement of his: 'I am the emperor and I want dumplings.' Various members of the royal family contended with the chancellor, Prince Metternich, and his main bureaucratic rival, Count Kolowrat, to set state policy, so that, in the end, no one was really in charge.

There are two unique aspects to this political life that was slowly emerging and very uncertain in all respects. First was the nature of the connection between liberalism and nationalism. As was true in Germany and Italy, nationalist demands were a key part of the liberal opposition in the Austrian empire. However, in the empire, there was not just one nationalist movement but many, and often conflicting, laying claim to the same territories and sometimes the same people as part of their nation: the Germans and Czechs in Bohemia, the Germans and the Italians in the Tyrol, the Hungarians and Croatians in Croatia (then a province of Hungary), the Poles and the Ukrainians in Galicia, to name just a few. Each of these nationalist movements generally had similar political demands, including the creation of a constitutional monarchy, or the abolition of noble privileges and of serfdom. But because these liberal demands were embedded in opposing nationalist frameworks, the potential political opposition was divided among itself, opening up promising possiblities for a strategy of 'divide and rule' on the part of the army and the state bureaucracy. In the 1840s, these divisions were still in many places beneath the surface of a modest public life, still heavily encumbered by censorship, but they would emerge suddenly and in very dramatic fashion during the 1848 revolution.

The second unique aspect of the emerging political life in the empire was the role of the nobility in the political opposition. One of the few public forums for politics in the empire before the 1848 revolution, were the old Provincial Diets, remnants of the eighteenth-century corporate society of orders, in which the nobility played the dominant role. More often than not, this role was itself a remnant of old regime politics, a provincial nobility opposing a centralizing, absolutist bureaucracy. The Hungarian Diet, the most powerful and active of these corporate, provincial legislatures, had played a leading

[390] role in such opposition during the old regime, and had continued to do so, well into the 1820s.

The ordinary Hungarian nobility, that had the right to vote in elections to the lower house of the Diet (the upper house was reserved for members of the titled, high nobility) was very large – 6 per cent of the entire population of Hungary, and perhaps 12–13 per cent of all native speakers of Magyar, the Hungarian language. When we consider that just 5 per cent of adult men in the July Monarchy had the right to vote, and that some 12–13 per cent of adult men in Great Britain possessed the franchise, after the passage of the Great Reform Act, we see that this group of nobles made up, by pre-1850 European standards, a large political public sphere. Increasingly, these nobles acted like the notables of western Europe, and began to espouse liberal ideas: a constitution valid for the entire Hungarian kingdom, to replace the different legal positions of the provinces, with their traditional, chartered privileges; legal equality for members of non-Catholic confessions, especially the Calvinists, a group well represented among the lesser nobility; an end to the society of orders and equality before the law, or the abolition of serfdom – albeit with compensation for noble landlords. In the twin cities of Buda and Pest (not yet connected by a bridge across the Danube), the major urban centre of Hungary, where the Habsburg viceroy and his central administration resided, a growing network of crypto-political organizations and associations brought these ideas before the public.

In the two decades after the 1820s, the oppositional forces in the Hungarian Diet followed this trend, moving from an old regime-style corporate opposition to the Habsburg government, to a more up-to-date liberal version. Originally under the leadership of a more moderate figure, István Széchenyi, the opposition strove, in liberal fashion, to cooperate with the Austrian government. By the 1840s, this willingness to cooperate had faded, and the new leader of the opposition, the lawyer, journalist, and talented public speaker, Lajos Kossuth, took a more intransigent line.

As was true everywhere in the Habsburg Monarchy, this attitude had unexpected consequences. The Hungarians wanted to create a unified Hungarian state, one and indivisible, on the model of the French Revolution; they wanted to make Magyar the official state language, replacing the Latin of the old regime. However, inhabitants of the provinces who were to be brought into this unified state did not see it that way. The German- and Rumanian-speaking inhabitants of Transylvania saw this programme not as national unification but as a trampling on their national rights. When the Hungarian Diet replaced Latin with Magyar as its official language, and addressed the Provincial Diet of Croatia in that language, the deputies to that Diet rejected Latin and promptly replied, instead, in Croatian. In an age of growing nationalism, the liberal programme of the Hungarian opposition to absolutist Habsburg rule would generate nationalist opposition to Hungarian rule.

In the Hungarian kingdom and the other eastern provinces of the monarchy, serfdom continued to exist and serfs made up a very large majority of the population. Liberal Hungarian nobles, who advocated the abolition of serfdom, were proposing to abolish an institution from which they benefited. The potential beneficiaries of this good deed might well have wondered about the validity of their benefactors' intentions. Such a remark is not cynical speculation, but is borne out by events in another eastern province of the monarchy, that would have a wide resonance across Europe.

Nobles were also a large proportion of the Polish population, and members of the nobility played a major part in Polish reform and revolutionary movements, through much of the nineteenth century. Following the failure of the Polish uprising against Russian rule in 1830, much of the political activity shifted to the Poles living in the Prussian kingdom and the province of Galicia, in the Austrian empire. In 1846, secret society members planned an uprising in these two states. The Prussian police uncovered the conspirators before they could act, but their counterparts in Galicia actually did carry out their uprising, and called on the bulk of the population, the serfs, to join in with them. Rather than doing that, the serfs turned on the noble conspirators and murdered them, slaughtering over a thousand noblemen, estate agents, and Catholic priests, connected with the nobility. The angry serfs asserted their counter-revolutionary sentiments. They rejected the radical revolutionaries, who were also their feudal lords, and insisted on their strong loyalty to the emperor, their rightful ruler, and, so they thought, their protector from noble exploitation. The peasants castigated the insurgents' nationalism, insisting that, unlike the noble revolutionaries, they were not Polish at all, but 'Austrians' or the 'emperors' peasants'.

The Galician uprising was front-page news for the day, and its results were read nervously by estate-owning oppositionists as far away as southern Italy. It demonstrated two points about politicization in 1840s Europe, one more general, and one more specifically Austrian. First, the growing trends of politicization and oppositional activity had not reached the inhabitants of the countryside, a majority of all Europeans. Peasants had their own ideas about politics, that did not necessarily correspond to what the educated classes and town-dwellers thought about it. Second, a crucial issue for the future of

[392] the Austrian empire – and other eastern European states – was the question of serfdom. Its further existence was becoming ever more doubtful; the political ramifications of its abolition would be enormous, and might well not benefit those noble radicals who proposed it – a point that would soon become crystal clear during the revolution of 1848.

Crisis years, 1845–47

The years 1845–47 were a period of serious economic crisis, that helped discredit and delegitimize governments, whether constitutional and liberal, or authoritarian and conservative, across Europe. In these circumstances, the oppositional political forces, what contemporaries called the 'party of movement', as opposed to the pro-status quo 'party of order', launched large-scale campaigns against the existing regimes, drawing both on the mood of popular discontent, and on the long-term growth of institutional forms of expressing it. The ultimate upshot of these campaigns would be the outbreak of a continent-wide revolution in 1848. In this section, we will look at the economic crisis and then consider three examples of political confrontation in 1847 – the Swiss Civil War, the meeting of the United Diet in Prussia, and the French banquet campaign – that directly led up to the revolution.

The economic crisis began in the agricultural sector, with the outbreak of the potato blight in 1845. The crop simply rotted away in the fields. Potatoes were very much the food of the poor, so the failure of this crop threatened the most vulnerable part of the population. Potates were also a product of the new, more efficient agriculture, a new world crop that could be grown in a relatively small space and could feed a large number of people, so providing an answer to the Malthusian threat of population outstripping food supply. Economically and agriculturally advanced areas, such as Ireland, Flanders, or northern France, were particularly threatened by the blight.

While the effects of the blight were ameliorated somewhat in 1846, the grain harvest was very bad, the worst in a generation. By the winter and spring of 1847, the food situation had reached its nadir. Bread prices had doubled (this on top of a price level that had already increased substantially since the 1820s); shortages were becoming increasingly apparent. A wave of food riots swept across Europe. Crowds blocked the movement of foodstuffs, stormed stores and markets, and demanded that potatoes, flour and bread be sold at affordable prices.

In contrast to similar years of disastrous harvests in the seventeenth and eighteenth centuries, or even to the previous crop disaster in 1816–17, this subsistence crisis did not bring with it widespread starvation. Death rates did rise slightly, but far less than they would in 1849, a year of bountiful harvests, but also of a cholera epidemic. Overall levels of agricultural production had increased considerably, so that even steep declines were not as catastrophic as previously. Transport had improved, so that grain could be brought to crisis regions from unaffected areas, such as North America or the Russian empire. Governments were more capable of taking action to ameliorate the situation. They restricted exports, purchased grain abroad, and sold flour from army storehouses. People died in large numbers only in Ireland, largely because the British government refused to take these steps under the impact of nineteenth-century liberal ideas, since they would have interfered with the workings of the free market and ruined the self-reliance of the Irish population. Mortality rose considerably, if to a more modest extent, in Belgium and the Netherlands, where governments followed similar economic policies.

The period of high food prices did not so much starve people to death as absorb all their purchasing power, leaving nothing over for manufactured goods and the goods and services of artisans. The harvest of 1847 was good, and food prices declined, but European economies slipped into recession. The business downturn proved worse than usual, since the early and mid-1840s had seen something of an industrial boom, characterized by borrowing large sums of money for railway construction and industrial expansion. With the recession, payments on the debts could not be made, and a chain of bankruptcies ensued; the still primitively organized credit market proved unable to deal with the situation. Business detoriorated further, and unemployment increased still more. The good harvests of 1847 and the following several years only exacerbated the crisis, since farmers received low prices for their crops and had trouble paying off the debts they had contracted during the previous period of near-famine. This sequence of dearth followed by recession, bankruptcy and unemployment, a combination of the worst of the economic crises of the old agrarian–artisan economy and the new capitalist and industrial one, set the backdrop to the political initiatives of the opposition in the years after 1845 and in the revolutionary period of 1848–49.

One example of such pre-revolutionary initiatives was the Swiss Civil War of 1847. The tacit division of Europe into a liberal west and a conservative centre and east, following the 1830 revolution, had run right through Switzerland. In addition to this, Switzerland was a country profoundly divided

[394] on religious lines, between its predominantly Protestant and its predominantly Catholic cantons. Since the Swiss revolution of 1830 had brought change only at the cantonal level, not to the institutions of the Swiss Confederation, tensions between liberal and conservative cantons, between economically advanced and more backward cantons and between Protestant and Catholic ones (these divisions usually overlapped, at least in part) continued unabated. Radicals would flee the conservative cantons for asylum in the liberal ones and try to mount invasions of their home territory from them.

Such disordered conditions continued until 1847, when a movement to prohibit the Jesuits in Switzerland led a group of Catholic, conservative, and mostly economically underdeveloped cantons – primarily the Alpine ones in the mountainous heart of Switzerland – to secede from the Swiss Confederation and form a secessionist league, a *Sonderbund*. The ensuing 'Sonderbund War' between the secessionist cantons and the rest of the Swiss Confederation was brief and almost bloodless, since the confederate armies, greatly superior in manpower, weapons and generalship, overpowered the secessionist ones. The civil war turned into a de facto revolution, as the conservatives running the conquered cantons were replaced with radicals, and the victorious cantons took steps to reform the Swiss Confederation, turning it from a loose union of sovereign cantons, into a united, federal, republican state.

The victory of the radicals in Switzerland provided a tremendous impetus for the forces of change throughout Europe, and for reasons that reached well beyond the Swiss borders. By themselves, the secessionist forces had little chance; they were counting on outside intervention, on the support of the conservative Great Powers, especially Metternich's Austria, to help their cause. But the Austrian government, just about bankrupt once again, as a result of the economic crisis, could not afford to intervene and Metternich was unable to convince the other Powers to join him in doing so. Such outside interventions had defeated many of the revolutions of 1820 and 1830; now they seemed impossible.

As the counter-revolutionary power of Metternich's Austria was sinking fast, the domestic situation in the other conservative, central European Great Power was approaching crisis. Frederick William IV of Prussia needed money to proceed with the state-sponsored building of railways in the economically less advanced eastern regions of his kingdom, where private enterprise would have difficulty in making a profit. Money was hard to come by in 1847, with Europe in the midst of a major credit crisis. The ruler's predecessor had promised, way back in the era of political turmoil after the war against Napoleon, not to raise taxes or take out loans without the consent of an elected legislature. The romantic conservative monarch would not hear of that, so [395] instead he summoned all the Provincial Diets in his kingdom to a United Diet, that would meet in Berlin in 1847 to vote him the necessary funds.

Contemporaries, thinking of politics in the terms of the French Revolution, could not help but be reminded of another monarch who had summoned a kingdom-wide representative body of the society of orders to his capital city in 1789, and what the consequences of that had been. Indeed, the leaders of the liberal opposition in Prussia, who were deputies in the United Diet used that historical precedent for their purposes, refusing to vote the king the necessary monies until he agreed to a constitution and an elected legislature. However, in an uncomfortably similar way to Louis XVI's refusal to cooperate with the National Assembly, Frederick William IV would not cooperate with the liberals of the United Diet. The body was adjourned at the end of 1847, leaving people free to think about what might happen next.

What is striking about the situation in Europe at the beginning of 1848 is the almost complete paralysis of the party of order. Conservatives in power apparently could think of nothing but defending the existing state of affairs. Such a determination to allow no change to occur was most pronounced in the tsar's empire. Nicholas I, who followed his brother Alexander I to the throne after the disturbing events of the Decembrist insurrection of 1825, had made cementing the status quo – absolutist, autocratic rule, the established Orthodox Church, and the society of orders, complete with serfdom – into the centre of his governmental policy. To do this more effectively, he even repealed some of the administrative reforms of his predecessor, taking back authority from the functional government ministries his brother had created, and recentralizing it in the private chancery of the emperor. Its 'third section', in particular, was in charge of the political police, who would ferret out and repress any challenge to the status quo.

This solution worked reasonably well in Russia, where civil society was still small and weak, and thus could be kept under control by the third section, and where the social and economic tensions emerging from population growth could be met, in part, by migration to newly conquered southern territories. It was not a course of action that was quite so effective elsewhere in Europe, yet rulers and their ministers could think of nothing else to do. Potential compromises with the party of movement were certainly an option, as the conservatives in Great Britain had done in the early 1830s. Oppositional initiatives in the German and Italian states, as well as in the Habsburg empire, were still largely led by liberals who would have welcomed the opportunity to cooperate with the monarchs and their bureaucrats in a programme of

[396] reform. As Frederick William IV showed, and as Pius IX demonstrated at about the same time in dealing with a similar consultative assembly in the Papal States, the willingness to engage in such a compromise was just absent.

Another possibility would have been to exploit weaknesses and internal divisions within the party of movement. Particularly in the Austrian empire, where a nascent liberalism was closely tied to different and competing nationalist movements, such a strategy would have had good chances of success. The central government did, cautiously, encourage and secretly subsidize Croatian nationalists, as a way of weakening the Hungarian opposition. The exact extent to which the government should engage in such activities was one of the main differences between Metternich and Kolowrat. Yet the divided and disunited Austrian government, in this, as in so many other issues, could not set a consistent course, but veered between a policy of trying to set one nationalist movement against another, and a policy of trying to suppress them all, equally.

Finally, there was the option being pursued by the oppositional Legitimists in France, and previously tried by the Carlists in Spain, of a connection between the culture of confessionalism, dynastic loyalties, and right-wing politics. Such an option was considered in prayer circles and religious sodalities across the continent, and many of the leaders of right-wing politics in the 1848 revolution would emerge from the lay and clerical adherents of awakened Protestantism and ultramontanist Catholicism. However, the impression of reformist and anti-restorationist sympathies of the new pope, Pius IX, made such an option difficult for Catholics. More than that, though, mobilizing such religious sympathies politically would mean taking part in the game of mass politics, accepting the existence of political actions and a civil society independent of the state, a step that conservatives, still in charge of absolutist regimes in so much of Europe, were unwilling to take. Ironically, it would only be the outbreak of the revolution they hated and feared, and did their best to prevent, that would give conservatives the option of mobilizing their supporters effectively.

In the end, all that remained to the party of order in Europe was the principle of legitimacy, the idea that the Great Powers would intervene to defend the existing rule of the princes. Tsar Nicholas I had never made any secret of his interest in doing so, from the time he ascended the throne. However, he generally would not act alone, outside his own possessions; it would take the actions of the Austrian government, since Napoleon's day the hub and co-ordinator of opposition to the forces of change in Europe. This is why the inability of Metternich to organize and finance an intervention in Switzerland was politically decisive: it showed that conservative and absolutist rulers could [397] no longer count on the principle of legitimacy to preserve their rule.

Ultimately, in this period of crisis, politically conscious Europeans looked to events in France, still the leading nation in Europe, and certainly still the continent-wide capital of the party of movement. There, the leaders of the opposition responded to their defeat in the legislative elections of 1846, by having recourse to a broader audience than the notables who had the vote. They launched a series of mass meetings against the government. To conform to the law, these were officially not meetings, but banquets, public meals, for which tickets were sold for a nominal sum, and an equally nominal amount of food and drink was provided – hence the name, banquet campaign. Speakers at these meetings denounced the government's corruption, the narrow and undemocratic franchise, the timid foreign policy, that would not use the nation's strength in support of movements of political opposition across Europe, and called for an alternative rule. Increasingly, there were references to France's first republican regime, and scarcely hidden calls for its repetition. These meetings continued throughout 1847 and into the beginning of 1848, when the demands expressed in them would be turned into reality.

The revolutions of 1848

Outbreak and spread

The combination of economic crisis, seeming paralysis of the party of order and oppositional political offensive left everyone in Europe who even occasionally thought about politics expecting large changes at the beginning of 1848. They were not long in coming. In January of that year, an uprising in the Sicilian capital of Palermo, planned by secret society members, proved a success, and the insurgents quickly gained control of the island of Sicily. The uprising spread to the Italian mainland, and after street fighting in Naples, the capital of the southern Italian Kingdom of the Two Sicilies, King Ferdinand gave in to the insurgents and agreed to replace his conservative government ministers with liberal ones, and hold elections for an assembly to write a constitution for his monarchy.

The southern Italian kingdom was at the very periphery of Europe, but the subsequent month would bring change to the political heart of the continent, in Paris. Participants in the banquet campaign sponsored by the opposition poured out of their banquets into the streets, demonstrating against the

[398] government. Clashes with the police and then the army led to the building of barricades – a signature event of 1848. During three days of street fighting in late February, much like 'the three glorious days' of July 1830, soldiers were reluctant to open fire, the National Guard went over to the insurgents, and the monarch was forced to flee the country. On 24 February 1848, the victorious insurgents converged on the Paris city hall, where leaders of the opposition, mostly journalists from Le National and La Réforme, proclaimed that France was once again a republic.

This was what everyone had been waiting for – whether with anxiety or anticipation – since the end of the revolutionary and Napoleonic era in 1815. Had it occurred at an earlier time, perhaps even as late as the 1830 revolutions, the result might have been a new European war between a revolutionary France and counter-revolutionary Great Powers. By the 1840s, though, as a result of the intensification and expansion of political life through the institutions of civil society, the upshot was a continent-wide wave of revolution. The proclamation of the republic was a signal for the intensification of the political campaigns of the opposition. Everywhere, there were banquets, mass meetings and street demonstrations. In the two central European Great Powers, the Parisian scenario was played out in full, with participants of mass meetings marching into the streets, clashing with troops, building barricades and engaging in street fighting. These struggles took place in Berlin, the Prussian capital, and Vienna the Austrian one, but also in a number of major provincial capitals of the Austrian empire: Venice and Milan, in the northern Italian provinces, and Cracow, in Galicia. Everywhere, the outcome was the same: wavering of the troops, whose loyalties seemed ever more uncertain, and then their withdrawal, leading to victories of the insurgents. As in southern Italy, the reactionary government ministers were replaced with liberal ones, and elections for a constituent assembly promised. The victory of the revolutionary forces was sealed by symbolic events: the flight of Prince Metternich, the architect of the Restoration, from Vienna to exile in London; the conservative Frederick William IV of Prussia standing to attention, with his hat removed, on the balcony of his castle, while the crowd paraded before him the coffins of the insurgents killed in the barricade fighting.

In the twin cities of Buda and Pest, centre of the administration of Hungarian provinces of the Austrian empire, the authorities were intimidated by the street demonstrations and gave into them without even risking a trial of strength on the barricades. This bloodless victory of the oppositional demonstrations was the rule in the smaller German and Italian states, in the Scandinavian countries, and in the distant Principality of Moldavia (today's

Moldova) then under nominal Ottoman sovereignty. The prince of Wallachia, the other of the two Danubian Principalities at the extreme southeastern end of revolutionary Europe, by contrast, attempted to suppress the revolutionary movement and was overthrown.

The revolutionary events had thus reached a substantial majority of the existing European states. There were a few, smaller exceptions. Little happened in the Iberian countries, still exhausted from their long-drawn-out revolutions and civil wars of the mid-1830s and early 1840s. Holland and Belgium were both constitutional monarchies, whose governments were not so different from those of France under the July Monarchy, and whose public life contained a similar mixture of political tendencies, including, on the left, both vaguely republican radicals and a nascent labour movement. Both countries were hard hit by the economic crisis of the years 1845–47, and had been the scene of a large number of bread riots and other subsistence disturbances. The revolution in neighbouring France threatened to spill over across the border, as had occurred in 1830. Large-scale street demonstrations in Holland, violent in Amsterdam, more peaceful and orderly in the Hague, showed the possibility of revolutionary change. Belgian radicals put their faith in an insurrection, that was to be sparked by a column of armed Belgians, previously resident in France, marching across the border.

However, the governments in both the Low Countries showed a strong mixture of flexibility and firmness, that helped contain the revolutionary events. The Dutch king appointed a commission, whose members were largely from the liberal opposition, to work out a new, more liberal constitution, including direct elections to the lower house of parliament, and a considerable strengthening of the parliament vis-à-vis the monarch, that enjoyed wide approval. The insurgent invasion of Belgium, encouraged by the government of the new French republic, not with the hope of revolutionizing its neighbour, but rather of getting unemployed Belgian workers out of the country, was an embarrassing failure. Not content with just repression, the Belgian government then introduced a number of reforms, in particular a sharp decline in the property qualification for the suffrage, that increased the electorate by 70 per cent. These reforms calmed the domestic situation.

The Scandinavian countries were also encompassed by the revolutionary wave. There were major street demonstrations in Copenhagen and Stockholm; and there would be considerable organized political activity in both Denmark and Norway (then an autonomous part of Sweden) in the course of 1848–49. The situation in Denmark was close to that of the smaller German and Italian states: the absolutist monarch quickly capitulated to the

[400]   demonstrators, appointing liberal ministers and calling for elections to a constituent assembly to write a constitution. By contrast, soldiers were ordered
to fire on the demonstrators in Stockholm, and the government was less
yielding. The Swedish royal government did propose to abolish the Swedish
Estates, and replace them with a more modern, bicameral legislature, with
the lower house elected by a property franchise, only by the time the proposal was put to a vote in 1850, the wave of revolution was over and the
Estates rejected the proposal, continuing their anachronistic existence for
another sixteen years.

   The dominant motif in the Low Countries and Scandinavia was thus, to a
greater or lesser extent, avoiding revolution by means of reform. Quite different were the circumstances in the two peripheral Great Powers, Russia and
Great Britain, whose governments were not inclined and were not required
to make any concessions. In Russia, neither the political opposition nor the
institutions of civil society in which it could act, had developed much in the
first half of the nineteenth century. 1848 did see an unprecedently large number
of peasant riots and disturbances directed against serfdom, even more than at
the previous high point, 1826, in the wake of the Decembrist uprising. This
clustering of opposition to serfdom does suggest that some news of the
Europe-wide revolutionary events had reached the tsar's empire, but there
proved to be no way to exploit it for political change. When necessary, troops
were deployed to suppress the angry serfs, and the handful of proponents of
organized political opposition in 1848–49 were either secret society conspirators, vainly hoping to plan an uprising, or isolated liberals, hoping, equally
in vain, that the ruler and his ministers would decide to cooperate with them.
Instead, they devoted their attention to suppressing revolutionary outbreaks
elsewhere: intervening against the revolutionary government in Wallachia in
the summer of 1848, adopting a threatening stance against the new, liberal
regimes in Germany, and, finally, suppressing the revolution in Hungary in
1849.

   By contrast, in Great Britain, the institutions of civil society were very well
developed and the political opposition sought to make use of them. The proclamation of the republic in Paris encouraged the British Chartists, as it had
forces of opposition everywhere in Europe, and the leaders of the gradually
declining movement gained energy for one last try. But their efforts, themselves not as impressive as the previous attempts at the movement's high points
in 1839 and 1842, were no more successful. A mass petition to Parliament,
supported by large, menacing public demonstrations – this time in London,
rather than in the industrial cities of the north – made little impression on the

authorities, who ignored the petition again, and made careful and coordinated use of police, soldiers and volunteer, property-owning constables, to
ensure that there would be no street fighting and barricade building in the
British capital as there had been in so many continental European ones.
Secret preparations for insurrections in industrial cities of northern England,
with substantial participation of immigrant Irish workers (their countrymen
in Ireland were too busy starving to death to take part in any revolutionary
activities), were broken up by the police. Thus the revolutionary wave of 1848,
like that of the 1790s, and the early 1820s, left the British Isles and the tsarist
empire largely untouched, if for different reasons.

A continent in revolution

Even without Great Britain and Russia the 1848 revolution encompassed
an enormous area, ranging from the Atlantic to the Ukraine, from the Baltic
to the Mediterranean. In fact, of all the waves of revolution in modern European history, from 1789 to 1989, it was the most widespread, covering the
greatest geographic area, and the most politically and socioeconomically
diverse group of states. As had been the case in previous revolutions, and
as would recur in the future, the events of 1848 were by no means limited to
the barricade fighting in the capital cities. Quite the opposite, the victories
of the insurgents were the signal for an enormous profusion of violent and
non-violent actions, of riots and mass meetings, of petitions and parades. The
combination of the expression of long-standing popular grievances and
challenging of the authority of the regime at the local level was very much
reminiscent of the events in the summer of 1789.

As was the case then, an important aspect of the mass movements of the
spring of 1848 were explosions of popular rage at institutions and individuals with whom they had long had strained relations. A major target was
the authority of the state. Tax collection was a particular point of anger, and
crowds, both rural and urban, threatened and beat tax collectors and customs
agents, burned down revenue offices and octroi barriers. Unloved state officials, from the lower levels of village mayors, forest watchmen, and gendarmes,
to the upper ranks of prefects and provincial governors, were assaulted and
driven out of office.

In areas of central and eastern Europe where serfdom or other forms of
seigneurial obligations existed, peasants rioted against their lords, refusing
to perform their labour services or pay their dues, burning charters of feudal
and seigneurial privilege – and sometimes the castles in which they were stored

[402]   – and also threatening and physically assaulting their lords, or the latters' estate managers. With these disturbances, serfdom and other forms of seigneurialism in the Austrian empire and the German states came to an end. Governments would issue decrees and legislatures pass laws to that effect, but they were just ratifying in legal terms the de facto result of these peasant uprisings. The one serious issue that awaited a decision was whether the nobility would receive compensation for their lost feudal and seigneurial privileges. Basically, they did, almost everywhere, but the terms of the compensation were more favourable for the peasantry than they had been in the previous efforts in this direction during the Napoleonic era. Peasants retained the land they themselves farmed and the governments generally compensated the nobles directly, using borrowed funds, and then paid off the loans by taxing the peasants. The yearly payments were modest, although in some parts of Austria or Bavaria they would continue into the twentieth century, and would only be finally terminated by the great inflation during and after the First World War.

Anti-seigneurial disturbances did not occur in the areas of western and southern Europe encompassed by the 1848 revolution, where seigneurialism had been completely abolished before 1815, but there was one form of peasant action that was found everywhere on the continent, namely the taking of the forests. Peasants streamed into the woods, chopping down trees as they pleased, seizing forest lands and defying the state officials who tried to regulate their use. From the Sila mountains in Calabria, to the forest and hill country of the Bukovina, at the eastern end of the Austrian empire, 1848 was the year that the peasants tried to regain control of the woods. The peasant struggle for the forests was a movement directed against both feudalism and capitalism, against seigneurial privileges that preserved the forests for the lords, and against efforts to bring capitalist property relations to the countryside by dividing woodlands held in common and by ending usage rights on other people's property, such as the right to gather wood. Forests were a crucial resource for the countryfolk and the combination of a growing population pressing on the wood supply, legal changes making it hard for peasants to use it, other users demanding an ever-greater share of this wood supply – ironmasters, for instance, still using charcoal to forge pig iron from iron ore – had created a stressed and difficult situation before the outbreak of the revolution. With the temporary collapse or discrediting of governmental authority at the outbreak of the revolution, the woods were an only too tempting target.

A characteristic feature of 1848, that revealed the gradual and social economic changes in the six decades since 1789, was the action and organization of the urban lower classes. Outworking artisans gathered together to threaten and intimidate the merchants who employed them, destroying their homes and storehouses, demanding that they pay better wages and offer more favourable working conditions – such as selling outworking weavers the looms they used. Craftsmen and labourers destroyed machines which were in competition with them, like the villagers of Weißenthurm, on the river Rhine, who earned their living guiding horses towing boats upstream. Threatened by the growing use of steamboats, they gathered on the shore and fired rifles on all steamboats that came by. Artisans demanded a return to the guild system; they attacked 'foreigners' and 'outsiders' competing with them – who could indeed be foreigners, such as the Belgians working in Paris or northern France (which is why the new republican government was happy to see these Belgians leave to try to overthrow their own government), or just people from the next village. In both the countryside and the city, debtors attacked their creditors; in a number of areas of central and eastern Europe, such attacks took on a strongly anti-Semitic character, as angry craftsmen and peasants went from assaulting their Jewish creditors to attacking all the Jews in the vicinity.

When we look at all these actions occurring throughout Europe in the spring of 1848, we can see some that continue an older tradition, particularly the peasant actions directed against feudal and seigneurial burdens. However, most of the actions demonstrate a popular response to the two big socioeconomic trends of the entire period of the age of revolution: the growth in power and influence of the market, and of the state. The forest riots, probably the single most common and widespread instance of collective violence in the 1848 revolution show this: peasants opposed government restrictions on wood cutting and on the types of trees that could be planted, typical examples of the state extending its reach. They also opposed the loss of their rights to cut wood on the property of others, as forest property owners found their own, increasingly commercial, uses for forest products – an example of the expansion of the reach of the market.

As peasants, craftsmen and labourers engaged in these sorts of actions, they did so while waving tricolour flags and chanting calls for liberty and equality, and for the constitution. This widespread understanding that a new governmental regime was at hand, a regime understood both in terms of memories from the years 1789–1815, and in terms of the political controversies of the 1840s, was another characteristic feature of the mass actions of the spring of 1848. The 'municipal revolution' that had taken place in the summer of 1789 was rather less common in 1848; better organized and centralized states,

[404]   working from central governments in the capital cities either dismissed local and provincial officials, or took them over in its service.

However, other features of 1789 were back with a vengeance. National or civic guards were formed everywhere in Europe. In 1848, as in 1789, these popular militias were, potentially, at least, a force for the restoration of order and the protection of property and also a core of future insurrections. Also as in 1789, there were widespread celebrations of freedom: the planting of trees of liberty, the raising of tricolour flags, nocturnal illuminations and torch-light parades, church services of thanksgiving. (As in 1789, but unlike in 1830, the clergy generally jumped on board the revolutionary bandwagon in 1848; anti-clerical riots and outbursts were limited to a few areas in the Austrian empire.) These ceremonies took place everywhere, from the capital cities to the most isolated mountain villages, helping to create an almost euphoric mood of liberation from decades of tyranny. It was, as contemporaries said, the 'springtime of the peoples'.

As the spring of 1848 gave way to summer, both the euphoria and the disorder gradually faded away. However, the mass movements of the spring did not so much disappear as change form. They were succeeded by an utterly unprecedented wave of communication, organization and assembly – the utilization of the institutions of civil society. The newly installed liberal governments of spring 1848 abolished previously existing censorship and other restrictions on the press. The number of newspapers doubled or tripled at least; 1848 saw the publication of the first ever Ukrainian-language news-paper. Increasingly, newspaper readership extended downward in the social spectrum to the urban lower classes – who certainly were newspaper readers before 1848 in Great Britain, and, to some extent in France, but nowhere else on the continent. Newspapers even began to circulate in rural areas. Since many denizens of the countryside were illiterate or not very good at reading, the practice of reading newspapers out loud in a group setting became increas-ingly common.

Newspapers stimulated an interest in public affairs and encouraged debate about them. Voluntary associations provided a forum for such debate and a means of taking action on the issues being debated. The 1848 revolution saw a profusion of associations, an often-noted feature being the labour associations. Members of different craft occupations formed associations, sometimes journeymen and masters separately, sometimes together. The unemployed formed their own groups, to press demands for public works. There were workers' associations, open to all of the urban lower classes, not just to members of a specific trade, mutual benefit societies, consumers' and producers' cooperatives. A few of these organizations were trade unions, and [405] engaged in strikes and collective bargaining, but the idea of cooperatives, of 'association', and the 'organization of labour', to use two phrases very popular in 1848, was much more common. Members of other occupations, such as schoolteachers, clergymen, professional groups, formed their own associations. Even soldiers did this, although army officers understandably feared such groups as subversive of military discipline, and did their best to repress them. Businessmen founded special-interest organizations, free traders and protectionists frequently squaring up to each other.

If these economically orientated groups were a new feature of the 1848 revolution, the formation of political clubs was reminiscent of the events of 1789 – only on a considerably larger scale. Then, such clubs had been primarily limited to France, and were found almost exclusively among the supporters of one political tendency, the Jacobins. In 1848, however, supporters of all political tendencies, from the radicals on the left, through the liberal, constitutional monarchists in the centre, to the conservatives on the right, formed their own clubs, as did several groups, such as the supporters of Louis-Napoleon Bonaparte in France, or the Catholics in Germany, whose politics spanned the whole left–right spectrum. Closely related to these political clubs were organizations such as gymnastics and choral societies, that had already existed before the outbreak of the revolution, but now expanded greatly in numbers and extent. Members of the different Christian confessions also formed their own religious associations which were sometimes related to political tendencies, and sometimes not. Political clubs in 1848 were very widespread in Europe – most common in the German states, but there were large numbers in France and Italy, and in portions of the Austrian empire. Even Norway, a country that experienced no revolution, but more peaceful reforms, had a substantial club movement.

These associations were the workhorses of revolutionary politics. Much like their Jacobin predecessors, they held debates, organized petitions to parliamentary bodies, sponsored public mass meetings and festivals. Also like the Jacobins, they organized on a supra-local level, creating regional and, ultimately, national federations of organizations. They had close relations to parliamentary deputies who shared their views; indeed, such deputies were often the leaders of the national federations. Clubs and newspapers were linked in similar ways, with editors and journalists often functioning as club leaders. Political clubs in 1848 held national congresses – an idea that the Jacobins had considered in the early 1790s but never carried out. These activities were all within the framework of the law, but, like their Jacobin predecessors, these

[406]   associations – particularly those of left-wing views – were involved in more violent or illegal action, such as the carrying out of a tax boycott campaign, or the planning of an insurrection.

It is hard to overestimate the extent of this activation of the three inter-related institutions of civil society – newspapers, associations and public meetings – during the 1848 revolution. A plausible estimate, for instance, would be that there were 1–1.5 million members of political clubs in the German states, about 10–15 per cent of the adult male population. There were hundreds of political clubs in France and Italy; French federations of consumers' and producers' cooperatives counted tens of thousands of members. In fact, this outburst of organization and activism in the 1848 revolution was a long-term high point. It would only be some fifty years later, at the turn of the century, that political or labour associations would recruit comparable numbers of members, and that politicized mass meetings would be so common and widespread.

One aspect of this whole process of the activation of civil society deserves special attention, namely the participation of women. Rather as was the case with the Jacobin clubs in the early 1790s, women were generally allowed – and frequently encouraged – to attend the meetings of associations (even conservative or Catholic groups were willing to admit women to their sessions), but usually were not permitted to speak or become members. Women did form their own organizations, at which they would speak in an all-female environment, and act, generally in support of men: by issuing addresses calling on men to engage in political action, by gathering money for nationalist causes and political prisoners, by pledging to buy products of national industry, by organizing festivities and sewing flags. Such women's groups also provided women with an opportunity to read newspapers together out loud and think about public events; this was, perhaps, the feature that most encouraged women to take an independent political role.

Rather like the women of the Chartist movement, women in continental Europe in 1848 generally did not act on their own behalf, or in support of women's issues. The major exception to this was in Paris, where there were political clubs that admitted both sexes equally to membership and allowed them speaking roles. Women in Paris also formed their own clubs and associations, and issued female-specific demands, such as public works programmes for the female unemployed, involving sewing, instead of road-work. In 1849, one Parisian feminist leader, Jeanne Déroin, even attempted to run for a seat in the legislature, only the government declared her candidacy invalid. The exceptional character of events in Paris only highlights the extent to which almost all the female political activity in 1848 might seem, by the standards of the twenty-first century, more than a little passive and subordinate to men. For contemporaries, however, it was remarkable and revolutionary: a substantial step forward in women's participation in public life. As was the case with men, women's political activity and involvement reached a high point in the 1848 revolution, that would not be reached again until the beginning of the twentieth century.

The course of the 1848 revolution: conflict, polarization and ultimate defeat

This broad process of mobilization and organization needs to be kept in mind when we consider the events of the 1848 revolution – itself, something of a misnomer, since important revolutionary events occurred in 1849, and the ultimate fate of the revolution was not completely sealed until 1851. We can divide the development of the 1848 revolution into four broad parts: (1) the initial struggles on the barricades in January–March 1848, and the coming to power of liberal regimes; (2) the generally unexpected development of political conflicts in these regimes during the spring of 1848; (3) a series of violent confrontations between May and November 1848, ending in the defeat of the revolutionary forces; (4) a new round of organization and agitation, but also of a growing political polarization, leading to a second wave of political confrontations, that peaked in the spring of 1849, but were not fully concluded in France (and given the central role of France in revolutionary events, thus in all of Europe) until December 1851.

As noted above, changes in regime rolled, wave-like, from one European country to another, between January and April of 1848. Whether rulers were willing to try to fight it out on the barricades, or whether they gave in without an armed clash, the result was everywhere the same: a liberal government ministry, that granted the basic civil liberties: freedom of speech, the press, association, assembly and religion. Elections were promised for a constituent assembly, that was to write a constitution to institutionalize and legalize this new political order. Only in France did this initial wave of revolution lead to the proclamation of a republic; elsewhere in Europe, as had been the case in 1789, monarchs remained on their thrones. As had also been true in 1789, these monarchs appointed new, liberal government ministers, but their old, conservative advisers (at least the ones not forced to flee the country) still retained a measure of influence, forming, as contemporaries said, a 'camarilla', an informal grouping sceptical of or downright hostile to the revolution.

[408]   In this situation, conflicts arose from two different directions. One was a result of the electoral process. Elections were held for a constitutent assembly in France, Germany, the Prussian kingdom, the Austrian empire, and in Denmark; similar elections were held in most of the Italian states and some of the smaller German states as well. The franchise for these elections was very broad, encompassing anywhere from a good one-third of adult males to virtually all of them. Participation rates were considerable as well: over 80 per cent of eligible voters cast their ballots in the April 1848 elections to the French constituent assembly. This figure was much higher than the 30 per cent or so of eligibles who voted during the 1789 revolution, and, in fact, was not matched in French elections until 1928.

Now, the large majority of voters, like the large majority of Europeans, lived in the countryside, and had little exposure to the campaigns of the pre-1848 political opposition, and little political experience of any kind, since voting, reading newspapers, or belonging to voluntary associations had been either uncommon or downright illegal before the revolution. The many organizations and associations that would be formed during the revolution, the many newspapers being printed and meetings held, however, were just getting under way in the spring of 1848, and were still largely confined to larger urban centres. Thus elections with a very broad franchise would be held among a population with little knowledge or understanding of politics.

This was a situation made to order for the notables, and for noble landlords and the clergy – groups who had the knowledge of public affairs and influence to exert. Elections to these constitutent assemblies, held largely without election campaigns or clearly defined parties putting up a slate of candidates, generally were decided by the notables and the clergy – and usually resulted in the election of deputies who were conservative or moderately liberal in political sympathy. A majority of the deputies to the constituent assembly that was to write a constitution for the new French republic, for instance, were supporters of a monarchy. Left-wing deputies were generally a distinct minority, and were only elected in areas – in parts of southern France, for instance, or in southwestern Germany – where the notables themselves had radical sympathies.

The outcome of the elections was a paradox. Elections held on terms favoured by radicals – supporters of a democratic franchise – had led to the radicals' defeat. Revolutions had created parliaments that were dominated by deputies who were opposed, on principle, to revolutions. This was a situation that clearly carried within itself the seeds of future conflicts, conflicts that would not be long in coming.

The second major direction of political conflicts involved competing [409] nationalist claims. As we noted in the previous chapter, nationalism was an integral part of the liberal and radical political programmes, and with the victory of the liberal and radical opposition in the barricade struggles of January–March 1848, nationalist demands quickly came to the surface. What liberals and radicals had not previously fully realized, however, was that the victory of liberal and radical movements in different European countries would lead to clashes of nationalist demands. The new liberal government in Denmark and the German National Assembly, dominated by liberal politicians, both laid claim, in nationalist fashion, to the province of Schleswig, which had a mixed German–Danish population. There was a similar conflict in the Prussian province of Posen (Polish: Poznàn) between the German- and Polish-speaking populations. Both had previously been part of a conservative Kingdom of Prussia, but now they would fight over whether to belong to a Polish or a German nation-state.

The major battleground for such national conflicts, however, was the Austrian empire. Insurrections in Venice and Milan destroyed the Austrian government's and army's hold on its northern Italian provinces. Responding to the appeal of the liberal provincial governments set up there, Charles-Albert, the king of Piedmont-Savoy, sent his army to occupy the area in the name of a future united Italy; smaller contingents from the other Italian states followed his lead. German-speaking nationalists in the empire, including many of the members of the new, liberal government created in Vienna after the victory of the insurgents on the barricades, wanted all or at least some provinces of the empire to be part of a united German nation-state. The provinces of Bohemia and Moravia were always counted among those to be integrated into Germany; the liberal Czech nationalists, who dominated the 'national committee' formed in Prague, however, saw Germany as a foreign country, and forcibly prevented any participation in elections to the German National Assembly. Instead, they created a sort of anti-German assembly, a 'Slavic Congress' that met in Prague. Polish nationalists in the province of Galicia, following their victory on the barricades in Cracow, wanted to see the province as part of a future Polish nation-state; to their horror and dismay, a newly formed 'Supreme Ukrainian Council' in the Galician provincial capital of Lemberg announced that at least the eastern half of the province did not belong to Poland at all.

For all the clashes in the Austrian lands, the major cockpit of the nationalities conflict was in the Hungarian half of the empire. Following the bloodless victory of the insurgents in Buda and Pest in March 1848, the Hungarian

[410]   Diet had met there, appointed a liberal government ministry for all the Hungarian provinces, proclaimed autonomy or home rule for this united Hungary (the Austrian emperor could, as king of Hungary, still be the head of state), and set elections for a Hungarian National Assembly, to write the constitution for this united Hungarian state. The liberal nationalists in the province of Croatia, however, had no interest in being part of a united Hungary: they held a special meeting of the Croatian provincial Diet, appointed a new government for Croatia, and scheduled elections for a Croatian National Assembly. Other national groups in Hungary, particularly the Serbs, Slovaks and Rumanians, did not actually form governments and call for National Assemblies, but they did hold enormous national mass meetings (the Rumanian one had tens of thousands of participants) to proclaim their national autonomy and independence from Hungarian rule.

There are two points worth noting about this clash of liberal nationalisms in the Habsburg empire, points that would be decisive for the fate of the revolution in both the empire and, in some ways, in all of Europe. First was the intersection of nationalism and feudalism. In the Hungarian province of Transylvania, the noble landlords – who were known for their particularly cruel and oppressive exploitation of the serfs – were Hungarians, who supported the Hungarian nationalist demand for an end to the special position of Transylvania, the result of traditional, chartered privileges, and its full integration into a united Hungarian nation-state. A substantial proportion of the Rumanian-speaking population, on the other hand, were serfs, who were, like serfs everywhere in the monarchy, rebelling against their lords. Although the liberal Hungarian government had proclaimed the abolition of serfdom, it is not entirely surprising that these serfs did not trust that government, especially since their own feudal lords were its strong supporters, and endorsed, instead, the ideas of Rumanian nationalist intellectuals. A similar situation existed among the Serbs of Hungary, and the Ukrainians of Galicia, where one stronger, better-organized nationalist movement, led by the nobility, confronted another, weaker one, that could count, however, on serf hatred of their lords for its support.

The second point about this nationalities conflict was that it was exploited by the civilian officials and army officers of the empire, most of whom, while paying lip-service to the new, liberal regime, remained loyal to pre-1848 conservative and absolutist ideas. Before the outbreak of the revolution, they had been reluctant, as part of their conservative principles, to endorse nationalism; ironically, it was the new revolutionary situation that enabled them to discard their scruples and take effective counter-revolutionary action. One of the very last acts of the conservative government ministers in Vienna before they were forced to resign was to appoint a new 'Ban' or provincial governor of Croatia. They chose an army colonel, Josip Jelačić, a man who was on good terms with the liberal Croatian nationalists, but who was, above all, a partisan of imperial rule. Jelačić would turn the Croatian nationalist movement, and the Croatian regiments in the Habsburg army into a counter-revolutionary force, determined to destroy the liberal Hungarian government and its aspirations for autonomy, to say nothing of its plans for social and political reform. Indeed, Habsburg officials and officers quickly offered tacit support and encouragement to all the anti-Hungarian and anti-Polish nationalist movements in the monarchy; the Supreme Ukrainian Council, for instance, was subsidized out of government funds by the provincial governor of Galicia, Count Stadion. Thus the many liberal nationalist movements in the conservative-absolutist, multinational Habsburg empire, rather than destroying that empire, ended up destroying each other and preserving the empire's existence.

Let us now turn to the conflicts that developed out of these clashes between nationalist movements, and between parliaments opposed to revolution, originating out of revolutions. The first victory of the counter-revolution was in the same place as the first victory of the revolution – in southern Italy, where in May 1848 King Ferdinand withdrew his troops from the war against Austria in the north, used them to coerce a liberal parliament that disagreed with him, and then sent his army to reconquer the rebellious island of Sicily. However, the first major victory of counter-revolution, that would shake the entire continent, like the first major victory of the revolution, would be in Paris. This conflict pitted the radicalized population of Paris against the politically moderate, monarchist constituent assembly meeting there.

Just as the oppositional forces of the July Monarchy had been divided between the politicized radicals, who sought to overthrow the government and establish a new Jacobin regime, and the socialists, who wished for peaceful reforms outside the political system, so the Parisian leftists and the members of the revolutionary provisional government were divided. On the one hand were the radicals, who quickly formed large numbers of political clubs, and demanded a Jacobin government. Afraid – correctly as it turned out – that elections to a constituent assembly would yield moderate or conservative results, they tried in vain to postpone these elections, until they, like their Jacobin predecessors, could control the state bureaucracy and build up a nationwide network of political clubs. On the other hand were the 'workers' (mostly craftsmen, both masters and journeymen, with some more modern factory workers

[412]   among them), who formed trade associations and pressed the government to finance producers' cooperatives, as socialist theories envisaged. The government did agree to sponsor 'national workshops', which were not socialist experiments at all, but public works projects for the unemployed.

When the moderate constituent assembly was elected, the Parisian radicals tried, following Jacobin precedent, to mobilize the clubs and overthrow it, to replace it with a more radical regime. Their effort in May 1848 failed, since the National Guard opposed them, and, just as significantly, the workers in the trade associations would not cooperate. The government cracked down on the clubs, dissolving many of them and arresting their leaders. It then turned, the following month, to the pseudo-socialist experiment, the national workshops, and prepared to dissolve them, and send the unemployed to the provinces to drain swamps. The workshop members and the trade associations responded by demonstrating against the government, clashing with the police and building barricades. The republican government, unlike the regime of Louis-Philippe, was ready to fight. It sent in the army and, especially the Mobile Guard, an elite branch of the National Guard – whose members were mostly unemployed workers, just like the insurgents on the barricades – and after three days of fierce fighting that left several thousand dead, destroyed the insurgent movement. Thousands of additional insurgents were arrested, tried, and deported to Algeria.

The June Days, as this conflict was known, was a dismaying spectacle, pitting two left-wing forces, a republican government, and a labour movement, against each other. Eugène Cavaignac, commander of the government's forces, and named prime minister after the suppression of the insurrection, was from an old Jacobin family, and was himself a veteran republican oppositionist. His older brother had even been, during the 1830s, a leader of the radical and conspiratorial Society of the Rights of Man. Cavaignac's republic, however, was a liberal republic, a regime of private property and the free market, rather than a radical Jacobin republic or a republic of social reform and socialist experiment. While in the French politics of June 1848, this distinction was a very real one, its significance for the broader outcome of the mid-century revolution should not be overemphasized. In the rest of Europe, any kind of republic was still a subversive extremely radical notion, and it was, above all, conservative, monarchist, counter-revolutionary forces who took delight in the victories of General Cavaignac. Indeed, it remained to be seen whether in France itself the general's triumph would not begin the process of undermining the republican form of government that he so passionately supported.

The second major conflict we can mention was centred in Germany and concerned the convergence of a clash of nationalist ideas, with a clash of political ones and a clash of Great Power politics. The arena of the conflict was the German National Assembly, a legislative body sitting in Frankfurt, the old capital of the German Confederation, writing a constitution for a united German nation-state. This assembly, unlike the French National Assembly of 1789 or the Convention of 1793 had no way of enforcing its will. There was no existing all-German government; the Assembly was to create it. For the liberal, constitutional-monarchist politicians, who dominated the assembly, this was no problem, because the individual central European states, that did have governments and armies, especially the Great Powers, Prussia and Austria, were being run by liberal governments, who were committed to cooperating with the National Assembly.

This cooperation proceeded relatively smoothly into the summer of 1848. One example of it concerned the nationalist demand for the incorporation of the province of Schleswig into a German nation-state. The German National Assembly had declared war on the government of Denmark, which was attempting to suppress the pro-German insurgents in Schleswig. While the Assembly had no troops, the individual German governments, Prussia in particular, did, and they sent them to fight the Danes – with considerable success, for they advanced beyond Schleswig into Denmark proper. This advance brought other Great Powers, Great Britain, and especially Russia, into action, since the latter feared a Prussia that would dominate the sea routes from the Baltic into the North Sea, an important outlet of Russian maritime commerce. The government of the tsar exerted heavy pressure on the Prussian government to end the war. The conservative camarilla, the informal advisers of the monarch Frederick William IV, endorsed the tsar's move, and the monarch made his moderately liberal government sign the Malmö armistice, in August 1848, renouncing the German national cause.

Such a decision marked the collapse of the liberal programme of cooperation between the National Assembly and the German monarchs. The decision was a slap in the face for German nationalism, and also a blow to the idea, particularly endorsed by radicals, that the National Assembly, elected by a democratic vote of all (well, most) adult men in Germany, was sovereign. The Assembly voted to denounce the armistice and seemed ready to face the consequences, including the possibility of a war with Russia: potentially, a great European war, whose radicalizing effects on a revolution had previously been well observed in 1792. However, moderates regained control of the situation and the Assembly reversed itself and endorsed the armistice,

[414] the actions of the king of Prussia, and, by implication, its own impotence. Radicals within and outside the Assembly tried, in Jacobin fashion, to invade and overthrow it. Prussian and Hessian troops, hastily called to intervene, faced insurgents who built barricades in the streets of Frankfurt. After brief but fierce barricade fighting, the 'September days', the insurrection was defeated.

The confrontations and victories of counter-revolutionary forces in the Austrian empire were more complex, confused and less definitive than elsewhere in Europe. Basically, the monarchy's bureaucrats and army officers – acting largely independently of the mentally retarded emperor and his liberal government ministers – played one national movement off against another, until most had been defeated and the authority of the monarchy restored in most parts of the empire. As early as April 1848, Habsburg troops bombarded the city of Cracow, and after barricade fighting there, destroyed the centre of the Polish nationalist movement. In June of that year, soldiers under the command of General Windischgrätz clashed with radicals in Prague; in the ensuing street fighting, occurring at the same time as the Parisian June Days, his forces were victorious. Czech radical leaders were arrested and the Prague Slavic Congress was dissolved. Finally, and most significantly, in July, soldiers led by General Radetzky, commander of Habsburg forces in northern Italy, emerged from their Alpine strongholds, to which they had retreated after being expelled from Milan and Venice, and, at the battle of Custozza, smashed the very ineptly led Piedmontese army. By August, they had reconquered all of the empire's northern Italian possessions, except for the island city of Venice.

These victories were eased by the cooperation of some nationalist movements, whose partisans engaged in fundamental miscalculations. The liberal German nationalists treated Windischgrätz and Radetzky as heroes, who had upheld their national cause against Slavic and Italian enemies – not understanding that the generals were absolutist conservatives, who would, at the right moment, turn on all radical or liberal nationalists. The liberal government of Hungary had allowed Hungarian army units to fight with General Radetzky against the Italians, hoping that such cooperation with the empire would strengthen the case for autonomy, and allow the government to deal with the dissident national movements in Hungary, not realizing that the reconquest of the northern Italian provinces was a precondition for military action against the Hungarian ones.

By late summer 1848, the Hungarian government in Budapest was the only one holding out against the central authority of the monarchy, now supported by a constituent assembly, meeting in Vienna. Throughout the summer of 1848, Habsburg generals and officials had been encouraging Serbian and Rumanian insurgents to oppose the Hungarian government. These efforts were quite successful, since the Serbian and Rumanian serfs did not need much encouragement to fight against their feudal landlords, most of whom were Hungarians. Indeed, in Transylvania, the situation developed into a full-scale civil war, complete with large-scale massacres, and what we might call ethnic cleansing, on both sides. In many ways, it was a mini version of the conflicts of western France during the 1789 revolution. Both conflicts pitted monarchist peasants, who seemingly were getting nothing from the reforms of the revolution, against landowners – middle class in France, nobles in Transylvania – who supported the revolution. Both were very bloody affairs. The Transylvanian civil war cost 40,000 lives, by far the greatest death toll in the 1848 revolutions.

Defeating the Hungarian government, though, would take more than badly armed peasant insurgents. The key to imperial plans was Ban Jelačić, as governor of Croatia, technically a subordinate of the Hungarian government, but really its opponent. In September 1848, he led his Croatian army units, in the name of the Austrian emperor, out of the province of Croatia, over the river Drava into the interior of Hungary. The Hungarian National Assembly wavered in its response; should it try, in liberal fashion, to reach agreement with the officials of the Austrian emperor – in his capacity as king of Hungary, still the official Hungarian head of state – or should it defy the emperor and go to war? Radicals in Budapest mobilized the population to surround the assembly. Quite in contrast to the German National Assembly, which was facing a similar situation at the same time, the Hungarian parliament – alone among such assemblies in Europe in 1848 – decided for the option of revolutionary war. It named the militant leader of the pre-revolutionary opposition, Lajos Kossuth, head of a National Defence Committee. Kossuth immediately took vigorous action to raise an army and prepare the country for war.

This Hungarian army defeated the troops of General Jelačić, and the Austrian government called on the garrison in Vienna to march to their assistance. This was the signal for an uprising in Vienna, as radical leaders there realized that a defeat of the Hungarian government would mean a victory of counter-revolution everywhere in the monarchy. With wide support in the Viennese population, they seized power in the city; the emperor, his ministers and the national assembly fled to Moravia. In October, the armies of Jelačić and Windischgrätz converged on Vienna: they stormed the city and after several days of street fighting defeated the National Guard and the

[416] radical militias. For good measure, they shot one of the insurgent leaders, Robert Blum, a deputy of the German National Assembly, demonstrating the Austrian government's low esteem for that body, just like its Prussian counterpart. Czech nationalists now rejoiced in the triumph of the emperor's forces over the German-speaking radicals in Vienna, not realizing that these victories marked an end to any reform movements, sponsored by any of the nationalities, in the empire.

Conservative forces followed up the triumph in Vienna by forcing the retarded Emperor Ferdinand to abdicate in favour of his youthful nephew Francis Joseph. Not long afterwards, the Austrian constituent assembly, still meeting in Moravia, was dissolved and its deputies sent home. The accession of a new emperor thus signalled a resurgence of the empire and of further attempts to rule in absolutist fashion; his long reign, until his death in 1916, would coincide with the monarchy's remaining existence, characterized by lengthy struggles over constitutions and the powers of parliaments and a never-ending battle with nationalist movements.

The string of victories of counter-revolution were rounded off by two relatively peaceful events in November 1848. In France, the constituent assembly, finished writing a constitution for the republic, including a strong, American-style president. Who should put forth his candidacy for this office, but Napoleon? Not the real Napoleon, but his nephew, Louis-Napoleon Bonaparte, who was chosen president of France with over three-quarters of the votes cast in the November elections. Louis-Napoleon was particularly strong in rural areas, with peasant voters who thought he was the original Napoleon, or imagined that he was so rich that he would pay for government himself, and abolish taxes. Leftist workers in Paris, Lyon, and other large cities, smarting under the defeat of the June insurgents, voted for Napoleon – as a blow at the main opposing candidate, General Cavaignac. So did conservative supporters of a restored monarchy, whether under a Bourbon or an Orléans dynasty, who saw Louis Napoleon as a stalking horse for their planned restoration, and a pliable and not too bright figure, who would do what he was told.

Finally, in Prussia, Frederick William IV, listening ever more to his conservative camarilla, decided the time had come to break with liberalism in his monarchy. He was opposed by the Prussian National Assembly, which was proving to be more of a left-wing body than its counterpart in Frankfurt. In November, the king appointed the arch-reactionary General Brandenburg as prime minister and sent 50,000 troops into Berlin to adjourn the insubordinate parliament. Thoroughly intimidated, the Civic Guard of Berlin offered no resistance. The Assembly called for a kingdom-wide tax boycott, in opposition to the monarch's efforts. Although this appeal was supported [417] in several of the monarchy's provinces, and led to near-insurrectionary clashes between radicals and the army, in the end the government was able to retain order. The Assembly was dissolved, but the government, cleverly and unexpectedly, decreed its own constitution – one that granted the monarch greater powers than liberals (to say nothing of radicals) would have liked, but that also marked a break with the previous tradition of absolutist rule. In this respect, the Prussian government proved more flexible and accommodating to new trends than its Austrian counterpart and rival, a stance that would have considerable consequences in subsequent decades.

By the end of 1848, conservative ministers were once more running the governments of the Great Powers, France, Prussia and Austria. While the constituent assemblies elected the previous spring continued to exist, and to work on constitutions or other legislation, they seemed powerless and their liberal leaders increasingly out of touch with political events. If, in spite of these developments, the revolutionary movement was not yet defeated, if, in fact, there would be a new round of revolutionary struggles in the spring of 1849 and a further reprise of them in France, in 1851, this was because of the process of political mobilization, using the institutions of civil society, outlined in a previous section of this chapter.

It was particularly the radicals who made use of this possiblity, to rally their followers and recover from some of their defeats. The autumn of 1848 saw the formation of nationwide federations of radical political clubs in France, Germany and Italy, and a vigorous campaign of political organization, particularly in rural areas. This campaign involved a certain political reorientation, we might say something of a merger of politically radical and socialist perspectives. Increasingly, leftists presented their plans for democratic and republican government as a means to resolve the bitter grievances the lower classes had demonstrated in the spring of 1848. The republic would bring lower taxes; in it, peasants could get wood from the forests and artisans could form producers' cooperatives. This campaign marked a turn in radical thought from the ideals of the Jacobins, a turn already apparent in the British Chartist movement. The republican and democratic form of government to which radicals aspired, would not so much reform individual morality and aim at an austere body of citizens, engaged in self-renunciation, rather, these new forms of government would aid the badly pressed lower classes; helping them to solve their social and economic problems.

Thus, we can see in the autumn of 1848 and winter of 1849 two opposed political mobilizations: a radical one, aimed at gaining a mass base of support; and a conservative one, also involving the formation of political clubs and a search for popular support, but primarily about securing a hold on the armed forces and the state officials to suppress any opposition. In these circumstances, the liberal forces that had dominated the revolution at an early stage quickly lost the ability to guide events: a political doctrine espousing a limited government chosen by the notables did not work well in the turbulent mass politics of the revolution.

There were a series of confrontations in the winter and spring of 1849 – with the one in France lasting until 1851. If we consider them, country by country, we can see the final fate of the 1848 revolution. Starting with Italy, although the revolution had been defeated in the northern provinces and in the south, the centre of the country became a stronghold of the radicals. Using their political clubs, they overthrew the rule of the grand duke in Tuscany, and of the pope in Rome. Pius IX was forced to flee the Holy City, and became, for the rest of his life an embittered enemy of even the most moderate kinds of political, social, or religious change. Under the guidance of radical veteran Giuseppe Mazzini, the radicals proclaimed a Roman Republic in the Papal States.

The key to the pre-1848 opposition in Italy and to the 1848 revolution itself had always been the opposition to Austrian rule in the north. This did not change in 1849, and under the impetus of the revolutionary movements in central Italy, Charles Albert, king of Piedmont-Savoy, decided once again to try his luck with an invasion, as he had the previous spring. Unfortunately, his army was no better prepared, and the Austrians crushed it at Novara. Austrian troops occupied most of central Italy; French troops, sent by Louis-Napoleon's conservative government reconquered Rome, after a powerful defence led by the insurgent military expert, Giuseppe Garibaldi, who began a spectacular career as an armed revolutionary, that would make him the most famous man in Europe in the early 1860s. However, such future fame could not be foreseen by the summer of 1849, as the revolution in Italy was crushed.

In Germany, the Frankfurt National Assembly finished writing its constitution for a united German state and proclaimed in March 1849, that the king of Prussia was to be its monarchical chief executive, the emperor. (The king was far from the Assembly's first choice, but since the conservative Austrian government had denounced the whole idea of a united Germany, there was no other appropriate monarch to whom they could turn.) Frederick William IV, although tempted by such an honour, ultimately rejected it. As a conservative, he could not accept an office created by a democratically elected legislature expressing popular sovereignty; also as a conservative, he could not bring himself to go against the historically based privileges of the Austrian emperor to be Germany's chief monarch. More practically, both his informal conservative advisers and the tsar made it clear that cooperation with the National Assembly would be politically unacceptable.

Having failed in their task, most of the deputies to the National Assembly gave up and went home. However, there developed a mass movement in support of the constitution written by the Assembly, led by the Assembly's radical minority and the German federation of radical political clubs. It might seem odd for radicals to favour a constitution creating an emperor – and naming a reactionary monarch to that office to boot – but when we consider the speeches given at mass meetings in this campaign, denouncing the Prussian king, and calling for a republic, we realize that the support of the monarchical constitution was largely a pretext, a way to gather support for more radical plans. There were, in the spring of 1849, mass meetings and demonstrations, sponsored and led by democratic political clubs, throughout Germany. Some of these went over into barricade building and street fighting; particularly, in the southwestern part of the country, a stronghold of the left, many soldiers joined the insurgents. Revolutionary governments were proclaimed in Saxony, Baden and the Palatinate. In the end, though, the armies of the king of Prussia proved strong enough to suppress this revolutionary movement.

The revolutionary movements in both Italy and Germany were a direct threat to the Austrian government, since a secession of its Italian provinces and a Germany united under Prussian rule would mean a decisive weakening of the position of the Habsburg monarchy, and incite its own revolutionary movements, regrouping at the time as was the case elsewhere in Europe, to another effort. Fortunately for the new emperor Francis Joseph, the troops under his veteran general Radetzky were more than a match for the Piedmontese army, and the king of Prussia, rather than taking the German nationalist movement as an ally against his traditional Austrian rival, suppressed it, instead. The internal problem of the Hungarians remained, though. In the winter and spring of 1849, Kossuth's government declared Hungary independent of Austrian rule, and the regrouped Hungarian armies launched successful offensives on all fronts. At one point in April 1849, it seemed as though the Austrian government would even have to flee Vienna, to escape Hungarian forces marching up the Danube.

In these difficult circumstances, the Austrian government appealed to the tsar for help. The slender diplomatic basis for this appeal was the Münchengrätz agreement of 1833, in which the Russian and Austrian governments had

[420] agreed, above all, to guarantee the European territories of the sultan and, secondarily, to cooperate against potential revolutions in Poland. All this had little to do with the Hungarian situation, which was covered, rather marginally, by a clause in the agreement concerning potential interventions against revolutions, on the request of a legitimate monarch. Tsar Nicholas I, who had been seeking an opportunity to intervene against the Europe-wide revolutions, since their inception at the beginning of 1848, was only too happy to accede to the Austrian request. The Russian intervention spelled the end of the Hungarian revolutionary government – the one in 1848 that was most like the French revolutionary government of the 1790s. Hungary was ultimately too small a nation to launch a great revolutionary war that would upset all of Europe as the French had done fifty years previously, but the Hungarians tried, and came suprisingly close to succeeding.

Finally, we need to consider France, the country where the age of revolution began, and where it would come to an end. Elections to the legislature in April 1849, while bringing a majority for the liberal and conservative adherents of a return to the monarchy had also brought suprisingly good results for the reorganized and reunified radicals. Contemporaries noted, in particular, their successes in rural areas in central and southern France, regions that had been, in the 1790s and again after 1815, centres of counter-revolution and White Terror. The radical deputies quickly challenged the government, when it sent troops to supress the revolution in Italy; their attempted mass demonstrations against the government in May 1849 were quickly and easily suppressed. Most radical political activity was prohibited, although it continued in legal and semi-legal forms.

If the conservative elements were in charge of France, they faced a different problem from any faced by their fellow conservatives elsewhere in Europe. The dominant conservatives wished to abolish the republic and return to a monarchy – feeling that only then would the revolution in France and all of Europe be truly defeated. But they disagreed about who should be the king: a Bourbon, heir to Charles X, overthrown in 1830, or an Orléans prince, heir to Louis-Philippe, overthrown in 1848. While the French conservatives and moderate liberals quarrelled about that, the president, Louis-Napoleon Bonaparte prepared for the return of a quite different dynasty. Using his executive powers and his role as commander-in-chief of the armed forces, he carefully incited that latent Bonapartism, those long-held sympathies for Napoleon, existing in France, while making sure that generals favourable to him held key military posts, and those who did not support him were sent off to Algeria. In December 1851, he launched his coup.

At first, there seemed to be little opposition, and Paris itself, centre of re- volutions, was quiet. But in rural areas of southern and central France, newly organized centres of radical sympathy, an uprising against the coup broke out. Waving red flags and chanting radical slogans calling for democratic government and social reforms, peasants and craftsmen – as well as some notables with left-wing sympathies – in villages and small towns gathered to march on departmental capitals. The poorly armed insurgents were no match for the army. Their defeat, paralleling the defeat of the insurgents in Italy and Germany two and a half years previously, marked the final end of the 1848 revolutions and of the whole age of revolution in European history.

Note

1. Quoted in James Epstein, *The Lion of Freedom: Feargus O'Connor and the Chartist Movement, 1832–1842*, (London, 1982), p. 13.

CHAPTER 9

THE AGE OF REVOLUTION IN EUROPEAN HISTORY

How revolutionary was the age of revolution?

Looking back from the vantage point of the middle of the nineteenth century, we can consider, briefly, the extent and nature of the changes occurring in the previous seven decades. We might wonder whether the changes were drastic, discontinuous and irreversible – 'revolutionary', in the meaning that the word acquired precisely in this era – or gradual, involving no sharp break with the past, and not definitive. Naturally, such a consideration could, and does lead to different conclusions when we look at different aspects of social, economic, political and cultural developments; as it does when we consider different regions of Europe.

It was in the realm of political participation that this era was at its most revolutionary. Both the possibilities for and the expectations of participation in public life expanded enormously. Revolutionary upheavals, particularly those following 1789 and 1848, were the major multipliers of political participation, but even countries where revolutionary efforts failed, such as Great Britain, or where they were basically lacking, such as the Scandinavian lands, nonetheless saw major changes in the public sphere. No longer reserved for an elite largely sanctioned at birth, public life had become an arena in which an ever-greater number of adult men, and even, sometimes, if to a lesser extent, women, could register their claims – often in drastic fashion. The focus and legitimation basis of public life had shifted from the absolute monarch, and the constituted bodies of the society of orders, to distinctly new entities, such as constitutions, elected legislatures and the nation.

Admittedly, these changes were most strongly felt in the British Isles and in northwestern and central Europe. Southern and eastern Europe rather lagged behind, with the latter area only first seeing a burst of popular political participation at the very end of the period, during the revolution of 1848.

Perhaps the one region that did not experience this change was the core provinces of the tsar's empire, where eighteenth-century autocracy continued into the nineteenth, and the possibilities for the expansion of political participation were felt at best feebly, and often not at all.

Less drastic but still considerable were the changes in the nature and structure of government. This was an age of growing claims by the state to legislate and regulate, to tax, conscript, police and imprison, to count and investigate – and to do it all in centralized and uniform fashion. Paradoxically, such claims could go along with a lessened and restricted area of competence for governmental action, a division of powers to check such actions, and a constitution setting forth areas of society and the economy quite outside of government control. To put it differently, a mid-nineteenth-century constitutional monarchy might claim a lesser radius of action than an absolutist monarchy of the end of the old regime, but within that reduced space it could be more effective and intrusive than its predecessor.

However, these many claims on public life could only be effectively implemented if there existed a well-trained and well-staffed government bureaucracy and police force. Here, aspirations and reality diverged, particularly in the states of central and eastern Europe, where state servants were present in relatively modest numbers. In the 1840s, there were far fewer police or government officials per capita in absolutist police states like Austria, Prussia or Russia, than in constitutional monarchies with guaranteed civil liberties, such as France or especially Great Britain.

Much the same can be said for those aspects of politics pertaining to relations between sovereign states, the realm of warfare and diplomacy, in which a pattern of drastic change coexisting with elements of continuity can be discerned. Above all, the 'Pentarchy', the five Great Powers, Great Britain, France, Prussia, Austria and Russia, remained the dominant influences on European warfare and diplomacy, except for a few Napoleonic years, when Prussia and Austria had been pushed into a marginal position. Admittedly, there were changes in the hierarchy of the five Powers: in the long term, this period saw the rise of the two peripheral powers, Russia and Great Britain, and the relative decline of the three continental powers. Positions of the smaller powers changed as well, mostly for the worse: Poland vanished; Spain and Sweden, still important states for military confrontations in the 1780s, at least on a regional basis, were diplomatically and militarily irrelevant, seventy years later.

There are, however, three more significant changes in international relations we can point to in this period. One is the decline of maritime warfare

[424]   and colonial competition among the Atlantic nations: still vigorous in the 1780s, it was won, decisively, by Great Britain in the following two decades. A second is the change in the nature of warfare brought about by the French Revolution and perfected by Napoleon: the mass conscript armies, whose common soldiers could fight on their own initiative, the order of battle in columns, instead of rows, the emphasis on mobility. It would be difficult to perceive the continuation of this development during the years 1815–50, since the European powers were not at war with each other, but it would be seen in the period of renewed warfare, running from the mid-1850s to the early 1870s.

The third, and most significant change in diplomacy was in its guiding principle. Under the old regime, raison d'état, the self-interest of absolutist rulers, had guided international relations, only modestly influenced by a fast-fading tendency to orient diplomacy on confessional lines. The French Revolution and the warfare proceeding from it, brought – often quite against the wishes and intentions of the elites running foreign policy – the newly developed sphere of popular politics into foreign affairs, as countries were forced to line up for or against the revolution. The guiding statesmen of the post-1815 era, particularly Austria's Prince Metternich, tried as hard as they could to keep the relations of the Great Powers aligned on a counter-revolutionary course. Raison d'état continued to be a major principle guiding international relations, but it was now quite heavily influenced – more heavily than confessional questions had influenced diplomacy at the end of the old regime – by the opposition between revolution and counter-revolution.

Turning from politics to society, we can see an equally revolutionary change in the movement from the society of orders to a civil society of property owners. The old regime patriarchal hierarchy of corporate groups with their chartered privileges, and of position set at birth, creating a constellation of status, affluence and power, was visibly evident in such organizations as the guild system and, above all, in the countryside, where most people lived, in serfdom and the seigneurial system of agriculture. Already largely undermined in the British Isles by the late eighteenth century, sometimes threatened by the reform projects of Enlightened absolutism, it came under direct attack in the French Revolution, and in the armed, Napoleonic export of the revolution's principles throughout continental Europe. The end of warfare in 1815 did not stop this questioning of the society of orders, which continued, virtually uninterrupted, during the subsequent decades, whether in peaceful gradualist, or abrupt revolutionary form. As the society of orders was placed in question, its successor, the civil society of property owners, with its characteristic features of equality before the law, public action through [425] voluntary organization, assembly, and the press, and the primacy of the un-restricted use of property and labour, steadily gained ground.

Here as well, we need to note regional differences. The impact of the French Revolution in France itself, in the Low Countries, Switzerland, Italy, and parts of western Germany had left the society of orders largely in ruins by 1815, and at least the outlines of a civil society of property owners apparent. To a somewhat lesser extent, this was the case in the Scandinavian lands as well. By contrast, in most of the German states, and on the Iberian peninsula, this transformation had only gone part way, and was completed, either via gradual reform, or sharp revolutionary transitions, in the decades of the 1830s and 1840s. In eastern Europe, in the eastern provinces of the Austrian empire, in the Danubian principalities, and in the core provinces of the tsar's empire, the society of orders remained largely intact until the 1840s. The 1848 revolu-tion destroyed one of its key features, serfdom and seigneurialism through-out the realm of the Habsburgs, but had no effect further east.

It is important to note that what had changed so drastically in this trans-ition was the basic principles of social organization and the use of property, not the content of social classes or the actual distribution of property owner-ship. These changed noticeably less. Most Europeans lived in the countryside and earned their living from agriculture in 1850 as well as 1780; landed prop-erty, which remained the primary basis of wealth, continued to be very un-equally distributed. Even revolutionary upheavals, coerced changes in the Napoleonic era, or anti-Napoleonic agrarian reforms, such as those in Prussia, produced relatively modest changes in the actual ownership of landed prop-erty, compared to the much more substantial changes they did produce in what it meant to own land, and the relationship of those who worked the land to those who owned it. Admittedly, there are exceptions here, primarily in Great Britain, where the industrialization and urbanization of the period, particularly in the years after 1820, did produce new social groups which were present in substantial numbers, such as the urban-industrial working class, or capitalist manufacturers. Such sharp changes, however, were very much more the exception than the rule on the European continent.

When we turn our gaze from society to the economy, we find that change was more modest still. In spite of that persistent and apparently ineradicable misnomer, the 'industrial revolution', developments in manufacturing – and in other sections of the economy – were anything but revolutionary. At the most basic level, that of demographic developments, population gradually increased, due to modest long-term changes in both birth and death rates, and the rate

[426]   of population increase, for all the difficulty it caused contemporaries, was one-half to one-quarter of what it has been in some underdeveloped countries during the second half of the twentieth century. In regard to another twentieth-century development, the lack of a practice of birth control (with perhaps some exceptions in parts of France) kept women tied to the cycle of reproduction, and told heavily against the possibility of revolutionary changes in women's lives. There were dramatic economic and technological innovations in this period – the planting of nitrogen-fixing crops in a new crop rotation, the use of steam power for transport, mining and manufacturing, the forging of pig iron with coking coal – but before 1820 they were implemented primarily in the British Isles, and before 1850 only to a modest extent in continental Europe. The major changes in the economy were gradual and incremental rather than sudden and drastic: increase and expansion of outwork, cultivation of market-oriented and new world crops, more roads, canals and navigable rivers. All of these were developments that had been under way in most of the eighteenth century, and, to some extent, since the middle ages. The dominant economic change, the increase in the influence of market forces and market relations in all branches of production, was itself a relatively slow and gradual process, albeit one with considerable influence on people's lives.

The best testimony to the slow, potentially reversible, and gradual nature of economic change is the way that total production barely kept pace with a growing population. The threat of a Malthusian disaster was only narrowly averted, and emigration – whether to overseas lands in the Americas and Australia, or to the lightly populated southern territories of the tsar's empire – played a crucial role in avoiding the worst. Such a conjunction suggests that changes in output were modest, and even where they were more substantial they tended to be noticeably inequitably distributed.

Turning to the realm of symbolic expression and interaction, the movement from the classical to the romantic cultural style was definitely perceived by artists, writers and intellectuals as a major, dramatic and revolutionary break, a discontinuity reflected in their lives as well as in their work. To a lesser extent, this change in cultural sensibility had a substantial effect on the educated public – although the older classical style certainly retained its partisans. Of course, the educated public was a small group, at most 5–10 per cent of the population; the influence of the new cultural style on the vast majority of farmers, craftsmen, labourers, small businessmen and the like was substantially more modest.

More important, and more truly revolutionary, was the challenge to [427] the culture of confessionalism mounted by the French Revolution, when the revolutionaries took the counter-culture of the Enlightenment out of the salons and learned journals and brought it to the centre of public life. This attack on the centrality of religion, taking visible form in the desecration of churches, the invention of a new calendar, and the creation of new forms and centres of cultic expression, was truly a cultural revolution, and one that had a dramatic and perceptible influence on the lives of ordinary people. This wave of secularization left its permanent mark in many places, and new secularized forms of transcendence, such as the cult of the nation, appeared, after the initial revolutionary tide had ebbed.

However, it would be easy to overstate the extent of such a secularization. Among Europeans of Eastern Orthodox or Moslem belief, the counter-culture of the Enlightenment made only a feeble appearance, and the cultural upheavals of the revolutionary era were primarily a distant rumour. Catholics, Protestants and Jews were much more strongly affected, and the institutions of the Catholic Church were severely shaken. Yet the connection between the clergy and the faithful remained unbroken, and new forms of religious expression and sensibility, particularly among Catholics, but to a lesser extent among Protestants as well, forms that made use of the new possibilities embedded in the growing civil society, rallied the faithful and reinforced the culture of confessionalism.

In many ways what made this an age of revolution, an era of rampant political instability, was precisely the interaction between drastic changes in some aspects of life and more modest ones, or even downright stagnation, in others. Placing the expansion of political participation, the development of new ideas about the appropriate foci of public life, and the spread of new cultural forms to articulate these ideas, and new institutions of civil society to realize them, in the context of governments that were making ever-greater demands on their subjects, and an economy that changed relatively little, leaving a growing population worse off, or at least fearful that this would be the case, was a recipe for recurrent revolutions. The revolutions themselves, however, generated a chaotic situation – whether the warfare and economic setbacks after 1789, or the clash of different and opposing nationalist movements in central and eastern Europe in 1848 – that prevented them from creating a new, more stable and more widely accepted social and political order. In this way, instability begat instability and from 1789 to 1848 Europe never seemed to come to rest.

[428] Looking forward: from the age of revolution to the second half of the nineteenth century

From this point of view, contemporaries of the mid-nineteenth century might have seen, with either hope or fear, a future of uninterrupted revolutions. One of the classic documents of the period, *The Communist Manifesto*, in fact looks forward to such a future of revolution, civil wars, and large-scale international warfare between revolutionary and counter-revolutionary governments. Yet this is precisely what did not happen in the decades after 1850, above all because the new political, social, economic and cultural forms, apparent, but never completely successfully implemented, in the age of revolution, would finally come into their own.

One example is the path of economic development. The decades after the middle of the nineteenth century would be prosperous ones, when rail networks, steamship lines and telegraph networks would expand the reach of the market throughout Europe. In this increasingly favourable environment, pre-1850 trends, such as the growth of agricultural specialization and the introduction of more productive systems of crop rotation would flourish. Industrialization on a substantial scale would spread from the British Isles to the western and central portions of continental Europe. Gradually rising standards of living, combined with an unprecedented emigration to North America would substantially reduce social tensions. Progress would become a slogan of the post-1850 era. Admittedly, this process was less pronounced in southwestern Europe – the Iberian peninsula and southern Italy – and even less apparent in the Balkans and great reaches of the tsar's empire, so that some of the social tensions of the age of revolution lingered longer there. They can be seen in events such as the Spanish revolutions of 1854–56 and 1868–74, or the massive agrarian upheavals and quasi-permanent state of insurrection found in southern Italy during the 1860s, as a consequence of the incorporation of the region into a united Italy, dominated by the northern kingdom of Piedmont-Savoy.

Such post-1850 disturbances, however, remained on the margins of Europe. For most of the continent in this age of progress, the constant impetus to social upheaval characteristic of the age of revolution would diminish and politics would lose something of its bitter and violent edge. Plans for total social and economic renovation, as formulated by the early socialists, would no longer seem quite so attractive. The social question, so hotly posed before 1850, would continue to be an important part of public life, but practical solutions in the form of trade unions, and the cooperative movement, or a growing influence of labour groups on political parties – even when workers did not have the vote – would take priority over revolutionary initiatives, or schemes for total moral renewal. More generally, the institutions of civil society would flourish as never before, but the consequences of their development would be more in the direction of different groups jockeying for position within an existing political and socioeconomic system, rather than working to overthrow it. In this calmed down and cooled off environment, political participation would not reach the levels of 1848; the notables, although not unchallenged, would be in a better position to guide and direct public life.

In all these respects, the third quarter of the nineteenth century would be the high noon of the civil society of property owners in Europe. The last remains of the society of orders would be abolished in the 1860s, with serfdom being done away with in Russia and the Danubian principalities, and the guild system reaching its end in the German and Scandinavian states. In an age of progress, when the market showed some of its most favourable sides – above all, the potential for increased standards of living, largely lacking before 1850 – previous forms of criticsm, whether Jacobin, communist, or social democratic in provenance, were muted and only marginally present. It would only be with the onset of another period of economic crisis in the last quarter of the century that the ideal of the civil society of property owners would be challenged once again.

Another reason for stability would be the increased power of the state. The major confrontations of the 1848 revolution, running from the Parisian June Days, through the barricade fighting in Frankfurt and Vienna, to the insurrections of the spring of 1849 and the French uprising of 1851 had all shown that insurgent irregulars were no match for organized, disciplined regular troops with good morale. This was a lesson not lost either on governments or revolutionaries. After 1850, governments would strive to preserve order, supplementing their control of the armed forces with an expansion of the police force on the model of Great Britain. Most major post-1850 European revolutions, from the Paris Commune of 1870–71, to the Portuguese revolution of 1974, would only occur when the power of the state and its control over the armed forces had been shaken by defeat in war. Only in 1989, with the total economic collapse of the communist states of eastern Europe, would widespread revolutions again occur that were not the direct result of military defeat.

Yet we can see after 1850 a similar development to the previous decades, the increased power of the state coinciding with a growth in constitutional

[430]   forms of government. 1848 marked a decisive breakthrough for constitutional government. To be sure, constitutions granted in the mid-century revolution in Austria and most of the Italian states were revoked in the 1850s. But by the end of the following decade constitutional government had returned, and absolutist rule in Europe was restricted exclusively to the realm of the tsar. In such circumstances, the post-1789 question of governments' political legitimacy remained – the way that their rule, their expanded intrusion into people's everyday lives, could be welcomed and greeted, not just accepted by threat of force. Here, one of the developments of the first half of the nineteenth century, as exemplified in the 1848 revolution, would point the way.

Nationalism had shown itself to be a powerful political force that could attract popular loyalties. In the first half of the ninteenth century, nationalism had largely been an oppositional force, one used against the existing states. In the two decades after mid-century, European statesmen would seek to meld nationalism and existing governments, to make it a force for the regime, rather than one directed against it. The dominant political figures of the years 1850– 70, the Piedmontese prime minister Emilio di Cavour, the French emperor Napoleon III, and, above all, the Prussian prime minister Otto von Bismarck, would show great skill in harnessing nationalism for the benefit of existing governments rather than letting it be used against the them.

All three of these statesmen, in acting to coopt nationalism, did not hesitate to use war as an instrument of policy. To be sure, the wars they fought were limited in extent, not the massive, decades-long confrontations of the revolutionary and Napoleonic era – a result that was in part conscious diplomatic calculation, in part the consequence of new strategies, expanding on the revolutionary and Napoleonic principle of the rapid mobility of mass conscript armies, by using the railway for troop movements, and in part just the luck of the battlefield. While preserving the basic structure of the Pentarchy, they would reshape it somewhat: the particularly powerful position of Russia, held since 1815, was demolished in the Crimean War of 1854–56; the question of whether France, Austria or Prussia would succeed to this position remained open and was not finally settled until the Franco–Prussian War of 1870–71, with the newly created German empire (a Prussia writ large) emerging as the most powerful nation in continental Europe. None of these events changed Great Britain's position as the dominant maritime and colonial power. The united Kingdom of Italy, created in the 1860s, laid claim to being a Great Power equal to those of the Pentarchy, but such a claim had little basis in the military and diplomatic realities of power politics.

Changes in the nature of such power politics were another important [431] aspect of this cycle of Great Power warfare, running from 1854 to 1871. The wars testify to a different, in some ways rather more cynical attitude toward power and power relationships, an attitude that would be part of a broader, cultural style. They demonstrated that the post-1850 era would see, to use a phrase coined by the German author Ludwig August von Rochau in 1853, the dominance of *Realpolitik* – of politics and policy based not on ideals or aspirations, but on the way power relationships really were, whether you liked it or not. The decades after 1850 would be an age of progress, but also an age of realism.

The era of revolutionary Europe had been one in which older forms of social, economic and political organization had been declining, sometimes gradually and peacefully, sometimes abruptly and violently, and newer ones had been emerging to take their place. A not very productive agrarian–artisan economy had been giving way to a market-oriented, more productive and, ultimately, industrialized one. A society of orders was in the process of being replaced by a civil society of property owners. Governments typified by the simultaneous clash and cooperation of absolutism and Estates were replaced with unitary, bureaucratically administered and constitutionally governed regimes. Dynastic and confessional loyalties were giving way to nationalist ones. The process of these multiple transitions had been difficult, characterized by impoverishment, disruption and disorder, but also by powerful expressions of ideals and aspirations, whether in classical or romantic cultural modes. The subsequent period of European history would see the end of this difficult transition, the establishment of a new economic, social and political, framework, under the sign of a culture of progress and realism.

ANNOTATED FURTHER READING

General works

There are a number of good general national histories that cover all or part of the period 1780–1850. In particular, I would mention Paul Langford, *A Polite and Commercial People: England 1727–1783* (Oxford and New York, 1989) and Norman Gash, *Aristocracy and People: Britain 1815–1865* (Cambridge MA, 1979); Gordon Wright, *France in Modern Times: from the Enlightenment to the Present*, 3rd edn. (New York, 1981); James Sheehan, *German History, 1770–1866* (Oxford, 1989); John Lynch, *Bourbon Spain, 1700–1808* (Oxford and Cambridge MA, 1989) and Raymond Carr, *Spain, 1808–1975*, 2nd edn. (Oxford, 1982); Stuart Woolf, *A History of Italy, 1700–1860* (London, 1979); C.A. Macartney, *The Habsburg Empire, 1790–1918* (New York, 1969); Isabel de Madariaga, *Russia in the Age of Catherine the Great* (New Haven and London, 1981) and David Saunders, *Russia in the Age of Reaction and Reform 1801–1881* (London and New York, 1992); H. Arnold Barton, *Scandinavia in the Revolutionary Era 1760–1815* (Minneapolis, 1986) and T.K. Derry, *A History of Modern Norway 1814–1972* (Oxford, 1973).

More general histories of this period, or part of it, such as Charles Breunig, *The Age of Revolution and Reaction, 1789–1850*, 2nd edn. (New York and London, 1977); J.L. Talmon, *Romanticism and Revolt: Europe 1815–1848* (New York, 1967) or Franklin Ford, *Europe 1780–1830*, 2nd edn. (London, 1989) are less impressive or not up to the latest scholarship. One general work, however, stands out as a remarkable intellectual challenge, E.J. Hobsbawm's *The Age of Revolution 1789–1848* (London, 1962). Although the reader of both books will quickly note that I do not agree with many of Hobsbawm's judgements, any serious consideration of the period must begin by taking account of his work.

Chapter 1

Useful works on society and social structure at the end of the old regime, include national studies, such as Pierre Goubert, *The Ancien Régime: French Society 1600–1750*, trans. Steven Cox (London, 1973); Béla K. Király, *Hungary in the Late Eighteenth Century: The Decline of Enlightened Despotism* (New York and London, 1969), or Rudolf Vierhaus, *Germany in the Age of Absolutism*, trans. Jonathan Knudsen, (Cambridge and New York, 1988). Studies of individual social groups include Mack Walker, *German Home Towns: Community, State and General Estate 1648–1871* (Ithaca and London, 1971); Rebecca Gates-Coon, *The Landed Estates of the Esterhazy Princes: Hungary during the Reforms of Maria Theresa and Joseph II* (Baltimore and London, 1994); T.J.A. LeGoff, *Vannes and its Region: A Study of Town and Country in Eighteenth-Century France* (Oxford, 1981); Olwen Hufton, *The Poor of Eighteenth-Century France 1750–1789* (Oxford, 1974); K.D.M. Snell, *Annals of the Labouring Poor: Social Change and Agrarian England, 1700–1900* (Cambridge and New York, 1985). A quite interesting article, describing the microcosm of an on old regime society is Charles Ingrao, '"Barbarous Strangers": Hessian State and Society during the American Revolution', *American Historical Review* 87 (1982): 954–76. Two short pieces on the eighteenth century Russian version of the society of orders, and its continuation into the nineteenth century, are Gregory L. Freeze, 'The *Soslovie* (Estate) Paradigm and Russian Social History', *American Historical Review* 91 (1986): 11–36, and Elise Kimberly Wirtschafter, 'Legal Identity and the Possession of Serfs in Imperial Russia,' *Journal of Modern History* 70 (1998): 561–87.

On the economy and economic development, see John Komlos, *Nutrition and Economic Development in the Eighteenth-Century Habsburg Monarchy* (Princeton, 1989); John Post, *Food Shortage, Climatic Variability and Epidemic Disease in Preindustrial Europe: The Mortality Peak in the Early 1740s* (Ithaca and London, 1985); Steven L. Kaplan, *Provisioning Paris: Merchants and Millers in the Grain and Flour Trade during the Eighteenth Century* (Ithaca and London, 1984). For the notion of proto-industry, see Peter Kriedte, Hans Medick, and Jürgen Schlumbohm, *Industrialization before Industrialization: Rural Industry in the Genesis of Capitalism*, trans. Beate Schepp (Cambridge and New York, 1981); a searching criticism of their ideas is to be found in R. Houston and K.D.M. Snell, 'Proto-industrialization? Cottage Industry, Social Change and Industrial Revolution', *Historical Journal* 27 (1984).

On government and administration, see Gail Bossenga, *The Politics of Privilege: Old Regime and Revolution in Lille* (Cambridge and New York, 1991),

[434] that is particularly useful in exploring the practice and political ramifications of privilege; Hilton Root, *Peasants and King in Burgundy: Agrarian Foundations of French Absolutism* (Berkeley and Los Angeles, 1987); Hubert Johnson, *Frederick the Great and His Officials* (Yale and New Haven, 1975); Bailey Stone, *The French Parlements and the Crisis of the Old Regime* (Chapel Hill and London, 1986), which contains a particularly useful introduction to the extensive literature on the French sovereign courts; James Allen Vann, *The Making of a State: Württemberg, 1593–1793* (Ithaca, 1984); Robert M. Schwartz, *Policing the Poor in Eighteenth-Century France* (Chapel Hill and London, 1988); P.G.M. Dickson, *Finance and Government under Maria Theresa 1740–1780*, 2 vols. (Oxford, 1987). Two shorter discussions of old regime government are P.G.M. Dickson, 'Monarchy and Bureaucracy in Late Eighteenth-Century Austria', *English Historical Review* 110 (1995): 333–67, and Judith Miller, 'Politics and Urban Provisioning Crises: Bakers, Police and Parlements in France, 1750–1793', *Journal of Modern History* 64 (1992): 227–62.

Owen Chadwick, *The Popes and European Revolution* (Oxford, 1981), actually has little to say about the French Revolution, but does offer an excellent and accessible account of the Catholic Church under the old regime. On religion and the Enlightenment, William J. Callahan and David Higgs (eds), *Church and Society in Catholic Europe of the Eighteenth Century* (Cambridge and New York, 1979) is a useful if uneven collection of essays. Gregory Freeze, *The Russian Levites: Parish Clergy in the Eighteenth Century* (Cambridge MA, 1977), describes clergy and religious life in the Orthodox world. Christina Rathgeber, 'The Reception of Brandenburg-Prussia's New Lutheran Hymnal of 1781', *Historical Journal* 36 (1993): 115–36, offers a very interesting discussion of Protestant piety in the late eighteenth century.

Works on the Enlightenment are legion. Three classics are Daniel Mornet, *French Thought in the Eighteenth Century*, trans. Lawrence M. Levin, (New York, 1929); Ernst Cassirer, *The Philosophy of the Enlightenment*, trans. Fritz Koelln and James P. Pettegrove (Princeton, 1951); Peter Gay, *The Enlightenment: An Interpretation*, 2 vols. (New York, 1966–69). An important political issue of the Enlightenment is discussed in J.Q.C. Mackrell, *The Attack on 'Feudalism' in Eighteenth-Century France* (London, 1973). For some more recent views, see the works of Robert Darnton, particularly *Mesmerism and the End of the Enlightenment in France* (Cambridge MA, 1968); *The Business of Enlightenment: a Publishing History of the Encyclopédie, 1775–1800*, (Cambridge MA, 1979) or

The Literary Underground of the Old Regime (Cambridge MA, 1982). Two recent general interpretations can be found in Roger Chartier, *The Cultural Origins of the French Revolution*, trans. Lydia G. Cochrane (Durham and London, 1991) or Dorinda Outram, *The Enlightenment* (Cambridge and New York, 1995).

The idea of eighteenth-century Great Britain as an old regime society is advanced by J.C.D. Clark, *English Society 1688–1832: Ideology, Social Structure and Political Practice during the Ancien Regime* (Cambridge and New York, 1985); a contrary, and perhaps ultimately more convincing account in Paul Langford, *A Polite and Commercial People: England 1727–1783* (Oxford and New York, 1989). Joanna Innes, 'Jonathan Clark's Social History and England's "Ancien Regime"', *Past and Present* 115 (1987): 165–200 offers a compact and detailed discussion of the idea of eighteenth-century Great Britain as an old regime society. An excellent account of the crisis of the Seven Years' War and a very useful discussion of the vexed topic of old regime government finances is in James C. Riley, *The Seven Years War and the Old Regime in France: The Economic and Financial Toll* (Princeton, 1986). On the reforms of Enlightened absolutism, H.M. Scott (ed.), *Enlightened Absolutism: Reform and Reformers in Later Eighteenth-Century Europe* (Ann Arbor, 1990) is an enlightening collection of essays, with very helpful bibliographies. This work can be supplemented by two aricles by P.G.M. Dickson on Joseph II and his reform policies, 'Joseph II's Reshaping of the Austrian Church', *Historical Journal* 36 (1993): 89–114 and 'Joseph II's Hungarian Land Survey', *English Historical Review* 106 (1991): 611–34.

Scott's collection of essays does not include a discussion of the reform era in France, for which see Steven L. Kaplan, *Bread, Politics and Political Economy in the Reign of Louis XV*, 2 vols. (The Hague, 1976); Cynthia A. Bouton, *The Flour War: Gender, Class, and Community in Late Ancien Regime French Society* (University Park, PA, 1993); Durand Echeverria, *The Maupeou Revolution: A Study in the History of Libertarianism, France 1770–1774* (Baton Rouge and London, 1985); William Doyle, *The Parlement of Bordeaux and the End of the Old Regime 1771–1790* (New York, 1974). Two briefer discussions of the difficulties of reform in France, with an emphasis on the political ramifications of the government's attempt to increase taxes, are Gail Bossenga, 'From Corps to Citizenship: The *Bureaux des Finances* before the French Revolution', *Journal of Modern History* 58 (1986): 610–42 and Michael Kwass, 'A Kingdom of Taxpayers: State Formation, Privilege and Political Culture in Eighteenth-Century France', *Journal of Modern History* 70 (1998): 295–339.

Chapter 2

The literature on the French Revolution is enormous beyond all measure. These are countless general histories; of English-language works that have appeared in recent years, perhaps the best is Donald Sutherland, *France 1789–1815: Revolution and Counterrevolution* (Oxford, 1986); also good is William Doyle, *The Oxford History of the French Revolution* (Oxford, 1989), while Simon Schama, *Citizens: a Chronicle of the French Revolution* (New York, 1989), sheds more heat than light. A much older, but simpler introduction is Albert Goodwin, *The French Revolution* (London and New York, 1953).

A useful overview of the early phases of the revolution is provided by Michel Vovelle, *The Fall of the French Monarchy 1787–1792*, trans. Susan Burke (Cambridge, 1984). On the pre-revolution, see Jean Egret, *The French Prerevolution, 1787–1788*, trans. Wesley D. Camp (Chicago, 1977). By far the best study of the Estates General and its transformation into a National Assembly, and a major work on the early period of the revolution is Timothy Tackett, *Becoming a Revolutionary: The Deputies of the French National Assembly and the Emergence of a Revolutionary Culture (1789–1790)* (Princeton, 1996). A short but handy account of the changing political universe in the early phase of the revolution is Michael P. Fitzsimmons, 'Privilege and the Polity in France, 1786–1791', *American Historical Review* 92 (1987): 269–95. On the fall of the Bastille and, more generally, on the role of the common people of Paris during the Revolution, George Rudé, *The Crowd in the French Revolution* (Oxford, 1959) is a classic. For the Great Fear, Georges Lefebvre, *The Great Fear of 1789: Rural Panic in Revolutionary France*, trans. Joan White, (New York, 1973), is the English-language edition of one of the great classics of revolutionary historiography. Clay Ramsay, *The Ideology of the Great Fear: The Soissonnais in 1789* (Baltimore, 1992), is a useful supplement, particularly good on the changes in the exercise of power at the local level. On the history of agrarian disorder in the revolution, John Markoff, 'Violence, Emancipation and Democracy: The Countryside and the French Revolution', *American Historical Review* 100 (1995): 360–86 offers an interesting perspective. More generally on the transformation of agricultural property and its effect on the rural population, see P.M. Jones, *The Peasantry in the French Revolution*, (Cambridge, 1988). A briefer account of peasants in the revolution is Peter McPhee, 'The French Revolution, Peasants and Capitalism,' *American Historical Review* 94 (1989): 1265–80. For the 'municipal revolution', see Lynn Hunt, *Revolution and Urban Politics in Provincial France* (Stanford, 1978). A classic discussion of the ideas of the Declaration of the Rights of Man can be found in George

Lefebvre, *The Coming of the French Revolution,* trans. R.R. Palmer, (Princeton, [437]
1967); more recent and much more sceptical views are in *The French Revolution and the Creation of Modern Political Culture,* ed. Keith Michael Baker, 4 vols. (Oxford, 1987–94), esp. vol. 2, or *A Critical Dictionary of the French Revolution,* ed. François Furet and Mona Ozouf; trans. Arthur Goldhammer (Cambridge, MA, 1989).

On the politics of the early phases of the French Revolution, particularly helpful is Barry M. Shapiro, *Revolutionary Justice in Paris, 1789–1790,* (Cambridge, 1993). For a short account of developing fronts in the National Assembly, see Timothy Tackett, 'Nobles and Third Estate in the Revolutionary Dynamic of the National Assembly', *American Historical Review* 94 (1989): 271–301. An interesting discussion of the work of administrative reform is in Ted Margadant, *Urban Rivalries in the French Revolution* (Princeton, 1992). Michael P. Fitzsimmons, 'The National Assembly and the Abolition of Guilds in France', *Historical Journal* 39 (1996): 133–54, addresses one of the major economic reforms of the National Assembly.

Jeremy Popkin, *Revolutionary News: The Press in France, 1789–1799* (Durham, NC, 1990) offers a good survey of the place of the periodical press in the revolution. On the Jacobin clubs, Michael Kennedy, *The Jacobin Clubs in the French Revolution,* 2 vols. to date (Princeton, 1982–) is unusually informative. Michael L. Kennedy, 'The Best and the Worst of Times: The Jacobin Club Network from October 1791 to June 2, 1793', *Journal of Modern History* 56 (1984): 635–66, is a short summary of his voluminous work. On the Civil Constitution of the Clergy, there is the important book of Timothy Tackett, *Religion, Revolution, and Regional Culture in Eighteenth-Century France: the Ecclesiastical Oath of 1791* (Princeton, 1986). Emigration and counter-revolution are analysed in Jacques Godechot, *The Counter-Revolution: Doctrine and Action 1789–1804,* trans. Salvator Attanasio (New York, 1971). For shorter discussions of the social and confessional context of counter-revolution, see Timothy Tackett, 'The West in France in 1789: The Religious Factor in the Origins of Counterrevolution', *Journal of Modern History* 54 (1987) 715–45; T.G.A. Le Goff and D.M.G. Sutherland, 'The Social Origins of Counter-Revolution in Western France', *Past and Present* 99 (1983): 65–87; and James M. Hood, 'Revival and Mutation of Old Rivalries in Revolutionary France', *Past and Present* 82 (1979): 82–115. Malcolm Crook, *Elections in the French Revolution: An Apprenticeship in Democracy, 1789–1799,* (Cambridge, 1996), is a detailed introduction to the theory and practice of balloting in the revolution. Works on the wars of the French Revolution and the new revolutionary army will be discussed below, in the bibliography to Chapter Three.

[438]   On the sans-culottes, Albert Soboul, *The Sans-Culottes: the Popular Movement and Revolutionary Government, 1793–1794*, trans. Remy Inglis Hall (Garden City NY, 1972), is a classic. Two more recent works, that modify some of Soboul's ideas are R.B. Rose, *The Making of the Sans-Culottes: Democratic Ideas and Institutions in Paris, 1789–92* (Manchester, 1983), and the important article of Richard Andrews, 'Social Structures, Political Elites and Ideology in Revolutionary Paris, 1792–94: A Critical Evaluation of Albert Soboul's *Les sans-culottes parisiens en l'an II*', *Journal of Social History* 19 (1985): 71–112. On the politics of the Convention, and the clash between Girondins and Jacobins, see Alison Patrick, *The Men of the First French Republic: Political Alignments in the National Convention of 1792* (Baltimore, 1972); David P. Jordan, *The King's Trial: The French Revolution vs. Louis XVI* (Berkeley, 1979) and Morris Slavin, *The Making of an Insurrection: Parisian Sections and the Gironde* (Cambridge MA, 1986). Donald Greer, *The Incidence of the Terror during the French Revolution: A Statistical Interpretation*, (Cambridge MA, 1935) remains a major study of the extent of the Terror. Further on the Reign of Terror and the civil war in France there are the many works of Richard Cobb, including *Reactions to the French Revolution* (Oxford, 1972) and *The Police and the People: French Popular Protest 1789–1820* (Oxford, 1972); Colin Lucas, *The Structure of the Terror: The Example of Javogues and the Loire* (Oxford, 1973); W.D. Edmonds, *Jacobinism and the Revolt of Lyon 1789–1793* (Oxford, 1990); Donald Sutherland, *The Chouans: The Social Origins of Popular Counter-Revolution in Upper Brittany, 1770–1796* (Oxford, 1982); Charles Tilly, *The Vendée: A Sociological Analysis of the Counterrevolution of 1793* (New York, 1967).

On the republic of virtue, and the Jacobins' political ideas, the collections of essays edited by Keith Baker and François Furet, mentioned above with regard to the Declaration of the Rights of Man, are very informative, if written from a distinct political point of view. Also of interest are Isser Woloch, *The New Regime: Transformations of the French Civic Order, 1789–1820s* (New York, 1994); Norman Hampson, *The Life and Opinions of Maximilien Robespierre*, (London, 1974); Michel Vovelle, *The Revolution against the Church: From Reason to the Supreme Being*, trans. Alan José (Columbus, 1991); Dorinda Outram, *The Body and the French Revolution: Sex, Class and Political Culture* (New Haven, 1989) and two works by Lynn Hunt, *Politics, Culture, and Class in the French Revolution* (Berkeley, 1984); *The Family Romance of the French Revolution* (Berkeley, 1992). For some philosophical reflections on the history and heritage of Jacobinism, cf. Ferenc Fehér, *The Frozen Revolution: An Essay on Jacobinism* (Cambridge, 1987). On the place of women in the Jacobin regime and, in the French Revolution, see, above all, Dominique Godineau, *The Women of Paris and Their French Revolution*, trans. Katherine Streip (Berkeley and Los

Angeles, 1998). For some broad interpretations, see the book of Dorinda Outram noted above, and the three very different points of view expressed by Joan Landes, *Woman and the Public Sphere in the Age of the French Revolution* (Ithaca, 1988); Olwen Hufton, *Women and the Limits of Citizenship in the French Revolution* (Toronto, 1992) and Lynn Hunt, 'Forgetting and Remembering: The French Revolution Then and Now', *American Historical Review* 100 (1995): 1119–35. A short empirical study is Timothy Tackett, 'Women and Men in Counterrevolution: The Sommières Riot of 1791', *Journal of Modern History* 59 (1987): 680–704.

Helpful for understanding the politics of the 'Great Terror' is Morris Slavin, *The Hébertistes to the Guillotine: Anatomy of a 'Conspiracy' in Revolutionary France* (Baton Rouge, 1994). Two books that provide particularly vivid portrayals of the Reign of Terror and of life under the revolutionary regime, are the novel of Anatole France, *The Gods Will Have Blood*, trans. Frederick Davies (New York, 1990 – but there are many other editions and translations) and R.R. Palmer, *Twelve Who Ruled: The Year of the Terror in the French Revolution* (Princeton, 1941). On the fall of Robespierre and the rule of the Thermidoreans, see Bronislaw Baczko, *Ending the Terror: The French Revolution after Robespierre*, trans. Michel Petheram (Cambridge, 1994).

A good, brief general history of the Directory is Denis Woronoff, *The Thermidorean Regime and the Directory 1794–1799*, trans. Julian Jackson (Cambridge, 1984). Lynn Hunt, David Lansky and Paul Hanson, 'The Failure of the Liberal Republic in France 1795–1799: The Road to Brumaire', *Journal of Modern History* 57 (1979): 734–59 offer a general interpretation of the ultimate lack of success of the Directorial Regime. On the White Terror and the increasingly chaotic situation in the provinces under the Directory, see Richard Cobb, *Reactions to the French Revolution* (Oxford, 1972); Gwynne Lewis and Colin Lucas (eds), *Beyond the Terror: Essays in French Regional and Social History, 1794–1815* (Cambridge, 1983); Gwynne Lewis, *The Second Vendée: The Continuity of Counter-revolution in the Department of the Gard, 1789–1815* (Oxford, 1978); Alan Forrest, *Conscripts and Deserters: The Army and French Society during the Revolution and the Empire* (Oxford, 1989) and Jonathan Devlin, 'The Army, Politics and Public Order in Directorial Provence', *Historical Journal* 32 (1989): 87–106. Government bureaucracy is discussed by Clive Church, *Revolution and Red Tape: The French Ministerial Bureaucracy 1770–1850* (Oxford, 1981); the Jacobin revival in the fine work of Isser Woloch, *Jacobin Legacy: The Democratic Movement under the Directory* (Princeton, 1970). The continued efforts at dechristianization and the creation of a new revolutionary culture are considered by Mona Ozouf, *Festivals and the French Revolution*, trans. Alan Sheridan (Cambridge MA, 1988) and Suzanne Desan, *Reclaiming the Sacred: Lay Religion and Popular Politics in Revolutionary France* (Ithaca, 1990). Michael Broers, *Europe under Napoleon 1799–1815* (London, 1996) has a good account of the coup of 18 Brumaire and the end of the Directory.

Chapter 3

Recent studies of soldiers and warfare in the revolutionary period include Alan Forrest, *Soldiers of the French Revolution* (Durham, 1990); Samuel Scott, *The Response of the Royal Army to the French Revolution* (Oxford, 1988); Jean-Paul Bertaud, *The Army of the French Revolution: From Citizen-Soldiers to Instruments of Power*, trans. R.R. Palmer (Princeton, 1988); John A. Lynn, *The Bayonets of the Republic: Motivation and Tactics in the Army of Revolutionary France* (Urbana, 1984) and Gunther Rothenberg, *The Art of Warfare in the Age of Napoleon* (London, 1977). A very handy history of the wars of the first and second coalition, with a useful bibliography, is T.C.W. Blanning, *The French Revolutionary Wars 1787–1802* (London, 1996). Paul W. Schroeder, *The Transformation of European Politics 1763–1848* (Oxford, 1994) covers the diplomacy of the period exhaustively, although not everyone may agree with his pro-Austrian interpretations. Two shorter discussions of British policy are Jennifer Mori, 'The British Government and the Bourbon Restoration: The Occupation of Toulon 1793', *Historical Journal* 40 (1997): 699–719 and Elizabeth Sparrow, 'The Swiss and Swabian Agencies, 1795–1801', *Historical Journal* 35 (1992): 861–84, this last a particularly interesting study of what we would today call covert operations.

The only English-language, general history of Europe and the French Revolution is R.R. Palmer, *The Age of Democratic Revolution*, 2 vols. (Princeton, 1959–64), with vol. 2, in particular, dealing with the decade after 1789. Although the author's thesis of a general 'western' or 'Atlantic' revolution has often been criticized, the work is a mine of useful information and offers what remains a challenging interpretation. Jacques Godechot, *The Counter-Revolution: Doctrine and Action 1789–1804*, trans. Salvator Attanasio (New York, 1971) offers a brief general, Europe-wide introduction to the debate on the French Revolution. Palmer's work is particularly helpful to the student because the English-language literature on individual European nations and the French Revolution is noticeably patchier than on the events in France. The British Isles are, of course, well covered: good works include Albert Goodwin, *The Friends of Liberty: The English Democratic Movement in the Age of the French Revolution* (Cambridge MA, 1979) – also good for the intellectual

debate on the French Revolution; Roger Wells, *Insurrection: The British Experi-*
ence 1795–1803 (Gloucester, 1983); Linda Colley, *Britons: Forging the Nation*
1707–1837 (New Haven, 1992). A good brief discussion of the responses of
the government and the forces of order in England to the revolutionary challenge is Clive Emsley, 'Repression, "Terror" and the Rule of Law in England
during the Decade of the French Revolution', *English Historical Review* 100
(1985): 801–25. For circumstances in Ireland, see Marianne Elliott, *Partners*
in Revolution: The United Irishmen and France (New Haven, 1982); Nancy J. Curtin,
The United Irishmen: Popular Politics in Ulster and Dublin 1791–1798 (Oxford,
1994) and Kevin Whelan, *The Tree of Liberty: Radicalism, Catholicism and the*
Construction of Irish Identity 1760–1830 (Cork, 1996).

On the Netherlands, there is the very detailed work of Simon Schama,
Patriots and Liberators: Revolution in the Netherlands 1780–1813 (New York, 1977);
a briefer study of the Low Countries is Janet L. Polasky, 'Traditionalists, Democrats and Jacobins in Revolutionary Brussels', *Journal of Modern History* 56
(1984): 227–62. Ernst Wangermann, *From Joseph II to the Jacobin Trials: Gov-*
ernment Policy and Public Opinion in the Habsburg Dominions in the Period of the
French Revolution (Oxford, 1959), discusses Austria, and T.C.W. Blanning, *The*
French Revolution in Germany: Occupation and Resistance in the Rhineland 1792–
1802 (Oxford, 1983), offers a case-study for Germany. Klaus Epstein, *The*
Genesis of German Conservatism (Princeton, 1966) has a good discussion of the
intellectual debate about the revolution in the German-speaking world. For
events in Poland, see the relevant parts of vol. 1 of Norman Davies, *God's*
Playground: A History of Poland, 2 vols. (New York, 1982). There is no English-
language book on the impact of the French Revolution in Italy; the student
might consult a more general national history, such as Henry Hearder, *Italy in*
the Age of the Risorgimento 1790–1870 (London, 1983), or Stuart Woolf, *A His-*
tory of Italy, 1700–1860: the Social Constraints of Political Change (London, 1979),
or three very informative essays: Michael Broers, 'Revolution as Vendetta:
Patriotism in Piedmont, 1794–1821', *Historical Journal* 33 (1990): 573–97;
his 'The Parochial Revolution: 1799 and the Counterrevolution in Italy',
Renaissance and Modern Studies 33 (1989): 159–74; and John A. Davis, '1799:
the *Santafede* and the Crisis of the *Ancien Régime* in Southern Italy', in John A.
Davis and Paul Ginsborg (eds), *Society and Politics in the Age of the Risorgimento*
(Cambridge, 1991), pp. 1–25. For political and intellectual developments
in a part of northern Europe relatively unaffected by the wars and upheavals
of the 1790s, Thomas Munck, 'Absolute Monarchy in Later Eighteenth-
Century Denmark: Centralized Reform, Public Expectation and the Copenhagen Press', *Historical Journal* 41 (1998): 201–24.

Chapter 4

The reader is fortunate in having two excellent general accounts of Napoleonic Europe: Stuart Woolf, *Napoleon's Integration of Europe* (London, 1991) and Michael Broers, *Europe under Napoleon 1799–1815* (London, 1996). Both have detailed bibliographies; Broers's list of English-language works is particularly to be recommended.

For warfare and diplomacy in the Napoleonic era, a recent overview is David Gates, *The Napoleonic Wars, 1803–1815* (London and New York, 1997). Also see the works of Paul Schroeder and Gunther Rothenberg, mentioned in the bibliography to the previous chapter, as well as Edward Whitcomb, *Napoleon's Diplomatic Service* (Durham, 1979); Brendan Simms, *The Impact of Napoleon: Prussian High Politics, Foreign Policy and the Crisis of the Executive, 1797–1806* (Cambridge, 1997); Gunter Rothenberg, *Napoleon's Great Adversaries: Archduke Charles and the Austrian Army 1792–1814* (Bloomington, 1982).

Generally, on France under Napoleon, including the religious settlement, the Napoleonic Code and the administrative system, see the history of Donald Sutherland, *France 1789–1815: Revolution and Counterrevolution* (Oxford, 1986), the relevant chapters in Broers's general history, or Louis Bergeron, *France under Napoleon*, trans. R.R. Palmer (Princeton, 1981). More specialized studies would include Irene Collins, *Napoleon and his Parliaments, 1799–1815* (London, 1979), and Margaret Darrow, *Revolution in the House: Family, Class and Inheritance in Southern France 1775–1825* (Princeton, 1989). Isser Woloch, 'Napoleonic Conscription: State Power and Civil Society', *Past and Present* 111 (1986): 101–29 is an unusually useful short discussion of a central element and equally central neuralgic point of the Napoleonic regime. A good general overview of Napoleonic rule in Germany can be found in James Sheehan, *German History 1770–1866* (Oxford, 1989); the relevant chapters from Mack Walker, *German Home Towns: Community, State and General Estate 1648–1871* (Ithaca and London, 1971) are very helpful, as is Jeffry M. Diefendorf, *Businessmen and Politics in the Rhineland, 1789–1834* (Princeton, 1980). The general works of Broers and Woolf both have a good focus on Italy; also of interest, and not just for military affairs, is Frederick C. Schneid, *Soldiers of Napoleon's Kingdom of Italy: Army, State and Society, 1800–1815* (Boulder, 1995) and Alexander Grab, 'Army State and Society: Conscription and Desertion in Napoleonic Italy (1802–1814)', *Journal of Modern History* 67 (1993): 25–54. Two shorter discussions of the civilian and military officials who ruled Napoleon's empire are Jean-Paul Bertaud,

'Napoleon's Officers', *Past and Present* 112 (1986): 101–29 and Stuart Woolf, [443]
'French Civilization and Ethnicity in the Napoleonic Empire', *Past and Present*
124 (1989): 96–120.

A good work on economic developments in Napoleonic Europe is Geoffrey
Ellis, *Napoleon's Continental Blockade: The Case of Alsace* (Oxford, 1981); the
same author's 'Rhine and Loire: Napoleonic Elites and Social Order', in
Gwynne Lewis and Colin Lucas (eds) *Beyond the Terror*: Essays in French Re-
gional and Social History, 1794–1815 (Cambridge, 1983) is an enlighten-
ing introduction to the notion of the notables. T.J.A. Le Goff and D.M.G.
Sutherland, 'The Revolution and the Rural Economy', in Alan Forrest and
Peter Jones (eds), *Reshaping France: Town, Country and Region during the French
Revolution* (Manchester, 1991), pp. 52–85, present a sceptical view of agri-
culture in the Napoleonic era. A stimulating essay is François Crouzet, 'Wars,
Blockade and Economic Change in Europe, 1792–1815', *Journal of Economic
History* 24 (1964); a brief general overview is Louis Bergeron, 'The Revolu-
tion: Catastrophe or New Dawn for the French Economy?' in Colin Lucas
(ed.), *Rewriting the French Revolution* (Oxford, 1991), pp. 118–31.

Biographies of the emperor himself are legion. Three that could be mentioned are Martyn Lyons, *Napoleon Bonaparte and the Legacy of the French Revolution* (New York, 1994); Jean Tulard, *Napoleon: the Myth of the Saviour*, trans.
Teresa Waugh (London, 1984); and the older but still stimulating Pieter Geyl,
Napoleon, for and against, trans. Olive Renier (New Haven, 1949).

On the various forms of guerilla warfare against Napoleonic rule, see Franck
Eyck, *Loyal Rebels: Andreas Hofer and the Tyrolean Uprising of 1809* (New York,
1986), and Don W. Alexander, *Rod of Iron: French Counterinsurgency Policy in
Aragon during the Peninsular War*, (Wilmington DE, 1985). A good short
introduction to the politics of the Spanish uprising against Napoleon, with
useful connections backwards and forwards in time is Richard Herr, 'The
Constitution of 1812 and the Spanish Road to Parliamentary Monarchy', in
Isser Woloch, (ed.) *Revolution and the Meanings of Freedom in the Nineteenth
Century* (Stanford, 1996), pp. 65–102.

On Prussia and its reform movement, see Brendan Simms, *The Impact of
Napoleon: Prussian High Politics, Foreign Policy and the Crisis of the Executive, 1797–
1806* (Cambridge, 1997) and Peter Paret, *Yorck and the Era of the Prussian Re-
form, 1807–1815*, (Princeton, 1966); Walter Simon, *The Failure of the Prussian
Reform Movement* (Ithaca, 1955) and Marion W. Gray, *Prussia in Transition:
Society and Politics under the Stein Reform Ministry of 1808* (Philadelphia, 1986).

For events on the margins of Europe, besides the general histories of Scandinavia and the Russian empire, noted in the initial general bibliography, see

[444] Wayne S. Vucinich (ed.), *The First Serbian Uprising 1804–13* (New York, 1982), although the hand of Serbian nationalism weighs quite heavily on a number of the contributions to the volume. Two shorter, and rather opposed discussions of patriotism and nationalism in embattled Great Britain during this period are Linda Colley, 'The Apotheosis of George III: Loyalty, Royalty and the British nation', *Past and Present* 102 (1984): 94–129; J.E. Cookson, 'The English Volunteer Movement of the French Wars, 1793–1815, Some Contexts', *Historical Journal* 32 (1989): 867–91.

Chapter 5

For the ideas of Thomas Malthus, one can start by reading his *Essay on the Principle of Population*, available in many different editions. A commentary on his ideas in their contemporary setting is offered by E.A. Wrigley, 'Malthus on the Prospects for the Labouring Poor', *Historical Journal* 31 (1988): 813–29, while David Grigg, *Population Growth and Agrarian Change: An Historical Perspective* (Cambridge and New York, 1980) is a recent empirical testing of Malthus's ideas, with particularly useful sections on eighteenth-and nineteenth-century Europe. More generally, on population trends in the period, see E.A. Wrigley and R.S. Schofield, *The Population History of England, 1541–1871* (Cambridge MA, 1981); David Levine, *Family Formation in an Age of Nascent Capitalism* (New York, 1977); Michael Flinn, *The European Demographic System, 1500–1820* (Baltimore, 1981); Michael Drake, *Population and Society in Norway 1735–1865* (Cambridge, 1969); Massimo Livi-Bacci, *A History of Italian Fertility During the Last Two Centuries* (Princeton, 1977); and W.R. Lee (ed.), *European Demography and Economic Growth* (New York, 1979). A briefer discussion of population trends is E.A. Wrigley, 'The Growth of Population in Eighteenth Century England: A Conundrum Resolved', *Past and Present* 98 (1983): 121–50.

A classic general economic history, with a particular emphasis on industrialization is David Landes, *The Unbound Prometheus: Technological Change and Industrial Development in Western Europe from 1750 to the Present* (Cambridge, 1972). Landes's work, it would be fair to say, is now somewhat outdated, but there is nothing comparable that can serve as a replacement. Some more recent works are Jordan Goodman and Katrina Honeymann, *Gainful Pursuits: The Making of Industrial Europe 1600–1914* (London, 1988); Sidney Pollard, *Peaceful Conquest: The Industrialization of Europe 1760–1970* (Oxford, 1981);

Clive Trebilcock, *The Industrialization of the Continental Powers 1780–1914* (London and New York, 1981); and Derek H. Aldcroft and Simon P. Ville (ed.), *The European Economy 1750–1914: A Thematic Approach* (Manchester and New York, 1994). This last-mentioned book has a particularly useful bibliography. Brian R. Mitchell, *International Historical Statistics: Europe, 1750– 1988*, 3rd edn. (New York, 1992) and Norman Pounds, *An Historical Geography of Europe 1800–1914* (Cambridge and New York, 1985) both contain a wealth of figures, although it is depressing how often their statistical series only begin in 1850.

Among the national economic histories, one stands out as a model work: M.J. Daunton, *Progress and Poverty: An Economic and Social History of Britain 1700– 1850* (Oxford, 1995). Almost as good is Cormac Ó Gráda, *Ireland: A New Economic History 1780–1939* (Oxford, 1994). Not at the same level, although still informative are Maurice Lévy-Leboyer and François Bourguignon, *The French Economy in the Nineteenth Century*, trans. Jesse Bryant and Virginie Pérotin (Cambridge and New York, 1980); Joel Mokyr, *Industrialization in the Low Countries, 1795–1850* (New Haven, 1976); David F. Good, *The Economic Rise of the Habsburg Empire 1750–1914* (Berkeley and Los Angeles, 1984); Iván T. Berend and György Ránki, *The European Periphery and Industrialization 1780–1914*, trans. Éva Pálmai (Cambridge and New York, 1982); William Blackwell, *The Beginnings of Russian Industrialization 1800–1860* (Princeton, 1968). Patterns of regional development are considered in Pat Hudson (ed.), *Regions and Industries: A Perspective on the Industrial Revolution in Britain* (Cambridge and New York, 1989). An imaginative, if at times downright weird, discussion of the impact of railways is Wolfgang Schivelbusch, *The Railway Journey: The Industrialization of Time and Space in the 19th Century* (Berkeley, 1986); a more sober account of railway building in France is Cecil O. Smith, Jr., 'The Longest Run: Public Engineers and Planning in France', *American Historical Review* 95 (1990): 657–92. For a fascinating and illuminating account of international finance in the first half of the nineteenth century, see Niall Ferguson, *The House of Rothschild: Money's Prophets 1798–1848* (New York and London, 1998).

Two broad surveys of agriculture are Slicher Van Bath, *The Agrarian History of Western Europe A.D. 500–1850*, trans. Olive Ordish (New York, 1963) and Wilhelm Abel, *Agricultural Fluctuations in Europe: From the Thirteenth to the Twentieth Centuries*, trans. Olive Ordish (New York, 1980); a more narrowly focused book is Hugh Clout, *Agriculture in France on the Eve of the Railway Age* (London, 1980). A most helpful discussion of the interaction of agricultural techniques and rural property and social relations is Jerome Blum, *The End of*

[446]   *the Old Order in Rural Europe*, (Princeton, 1978). The difficulties of trying to reform or eliminate serfdom in one of its strongholds are explicated by Edgar Melton, 'Enlightened Seigneurialism and its Dilemmas in Serf Russia 1750–1830', *Journal of Modern History* 62 (1990): 676–708.

For protoindustry and outworking, besides the works cited in the bibliography to Chapter One, see Maxine Berg, Pat Hudson and Michael Sonenscher (eds), *Manufacture in Town and Country before the Factory* (Cambridge and New York, 1983); Gay Gullickson, *Spinners and Weavers of Auffay: Rural Industry and the Sexual Division of Labor in a French Village, 1750–1850* (Cambridge and New York, 1986); Christopher H. Johnson, *The Life and Death of Industrial Languedoc, 1700–1920* (Oxford and New York, 1995); J.K.J. Thomson, *A Distinctive Industrialization: Cotton in Barcelona, 1728–1832* (Cambridge and New York, 1992); Edgar Melton, 'Proto-Industrialization, Serf Agriculture and Agrarian Social Structure: Two Estates in Nineteenth-Century Russia', *Past and Present* 115 (1987): 68–100. L.D. Schwarz, *London in the Age of Industrialization: Entrepreneurs, Labour Force and Living Conditions, 1700–1850* (Cambridge and New York, 1992), is an unusually good and multi-faceted discussion of economic developments in a large city, where many forms of artisanal work went along with limited industrialization.

On social change and social structures, two general works are Dominic Lieven, *The Aristocracy in Europe 1815–1914* (New York, 1992) and Pamela M. Pilbeam, *The Middle Classes in Europe 1789–1914: France, Germany, Italy and Russia* (Chicago, 1990), and the massive collection of essays in Jürgen Kocka and Alan Mitchell (eds), *Bourgeois Society in Nineteenth-Century Europe* (Oxford and Providence RI, 1993). A briefer account is Jürgen Kocka, 'The Middle Classes in Europe', *Journal of Modern History* 65 (1995): 703–800. France is particularly well served by general studies. There are two recent social histories, Peter McPhee, *A Social History of France, 1780–1880* (London and New York, 1992), and Christophe Charle, *Social History of France in the Nineteenth Century*, trans. Miriam Kochan (Oxford and Providence RI, 1994). The former is more detailed, the latter more impressionistic, but more subtle, and containing an excellent biography. Annie Moulin, *Peasantry and Society in France since 1789*, trans. M.C. and M.F. Cleary (Cambridge and New York, 1991) and Gérard Noiriel, *Workers in French Society in the 19th and 20th Centuries*, trans. Helen McPhail, (New York and Oxford, 1990), are accounts of two major social groups. See also, David Higgs, *Nobles in Nineteenth-Century France: The Practice of Inegalitarianism* (Baltimore, 1987). Adrian Shubert, *A Social History of Modern Spain* (London, 1990), is a helpful overview. F.M.L. Thompson (ed.), *The Cambridge Social History of England*, 3 vols. (Cambridge and New York,

1990), is a massive work for England, with extensive bibliography. The [447] one book that deserves to be mentioned separately is the towering work of E.P. Thompson, *The Making of the English Working Class* (London, 1963, but in many editions since), that is an essential read, not just for the study of the working class itself, but for an infinite number of aspects of British society and politics, between 1780 and 1830.

Similar English-language accounts of the social history of other European countries are lacking. Students, however, can turn to a number of useful monographic studies of individual cities, regions, or occupations, which are available for England and France as well, of course. To mention just a few of these sorts of study: John Foster, *Class Struggle and the Industrial Revolution: Early Industrial Capitalism in Three English Towns*, (New York, 1975); Theodore Koditschek, *Class Formation and Urban-Industrial Society: Bradford, 1750–1850* (Cambridge and New York, 1990); Robert James Scally, *The End of Hidden Ireland: Rebellion, Famine and Emigration*, (Oxford and New York, 1995); William H. Sewell, Jr., *Structure and Mobility: The Men and Women of Marseilles 1820–1878* (Cambridge and New York, 1985), and, by the same author, 'Social Change and the Rise of Working Class Politics in Nineteenth-Century Marseilles', *Past and Present* 65 (November 1974): 75–109; William Reddy, *The Rise of Market Culture: the Textile Trade and French Society, 1750–1900*, (Cambridge and New York, 1984); Catherina Lis, *Social Change and the Labouring Poor: Antwerp, 1770–1860*, trans. James Coonan, (New Haven, 1986); Michael J. Neufeld, *The Skilled Metalworkers of Nuremberg*, (New Brunswick NJ, 1989); David W. Sabean, *Property, Production, and Family in Neckarhausen, 1700–1870* (Cambridge and New York, 1990); James H. Jackson, Jr., *Migration and Urbanization in the Ruhr Valley, 1821–1914* (Atlantic Highlands NJ, 1997); Marta Petrusewicz, *Latifundium: Moral Economy and Material Life in a European Periphery*, trans. Judith C. Green (Ann Arbor, 1996).

On women, women's conditions, women's work, and women's role in society, Gay Gullickson, *Spinners and Weavers of Auffay*, David Sabean, *Property, Production and Family in Nectkarhausen*, and L.D. Schwarz, *London in the Age of Industrialization*, noted above in the bibliography to this chapter, and K.D.M. Snell, *Annals of the Labouring Poor: Social Change and Agrarian England, 1700–1900* (Cambridge and New York, 1985) and 'Proto-industrialization? Cottage Industry, Social Change and Industrial Revolution', *Historical Journal* 27 (1984), are particularly informative. Other works on the topic are Louise Tilly and Joan Scott, *Women, Work and Family* (New York, 1974); Leonore Davidoff and Catherine Hall, *Family Fortunes: Men and Women of the English Middle Class, 1780–1850* (Chicago, 1987); Pat Hudson and W.R. Lee,

[448]   *Women's Work and the Family Economy in Historical Perspective* (Manchester, 1990)
and Anna Clark, *The Struggle for the Breeches: Gender and the Making of the British
Working Class* (Berkeley and Los Angeles, 1995). Two very handy articles on
women's work are Jean H. Quataert, 'The Shaping of Women's Work in
Manufacturing: Guilds, Households and the State in Central Europe, 1648–
1870', *American Historical Review* 90 (1985): 1122–48 and Deborah Valenze,
'The Art of Women and the Business of Men: Women's Work and the Dairy
Industry c. 1740–1840', *Past and Present* 130 (1991): 142–69. David Levine,
'Industrialization and the Proletarian Family in England', *Past and Present* 107
(1985): 168–203, offers a short survey of the impact of industrialization on
family life.

Some idea of the difficulties involved in trying to work out real wages and
relating real wages to standards of living can be gathered from two collections of essays: Peter Scholliers (ed.), *Real Wages in 19th and 20th Century Europe: Historical and Comparative Perspectives* (New York, Oxford and Munich,
1989) and Peter Scholliers and Vera Zamagni (eds), *Labour's Reward: Real Wages
and Economic Change in 19th- and 20th-century Europe* (Aldershot and Brookfield
VT, 1995). Most of the essays in the two volumes deal with the years
after 1850, when modestly reliable statistical material is easier to find.
M.J. Daunton's *Progress and Poverty*, noted above in the bibliography to this
chapter, includes an excellent account of the standards of living controversy
and an informative bibliography. A very succinct local study is the article of
L.D. Schwartz, 'The Standard of Living in the Long Run: London 1700–
1860', *Economic History Review* 2nd ser., 38 (1965): 24–41. Vol. 34, No. 2
(1986) of the *Scandinavian Economic History Review* is a special issue with a
number of essays devoted to the standard of living in the Scandinavian
countries between 1750 and 1914.

For some ideas about the periodization of economic and social change,
see David Pinkney, *Decisive Years in France 1840–1847* (Princeton, 1986), and,
especially, the stimulating and thought-provoking essay of E.A. Wrigley, *Continuity, Chance and Change: The Character of the Industrial Revolution in England*
(Cambridge, 1988). On the economics of the Great Famine, there is the relentless study of Joel Mokyr, *Why Ireland Starved: A Quantitative and Analytical
History of the Irish Economy, 1800–1850* (London, 1985); a simpler introduction to the topic can be found in Cormac Ó Gráda, *The Great Irish Famine*
(London, 1989). On the Poor Law of 1834, see Anthony Brundage, *The Making
of the New Poor Law: the Politics of Inquiry, Enactment, and Implementation, 1832–
1839* (New Brunswick, 1978); Philip Harling, 'The Power of Persuasion:
Central Authority, Local Bureaucracy and the New Poor Law', *English*

Historical Review 107 (1992): 30–35; and the collection of essays, Derek Frasier (ed.), *The New Poor Law in the Nineteenth Century* (New York, 1976). On French social policy in the period, Katherine A. Lynch, *Family, Class and Ideology in Early Industrial France: Social Policy and the Working Class Family, 1825–1848* (Madison, 1988) can be recommended; for Germany, see Herman Beck, 'The Social Policies of Prussian Officials: The Bureaucracy in a New Light', *Journal of Modern History* 64 (1992): 263–98. Lenore O'Boyle, 'The Problem of an Excess of Educated Men in Western Europe 1800–1850', *Journal of Modern History* 42 (1970): 472–95, discusses unemployment among the educated. Dudley Baines, *Emigration from Europe, 1815–1930* (Cambridge, 1995) is a general overview of transatlantic migration.

Chapter 6

The diplomatic history of the period is well covered in Paul Schroeder, *The Transformation of European Politics 1763–1848* (Oxford, 1994). A short version of his argument is Paul Schroeder, 'Did the Vienna Settlement Rest on a Balance of Power?' *American Historical Review* 97 (1992): 683–706. For military aspects, one can consult Geoffrey Best, *War and Society in Revolutionary Europe, 1770–1870* (Oxford, 1986). Useful works on the state include Stanley Palmer, *Police and Protest in England and Ireland, 1750–1850* (Cambridge and New York, 1989); John A. Davis, *Conflict and Control: Law and Order in Nineteenth-Century Italy* (Atlantic Highlands, 1988); Alf Lüdtke, *Police and State in Prussia, 1815–1850*, trans. Peter Burgess (Cambridge, 1989); Howard C. Payne, *The Police State of Louis Napoleon Bonaparte, 1851–1860* (Seattle, 1966) (the first chapter on pre-1850 circumstances is very useful); and David Laven, 'Law and Order in Habsburg Venetia 1814–1835', *Historical Journal* 39 (1996): 383–403. Michel Foucault's work on prisons is *Discipline and Punish: The Birth of the Prison*, trans. Alan Sheridan (New York, 1977); a very different interpretation is given in Peter Spierenburg, *The Spectacle of Suffering: Execution and the Politics of Repression* (Cambridge, 1984). On the idea of civil society, there is the seminal book of the philosopher Jürgen Habermas, *The Structural Transformation of the Public Sphere: an Inquiry into a Category of Bourgeois Society*, trans. Thomas Burger and Frederick Lawrence (Cambridge MA, 1989). Two other books on the origins and application of the concept and the social order to which it refers are Marvin Becker, *The Emergence of Civil Society in the Eighteenth Century* (Bloomington, 1994) and Norbert Waszek,

[450] *The Scottish Enlightenment and Hegel's Account of 'Civil Society'*, (Dordrecht, 1988). Ernst Gellner, *Conditions of Liberty: Civil Society and its Rivals* (New York, 1994), is one of many discussions of the recent revival of the term. Some useful empirical studies of different aspects of civil society (all with helpful bibliographies) are Harold Perkin, *The Origins of Modern English Society 1780–1880* (London, 1969); Charles Tilly, *The Contentious French* (Cambridge MA, 1986), and by the same author, *Popular Contention in Great Britain, 1758–1834* (Cambridge MA, 1995); Irene Collins, *The Government and the Newspaper Press in France 1814–1881* (London, 1959); Leonore Davidoff and Catherine Hall, *Family Fortunes: Men and Women of the English Middle Class, 1780–1850* (Chicago, 1987). Two briefer studies of important aspects of civil society are William M. Reddy, 'Condottieri of the Pen: Journalists and the Public Sphere in Postrevolutionary France (1815–1850)', *American Historical Review* 99 (1994): 1546–1570; and Mark Harrison, 'The Ordering of the Urban Environment: Time, Work and the Occurrence of Crowds, 1790–1835', *Past and Present* 110 (1986): 134–68. On mutual benefit societies and the role of the urban lower classes in civil society, see William H. Sewell, Jr., *Work and Revolution in France: The Language of Labor from the Old Regime to 1848* (Cambridge, 1980). For the work of Daniel O'Connell, see James Reynolds, *The Catholic Emancipation Crisis in Ireland, 1823–1829* (2nd edn., Westport CT, 1970); or Feargus O'Ferrall, *Daniel O'Connell* (London, 1981).

Studies of conservatism include Robert Berdahl, *The Politics of the Prussian Nobility: The Development of a Conservative Ideology, 1770–1848* (Princeton, 1988); René Rémond, *The Right Wing in France*, trans. James M. Laux, 2nd edn. (Philadelphia, 1969), or J.C.D. Clark, *English Society 1688–1832: Ideology, Social Structure and Political Practice during the Ancien Regime* (Cambridge and New York, 1985). An informative short piece, particularly helpful for the conservative critique of capitalism is David Eastwood, 'Robert Southey and the Intellectual Origins of Romantic Conservatism', *English Historical Review* 104 (1989): 308–31. Informative biographies of three very different prominent conservatives are David Barclay, *Frederick William IV and the Prussian Monarchy, 1840–1861* (Oxford, 1995), Guillaume de Bertier de Sauvigny, *Metternich and his Times*, trans. Peter Ryde (London, 1962), and Janet M. Hartley, *Alexander I* (London and New York, 1994).

For liberalism, see Pierre Manent, *An Intellectual History of Liberalism*, trans. Rebecca Balinski (Princeton, 1996); Alan S. Kahan, *Aristocratic Liberalism: the Social and Political Thought of Jacob Burckhardt, John Stuart Mill, and Alexis de Tocqueville* (Oxford and New York, 1992) and James Sheehan, *German Liberalism in the Nineteenth Century* (Chicago, 1978). Guy Howard Dodge, *Benjamin*

Constant's Philosophy of Liberalism: a Study in Politics and Religion (Chapel Hill, 1980) is one of many accounts of a major liberal theorist of continental Europe. On Friedrich List and his ideas, see William O. Henderson, *Friedrich List, Economist and Visionary, 1789–1846*, (London, 1983); for their application in eastern Europe, Andrew Janos, *The Politics of Backwardness in Hungary* (Princeton, 1982). A very useful short account of the differences between liberals and conservatives in theory and practice is Iván Zoltán Dénes, 'The Value Systems of Liberals and Conservatives in Hungary', *Historical Journal* 36 (1993): 825–50.

Some works on radicalism in the first half of the nineteenth century might include Clara Lovett, *The Democratic Movement in Italy 1830–1876* (Cambridge MA, 1982), Roland Sarti, *Mazzini: A Life for the Religion of Politics* (Westport CT, 1997); Alan Spitzer, *The Revolutionary Theories of Louis-Auguste Blanqui* (New York, 1957); Pamela Pillbeam, *Republicanism in Nineteenth-Century France, 1814–1871* (New York, 1995). A charming article on artisans and radicalism is E.J. Hobsbawm and Joan Scott, 'Political Shoemakers', *Past and Present* 89 (1980): 86–114. Informative introductory essays on radicalism in England (with bibliographies for further reading) are Gareth Stedman Jones, 'Rethinking Chartism', in his *Languages of Class: Studies in English Working Class History 1832–1982* (Cambridge, 1983); Ian McCalman, 'Popular Constitutionalism and Revolution in England and Ireland', in Isser Woloch (ed.), *Revolution and the Meanings of Freedom in the Nineteenth Century* (Stanford, 1996) and James Epstein, 'Understanding the Cap of Liberty: Symbolic Practice and Social Conflict in Early Nineteenth-Century England', *Past and Present* 122 (1989): 75–118. See also, D.G. Wright, *Popular Radicalism: The Working Class Experience* (London, 1988) and Edward Royle and James Walvin, *English Radicals and Reformers 1760–1848* (Lexington KY, 1982).

Helpful works on romanticism would include Lilian B. Furst, *The Contours of European Romanticism* (London, 1979); Hugh Honour, *Romanticism* (New York, 1979); Rupert Christiansen, *Romantic Affinities: Portraits from an Age, 1780–1830* (London, 1988) or Maurice Cranston, *The Romantic Movement* (Oxford and Cambridge MA, 1994). For religious developments in the first half of the nineteenth century, the Catholic Church is discussed in Rogert Aubert, Johannes Beckman, Patrick J. Corish and Rudolf Lill, *The Church between Revolution and Restoration*, trans. Peter Becker (London, 1981) and vol. 7 of Hubert Jedin and John Dolan (eds), *History of the Church* (New York and London, 1964–). Owen Chadwick's book, *The Popes and European Revolution* (Oxford, 1981) has a good but brief discussion of the Catholic Church in the Restoration era. On Protestantism, see Nicholas Hope, *German and Scandinavian*

Protestantism, 1700–1918 (Oxford, 1995), or W.R. Ward, *Religion and Society in England 1790–1850* (New York, 1973). Gregory Freeze, *The Parish Clergy in Nineteenth Century Russia; Crisis, Reform, Counter-Reform* (Princeton, 1983) offers an introduction to the world of Orthodoxy.

Although there has been a lot written on nationalism, most of it is not very good. Two helpful works would include Miroslav Hroch, *Social Preconditions of National Revival in Europe*, trans. Ben Bowkes (Cambridge, 1985) and George L. Mosse, *The Nationalization of the Masses* (New York, 1975). See, as well, Linda Colley, 'Whose Nation? Classes and National Consciousness in Britain 1750–1830', *Past and Present* 113 (1986): 97–117. For the early socialist movement and its theorists, see Frank Manuel, *The Prophets of Paris*, (Cambridge MA, 1962); Christopher H. Johnson, *Utopian Communism in France: Cabet and the Icarians 1839–1851* (Ithaca, 1974); Barbara Taylor, *Eve and the New Jerusalem: Socialism and Feminism in the Nineteenth Century* (New York, 1983) or Claire G. Moses, 'Saint-Simonian Men/Saint-Simonian Women: The Transformation of Feminist Thought in 1830s France', *Journal of Modern History* 54 (1982); 240–67. Works on Karl Marx and Friedrich Engels are legion; two that might be relevant are David McLellan, *Marx before Marxism* (New York, 1970) and Oscar Hammen, *The Red '48ers: Karl Marx and Friedrich Engels* (New York, 1969).

Chapter 7

An excellent study of the *fédérés* of 1815, and one that sheds much light on the hundred days and on the basic nature of politics in Restoration France is R.S. Alexander, *Bonapartism and the Revolutionary Tradition in France: The Fédérés of 1815* (Cambridge and New York, 1991). A briefer version of this is his 'The Fédérés of Dijon in 1815', *Historical Journal* 30 (1987): 367–90. For the aftermath to the Hundred Days, see Gwynne Lewis, 'The White Terror of 1815 in the Department of the Gard: Counter-Revolution, Continuity and the Individual', *Past and Present* 58 (1973): 108–35. For the political agitation in Great Britain during the years 1815–21, see John Belchem, *'Orator' Hunt: Henry Hunt and English Working-Class Radicalism* (Oxford, 1985); Iain McCalman, *Radical Underworld: Prophets, Revolutionaries and Pornographers in London, 1795–1840* (Cambridge and New York, 1988). Three shorter pieces on this period are Thomas Laqueur, 'The Queen Caroline Affair: Politics as Art in the Reign of George IV', *Journal of Modern History* 54 (1982): 416–66;

Ian McCalman, 'Ultra-radicalism and Convivial Debating Clubs in London, 1795–1835', *English Historical Review* 102 (1987): 309–33 and John Belchem, 'Henry Hunt and the Evolution of the Mass Platform', *English Historical Review* 93 (1978): 739–73. More general overviews can be found in D.G. Wright, *Popular Radicalism: The Working Class Experience* (London, 1988) and Edward Royle and James Walvin, *English Radicals and Reformers 1760–1848* (Lexington KY, 1982).

André Jardin and André-Jean Tudesq, *Restoration and Reaction, 1815–1848*, trans. Elborg Forster (Cambridge and New York, 1983) is a most useful survey of political life in France during the Restoration and the July Monarchy. James Roberts, *The Counter-Revolution in France, 1787–1830* (New York, 1990) is also helpful for the years 1815–30. On the specific crisis of the early 1820s, see Alan Spitzer, *Old Hatreds and Young Hopes; the French Carbonari against the Bourbon Restoration* (Cambridge MA, 1971) and Sylvia Neely, *Lafayette and the Liberal Ideal 1814–1824: Politics and Conspiracy in an Age of Reaction* (Carbondale and Edwardsville IL, 1991). Richard Herr's essay, 'The Constitution of 1812 and the Spanish Road to Parliamentary Monarchy,' in Isser Woloch, (ed.) *Revolution and the Meanings of Freedom in the Nineteenth century* (Stanford, 1996) pp. 65–102, is a good guide to events in Spain; for an English-language account of the 1820 Italian revolutions, one must turn to textbooks, such as Harry Hearder, *Italy in the Age of the Risorgimento 1790–1870* (London, 1983). The best English-language discussions of events in central Europe are also in general histories, such as James Sheehan, *German History 1770–1866* (Oxford, 1989) or Thomas Nipperdey, *Germany from Napoleon to Bismarck, 1800–1866*, trans. Daniel Nolan (Princeton, 1996). For the Greek revolution and war of independence against Turkish rule, see Richard Clogg, *A Concise History of Greece* (Cambridge, 1992) and Giannes Koliopoulos, *Brigands with a Cause: Brigandage and Irredentism in Modern Greece, 1821–1912* (Oxford, 1987). Adam Ulam, *Russia's Failed Revolutions: From the Decembrists to the Dissidents* (New York, 1981) has a good chapter on the secret societies and conspirators in Russia. On Philhellenism there is William Clair, *That Greece Might Still Be Free: The Philhellenes in the War of Independence* (Oxford, 1972).

For the events leading up to the 1830 revolution in France, and the revolution itself, see Jardin and Tudesq, *Restoration and Reaction*, James Roberts, *The Counter-Revolution in France*, David Pinkney, *The French Revolution of 1830* (Princeton, 1972) and Pamela Pillbeam, *The 1830 Revolution in France* (New York, 1991). Clive Church, *Europe in 1830: Revolution and Political Change* (London, 1983) is a model work, that covers the continent in detail and has a very useful bibliography. On the political crisis of 1828–32 in Great Britain and

[454]   the Great Reform Bill, see John Belchem, *'Orator' Hunt*, Edward Royle and
James Walvin, *English Radicals and Reformers* and D.G. Wright, *Popular Radical-
ism*; Frank O'Gorman, *The Emergence of the British Two-Party System, 1760–1832*
(London, 1982); John Cannon, *Parliamentary Reform 1640–1832* (Cambridge,
1973); John A. Phillips, *The Great Reform Bill in the Boroughs: English Electoral
Behaviour, 1818–1841* (Oxford, 1992); E.J. Hobsbawm and George Rudé,
Captain Swing (New York, 1968); Michael Brock, *The Great Reform Act* (London, 1973), and Joseph Hamburger, *James Mill and the Art of Revolution* (New
Haven, 1973). Both the extent of the reforms in the Reform Act and the relationship of pre- to post-reform politics have been debated at length in recent
years. For a sampling of different views, see Philip Harling, 'Rethinking "Old
Corruption"', *Past and Present* 142 (1995): 127–58; Frank O'Gorman, 'Campaign Rituals and Ceremonies: The Social Meaning of Elections in England
1780–1860', *Past and Present* 135 (1992): 79–115; W.D. Rubenstein, 'The
End of "Old Corruption" in Britain 1780–1860', *Past and Present* 101 (1983):
55–86, or L.G. Mitchell, 'Foxite Politics and the Great Reform Bill', *English
Historical Review* 103 (1993): 338–64. On the post-1830 role of Paris as a
Europe-wide centre of oppositional politics, there is Lloyd S. Kramer, *Thresh-
old of a New World: Intellectuals and the Exile Experience in Paris, 1830–1848* (Ithaca
and London, 1988).

Chapter 8

The political events of the early 1830s are well covered by the books on the
1830 revolution and the Great Reform Act, mentioned in the bibliography
to the previous chapter. Additionally, Mark Brown, 'The Comité Franco-
Polonais and the French Reaction to the Polish Uprising of November
1830', *English Historical Review* 93 (1978): 774–93, discusses the politics of
international revolutionary solidarity (or lack of it) and broader support for
the Polish cause. Although there is still no complete modern history of the
Chartist movement, the literature on it has become very extensive. A small
selection of works on this topic would include two general histories, David
Jones, *Chartism and the Chartists* (New York, 1975) and Dorothy Thompson,
The Chartists: Popular Politics in the Industrial Revolution (New York, 1984).
Among the more specialized studies, one could mention Jutta Schwarzkopf,
Women in the Chartist Movement (New York, 1991); James Epstein, *The Lion of
Freedom: Feargus O'Connor and the Chartist Movement, 1832–1842* (London,

1982); David Goodway, *London Chartism 1838–1848* (Cambridge, 1982); [455]
Gareth Steadman Jones, 'Rethinking Chartism', in his *Languages of Class: Studies in English Working Class History 1832–1982* (Cambridge, 1983). Theodore Koditschek, *Class Formation and Urban-Industrial Society: Bradford, 1750–1850* (Cambridge and New York, 1990) and John Foster, *Class Struggle and the Industrial Revolution: Early Industrial Capitalism in Three English Towns* (New York, 1975), also have very useful material on Chartism. For a view of Chartism in the continuity of radical political movements in England, see T.M. Parsimen, 'Association, Convention and Anti-Parliament in British Radical Politics', *English Historical Review* 88 (173): 504–33; by contrast, John Belchem, 'Chartism and the Trades 1848–1850', *English Historical Review* 98 (1983): 558–87, portrays more of the novel elements in Chartism. Still another version of the relationship between Chartism and radicalism can be found in Michael Winstanley, 'Oldham Radicalism and the Origins of Popular Liberalism 1830–1852', *Historical Journal* 36 (1993): 619–43.

For Europe in the 1840s, and the campaigns of the political opposition, see Lloyd Lee, *The Politics of Harmony: Civil Service, Liberalism and Social Reform in Baden, 1815–1850* (Newark DE, 1980); Dagmar Herzog, *Intimacy and Exclusion: Religious Politics in Pre-Revolutionary Baden* (Princeton, 1996); Bruce Haddock, 'Political Union without Social Revolution: Vincenzo Gioberti's *Primato*', *Historical Journal* 41 (1998): 705–23. Several essays discuss reforms and political alignments in Great Britain of the 1830s and 1840s: Michael J. Turner, 'The "Bonaparte of Free Trade" and the Anti-Corn Law League', *Historical Journal* 41 (1998): 1011–34; Anna Gambles, 'Rethinking the Politics of Protection: Conservatism and the Corn Laws 1820–1852', *English Historical Review* 113 (1998): 928–52; Ian Newbold, 'Sir Robert Peel and the Conservative Party, 1832–1841: A Study in Failure', *English Historical Review* 98 (1983): 128–57; Alan Heeson, 'The Coal Mines Act of 1842, Social Reform and Social Control', *Historical Journal* 24 (1981): 69–88. H.A.C. Collingham and R.S. Alexander, *The July Monarchy: A Political History of France 1830–1848* (London and New York, 1988), are also helpful for understanding political developments in France from the 1830s until the revolution of 1848. James Sheehan, *German History, 1770–1886* (Oxford, 1989); Thomas Nipperdey, *Germany from Napoleon to Bismarck, 1800–1866* (Princeton, 1996); Henry Hearder, *Italy in the Age of the Risorgimento 1790–1870* (London, 1983); and André Jardin and André-Jean Tudesq, *Restoration and Reaction* (Cambridge and New York, 1983) also have good accounts of developments in the 1840s. Most works on the revolution of 1848 also include accounts of the pre-revolutionary crisis. Although not terribly successful, Joachim Remak,

[456] *A Very Civil War: The Swiss Sonderbund War of 1847* (Boulder CO, 1993), is the only English-language work on the topic. A better – if very brief – account can be found in Gordon Craig, *The Triumph of Liberalism: Zurich in the Golden Age, 1830–1869* (New York, 1988). Two accounts of subsistence-related riots and disturbances on the eve of the 1848 revolution are Manfred Gailus, 'Food Riots in Germany in the Late 1840s', *Past and Present* 145 (1994): 157–93; Roger Price, 'The Techniques of Repression: The Control of Popular Protest in Mid-Nineteenth Century France', *Historical Journal* 25 (1982): 859–87.

Everything one might ever want to know about the revolution of 1848 is contained in Dieter Dowe, Heinz-Gerhard Haupt, Dieter Langewiesche and Jonathan Sperber (eds), *Europe in 1848: Revolution and Reform*, trans. David Higgins (New York and Oxford, 2000). For a shorter version, the most recent general history, with a detailed bibliography, is Jonathan Sperber, *The European Revolutions, 1848–1851* (Cambridge and New York, 1994). A few of the important works on the 1848 revolution in France are: Maurice Agulhon, *The Republican Experiment 1848–1852*, trans. Janet Lloyd (Cambridge, 1983); by the same author, *The Republic in the Village: The People of the Var from the French Revolution to the Second Republic*, trans. Janet Lloyd (Cambridge, 1983); John Merriman, *The Agony of the Republic: The Repression of the Left in Revolutionary France 1848–1851* (New Haven, 1978); Ted W. Margadant, *French Peasants in Revolt: The Insurrection of 1851* (Princeton, 1979); Peter Amman, *Revolution and Mass Democracy: The Paris Club Movement in 1848*, and William H. Sewell's *Work and Revolution in France*, noted in the bibliography to Chapter Five.

English-language works on the 1848 revolution in the rest of Europe are rather sparser. For Germany, the old classic, Theodore Hamerow, *Restoration, Revolution, Reaction: Economics and Politics in Germany, 1815–1871* (Princeton, 1958) is now quite outdated. More recent studies would include Frank Eyck, *The Frankfurt Parliament 1848–1849* (New York, 1968), and Jonathan Sperber, *Rhineland Radicals: The Democratic Movement and the Revolution of 1848–1849* (Princeton, 1991). James Sheehan, *German History, 1770–1886* and especially Thomas Nipperdey, *Germany from Napoleon to Bismarck, 1800–1866* have good coverage of the 1848 revolution in Germany. For Italy, there is, above all, Paul Ginsborg, *Daniele Manin and the Venetian Revolution of 1848–49* (Cambridge, 1979); Clara Lovett, *The Democratic Movement in Italy 1830–1876* (Cambridge MA, 1982), has some useful chapters on 1848. Also see Marion S. Miller, 'Communes, Commerce and *Coloni*: Internal Division in Tuscany 1830–1860', *Historical Journal* 21 (1978): 837–61. Istvan

Deak, *The Lawful Revolution: Louis Kossuth and the Hungarians, 1848–1849* [457]
(New York, 1979) is by far the best English-language account of the 1848
revolution anywhere in the Austrian empire. Another important work on the
empire in 1848 is Alan Sked, *The Survival of the Habsburg Empire: Radetzky, the
Imperial Army and the Class War* (London and New York, 1979), that also throws
a good deal of light on the 1848 revolution in Italy, the role of the armed
forces in the revolution, and the diplomacy of the 1848 revolution. Some
other works one could read on 1848 in the Habsburg lands are John Rath,
The Viennese Revolution of 1848 (Austin, 1957); Stanely Pech, *The Czech
Revolution of 1848* (Chapel Hill, 1969) and Lawrence Orton, *The Prague Slav
Congress of 1848* (Boulder CO, 1978). For Great Britain, see John Saville, *1848:
The British State and the Chartist Movement* (Cambridge, 1987) and the rather
more optimistic essay of Roland Quinault, '1848 and Parliamentary Reform',
Historical Journal 31 (1988): 831–51. J.H. Seddon, *The Petrashevtsy: A Study
of the Russian Revolutionaries of 1848* (Manchester, 1985), describes the very
feeble revolutionary movement in the tsar's empire. On the diplomacy of
the 1848 revolution, there is Lawrence Jennings, *France and Europe in 1848*
(Oxford, 1974); Werner Mosse, *The European Powers and the German Question
1848–1871*, 2nd edn. (Cambridge, 1969), and Alan Sked, *The Survival of the
Habsburg Empire*.

Chapter 9

A good place to begin a consideration of the relationship of the age of revolution to the later nineteenth century is with the general national histories
listed in the bibliography to Chapter One, and the general economic histories given in the bibliography to Chapter Five. Two other general histories
that are useful for a comparison of pre- and post-1850 developments are
David Blackbourn, *The Long Nineteenth Century: A History of Germany, 1780–
1918* (Oxford and New York, 1998) and Theodore Zeldin, *France, 1848–
1945*, 2 vols. (Oxford, 1973–77). Among the specific studies that thematize
the difference between pre- and post-1850 conditions, I would mention
Raymond Grew, *A Sterner Plan for Italian Unity: The Italian National Society and
the Risorgimento* (Princeton, 1963); Theodore Hamerow, *The Social Foundations of German Unification*, 2 vols. (Princeton, 1969–72); Jonathan Sperber,
Popular Catholicism in Nineteenth Century Germany (Princeton, 1984); Margot
C. Finn, *After Chartism: Class and Nation in English Radical Politics, 1848–1874*

[458] (Cambridge and New York, 1993); Eugenio F Biagini, *Liberty, Retrenchment and Reform: Popular Liberalism in the Age of Gladstone, 1860–1880* (Cambridge and New York, 1992); Paul W. Schroeder, *Austria, Great Britain, and the Crimean War: The Destruction of the European Concert* (Ithaca, 1972). On a broader scale, the general accounts of Eric Hobsbawn, *The Age of Capital 1848–1875* (London, 1975); *The Age of Empire 1875–1914* (New York, 1987); and *The Age of Extremes: A History of the World, 1914–1991* (New York, 1994) provide food for thought about the age of revolution and its place in modern European history.

INDEX